Kill Caesar!

Kill Caesar!

Assassination in the Early Roman Empire

Rose Mary Sheldon

ROWMAN & LITTLEFIELD
Lanham • Boulder • New York • London

Published by Rowman & Littlefield
An imprint of The Rowman & Littlefield Publishing Group, Inc.
4501 Forbes Boulevard, Suite 200, Lanham, Maryland 20706
www.rowman.com

Unit A, Whitacre Mews, 26-34 Stannary Street, London SE11 4AB,
United Kingdom

British Library Cataloguing in Publication Information Available

Library of Congress Cataloging-in-Publication Data Available

ISBN 978-1-5381-1488-9 (cloth : alk. paper)
ISBN 978-1-5381-1489-6 (ebook)

♾™ The paper used in this publication meets the minimum requirements of
American National Standard for Information Sciences—Permanence of Paper
for Printed Library Materials, ANSI/NISO Z39.48-1992.

Printed in the United States of America

DMS

John MacIsaac

Remember that to change your mind and follow him who sets you right is to be nonetheless freer than you were before.

—Marcus Aurelius, *Meditations* 8.16

Contents

Contents

Preface

Roman emperors had a penchant for expiring, or so one of my students once observed. This led me to count the actual number of assassinated Roman rulers and, when I came up with the shocking figure of 75 percent, I was amazed. Today one can look at the list of Roman emperors on Wikipedia and see the manner of all their deaths. Not only is the 75 percent figure correct but it is the highest rate of any monarchy anywhere in all of history. Many people have noted the phenomenon; only a few have tried to explain it. Until now, no one has written a book on whether or how it could have been prevented.

There have been many books on related topics. Fik Meijer, for example, has written on how each Roman emperor met his end.[1] Franklin L. Ford has written a classic book on political assassinations throughout history, beginning with Julius Caesar.[2] Walter Scheidel has compared the Roman imperial monarchy to others around the world and has indeed confirmed the statistically high rate of attrition among Roman rulers.[3] Fergus Millar has written about the emperor's entourage and what sort of people surrounded him, which is an important concept, since killing an emperor required access.[4] Finally, there has been at least one dissertation on this under-researched subject.[5] Why this should be is still a mystery to me; since there have been so many attempts at killing Roman emperors, I reluctantly concluded I would have room to discuss the internal security of only the first five Julio-Claudians in one reasonably sized book.

No one doubts that the Julio-Claudian emperors had a great deal of opposition. The principate was new; Augustus introduced an autocracy that had never before existed in the republic. Challenges to the new emperor's authority have been studied along with identifying groups that acted in opposition to the new regime.⁶ While identifying the malcontents is important, here we will focus on how these groups or individuals were watched and neutralized. To realize the extent to which the topic of internal security has been ignored, one merely has to look at any biography of Julius Caesar and notice that the index contains no entry for security, internal security, bodyguards, or intelligence. If this can be true of Caesar's assassination, the most famous of them all, then what is being missed with the less famous assassinations or the attempts that were not quite as successful?

Not all opposition or discontent was aimed at removing the emperor. There were certainly people unhappy with the prevailing social and economic conditions or with Roman occupation in general. Revolts in the provinces, for example, were usually triggered by fiscal burdens or by the greed and corruption of individual Roman governors. Disturbances by the city mob usually followed food shortages. These were issues the emperor had to deal with, but they generally did not threaten his life. Mutinies by the legions were another matter. Since the armies were the mainstay of imperial power, any revolt by an army could potentially overthrow an emperor. Thus the revolts of troops in Germany and Pannonia after the death of Augustus or of the Illyrian legions on the accession of Claudius were a serious threat.⁷

The men who truly had the chance to kill the emperor came from one class only: the politically and socially prominent men of Rome and the Senate. These were the men who had personal access to the emperor. Many of them opposed the princeps, and they claimed to oppose the system of government he represented. Not all nobles were complicit, of course, and to speak of "senatorial opposition" may be an oversimplification. Nevertheless it is within this milieu that assassins arose and the emperor had to carefully watch both his so-called friends and his enemies. Why would any Roman want to kill the most important citizen in Rome and, if successful, what would this mean for the stability of the empire? The threat to the emperor came from the upper classes, including his own family members. The leader of a conspiracy had to be from the upper classes because the major reason for killing an emperor was to take his place, and this could be done only by a person of high enough rank and birth to qualify for the position. This has led at least one scholar to ask if dissident behavior ran in families.⁸

Was assassinating an emperor all that simple? The question itself brings us within the purview of intelligence studies, because keeping an emperor alive was a matter of internal security. While some may question whether *intelligence* is an anachronistic term used in a Roman context, the fact is that the emperor's safety must have required a large amount of "intelligence" (meaning timely and relevant information that has to be delivered beforehand to users) on possible threats and surveillance of the groups from where these threats might come, regardless of what they called it or how they collected and processed it. Places where the emperor went had to be guarded, crowds had to be kept under control, and even those within the palace were put under scrutiny. Although we now have many more studies on Roman intelligence, not one of them has focused on the most important internal security problem of them all: how to keep people from making attempts on the emperor's life.[9] Nor have recent books on the Roman army or policing in the Roman Empire answered our question, since they have focused on empire-wide security, an interesting but separate problem.[10] There have been studies on the various components of Roman internal security—for example, the informers known as *delatores*. Too often these men have been portrayed as merely nasty informers, men without scruples who simply turned in innocent men to make money, but in the absence of public prosecutors they actually formed an important way in which the emperor might detect conspiracies.[11]

One group that often gets blamed for the high rate of imperial assassinations is the Praetorian Guard. Many have asked the obvious question: If the emperor had nine thousand soldiers acting as bodyguards, how could people get close enough to kill him? And yet they did. A common erroneous assumption is that members of the Guard were always in on assassination attempts. This was true only in a very few cases. A recent study of the Praetorian Guard has shown that the troops were generally loyal, efficient, and effective.[12] We must not think of them as the "emperor-makers" of popular imagination. That brings us back to our original question: Who was killing all these emperors?

In spite of the fact that the early empire is one of the best documented periods of Roman history, conspiracy is never the part that gets documented very well. It is exactly the gaps in the narratives that cause conspiracy theories to grow. Unfortunately some modern authors will take the most conspiratorial view because it sells books or answers "all the questions"—the true sign that we are dealing with a conspiracy theory and not history, because in true history, all the questions are never answered, nor can they be.[13] It is in the gaps that historians must conjecture about what really happened, and even they often disagree.

Deciding which conspiracies are real and which are just literary creations is difficult. Even when we have eyewitnesses, their motives are suspect. Conspiracies are based on secrecy and silence and leave little trace. The ancient evidence is too fragmentary for any certainty to be reached, which explains why modern scholars can disagree on what actually took place. Ancient historians were not held to our modern standards of accuracy.[14] They wrote to prove a moral point, to blacken enemies, or

just to tell a rousing good story. And what could be more rousing than
sex, betrayal, espionage, and a good murder mystery? In the absence of
real evidence, people will tell stories about what they think happened.
This is how conspiracy theories are born; they are usually based on belief,
not fact.

As Victoria Pagán has written, "Conspiracy is an ideal circumstance in
which to observe how an historian confronts the limits of knowledge."[15]
The ancient sources are always fragmentary and contradictory regardless
of the topic. Some gaps were caused by lacunae created in the transmission of the ancient texts, and some are caused by those things the historians chose not to discuss. Others become evident when the author had
no sources to work from. All of the missing parts affect the way we read
the story. Pagán has pointed out that if eighteen and a half minutes of
the Watergate tapes or four minutes of the Zapruder film can obscure
our view of the two most famous events of twentieth-century America,
imagine what two lost books of Tacitus can do.[16] Added to this is the
fact that few writers in antiquity ever wrote without antipathy or parti-
sanship. Ancient historiography prioritized rhetoric, moralization, and
literary emulation, not accuracy.[17] We must get beneath their tendentious
motives. The sources are never as reliable as we would wish, and there
are many chronological and prosopographical problems (those related to
family connections) that have had to be relegated to the footnotes. The
sources have been exhaustively analyzed by the classical scholars who
have written recent biographies of the Julio-Claudian emperors, yet even
these historians realize that writing a true biography of an emperor is a
nearly impossible task due to the fragmented nature of the sources, let
alone their bias.[18] These authors have discussed the personalities of the
emperors, the inner workings of their regimes, and the reliability of the
sources. Yet still, there is no agreement on even these details, let alone
the hidden details of conspiracies. Some authors treat conspiracies as
believable; others reject them as unreliable stories added to entertain the
reader. Many dismiss attempts on the emperor's life as "minor" or "unimportant" simply because they were unsuccessful. We can be sure the
emperor—the target—did not feel this way.

We are also fortunate that we can draw on recent studies on conspiracy
theory not only as a historical genre but as a theme in Latin literature.[19]
Victoria Pagán has observed that, although the term *conspiracy theory* was
not a part of the vocabulary of the ancient Romans, conspiracy formed a
substantial part of the Roman mindset and is a major theme in Latin literature. The ancients wrote about conspiracies of all types, not just those
aimed against removing an emperor. The fact that these usually involved
a woman, a slave, and a foreigner also suggests there are themes of which
we need to make ourselves aware. Modern historians have been all too

prone to internalizing the Roman bias against marginalized groups like women and slaves.[20] They are more likely to accept the lascivious tales about the sex life of Agrippina than they are to look for the conspiracy that such tales were used as cover-up. They also make value judgments, conscious or unconscious, against spies, informers, soldiers, adulterers, and murderers.[21] There is no getting around that Roman history is the story of the ruling class from the perspective of elite male historians writing for their peers.[22] This is the same class that produced the conspirators. How can we expect to get an accurate picture of the conspirators from a group whose disloyal activities might give them a motive to cover their own tracks? Literary themes often portray the late emperor as a tyrant who needed to be killed in the name of "liberty," or as a madman who needed to be removed for the good of the state, but never because of the raw ambition of the participants.

Conspiracies are not easy to trace under the best of circumstances. They are born in secrecy and are sometimes suppressed in secret. No emperor wanted to admit that he was in a constant state of having his life threatened. Rather, he wanted to present the image that everyone loved him and the state was both stable and safe. The emperor and his security staff had to detect the plans of a small, dedicated group acting clandestinely and eliminate the group before it struck. Beginning with Augustus, emperors had a wide range of institutions to draw from—men who could be used to detect and eliminate potential threats. There was no central institution like an FBI to do this, but multiple groups could be called upon to investigate a possible threat. On the orders of the ruler, they might throw out a very wide net, and there was a risk that innocent men might be implicated. If the list of suspects became too long or the executions too many, this could create new problems for the emperor: those who survived could decide to remove an increasingly suspicious emperor before the net reached them. It is difficult to say whether an emperor was paranoid or whether others really *were* out to get him. There was only one certainty: you had to get the emperor on the first try; you would not be given a second chance. Once you were caught, all your friends, allies, and family would fall under suspicion and perhaps be taken down with you.

Fear of conspiracy and assassination is inherent in the office of any autocrat. Once Augustus established the principate as the rule of one man, keeping the emperor safe became job number one for himself and his security staff. Since the principate was an evolving institution, tracing how the increasing centralization of power caused a pushback by those classes losing power is the constant backdrop of this story. It is the tale of the system Augustus created and the institutions he designed to keep himself and his successors safe. Judging by the result, the system may seem inadequate. Three of the Julio-Claudian emperors were assassinated, and there were multiple stories circulating that the other two were also murdered. Perhaps we should be asking how the Romans could have kept alive a man that so many people wanted dead. What made Roman emperors such constant targets, and could a determined assassin ever be stopped? Without anachronistically comparing what the Romans did and modern security procedures, we will examine the question asked by Miriam Griffin, in her excellent biography of Nero: Why was it so difficult to succeed as princeps?[23]

There are many subtopics of great importance to the history of the principate that could not be discussed here in detail. These topics have been covered by professional ancient historians over the last decades. This is not a book on foreign policy, Roman military history, senatorial relations, patron-client relations, prosopography (i.e., a description of a person's social and family connections, career), or Latin historiography, although all of them are interesting and relevant topics. My focus is Roman internal security during the reign of the Julio-Claudians. I have made copious references in the notes to books on these other subjects in order to give the reader food for thought, to show the foundation upon which I have based my conclusions, but also to give due credit to those whose ideas and works I have built upon. Many academic controversies have been relegated to the notes, along with analysis of the literary, inscriptional, and numismatic evidence. The originality of this work comes from its viewpoint, not in the discovery of new sources or interpretations of the old. This book was written for the intelligence professional with little or no knowledge of ancient history and its literature and for the general reader with an interest in Roman history or intelligence history. I still hope it will give classicists some things to consider.

Studying intelligence history as the "missing dimension" tends to give one a cynical view of the world. Truth be told, there is something inherently unsavory about a conspiracy. It involves betrayal and violence. It reveals the dark underbelly of Roman society and Roman politics at its worst. It shows the discriminatory nature of the Roman class system and the worst side of human nature. It is not my intention, however, to portray a Machiavellian approach to maintaining power or to present the story of the Julio-Claudians as one big conspiracy theory. Worldview dictates whether one sees wide-scale policing as part of Rome's military and administrative grandeur or something more sinister. My goal is not to glorify the Praetorian Guard or sing the praises of a highly policed state but simply to explain the mechanisms by which the emperor's life was protected. The only judgment to be made is whether internal security mechanisms surrounding the emperor were effective or not. If the emperor is assassinated, the mechanism has failed.[24] This may seem to avoid the bigger issues of the effect such security services have on the personal liberty of the individual senator or citizen, but that would be a topic for an entirely different book. Still, I have tried to touch upon how autocracy affects freedom of speech and what happens when even just withdrawing from public life gets interpreted as treason.

There is nothing new or original about noting the fear and paranoia that exist in royal families and the drama that revolves around successions. A Roman ruler needed to stay alive in spite of his relatives, friends, colleagues, and even the people tasked with protecting him. There are numerous motives for wanting to kill an emperor—some personal, some professional, some perhaps even irrational—but there should be only one response on the part of a professional security detail, and that is to prevent it from happening. So we are brought full circle back to our original question: Why did this security fail 75 percent of the time in the Roman Empire?

Acknowledgments

It is a cliché of the acknowledgment process to say that one cannot fully acknowledge let alone reciprocate all of the debts one has incurred in producing a book. Still, the numerous debts I owe people are hereby listed with a tremendous amount of gratitude.

First, I thank Susan McEachern at Rowman & Littlefield for having faith in the project when many others lacked it. Also at Rowman I thank Katelyn Turner and Janice Braunstein for helping shepherd the manuscript through production. The anonymous readers assembled by them all contributed useful suggestions for improvement of the manuscript. I am especially grateful to Adrian Goldsworthy for his suggestion that I add a chapter on the Roman Republic.

It is particularly important when a project is still the seedling of an idea that people who nourish the seeds are thanked. Ralph Sawyer and his panel at the Society for Military History annual meeting in New Orleans, March 2012, gave me the opportunity to present my first paper on the subject of killing Roman emperors. It allowed me to work out some of this material and begin the process of thinking about how to organize what turned out to be a huge topic. My thanks go to all my cadets who allowed me to practice on them in Roman history class, and thanks to Col. Timothy Dowling, who allowed me to practice on a larger audience in our world history lecture.

Since my arrival at VMI, I have been indebted to the staff of Preston Library—all the people in reference, interlibrary loan, and acquisitions who helped me assemble the wide variety of documents in multiple languages that were needed to complete a project such as this. I am always indebted to Chad Dunbar, Carrie Miller, and Stephen Hayden, of VMI's IT department, without whose help nothing would ever be retrieved from my computer.

So many people gave of their time and expertise in fields in which I am not an expert: Adrienne Mayor on poisoning and Elizabeth Kosmas on medical symptoms; Ted Lendon on various aspects of the Roman army and the Roman Empire; Liane Houghtalin on all things numismatic; Julie Brown and Tom Panko at VMI for their help with this graphically challenged author. Special thanks go out to Dr. Chrystina Haüber of the Department für Geographie, Facultät für Geowissenschaften at Ludwig Maximiliens Universität, Munich, for her expert advice on sculptural evidence and Augustus, and decades of general good advice and friendship. As luck would have it, we were working simultaneously on topics that overlapped. I greatly regret that Prof. Garrett Fagan did not live to see the finished project, but he generously made his dissertation available to me just before he died.

Thanks to my colleagues Megan Herald and Vera Heuer, who read parts of the manuscript and made helpful suggestions. Because of their experience at BWXT, Brian Phillips and Jeffrey Aubert know more about installation security than I will ever know. Their proofreading skills have also become more important than ever, since auto-correct has become not a friend but an aggressive enemy. Every time it changed *public* to *pubic* I cringed in fear that I might miss the correction and lead some reviewer to think it was a Freudian slip. Auto-correct is particularly bad on classicists. It changes the *Ides* of March to *Ideas*, and every word that ends in *-io* gets changed to *-ion*.

I am especially indebted to Prof. Alan Baragona of James Madison University, a literary scholar and wordsmith extraordinaire. He has helped me to achieve all the clarity that correct punctuation can provide. All remaining dangling modifiers or comma splices remain my own.

I thank the Dean's Office at VMI for giving me a sabbatical leave in the fall of 2013 to do a major part of the work on this book and to BG Jeffrey G. Smith Jr. for sitting in on my lecture and encouraging my work.

As we reach a certain age, we look back on the people with whom we have studied and hope that our work does justice to their training. Having just lost a mentor this year when Prof. John P. Karras of the College of New Jersey passed away, I am acutely aware of how important it is to thank people while they are alive, but I also think of the people no longer with us who contributed to my ability to do research. My thoughts go back to Hunter College and the City University of New York Graduate Center, to William G. Sinnigen, JoAnn McNamara, and Naphtali Lewis; at the University of Michigan, John Eadie, Chester G. Starr, and Roger Pack; in Rome, Silvio Panciera; in Perugia, Mario Torelli. To all the scholars whom I have not met but whose work I have used in this book, I hope I have quoted them correctly, accurately portrayed their views, and been gracious in my disagreements.

My goal in this book, as in all my others, has been to identify in broad terms intelligence themes in the ancient world in the hope that specialists will continue to illuminate these issues and perhaps dig even deeper than I have.

Finally, to my husband, Jeffrey Aubert, I am grateful we both made it through 2017 alive and are here to see this book in print; I owe him more than is fit for public declaration.

Abbreviations

ANCIENT AUTHORS

Andoc.	Andocides, in *Minor Attic Orators*
Appian, *BC*	Appian, *Civil Wars* [*Bella civilia*]
Asc. Ped.	Asconius Pedianus, *Asconius: Commentaries on Five Speeches of Cicero*
Aul. Gell., *NA*	Aulus Gellius, *Attic Nights* [Noctes Atticae]
Aur. Vic., *Epit. de Caes.*	Aurelius Victor, Sextus, *Epitome de Caesaribus*
Auson., *De Caesar.*	Ausonius, *De Caesar*
Cicero	
ad Fam.	*Epistolae ad familiares*
Att.	*Epistolae ad Atticum, Letters to Atticus*
Cat.	*In Catilinam*
de Har. Resp.	*De Haruspicum Responsis*
de In. Rhet.	*De Inventione Rhetorica*
de Leg.	*De Legibus*
de Lege Agr.	*De Lege Agraria*
de Off.	Cicero, de Officiis
pro Reg. Dei.	*Pro Rege Deiotaro*
de Rep.	*De Re Publica*
Phil.	*Philippics*
Dig.	Justinian, *Digest of Justinian*
Dio	Dio Cassius, *Roman History*
Diod.	Diodorus of Sicily [Diodorus Siculus]

Diog. Laert.	Diogenes Laertius
Dion. Hal.	Dionysius of Halicarnassus, *Antiquitates Romanae*
Epictetus	Epictetus, *Discourses*
Eutropius, *Brev.*	Eutropius, *Breviarum*
	Fasti Amniternini (dating to the reign of Tiberius and found at Amiternum [now San Vittorino] in Sabine territory. CIL IX 4192); with picture of the inscription and references: http://arachne.uni-koeln.de/item/objekt/219432
Fasti. Ost.	*Fasti Ostienses*
Fasti Val.	*Fasti Vallenses*
Herodian	Herodian, *History*
Hyginus	Pseudo Hyginus, *De Munitionibus Castrorum* (*The Fortification of the Roman Camp*)
Josephus, *AJ*	Josephus, *Jewish Antiquities* (Latin abbreviation)
Juvenal	Juvenal, *Satires*
Livy	Livy, *From the Founding of the City*
Livy, *Per.*	Livy, *Periochae* (the later books of Livy are lost; they exist only in summaries called the *Periochae*)
Macrobius, *Sat.*	Macrobius, *Saturnalia*
Nic. of Dam.	Nicolaus of Damascus, *Life of Augustus*
Philo	Philo Judaeus
in Flacc.	*In Flaccum*
Leg. ad Gaiam	*Legatio ad Gaiam*
PIR	*Prosopographia Imperii Romani*, saec. I, II, III ediderunt P. von Rohden et H. Dessau. Berlin: Reimarus, 1897–1898
Pliny, *HN*	Pliny the Elder, *Natural History* [*Historia Naturalis*]
Pliny, *Paneg.*	Pliny the Younger, *Panegyricus*
Plut.,	Plutarch, *Lives* (comprises all Plutarch citations except the following)
de Garul.	Plutarch, *De garulitate*
Sallust, *Bell. Cat.*	Sallust, *Bellum Catilinae*
Schol. *Iuv.*	Juvenal, *Scholia in Iuvenalem Vetustiora*. Leipzig: Teubner, 1931
Seneca, *Contr.*	Seneca the Elder, *Controversiae*
Seneca	Seneca the Younger
Apoc.	*Apocolocyntosis*
Cons. Marcia	*To Marcia, on Consolation* [*de Consolatione ad Marciae*]

Constant.	*De Constantia Sapientis*
Contro.	*Controversiae*
de Bene	*De Beneficiis*
de Brev. Vit.	*De Brevitate Vitae*
de Clem.	*De Clementia*
Epis.	*Epistulae*
Ira	*De Ira*
Tranquil	*De Tranquilitate Animi*
SHA	*Scriptores Historiae Augustae*
Suet.	Suetonius, *Lives of the Caesars* (comprises all Suetonius citations except the following)
de Gramm.	*De Grammaticis*
Div. Aug.	*Divus Augustus* [Life of Augustus Caesar]
Div. Jul.	*Divus Julius* [Life of Julius Caesar]
Vita Lucani	*Life of Lucan*
Tacitus	
Ann.	*Annals* [*Annales*]
Dial.	*Dialogus de Oratoribus* (A Diologue on Oratory)
Hist.	*The Histories* [*Historiae*]
Thuc.	Thucydides, *The Peloponnesian Wars*
Val. Max.	Valerius Maximus, *Memorable Doings and Sayings*
Vell. Pat.	Velleius Paterculus, *The Roman History*
Zon.	Zonaras, *Epitome Historiarum* [*Epitome of Histories*]

MODERN WORKS

AC	*Acta Classica Universitatis Scientiarum Debreceniensis*. Debrecen, Hungary: Debreceni Egyetem.
Acme	*Acme: Annali della Facoltà di Filosofia e Lettere dell'Università degli studi (Statale) di Milano*. Milano.
AE	*L'Année Epigraphique*. Paris. Presses Universitaire.
AH	*Ancient History*. Sydney: Macquarie University, Ancient History Association, University of New South Wales.
AHB	*Ancient History Bulletin*. Calgary, Alberta: University of Calgary, Department of Classics.
AJA	*American Journal of Archaeology*. New York. Archaeological Institute of America.
AJAH	*American Journal of Ancient History*. Piscataway, NJ: Gorgias Press.
AJPh	*American Journal of Philology*. Baltimore: Johns Hopkins University Press.

Akroterion	*Akroterion: Quarterly for the Classics in South Africa.* Stellenbosch: Department of Classics, University of Stellenbosch.
ANRW	*Aufstieg und Niedergang der Römischen Welt: Geschichte und Kultur Roms in Spiegel der neueren Forschung.* Berlin: de Gruyter.
AntCl	*L'Antiquité Classique.* Brussels: Association L'Antiquité classique
Athenaeum	*Athenaeum: Studi di letteratura e storia dell'antichità.* Como: New Press
BIDR	*Bullettino dell'Istituto di Diritto Romano.* Milan: Giuffrè.
BMCR	*Bryn Mawr Classical Review.* College Hall, Bryn Mawr College, Department of Classics.
CAH	*The Cambridge Ancient History.* 12 vols. Cambridge: CUP.
CAH²	*The Cambridge Ancient History.* 2nd ed. 14 vols. Cambridge: CUP.
CB	*The Classical Bulletin: A Journal of International Scholarship and Special Topics.* Wauconda, IL: Bolchazy-Carducci.
Chiron	*Chiron: Mitteilungen der Kommission für Alte Geschichte und Epigraphik des Deutschen Archäologischen Instituts.* München: Beck.
CIL	*Corpus Inscriptionum Latinarum.* Berlin: Brandenberg Academy of Sciences and Humanities.
CJ	*The Classical Journal.* Ashland, VA: Randolph-Macon College, Department of Classics, Classical Association of the Middle West and South.
ClAnt	*Classical Antiquity.* Berkeley: University of California Press.
CP	*Classical Philology: A Journal Devoted to Research in Classical Antiquity.* Chicago: University of Chicago Press.
CQ	*Classical Quarterly.* Oxford: Oxford University Press.
CR	*Classical Review.* Oxford: Oxford University Press.
CUP	Cambridge University Press
CW	*Classical World.* Pittsburgh, PA: Duquesne University, Department of Classics, Classical Association of the Atlantic States.
EMC	*Échos du monde classique: Classical Views.* Calgary, Alberta: University of Calgary Press.
Epigraphica	*Epigraphica: Periodico internazionale di epigrafia.* Faenza: Lega.
Et.Cl.	*Les Études Classiques.* Namur, Belgium: Facultés universitaires.

G&R	*Greece and Rome.* Oxford: Clarendon Press.
GGA	*Göttingische gelehrte Anzeigen.* Göttingen: Vandenhoeck und Ruprecht.
Gnomon	*Gnomon: Kritische Zeitschrift für die gesamte klassische Altertumswissen-schaft.* Munich: Beck.
Henze, *AFA*	Henze, Wilhelm, *Acta Fratrum Arvalium.* Berlin: George Reimarus, 1874.
Hermes	*Hermes: Zeitschrift für klassische Philologie.* Stuttgart: Steiner.
Historia	*Historia: Zeitschrift für Alte Geschichte.* Stuttgart: Steiner.
HSCPh	*Harvard Studies in Classical Philology.* Cambridge, MA: HUP.
HUP	Harvard University Press
ICS	*Illinois Classical Studies.* Champaign, IL: Stipes Publishing.
ILS	Hermann Dessau, *Inscriptiones Latinae Selectae*
JRS	*The Journal of Roman Studies.* London: Society for the Promotion of Roman Studies.
Klio	*Klio: Beiträge zur Alten Geschichte.* Berlin: Akademie Verl.
Labeo	*Labeo: Rassegna di Diritto Romano.* Napoli: Jovene.
Latomus	*Latomus: Revue d'études latines.* Brussels : Latomus.
LEC	*Les études classiques.* Namur: Société des Études Classiques.
MAAR	*Memoirs of the American Academy in Rome.* Ann Arbor: University of Michigan Press.
MH	*Museum Helveticum*
Mnemosyne	*Mnemosyne: Bibliotheca Classica Batava.* Leiden: Brill.
NC	*Numismatic Chronicle.* London: British Museum, Department of Coins and Medals, Royal Numismatic Society; Spink.
OCD	Hornblower, Simon, and Antony Spawforth. *The Oxford Classical Dictionary.* 3rd ed. Oxford: Oxford University Press, 1996.
Op. Epig.	*Opuscula Epigraphica.* Rome: Università degli studi (La Sapienza).
OUP	Oxford University Press
Pallas	*Pallas: Revue d'études antiques.* Toulouse, France: Pr. Universitaires du Mirail.
PBSR	*Papers of the British School at Rome.* London: British School at Rome.
Phoenix	*Phoenix: Journal of the Classical Association of Canada = Revue de la Société canadienne des études classiques.* Toronto, Ontario: University of Toronto Press.
PIR	*Prosopographia Imperii Romani Saec I. II. III.* 1st ed. Berlin, 1897–1898.

PIR²	E. Groag, and A. Stein, eds. *Prosopographia Imperii Romani Saec I. II. III.* 2nd ed. Berlin, 1933–2015.
PUP	Princeton University Press
R-E	J. B. Metzler, ed. *Paulys Real-Encyclopädie der classischen Altertumswissenschaft.* Stuttgart, 1894-1963.
RAL	Atti della Accademia Nazionale dei Lincei, Classe di Scienze Morali, Storiche e Filologiche. Rendiconti. Roma: Accademia Nazionale dei Lincei.
RBPhil	*Revue Belge de philologie et d'histoire = Belgisch tijdschrift voor lologie en geschiedenis.* Brussels: Société pour le progrès des études philologiques et historiques.
RDM	*Revue des deux mondes.* Paris: Société de la Revue des Deux Mondes.
REL	*Revue des Études Latines*
RhM	*Rheinisches Museum für Philologie.* University of Köln, Sauerländer Verlag.
RIDA	*Revue internationale des droits de l'antiquité.* Brussels: Service des publications des Facultés universitaires Saint-Louis.
Röm. Mitt.	*Römische Mitteilungen. Mitteilungen des Deutschen Archäologischen Instituts, Römische Abteilung = Bullettino dell'Istituto Archeologico Germanico, Sezione romana.* Mainz: Von Zabern.
Staatsr.	Mommsen, Theodor. *Römische Staatsrecht.* 3 vols. Leipzig: S. Hirzel, 1887–1888.
Syll. Class.	*Syllecta classica.* Iowa City: University of Iowa, Department of Classics.
TAPA	*Transactions and Proceedings of the American Philological Association.* Baltimore, MD: Johns Hopkins University Press.
WJA	*Würzburger Jahrbücher für die Altertumswissenschaft.* Würzburg: Schöningh.
WS	Wiener Studien: Zeitschrift für Klassische Philologie, Patristik und lateinische Tradition. Wien: Verlag der Österreichischen Akademie der Wissenschaften.
YUP	Yale University Press
ZPE	*Zeitschrift für Papyrologie und Epigraphik.* Bonn: Habelt.
ZRG	*Zeitschrift der Savigny-Stiftung für Rechtsgeschichte. Romanistische Abteilung.* Wien: Böhlau.

The Emperors from Augustus to Nero

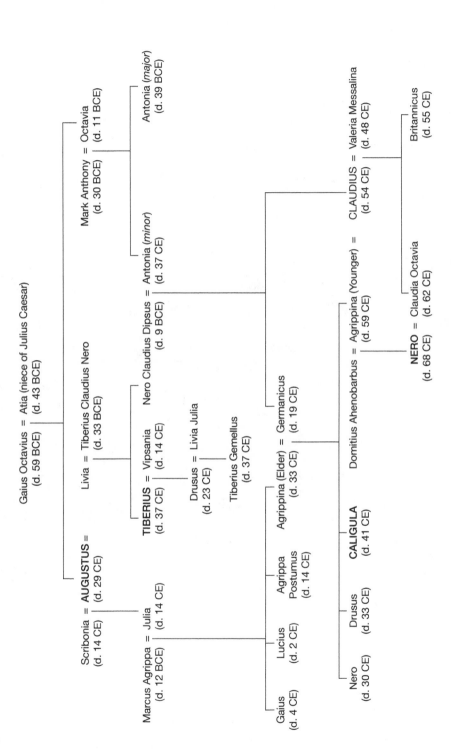

Conspiracies against the Julio-Claudian Emperors

Date	Conspirators	Reference
Augustus		
31/30 BCE	Aemilius Lepidus the Younger	Dio 54.15.4; Appian, *BC* 4.50; Livy, *Per.* 133; Vell. Pat. 2.88; Suet., *Div. Aug.* 19.1; Seneca, *de Brev. Vit.* 4.6
26 BCE	Cornelius Gallus and M. Egnatius Rufus	Dio 53.23.5ff.; Suet., *Div. Aug.* 19; Vell. Pat. 2.91–93; Dio 53.24
23/22 BCE	Fannius Caepio and L. Murena	Dio 54.3.2–4; Vell. Pat. 2.91.2; Suet., *Div. Aug.* 19.1; Suet., *Tib.* 8; Tacitus, *Ann.* 1.10.4; Seneca, *de Brev. Vit.* 4.6
19 BCE	Egnatius Rufus	Vell. Pat. 2.91.3–4
18 BCE	A few men executed	Dio 54.15.1, 4
	Telephus	Suet., *Div. Aug.* 19.2
	Camp orderly with knife	Suet., *Div. Aug.* 19.2
16 BCE	Cn. Cornelius Cinna Magnus (Pompey's grandson)	Dio 55.14.1 (before 5 BCE); Seneca, *de Clem.* 1.9.2ff. (16–13 BCE?)
9 BCE	Unnamed Conspirators	Dio 55.4.3
2 BCE	The Julia (daughter) Scandal: Iulus Antonius, Decimus Junius Silanus, T. Quinctius Crispinus, Appius Claudius Pulcher, Cornelius Scipio, and Ti. Sempronius Gracchus	Seneca, *de Brev. Vit.* 4.6; Dio 55.10.15; Pliny, *HN* 7.149

(continued)

Date	Conspirators	Reference
6 CE	Plautius Rufus (Publius Rufus, pamphleteer)	Dio 55.27.1–3; Suet., *Div. Aug.* 19.1; *Schol. Iuv.* 6.158
9 CE	Julia (granddaughter), Lucius Aemilius Paullus (husband), and Agrippa Postumus	Suet., *Div. Aug.* 19.2, cf. 65.4; Vell. Pat. 2.112.7; Tacitus, *Ann.* 1.3.4; Dio 55.32.1
14 CE	Livia (with figs)	Dio 56.30.1–3
Tiberius		
14 CE	Legionary Revolt Three legions under Q. Junius Blaesus, Pannonia. Four legions under A. Caecina Severus on the Rhine, All declared for Germanicus.	Tacitus, *Ann.* 1.16.1–4 and 1.31.1–4; Dio 57.5.1; Suet., *Tib.* 25.2, in Suet., *Cal.* 1.1; Vell. Pat. 2.125.2
16 CE	Clemens's failed attempt to rescue Agrippa Postumus from Planasia and revolt against Augustus with Lucius Audasius and Asinius Epicadus.	Suet., *Div. Aug.* 19.2, cf. 65.4; Tacitus, *Ann.* 2.39–40; Dio 57.16.3–4; Suet., *Tib.* 25.1
16 CE	Conspiracy of M. Scribonius Libo Drusus, Praetor in year 16.	*Fasti Amiternini*, CIL IX 4192; Tacitus, *Ann.* 2.27–32; Dio 57.15.4. Cf. Suet., *Tib.* 25.1; Vell. Pat. 2.129.2, 130.3
21 CE	Gaius Silius and Titius Sabinus Plot to put Nero on the throne	Tacitus, *Ann.* 4.68–70, 6.4; Dio 58.1, 1b-3; Pliny, *HN* 8.61.145
31 CE	Sejanus	Josephus, *AJ* 18.180–82; Suet., *Tib.* 55, 65; Suet., *Cal.* 12.2; Dio 58.6–19; Tacitus, *Ann.* 4.1

Date	Conspirators	Reference
37 CE	Tiberius dies. Tacitus and Dio: Macro and Caligula smothered him. Suetonius: poisoned by Caligula and smothered. Suetonius: Seneca attributed it to a natural death.	Tacitus, *Ann.* 6.50; *Tib.* 73.2; *Cal.* 12.2–3; Josephus, *AJ* 18.225; Dio 58.28.1–4
Caligula		
37 CE	Caligula ill. Macro, Silanus, and Gemellus plot to replace him.	Dio 59.8.1, 10.6; Suet., *Cal.* 23.3; Philo, *Leg ad Gaium* 14; Philo, *in Flacc.* 16
39 CE	Lepidus and Gaetulicus Both consuls, a large number of senators and the sisters. sisters	Dio 59.21.4, 22.5. Henze, *AFA* 49.6–8 Suet., *Cal.* 24.3; Suet., *Claudius* 9.1
40 CE	Sextus Papinius and Anicius Cerialis	Tacitus, *Ann.* 16.17.6; Dio 59.25.5ff.
40 CE	Betilinius Bassus and Betilinius Capito	Dio 59.25.6–7; Seneca, *Ira* 3.18.3
40 CE	Julius Canus and the Philosophers	Seneca, *Tranquil* 14.4–10; Sen. *Epi* 73.1, 103.5; Tacitus, *Ann.* 3.51.3; Boethius, *Consol. Phil.* 1.4.94
40 CE	Scribonius Proculus	Dio 59.26.1–2; Orosius 7.5.10; Suet., *Cal.* 28
41	Cassius Chaerea Aemilius Regulus, Annius Vinicianus, Valerius Asiaticus, G. Cassius Longinus, P. Nonius Asprenas, and L. Norbanus Balbus.	Josephus, *AJ* 19.18ff. Tacitus, *Ann.* 1.32.2; Suet., *Cal.* 56ff.
Claudius		
42	Governor of Dalmatia	Dio 60.15–16; Pliny, *Ep.* 3.16

(continued)

Date	Conspirators	Reference
	Annius Vinicianus (son-in-law of Corbulo) Furius Camillus Scribonianus, and Q. Pomponius	Suet., *Claudius* 13.2 and 35.2; Tacitus, *Ann.* 12.52, 13.43.2; Tacitus, *Hist.* 1.89.2 and 2.75; Orosius, 7.6.6–8
43	Equestrian thrown from Tarpeian Rock for plotting against emperor; he was detected by the father of Otho.	Dio 60.18.4; Suet., *Otho* 1.3
46	Asinius Gallus (grandson of Asinius Pollio), who is thereupon banished.	Suet., *Claudius* 13.2
	T. Statilius Taurus Corvinus, consul.	Dio 60.27.5
47	Gnaeus Nonius arrives with morning callers, armed with a sword.	Tacitus, *Ann.* 11.22.1
48	"Marriage" of Messalina with Gaius Silius Eight senators, Prefect of the Vigiles, equestrians, the Praetorian Prefect, and an actor (all prosecuted for collusion).	Tacitus, *Ann.* 11.5–7
48	Claudius poisoned by Messalina	Suet., *Claudius* 44.2; Tacitus, *Ann.* 12.66–67; Josephus, *AJ* 20, 148, 151; Dio 61.34; Pliny, *HN* 11.73.189, 22.46.92
Nero		
65	Pisonian conspiracy Senators: Gaius Calpunius Piso, Plautius Lateranus, Flavius Scaevinus	Dio 62.24.1–29.4; Suet., *Nero* 36.1ff.; Tacitus, *Ann.* 15.48–74

Date	Conspirators	Reference
	Military: L. Faenius Rufus, Praetorian prefect; Sulpicius Flavus, tribune of the Praetorians; C. Gavius Silvanus, praetorian tribune; Statius Proximus, Maximus Scaurus, Praetorian/centurion; Paulus Venerus, Praetorian/centurion; Sulpicius Asper	
66	Vinician Conspiracy, Beneventum Annius Vinicianu, Crassus Frugi, Antistius Vetus, Sulpicius Camerinus Military people under suspicion. Nero eliminates: Corbulo (Syria); Scribonii brothers (Germany); Barea Soranus, proconsul of Asia, friend of Rubellius Plautus; Cassius Longinus; Annius Pollio	Suet., *Nero* 36.1
68	Revolt of Vindex Lucius Verginius Rufus, Vindex Servius Sulpicius Galba	Dio 63.22–29; Suet., *Nero* 40–49 Suet., *Galba* 9.2 Plut., *Galba* 4; Pliny, *Letters* 9.19

Introduction

From the end of the sixth century BCE until two-thirds of the way through the second century CE, Rome's political officials seemed virtually immune to assault. How ironic then that the most famous day in the history of the republic is the Ides of March. We know more about that day than any other in Roman history because it was the day Julius Caesar was murdered. After his assassination, killing the chief executive officer became almost routine.

Augustus, always mindful of Caesar's fate, founded a Roman monarchy far more autocratic than the dictatorship that Brutus, Cassius, Cato, and Cicero had so bitterly opposed and died trying to prevent. He introduced a series of institutions guaranteed to keep the Roman state stable and prevent the forcible removal of its leader. He created a variety of bodyguards—the most prominent being the Praetorian Guard, whose job it was to keep him safe—and he created the urban cohorts and the *vigiles*, the night watchmen who doubled as a fire brigade, to keep the city of Rome safe. Under Augustus, whose rule began in 27 BCE, there were between seven and eight thousand troops stationed in Rome; the number rose rapidly, reaching about thirty thousand by the end of the century. Yet, with all these guardians, there were continued attempts on the lives of the emperors, many of them successful. Three of the five Julio-Claudians died by assassination.

Why did the Roman security system fail so miserably? More importantly, how did the killing of Roman emperors affect the state and its stability? The great irony is that the root causes of the problem lay within the system that Augustus, the great architect himself, designed.

No government, whether monarchical or democratically elected, can be expected to tolerate assassination as a form of political opposition. Conspiracies are violent, and they have unforeseen consequences. A conspiracy to kill a Roman emperor was dangerous and threatening morally, politically, economically, and socially. Conspiracies can unleash unseen forces that spring out against legitimate authority. Assassins may strike anywhere, and they may inspire others to rise up in revolt. Conspiracies aroused fear in those in power who faced being overthrown and in those who conspired and risked being discovered, punished, or even executed. Yet time after time, people came forward who were willing to sacrifice their own lives to remove an emperor.

When news of a conspiracy became public, the populace might begin to question what exactly was going on in the palace or doubt whether the government was in good hands. Conspiracies were worrisome events that threatened the social and political fabric of Rome. Ancient conspiracy narratives functioned to show readers that the perpetrators were being caught and punished. People wanted to be assured that such attempted murders were exceptional events, that the state was secure, and that someone was firmly in control. While watching the upper classes savage each other might be amusing to the lower classes, such behavior could ultimately lead to a civil war in the Roman state, and this would impact everyone negatively.[1]

Many factors led to the uncertainty of an emperor's life and the instability of the Julio-Claudian dynasty: the lack of an acknowledged hereditary principle, the lack of a law of succession, the hostility of members of the upper classes to the new autocratic regime, anger over their loss of status and the concomitant rise of *equites* and freedmen, and, finally, the existence of many possible successors from both within and outside the Julio-Claudian line. The intermarriage of Roman nobles produced multiple, alternative candidates for the throne, and these nobles were highly ambitious.[2] Once Augustus set up the principate, the aristocracy had to adjust to rule by one man. The old powerful families looked back to the good old days when they were the ruling magistrates and the consuls were the true heads of state, and they began to realize what they had lost. The hostility this engendered toward the emperor often surfaced as murder or attempted murder. Anyone with a high enough social status could imagine himself on that throne in place of the man who actually got there. Many people remembered Augustus in his earlier days when his actions against his enemies, like Antony, made him little more than a mass murderer, so why would anyone else hesitate to take his position by violence? This state of affairs created a terrible instability in the principate right from the beginning. Senators needed the strength to ride out the results of an attempt on the throne.[3] If the emperor died, someone had to take his place; this meant a candidate being proclaimed, approved by the army, and confirmed by the Senate. If more than one candidate emerged, as happened after the death of Nero in 68 or Commodus in 192—then a civil war would break out.[4]

Family relationships were of utmost importance in this story. The republican aristocracy consisted of a group of families whose names, connections, and family fortunes were passed down along with their tradition of holding offices and serving in the military. Such relationships acquired great political significance that could either support the position of a reigning emperor or destabilize it. Even within the emperor's own family there were many pretenders to the throne. Sons, daughters, and wives all played a crucial role in the question of succession, along with children from a previous marriage and eventually grandchildren. Sometimes these heirs got impatient or were manipulated by those hoping to marry someone within the emperor's bloodline or be regent for his minor children. The ultimate reality was that emperors were usually killed by men who were after their job. If the assassin was successful, he or, more likely, the man he was working for, would become the next emperor either to found a new dynasty or just continue the old one. If a change of rulers went smoothly, it could provide a certain continuity in government policies. It gave an air of legitimacy to the successor. Although it was the job of security services to protect an emperor, it was not their job to provide for the transition after a coup. They only had to protect the living emperor. An interregnum put them in a dubious position. It was not impossible for a praetorian prefect or an urban prefect (head of the three cohorts of soldiers who policed the city of Rome) to be carried over to a new regime, but there was never a guarantee. Successive praetorian prefects would find themselves having their loyalty tested as pretenders tried to co-opt them into the plot.

How do we document these conspiracies? As Sir Ronald Syme has written, "Conspiracy alleged, proved, or punished, is an elusive theme."[5] Detecting a conspiracy to remove an emperor is difficult but not impossible. Because conspiracies involve secret events, many acts will always remain in the shadows. This makes more guessing than usual a necessary hazard. One of the reasons we hear so little about these events is that the sources are frequently biased in favor of a senatorial order. Writers like Cassius Dio, Tacitus, and Suetonius tended to cover up or at least justify conspiracies from their own order. This meant leaving out details that would mark some of their colleagues as guilty. There is also the problem of "spin." Narratives might have been written by someone who thought the conspirators were defending liberty and had a just cause in overthrowing an unjust or cruel or even insane emperor. They offer us little detail on the course of events and leave much doubt as to whether there was an actual conspiracy or whether the condemned were just denounced by unscrupulous prosecutors who were after their estates. We are not told their motives or their methods. What they cannot cover up, however, is that the serious threats against the emperor did not come from the "people." There are no firebrands or revolutionaries in this story. The threat came directly from other people who wanted to be emperor in his place.

Even when a historian like Tacitus tried to bring into the open the closed and secret events of Roman history, he did not have all the evidence at his disposal. The secret of what was being planned was usually revealed only after an assassination. The success of an attack, while it was happening, depended on keeping information from leaking out. Ancient historians did not even have access to what little information was available at the time. Added to this is the problem that their writings were not held up to the kind of scrutiny modern historians are expected to display. They could borrow stories out of context or make up stories for effect. Roman historians described events they did not witness, or they used a conspiracy as an explanation in the absence of real information. They traded in gossip and what was being said at the time. They knew their readers enjoyed conspiracy theories. As Syme has asked, what does the historian do when confronted with fiction as well as deceit?[6]

What makes a conspiracy theory different from a real conspiracy, however, is that real conspiracies, like life, are messy. Things do not go as planned. People are delayed; they show up at the wrong place or at the wrong time. Weapons break, or what is supposed to be a fatal blow misses its target. A conspiracy theory can be spotted immediately because it accounts for all the loose ends, and everything fits neatly. People like such theories because they challenge the authoritative view. It makes people feel "in the know" as opposed to the herd that believes the "official story." Modern historians have sometimes overcorrected in the other direction. Many commentators refuse to believe that anything except a completely successful coup can constitute a real conspiracy. They dismiss many conspiracies as mere gossip in a way that reminds us of the Emperor Domitian's remark that emperors were unhappy because, when they discovered a conspiracy, no one believed them unless they had been killed.[7]

We are left with the problem that little can be taken at face value either in the literary or material record, and this is so much more true when we're dealing with conspiracy. With our truncated sources, piecemeal evidence, and literary constructs, it will never be possible to establish the precise motives or the moves of all the participants in an assassination attempt. All we can do is make an educated guess about who was involved and what their aims were. We must assess cui bono in each case. Who would benefit from the emperor's death? If he were killed, who would be his successor and what would be that person's claim to legitimacy? If we trace what the participants did and what the outcome was, rather than trying to discern what they were thinking or what their motives were, we get a better idea of what was going on. We must pay special attention to where the security services were and what they were doing. We are sometimes left with having to judge whether there was a legitimate threat by how violently the emperor reacted in response.

One aspect of the literature that has changed over the last two decades is our interpretation of the role women played in these conspiracies. Commentators have been reluctant to see women as active participants in political matters. When they do participate, they are seen as demented, power-hungry women with voracious sexual appetites.[8] More recent scholars, both male and female, have been able to peel back the layers of sexual accusation and innuendo to reveal some very real and active political intrigue.[9] Women were key players because they carried the imperial bloodline that originated with Augustus himself and, therefore, could provide a usurper with the opportunity to ally himself with a woman of the palace. Women like Agrippina, however, were much more than passive breeders. They actively plotted to put their male relatives or lovers on the throne. Even nonimperial women could play a role in a conspiracy by carrying information, hiding conspirators, or poisoning those about to testify. Espionage has always been an equal opportunity employer.

This is not the story of the emperors' lives, their personal foibles, their sexual predilections, their physical disabilities, or their moral shortcomings. For that we can always read Suetonius! The personality of the emperor and what was written about him afterward can be more of a hindrance than a help. Yes, there may have been some people who hated him or thought him demented, but that does not mean that he *was* demented. People will justify their actions after the fact by portraying themselves as aiming at loftier goals like freedom or liberty or justice and portraying their victims as evil.

This is the story of the people whose job it was to protect the emperor. Even bad emperors had the right to be protected. They might find themselves protected by bad people or at least people whose motives were unsavory, but nevertheless they needed to be protected. Few historians try to see things from the point of view of the *delatores*, the professional informers who brought intelligence of conspiracies to the emperor's attention in the absence of a public prosecutor. After all, they, too, were senators trying to survive. People tend to focus on their "immoral activities" and have little sympathy for men thriving under a dictatorship. They are perpetually portrayed as unrepentant villains. An imperial politician could embark on a career as a *delator* out of loyalty to the emperor, out of ambition and the desire for influence at court and political power, or just for personal enrichment. It could be all three.

One has to examine not just the emperor's ability as emperor, but the security problems built into the principate itself. It was the system that created the guards, the informers, the sycophants, and even the assassins. There were fewer and fewer avenues by which a senator could gain influence while the emperor controlled most of the governmental mechanisms. It took a very strong will, a sense of commitment, and a great deal of political skill to survive in that atmosphere, and those who did managed to impress their contemporaries and even occasionally arouse grudging admiration from among their foes.[10] It was a dangerous game to play because, whether hero or informer, one could suffer a precipitous decline. One can only imagine what happened to a *delator* who found himself turned over to his imperial colleagues after an unsuccessful prosecution. We know what happened when one stood up to an emperor; speaking truth to power is dangerous in any age.

The Julio-Claudians are certainly not great examples of stable leadership. This book will not attempt to exculpate their folly or viciousness, but no matter how eccentric a ruler is, assassinating him is treason. There were different visions of how the principate should be run, but those emperors who attempted to change the pattern often paid for it with their lives. This does not necessarily mean they were lunatics who had to be removed, but it may have seemed that way to the people closest to them at the time. It should come as no surprise that the atmosphere around the court of the Julio-Claudians and the Senate could be dangerous and unpleasant. Neither the senators who dared oppose the emperor nor those who remained quiet could escape being caught in a dilemma. Though both loyalist and informers were "forced to practice every kind of adulation, they, nonetheless, never appeared either servile enough to the authorities, or free enough to us."[11] Using deceit and flattery to get along politically was not restricted to the republic or empire or, for that matter, the ancient world. In the ancient Roman world, as in the world today, sycophancy was a means of survival.

Closeness to the emperors was a double-edged sword. If you were one of his friends or close advisors, you had access to his presence. That presence is what your influence and position relied upon, but it also put you in a position to be the one to kill the emperor or to be approached by someone who wanted to kill him. Nor could these associates rely on the loyalty of the emperor, who had no qualms about repudiating his *amici*. It might be for personal reasons, jealousy over a woman, dynastic policy, or political factors. Epictetus writes about what it was like to dine with the emperor and worry whether it was your last meal and whether you would lose your head shortly thereafter.[12] Losing the friendship of the emperor was a death warrant. Knowing this, disgraced *amici* could be driven into a conspiracy to kill the emperor first. If they were accused of having conspired first, they would either perish at the hands of an executioner or be forced to die by their own hands.[13] It must be noted that men who committed suicide were not necessarily guilty, nor is it certain their guilt would have been established had they stood trial. In some cases, even after the suicide, the trial proceeded.[14] Some always managed to survive. Lucius Vitellius is often given as an example of a man who was threatened with ruin but managed to ingratiate himself with Caligula; acted as a principal advisor to Caligula's successor, Claudius; successfully maintained his influence under both of Claudius's wives, Messalina and Agrippina; even in his old age maintained enough influence to avoid a treason charge; and then launched his son onto the imperial throne.[15] Vitellius was, however, an exception.

There are so many conspiracies just against the Julio-Claudian emperors that there is hardly room to discuss them all in great detail. Episodes that are described here in only a few pages could easily be given their own book. An example of this is the prosecution of M. Scribonius Drusus Libo, who was prosecuted in 16 CE and is often dismissed as a harmless fool and the victim of greedy prosecutors. Yet, as Andrew Pettinger has shown in his recent book *The Republic in Danger*, there may have been a very real conspiracy to kill the emperor behind this story. I suspect many more such books could be written about other conspiracies, and I encourage other scholars to dig deeper into these matters.

In the meantime, let us take a closer look at the first five emperors, the Julio-Claudians, and see why three of the first five emperors could be murdered so easily and why the other two had assassination stories circulated about them. Who were the men that constituted the system of defense against such assassinations? Were there enough of them? Were they competent? Were they loyal? What made the Roman imperial security system fail for three-fifths of the Julio-Claudian dynasty?

1

The Republic

The Roman Republic managed to exist for nearly four hundred years without a politically motivated assassination of a leading public figure, that is from its founding in 509 BCE to the assassination of Tiberius Sempronius Gracchus in 133 BCE. That is an amazing record, and one that stands in stark contrast to the violence of the Late Republic and the empire.[1] This is not to say that the early Republic was without violence. Even in legend, three of the seven kings had been murdered, and the first one, Romulus, had killed his brother, Remus.[2] The last Tarquin was killed by the Elder Brutus. Once the republic was established in 509 BCE, however, the Romans showed their genius by creating conservative yet flexible institutions that could accommodate conflicting social demands before they broke out in violence. Roman citizens came to revere the old virtues of loyalty, unselfishness, and rational organization as the very embodiment of the *res publica*, and this seemed to keep their elected officials safe.[3] The system depended on good faith (*fides*), honesty, and responsibility.[4]

The Romans of the Early and Middle Republic showed restraint as much by custom as by legislation and this offered great security to their governmental representatives. Like all humans, the Romans indulged in brawls, vendettas, and occasional group attacks, including the stoning of individuals condemned by public opinion for private transgressions, but in the public sphere, their leaders were not usually the target of personal vendettas or lynch mobs. Their respect for civil law and established procedures kept their political officials relatively free from assault.[5] A less generous view might point out that the social order in Rome was maintained through the use of violent oppression, but we just do not get that view from Roman historians who were members of the upper classes. There was probably more conflict than was recorded.[6]

Much of early Roman history, as received from writers like Livy and Dionysius of Halicarnassus, is idealized. The Romans imagined a distant time when a single patrician could disperse an angry mob through the force of his moral authority.[7] Perhaps their past was not quite that ideal, and the restraint in behavior towards figures of public authority was a little more complicated. It stemmed from a whole web of mutually reinforcing attitudes towards violence in the conduct of Roman business. The Romans seem to have had a widely shared sense of the need for restraint. Although they recognized that violence could be used to remove a potential tyrant, they, unlike the Greeks, did not honor the memory of tyrant slayers like Harmodius and Aristogeiton.[8] The Romans distrusted the legendary assassins and would-be heroes of the past. So how, then, did this Rome, idealized or not, evolve from a peaceful Republic into a murderous Empire? How did they go from a system of law among equals to a world of measureless ambition and a dreadful lust for power?

PUBLIC ORDER

Who kept Rome and its ruling magistrates safe during the republic? Rome was quite different from other pre-modern states in that the higher magistrates held both civil and military responsibility, and yet they were not allowed to use military means to maintain law and order or protect themselves.[9] Lacking a police force in any modern sense, they were even forbidden to mobilize a military force as a last resort.[10] In fact, Republican Rome had no standing army, only a militia that was, until the mid-second century BCE, dissolved and then newly recruited annually.[11] There was no special magistracy chiefly or exclusively responsible for maintaining public order. During the first centuries of the republic, new offices were created as functions were delegated out in a division of labor, but it was always the chief magistrates who retained the overall authority and commanded the most powerful means for enforcing obedience and therefore would be the target for any attempt to overthrow the government.

Although public order is a separate subject from assassination, political violence, riot, and civil war create the atmosphere in which violence against a leader can occur. A ruler losing control is not a safe ruler. Scholars investigating public order in the Roman Republic have all stressed the absence of a modern-style police force, but the absence of police *per se* does not imply a lack of public order.[12] Censors oversaw public morals, praetors issued legal injunctions, aediles policed markets and other public spaces, and tribunes of the plebs could arrest anyone who was abusing a citizen. A trio of minor magistrates called the *triumviri*, or *tresviri capi-tales*, were specialized police officials who administered Rome's jail, and executions were held there. Because they supervised a modest nocturnal patrol, they were also known by the alias *nocturne*, and they seemed to have exercised jurisdiction over minor crimes, arresting and dispensing summary justice to slaves and lower-class citizens in the Forum near the jail.[13] The absence of a law-enforcement agency and even any demand for one reflected the assumption that, in cases in which public order was not an issue, citizens were themselves able and prepared to protect their own lives and property. An aristocrat's usual entourage of slaves and freed-men would serve as a bodyguard in public places.[14] It was the duty of every citizen to exercise self-control and to ensure that his fellow citizens did likewise. A secure state was to everyone's advantage.

The two consuls possessed a major means of law enforcement called *coercitio* that was used to enforce obedience without instituting legal proceedings.[15] The powers of the chief magistrates included the ability to scourge or execute citizens, to arrest, imprison, or fine them.[16] The most severe measures, scourging and decapitation, were banned once the ple-beians had succeeded in establishing a means of appeal to the popular as-sembly instead of being subjected to the arbitrary action of the magistrates. After that point, citizens had an absolute protection against coercion. This protection was called *provocatio*, and it allowed any citizen to appeal any punishment.[17] To a great extent, magistrates relied upon the acceptance of their authority and not so much on threatening or applying coercion.

WHO GUARDED THE MAGISTRATES?

Among the permanent staff at the disposal of the consuls were the lictors. These were priests who carried the *fasces*, a bundle of rods with a project-ing axe blade that served as instruments as well as symbols of physical coercion (*insignia imperii*). They are thought to have been of Etruscan origin.[18] We are told these symbols produced terror in Roman subjects overseas, but in the city of Rome itself, the axe blade was removed.[19] Magistrates with *imperium* never appeared in public without their lictors, not even when on personal business.[20] The dictator had twenty lictors at his disposal; consuls were accompanied by twelve lictors, city praetors were allowed two to six.[21] The lictors walked in single file in front of the magistrate. There was a rule that no one was allowed to step between the last lictor and the magistrate. Only a minor son could walk in front of his father, the consul. This arrangement is interpreted by scholars to have created a "taboo zone."[22] Thus, rather than constituting an effective body-guard, the lictors served primarily a symbolic function. They represented the magistrate's legitimate claim to reverence and obedience.[23] This was the only line of defense they had; magistrates were not allowed to use public slaves or privately recruited staff against citizens.[24]

Lictors were never used to disperse a crowd; they were not allowed to use their rods (*virgae*) indiscriminately when applying physical force. Confronted by a crowd, a magistrate might identify a ringleader to the lictors and punish that person as an example.[25] Only then were their rods untied on the magistrate's explicit order, and only when the perpetrator had already been seized, stripped of clothing, and bound to a stake. If the aggressor was backed by a crowd that did not back down, lictors would be useless. Livy was right when he said that the lictors' power consisted solely in the plebeians' respect for them.[26]

It was the job of the lictors to clear the way for the magistrate and to exact due reverence from the crowd. This showed the deference of the citizens to the authorities. In turn, when the crowd wanted to show their anger, they would seize the *fasces* and break them, showing their disregard for the magistrate's authority. Such angry crowds are reported during the Struggle of the Orders in the fourth century, as well as the Late Republic.[27] Their flagrant disregard for authority also shows how useless the lictors were to prevent violence by a mob that really wanted to do harm to a magistrate rather than just to his symbols.

Since the lictors were chiefly symbolic and as a group were too small and inefficient by the standards of a modern police force to provide much protection, then who else could protect the magistrates? There was a veritable ring of other people surrounding consuls. The magistrates were regularly accompanied by privately recruited helpers, retainers, and clients, even though these people were not employed as bodyguards.[28] Magistrates were also accompanied by groups of functionaries called *apparitores*, who assisted them in maintaining order at public assemblies, at trials in the Forum, in front of the Senate's meeting place, and during public festivals.[29] During the empire, they would continue to accompany the emperors as they did the city magistrates of Rome and the provincial governors. Still, none of these men was formally trained for security functions.[30]

In spite of the lack of formally trained bodyguards, it would seem that controlling crowds at public events and keeping the magistrates safe presented early Rome with no real problem. This seems ironic, since so much of Roman business was transacted in open spaces that gave a potential assassin access to their leaders. The Roman business of government was transacted publicly, in the Forum and the *comitium*. It was here that rulers and the ruled met, presumably in safety.[31] We are presented with a picture where magistrates needed no protection from their subjects, so the Senate could meet regularly with the doors left open. Special guards were only considered necessary under extreme circumstances, as in December

63 BCE during the Catilinarian conspiracy. No one ever considered banning the public from the area around the Senate's meeting places. In other words, the Roman political process included mass meetings that were, by definition, noisy and sometimes disorderly, but this did not require the authorities to take precaution against popular violence.[32] In this early period, the possibility of an attack from the ruling class itself seemed impossible, and those ruled could be managed well enough.

CONSPIRACIES AGAINST THE GOVERNMENT

Running concurrently with this idealized view of a peaceful Rome, however, there are also hints of a constant fear of threats to overthrow the government. Why else would Romulus need three hundred bodyguards, not to mention the existence of ever-present informers? Roman law certainly made provisions for treasonous behavior. The Roman Republican government seemed to be always on the lookout for possible conspiracies. It distrusted any assembly of people that was not in full view of the magistrates.[33] Night meetings were allegedly banned by Rome's earliest law code, the Twelve Tables.[34] Clandestine meetings in private houses were the start of many an attempt to overthrow the government, starting with a move to restore the Tarquins to power in the very first year of the republic, the establishment of a tyranny by Spurius Maelius in 439, and the attempt by patrician Marcus Manlius Capitolinus in 384 BCE to get debt relief for the poor.[35] The authenticity of these stories has been rightly questioned. The overall implication is either that the annalistic tradition reflects an almost neurotic sensitivity on the part of the authorities to the putative danger of conspiracies or that these stories reflect the kind of paranoia felt in later ages that are then retrojected into early republican history.[36] Even the most famous attempt to overthrow the republican government would not happen until 63 BCE, when the plot of Catiline was uncovered by Cicero and reported before the Senate.[37] Even a massive conspiracy such as that had to be detected by private contacts of Cicero's in the absence of any Roman FBI.

Without a police force, a secret service, or even the use of the army within the city limits, other types of countermeasures had to be devised to root out threats to the government and its leading magistrates. The best source for the detection of such conspiracies would in most cases be information supplied by a fellow conspirator or one of his intimates, as happened with Cicero through Fulvia, the girlfriend of one of Catiline's accomplices. Lacking this, another measure was to offer a reward for information leading to the arrest of the conspirators and protection against revenge for the informant.[38] Citizens could receive money; slaves received both liberty and money.[39] We can see how seriously Roman authorities took such a method, because offering liberty to slave informers meant interfering with the property rights of slave-owners not even involved in the case, even though such owners would be compensated financially by the state for the loss of property.[40] This practice would also provide an incentive for the denunciation of masters by slaves, which was a violation of a long-established rule that slaves could not give evidence against their masters in court.[41] Even the testimony of women could be taken seriously when they offered information that might lead to the unmasking of a conspiracy, as in the case of Hispala Faecenina in 186 and Fulvia in 63 BCE.[42] Of course, informers took the risk that the veracity of their statement might be questioned or might implicate them in the plot, as happened to Lucius Vettius in 59 BCE when he reported an alleged attempt on Pompey's life.[43]

The magistrates' role in maintaining order enhanced the mechanisms of social control that underlay the authority of both the magistrates and the Senate—that is, the military discipline that was so important in a society that was constantly at war. Citizen-soldiers were subject to the power of their commanders, who would punish any conduct that could undermine military discipline.[44] It is not surprising, then, that one of the uses of laws against treason was to control rebellious governors who might attempt to march on Rome and effect a change of regime. The *Lex Cornelia de Maiestate* was a Roman law passed under Sulla during his dictatorship from 81–80 BCE. The law was meant to control governors and their forces in the provinces. It stated among other things that a governor could not leave his province during his time in office, with or without his army. It was just four years later that Lepidus left his province in Cisalpine Gaul with his army and marched toward Rome.

The central legal keystone for preventing and punishing treason was the *Lex Maiestatis*. This term refers to several ancient Roman laws throughout the Republican and Imperial periods that dealt with the Roman people, the state, and later the emperor.[45] Most of the offenses defined as treason were exclusively those committed in military service. The crime of *perduellio* defined as a public enemy anyone who bore arms against the state. Traitors were considered public enemies. The law of the Twelve Tables made it punishable by death to communicate with the enemy or betray a citizen to the enemy. The punishment for *perduellio* was denial of "water and fire" (*aquae et ignis*), which meant, in effect, banishment. The crime was tried by two officials (*duumviri perduellionis*) before a special tribunal (*quaestio*) that was, perhaps, the earliest permanent criminal court existing in Rome.[46]

Eventually, *perduellio* gave way to laws of *maiestas*. The *Lex Julia Maiestatis*, passed under either Julius Caesar or Augustus, continued to be the basis of the Roman law of treason until the latest period of the empire.[47] The law seems to originally have dealt chiefly with military matters, as did the earlier laws, but something changed in the Late Republic. Appian writes, "No sword was ever brought into the assembly, and no civil bloodshed ever took place, until Tiberius Gracchus, a tribune of the *plebs* . . . was the first to be killed in political strife; and many others with him."[48] After the murder of the Gracchi, the Roman Republic extended the policing role of the state, the power of certain leaders, and the role of the military in enforcing the state's will. People who were considered a threat to the state were suppressed in a variety of ways. In 121 BCE the Senate gave the consul Opimius special authority to suppress Gaius Gracchus, and his main instrument for doing this was a body of Cretan archers he had at hand. The so-called final decree of the Senate, what the modern scholarly literature calls the *Senatus Consultum Ultimum* (SCU), was used sporadically in the crises of the first century BCE, and it was not unheard of to use mercenary soldiers to enforce it.[49]

THE BREAKDOWN OF THE ORDER

Breaches of public order in the Early and Middle Republic may have been exceptional, but by the Late Republic they had become a regular feature in Roman politics. Violence was increasingly taken for granted as a political tool, and rioting more or less replaced the ballot box.[50] Most distressingly, this violence would come to include assassination of their own leaders. The reasons for this violence have been discussed by historians in great detail elsewhere, but suffice it to say that the cause was a general sociopolitical disintegration that contributed to a disregard for fundamental constitutional conventions.[51] Although there had been violence during the fourth-century Struggle of the Orders, it was the bludgeoning of Tiberius Gracchus and hundreds of his supporters that would be remembered as the "first political dispute since the fall of the monarchy to be settled by bloodshed and the death of citizens."[52] Only a decade later Gaius Gracchus would be murdered, and this time the bodies of thousands of his followers would clog the Tiber. Sulla would organize a reign of terror and the first organized purge of political enemies in Roman history.[53] Violence demonstrated itself at trials, at election time, and even in clashes within the assembly itself. Plutarch writes that Caesar's followers would "defile the rostra with blood and corpses . . . leaving the city to anarchy like a ship drifting about without a steersman." This caused many to suggest that the only cure for the illnesses of the state was monarchy.[54]

The time eventually came, however, when controlling violence through only the traditional display of magisterial authority was no longer possible.

One could no longer silence a crowd by declaring one knew better than the people what the state's interest was—as the consul Scipio Nasica reportedly did in 138 BCE.[55] Although Vergil still echoed the idea that a man with dignity and gravitas should be able to silence a crowd or even a riot, magistrates were allowed ad hoc bodyguards to ensure undisturbed trials, legislation, and elections.[56] Such bodyguards were not supplied by the state, however, and were probably recruited from among the magistrate's clients and personal followers.[57] Magistrates could also appeal for assistance from citizen volunteers.[58]

The Roman Republic functioned well as long as the ruling class adhered to a basic code of conduct. From the time of the Gracchi on, however, there was a growing disregard for traditional norms and conventions. The introduction of violence as a political tool was a radical change, and yet there was still no permanent police force to mediate. This is because despite the deep-rooted social and religious taboos against political violence, its use was being institutionalized by the ruling class; deciding which magistrate would command such a police force would require almost a total reconstruction of the constitution.[59]

The post-Sullan laws on violence made prosecuting violent offenses a little easier.[60] Under Late Republican law, attacks on a magistrate or the occupation of a public place with an armed gang became punishable offenses.[61] By declaring that certain actions had threatened the security of the state, the Senate could allow prosecutions under this law even if political violence did not immediately affect magistrates or public property.[62] Such legislation was aimed at any identifiable organizers of violent action, whether they were politicians or organizers of gangs. One notices that the clauses concerning the carrying of arms with offensive intent could be applied to any participant in the event, and the law criminalized not just the completed act but also intent. This seemed to be aimed especially at urban gangs.[63]

In certain circumstances the carrying of weapons could be prosecuted under the laws against violence. In some extreme situations, carrying weapons of any kind within the city was banned—for example under Pompey in 52, Antony in 47, and the consuls after Caesar's murder in 44 BCE.[64] These republican laws were not aimed at bystanders but were used specifically against politicians and mob organizers.[65] The laws did not prove entirely effective, although a few convictions were achieved after the Catilinarian conspiracy and the events of 52 BCE.[66]

As the government attempted to legitimize the suppression of sedition even by killing its own leaders, its efforts were consistently met by a public that asserted that there was an inviolable right of the Roman citizen to not have a death sentence inflicted on anyone without a formal trial. The Senate might pass an SCU calling on the responsible magistrates to undertake all appropriate measures to preserve the integrity of the state, but senatorial decrees did not have the force of law.[67] The state suffered as the struggle for power between generals such as Marius and Sulla escalated. There were overlapping conflicts between individual magistrates, between magistrates and the Senate, between senators and equestrians, and between old and new citizens, causing the Senate to develop a pattern of crisis management. The government's need to "protect itself" evolved into declaring emergencies, calling up troops, identifying public enemies, and then killing them with impunity. Struggles for power were now decided by military force. Citizens were killed not in open sedition but simply put on a blacklist at the behest of the latest dictator and hunted down.

In the mind of republican leaders there was a line of reasoning that came to justify their acts of political violence, at least to a certain degree: they said they were expressing the legitimate will of the people.[68] They acted when the political order as a whole, meaning especially the Senate's key position, was in jeopardy. The Senate did not have the option of massive repression, and any large-scale action it took would require cooperation from a substantial number of citizens who would perceive the situation as a state emergency.[69] The murder of a tribune in office would certainly elicit an angry reaction on the part of the populace. It was the tribunes who made an effort to identify those responsible for the death of Tiberius Gracchus and his followers, and they were the ones who summoned senators before the people. The senator responsible, Scipio Nasica, later openly admitted his responsibility for their deaths, declaring that he had recognized Gracchus's tyrannical aspirations, but the people had not.[70]

All these trends escalated until the 60s and 50s of the first century BCE, when Rome saw waves of political violence that could no longer be controlled. The government found itself paralyzed by power struggles within the nobility. The post-Sullan era witnessed the development of new methods of organizing the plebs and instituting social protest.[71] In the end, the republican system of maintaining law and order collapsed. The methods of crisis management that had been developed in the late second century no longer worked. The ruling classes were unable to agree on emergency measures, and the urban masses could not be kept in check merely by means of patronage and social control. Ordinary Romans no longer showed the deference to their superiors that had once restrained them from actual confrontation. In extreme situations of popular unrest, public order could be restored only by using the military and sacrificing the fundamental principles of the republican constitution.[72]

During the domination of Caesar and the Triumvirate, those in power, regardless of their response to the actual demands of the people, did not hesitate to employ troops when they needed to put down riots and restore order. This led to the killing of hundreds of people. They could arrest ringleaders on the spot and stage spectacular executions intended to intimidate the masses.[73] Strangely enough, the decision on what to do in each case depended on the calculation of whether the riots were useful for their own ends—for example, to justify declaring martial law—or whether the use of violence might involve a threat to the leaders' own position. The powerful were bound by no scruples as to the use of violence or concern for the civil rights of citizens. Executions were carried out without trial or any pretense to judicial justification.[74] Such actions were viewed by senators, and especially Cicero, as necessary to maintain the state's authority.[75] The use of soldiers in the capital during the civil-war period was not a legitimate method of maintaining public order because, first of all, their use was illegal, and second, the soldiers could not be kept under control. During the famine of 41–39 BCE, for example, soldiers broke into houses and took to robbing and plundering.[76] During the proscriptions of 43, they were simply instruments of the political will of their leaders.[77] The republic's constitutional principles were simply ignored.

THE IDES OF MARCH

The disintegration of the old order and the use of violence to prevent it led to what is perhaps the most renowned assassination in history: the murder of Julius Caesar. As Mary Beard wrote in 2015, "The assassination of Julius Caesar . . . has provided the template, and sometimes the awkward justification, for the killing of tyrants ever since."[78] The deed was carried out not by an angry mob or a deranged killer, but by Rome's most elite citizens. They were senators from some of the most noble families of ancient Rome.[79]

Caesar had recently been declared dictator for life, and senators began to fear he would overthrow the Senate in favor of a tyranny. Kings had been an object of hatred since Tarquinius Superbus had been removed, and to be accused of wanting to be king was a veritable death sentence.[80] Suetonius reports that there were several plots formed to kill Caesar; they were made up of groups of two or three, but eventually they coalesced into one group.[81] Then they debated the problem of method. In one scenario, the conspirators would break into two groups. One would hurl him from the bridge, that is, the temporary bridge of planks called the *pons suffragium* over which voters passed to cast their ballot.[82] As Caesar summoned the tribes out to vote, the second group would be waiting below the bridge and, when Caesar was pushed off, they would kill him. Other plans involved waiting for him on the Sacred Way or at the entrance to the theater. The plan they settled on, and which ultimately succeeded, was to attack him in the Senate on the Ides of March in the Curia of Pompey. This was the conspiracy led by a number of Roman senators including Gaius Cassius Longinus, Marcus Junius Brutus, and Decimus Brutus.

As dictator, Caesar should have had many levels of security around him, with people who could have guarded him against such a conspiracy: lictors, the Spanish Guard, private bodyguards, and regular soldiers.[83] But Caesar's attitude toward these figures was rather hostile. When warned by loyal supporters that he should provide himself with even more bodyguards, he refused. He said nothing was more miserable than having oneself guarded; only someone who was afraid needed that. It was better to look death in the eye than live in constant fear of it. Unfortunately for Caesar, that was exactly what he was about to do, but then he had also said the best death was one that came suddenly and unexpectedly.[84]

The sources are filled with stories of bad omens.[85] Because of her ominous dreams, his wife, Calpurnia, begged him not to go to the meeting. Dio claims that on the morning of the meeting they had to send Decimus to Caesar's house to convince him to come.[86] In this sense, Decimus was the lynchpin of the operation—no Caesar, no assassination.[87] Each ancient author interprets these events differently. Nicolaus of Damascus says Caesar was duped by a brazen and audacious snake, a liar, in Decimus. Plutarch says he put his fate in the hands of another man, which made him a follower, not a leader (and we might add, it is bad internal security). Appian says he was worried about appearances and felt he had to go to the meeting. Suetonius and Dio accuse Caesar of being arrogant because he ignored the warnings of the gods. Appian accuses him of the opposite; he portrays Caesar as the ultimate risk taker. Caesar went *exactly* because it was dangerous; he could not resist one more roll of the dice.[88] The ominous warnings continued. Before a meeting of the Senate could be held, the magistrates had to conduct the customary sacrifices, and the soothsayers had to take the auspices. Even these were unfavorable; several sacrificial victims were offered, but when the entrails were examined the omens were always bad.[89] Once again Caesar's friends talked him into putting off the meeting, but Decimus scorned the superstitious rites and talked Caesar into going in spite of the bad omens.[90] Caesar laughed off most of the omens anyway, since he did not believe in such superstitions. Spurinna had warned him to beware the Ides of March. When he saw Spurinna in the crowd that day, Caesar joked that "the Ides of March have come," but Spurinna replied, "Aye, but not gone."[91]

The assassins had made careful preparations. They had staged gladiatorial games in Pompey's Theater with gladiators provided by Decimus Brutus. Some gladiators were held back in reserve nearby in case their services should be needed.[92] The conspirators also had to neutralize Mark Antony who, having vaguely heard of a plot underfoot from Servilius

Casca the night before the event, went to head Caesar off at the steps of the Forum. The senators separated Caesar from Antony by having an old friend, Trebonius, chat up Antony on the steps.[93]

Much to the dismay of his counselors, Caesar had long since dismissed his Spanish Guard of two thousand men. When he walked through the Forum, he was accompanied by only his twenty-four lictors and a small entourage. As they proceeded, they would have been joined by public officials and a large, diverse crowd of citizens, foreigners, freedmen, and slaves. If the danger to Caesar had come from the general public, this would have been a dangerous milieu, but most of these people were well-wishers, gawkers, or just people trying to hand him petitions or letters. One of these petitioners was Artemidorus of Cnidus, who handed Caesar perhaps the single most important piece of intelligence Caesar could have gotten: he gave Caesar a small scroll and told Caesar to read it himself—immediately. It contained a list of the conspirators who were about to kill him. Caesar tried more than once to read the scroll, but the mob of people kept interrupting him. He still had the scroll in his hand, unopened, when he entered the Senate.[94] The intelligence cycle had therefore been completed, but the ruler did not act on it.[95]

All the senators had gone inside, as had the *capsarii*, the slaves who carried the *capsae*, the baskets containing scrolls. What Caesar did not know was that hidden in these baskets were the daggers the assassins would use. Swords would have been too big to hide and an inappropriate weapon for close-quarter killing. If the baskets were any heavier for it, the slaves said nothing. There was nothing left except for Caesar to go in, around noon.

Caesar had to leave his bodyguard outside, but he still had allies around him in the Senate. Among the new senators he had appointed were centurions who could have jumped to his defense even if they were not armed. The attack on Caesar was, however, well planned. Sixty men could not have approached Caesar at once without raising suspicion. Instead, about a dozen conspirators gathered around the seated dictator, with others poised to join them in a second wave. The five ancient sources are generally in agreement as to what happened, although they sometimes differ in detail.[96] Lucius Tillius Cimber presented Caesar with a petition to recall his brother from exile.[97] The other conspirators crowded around to offer their support. Cimber grabbed Caesar's toga and tried to pull it down from his neck.[98] This was the signal for the others to attack. Caesar shouted, "Why, this is violence!" (*Ista quidem vis est!*).[99] The honor of the first blow went to Casca, who pulled a dagger and aimed at the dictator's neck, but he missed and struck him instead in the chest. After all, Caesar was a moving target.[100]

Four of the five ancient sources agree that Caesar tried to defend himself. Dio says there were too many attackers for Caesar to say or do anything in response.[101] Nicolaus of Damascus says Caesar stood up to defend himself.[102] Plutarch says Caesar turned around and grabbed Casca's dagger by the handle.[103] Appian says he hurled away Casca with great violence and stabbed him with his stylus. No two sources agree on what Caesar shouted during this time if anything at all.[104] The one Latin phrase we do know does *not* appear in the ancient sources is *Et tu, Brute*, a Renaissance invention by Shakespeare (Julius Caesar 3.1.770). Suetonius and Dio claim that after Brutus struck him, he exclaimed (in Greek), "*Kai su teknon*," which means "You, too, child?" but the ancient sources doubt its authenticity, and a lively scholarly debate has raged over what he meant if he did say it.[105]

The conspirators now surrounded Caesar in a circle, as the rest of the blows came fast and furious. Casca's brother Gaius stabbed him in the ribs, Cassius slashed him across the face, Decimus stabbed deep under the ribs, but several of them missed and hit other conspirators instead.[106] Although the ancient sources do not agree on what Caesar said, they all agree, except for Nicolaus of Damascus, on what he did. He pulled his toga over his head.[107]

If anyone wanted to claim afterward that he stabbed Caesar, he either had to move quickly or stab a dead body. Caesar was stabbed twenty-three times, although the physician Antistius would later state that only the second blow was fatal.[108] The conspirators had asked Cicero, who was not in on the conspiracy, to take the lead and bring the rest to order. Instead, panic ensued, and everyone fled, including Cicero. They had originally planned to kill Caesar and drag his body to the Tiber, confiscate his property, and revoke his decrees. Instead, according to Suetonius, they all ran off while Caesar lay there, lifeless, for some time, and finally three common slaves put him on a litter and carried him home, with one arm hanging down.[109]

The plan had worked efficiently. They had killed Caesar on the Ides of March because they knew he would be leaving Rome shortly for more campaigning and they would lose their opportunity. They picked the perfect venue where they could outnumber and overpower him. Although the information had leaked out and too many people knew about the plot, Caesar still walked into the trap. Proof that he had been betrayed by his own friends can be seen in the fact that several of his assassins were named heirs in his will and made guardian of his son, in the event he should ever have one.[110] Hardly any of the assassins survived him by more than three years. Some died natural deaths; some took their own lives with the very dagger they had used to kill Caesar.[111]

As often happens, the result of the assassination could not be fore-
seen by the assassins. Caesar's death did not bring back the republic
but precipitated its end. The interests of an arrogant aristocracy did not
coincide with those of the Roman citizen body as a whole. The Roman
lower classes, with whom Caesar was popular, became enraged that a
small group of aristocrats had sacrificed their leader. The assassins may
have been motivated by the high-sounding cause of "liberty," but, in
reality, this amounted to little more than an excuse for elite self-interest
and the continued exploitation of the underclass. Antony, who had been
drifting apart from Caesar, capitalized on the grief of the Roman mob
and threatened to unleash them on the senatorial elite, perhaps with the
intent of taking control of Rome himself. To his surprise and chagrin,
however, Caesar had named his grandnephew Gaius Octavius his sole
heir, bequeathing him the immensely important name of Caesar as well
as making him one of the wealthiest citizens in the republic. Octavius
became *Gaius Julius Caesar Octavianus*, or Octavian, the son of the great
Caesar, and consequently also inherited the loyalty of much of the Roman
populace. Only eighteen at the time of Caesar's death, Octavian proved to
have considerable political skills and would be the man who created the
military dictatorship they thought would die with Julius Caesar.

THE AFTERMATH

The entire system of internal security in the republic had depended on the
balance between the authority of the upper-class magistrates and the acceptance of that authority by the lower classes. The strong social cohesion
of the Early and Middle Republic was based on *mos maiorum*—the traditions and norms passed down from the ancestors.[112] There was a military
discipline imposed almost permanently on the society as a whole; there
were the sacred aura of the magistracies themselves, the role of the state
cults, and the disciplining effects of patronage. All around them the public saw buildings, statues, triumphs, and funerals that represented the
success of the senatorial system and its ability to keep order over a public
that had no general access to weapons.[113] Perhaps because of their need
for control, the nobility's feeling of vulnerability to conspiracies never
went away. This fear materialized in the last generation of the Roman
Republic when the magistrates were faced with instances of open rebellion. They were stymied because the Senate could not simply order mass
repression.[114] Ironically, the inability of the authorities to cope with major
disturbances resulted from the paralysis in government caused by power
struggles within the nobility itself. The cultural hegemony of the ruling
class was being shaken, and thus the social preconditions of the republi-

can system for securing public order no longer prevailed. The estrangement of large parts of the urban population from the nobility rendered obsolete the system of crisis management that had worked until 133. Once the government started using troops to control the public, the old republican system broke down. The aristocracy was no longer able to cope with genuine mass protest without sacrificing the fundamental principles of republican government.[115] With no police force in the republic, and no measures developed to facilitate law enforcement, the only recourse was to use professional troops, and that led to a military dictatorship.[116]

The unrestrained violence of the Late Republic ended in the death of its leader and the birth of an autocracy. The ultimate irony is that Roman leaders who were not aiming at dictatorship for themselves used force in a way that would destroy the political framework of their position.[117] Conspiracy (*coniuratio*) now came to denote not the overthrow of the republic but the overthrow of one man. The assassination of Julius Caesar became the model for the effective removal of a tyrant, but it did not remove the tyranny. The civil war had brought an end to centuries of aristocratic power sharing and left a single ruler in its place. When the civil war was over, Octavian, as Augustus, would be challenged for trying to establish the same autocracy as Caesar while pretending that power was still shared by the princeps and the Senate. This divorce of appearance from reality was always fraught with danger, as Augustus and his successors were to discover. Each of his successors made the reality a little more visible, and each of them accordingly had, for this very reason, to try to avoid the fate of Caesar.

2

The Augustan System
Fume et Specule

Trying to hold supreme, permanent power was what had gotten Julius Caesar killed; Augustus had no intention of following that pattern. Augustus's challenge was to legitimize his autocratic rule under the forms of traditional republican law and establishing the legal, political, and cultural foundations for a monarchy that would continue after his death.[1] Unlike Caesar, Augustus would not dismiss the *res publica* as "nothing"— a mere name without form or substance—nor was he going to repeat Caesar's mistake of appointing himself dictator for life.[2] He never abolished the institutional apparatus of the republic; he just wanted to stay in power over it. The result was a balancing act, a hybrid creation called a *principate* that had the form of the republic but was headed by a monarch.[3] It was done by smoke and mirrors—*fume et specule*. This is nothing new: hypocrisy is a common weapon of power. As princeps, Augustus had to seem less an autocrat and yet stay totally in charge. He had to make one-man rule a permanent fixture at Rome yet make it seem nonhereditary.[4] This arrangement also made it easier to subvert the government. One did not need to overthrow a republic to gain power; just killing the autocrat would suffice.

The constitutional arrangement known as the principate was a complicated phenomenon, and it continues to inspire heated scholarly debate.[5] Writing about the sources of Augustus's power, both constitutional and military, was a virtual industry in the twentieth century. Yet there seems to be no more of a consensus today than there was in antiquity.[6] Suetonius recognized it as a *novus status*—a new creation cleverly combining one-man rule behind a republican façade.[7] Most traditional republican institutions remained intact, and certainly the presuppositions of republican political life did not disappear overnight, but they were also being transformed into channels of personal power for the emperor.[8] The association of his family with political offices was unprecedented, and a remarkable transformation of Rome was taking place as it went from a state led by elected magistrates whose office was time-limited to one that was dominated by a single family.[9] As A. Wallace-Hadrill has written, "Nobody could doubt monarchy as a *fact* after Actium."[10]

Augustus did not have the option of sweeping away the accumulated tradition of five centuries of republican government, but then again there is little evidence that he was an original thinker or an ideological mastermind. He was a traditional Roman brought up in a conservative, hierarchical culture.[11] It is no surprise that he used traditional terms and ideas to describe his near monopolization of military command. As Fred Drogula showed in 2015, Augustus manipulated the traditional concepts that had shaped and defined provincial command to give himself a radically new but traditional-sounding position as Rome's main commander or *imperator*.[12]

More than anything else, an autocrat's government needs to protect itself and its hold on power. Those who claim Augustus changed very little seem to ignore the fact that the principate had something quite new: a centralized officialdom of its own with new institutions for internal security. Many still believe that Augustus did not need to create any institutions outside of the *mos maiorum* (ancestral customs), because the ones that already existed would serve his purpose well enough.[13] To the contrary, there *were* new institutions in charge of policing, maintaining military control, and guarding the emperor and his regime. The republican system had been simply inadequate for guarding and maintaining an autocratic government. Although the ideology was the "restored republic," the new government was the very opposite: an autocracy with a new security system. All significant political and military powers were placed in the hands of Augustus.[14] For example, to cement his position in 23 BCE, Augustus assumed tribunician power, which was thereafter renewed annually. As both consul and proconsul, he advertised his power to assure the general public that he would protect them. What Augustus and, later, his successors did that was different was to extend this tribunician power to denote heirs to the principate. This power also served as a constitutional expedient by which to manage the Senate.[15] Augustus assumed personal patronage of the entire army, and this army served as a main guardian of internal stability. His highest priority was to ensure that nobody could use military power to challenge or disrupt the regime. While Augustus did an impressive job of wrapping his new arrangements in the cloak of republican tradition, we should not think that he genuinely tricked the aristocracy into believing that they were living in a restored republic. Nor was there room for an all-powerful protector within the old republican system; he placed himself outside of it.[16]

Most scholars recognize that the creation of the principate was gradual. Some still believe there was no intent to put all power in Augustus's hands, but this is wrong.[17] Augustus knew the general outline of what he was planning to do. The fact that he met more opposition than he expected to encounter created crises. Being both lucky and skillful, however, Augustus was able to handle whatever opposition was put in his way and even turned such incidents to his advantage. His plan, nevertheless, always included holding overwhelming force and the overwhelming moral position. His attempts to establish a dynasty, his dependence on the army, his promotion of the cult of personality, particularly in the provinces, and his accumulation of a vast wealth all translated into power. There was no doubt in Tacitus's mind that Augustus was aiming at total power right from the beginning.[18] The emperor's authority could not be challenged. Any attempt to overthrow the emperor could only be done by someone attempting to become the new emperor or acting on behalf of that person, and this meant killing the old emperor.

SPQR: THE SENATE AND THE ROMAN PEOPLE

The political history of the principate is an account of the relationship between the reigning emperor and other individuals or groups who played a role in public life.[19] Although the creation of the principate brought peace and benefited a good many people, most threats to the emperor came from the class that would lose the most under the new system: the old republican nobility. The traditional republic had been run by the *nobiles*, but this type of government had already disappeared by the 80s BCE. Such a system would be an anachronism in a world empire.[20] Julius Caesar knew how outdated and essentially meaningless restoring it would be. All claims to "restoration" are little more than rhetoric, but this does not mean people would not try to regain their traditional roles or use a "restoration of the republic" as a rallying cry. Augustus might portray his career as a continuation of the republic, but several things had changed. The most important of these changes was the relationship between himself and the Senate. For a Roman aristocrat the true republic existed only when the senatorial class shared control, guiding magistrates elected through open competition and changing regularly, so that plenty of people won the chance for high command and profit. This was "liberty" to a senator; and it was now clearly dead. There was no realistic chance of turning back the clock to the "liberty" of earlier times. How, then, did the Senate and the ruling class react to their shrinking role in governing Rome?[21]

Even a sole ruler cannot rule alone. Augustus's security rested on finding a balance between the two extremes of obliterating the nobility altogether or allowing them so much influence that they posed a threat to his survival and power. The encroachment on their traditional prerogatives should have been alarming to senators, even if the name "dictator" or "monarch" was not used by their new leader. Senators were gradually losing their influence, and both they and Augustus were aware of it.[22] Augustus was establishing an autocracy, sanctioned by law, in the guise of the old republic, but he still needed an oligarchy to run his empire.

How would the Senate react to this new reality? Would the senators fight to get their old privileges back? Would they collaborate or become the opposition? The Senate was now composed of a majority of Augustan partisans in whose best interest it was to participate in a conspiracy of reticence about the gap between fact and theory. The new "nobility" comprised a mixed bag of ancient Roman families and new nobles elevated by Augustus from both Roman and Italian stock. From the senatorial perspective, the old idea of communal service was now transformed into service to the ruling emperor, who would be seen as the state incarnate.[23] It was up to the emperor whether or not he wanted to recognize the "ancestral customs" (*mos maiorum*), and Augustus made every effort to portray himself as a champion of tradition and not appear as a dictator.

SECURITY AND THE STATE

Whether one thinks Augustus's power was maintained more by military or constitutional means, both were necessary for maintaining power. His most basic responsibility was to remain in control and safe. Even naked despotism is vulnerable, so if Augustus wanted his rule of the "restored republic" to be permanent and unchallenged, he would have to set up a security system that could make this happen. Augustus's security concerns underlie much of his ideology. Some of Augustus's security came from protections that were already in place during the republic. He added to these by devising a new armory of potent, dangerous weapons with which to control any thought or behavior that might be a threat to his regime. These weapons were kept well polished by his successors. His arsenal included personal bodyguards, secret police, intelligence assets, various laws against the employment of force and against treason, and the perfection of necessary punishments for these crimes. Most importantly, he had to control any political expression that favored a return to the republic or even used that idea as a challenge to his position.[24] Augustus was aware of the fact that too many people wanted him dead, and they could use the cry of "liberty" to justify an assassination attempt. In addition to the people who wanted him dead in the name of saving the republic, there were people who simply wanted him dead in order to take his job.

The first line of Augustus's defense was ideological. From republican times Augustus could draw on the idea of the inviolability of his person. As consul he was protected by lictors, and by holding the tribunician power, he was considered sacrosanct. Next came his political and artistic program to rally support behind his new form of government. He tried to make it seem unthinkable that anyone would oppose the emperor, let alone try to harm him. For this new system of government to succeed, especially his program of rejuvenation, he had to gain not only men's bodies, but their minds. Because of Augustus's eye for detail, he implanted his program in public opinion and tried to prevent the vocal or physical expression of discontent. Upon this base, his successors could build a mighty structure of propaganda and control. Augustus thus shaped a great appeal to public opinion and extended it far beyond the mere security of his personal position, though that aspect was never forgotten.[25]

Still, there were people who were not taken in by this new regime and went so far as to try to eliminate the princeps. Access is the key to assassination, so because of the openness of Roman politics, many senators could get physically close enough to the princeps to do him harm. Senators were theoretically not allowed to carry arms in the house, but they clearly did not always adhere to the rule. Augustus took to wearing a cuirass (breastplate) under his clothes at Senate meetings, although he doubted its real effectiveness. He even had senators searched before they came into his presence.[26] The general public, on the other hand, rarely got to see the emperor except at the games. For most provincials the emperor existed more as an idea or a symbol than as an individual. In the minds of many of his subjects he was almost a fiction; many provincials probably did not even know who the emperor was.[27]

Ideology alone would not protect the emperor. The military and police units would have to be added. These security organs would become the greatest argument for the existence of the change that would cost so many people their lives and liberty. Although no one institution was responsible for all security, each element contributed both to the safety of the emperor and the creation of a radically different Roman state.

POLICING THE EMPIRE

It seems odd to us that republican Rome had no police force, but it went against the ideology of the city-state for one to be subject to armed violence in one's own city.[28] Scholars had previously written that the Roman citizens, like other ancient peoples, relied on self-help or "community self-regulation." In the republic, this had been basically true, but in the empire there were new enforcement tools.[29]

State policing expanded significantly in the first three centuries of the empire, and Augustus began this trend. This was certainly true of military policing, whose expansion was a logical outgrowth of the accretion of the state's security needs in Rome, Italy, and the provinces. Expanded policing was not created to make ordinary people's lives safer or more stable. The police were not established to protect and serve; they were there to safeguard elites and to keep the emperors in power. If they actually benefited others, it was strictly incidental.[30]

Modern policing was an innovation of the eighteenth and nineteenth centuries. Nippel has correctly pointed out that Rome lacked a "strong politically impartial police force" or a "specialized impartial law-enforcement agency."[31] Rome needed state involvement in public order because there was a regime to keep in power, and the emperor's involvement in public order was real and direct. The new regime used soldiers as police to enforce its will, and it was Augustus who started the trend of using soldiers for regular policing purposes. Fuhrmann has shown that Augustus's principate was foundational for the history of Roman imperial policing and public order. Augustus not only had an impact on public order in Rome, Italy, and the provinces during his lifetime but also concretely molded the way his successors would exercise power. We should not make the logical mistake of assuming Augustus meant to set up a full-blown police state; not everything that occurred later was planned by Augustus. The security measures he laid down in Rome and Italy, however, continued growing and eventually became a full-fledged military police apparatus that reached into every province of the empire.[32]

FROM *LICTORES* TO *SPECULATORES*

When Augustus emerged as sole ruler of the empire, he was provided with no publicly employed persons to assist or escort him.[33] Keeping the emperor safe meant being close to the emperor's person. He had to rely on groups already in existence during the republic. One group that followed him in public were the lictors. As we saw in chapter 1, the number of lictors attending a magistrate was a very public measure of a man's importance in republican Rome. This continued into the empire. Augustus maintained the privilege of having "twelve *fasces* at all times and everywhere."[34] As we have also seen, however, these men were not bodyguards. The original purpose of the lictors remained the same: it was to clear the path of the magistrates they served, using their rods of authority to get people out of the way.[35]

For an actual protective force we must look to a new element of the reconstituted army used by Augustus and his first-century successors. It was an elite body of Praetorian horsemen, known as the *speculatores Augusti*, who formed the emperor's bodyguard.[36] The *speculatores* of the first century were called "Augusti" (i.e., the emperor's own) to set them apart from the *speculatores* of the provincial armies.[37] Their special weapon was the *lancea*, a long, knobbed lance that could protect the princeps.[38] They escorted the emperor through the crowded streets and stood behind him at banquets.[39] Their numerical strength is thought to have been around three hundred men.[40] It has been suggested that Augustus did not want to use his German bodyguard (see below) lest he appear to be unleashing "foreigners" against citizens, like some tyrant relying on ruthless barbarians.[41] The *speculatores*, being older men, may have taken greater care toward the emperor, toward other soldiers, and toward the people.[42]

THE GERMAN BODYGUARD

Augustus inherited from Julius Caesar the custom of having a private bodyguard of foreign troops.[43] In Gaul, Caesar had had a guard of four hundred German cavalry.[44] Later he had Spanish bodyguards, whom he famously dismissed shortly before his murder,[45] relying instead on the informal protection of the senators and equestrians. In the end, what this did was facilitate his own assassination.[46] Augustus was not going to leave any such weakness in his security detail. Military bodyguards became the norm for Augustus and his first-century successors.[47] Augustus added a new ring of security by hiring a force of Germanic bodyguards, the famous *Germani corporis custodes*.[48] Since Julius Caesar had first used Germans as an escort, it seems likely Augustus got the idea from him. Augustus preferred Batavians; he had used them against Antony and was much impressed by their skill, especially the cavalry.[49] He probably had his legate in Lower Germany pick them from allied tribes who had proven their horsemanship and fighting skills.[50]

The *Germani* were quite separate from the Praetorians, and they have been referred to as the emperor's "private militia." Little is known about their organization. The five hundred bodyguards were formed up in five centuries, each one commanded by a centurion.[51] Tacitus claims that

Germani were used as bodyguards because they were foreigners and therefore had no personal investment in Roman politics.[52] During the Julio-Claudian period the *Germani* and the Praetorians complemented each other in the task of ensuring the emperor's safety. Perhaps Augustus felt safer when protected by two rival corps rather than one.[53] Augustus placed the fort of the *Germani* north of the Tiber, far from the Forum and the Senate, but this did not disguise the fact that Rome now had a single ruler, and this ruler had a military guard.

The *Germani* remained an invaluable element of internal security for Augustus until the Varian disaster in 9 CE, when the Cherusci tribe wiped out three Roman legions at Kalkriese.[54] According to Suetonius, Augustus disbanded his German bodyguard because their nearness to the emperor made them a threat, should any one of them waver in their allegiance to Rome as had the Cherusci.[55] Some of the *Germani* certainly remained and are well attested in inscriptions and literature. The unit reappeared in 14 CE, when it was sent north with Drusus to assist in quelling the revolt in Pannonia after the death of Augustus.[56] The fact that the ancient sources rarely mention Augustus's horse guard may be because the princeps wanted to keep such a monarchical institution in the background.[57] Tyrants of old had used their bodyguards to oppress the populace. Cicero rightly complained when Caesar came to visit him with two thousand armed men; the sheer number was enough of an intimidation to any senator or group of senators.[58] So although they are not attested to as taking an active role in events, their presence must have had an appreciable effect on the atmosphere of the court, and their importance can be seen when Nero withdrew them from his mother, Agrippina.[59]

THE PRAETORIAN GUARD

Perhaps the most famous feature of the new regime, from the point of view of internal security, was the Praetorian Guard. It became the most blatant symbol of the military force that sustained imperial power.[60] Although Augustus created this elite unit of soldiers to protect himself and his family, the idea of an imperial Praetorian Guard was not entirely his invention. Since the Middle Republic, commanders on campaign had selected and pulled together a bodyguard. By the first century BCE, the term *cohors praetoria* was being applied to this type of unit.[61] There is an important distinction, however, between the republican guard and what Augustus created. Under the republic such troops were not allowed into the capital, but under Augustus the Praetorians were made a permanent force, and he kept a large number of them in Rome itself; this signaled the beginning of a new era.[62] This corps of Praetorians would become one of the most controversial parts in the story of Roman internal security as their functions were transformed from guarding to policing. The Guard, and especially its prefect, became major players in the safety or the removal of Julio-Claudian emperors.[63] Their gradual politicization is usually given as a reason for occasional disloyalty of a prefect or a ranking officer in the early empire.

Right from the beginning, the Praetorians were marked out as an elite force; they were the most privileged group in the military.[64] The privileged position of a new armed guard was probably not lost on the government of Rome nor its population; the Guard was given double pay as soon as the formal vote for Augustus's powers as princeps occurred in 27 BCE.[65]

Augustus initially directed the Praetorian Guard himself, but in 2 BCE he delegated the task instead to two equestrian prefects. Having two prefects was seen as a safeguard against corruption and plotting, although, as Nero would later find out, this simply did not work. It only meant that an extra man had to be co-opted into any plot.[66] The rationale for moving control over the Guard from the emperor to the prefects is unknown, but surely it has something to do with having to delegate the day-to-day command of the Guard to someone else because of the sheer number of duties the emperor had himself and the many activities with which the Praetorian Guard were involved. Orders probably still came from the palace, and the emperor maintained overall control of the Guard since it would always remain his personal army.[67] The loyalty of the Praetorian cohorts to the emperor is also shown by the inclusion of the emperor's image on their standards. This was not done by the legions, where the image was carried separately.[68]

Because this was a new institution, there would be adjustments to both practice and form, but it is clear the position would continue to grow in importance.[69] In this early period, the power later associated with the Guard was still developing. The position was always as much political as military, if for no other reason than the way these people were chosen: by patronage.[70] We do not even know if the prefect was armed in the presence of the emperor. The relationship between the emperor and the prefect had to be close, and the prefect had to be a man he trusted.[71] Under Augustus, the prefects accompanied the princeps into the Senate. Tiberius later abolished the practice, but Claudius reinstated it.[72] This is one of the reasons Augustus chose equestrians for the job; their modest status made them less likely to be ambitious enough to make a move on the throne. This may also be the reason there were two prefects: to keep power from being concentrated in the hands of one man.[73]

Although their primary function was to provide protection for the emperor and his family, the Praetorians were also assigned other duties relating to imperial security. Augustus built their force up into a formidable army of nine cohorts, each a thousand strong. He kept three cohorts in the city and billeted the others in neighboring towns.[74] This meant that not only did the emperor have a force to guard the palace but he also had an army big enough to guard the city of Rome and its environs in case he needed to travel. Its day-to-day purpose was to reinforce the emperor's control of Rome's one million inhabitants. The Guard could also be used as a strategic military force sent to deal with problems where other measures had proven ineffective or where there was a need for covert activity.[75]

Having a military force this large so close to the capital meant that Augustus could use the Praetorians for any administrative job that required large numbers of trained personnel. They could fight fires, provide security and crowd control for the games, guard the palace, or conduct political espionage.[76] They could be used for covert activities from time to time. Although they wore their formal regalia for ceremonial occasions, they could also work in civilian clothing while still armed.[77] In its early history, a division of their own *speculatores* became specifically associated with such clandestine activities.[78]

The Guard could be used in whatever ways the government deemed necessary, because Augustus was in control and he relied on the military to support this new structure.[79] Most importantly, the Praetorians were at the heart of the security around the palace, with the emperor himself giving the watchword to the cohort on duty. They guarded him in the city of Rome, and they accompanied the emperor on all his journeys and military campaigns.[80]

We know very little about the day-to-day workings of the Praetorian Guard during the reign of Augustus, mostly because we lack any contemporary and comprehensive source for his reign. Nowhere in Augustus's *Res Gestae*, his list of achievements, does he mention founding the Guard, but this was because Augustus was good at hiding how his power was maintained.[81] Since keeping troops in the city was a relatively new phenomenon, the lack of information about the responsibilities of the Praetorian Guard in running the new security state should not be surprising.[82] We do know that from Tiberius onward, emperors attended the Senate's meetings with its official permission and only in the company of Praetorian officers.[83] An emperor who visited a private residence without a military escort was demonstrating his trust in his host.[84]

Not only was it important to guard Augustus's life, but, since he was trying to introduce a new dynastic system, he also had to ensure the succession by keeping his heirs safe. Separate detachments were assigned to princes of the imperial dynasty, and the new practice of deploying young men of the imperial house in pairs to different parts of the empire meant these potential heirs had to be kept safe no matter where they were.[85]

Certainly from the point of view of his personal safety, the emperor was so well protected by his Praetorian Guard that only persons familiar with court procedure had any chance of delivering a personal attack. They maintained the security perimeter around the palace, closely escorted him within his residence, especially in formal situations, and would have guarded his private rooms.[86] Because of this proximity to the emperor, the Guard and its prefects occupied a key position in the imperial government. They could both keep the emperor safe or become involved in plots to remove him. As the empire progressed, the Praetorian Guard would find itself involved, or at least suspected of involvement, in a number of court intrigues and conspiracies. As the following chapters will show, the loyalty of the Praetorian Guard as a whole was especially at issue when the succession to the throne was disputed.[87] The history of the Praetorian Guard became closely intertwined with the early history of the principate. The presence of a considerable number of troops in Rome whose loyalty was to Augustus, and Augustus alone, was a clear indication that the old republic was gone and something new and imperial had taken its place.[88] With this kind of control and the protection of the Praetorian Guard, how could anyone expect to hatch a plot against an emperor in an atmosphere like this? And yet they did—quite successfully.

THE URBAN COHORTS

The ring of security did not end with the *Germani* and the Praetorian Guard. Augustus supplemented the nine Praetorian cohorts with three more urban cohorts. They were numbered in sequence with the Praetorians (I–IX), the urban cohorts being X, XI, and XII.[89] They were not as privileged as the Praetorians, receiving only half the pay. This would make them intermediate in pay and in terms of service somewhere between the Praetorians and the legionaries.[90] The size of an urban cohort is uncertain, but scholars have suggested that a figure of five hundred seems plausible.[91] During the first century the urban cohorts were under the command of the city prefect, the *praefectus urbi*. Augustus tried several experiments that met with senatorial opposition. The office was made a permanent institution as late as the last year of Augustus or the early years of Tiberius. The position was usually filled by a senator of consular rank, but granting the city prefect command over three legions was probably not just a political gesture toward the Senate and the nobility.[92] Augustus wanted to give the magistrate responsible for the security of the city an effective means of control, ready at hand, especially when the emperor was not present.[93] Whether the emperor closely supervised the urban prefects' activities or allowed them latitude varied from time to time.[94]

The exact relationship between the urban cohorts and the Praetorian cohorts in Rome's security scheme is also unclear to us. Were the urban cohorts created just to provide more policing support? This might have been necessary when the emperor was out of Rome and had taken the Praetorians with him.[95] Some Praetorians always accompanied the emperor out of town, but the soldiers of the urban cohorts usually remained in the city.[96] There is just not sufficient evidence, however, to prove that the urban cohorts were the day-to-day police force of Rome.[97]

As with the Praetorians, there was a very close, personal relationship between the emperor and his urban troops. This can be seen in the oath taken by the soldiers in the city. Because of their proximity to the emperor, the Praetorian and urban cohorts were both expected to take a special oath that confirmed their allegiance to the emperor and his household in a way that bound them more directly to him than were the provincial armies.[98]

We should not think of the Praetorian Guard and urban cohorts in imperial Rome as modern police forces. They did, however, become an important element in the proliferation of institutional security forces, especially later in the second and third centuries. It is also possible that the new enforcement agencies under Augustus had more comprehensive duties and executed them more efficiently than our sources reveal.[99] Still, in comparison to the Republican period, a dramatic change had occurred with respect to the government's capacity to control the population with a permanently available force of militarily trained and disciplined men. What level of control they exerted probably depended on the emperor's perception of the situation. An emperor concerned about his popularity with the masses would be reluctant to resort to repression of popular demonstrations unless he considered his own position to be in jeopardy. Augustus's first attempt to create a police chief or city prefect to control Rome collapsed. The first holder of the position, M. Valerius Messalla Corvinus, resigned the position after three days because he claimed he did not know how to exercise a power that was so contrary to traditional citizen spirit.[100] But future holders of the office did not have any such qualms, and the position continued to grow in importance. The urban prefecture became one of the top posts of a senatorial career.

THE *VIGILES*

Yet another organization founded by Augustus to enhance the security of the city of Rome was the *vigiles*, a permanent fire brigade that provided a necessary service to a city that was constantly endangered by fires in the urban slums.[101] The *vigiles* started out as a body of six hundred state slaves whom Augustus had set up in 22 BCE and placed under the command first of the aediles and later of the *vicomagistri*.[102] Augustus's initiative may have been a reaction to the activities of the ambitious aedile, Egnatius Rufus (see chapter 3), who had achieved particular popularity by employing a privately recruited firefighting squad.[103] The *vigiles* achieved their final form after a devastating conflagration in 6 CE. The new organization was designed as a paramilitary corps of seven cohorts of night watchmen (four thousand men, total) distributed so that each cohort was responsible for two of the regions of the city.[104] These men were no longer slaves but were recruited among freedmen, who then qualified for Roman citizenship after six or, later, three years of service. Their command was entrusted to an equestrian prefect—the so-called *praefectus vigilum*.[105] The important point here is the movement away from the traditions of a city-state, which relied on popular self-help, to a militaristic solution that put force into the hands of a nonelected officer.[106]

In addition to fire prevention, the *vigiles* had other duties They supervised building regulations and obligatory protective measures such as going on regular nightly patrols and pursuing thieves or runaway slaves.[107] Their numbers were not large enough to perform such functions regularly to any significant degree.[108] In an overcrowded city with a low technological standard of firefighting that precluded the effective use of water, they would have been busy enough with their tasks as a fire brigade without having to take on regular policing duties.

Although their original charge had nothing to do with protecting the emperor, the *vigiles* could be used by the princeps as an internal security force. Although Augustus may have thought of employing the *vigiles* as a sort of riot police if necessary, we have no evidence that they were really used in this way during his reign.[109] Still, any security force can be called up in emergencies on an ad hoc basis, especially when the security of the emperor is at stake. The best example of this came in 31 CE during the reign of Tiberius, when the *vigiles* were ordered to secure the Senate's proceedings against the attempted coup of the Praetorian prefect, Sejanus. This was done because of a lack of confidence in the urban cohorts' readiness to oppose the Praetorians.

DELATORES

Although without a formal intelligence service, Augustus still needed to discover what was going on in Rome and to detect plots against his life or family members. Perhaps the most controversial of the tools he had at his disposal were informers and accusers called *delatores* and *accusatores*.[110] Although the sources depict them as unique to the early principate, they

would have been at home in the republic or the Late Empire as well, because when a government needs intelligence, people will appear who can
provide it, especially if they are well paid.[111]

The *delatores* are often portrayed as appearing because of the oppressive rule of one man—that is, as a group of vicious informers who would
attack anyone they suspected as disloyal toward their emperor. Their
reputation was so bad that even modern historians have avoided discussing them until recently, and the picture we get of them is frequently
distorted.[112] More recently, however, they have gotten more scholarly
attention that has put them in their larger historical, social, and political context.[113] The political and legal structure under which prosecutors
worked changed under the new autocratic government. What was lacking in the new system was a state system of prosecution, and this is the
gap that allowed private accusers and informers to flourish.[114]

Informing has always been a morally dubious undertaking, and those
who indulged in this type of activity do not fare well in the sources.[115]
Yet, as Steven Rutledge has pointed out in his study *Imperial Inquisitions*,
one need not postulate a sinister world filled with amoral men who acted
as instruments of constant repression. The picture we are handed of *delatores* comes from senatorial sources like Tacitus, and they are as much
a literary creation as a reality. *Delatores* get a bad name because they
are portrayed in Tacitus as snitches, social climbers who informed for
money, and generally people of lower social status than the people they
accused.[116] These people were not, however, back-alley snitches (the CIs
of TV police procedurals) and lowlifes. These were upper-class Romans,
senators even, who collaborated with the regime because they felt that
their own interests were closely tied to the imperial court. Some of them
were considered great orators in their own right.[117] In this context, informing could be a positive thing. It was a means of social advancement and a
tool used by prosecutors throughout Rome's history, not just a source of
malicious accusation.[118]

Volunteer informing against suspected offenders was extensive.[119]
These people provided information on treasonable activities and, in return, would receive a portion of the guilty man's estate upon conviction.
The apex of the legislation that enabled such public accusation came from
Augustus, not Caligula or Nero.[120] There seems to have been an entire
web of imperial agents under Augustus. Indeed, informers were just one
of many levels of intelligence gathering available to the new emperor.
Trying to trace how this machine worked after 27 BCE, however, is quite
difficult.

Augustus was generally popular, and he did not have to spy on the
level of, say, a Herod of Judaea, but there are hints of secret agents scattered at home and abroad. Maecenas, as prefect of the city, probably used

agents of this type to ferret out the plot of Lepidus the Younger, "quietly and carefully concealing his activity" so that he could crush it without any disturbance.[121] Augustus's secret agents did more than carry intelligence; they were also authorized to assassinate enemies of the state. During the civil war, Augustus had used men to dispatch undesirable persons with a minimum of fuss. The tribune Offilius, who stirred up the soldiers after the victory of Mylae in 36 BCE, for example, disappeared the next day, and "it was never known what became of him."[122] Another opponent, the praetor Q. Gallius, was accused of trying to assassinate Octavian. He disappeared at sea in 43 BCE, ostensibly on his way to Antony, but a hostile rumor asserted that he never made it to his ship alive.[123]

Being an accuser was a dangerous job. The *delatores* inspired enough fear to deter their enemies from any action aimed at their ruin, but they were safe only insofar as they kept the emperor's favor.[124] Tacitus gives the example of Tiberius, who grew weary of the *delatores*, so, if new ones presented themselves, he would sacrifice the old ones.[125] They were too close to the emperor to be friends with anyone else, and thus the death of the emperor would put them in immediate peril.[126] In fact, the fall of anyone in power who had protected them could seal their fate. Inspiring fear to make a living was a very dangerous game because that fear could often backfire on them. When Sejanus fell, it was the senators who gloated over disposing of his henchmen, whom they had dreaded for years.[127]

Who exactly posed a threat to the emperor is highly debatable. People perceived as the "opposition" were prosecuted for libel, magic practices, and astrological consultation, although these did not seem to pose an imminent threat to the emperor's life. Actual sedition (*maiestas*) was another story since this did pose a threat to the stability and security of the state.[128] A charge of treason discouraged others from coming to the defense of the accused. A *delator* could also interrogate the defendant's slaves and use evidence extracted under torture, which made it very likely *something* would be found. Furthermore, juries would be reluctant to acquit someone accused of high treason.[129]

Thus *delatores* were not just people who made malicious accusations for profit and power at the expense of others. They were a necessary part of the government's system of law enforcement and prosecution; they were a function of the executive branch of government.[130] As long as there were threats against the emperor and his regime, an emperor would be willing to pay handsomely for information. There are always people willing to serve that purpose and who will portray their behavior as patriotic.[131] How one views such people depends on where one stands. To the emperor they were a source of needed intelligence and an important part of the internal security apparatus. From the point of view of the Senate, on the other hand, *delatores* were an oppressive institution and one of the instruments emperors used to eliminate the old republican aristocracy. The emperor faced many forms of opposition and resistance from this class, and he needed to detect and eliminate any conspiracies that might turn into actual threats to his life. The need for state security and for the oversight of the workings of government and its members meant that there would always be a need for the service of prosecutors, not just during the early principate.[132]

TREASON LAWS

Another mechanism Augustus used to eliminate any threats against his position was the law against *maiestas*. Any attempt to kill the emperor was, of course, treason, but under Augustus the definition of treasonous activity was expanded.[133] To break an oath by Augustus, to deface his image, to violate the sanctuary of his statue was to show disrespect to his greatness, his *maiestas*. Although Augustus was famous for ignoring such slights, at the grassroots level, this accusation had enormous consequences. If you could show that your rival was guilty of abusing Augustus, you could show he was an enemy of the whole order that depended on Augustus. Disrespect to the divine *maiestas* was the ultimate treachery. The charge was rapidly assimilated to the existing legislation against contempt for the majesty of the Roman people.[134]

The offenses specifically covered by this law were logical parts of state security: the raising of a force against the state; the killing of a magistrate or of a person holding power (*imperium* or *potestas*); the support of public enemies; the encouragement of unrest in the army, including desertion and flight; plus a great many other such matters.[135] The law was couched in terms of offenses against the Roman people. Since Augustus was the representative of the people, the concept of *maiestas* could be used to protect his personal position. He was endowed by the law with various public powers, especially those of the sacrosanct tribunes. We know from Seneca the Elder that various men argued forcefully against this critical point, but their effort to secure the limitation of *maiestas* to issues of state security was foredoomed to failure.

Both in scope and in means of punishment, the concept of *maiestas* was rapidly expanded under Augustus into an all-inclusive tool whereby he could suppress any type of criticism of his essentially autocratic system.[136] *Maiestas* laws became a mighty weapon in the arsenal of absolutism throughout the history of the empire. *Delatores* played a large part in implementing these laws.[137] Under later emperors the penalties grew harsher, and the laws' scope broadened to cover a wide variety of offenses, not the least of which was disloyalty to the supreme representative of the Roman state. Both Tacitus and Dio depict excessive *maiestas* prosecutions as instruments of terror by which the emperors cowed their opposition, real or imagined.[138]

KEEPING THE GODS ON OUR SIDE: THE IMPERIAL CULT

A great deal of the epigraphic and literary evidence from the empire attests to the fact that the world seems to have been waiting for a savior, and the Romans were encouraged to believe they had found one in Augustus. Simon Price has written that "the imperial cult, along with politics and diplomacy, constructed the reality of the Roman Empire."[139] In the west, where there was no tradition of ruler worship, there was the imperial cult that simply focused on loyalty to Rome. In the eastern provinces, people went even further in consecrating the new emperor.[140] They were worshiping a ruler who protected humankind by his acts. He was a "benefactor" and a "savior." He kept the empire safe and he, in turn, needed to be kept safe. The suggestion is that he was protected by a divine force and thus inviolable. The worship of the Caesars could be used to promote political loyalty and stability, but was it of any use in internal security? Although it was a great influence in the arts and letters of the empire, the imperial cult probably did little to keep the emperor safe.[141] Since emperors could accept or refuse cult worship as they wished, religious devotion was not an indispensable part of imperial power.[142] The imperial cult was driven by the subjects of the Roman Empire, not by the emperor. Expressions of devotion to the emperor might reflect loyalty, but they were not a very effective means of protection. It would not make him as safe as, say, a Chinese emperor, whose mandate from heaven meant killing him was a threat to society as a whole.[143]

CONTROLLING LOYALTY

As if all these layers of security were not enough, protecting the new regime went beyond just hiring more security forces. Augustus had to maintain concentric circles of loyalty within the population itself. Job number one was to keep the upper classes busy and loyal.[144] Augustus controlled them by packing the Senate with his supporters. The more recalcitrant nobles had been removed by civil war and proscriptions, and those who were left got the message quickly. The lower classes could be diverted with bread and circuses. His greatest support, however, came from the middle classes of Italy, who had risen economically into powerful positions during the previous two centuries.[145] This group had no problem with giving up the political liberty it had never really enjoyed any way. Augustus admitted new men from this class into the senatorial aristocracy.[146]

Along with the concept of the inviolability of his person came his program to rally support behind his new form of government. He tried to make it seem unthinkable that anyone would oppose the emperor, let alone try to harm him. For this new system of government to succeed, especially his program of rejuvenation, he had to gain not only men's bodies but their minds as well.[147] Because of Augustus's eye for detail, he implanted his program in public opinion and tried to prevent the vocal or physical expression of discontent. Upon this base, his successors could build a mighty structure of propaganda and control. Augustus manipulated public opinion and extended his control far beyond the mere security of his personal position, though that aspect was never forgotten.

Although Augustus's power was based on his control of the military and policing forces, the importance of rhetoric and symbolism should not be underestimated.[148] Like all autocracies the Augustan regime penetrated intimately into the social life, thought, and personal morality of his subjects.[149] Augustus's message was addressed to all levels of society from slaves, freedmen, and provincials to the upper classes of Rome and Italy. Augustus was able to exert control over knowledge in just about every major area of Roman cultural activity: religion, the calendar, public speaking, the law, and even the proper use of Latin.[150] The new message of the Augustan program was disseminated through Roman society at many different levels of understanding including sculpture, architecture, coinage inscriptions, and literature.[151] Augustus's skillful use of all these avenues of communication has been pointed out before by scholars in their many detailed analyses of the literature and art of the Augustan Age.[152] Augustus's talent was in his deft interweaving of himself into the patriotic and religious institutions of Rome and the empire, and other subtle devices. Through poets and artists he carefully founded his legend of Rome.[153]

Augustus controlled the message not only through his own direction but also by squelching any contrary message. He could not control what his contemporaries wrote, but he could burn what he did not like. The first thing an autocrat does is to limit freedom of speech, and Augustus was no exception.[154] Augustus's government, like most modern governments, "habitually and effectively suppressed general circulation of embarrassing, unpalatable facts," as Dio Cassius makes very clear.[155] This was a one-way imposition of the rules from the top, and only Augustus knew the rules of where the limits were.[156] The downside to allowing people to communicate, coordinate, and interact freely is the possibility that they will protest the current political order. Augustus would not tolerate direct opposition, and he was also sensitive about his own dignity since this was one of the main bases of his position and had political ramifications. Augustus had to remain above the fray, untouchable, and, above all, revered. One should not even think of hurting him or his regime. Seneca pointed out that things were not so bad in the early empire that a slight against the emperor's dignity would cost someone his life, but "it would cause him trouble."[157] Anything that undermined the image of the imperial house as a unified and model family could not be tolerated.[158] Public admiration for Caesar's assassins could become a death sentence for a senator. Asinius Pollio wrote about Augustus, "It is not easy to write against one who can proscribe you." This line was remembered for centuries.[159]

There is still disagreement over how much censorship actually occurred under Augustus. Anthony Everitt, in his biography of Augustus, claimed that "speech remained free."[160] Ronald Syme, on the other hand, spoke of "stern measures of repression against noxious literature" and "public bonfires."[161] Augustus took strict measures to prevent what he regarded as scurrilous writings, ordering the burning of books and the punishment of some authors. Dio, who records this, does not mention any writers by name and still less suggests that they were composing works against Augustus or his family, but Seneca tells us the first person to suffer the destruction of books by fire was the free-speaking advocate and historian Titus Labienus. It may be that this was also when Cassius Severus was tried and condemned under the *maiestas* law. Labienus committed suicide, and Severus was exiled first to Crete and then to the desolate island of Serriphos in the Aegean.[162] Augustus tightened the conditions under which exiles could live after being removed from Rome. He grew harsher in his treatment of those who had not complied with his notion of how Rome should be or how a Roman should behave. Woe to the orator who strayed very far from what the emperor wanted to hear.[163] The iron fist did not have to be visible. Augustus had so many people in public life trying to please him—people who were willing to make his agenda their own—that he could achieve his purposes indirectly without exercising too much of his authority. Still, Dio Cassius, two centuries after Augustus, quite correctly judged that never again did Rome have complete freedom of speech after the Battle of Philippi.[164]

POLICING THE MOB AND THE USE OF FORCE

Augustus's security reforms in Rome have left a clear mark.[165] It was Augustus who started the trend of using soldiers for regular policing purposes.[166] Augustus's program was aimed at controlling the population. The citizen body might be rabble in Augustus's eyes, but he had to keep them safe and obedient and, from the point of view of personal security, away from himself, especially if they were in an agitated state.[167] He did this through public works, *largesses,* games, festivals, amnesty, food in abundance, and safety from invaders and evildoers. While soldiers had been present as spectators at the games in the Late Republic, Augustus introduced a formal separation between soldiers and the populace.[168] We are not entirely clear about whether this division refers to the seating arrangements in the theater (i.e., soldiers seated apart from the rest of the crowd) or, given the use of Praetorians as security, to a command post being established for those present to maintain order. Post-Augustan evidence and commonsense security would point to the latter. The presence of soldiers in the theater as the imperial bodyguard, later developing into a full-blown security detail, necessitated physically separating the audience from the Praetorians.[169]

The theater was a place where violent activity often broke out, and the presence of soldiers would have been useful for keeping order, especially if the emperor were present.[170] Valerius Maximus, writing during the reign of Tiberius, refers to the theater as a military camp (*urbana castra*) in the city, indicating that soldiers were highly visible.[171] Under Tiberius there was an increase in violence in the theater and, on one occasion, members of the audience were killed as well as Praetorians and a centurion. A tribune of the guard was injured trying to keep order and stop any further attacks on the magistrates present.[172] It is clear from incidents like these that Praetorians were there to take part in the policing of the crowd, since by then security at these venues was one of their administrative duties.[173]

Augustus's expanded use of the army and police, particularly in internal matters, shows the changing relationship between the state and the use of violence. The unorganized masses, lacking popular leaders of stature, were powerless against well-armed troops loyal to the ruler. As long as the army was loyal to the emperor, it was not difficult to spread confusion among the agitated masses and disperse them with rods and drawn swords.[174] There was never a full-blown riot that stormed the palace, so unless Augustus put himself near a crowd at a public performance, he was generally safe.

Although the police system inaugurated by Augustus reduced the intensity of the public demonstrations, it could not wipe them out entirely. In 22 BCE, a great popular protest occurred over the perception that Augustus was becoming dictator for life. The populace did not care about the subtleties of his compromise with the Senate. He might call himself "first citizen," but they saw through the charade. Augustus was able to stop the outbreak only by a dramatic public appeal in which he tore open his toga and threatened to commit suicide.[175] His popularity won out over their democratic sensibilities.

THE NEW ROME

There are many differing opinions about Augustus, who he was, what his intentions were, or what kind of government he founded. There were already differing interpretations of Augustus's reign in the first century CE.[176] Historians, both ancient and modern, have told hostile tales of Octavian's cruelty or Augustus's hypocrisy and lack of scruples. What matters for this study is not his personality, his personal morals, or his intentions but simply that he crafted a system of one-man rule, and this required him to protect himself and his regime.[177]

The most fundamental change in the new Roman world under Augustus was that the state—that is, the business of the Senate and people of Rome—was now guided by one person.[178] Augustus's policy was recognized for what it really was—the establishment of a hereditary monarchy built around his family.[179] Although the dictatorship of Julius Caesar in 44 BCE and that of Sulla in the late 80s put power in the hands of one man, even Sulla had walked away from his dictatorship. Augustus and his successors were permanent monarchs.[180] No previous Roman since the time of the kings had been in a position to appoint a successor or even thought of doing such a thing. The great figures of the Roman Republic certainly promoted the interests of their families, but there was no question of a succession of the sort that caused such problems for Augustus in the last twenty years of his life. Although the dynasticism of his early years was tentative, his intentions were clear. Augustus founded a Roman monarchy far more autocratic than Julius Caesar aimed at, and this second Caesar would not be eliminated through carelessness of his own security, as had been the first.[181]

That people opposed him is not in question; therefore, retaining power and keeping away potential assassins was Augustus's first priority. A man who wears a cuirass under his toga to prevent himself from being assassinated knows there are plots afoot.[182] And a man who was rumored to have personally torn out the eyes of a senior official whom he suspected of plotting against him certainly had a very personal sense of his own security.[183] Augustus introduced a series of institutions guaranteed to keep the Roman state stable and prevent the assassination of the emperor. He obviously succeeded because he ruled for forty years and outlived his daughter's grandson.[184]

Augustus may have claimed that he remained in his supreme position by "universal consent," but the fact was he ruled because he commanded large numbers of seasoned troops and had already demonstrated that he would not hesitate to use them to protect himself. The law can place a man at the head of the government and even maintain him there, but it cannot make people accept him emotionally. The security services must protect him against those who would remove him in spite of the law. The price to be paid for this new security was a large military force present in the capital. Although we cannot always identify which unit was operating, we can certainly state that the imperial presence always had a military aspect to it. We do not even know the precise functions of the different units that accompanied him, carried messages, carried out executions, or brought persons to the emperor.[185] Even estimating conservatively, by 6 CE Augustus had nearly ten thousand security personnel policing Rome, approximately one per hundred inhabitants of the city. All of this policing was carried out in the interests of maintaining those in power, not of protecting the weak or making Rome safe for tourists.[186] The constant presence of armed soldiers had an important influence on what it meant to appear before the emperor and lent an increased immediacy and force to any sign of imperial displeasure. Their presence must have added fear, and they would, of course, play an important role in the accessions of Claudius in 41 and Nero in 54.

The new security apparatus set up by Augustus was designed to keep in check the strong sentiment among the upper classes against absolute rule and make quite sure that Augustus did not suffer Caesar's fate. He lived long enough to accustom people to the idea of the dynastic succession without ever having to admit he was a king. Augustus devised a formula by which he could reconcile the members of the ruling class to cooperate with him in "maintaining this new order as servants of the republic and heirs to a great tradition, not as mere lieutenants of a military leader or subservient agents of arbitrary power."[187]

Recognizing the importance of the senatorial class as a political elite that spawned the opposition to the emperors is an important concept when discussing internal security. It will remain a theme throughout the Julio-Claudian era.[188] Augustus could not rule by himself; he needed the cooperation and help of a new ruling class. One elite was replaced with another elite as the old *nobiles* were replaced by a new governing class from Rome, Italy, and the provinces.[189] This resulted in a political and social transformation of the Roman Empire. A large part of the governing class had to be complicit. What opposition dared stand up against them would be ruthlessly eliminated. Even their friends would remain silent when someone ran afoul of the powerful. The final years of Augustus's principate had seen a general strengthening of the power of the princeps at the expense in particular of the Senate.[190] Augustus needed either the cooperation of the Senate or its complete subjection. Augustus went for the former; Nero went for the latter.

Most people went along with Augustus because they had survived decades of civil war and they wanted peace. The principate was supposed to bring stability with it. The vast majority of people wanted safety for themselves, their families, and their property. They wanted protection from their enemies, both domestic and foreign. They wanted some guarantee against famine, a promise of economic success, and to be allowed to get on with their own lives.[191] The upper classes may not have regarded the "restored Republic" as anything but a "fraudulent façade," but they had no choice but to reconcile themselves to it.[192] All physical defiance of Augustus's power would fail. The power of the throne had become, in the words of A. H. M. Jones, "ubiquitous and irresistible."[193] The *nobiles* who had lost the most had to suffer in bitter impotence, but they could get vindictive.

Once the government sets up a security apparatus, it very rarely, if ever, gets rid of it. Augustus set the precedent of using soldiers to enhance security in the city and around himself. In Rome and Italy, emperors would continue to use military and police forces to maintain their own power. It does not matter really whether one believes the empire was kept together by brute force or loyalty, by the image of the emperor as benefactor of his people or by propaganda. The emperor's new system worked and survived his reign.[194] Seneca may have idealistically believed that "an emperor is kept safe by benefaction: he has no need for guards—weapons he keeps for decoration,"[195] but, as Jon Lendon has realistically suggested, it was not the image of Augustus, the patron-client relationship, or even the tribunician sacrosanctity that haunted the minds of potential assassins; it was "the glowering German bodyguards."[196] No conspirator against the emperor ever slept less well at night because the emperor technically had tribunician sacrosanctity. As one orator later told Trajan, "For an emperor, the laws are no protection against betrayal." This is why Augustus worried less about what people said than what they did. As he once told Tiberius, "My dear Tiberius, you must not . . . take it to heart if anyone speaks ill of me, let us be satisfied if we can achieve it that nobody is able to do us any harm."[197]

This is not to suggest that Augustus created a full-blown police state. Augustus merely instituted the principate and established its form in broad outline. This allowed his successors latitude with regard to its inner content. Emperors after Augustus would continue to rule with an eye to personal charm and public relations as well as brute force. Emperors had to maintain a delicate balance between gaining the goodwill of the masses while also avoiding the public humiliation of members of the upper classes.[198] The emperor could command obedience by means of a cult of the personality crafted by propaganda; he ruled by manufactured charisma.[199] This image has caused at least one modern capitalist tycoon to see Augustus as the CEO of the Roman Empire, a great leader, a model for modern business managers.[200] Unfortunately, most of the succeeding Julio-Claudian emperors were not nearly as charismatic or as successful.

As one historian of Augustus has pointed out, not everything that happened under Augustus happened because of Augustus; there were unplanned consequences.[201] He may not have set up a tyranny, but the structures he created made a tyranny possible. Augustus's regime did not set up any system of checks and balances against imperial authority or against the security services becoming politicized. None of his successors was as good as Augustus at maintaining the balance between tradition and innovation, between the liberties of the republican period and maintaining security. In the end this imbalance would result in the loss of the functions of the Senate, magistrates and law, and the independence of the leading men.[202] Republican sympathies would fade as the generation of men who remembered the republic disappeared. Under all the Caesars, politically significant persons of wealth, family, or culture had to watch what they did or said. As the importance of the security services rose, politics in Rome would not move in the direction of more freedom.

3

Augustus and the Opposition
Attempts on the Life of the Emperor

No emperor was spared assassination attempts, not even the first one. Whatever popularity Augustus enjoyed with the populace, it was not shared by certain elements of the Senate or certain members of his family. Augustus, the grand old man of the Roman Empire, its founder and the model for all future emperors, spent a considerable part of his reign fighting off assassination attempts—seven of them, to be exact. There was opposition to both Augustus personally and his new system of monarchy from the very beginning. Resistance in the Senate was a reaction to the purges of its members, against the assumption of extraordinary offices by Augustus or his associates, and against legislation that negatively affected the Senate's social or financial privileges.[1]

Levick rightly concluded there was a considerable amount of discontent that found expression from time to time among different groups, embracing all classes of society: the army, the senators, the provincials, and, not the least, Augustus's own family.

Yet Levick goes on to say there were no *real* conspiracies.[2] But what is a "real" conspiracy? Modern historians have often played down the threats to Augustus as "minor," suggesting they were unimportant. Crook, for example, wrote that the opposition to Augustus was "exaggerated."[3] Similarly Raaflaub and Samons called the opposition to Augustus "scattered, isolated, ineffective, and, overall, minimal."[4] Pat Southern talks about resistance not "escalating into warfare," but this is not the same thing as saying there were no attempts on Augustus's life. It is also a very high standard by which to judge "opposition." Rogers said the conspiracies against Augustus were numerous but not serious and they were usually caught in the early stages.[5] But this is exactly why they did not become serious, because Augustus's security apparatus detected them before they struck. Had they not been stopped in the early stages, they might indeed have become "serious." It speaks well of Augustus's internal security system that conspiracies were detected and quashed before they ended in regime change.

Is there any such thing as a "minor" attempt on one's life? Can only a successful assassination convince historians of a serious plot underfoot?[6] It would be naïve to assume Augustus could make such great changes in Roman society, take away the freedoms senators had enjoyed for centuries, and keep everyone happy. This is not to suggest Augustus lived in constant fear for his life, but he did take threats seriously, and he got more ruthless as his reign progressed. He became less and less magnanimous in the punishments of suspected conspirators. As we saw in the last chapter, Augustus had set up a series of organizations dedicated to keeping himself safe and in charge, so it should come as no surprise that they worked efficiently. The emperor always had the advantage of the better intelligence assets and effective internal security organs.[7] The attempts on the life of the emperor were not outright revolts or major uprisings, but they were nevertheless serious. It only takes a small group of dedicated, discontented men willing to effect an assassination to kill a leader. Southern's assertion, for example, that Augustus did not upset enough people for the discontented elements to combine and form "a well-organized universal conspiracy" is misguided, as is Levick speaking of the lack of "programmatic opposition."[8] A conspiracy, by definition, does not need to be large or universal or programmatic. In fact, conspiracies work better if they are small but well organized. They do not require the entire Senate or even a large faction. They do not require an entire social class to be in a state of unrest. Luckily for the emperors, most of the assassination attempts against the Julio-Claudians were rarely well organized—even the successful ones. The Julio-Claudian emperors were not toppled from power by large armies or massive popular movements. They were removed by individual assassins backed by small groups of partisans, usually for personal reasons of revenge or ambition. And what constitutes a threat may be entirely subjective and based on a ruler's sense of his own security.[9]

Three of the major conspiracies that were aimed at removing Augustus were those of M. Aemilius Lepidus the Younger (30 BCE), L. Murena and Fannius Caepio (23 BCE), and Egnatius Rufus (19 BCE). These must have weighed heavily on Augustus, as is suggested by Pliny the Elder, who cites the emperor as a superb example of the limitations of human happiness.[10]

LEPIDUS THE YOUNGER, 30 BCE

The conspiracies had started right after the battle of Actium in 30 BCE, even before Octavian returned to Rome and assumed the title of Augustus. M. Aemilius Lepidus (Lepidus the Younger) was the son of the former triumvir.[11] He was accused of planning to assassinate Octavian and starting a new civil war. As far as we can tell, he gave no thought to the situation that would follow Octavian's assassination. He may have assumed that with the death of the autocrat, the republic would revive spontaneously.[12]

The plot appears to have been detected early and then suppressed. Maecenas, as prefect of the city, probably used agents to ferret out the plot "quietly and carefully concealing his activity" so that he could crush it without any disturbance.[13] Lepidus was either executed by Maecenas or sent on to Octavian at Actium. Except for his closest relatives, there seems to have been no other persons involved. Whether this was anything other than an isolated action by a man with a personal grudge or something more has been debated.[14] It has even been suggested he was innocent and framed by Maecenas on the orders of Augustus to eliminate one more "redundant pawn or hostage."[15]

MURENA AND CAEPIO, 23 BCE

Despite the prosperity and peace that the Augustan settlement brought, a considerable element of the ruling class found the loss of political liberty that went with it unacceptable. Many were angered to the point of joining conspiracies.[16] An example of Augustus's intrusion into senatorial affairs can be seen at the trial of M. Primus, the former governor of Macedonia. He was accused of attacking the Odrysae tribe against Augustus's instructions. When the emperor showed up uninvited into the court proceedings and gave evidence damaging to Primus, there was an explosion of indignation.[17] In an early example of jury nullification, many of the jurors voted for acquittal just based on this outrage, while L. Licinius Varro Murena, the defendant's lawyer, joined with Fannius Caepio, among others, to form a conspiracy against Augustus.[18]

We know nothing about the leader Caepio except that he is described as "very bad" and from a family that held republican sentiments.[19] We are told he was noted for his freedom of speech (*parrhesia*)—the characteristic virtue of a free citizen as opposed to a subject under tyranny. In contrast, L. Licinius Varro Murena was brother of A. Terentius Varro Murena, the *consul ordinarius* of 23,[20] making the conspiracy one from the highest ranks of government. Augustus's heavy-handed intrusion into the trial of M. Primus showed exactly how little Augustus had given up when he relinquished the consulship but retained his tribunician power and *imperium proconsulare maius*. Many believed this much power in the hands of one man at the expense of the Senate had to be stopped. What the conspirators wanted other than the assassination of Augustus is often unclear.[21]

Augustus's intelligence network uncovered the plot by means of a freedman named Castricius, but the conspirators escaped.[22] Murena had been warned by his sister Terentia, wife of Maecenas, and he fled. Augustus's soldiers captured Caepio and killed him along with some other conspirators who resisted arrest. They were both tried *in absentia* and convicted; Tiberius was the prosecutor. Murena was later captured and executed without getting to testify in his own behalf at the trial. Murena's disgrace may have affected the standing of his brother-in-law, Maecenas.[23] According to Dio's account, there were others involved in the conspiracy, but we remain ignorant as to their identities.[24] There were public displays of sympathy for the conspirators even after their conspiracy was crushed. Augustus celebrated his delivery from the plot to knife him, but he was furious at the lack of unanimity in the condemnation.[25] Fannius, Caepio's father, in open defiance of the emperor, freed one of the two slaves who had assisted his son in his attempt to escape arrest, and he crucified the one who had betrayed him.[26] At the trial of the conspirators, in an echo of what had happened at the trial of Primus, there were votes of acquittal. This was a stinging denunciation of the princeps, since it was his very life that had been threatened and since the plotters had confessed their own guilt by fleeing before the trial.[27] Augustus responded by ruling that, in the future, all verdicts in such cases had to be unanimous and that there would be no secret ballots allowed. He authorized sacrifices to be made commemorating the suppression of the plot.[28]

M. EGNATIUS RUFUS, 19 BCE

M. Egnatius Rufus was another accused conspirator about whom we know little in the way of background.[29] He seems to have been a compulsively ambitious man. He had been a colleague of the emperor's nephew and son-in-law, Marcellus, in the aedileship of 23.[30] He exploited the aedile's function of fighting fires to amass widespread favor among the populace. Contrary to law, he ran for the praetorship for the next year (22) while still aedile and by virtue of his popularity.[31] Showing a dangerous disregard for the emperor's authority, he slighted Augustus by proclaiming that it was he himself who handed over to his successor a city unscathed and intact.[32] That he was popular can be seen in the measures Augustus put into action to thwart him.[33] To prevent a recurrence of a similar use of the aedileship, Augustus entrusted the curule aediles with the supervision of fighting fires and put a body of six hundred public slaves under their command.[34] He also encroached on Egnatius's praetorship by limiting the frequency and size of entertainments the praetors could give, together with their personal expenditures on them.[35]

In 19 Egnatius illegally stood for the consulship, even though two years were supposed to elapse between the praetorship and the consulship.[36] In his attempt to climb the *cursus publicus*, he had encumbered himself with debt and committed crimes that would bring him to ruin as soon as Augustus returned. When his candidacy was rejected, there were popular riots. According to Dio, Egnatius and his supporters turned to arms, and there were murders.[37] Egnatius formed a plot against Augustus in self-defense before the emperor could catch up with him.[38] The Senate voted a bodyguard for the sitting consul, Saturninus, which he refused, and envoys were dispatched to Augustus, who was on his way back to Rome from the East. Augustus appointed Q. Lucretius to the open consulship as he hastened back to Rome.[39] Egnatius and his accomplices were imprisoned and executed on orders of the Senate, presumably with the emperor's agreement.[40] We do not know how many senators sympathized with Egnatius, and we know nothing of his personal background. Although his aims and motives are obscure, some modern scholars see him as a kind of people's champion on the model of Clodius and other tribunes of the Late Republic. What seems clear is that he and his colleagues were protesting against the erosion of senatorial independence and asserting the rights of the senators to their traditional links with the Roman people.[41]

Augustus showed his confidence at being "in control of all affairs" by not acting defensively and hiding in the palace. He was not paranoid, but neither did he give people easy opportunities to make an attempt on his life or his position. He did not tolerate people becoming so famous or popular that they might become an alternative source of power. Once he had eliminated Antony, he was especially sensitive about Egypt being used as a power base. So when C. Cornelius Gallus started setting up statues to himself in Egypt, he was quickly eliminated.[42] The Senate tried Gallus in 28 BCE, found him guilty of *maiestas*, confiscated his property, and sent him into exile. He committed suicide in 27 BCE. But Gallus had not conspired so much as made too much of his success.[43]

CN. CORNELIUS CINNA MAGNUS

Sometime during Augustus's sojourn in Gaul, Seneca relates a story that Pompey the Great's grandson, Cinna, formed a plot against the emperor.[44]

The plan was to assassinate him while he was making a sacrifice, but the plot was discovered, and Cinna would have been executed except for the intercession of the empress Livia, who convinced her husband that severity in punishment would not deter assassination attempts and that he should pardon his enemy. Augustus agreed and, after a private audience with Cinna, dismissed him unpunished. Seneca claims that by this act he won the young man's loyalty to such a degree that he was able to reward the young man with a consulship in 5 CE and that there was no further plotting on Cinna's part. With good reason, this story has been doubted as improbable, especially when one considers the severity of the punishments against Lepidus, Murena, Caepio, and Egnatius Rufus.[45]

There may have been other plots, but they are much less well documented. There was the plot of a slave named Telephus, who either was driven by delusions of grandeur or was doing someone else's bidding.[46] He was set to attack both Augustus and the Senate under the delusion that he would be emperor. Then there was a bizarre intrusion into the palace by an Illyrian camp orderly armed with a hunting knife. It is hard to tell if he was insane, because he gave up no confession, even under torture.[47] Sources give no comment on how either of these men got access or who was guarding the palace. Besides the reports of individual conspiracies, Dio Cassius makes several general statements about the frequency of plots against Augustus.[48] His report on a purge of the Senate in 18 BCE talks about "plotting against both the emperor and Agrippa" and the accusation and punishment of several men for real or alleged conspiracies against the emperor but with no names or details given.[49] Thus we have no way of knowing if these conspiracies were historical or how serious the attempts were to remove the emperor.

A FAMILY AFFAIR

As far as we know, there was no major plot against the princeps for the next seventeen years after Egnatius Rufus's execution. Augustus had fortified his position and successfully identified himself in the minds of the people with the welfare of Rome. The official poetry (like Horace's *Carmen Saeculare*), dynastic works of art, portraiture and legends on coins, and imperial titulature were a constant reminder of who was in charge and that this arrangement was permanent.[50] Such means of imperial communication were meant to send a message discouraging any designs by his enemies to remove Augustus. At the same time the principate, as an institution, was growing and consolidating its control over every aspect of the empire, which also made the existence of an opposition more difficult.

The establishment of a "dynasty" was a means of perpetuating Augustus's own memory and assuring the permanence of his life's work. Anyone who thought about cutting him down prematurely like Julius Caesar and perhaps taking his position had to contend with a long line of possible heirs and regents, among them Marcellus, the eldest son of his sister Octavia; his grandsons, Gaius Caesar and Lucius Caesar; his son-in-law, Agrippa; his grandson, Agrippa Postumus; and Germanicus, the husband of Agrippina, Julia's daughter.[51] One could no longer overthrow the regime simply by removing its head. A conspiracy against the princeps with the idea of restoring the republic was no longer feasible since it meant not only killing Augustus, but removing the vast institution that he had created, along with everything it represented.

The fact that Augustus was attempting to transfer rule of the empire on a dynastic basis, however, also put him at risk from anyone who was related to him by blood or marriage. The conspiracies from the end of his reign, and indeed some that carried over into the reign of Tiberius, came right from his own household. Although the emperor did not yet live in a palace, "palace politics" certainly describes the power struggle that went on within his family and the "court," made up of advisors, relatives, friends, and hangers-on.[52]

Although ultimate power was concentrated in the hands of Augustus, in 2 BCE the spotlight turned to the women who stood closest to the throne. They held the key to the succession since they produced the heirs and the bloodline.[53] Augustus, who had passed a series of laws in 18–17 BCE aimed at moral reform even to the point of banning adultery, was an emperor trying to depict himself as promoting behavior that conformed to the most traditional moral ideas of the republic. But in one of the great examples of karma, he discovered that his daughter, Julia, seemed to be involved with half of *la jeunesse dorée* of Rome. The scandal sparked off the most dramatic series of trials in his reign. They would result in his daughter being disowned and a good number of disaffected senators being executed for treason.[54] Certainly their behavior was seen as undermining the conservative ideal Augustus was promoting, but although the ancient sources portray the participants as merely the disgraced lovers of Augustus's daughter, there is a widespread scholarly view that their plots may have involved assassinating the emperor and replacing him with another well-born aristocrat.[55]

Just as Augustus's government was a revolutionary new order, the role of imperial women was changing. As much as the upper classes would have liked to enforce the traditional roles of women, women's behavior was often undermining the conservative ideal. Although women could not aspire to rule themselves, they had influence as patrons. They were close to the Praetorian Guard, to the new imperial staff of freedmen, and of course they held a key role in the succession. Gender relationships were having a much greater bearing on the power structures of the principate.[56]

Power struggles within the imperial family included both relatives and outside supporters, and this secret struggle for influence and power grew complicated and menacing. Conspiracies from within a family are most dangerous because the family members have access to the palace and to the princeps. In Augustus's case, he was plagued by problems that revolved around both his daughter and granddaughter. If the moral program of Augustus's New State was designed to keep women in their place, it was a grand failure.

JULIA, THE DAUGHTER, 2 BCE

Julia was the most prominent pawn in Augustus's game of succession. Having had marriages of state arranged for her with Marcellus, Agrippa, and then Tiberius, one could see why she might harbor resentment toward her father and perhaps had her own opinion on who should be on the throne, since she held the key. Beneath the crisis that shook the palace and led to the punishment of Augustus's daughter and her paramours lay not just the charge of profligacy but also conspiracy. Through Julia, the conspirators hoped to get into a position from which they could, after Augustus's death, whether natural or induced, take over effective control of the empire. Some believe the fight split along the line between the Julians and the Claudians, the two branches of the imperial family descended from Augustus (the Julians) or his wife Livia (the Claudians).[57]

There is a debate over whether the conspiracy was about policy disputes or actual regime change,[58] but if Julia were indeed in the middle of a plot to put someone else on the throne in place of her father or Tiberius, it surely would have necessitated doing some harm to one or more members of her family.[59] The natural figurehead for any succession plot by a Julian faction would inevitably be the two Julias (daughter and granddaughter of Augustus) and Agrippa Postumus, the elder Julia's son by Agrippa. It is no wonder that the other faction, Tiberius and his supporters, would devote so much time and ingenuity to neutralizing all three of these people. Historians both ancient and modern have suggested there was some scheme to remove Augustus in favor of Gaius Caesar and Lucius Caesar or to remove Gaius and Lucius in favor of Iullus Antonius, the son of Mark Antony and his third wife, Fulvia.[60] Some scholars, like Ronald Syme, emphasized the role of Iullus, while others see Julia as the motivating force; we will never know for sure.[61] Certainly Julia and her young sons would have much to fear if Augustus were incapacitated and Livia were given free rein, since she would obviously favor her son, Tiberius.[62] The question has certainly been raised as to whether it was Livia who ratted Julia out.[63] Perhaps Julia saw an alliance with Iullus as a way of escaping her marriage to Tiberius and her dominating father. With Iullus as emperor and her as consort, the succession of her sons would be more secure than if Augustus died and Livia raised her son, Tiberius, to the throne.

More than one modern author has suggested that Julia's affairs were more than just private scandal but also a convenient political smoke screen for Augustus.[64] Others have argued that the sexual exploits are not even true—rather, the work of those who wrote about those who suffered disgrace, death, or exile. The accusation of adultery was used through Roman history to discredit women of high rank.[65] The official charge against Julia, publicized in a letter to the Senate, was adultery and excessive immorality, but Syme and many others believed this was only a pretext.[66] The real charge may have been treason. Many of her lovers were men from old republican families like the Scipios and the Gracchi, or Iullus Antonius, son of Mark Antony, who may have wished to avenge his father's fate. The fact that Augustus considered the death penalty for his own daughter suggests the seriousness of the situation. Only some of the evidence of Julia's scandalous behavior was brought before the Senate. She was convicted and exiled to the barren island of Pandateria, where she was accompanied by her mother, Scribonia.[67] She was forbidden wine or fancy food, and no freedman or slave was allowed to contact her without Augustus's permission. The Roman people protested, but Augustus was adamant, and Augustus never saw her again.

Her confederates did not fare as well. The lightest sentence went to Decimus Junius Silanus, who was excluded from the emperor's friendship, which he interpreted as a sentence of exile and so left Rome.[68] Iullus Antonius was convicted of high treason and adultery and was executed.[69] T. Quinctius Crispinus, Appius Claudius Pulcher, Cornelius Scipio, and Tiberius Sempronius Gracchus were also convicted and relegated for treason or adultery or both.[70] Gracchus was exiled to Cercina, off the southeast coast of Tunisia, where he remained for fourteen years. When the soldiers showed up to execute him, they found him waiting, and he offered his neck to the executioners, or at least this is what Tacitus tells us. He also reports that the execution order was not given by Tiberius, but by Lucius Asprenas, proconsul of Africa. This version of the story may have been circulated by Tiberius to remove the blood from his own hands.[71]

Those who believe this was a conspiracy against Augustus cite Pliny the Elder, who speaks of Julia's "plots against her father's life," and Dio, who explicitly says Iullus was executed because of his designs on the monarchy.[72] We do not know whether these sentences were part of the ongoing conflict within the palace over designating successors and the future course of the principate or if they were just meant to save face for an imperial family embroiled in scandal. Syme felt the punishment was certainly too great for just imperial embarrassment. It does not matter if any of them were Julia's lovers. The later reports of her revels were probably propagated by rumor. Without solid evidence, one can only explore cui bono—that is, who would benefit the most from Augustus's death? Had he been killed, who would have been his successor at that point, and would anything have changed? Iullus Antonius was sentenced to death because his family and prestige were strong enough to make him a genuine threat to Augustus and his grandsons.

There was no trial for Julia herself; the charge of adultery did not require one, as the charge of *maiestas* would have. In this way, Augustus made sure the whole story never reached the public, regardless of whether it was treason or adultery.[73] He put a high premium on preventing an open debate in the Senate. Unlike later emperors who sent the Praetorians to deliver sentences of death or exile, in Julia's case it was probably a trusted member of the imperial household—possibly even Livia herself—who went to Julia's home with the instructions to pack a few things, take the slaves, and be gone by the next day.[74] Her sentence was commuted somewhat in 4 CE, when she was allowed back onto the mainland, where she lived in Rhegium under less restricted circumstances. When Augustus died, however, Tiberius kept her under house arrest, saw to it that she was deprived of any possible inheritance, and allowed her to virtually starve to death.[75]

JULIA, THE GRANDDAUGHTER, 8 CE

Ridding himself of Julia did not solve Augustus's problem. Another supposed plot was centered around Augustus's granddaughter, Julia, and her husband, Lucius Aemilius Paullus, who may have been gathering the remnants of her mother's faction around her.[76] The participants are named in a list of conspirators by Suetonius that includes one P. Plautius Rufus, who is often identified with Publius Rufus, a man responsible for inciting rebellion against Augustus by a campaign of subversive pamphlets in Rome two years earlier (6 CE).[77] Scholars have argued that this plot was another episode in the struggle over the succession within the imperial house, between, on the one hand, Tiberius and his supporters and, on the other, those who were promoting the claims of the Elder Julia's children, Agrippa Postumus and Julia the Younger.[78]

Augustus's granddaughter Julia was exiled in 8 CE to Trimerus on the charge of adultery. Augustus ordered that the child she gave birth to there be killed by exposure; Paullus was exiled or executed.[79] Augustus dealt with Julia's brother Postumus so harshly that modern commenters have assumed he must also have been involved in the plot against Augustus.[80] The charge of treason is very explicit in Pliny, but treason can cover almost anything that displeases the emperor.

The princeps disowned Agrippa Postumus, returned him to his family, the Vipsanii, and removed him to the town of Surrentum (Sorrento) on the Amalfi Coast. In 9 CE he was transferred to the island of Planasia, between Corsica and the Italian mainland, and a decree of the Senate declared that he would stay there until he died. He lost his place in the imperial family, the wealth he had inherited from his father Agrippa, and his freedom.[81] There was a rumor of a failed attempt to rescue him and Julia the Elder and bring them both "to the armies" in Germany, but this has been doubted.[82] The two plotters mentioned are Lucius Audasius and Asinius Epicadus. Another story in Tacitus tells us Augustus paid a highly covert visit to Planasia in 13 CE to apologize to Postumus and put him back in the succession, but most modern historians reject this story and believe Augustus never changed his mind.[83] Soon after the death of Augustus, Postumus was executed by his guards. It was said that Augustus ordered the execution in his will; others said that Tiberius and Livia were behind it, although Tiberius would later disavow all knowledge of the deed.[84]

Julia's offense may not have gone beyond angry words or illicit communication with her brother. This would have been enough, however, to get informers talking, and when it got back to the princeps, there was a very stiff price to pay.[85] The charges of sexual promiscuity were made against Julia as they had been against her mother by their political enemies. The charges have often been accepted by censorious male critics; the campaign of slander was so successful that not even Tacitus could get a clear picture of her personality and activities after the fact. The insistence by Augustus on official secrecy about the real reason is understandable considering the disturbed political climate of the time.[86]

As for how far this supposed revolution went or who all the actors were, we are in the dark. The exile of the poet Ovid may be tied in with this affair.[87] Perhaps he and his friends in high society had seen something and not reported it. Historians have referred to this attempt on Augustus as ad hoc rather than the result of systematic opposition, but opposition does not need to be systematic to be effective. A conspiracy needs planning, timing, access, and good execution. A family plot of disgruntled relatives could manage this, but even if they were less than efficient, they were still a danger. There is a reason Augustus referred to his family members as "my three boils and carcinomas."[88]

We should not minimize the threats to Augustus and his plans for succession. If there is any pattern to be discerned here, it seems that all the plots originating outside of the center of power itself were concentrated in the first twelve to fifteen years of Augustus's reign. These were aimed at preventing Augustus from gaining sole power. Afterward, with two dubious exceptions, the plots seem to have originated within the imperial family and his own entourage, and they were aimed at preventing him from passing the power on.[89] Even with the limited evidence we have, we can see that these few conspiracies may be just the tip of the iceberg.[90] The recurring theme here is that there was always a real danger to the princeps from shadowy figures working behind subterfuge and court intrigue.[91] That Augustus survived as long as he did may be due to his extraordinary vigilance or luck or even the incompetence of the conspirators. If anything attests to the efficiency of Augustus's security team, it is how few people were willing to join the conspirators, probably out of the fear of joining them and being caught. Augustus had made clear what the price of that would be.

THE DEATH OF AUGUSTUS

Augustus managed to die in bed of natural causes—or so we think. Suetonius describes him kissing Livia and lovingly telling her, "Goodbye Livia. Never forget our marriage."[92] Yet rumors began immediately that Livia had poisoned him to speed up the succession for her son, Tiberius. The poisoning myth has been popularized in modern times by Robert Graves in his *I, Claudius*. There was nothing particularly suspicious about Augustus's death. He was an old man even by modern standards, so why would anyone spread the rumor that there was a conspiracy to kill him? The accusations against Livia should be set in the context of two Roman realities: fear of poisoning and the stereotype of the scheming stepmother who would do anything to advance the interests of her son.[93] Given Livia's reputation as a ruthless woman, perhaps her involvement should not be ruled out entirely. In a time before ubiquitous CSI teams, eliminating enemies with poisoned mushrooms or tainted fish and getting away with it was not all that difficult.[94] Augustus had always wished that he could die a natural and peaceful death, called *euthanasia* in Greek. This has given biographers license to suggest that Livia may have poisoned him to alleviate his suffering and give him his euthanasia in the more Kevorkian sense of the word.[95] In the end, the rumor may reflect nothing more than the palpable unease of Roman aristocratic males in the presence of a powerful woman.[96]

There is no reason to suspect that Livia had to do anything to ensure her son's succession, although the issue had dominated the last years of Augustus's life. He had made plentiful preparations for the smooth transfer of power to Tiberius, and there is no sign in anything else he did in his last months to suggest that he had changed his mind. Tiberius had the *imperium* given to him in the previous year, along with the tribunician power. Once Augustus was declared a god, Tiberius was declared *divi filius*, son of the deified one.[97] Tiberius had all the powers and the titles that Augustus had held. Still, the death of a long-term leader—a man called *pater patriae*—could still become a political tinderbox.[98] Although the transition worked as Augustus had planned, still the succession was never a sure thing legally, and this was the first time it had been done. Perhaps this caused the rise of rumors about Livia and her machinations on behalf of her son Tiberius.

Livia probably had a hand in making the transition of power to her son as smooth as possible. Tacitus tells us that once Augustus had passed, she acted in concert with the Praetorian Guard to make certain that the news of the emperor's death was delayed until such time as the transition of power was secure.[99] Tiberius was on the way to Dalmatia at the time, and it is not clear from the sources whether he returned to find Augustus alive or dead.[100] The empress stationed Praetorians around the house in Nola so that no one could approach. It is likely as well that *speculatores* were used to convey the message of Augustus's decline to Tiberius, given the need for strict secrecy.[101]

Tiberius could not take public acquiescence on his accession for granted. He accompanied Augustus's body on its ceremonial return to Rome, just as twenty-two years before he had accompanied the body of his brother, Drusus, on its journey back from northern Germany. Velleius Paterculus refers to fear of disorder confirmed by the posting of large numbers of troops at Augustus's funeral.[102] Tacitus, too, mentions the armed guard at the funeral, and he makes clear there were threats to the succession.[103]

The first emperor's reign had been a series of ongoing security challenges, and Tiberius's reign would be no different. Pliny the Elder lists Augustus's concerns:

> the disgrace of Agrippa's banishment, the many plots against his life, the charge of causing the death of his children . . . his daughter's adultery and the disclosure of her plots against her father's life . . . another adultery, that of his granddaughter . . . afterwards the intrigues of his wife and Tiberius that tormented his last days.[104]

Dio made no attempt to hide the fact that conspiracies against the emperor usually originated among the upper classes, even though their motives may have been lofty. It was this that Tiberius would inherit.[105] The focus of political intrigue had shifted decisively from the open forum of the republic, to the circles that reached into the emperor's household.[106]

Augustus's political career had lasted for fifty-eight years, and he reigned longer than any other Roman emperor. This suggests he was successful at maintaining the internal security of his regime. Throughout all that time he survived within a very dangerous and competitive political culture. There had been previous Roman leaders who were as ruthless as Augustus, but none was so professional in the art of politics.[107] In his rise to power he was brutal in disposing of his enemies, and he became particularly skilled in picking them off one by one. Once he had achieved the summit of power, he became more surgical, but he nevertheless built up a highly effective intelligence network and security team. He was more than happy to launch a preemptive political strike on anyone who even raised the possibility of opposition to his power, and he had built the apparatus that should have helped both him and his successors achieve security.

Augustus had had to keep under arms a sufficiently large force to make any subsequent opposition of this nature a most foolhardy gamble. He created new security contingents to safeguard his own power and, at the same time, to make Rome's inhabitants feel more secure. These two motivations are not mutually exclusive. Augustus wanted to give Rome prosperity, peace, and harmony; in the end, he gave them a regime with seemingly stable leadership, the semblance of liberty, and enough distractions for them not to notice any cracks in the façade. His successors would get to make that system more autocratic.

4

The Reign of Tiberius

Examining the reign of Tiberius gives us the opportunity to see if the Augustan system would work without Augustus. The transition from a representative republic to an autocratic empire was still in its infancy, but the one constant was that whoever became emperor would need an internal security system to keep himself alive and in charge. Tiberius kept all of Augustus's policies strictly in place, including his policing and military innovations. Tiberius had the Praetorian Guard, the urban cohorts, a personal bodyguard, the lictors, the *vigiles*, all the informers he needed, plus a military presence in Rome at his disposal. Would all of these layers of security be enough to keep him safe? He certainly needed them, because, thanks to his unpopularity and his overly ambitious friends and family, he spent most of his reign fending off conspiracies and prosecuting treasonous acts.[1]

Tiberius's very accession was said to have been a sanitized version of the truth. The rumor spread that Livia dispatched her husband to ensure the accession of her son before Agrippa Postumus was reinstated as heir. Such stories can probably be dismissed, because there was no real motive for her to speed up the passing of Augustus.[2] Tiberius had been publicly designated his rightful successor, and he had been given all the powers he needed before Augustus's death. Tiberius, as the last man standing, was given all the requisite powers by Augustus and had become *de facto* emperor by 13 CE. This ensured that, when Augustus died in 14 CE, Tiberius was able to present documents to the Senate that officially named him as Augustus's legal successor, thereby guaranteeing the continuity of the monarchy.[3] All of Augustus's other heirs, except Agrippa Postumus, were dead, and Postumus was considered enough of a threat to the incoming administration to justify his murder shortly after Tiberius's accession.[4] He was the last link that stood between the descendants of Livia and a true monopoly of power.[5] Tiberius also saw to it that his former wife, Augustus's daughter Julia, was deprived of all income and starved in Rhegium. He believed that there were still efforts being raised on behalf of her and Postumus.[6]

Augustus had set the precedent that his chief heir was also his political successor, but being named ruler in a smooth transition and holding on to the throne are two different things.[7] There was still uncertainty in how the role of princeps would be filled by a new player with a different vision of the principate. There were many reasons someone might want Tiberius dead, including not wanting a princeps at all. There were still people alive who remembered the republic, with its elected officials, a Senate with some independent power, and a tradition of hating tyranny. If the emperor were eliminated, perhaps Rome could go back to the "good old days." This was an unlikely scenario, but not an unimaginable one in the minds of people with republican sympathies. More realistically, there were those who might be able to resign themselves to one-man rule but just not with Tiberius as that man. An extreme dislike of Tiberius personally would be enough motivation for some people to start a conspiracy or become involved in an already existing one. Such people might plot to put someone else, including themselves, on the throne.

Like Augustus, Tiberius had to watch the same constituencies to be safe: the aristocracy, the armies, the populace, and his own extended family. Tiberius was particularly conservative on the subject of imperial women. He limited any display that was suggestive of female power within the imperial order. He constrained the life of his mother, Livia, by refusing the honors voted to her by the Senate and by preventing her from playing a prominent role on state occasions.[8] The most dangerous threat to Tiberius, however, came from his own security service. What happens if you are betrayed by the very people being paid to keep you safe? This is a problem that would raise its ugly head in the reign of Tiberius and become a concern for future emperors.

THE POPULACE

One of the things that helped keep Augustus alive was his popularity with the people. Tiberius shared no such popularity, and this made his job much harder. A large part of controlling the populace was having them love you or at least your official image. It would be difficult to find two men more different than Tiberius and Augustus in that department.

Augustus was affable and outgoing; he liked the humbug of the imperial façade, and people loved him for it. Tiberius was a conservative and old-fashioned soldier with an interest in Roman law. He was intelligent and shrewd but is often described as being morose, with attacks of melancholy and depression.[9]

Tiberius was bitterly conscious of his own unpopularity, and frankly, he had no use for the public in general. Gaining popularity was not even part of his program.[10] He made no attempt to present a winning side of himself to the masses; in fact, his very first act as princeps was to effectively deprive the people of their rights as electors. He transferred election of the magistrates to the Senate. Nor did Tiberius make any attempt to appeal to the populace through the mass media of antiquity—coins and inscriptions. They probably would not have liked what he had to say, anyway, and it was an omission that added to his reputation as being arrogant.[11] His reign has been described as an "austere and oligarchic programme" run by an urban palace clique.[12] A man who stands for the rule of an elite and the reduction of the people to a position of respectful docility cannot, in the nature of things, expect to command mass support, but then he did not really need it. Tiberius had a following of his own. Besides the ranks of the legions he had commanded, he had his friends, men who shared his views, and those who enjoyed his patronage or hoped to benefit from it in the future.

In the larger scheme of things, the succession to the empire should not rely on personality. Even dour men can be good emperors. Tiberius saw his job not as winning over hearts and minds, but simply keeping the urban plebs in line. Although there were regulations in place, mobs could become unruly. He would not hesitate to send a regiment of soldiers to quell an unruly crowd or inflict punishment on the people.[13] Tiberius saw no reason to join the crowds in their amusements. He did not care much for theatrical performances, and he hated the circus. He only attended them for a short time until he realized that spectators would use them as occasions to bring pressure on him to do things he might not have wanted to do. He limited the number of shows and reduced the number of gladiatorial contests to be given in any one festival. Personally, he adopted an ostrichlike policy of not appearing at performances, thus avoiding the pressure applied to him by the crowd or the possibility that he could be killed there.[14]

Keeping the urban plebs under control could be a dangerous task. At a food riot that broke out in 15 CE, some ordinary citizens were killed along with a centurion and several soldiers.[15] The plebs generally caused no trouble except in times of extreme stress, such as food shortages. Tiberius reacted to such events with speed and decision, and he made every effort to satisfy the needs of the people. He was conscientious in maintaining grain supplies in the face of widespread shortages. He acted quickly and effectively when it came to fires in Rome in 16, 27, and 36, and made earnest, if not effective, efforts to curb the Tiber floods.[16] He worked hard and resented being accused of negligence.[17] From the point of view of the general public, Tiberius was unliked, but he was generally kept safe from their behavior.

THE SENATE

Although Tiberius had all the essential powers he needed to make him princeps by August of 14 CE, what he really wanted and needed in addition was the moral sanction of the Senate for his regime.[18] Even though one of his first acts was to transfer the power to elect magistrates from the people's assemblies to the Senate, this did not lead to an improvement in his relations with the senators. The principate of the deified Augustus had become a subtle tyranny, yet here was an emperor trying to play a lesser part in government by giving some power back to the Senate. Tiberius vowed to do his part and carry out the duties that were entrusted to him by the Senate, but he wanted them to take an active part, also.[19] Some senators may have liked this; others thought it impracticable. Some just did not like Tiberius; many simply did not understand what he was proposing. What Tiberius did not seem to grasp was that power is indivisible. Once you gather it into one pair of hands, it rarely gets redistributed back throughout the body politic. In the end, Tiberius failed to get the senators to acknowledge that the burden of government lay ultimately on them. Too much had changed. Tiberius needed to be in charge and stay in charge. If he showed any weakness or tendency to shirk his responsibilities, there were other ambitious people who would be happy to take his place. The voluntary restriction of his own power or authority could only make him more vulnerable. He might discourage servility, flattery, and the "cult of personality" as a matter of taste, but in the end his success as a princeps would be his individual ability to maintain power with the support of a constitution that was wholly inadequate and a security force that was not entirely loyal.

THE ARMIES

Tiberius made the place of the armies clear. One of his first acts was to make the Praetorian Guard and the legions swear an oath of allegiance to him. Still, an interregnum is always the most dangerous time for a new emperor. Although Augustus had made the succession as clear as possible, there was a period of eight weeks following Augustus's death during which Tiberius had to consolidate his power.[20] He had to be on guard for both armies in revolt and conspiracies at home. The first fear came to pass rather quickly. Three legions under the command of Q. Junius Blaesus in Pannonia and four legions stationed in summer quarters on the Rhine under A. Caecina Severus broke out in revolt. The stated motivations were demands for an increase in pay and bounties and for improving and shortening their conditions of service. There was also an idea current on the Rhine frontier that the legions might declare themselves in favor of their commander in chief Germanicus in place of Tiberius.[21] This turned out not to be the case, but it was a threat Tiberius could not ignore. As a former commander with a great career of military experience behind him, Tiberius could have gone to put down the revolts himself, but he dared not leave the capital and risk exposing his person. This was the great dilemma of all emperors—they could not be in two places at once. They could stay in Rome and control the senatorial plots and palace conspiracies or take to the provinces to control the legions. No one really solved the problem; each emperor chose his own way.

Tiberius had the *imperium*, but it was what he did with it that mattered. The emperor had to work quickly to have the legions brought under control before he could do anything else. As a soldier he knew he had to seize the initiative and deal with any opposition decisively before it got too strong. He immediately dispatched his son, Drusus Caesar, to Pannonia, along with L. Aelius Sejanus, who brought a detachment of the Praetorian Guard, some cavalry, and a few leading men to watch over the son.[22] The mutiny was successfully put down.

THE CONSPIRACY OF
M. SCRIBONIUS LIBO DRUSUS, 16 CE

No sooner had the military situation been taken care of than Tiberius was threatened with his first conspiracy from the ranks of the aristocracy. On September 13, 16 CE, M. Scribonius Libo Drusus, praetor in 16 or 15 and brother of the *consul ordinarius*, was brought to trial by a group led by four senators on a charge of plotting against the lives of Tiberius, Germanicus, Drusus, and other leading men of the state.[23] What he hoped to achieve is unclear. He had blood ties to the imperial family, but sources like Tacitus depict him as a pitiable young man, vapid and extravagant—a dull-witted young aristocrat with resplendent family connections. Seneca describes him as "stupid as he was noble."[24] Hardly a replacement for the princeps, but this did not stop him from representing what Rogers called "the inane and irresponsible opposition to the emperor."[25]

Libo was turned in by one of his closest friends, Firmius Catus. Catus made contact with Tiberius through an intermediary, Vescularius Flaccus, an equestrian friend of the princeps.[26] The evidence brought forward, as preserved for us by Tacitus, consisted of papers showing among other things that Libo had consulted astrologers. The charges rested entirely on a notebook with the names of the members of the imperial family with cryptic signs next to them. It was believed Libo thought he could eliminate members of the imperial family by black magic. As ridiculous as it seems to us, astrology and magic were taken seriously at the time.[27] Even the wearing of an amulet or the consulting of a haruspex could result in a harsh penalty.[28] The document was in his own handwriting. Libo was unable to find anyone to act as his counsel and, on the night after making an appeal to the princeps through P. Sulpicius Quirinius and receiving the reply that he should approach the Senate, he committed suicide. The trial continued anyway, and Libo was convicted.[29]

Andrew Pettinger is only the most recent scholar to suggest that beneath this seemingly ridiculous episode there was a senatorial conspiracy to murder Tiberius, Germanicus, and Drusus Caesar and seize the throne. Libo was simply a tool who was sacrificed when the plot was prematurely uncovered. Pettinger looks for disparities between the ancient accounts and finds that all agree;[30] it is only Tacitus's account that stands alone in representing Libo as an innocent victim of Tiberius.[31]

The scholars arguing for a conspiracy believe there was a senatorial conspiracy that was prematurely thwarted, and Libo was the sacrificial lamb. That would explain the charge of treason. In any event, the prosecutors received their rewards; Libo's property was divided among them, and praetorships were granted to those who were senators.[32] Of Libo's accomplices who were punished, one was thrown from a cliff and the other was scourged to death outside the Esquiline Gate.[33] Libo's image was ordered excluded from the funeral processions of his descendants, and the assumption of the cognomen Drusus was henceforth denied to the Scribonii. Days of thanksgiving were offered in celebration of his detection and death.[34]

This was the first supposed conspiracy against Tiberius that was publicly investigated. The swiftness with which the trial was held and Libo's property confiscated hinted at the shape of things to come. Both the senators and the princeps watched each other closely during the trial. The Senate realized that its own members had been marked for death by Libo. The result seemed to produce servility in the Senate and a new independence for Tiberius. It certainly contradicted Tiberius's illusion that he was "just another senator." Whatever imperial indecisiveness he had exhibited elsewhere, Tiberius dropped it in the presence of the Senate when the subject was his own security.

THE CONSPIRACY OF CLEMENS

Another attempt to interfere with the succession occurred when one of Agrippa Postumus's former slaves, Clemens, tried to impersonate his dead master and raise a rebellion against Tiberius. Clemens was involved in the earlier attempt to rescue Postumus from Planasia in 14 CE. He arrived in Planasia too late to save Postumus, but he stole his murdered owner's ashes, went underground in Cosa for a year, grew his hair and beard to look like his former owner's, and then spread the rumor that Agrippa was alive. Then in 16 he assembled a crowd of supporters at Ostia with the aim of overthrowing Tiberius.[35]

We do not know who else may have been supporting him behind the scenes. Some have argued that the group around Clemens was large and that this attempt was not just the isolated plotting of an overbold ex-slave.[36] Paladini argued that it was fear of offending the senatorial oligarchy that discouraged Tiberius from investigating the affair more thoroughly.[37] Was he afraid of what he would find? In the end, Tiberius did what he had to do to neutralize the threat without starting a full-blown senatorial witch hunt. Deciding how to strike back may have put Tiberius in a quandary in that sending troops to intervene might seem like overkill, but to ignore a nascent coup was also dangerous. He turned instead to a trusted agent, Sallustius Crispus, who sent two of his retainers to capture Clemens and bring the freedman secretly to Rome. Clemens refused to reveal the names of his confederates and told Tiberius he had as much right to call himself "Agrippa" as Tiberius had to call himself "Caesar." Tiberius thought it best to hush up the whole affair. Clemens was quietly executed, and although it was said that many distinguished persons might have been involved, no inquiry was held.[38]

LA FAMIGLIA: GERMANICUS AND
THE SUCCESSION PROBLEM

Minor conspiracies like Libo's and the false Agrippa's are usually dismissed since they were carried out by people unlikely to be successful at either killing the emperor or replacing him themselves. It is assumed they posed no real threat to the emperor, but we cannot be sure how many people were involved and who was really behind the attempted coups. To have a successful change of regime, one of these unknown people would have to have been the next candidate for the throne. There were people both in the imperial family and the Senate who might want that throne and had enough ambition to want to pursue power during the lifetime of Tiberius. These were the people whom the emperor had to watch most closely.

Unlike Tiberius, both Germanicus and his wife enjoyed and courted the favor of the populace. We are led by Tacitus to believe that this popularity plus his military successes in Gaul, Germania, and Armenia made Tiberius jealous of his popular nephew.[39] As commander in chief in Germany with eight legions at his disposal, as the designated successor to the throne, and as the bearer of Tiberius's special commission to the East, Germanicus was certainly in a position to promote his own career, but this is not the same thing as being overly ambitious to the point of treason. The problem with the sources is that we cannot tell for sure whether anyone was plotting to put Germanicus on the throne or if Tiberius's paranoia made him perceive every move as a calculated threat.[40] We do not even know for certain whether Germanicus's death was by natural causes or a murder. If Tiberius truly viewed Germanicus as his rival, the outcome would be predictable. Between Germanicus almost neurotically trying to avoid doing anything that might excite the suspicions that he felt Tiberius had about him, on the one hand, and a paranoid emperor looking for any excuse to mistrust him, on the other, lies the truth, which is unrecoverable.[41] Certainly popular rumor at the time regarded Germanicus as a marked man.[42]

Germanicus's commission to the East brought the problem to a head. Germanicus was sent to the East when the Parthians expelled their king, Vonones, a Roman appointee. To keep an eye on Germanicus, Tiberius appointed Cn. Calpurnius Piso, governor of Syria, to help head off any rash attempts at military glory by his nephew.[43] Piso, instead, jumped on every indiscretion that Germanicus committed. For example, when Germanicus and Agrippina were offered gold crowns by the king of Nabataea at a banquet, Piso refused his, saying there was a difference between the son of a Parthian king and of a Roman princeps.[44] Germanicus formally renounced his friendship with Piso and ordered him out of the province. The rivalry escalated from the sphere of personal attacks to the stage where it began to affect policy decisions.[45] When Germanicus ordered troops be sent to Armenia, Piso refused and countermanded Germanicus's orders.[46]

Piso was on the island of Cos in 19 CE when Germanicus suddenly fell ill. In Germanicus's tent they found objects "designed to bring about the young princep's death by magic." We do not know how they got there.[47] Germanicus accused Piso of murder as he lay dying. His legates exposed his dead body to demonstrate signs of poisoning. Later a notorious poisoner named Martina was arrested and sent to Rome, but she exercised her art on herself at Brundisium. When Piso got the news of Germanicus's death, he had to decide whether to return to Rome to fight the charges or return to Syria to reclaim his province. He decided to return to Syria, but he was captured in Cilicia and returned to Rome under arrest to face charges of murder, treason, and extortion.[48]

Tiberius tried to secure a fair trial for Piso, even though we are told Piso threatened to implicate Tiberius in the plot against Germanicus. Whether the governor actually could connect the princeps to the death of Germanicus is unknown. When it became evident that the Senate was against him, and with the mob already dragging his statue to the Gemonian steps, Piso saw the handwriting on the wall and committed suicide.[49]

Whatever the truth of Germanicus's death, his wife Agrippina's mourning became a focus for every discontent that until then had been festering beneath the surface of the Tiberian regime. The return of Germanicus's ashes sent the population of Italy and Rome into paroxysms of grief.[50] Although Tiberius sent two cohorts of the Praetorian Guard to escort the ashes back to Rome, when the ashes arrived, neither Tiberius nor Livia attended the internment. Considering the public demonstrations, it is no wonder he stayed safely inside. It is difficult to estimate Tiberius's reaction to the death of Germanicus. Perhaps he felt some relief; he may have neither liked nor trusted him or Agrippina, but there is no reason to believe he had ever tried to disinherit him or have him murdered. That, however, did not stop public rumors. That Tiberius's son, Drusus, would take Germanicus's place in the succession was confirmed in 21 CE, when he was made the emperor's consular colleague for the second time. Tiberius wrote to the Senate and asked for his son to be given the tribunician power.[51] Unfortunately for Tiberius, as long as Agrippina lived, she would be pushing her sons toward the throne in place of Drusus.[52]

SEJANUS, TIBERIUS, AND THE SUCCESSION

The biggest conspiracy in the reign of Tiberius was the emperor's supposed betrayal by his own head of security, the Praetorian prefect Lucius Aelius Seianus, commonly known as Sejanus. The fall of Sejanus, according to Tacitus, was the turning point of Tiberius's life and principate. How Tiberius handled it would decide the succession, produce a new head of security, and result in the death of many a famous Roman.[53]

Sejanus had been a soldier, friend, and confidant of Tiberius. An equestrian by birth,[54] Sejanus rose to power as prefect of the Praetorian Guard, of which he was commander from 14 until his death in 31 CE. As we saw in chapter 1, the Praetorian Guard had been formally established under Emperor Augustus, but Sejanus introduced a number of reforms that saw the unit evolve beyond a mere bodyguard into a powerful and influential branch of the government involved in public security, civil administration, and ultimately political intercession. These changes would have a lasting impact on the course of the principate.[55] In 20 CE, for example, Sejanus took the scattered encampments inside the city and centralized them into a single garrison just outside Rome.[56] By concentrating the cohorts into a single camp outside the city, he increased the political potential of the Guard and secured the allegiance of the troops for himself.[57] He increased the number of cohorts from nine to twelve,[58] one of which now held the daily guard at the palace. He abolished the practice of joint leadership between two prefects, and he himself rather than the princeps appointed the centurions and tribunes.[59] With these changes in effect, Sejanus now commanded the complete loyalty of a force of around twelve thousand soldiers, all of whom were at his immediate disposal. Romans would notice the change from Augustus's time immediately when Tiberius occasionally summoned the Guard to drill in front of the assembled senators as a visible demonstration of his power.

Not only was Sejanus a trusted advisor to Tiberius but by 23 he was exerting a considerable influence over the decisions of the emperor, who referred to Sejanus as his "partner in my toils" (*socius laborum*).[60] By this time he had been raised to the rank of praetor, a position that was not normally granted to Romans of the equestrian class.[61] A statue had been erected in his honor in the Theatre of Pompey, and in the Senate his followers were advanced with public offices and governorships[62] while at the same time potential political opponents were eliminated.[63] A major token of Tiberius's esteem was the betrothing of Sejanus's daughter, Junilla, to the son of Claudius, Claudius Drusus. At the time the girl was only four years old, but the marriage was nonetheless prevented when the boy *accidentally* died a few days later of asphyxiation.[64] Just the idea of such a union aroused much adverse feeling. Sejanus's privileged position caused resentment among the senatorial class and the imperial family because they felt a marriage into the imperial family was above his station. It particularly earned him the enmity of Tiberius's son, Drusus Caesar.[65]

The history of Sejanus and Drusus dated back to at least 15 CE during the military revolt in Pannonia.[66] Despite the successful quashing of the revolt, the following years witnessed a growing animosity between the two. Although Drusus was being systematically groomed as the successor to his father, in practice it was Sejanus who was the second man in the empire, and he was eager to further expand his power.[67] We do not really know what Sejanus's ultimate goals were, since the sources, once again, are ambiguous. Tacitus suggests that Sejanus exploited Tiberius—deluding his master into courses of action that would guarantee his own advancement.[68] Suetonius, on the other hand, states that Tiberius used Sejanus as a pawn and set him against Agrippina and her son.[69] Perhaps both Tiberius and Sejanus had the same goal—to stop Agrippina's single-minded obsession with advancing her sons.

If Tacitus is right, Tiberius was making the worst security mistake one can make: relying on friendship rather than verification. Sejanus played upon Tiberius's gnawing fears and suspicions, and Tiberius believed his accusations, demanding neither proof nor even plausibility. Blind confidence was all that a man like Sejanus needed.

THE DEATH OF DRUSUS

With his ambitions by marriage thwarted, it seems Sejanus turned his attention toward eliminating Drusus. In attacking Tiberius's son, he may have, for the first time, let his personal hopes override his loyalty to the emperor. By 23 the enmity between the two men had reached a critical point. During an argument Drusus had struck the prefect with his fist, and he openly lamented that "a stranger was invited to assist in the government while the emperor's son was alive."[70] With Tiberius already in his sixties, there was a real possibility of Drusus succeeding his father in the near future. To secure his own position, Sejanus secretly plotted against Drusus and succeeded in seducing his wife, Livilla.[71] It is alleged that, with Livilla as his accomplice, Drusus was slowly poisoned but appeared to die of seemingly natural causes on September 13, 23.[72] This played right into Agrippina's hands, for once Drusus was dead, the succession reverted back to the family of Germanicus. Her sons, Nero Caesar, Drusus Caesar, and Caligula, were presented to Tiberius as his heirs.[73]

The loss of his son was a major blow to Tiberius, both personally and politically. Over the years he had grown increasingly disillusioned with the position of princeps, and by sharing the tribunician powers with Drusus in 22, he had prepared to shed some of his responsibilities in favor of his son.[74] With these hopes now dashed, Tiberius left his administration more than ever in the care of Sejanus. If Sejanus was actually aiming at the throne, Agrippina's sons, Nero Caesar, Drusus Caesar, and Caligula were a direct threat to his power and "in the way."[75] The atmosphere around the palace fairly seethed over the competition for the throne. Agrippina, guarding her sons' interest, had become involved with a group of senators who opposed the growing power of Sejanus. Yet her relations with Tiberius were equally tense because she still believed that he was responsible for the death of Germanicus.[76] The climate was further poisoned by the hatred that Tiberius's mother (Augustus's widow), Livia Drusilla, felt for her, since Agrippina's ambition to be the mother of emperors and Rome's "first lady" was an open "secret."[77]

Sejanus, ever trying to improve his position, attempted to marry into the Julio-Claudian family again. Having divorced Apicata two years earlier, he requested marriage with Livilla in 25, possibly with an eye toward placing himself, as an adopted Julian, either in the position of a potential successor or at least regent for a young prince.[78] Although many writers try to paint Sejanus as after the throne itself, his motives are not that clear. Tacitus speaks of his desire to secure imperial power for himself, but this is vague.[79] Sejanus's ambitions were blocked by any man who could occupy the place of guardian to a prince and by any prince old enough to not need a guardian. The only slot he could aspire to was guardian to a prince too young to rule. Therefore, the adult princes were his roadblock.

Tiberius, being no fool, denied his request for marriage, warning Sejanus that he was in danger of overstepping his rank.[80] Faced with this sudden denigration, Sejanus changed his plans and began to isolate Tiberius from Rome. By fueling his paranoia toward Agrippina and the Senate, he encouraged the emperor to withdraw to the countryside of Campania, which he did in 26, and finally to the island of Capri, where Tiberius would spend the remainder of his life until his death in 37 CE.[81] With the emperor guarded by the Praetorians, Sejanus tried to control all the intelligence that passed between Tiberius and the capital.[82]

Despite the withdrawal of Tiberius from Rome's political scene, the presence of the dowager empress, Livia, seems to have checked Sejanus's overt power for a time. According to Tacitus, her death in 29 changed all that.[83] The chronology of what happened to Agrippina's family after Livia's death is confused, and there are contradictory versions of what occurred.[84] Sejanus began a series of purge trials of senators and wealthy equestrians in the city, removing those capable of opposing his power, as well as extending the imperial (and his own) treasury. Sejanus's technique was to employ *agents provocateurs* to arouse suspicions. Networks of spies and informers brought the victims to trial with false accusations of treason, and many chose suicide over the disgrace of being condemned and executed.

There seems to have been an endless series of plots against the aging, absentee emperor. Between the conviction of Agrippina and Nero Caesar (in late 29 or early 30; see below), and the fall of Sejanus in mid-October 31 there occurred several cases of treason. The chronology is uncertain due to the fragmentary nature of Dio's text, which, in the absence of the relevant books of Tacitus's *Annals*, is our principal source. We cannot even list the trials in order, but the defendants concerned included Gaius Asinius Gallus, a prominent senator and opponent of Tiberius who was linked to Agrippina's faction.[85] Tacitus doubted whether the suicide of Gallus was voluntary, and Tiberius was said to have regretted the fact that Gallus killed himself before he could be tried or acquitted.[86] Gnaeus Domitius Ahenobarbus, the father of the future emperor Nero, also faced arrest for involving himself in one of these schemes. He got lucky in that Tiberius died before he could be brought to trial. He escaped execution to be thrust back into the limelight as the emperor Caligula's brother-in-law and, nine months later, father of a new potential heir to the Julio-Claudian line, Nero.[87]

Meanwhile two influential nobles, Gaius Silius and Titius Sabinus, probably with accomplices unknown to us, formed a plot to place Drusus's elder brother, Nero Caesar, on the throne.[88] Silius had a military reputation and could probably have commanded the support of the armies formerly under Germanicus's authority, some of whose soldiers had wanted to raise his father to the throne a decade before. The plot became known to Sejanus. The prefect, having removed Tiberius's son, Drusus Caesar, from his path to the throne, now, according to Tacitus 4.12, was given the opportunity of getting Germanicus's three sons out of the way. The plot gave him the perfect opportunity to move against the eldest son of the house of Germanicus, and (if this was indeed his motive) to move closer to the throne himself—all this while also entrenching himself in Tiberius's favor and confidence by loyally protecting the emperor. There was a revolt forming, and he had to prevent this by eliminating two of the outstanding leaders of the movement. There immediately followed an indictment for high treason of Silius and his wife, Sosia. They committed suicide in 24.[89]

By 27 Sejanus's sustained attack upon Agrippina and her family came to its denouement. The prefect placed Nero Caesar and his mother, Agrippina, under military surveillance by Sejanus.[90] Every act or word of Nero was reported to Sejanus through Nero's wife, Julia, her mother, Livilla (Livia Julia), or by his secret agents. In 30 Agrippina and her two sons, Nero and the younger Drusus, were openly denounced by Sejanus. The reason that treason was not part of the charge is that the party may have been so strong that overt rebellion might have broken out. One also had to maintain the family name, whether they deserved it or not. Even when the indictment was read to the Senate, people were either dumbfounded or terrified. A goodly number of the Senate's members may have been sympathetic or even complicit in the movement.[91] Propaganda pamphlets claiming to be the opinions of consular senators began circulating in the Forum, denouncing Sejanus. Sejanus informed the emperor that the Senate refused to indict Agrippina and Nero Caesar. Eventually Tiberius asked for a trial to be held; we are ignorant of the proceedings.[92] Both were convicted and sentenced to exile. Nero's conviction was followed by his denunciation as an enemy of the state by the Senate, and he was confined to the island of Pontia.[93] Agrippina was removed to Pandateria, where, according to Suetonius, she was force-fed to prevent suicide and was beaten by a centurion so savagely that she lost an eye.[94] She had been a significant figure in dynastic politics during her entire adult life, and she became an even more potent symbol in the propaganda of her sole surviving son, Gaius, after her death.[95] Her memory would be rehabilitated and extravagantly honored by Caligula, as Gaius is more commonly known, both because she was his direct connection to Augustus and because of the personal qualities that had won her the support of many opponents of Tiberius during her life.

Caligula, as the last remaining son of Germanicus, managed to survive the purges of Sejanus only because Tiberius called him to Capri for safekeeping in 31.[96] It is anybody's guess why Tiberius allowed Caligula to survive. It has been suggested that the old emperor derived a grim satisfaction from watching the young man's struggle to be sycophantic to him every day in the hothouse atmosphere of the imperial court, which by then had been transferred to Capri, in the Bay of Naples.[97] This made him one of only two remaining heirs, the other being Tiberius Gemellus, son of Drusus the Younger. Caligula knew, that if Tiberius's place were ever taken by Sejanus, he would be doomed: his elder brothers and mother, who had backed Nero Caesar, were already dead or disgraced. Caligula, like his brothers, found himself assailed by agents of Sejanus, and duly reported this fact to his grandmother, Antonia.[98] Caligula had lived in Antonia's house from Livia's death in 29 until he was summoned to Capri sometime after his eighteenth birthday on August 31, 30 CE.[99] According to Josephus, it was Antonia, the mother of Livilla, who finally alerted Tiberius to the growing threat Sejanus posed, possibly with information provided by Satrius Secundus, in a letter she dispatched to Capri in the care of her freedman Pallas.[100] According to Juvenal, a letter was sent from Capri with the orders to execute Sejanus without a trial.[101]

With Tiberius not having been seen in Rome since 26 and with most of the political opposition crushed, Sejanus felt his position was unassailable. In 31, despite his equestrian rank, he shared the consulship with Tiberius *in absentia* and finally became betrothed to Livilla.[102] He had worked himself up to become the most powerful man in the empire. Tiberius was up to date on his intelligence. Once he realized to what extent Sejanus had already usurped his authority in Rome, he finally took steps to remove him from power, but an outright condemnation could provoke Sejanus to attempt a coup, so these things would have to be handled delicately. Once Tiberius ascertained that support for Sejanus was not as strong as he had feared, he chose another member of his security team, Naevius Sutorius Macro, previously prefect of the *vigiles* (Roman police and fire department), to be his point man, replace Sejanus, and effect Sejanus's downfall.[103]

On October 18, 31, Sejanus was summoned by a letter from Tiberius to a Senate meeting held ostensibly to bestow tribunician powers upon him. Sejanus entered the Senate at dawn, but while the letter was being read, Macro assumed control of the Praetorian Guard, and members of the *vigiles* led by Graecinius Laco surrounded the building.[104] The senators at first congratulated Sejanus, but when the letter, which first digressed into completely unrelated matters and then suddenly denounced him and ordered his arrest, he was immediately surrounded and escorted to prison. There he was strangled and his body unceremoniously cast down the Gemonian stairs, where the crowd tore it to pieces.[105] Tiberius was notified on Capri by a prearranged fire signal.

THE AFTERMATH

The excision of the traitor had been done expertly, but it could have easily gone the other way. The Guard, rather than follow its commander of seventeen years, stayed loyal to the emperor. It accepted Macro's donative (cash bonus) and then went on a rampage against the property of Sejanus and his friends, who were accused of actually having conspired with Sejanus.[106] Tiberius had a boat moored nearby to carry away Memmius Regulus, who had carried the letter to the Senate and put up the motion for Sejanus's death, to an overseas province, in case the Senate turned against him.[107]

Following the issue of *damnatio memoriae* by the Senate, Sejanus's statues were torn down and his name obliterated from all public records. Then his family and faction were eliminated.[108] On October 24, Sejanus's eldest son, Strabo, was arrested and executed. Upon learning of his death, Apicata committed suicide on October 26 but not before addressing a letter to Tiberius claiming that Drusus had been poisoned with the complicity of Livilla.[109] The accusations were further corroborated by confessions from Livilla's slaves, who admitted to having administered the poison to Drusus.

Although Rome at first rejoiced at the demise of Sejanus, the city quickly plunged into more extensive trials, as Tiberius relentlessly persecuted all those who could in any way be tied to the schemes of Sejanus or had courted his friendship. Livilla herself committed suicide or, as legend would have it, was forcibly starved to death by her own mother, Antonia Minor. The remaining children of Sejanus, Capito Aelianus and Junilla, were executed in December of 31. According to ancient historians, because there was no precedent for the capital punishment of a virgin, Junilla was raped before her execution, with the rope around her neck.[110] Their bodies were likewise thrown down the Gemonian stairs. At the beginning of the following year, *damnatio memoriae* was passed on Livilla.[111] A clean sweep had been made of the immediate family. Collateral relatives had to wait a while longer. The senatorial ranks were purged; the hardest hit were those families with political ties to the Julians. Even the imperial magistracy was not exempted from Tiberius's wrath. Arrests and executions were supervised by the new Praetorian prefect, Naevius Sutorius Macro. The political turmoil would continue until Tiberius died in 37.

Exactly what caused Sejanus's sudden downfall still remains a matter of debate. It was widely believed in antiquity that Sejanus was guilty of some form of treason and that he was a serious threat to Tiberius.[112] But could this attempted coup d'état not be a coup at all? Scholarly investigations over the last fifty years have tended to portray Sejanus more as a victim than a conspirator.[113] Because the accounts we do have differ, and with the fifth book of Tacitus largely lost, we will probably never know to what extent Sejanus was manipulated by Tiberius or whether it was the other way around. Modern authors who follow Suetonius assert that Sejanus was merely an instrument of Tiberius to hasten the downfall of Germanicus and his family and that he was quickly disposed of once he ceased to be useful. Tacitus refers to the conspiracy in the parts of the *Annals* that survive, but he gives no clear indication of its aims or intended victims.[114] Dio claims the real conspirator was Tiberius, who distrusted the intentions and growing political influence of his favorite.[115] It has even been suggested that the army commanders on the Rhine were involved.[116] Both the Praetorian Guard and the Syrian legions were rewarded, but whether it was for their refusal to take an active part in the conspiracy or simply for their acquiescence is unclear.[117]

Many modern historians consider it unlikely that Sejanus plotted to seize the imperial power for himself and, if he had planned so at all, rather might have aimed at overthrowing Tiberius to serve as a regent to Tiberius Gemellus, son of Drusus, or possibly even Gaius Caligula.[118] On the other hand, ambition has been known to make people delusional about their chances. Even as regent, his power would not last long. And his persecution of Caligula's mother and brothers should have given him real cause to fear for his future if Caligula became princeps. Perhaps he felt he needed to move quickly once Tiberius promoted Caligula's status in 31, recognizing him as his successor.[119]

Still, despite our lack of sources, we can count approximately fifty persons involved in the aftermath of Sejanus's downfall. This is more people than were implicated in the Pisonian conspiracy against the emperor Nero in 65 CE, and we have the full narrative of that event.[120] In the end, it does not matter what the real reason was. It is only important that Tiberius felt threatened and struck back. So large a number of people could not have been involved in a conspiracy and kept it quiet. Tiberius may have been settling some personal scores, possibly over the death of his son Drusus.[121]

The fact that all of the police and military personnel stayed loyal to Tiberius shows that his security system was working well. How this most unpopular of emperors used his security staff or whom they were used against is open to interpretation. In the mind of Tiberius, the only consideration had to be security; he needed no further justification. No doubt he thought the net needed to be cast out a bit farther than the Senate would have liked, but this was the prerogative of the chief executive.

THE DEATH OF TIBERIUS

After the trouble with Sejanus was cleaned up, Tiberius's last four years were relatively uneventful. He continued to do his duty plainly and straightforwardly, although from Capri. Illnesses and a fear of betrayal made him even more suspicious than he already was, and he had become a bitter man.[122] The countless trials for *maiestas* had alienated the Senate completely. His only contact with Rome was by correspondence, and this was mainly in order to have people he suspected of being ill-disposed toward him put on trial. Suetonius would have us believe Tiberius's days on Capri were filled with sexual perversions.[123] None of that really mattered. What mattered was the succession.

All of the arrangements he had made for his succession, as vague as they were, had come to naught. Tiberius had tried to continue the dynasty on lines laid down by Augustus. When that failed, he had tried giving power to Sejanus, possibly in hopes of keeping Caligula out of the running in favor of Gemellus; that also backfired.[124] In the end Tiberius was left with only two plausible heirs: Gaius Caligula, the son of Germanicus, who was twenty-five, and Tiberius Gemellus, son of Drusus, who was eighteen.[125] They were young, and Tiberius was by now past seventy. The idea that he would live long enough to pass the empire to two mature and well-trained princes that could both administer the empire in war and peace was unachievable. From a strictly legal point of view, all he could do was appoint an heir, and he bequeathed his estate jointly to Caligula and Gemellus.[126]

On March 16, 37 CE, Tiberius died in a villa in Misenum of an unknown sickness. He suffered from stabbing pains in his side and a high fever. Most scholars think he died of natural causes, but it seems that no emperor dies without a conspiracy theory to surround him. There are at least three conflicting accounts of his death, two of them attributing it to murder.[127] Tacitus tells us that a famous doctor, Charicles, was the emperor's occasional physician and was consulted during the last weeks of Tiberius's life.[128] During the visit, Charicles gave the emperor his hand out of courtesy, but in reality he was trying to do a quick check of his pulse. When Tiberius noticed this, he wanted to show the doctor that there was nothing wrong with him. He had a dinner prepared for himself, and he stayed at the table longer than usual. Nevertheless Charicles assured Macro, the prefect of the Praetorian Guard, that life was draining slowly out of the emperor and it would be a matter of days before he gave up the ghost.[129]

After that, everything was set into motion to prepare the provincial governors for the final farewell. On March 16, Tiberius's breath grew labored, and it was thought that death was imminent. Caligula entered the villa, thinking the moment had come for him to assume the reins of power. He was already being congratulated, but the jubilant mood turned sour when word came that Tiberius had opened his eyes and had asked for something to eat. There was general confusion, and no one knew exactly what to do. According to Tacitus, Macro kept a cool head. He went into Tiberius's room, gave the order to throw the covers over him, and suffocated the emperor.[130]

In the elder Seneca's account, written less than four years after the event, Tiberius, who knew that he was dying, took off his signet ring to give it to someone, but then changed his mind, put it back on his finger, and lay motionless for some time with his left fist clenched. Of course, how does anyone know this if Tiberius was alone? Suddenly he called for his servants, but no one came, so he got out of bed. The effort was too much for him; he collapsed near the bed and died on March 16, 37 CE, according to Seneca, of natural causes.[131]

A third version of the events by Suetonius openly speaks of murder, claiming that he had been poisoned by Caligula, who had set his sights on the throne and thought things were taking far too long. In this scenario Tiberius was the victim of a slow-acting, undetectable poison.[132]

Whatever the cause of death, once Tiberius had passed, Macro had Caligula saluted as *imperator* by the armed forces at Misenum as he arrived from Capri. When the news of the emperor's death was made public two days later, the people took to the streets crying out, "Throw Tiberius into the Tiber" and "May Mother Earth and the gods of the underworld give him a place among the damned."[133] Yet others threatened to avenge themselves on his corpse. In spite of the people's hatred, the soldiers brought his body to Rome. He was cremated in a solemn ceremony and interred in the Mausoleum of Augustus. He was *not* deified by the Senate, an honor reserved for emperors who met with the Senate's approval.

LEGACY

Tiberius is often portrayed as an old republican who objected to the principate and the freedoms Augustus had taken away.[134] He was nothing of the sort. He knew he was the head of state, and the state went on forever.

The way he handled his own transition of power and maintained his position with his new security service made the new imperial structure permanent. He maintained the Augustan constitution, avoided innovations, and turned the principate from a sham into what it purported to be: an autocratic government. He may have failed in his attempt to make the Senate take on more responsibility, but despite his unpopularity with the Senate and the Roman people, he managed to keep himself alive and on the throne. We will never be able to determine how many of the conspiracies against him, real or imagined, actually threatened his position, not even the supposed conspiracy of Sejanus. There is no conclusive proof in the sources that Tiberius ever intended to set aside the Julio-Claudian line for an ambitious outsider like Sejanus. It was loyalty to the dynasty that kept the armies quiet, and Tiberius would have been foolish to think they would tolerate a master who, for all his aristocratic connections by marriage, was the son of an *eques*.[135]

Despite his conservative outlook, developments occurred during his regime that would have a profound effect on the security of future emperors and the history of Rome. The reforms of Sejanus, most significantly the founding of the Castra Praetoria,[136] essentially established the Praetorian Guard as the powerful political force for which it is primarily known today. Henceforth the entire Guard was at the disposal of the emperors, but the rulers were now equally at the mercy of the Praetorians. The reality of this was seen in 31 when Tiberius was forced to rely upon the *vigiles* against the soldiers of his own Guard. Although the Praetorian Guard proved faithful to the aging Tiberius, their potential political power had been made clear.[137] The power Sejanus attained in his capacity as Praetorian prefect proved Maecenas right in his prediction to Augustus that it was dangerous to allow one man to command the Guard. There is an entire literary corpus of works on Sejanus as the avatar of ambition, not to mention a long list of the people he destroyed.[138] Cassius Dio noted that, after Sejanus, no other prefect except Gaius Fulvius Plautianus, who commanded the Guard under Septimius Severus, would rise to such influence.

Tacitus chastises Tiberius for his interpretation and overuse of the laws of *maiestas*. While it is true that the Julian law could encompass a wide range of charges—insult, slander, adultery, and so forth—he ignored perceived slights to the emperor's dignity, but attacks on his life could not be allowed. How many times you use such a law depends on how many conspirators you think you have working against you. Where does self-defense end and paranoia begin? The vague nature of the *maiestas* laws made it possible to prosecute anyone who "diminished the majesty of the Roman people," whatever that was taken to mean. This made it a particularly flexible weapon in the political game and could provide opportunities for malicious political prosecution. The fact that so many people were executed or committed suicide in the reign of Tiberius in part accounts for his reputation for misuse of ancient precedents for his own cruel ends. Tiberius is accused of taking on capital jurisdiction, using the Senate for trials, and inflicting penalties far beyond what the law had previously allowed.[139] Tacitus defends the aristocratic point of view of the senators and paints Tiberius as demented. Others see these trials as the measure of the malice and stupidity with which Tiberius had to contend in his dealings with the Senate.[140]

Tacitus chooses his examples of prosecution carefully to highlight the rise of informers. These were cases in which the defendants were persons of distinction and Tiberius took part in the prosecution.[141] It is unfair, however, to blame Tiberius entirely. In the absence of modern forms of investigation and prosecution, the principate eagerly relied on professional informers. Added to this was the reluctance of friends and family to assist defendants for fear that they might seem accessories to treason and the Senate's sycophantic readiness not merely to condone such abuses, but to initiate such abuses themselves.[142] Tiberius had not created this situation, nor could he conjure it out of existence. He stepped in to prevent abuse in several cases, exploitation in others, or the irresponsible application of the law. He could do nothing more. He could not simply abolish the law of treason and leave his own life at risk. It was impossible to check ahead of time if a man were an honest and loyal citizen or a *delator* who had spotted a likely victim. The charges had to be brought forward publicly, thus setting the deadly wheels in motion. There was no independent safeguard that could keep a close check on the merits of individual cases and throw out those that were patently malicious or absurd. Tiberius, in spite of the tenacity of the informers and the spinelessness of the Senate, did his best to see that justice was not mis-served.

The emperor seems to have adopted a detached attitude toward the informers, judging their performances while he remained at Rome. After all, they were doing him a service.[143] *Delatores* may have been hated under the principate, but an emperor could not really do without them. No matter how much the later emperors tried to stamp out *delatores*, they would reappear, offering news of a new conspiracy.[144] Since rewards for successful prosecutions were in proportion to the seriousness of the offense, they varied at the discretion of the Senate. Provision was made in the *Lex Julia Maestatis* as in other laws. One quarter of the defendant's property was the standard material reward, but there were probably others. Nor were *delatores* marginal, back-alley snitches. They came from the senatorial classes. Under some statutes the accusers were entitled to take the insignia of the victim and his seniority.[145] So in the case of Libo Drusus, for example, the four accusers received praetorships *extra ordinem*, and the entire property was divided between them. They could also be given priesthoods (perhaps in the college or colleges in which the accused had belonged). What we have thus is a class of men who acquired not only the favor of the emperor but also standing and wealth through the practice of prosecution. They received much opportunity during the reign of Tiberius, and they continued to be maintained under other emperors, especially those whose fear and paranoia made them tyrannical.[146] Tiberius has been blamed for actively encouraging them, notably by refusing to deprive them of their rewards even when defendants committed suicide. He also backed certain individual prosecutions.[147] Part of this was a political phenomenon. Senatorial life was competitive, and crawling up the *cursus honorum* on the back of someone else was nothing new. Part of this was also a social phenomenon wherein new men were fighting against the conservative prejudice that had previously kept them in their place. There had been a tremendous amount of social mobility under Augustus, but that was now coming to an end, and some families found themselves in financial difficulties and unable to improve their status.[148]

Pursuing one's enemies ruthlessly in the courts was one of the less appealing aspects of republican freedom. Tiberius prided himself on his knowledge of Roman law. He respected the law and wanted an even-handed administration of justice. He sat in with jurists, advised consuls, and in his early career, even according to Tacitus, admirably administered the laws.[149] The *Lex Julia Maiestatis* was the major exception and with good reason. This was the law under which treasonous persons would be tried. As the principate was only on its second princeps, certain adjustments needed to be made based on the experiences of an emperor who had watched his family be subjected to assassinations and attempted assassinations. There were changes in both the penalties and the rewards for the accusers. The fact that the period following the execution of Sejanus held the most prosecutions speaks volumes about how Tiberius felt he needed to handle threats to his power or life.[150]

The biographies of Suetonius and the embellishments of Robert Graves in *I, Claudius* notwithstanding, there *were* plots by people from both inside his family and outside of it.[151] Tiberius was able to protect himself from the plebs, the Senate, and his own family, which is no small feat. From the point of view of internal security, Tiberius's approach is often described as "paranoid," but if half the plots against him were real, he was certainly justified in being overly suspicious—and a bit tired of it all after more than twenty years. He did not kill everyone who crossed him or even everyone who plotted against him. Although he admired the virtue of *clementia* (clemency), he was also pragmatic.[152] He extended clemency to those who opposed his rise to power. He continued to offer it to lesser political offenders. He showed forbearance toward the antics of Agrippina, knowing that he could have had her executed and her body thrown on the Gemonian steps.[153] Tiberius's clemency, shown to defeated and convicted rivals, came from a position of strength. In the whole twenty-two years of Tiberius's reign, half the people accused of treason escaped conviction, while the four innocent people who were condemned were victims of the excessive zeal of the Senate, not of the emperor's tyranny.[154] Tiberius made the best of a bad situation; he had to keep the Senate happy by discerning actual treason from mere abuse or lesser crimes. As we shall see in the next chapter, his successor, Caligula, would show neither tolerance nor mercy—but he would not survive his own principate.

5

The Conspiracy That
Killed Caligula

The reign of the emperor Caligula[1] presents us with the first full-blown conspiracy that resulted in an assassination, and it is one of the best documented events of the Julio-Claudian era.[2] Whatever security measures were taken, they failed to keep the ruler alive. As suggested in chapter 1, there were four constituencies an emperor had to keep under control to be safe: the aristocracy, the military, the populace, and his own family. By the end of his reign, Caligula had lost all four, so, in a sense, we should not be surprised he ended up dead.

Much has been made of Caligula's character flaws—his cruelty, his sexual exploits, his eccentricities, and his paranoia. One can turn to any biographer for descriptions of bizarre behavior, suggestions of illness, or even insanity.[3] Distinguishing the line between outrageous behavior and insanity, however, is not the task of the historian. In the end the exercise is futile anyway, because we are not dealing with an objective portrait of a ruler but are faced with a case of ancient character assassination. It was part of the ancient literary tradition to suggest that Caligula had to be killed because he had become unhinged. Recent biographers have tried to salvage from the biased sources a more realistic picture of the third emperor as simply a willful, indiscreet autocrat with sadistic tastes, and they try to find some method in his madness.[4] It would be surprising if Caligula had not become unhinged considering he spent his childhood surrounded by conspiracies and murder and that they continued long into his own reign. Under these circumstances it is understandable that he might lash out against the aristocracy and the military elements that allied with his family almost from the beginning to have him killed.[5]

The atmosphere in which Caligula was raised was enough to make anyone paranoid. He was the son of Germanicus, whose own death was suspected as a murder. His mother Agrippina and all his brothers were done away with because of the machinations of Sejanus and the suspicions of the emperor Tiberius. Now the young boy was called to live on Capri with the very man who had presided over the murder of most of his close relatives. He had to learn how to protect his position from continuous threats against his life.

Caligula's efforts to stay alive and make it to the throne were aided and abetted by his head of security, the Praetorian prefect Macro. Caligula was the popular heir apparent, and he realized he would need the support of the military once he came to power.[6] We are told by Philo that Macro saved Caligula's life several times on Capri, showing that conspiracies were his constant reality. Some of the *maiestas* trials under Tiberius were against men who had plotted against Caligula.[7]

THE SUCCESSION PROBLEM

The weak point in the Augustan system was the succession problem, and that flaw plagued Caligula as much as it had his two predecessors. There was no legal way for Tiberius to pass on the principate. In his will, he designated as his heirs his young grandson, Tiberius Gemellus, and his grandnephew, Caligula. Neither of these two young men held any office that might mark them as the next princeps. All that legally distinguished them from any other claimant was their kinship to the Julio-Claudian line and their designation as Tiberius's heirs. Tiberius did not intend for Gemellus, his grandson by blood, to be passed over. On the other hand, how could he expect Gemellus to survive against Caligula? Tiberius was aware of the weakness of his grandson Gemellus in comparison to the much older and more popular Caligula, who was the choice of the army and the darling of the masses even during the lifetime of Tiberius.[8] Caligula held, as the son of Germanicus, tremendous popularity and also enjoyed prestige as a direct heir of Augustus, but the fact is he came to power through ill-defined and probably illegal means.[9]

On the same day that Tiberius died, the Praetorian Guard in Misenum proclaimed Caligula *imperator*. They administered the loyalty oath to the new princeps, and it is interesting that in the oath Caligula is referred to as *imperator*—a title that shows acclamation by the troops.[10] He was not called *Augustus*, which was a title that could only be bestowed by the Senate. A crowd broke into the Curia and compelled the senators to annul Tiberius's will, disenfranchise Gemellus, and give full and absolute power to Caligula.[11] On the instigation of Macro, the Senate did just that and proclaimed Caligula as both sole heir and the next emperor.[12] By the time the Senate declared for Caligula, however, he had already taken *de facto* power through a first-ever coalition between the claimant to the throne and the Praetorian Guard. The Senate was so happy to be rid of Tiberius that they complacently handed over supreme power to a personable but totally inexperienced young man who was being micromanaged by the head of state security. Macro had insured the support of both the military commanders and the provincial governors. Having the head of security given this much power set a dangerous precedent.

There must have been a number of people in the Senate who resented being maneuvered into handing over both the trappings and the reality of power to an untrained twenty-five-year-old, especially one being handled by Macro, but Caligula and his handler knew where the power lay. When it came time to dispense the legacies that Tiberius had left—that is, the thousand sesterces each he had promised the Praetorians—the new emperor doubled them. Caligula became the first emperor to acknowledge his debt to the Praetorians for his accession. Two of Caligula's immediate successors, Claudius and Nero, would also be acclaimed by the soldiers before being recognized by the Senate.[13]

AN AUSPICIOUS BEGINNING

During the first six months of his reign, Caligula behaved with remarkable restraint and modesty.[14] In 38 CE he tried to restore popular elections, although with no success.[15] Candidates could not be found who would risk standing for elections; the people remained passive, perhaps for their own protection.[16] And in the end, why would anyone waste their energies voting for magistrates who were powerless?[17]

Caligula seemed secure enough at the beginning of his reign to abolish some of the charges that had been Tiberius's main weapon against his enemies. Some believe this was the law of *maiestas* but, as P. A. Brunt has argued, no government in any age suspends the law under which an assassin could be prosecuted.[18] There had been fear and resentment under Tiberius because he used the statute in ways it was not originally intended. Used too liberally, the law could be used to prosecute anything from insulting the emperor to outright treason. As popular as it was to get rid of the charge, this was the one law that covered attacks against the princeps and guaranteed the security of the state. Caligula wanted to show that there was no need to fear any retribution from him due to malice against those who meant the emperor no harm or who, in the past, had hurt his relatives. He announced he would not be one who had "ears for *delatores*." He made a great public show of burning the papers and letters relating to those cases in the Forum, swearing he had never read or even touched them.[19] He was generous in doing away with many such cases, putting aside all of those still pending, and calling back from exile all those people already condemned.

Caligula's actions seem genuine on the surface, but no emperor can live without the protection of laws against treason, and there were certainly hints of machinations against Caligula from the very outset. His reaction to these seem a bit naïve. Suetonius records that soon after his accession he made a show of refusing to accept a document with evidence of some sort of plot against him, claiming that he had done nothing to make anyone hate him and that he had no time for informers.[20] Realistically, if there is a plot against the emperor, the one thing he really *would* want is an informer. Besides, people do not have to hate you to want to kill you; they can kill you simply because they want your job. Factions do not really form on love and hate but on common interests. They form on the desire for power or loyalty to bloodlines. Hatred may motivate the person who actually strikes the blow, but that person is usually supported by people who have a whole other agenda. In short, the abolition of *maiestas* charges became a formality, like an amnesty, at the beginning of each reign, but the gesture was probably more symbolic than practical. Neither Caligula nor any other emperor should leave himself exposed to the dangers of sedition.[21] If the threat were real, he would have to face it sooner or later. Threats would come from the same constituencies that threatened the first two emperors. Keeping good relations with them all would be Caligula's challenge.

CALIGULA'S ILLNESS AND THE AFTERMATH

The honeymoon period of the first six months of the new regime came to a crashing halt in the summer of 37 when Caligula came down with a serious illness.[22] The ancient sources seem to suggest this was a turning point in Caligula's reign, and at least one writer, Philo, implies a causative link between his illness and his subsequent behavior. Modern historians have been less likely to see any dramatic shift in his behavior.[23] Even if there was a change in his behavior, it might not have been because his illness had a lasting physical effect or unhinged him in any way. Having survived the illness and seen what was done in his absence, perhaps he decided to take control of his life and run the state in a way that has caused later historians to call him autocratic. Although it has been asserted that "Caligula's fear of a conspiracy against him began after his illness in 37," one need only look at the previously mentioned *maiestas* trials arranged by Macro on his behalf before Caligula came to the throne to see that his fear of conspiracies began early and remained almost continuous.

They were not just the result of illness or paranoia; they were the result of actual attempts to take his job and his life. The earliest plots against Caligula are poorly documented, and we will probably never know all the participants or all of their motives because of the vagueness of the sources.[24] Suetonius, for example, comments that before the final plot that killed the emperor, there were "one or two others" and that the prefects of the Guard were implicated in some conspiracy or other.[25] Josephus says only that conspiracies were "commonly formed against him."[26]

THE PLOTS BEGIN:
37 CE GEMELLUS, SILANUS, AND MACRO

Shortly after Caligula's recovery, the spirit of universal goodwill disappeared with a series of forced suicides. First came Gemellus, then Caligula's father-in-law, Silanus, and finally the Praetorian prefect himself, Macro. The sources are frustratingly reticent about the details; we are not even certain of the dates.[27] Even the simple premise that these events might be related is unprovable, but one can make a reasonable guess about the cause by looking for the motive. In what ways were all three men a threat to Caligula?[28]

During Caligula's illness, someone had to act in his place. Had a group, possibly including old enemies of Germanicus's family, anticipated Caligula's death and started working toward putting Gemellus on the throne? The charge against Gemellus, made in late 37, was exactly that: "anticipating the death of the *Princeps*" and waiting for the chance to benefit from it.[29] Philo flatly states that the charge of conspiracy was false. Suetonius tells a more convoluted story about Gemellus having to take medicine for a chronic cough, and the smell of the medicine led to the charge that he was taking an antidote against poison.[30] Whatever really happened, Caligula may have interpreted his actions as dictated by ambition rather than necessity or circumstance. If Gemellus had a party of supporters around him, it must have been a very small and not terribly powerful one.[31] In the end, the poor young man's only sin may have been being the one viable candidate for the throne in the case of Caligula's death. Soldiers were dispatched to make him commit suicide, but the pathetic boy did not even know what to do with the sword they handed to him, and he had to be helped.[32] We will never know if there was a nascent conspiracy, but the public did not criticize Caligula for this execution or the ones that followed. Caligula believed he was acting for "reasons of state." This kind of dynastic elimination is an integral part of any hereditary succession; one only need remember the elimination of Agrippa Postumus under Tiberius or that of Britannicus under Nero.[33]

We are equally in the dark about the fall of Caligula's father-in-law, Marcus Junius Silanus. Both Silanus and Macro had been the men who had ushered in Caligula's reign and tutored him in the ways of the principate. We know of no link between Silanus and Gemellus. Neither Philo nor Dio say anything that would suggest what led to Silanus's downfall except perhaps that the emperor resented his father-in-law's attempts to guide things along.[34] An anecdote that appears in Tacitus suggests that there was a man named Silanus plotting against Caligula but, if the father-in-law had been the figurehead of such a conspiracy, there would have had to be an open trial in the Senate. That never happened because Silanus committed suicide with his own razor.[35] Silanus's daughter, Junia Claudilla, had predeceased her father; she died in childbirth in 36 or 37. Caligula's suspicion that there had been some kind of plot underfoot may have turned the emperor's mind to the subject of producing an heir for the succession. He married his second wife, Livia Orestilla, in 37 CE. The fact that Caligula abducted her during her wedding to another man, Gaius Calpurnius Piso, did not solve the succession problem. She continued to see Piso on the sly, which disqualified her as the mother of possible imperial offspring.[36]

In the first part of 38 CE, Caligula eliminated his staunchest supporter and head of security, Macro. Philo records that Caligula contrived charges against the prefect because, among other things, he was tired of being reminded of the role Macro had played in the succession, in particular in ensuring the loyalty of the Praetorians after the death of Tiberius.[37] Philo attributes his fall to acting as guide and mentor to an emperor now tired of listening to others. Caligula is quoted as saying, "*Tolmai tis didaskein?* (Who dares teach me?)"[38] Macro had brought the army over to him and saved him from many an error, but now he was to pay the price. There is no hint of any conspiratorial activity in Philo, although Dio does imply that several other people were executed at the same time. It is tempting to speculate that Macro's fall was a result of conspiratorial dealings with Gemellus or Silanus and others.[39] Had they thought Caligula was going to die because of his illness, Macro would have positioned himself with the new princeps exactly as he had done with Caligula. If the Praetorian prefect, a new prince, and a senior family member had made plans about what would happen if Caligula died, then when Caligula recovered he may have interpreted these discussions as possible treason. In the end, we have no way of proving this conjecture.

Caligula acted very carefully and deliberately. He had Macro appointed prefect of Egypt—possibly a ploy to keep him occupied and unsuspecting, much like giving Sejanus the tribunician power.[40] Such a transfer would remove him from the command that had the potential to do the greatest harm to the emperor and would isolate him from the capital and, perhaps more importantly, from the soldiers there. Macro, however, never made it to Egypt. The charges came down as an accusation of adultery, specifically *lenocinium*, which means "pandering." The fact that Caligula was having an affair with Macro's wife, Ennia, and supposedly with Macro's approval, would support this charge. Macro may have originally thought this would buy him favor with the emperor, and Caligula went along with it since he needed the support of the Praetorian prefect. If this was indeed the arrangement, it had now outlived its usefulness.[41] As we will see many times over, however, charges of sexual misconduct were often substituted for charges of treason in order for the administration to cover up any hint of instability or unpopularity of the emperor.[42]

The actions against Macro and Ennia were kept a secret. Perhaps by covering up the charges of disloyalty with accusations of sexual misconduct, the emperor could disguise how precarious his political position was.[43] Early in 38 CE the prefect and his wife committed suicide, possibly to keep their estate intact. If the charge had really been treason, Macro's estate would have been confiscated. We know this did not happen, because Macro was able to leave enough money to build an amphitheater in his hometown of Alba Fucens.[44]

There is no indication that the Praetorian Guard itself was in any way implicated in Macro's downfall, and there is no record of its reaction to his removal. The hasty nature of Macro's death has suggested to some scholars, however, that there was some suspicion of the office itself on the part of the emperor. Neither when a new Praetorian prefect was appointed nor who it was are known at this point.[45] After Macro's death, however, Caligula probably felt that putting control of the Praetorian Guard in the hands of one man was dangerous. It may have been at this time that the command of the Guard was divided in two. None of the sources specifically mentions a formal change, but they do refer to the dual Praetorian prefects later under Caligula.[46]

LEPIDUS, GAETULICUS, AND THE SISTERS

Conspiracies against Caligula continued from the autumn of 39 onward until another raised its ugly head on January 24, 41. With Macro and Gemellus gone, another threat arose and centered around two influential men: Marcus Aemilius Lepidus, the emperor's most important senatorial confidant, and Cn. Cornelius Lentulus Gaetulicus, the commander in Upper Germany.[47] Other participants included members of Caligula's immediate family, his two sisters, Agrippina and Livilla. Tacitus claims Agrippina entered into an affair with Lepidus "out of her lust for power," but if Lepidus and the sisters plotted to overthrow Caligula, it could only have been because they both thought it would serve their own best interests politically.[48] Caligula's marriage to Caesonia in the summer of 39 might have provided them with such a motive.[49] Caesonia gave birth to a daughter, thus producing legitimate offspring and removing Agrippina and Livilla and their children from possible succession to the throne. Lepidus's wife, Drusilla (also the emperor's sister), was already dead, so Lepidus's only connection to the imperial family would be through the two remaining sisters.[50] Nobody involved seemed to object to the principate as an institution; they objected only to the reigning emperor and perhaps wanted the position themselves.[51]

Also privy to the plot were a large number of senators, including both of the consuls, who had taken office on July 1. Any plot to overthrow Caligula would also need military backing, which is why Lepidus allied himself with someone in command of legions. There is a single line in Suetonius's *Life of Claudius* that tells us of the exposure of the "conspiracy of Lepidus and Gaetulicus." Since Gaetulicus had command over four legions and indirect influence over another four, plus the two new legions, the XV and XXII Primigeniae, which were being raised in connection with a planned invasion of Britain, we may now have the military link we need. It is the only reference in the sources that suggests any kind of collaboration between the two men, and there has been no end to the speculation about what form their cooperation might have taken.[52]

The conspirators had everything they needed for a successful coup: military backing in the empire, broad support among the aristocracy, consular authority, and the emperor's closest relatives. To this they could add all the virtues of simplicity and surprise. They had a presumptive future emperor and empress at hand and state supporters to recognize them. Agrippina's son Nero even offered a successor in the next generation. As far as conspiracies go, this was the best set of circumstances one could have. Now all they had to do was kill Caligula. If they succeeded in assassinating him far from his court, they could march on Rome at the head of Gaetulicus's legions to ensure Lepidus's acceptance by both the Senate and the Praetorian Guard.[53]

As often happens in such affairs, however, things did *not* go as planned for the conspirators. Our sources do not reveal who acted as Caligula's spies, but they betrayed the plot. His agents were probably not able to uncover the complete extent of the conspiracy. Evidently only Gaetulicus and the senatorial circles in Rome fell under suspicion at first. Caligula's response was swift and effective. Without wasting much time investigating the charges fully, Caligula had both Lepidus and Gaetulicus executed.[54] In the early days of September, he also removed the two consuls from office and ordered his minions to break their *fasces*, the bundle of rods that symbolized their office and the power connected to it.[55] One of the consuls committed suicide.[56] It may be at this same time that the Senate's hold on the last military unit that had remained formally under its control was taken away—the legion in the province of Africa. Caligula replaced its commander.[57]

There has been a great deal of discussion over the events surrounding Gaetulicus's death. He was eliminated in 39 during the emperor's planned military campaigns against Britain and Germany.[58] The emperor traveled north to Mevania on the banks of the Clitumnus River, accompanied by a detachment of the Praetorian Guard. This spot was famous for its oracles and, in this case, the oracle advised him to reinforce his German bodyguard. Suetonius claims that Caligula's expedition to Germany was in part intended to recruit a Batavian bodyguard, suggested perhaps by the fact that he brought such a unit back with him, but it certainly was not the main motivation.[59] There was no need for Caligula to move quickly, say, to surprise Gaetulicus, because he could not have possibly kept his movements secret, and there is no evidence to suggest he was in Germany when Gaetulicus was eliminated. It may well be that Caligula stayed in Mevania, protected by the Praetorians, and sent agents including Servius Sulpicius Galba to Germany to eliminate Gaetulicus before the emperor's arrival. Once he knew Gaetulicus was dead, he could proceed to Germany, where he replaced Gaetulicus with Galba. This re-creation is speculative, but it makes sense from a security point of view.[60] By October 27, 39, the conspiracy of Gaetulicus had been exposed and suppressed, and the commander had been executed along with some other men.[61]

The full scope of the conspiracy apparently came to light only after Gaetulicus was executed. Perhaps he was tortured first or just gave up names in an attempt to save his own life.[62] There may also be a good case for the connection between the executions of Calvisius Sabinus, the Governor of Pannonia, and Gaetulicus. They had both been consuls in 26. The possible combination of Sabinus's two Pannonian legions and those under Gaetulicus's direct or indirect charge could have put the possible conspirators in charge of about half the available legionary troops in the empire.[63]

In the end, we will never know the exact thing that precipitated Gaetulicus's plot because the sources tell us nothing. Punishment of the conspirators suggests ambition. Lepidus, Agrippina, and Livilla were found guilty as accessories to the plot to assassinate the emperor. Lepidus was executed, and the two sisters were banished to the Pontine islands.[64] The emperor produced letters he claimed were from both women, in their own handwriting, revealing their share in planning the conspiracy.[65] Caligula forced Agrippina to take the urn with the ashes of her lover Lepidus back to Rome, carrying it against her body for the whole journey.

It was a macabre restaging of the journey that her mother had made with their father's ashes twenty years earlier.[66]

Caligula distributed money to the soldiers as a reward for their continued loyalty to him and sent the three swords with which the plotters planned to kill him to Rome, where they were placed in the temple of Mars Ultor (Mars the Avenger). The sending of the daggers to the temple suggests Caligula thought he had survived a serious threat on his life. The charges of adultery could be the usual cover-up for political intrigue with the claim of sexual indiscretion.[67]

In a letter, Caligula informed the Senate of the assassination he had narrowly escaped and forbade the senators to vote honors for any of his relatives in the future. The dating of these events and the nature of the conspiracy can be seen from a fragmentary inscription of the priestly college known as the Arval Brethren. On October 27, 39, they performed a sacrifice to offer thanks that "the nefarious plans of Gnaeus Lentulus Gaetulicus against Gaius Germanicus" had been detected.[68]

Caligula took measures to reorganize the troops in Germany. Several commanders of forces deployed to Germany from other provinces in the empire received dishonorable discharges because they had arrived on the scene too late. Evidently they were suspected of having held back intentionally, waiting to see if Gaetulicus's uprising would be successful. Caligula attempted to decimate one of the legions that twenty-four years earlier had temporarily rebelled against his father, Germanicus, over pay and conditions of service, even though there would be almost no one still in that legion who would remember those events. When one of the legions threatened to rebel against him, he beat a hasty retreat from the camp.[69]

On returning to Rome, Caligula embarked on a series of trials of prominent people for treason. He was accused of doing this just to confiscate their property, but we can only imagine Caligula's state of mind when he found out that not only the senatorial order but even his own sisters were out to kill him. His siblings were the people who had been closest to him personally, and no one would have been surprised if he had put them to death. The comparatively mild treatment they received may perhaps point to the close relationship they once shared. Legal proceedings were taken against individuals who could be shown to have had conspiratorial contacts with Caligula's sisters or the men who had been executed. In addition to the consuls, who had already been removed from office, several aediles and praetors had to resign from office and stand trial.[70] Even men not involved in the conspiracy must have felt a bit queasy at this point. The aristocracy feared the emperor would take further measures, and one never knew how far out that ring would extend.[71]

The conspiracy of Agrippina, Livilla, and Lepidus had presented Caligula with the same threat that had plagued his imperial predecessors and that would also plague his successors. The very people who made up the emperor's closest circle were also the ones who could endanger his security. Precisely because they were close to the emperor or could deny access to the emperor for others, they had power that could be turned against him. In a sense the emperor had to be most mistrustful of the very people he was supposed to be able to trust. This is why emperors came to rely on freedmen and members of the equestrian class to fill politically sensitive positions. Caligula systematically exploited the advantages that this group offered. After Lepidus was executed and the emperor's sisters banished, we hear nothing more of Roman aristocrats who acquired influence and wealth as members of Caligula's inner circle or through personal ties to him. The emperor used freedmen to keep himself informed of plots. It was Gaius Julius Callistus who may have informed Caligula of the conspiracy against him.[72] In the aftermath, according to Josephus, Callistus inspired fear in people because of the power and influence he achieved with the emperor.[73] Another freedman, Protogenes, had the same investigative powers—he recorded the behavior of six hundred members of the aristocracy and the intended punishment for each in books labeled "Sword" and "Dagger."[74] An Egyptian slave named Helicon was always at the emperor's side and acted as an unofficial bodyguard.[75]

These men, along with the emperor's new wife, Caesonia, were his new inner circle. He removed all aristocrats from his inner circle and therefore from the political nerve center of the empire.[76] Internal security and the emperor's need for personal safety were dictating policy and affecting Rome's traditional political institutions. Officers of the Praetorian Guard were authorized to collect taxes and unpaid tribute. Caligula was using his security staff and those left whom he felt he could trust to run the palace.[77]

THE PLOTS CONTINUE, 40 CE: SEXTUS PAPINIUS, ANICIUS CERIALIS

Upon his return from Germany, Caligula was met by a senatorial delegation feigning enthusiasm and urging him to make haste. He is said to have replied, "I'm coming, I'm coming, and this will be with me!" with a gesture toward his sword.[78] By 40 CE Caligula was no longer a very popular emperor, even among the people of Rome. A crowd at the circus, for example, showed signs of contempt for the emperor, who immediately commanded his soldiers to attack the spectators, many of whom were killed; thereafter, the crowd remained silent.[79] He was later voted a security guard for himself and his statues.[80] He spent a great deal of time outside of Rome due at least in part to fear of assassination. It was probably around this same time that he began to insist on the official cult of himself, or of his genius, in Rome. He hoped that fostering popularity for himself among the people might protect him from what he perceived as the growing threat from the nobility.

Caligula was right about his presence in Rome making him more vulnerable to treason. In a very short time another plot was formed, detected, and crushed. The identification of the members of this conspiracy is difficult. Tacitus does not name any of the members but does say that there was a conspiracy, and he recounts incidents from the inquisition and punishment of the suspects.[81] Two of the men were Anicius Cerialis and Sextus Papinius (inaccurately identified by Dio as Cerialis's son).[82] We are told they were both tortured by Caligula, but Cerialis maintained his silence while Papinius was convinced to name names by the promise of a pardon. One would think the torture, rather than just a promise that could be revoked, would make him talk. According to Dio, on the testimony of Papinius, Cerialis and others were executed in Papinius's presence.[83] Some historians believe Papinius betrayed some of the other conspirators besides Cerialis. Other historians question the story entirely since there was an Anicius Cerialis forced to commit suicide in 66 on suspicion of disloyalty to Nero, and he was described as having earlier *betrayed a conspiracy to Caligula*. If this was the same man, then he was not executed and had a record of sycophantic collaboration. It is no wonder he aroused little sympathy.[84]

MORE PLOTS IN 40 CE:
BETILINIUS BASSUS AND BETILINIUS CAPITO

Still another group of conspirators rose up that included Betilinius Bassus, a quaestor, and his father, the procurator Betilinius Capito. Dio provides most of the details, although Seneca writes of the group, too.[85] Their deaths belong to the same conspiracy that included a man named Papinius. It is tempting to conclude that these men were those who were said to have been betrayed by Cerialis.[86] It is Dio who adds the detail that Capito was forced to be present at his son Bassus's execution.

Although not personally guilty of any crime, when Capito asked that he be allowed to close his eyes, Caligula ordered him executed. In an attempt to save his own life, Capito offered to disclose the names of others in the conspiracy. Dio implies very strongly that the people identified by him were, in fact, involved in a conspiracy—namely, the prefects of the

Praetorian Guard and the powerful freedman Callistus. Whether this was true or whether Capito was just naming people of influence, we do not know. It might have worked until Capito went too far and added Caesonia, the emperor's wife, to the list of the accused![87]

And where was the Senate in all of this? When A. Titus Rufus accused the Senate of thinking one way and voting another, he was forced to commit suicide. He was openly calling them to rally against Caligula, but those who did preferred to do so in secret.[88]

THE PLOTS OF 40 CE: THE PHILOSOPHERS

Among the others accused in this early phase of conspiracies was Julius Canus, a Stoic philosopher. Canus is the first identifiable example of what was to become a familiar type on the imperial scene under the Julio-Claudians: courageous Stoic opposition.[89] Seneca's description of Canus's death suggests that there was a senatorial trial involved.[90] Another member of the senatorial order to die was Julius Graecinus, the father of Agricola, the famous general from Britain. Graecinus was a philosopher and possibly a Stoic. All Seneca says is that he was a *vir egregius* (a man of distinction) and that he was a better man than it suited a tyrant to be. Tacitus relates the execution to his refusal to prosecute Silanus, although he survived the trial of Silanus by two years.[91]

Senators as a group seem to have shown a distinct lack of zeal in protecting those willing to take a stand against Caligula. One exception is Pomponius, a man of Epicurean leanings, who held a number of political offices and was of consular rank; he was betrayed by a disloyal friend, Timidius.[92] The main witness was Quintilia, a beautiful actress and Pomponius's mistress. She was tortured, but held firm, suffering horrific punishment that left her disfigured. Caligula was so moved by her courage and wrecked body that he gave her a gift of money as compensation, put by Suetonius at 800,000 sesterces.[93] Pomponius did not match Quintilia's bravery. During her interrogation, it is said, she gave a secret signal to reassure Cassius Chaerea, the Praetorian tribune, a gesture that suggests that her lover was, in fact, involved with the conspirators. Cassius Chaerea was the protagonist in the final phase of the attempt on Caligula's life, and the tradition that he and Quintilia were involved together strongly suggests to some that the supposed "earlier" and "later" conspiracies were both part of the same operation.[94]

The orator and Stoic philosopher Lucius Annaeus Seneca also seems to have been on the fringe of the conspiracy.[95] At least he was close to the people who fell from grace. He was condemned to death but spared, according to Dio, because Caligula learned through a female associate that he was in an advanced state of consumption and would die soon anyway.[96]

STILL MORE PLOTS OF 40 CE: SCRIBONIUS PROCULUS

By 40–41 the senatorial order was scared to death of the emperor, and Caligula was on a rampage looking for conspirators. His investigations did smoke out one figure about whom very little is known, the senator Scribonius Proculus. The emperor's tactic seems to have been to isolate him. Caligula called a meeting and declared an amnesty for him, but now everyone around him feared for themselves, and the incident resulted in an outbreak of abject sycophancy. Protogenes, a freedman, was used to set Proculus up for execution at a meeting of the Senate. Protogenes entered the Senate one day on some pretext, and when senators greeted him, he rebuked Proculus for addressing him. This was evidently a pre-arranged signal, since a number of senators now set upon the man and brutally murdered him. He was hacked to pieces and a large number of senators were involved in the savagery. According to Suetonius, he was stabbed with pens! His limbs and entrails were then dragged through the streets and piled up before the emperor. It seems as if every senator was prepared to save his own skin at the expense of another.[97]

This was the third conspiracy within a year and a half. The death of Proculus marked a setback to that small element in the Senate prepared to stand up against Caligula. The remaining senators scrambled to ingratiate themselves with him. Several security steps were taken. Caligula was granted the right to sit on a higher platform in the Senate house, which prevented access to his person, and he was allowed to have a bodyguard when attending Senate meetings.[98] For his security Caligula, like Augustus, relied mainly on a special corps of Germans, noted for their physical strength and brutality.[99] The special unit assigned to guard even Caligula's statues seems to suggest that matters had taken a particularly serious turn.[100] It may be at this same time that Caligula increased the number of the Praetorian Guard from nine cohorts to twelve.[101]

THE HOUSEHOLD STAFF, THE WIFE, AND
THE PRAETORIAN GUARD

The opposition to Caligula from certain quarters of the nobility was not especially surprising, and much of the time he could counter it by playing on the ambitions and insecurities of individual senators, pitting one member against another. That and his formidable security details should have kept him safe. But here the emperor made one of his biggest mistakes by losing the support of his own household. When Betilinius Capito, in order to save his own life, named other conspirators, he included the freedman Callistus, the two Praetorian prefects, and the emperor's wife Caesonia.[102] Scholars have seen the inclusion of the emperor's wife as unlikely but the others as credible.[103] Josephus writes that Callistus, Caligula's most trusted and feared advisor, came over to the plot out of fear for his own life. It was rumored he had been ordered to poison Claudius but had dragged his feet. He now attached himself to Claudius so that, in the event of Caligula's death, he would still have imperial backing.[104]

What made this conspiracy particularly dangerous was the inclusion of the prefects of the Guard.[105] Josephus provides the name of one of them, Marcus Arrecinus Clemens, father-in-law of the future emperor Titus.[106] We do not have the name of the other prefect, let alone knowledge of whether he was part of the plot. We know there were at least three other tribunes of the Guard involved: Cornelius Sabinus, Papinius, and Julius Lupus, who was related to the prefect, Clemens.[107] The fact that four tribunes of twelve were involved in the plot, and one of them was a relative of the prefect, reveals the strength of the conspiracy. Clemens himself was approached by the conspirators, but he did not agree to participate directly, claiming his age as an excuse.[108] He has been called shrewd for distancing himself from the actual deed, but he was still in danger, because merely knowing of an assassination attempt and doing nothing about it would mean a violation of his oath to protect the emperor. How could any successor have retained either prefect in that position, knowing what they had done? In fact, they would both be removed from office by Claudius but allowed to live.

Dio suggests that the individuals named by Capito were, in fact, innocent of the charges against them.[109] Caligula, however, was so obsessed by his suspicions that he supposedly drove a wedge between them, ingratiating himself with one and then with the other. After a while they became so indignant they eventually betrayed him. This, too, seems implausible and the insistence that the emperor's staff was not originally involved in the plot may spring from a desire to enhance the role of the senatorial conspirators and to put Capito in a good light, as not giving away real participants.

THE FINAL BLOW: CASSIUS CHAEREA

Tacitus noted that the emperor Caligula was murdered in "secret treachery" (*occultae insidiae*), but not much else is agreed upon.[110] There is no need to create one big, unified conspiracy by tying together what may have been separate operations. It could well be that Josephus was right when he commented that the conspirators were operating in ignorance of one another.[111] It is enough to say that more than one faction wanted Caligula dead. A conspiracy, unlike a straightforward military coup, can be a complex series of events that can involve individuals with disparate aims and ambitions united only by the common determination to be rid of a particular ruler. The more widespread the dissatisfaction, the greater the number of individuals likely be involved. Branches of the conspiracy could act almost independently, and part of it might be exposed without betraying the central core, which could continue its plotting.

Caligula's final weeks are more fully documented than any other period of his life because of the detailed account provided by Josephus in his *Antiquities*. Unfortunately, Josephus is frequently confused, and his report is vitiated by the corrupt state of the manuscripts. In Josephus and the other sources, the actual execution of the deed is engineered by, not surprisingly, military figures, the most prominent of whom was Cassius Chaerea, a tribune of the Praetorian Guard.[112] In Josephus's portrait Chaerea is depicted as a noble idealist, motivated by a profound commitment to republican liberties, but this has been challenged.[113] Moreover, Josephus makes him not merely the actual agent of the deed, but the inspiration and organizational power, serving a useful moral purpose as a virtuous man helping to carry out the will of the gods. The only fact that all the sources, including Josephus, agree upon is that Chaerea had a personal grudge against Caligula. To those other than Josephus, the senators egging him on were the real plotters.[114]

Dio tells us of his personal motive for the murder. Supposedly Caligula had regularly made him the butt of jokes, teasing him as weak and unmanly.[115] Chaerea had been given unpopular tasks like collecting taxes and demanding late payments. When he did not perform these duties properly, Caligula accused him of cowardice and insufficient manliness and began making jokes at his expense.[116] He was also employed in cases of murder and torture and endeavored to carry out his tasks viciously, not wanting to be accused of weakness.[117] In other words, Chaerea was the man who did Caligula's dirty work. The emperor took advantage of his decency and abused Chaerea for his own amusement.[118] Perhaps the fate of so many victims made Chaerea bring up the possibility of eliminating the emperor with the Praetorian prefect, Clemens, and another tribune, Papinius. If fear for their lives now gripped even the Praetorian Guard, then the system had broken down. All it would take is for all of these threats to come together in one coordinated effort to remove Caligula. Chaerea had many opportunities to simply kill the emperor himself, since he was frequently in his presence. The fact that he held back and waited for orders suggests others were taking the lead and that this was supposed to be a regime change, not just a revenge killing. Had Chaerea just killed the emperor at an opportune moment, it could be passed off as an ancient example of workplace violence. Word finally came down to Chaerea that the most favorable opportunity would be at the theatrical performances in honor of Augustus scheduled for January 21–24 on the Palatine Hill.

The sources mention a strikingly large number of aristocratic names, and there are even four different leaders from which to choose. After identifying the core group, Dio goes on to say that "nearly all the people around the emperor were won over," although this seems unlikely: there are always factions.[119] A conspiracy made up of so many people with many others in the know would not have remained secret for long. We can suggest a reason that so many named are connected to the assassination: Caligula's name was blackened after his death, and everyone wanted to be in favor with the new emperor, Claudius, who above everyone else was responsible for the blackening. By buying into the newly rewritten "history," they could wipe out the memory of the inglorious role they had played as hypocritical sycophants.

Among the participants mentioned was Chaerea's right-hand man in the actual execution of the deed: another tribune, Cornelius Sabinus.[120] Josephus mentions at least two senatorial conspirators, one Aemilius Regulus of Cordoba, otherwise unknown, who simply disappears from the narrative after Caligula's death.[121] A much more sustained role is given by Josephus to the senator Annius Vinicianus.[122] According to Josephus, Vinicianus was motivated partly by his friendship for the executed Lepidus and partly, we are led to believe, by the realization that he himself was a potential target of the emperor's anger. Josephus suggests that Chaerea and Sabinus approached Vinicianus and presented their plan. If this was the order in which it happened, then it would have given the senators who were looking for a patsy in the person of someone with a grudge to do the actual dirty work while reserving plausible deniability for themselves should the plot be exposed prematurely. Regardless of who initiated the plot, Vinicianus seems to have played the role of providing a liaison between the plotters in the Praetorian Guard and the element of the Senate who supported them.[123] Josephus has Vinicianus praise the undertaking and pronounce that he was ready, if necessary, to follow Chaerea's lead. It is more likely that Chaerea was the dupe of much more powerful figures who, for the most part, remained in the background. Several modern scholars see an important role for Vinicianus, considering him the heart of the plot from the outset, motivated not by a desire to restore the republic but by the determination to stage a takeover by exploiting ill-feeling against Caligula.[124]

Another senatorial figure with some role in the conspiracy was Valerius Asiaticus. He was from Vienne and the first Narbonese to attain the consulship.[125] Seneca describes him as a personal friend of Caligula's, but Asiaticus also developed a personal grudge against the emperor. Seneca tells how Caligula's taunts at public banquets over his wife's lack of prowess in bed drove Asiaticus into the arms of the conspirators.[126] Asiaticus's later conduct gives weight to the possibility of his involvement, since after Caligula's death he responded to furious popular demands for the assassin's identity by declaring that "he wished it were he."[127]

Another possible participant was Gaius Cassius Longinus, suffect consul in 30 and a governor of Asia. Dio tells us that Caligula recalled him after supposedly being warned by an oracle to beware of a Cassius—which in the end turned out to be correct, but it was Cassius Chaerea, not Cassius Longinus.[128] There were two senators involved in the plot who lost their lives along with Caligula, but little is known about them. Publius Nonnius Asprenas, the suffect consul of 38, was the first to be cut down by the Guard after the assassination, and Lucius Norbanus Balbus was killed alongside Caligula.[129]

DEATH ON THE PALATINE

A large part of any assassination is choosing a place that makes the deed efficient, while leaving an escape route that works for the assassins. The killing of Caligula took place on the final day of the festival games in honor of the divine Augustus. The games were held before an invited audience of several thousand people in a temporary wooden "theater" on the Palatine Hill.[130] A group of seats at one side of the auditorium was reserved for Caligula and his special guests. From this restricted area, a corridor led toward a palace door. Of all places to choose for an assassination, why a public occasion on the Palatine? Thousands of people would be assembled, including the leading senators and their wives and children. Members of the Praetorian Guard were there, plus the German bodyguard. Attempting such an assassination in public would seem to have entailed incalculable risks. Assassinating him in his bed or at a private audience or while alone in the palace or even at a private banquet would have been easier. Chaerea had suggested pitching the emperor off the roof when he was distributing money to the populace, which was not such a bad idea, but he was vetoed, once again suggesting there were others running the show.[131]

The theater had one exit into the city and one into the imperial palace. Caligula entered the temporary theater on the Palatine in the morning when it was already crowded. He seemed in high spirits. No special seats had been set aside that day for guests, so everything was a jumble of confusion with senators and *equites*, freedmen and slaves, men and women all jockeying for position. This seems to have amused the emperor. He started the day's procedures with the sacrifice of a flamingo in honor of Augustus, and when he struck the bird the blood spurted out, spattering the emperor's own toga.[132] After the sacrifice he took his seat, eating and drinking with his companions. The consul Pomponius Secundus, who knew about the plot, was sitting servile at his feet, eating enthusiastically.[133] Fruit had been dispersed among the spectators, which attracted exotic birds, and afforded much entertainment as the public scrambled to catch the creatures.[134] Among the spectators behaving with more dignity was the consular Cluvius Rufus, usually identified with the historian of that name. In a famous exchange, he was asked by another senator, Bathybius, if he had heard of the planned revolution. Cluvius admonished him with words from Homer: to be silent lest anyone else hear of it.[135] If the story is true, and it may only have been an attempt by Cluvius afterward to range himself on the side of the angels, it means that knowledge of the conspiracy was widespread enough for it to be the subject of casual gossip in the theater. How could this be without Caligula's agents getting wind of it?

The assassins, mostly officers of the Praetorian Guard, were on duty in the corridor between the theater and the palace. They had a long, nerve-racking wait, and there were contingencies that had not been expected. For example, Caligula was in the habit of leaving the show at midday to bathe and have lunch before returning. This day, however, he had had a stomachache, perhaps from the excesses of the previous night, and so, against their expectations, he did not get up and return to the palace for lunch. Vinicianus tried to leave so he could urge Chaerea and the assassins to enter the theater and murder Caligula there before the opportunity slipped away. Before he could take his leave, however, Caligula tugged at his toga in a friendly manner and asked where he was going; Vinicianus was obliged to sit back down and pretend nothing was happening.[136] It was apparently Nonius Asprenas who finally persuaded Caligula to leave; he may have been tasked with decoying the emperor into the passageway where he would be killed. He got the emperor moving just in time, according to Josephus, since Chaerea was on the point of abandoning the original plan and of returning to the theater to take his chances at assassinating Caligula where he sat.[137] The more they waited, the more the conspirators became tightly wound.

When the theater door opened, it was not the emperor who stepped out, but his uncle Claudius, his brother-in-law, Marcus Vinicius, and the wealthy Valerius Asiaticus who were at the front of the entourage leading Caligula into the trap. On the pretext that the emperor wanted a moment of peace and quiet, the plotters kept the rest of the retinue from following. The three of them hurried past the assassins along the main corridor to the palace. We can assume that the Praetorian officers were surprised by the appearance of this trio instead of the emperor, because Josephus tells us the guards briefly considered whether they should block their path but then decided there was no problem. Were these three in on the plot, or were the Guards just surprised at the order in which people emerged from the theater? The plotters should have allowed for a contingency of someone other than the emperor emerging first into the corridor. They probably thought that no one would have been bold enough to push past the egomaniac Caligula to get to lunch, no matter how hungry they were.[138]

One explanation for Claudius's behavior is that he knew in advance what was going to happen. Either he and his two companions were active participants in the plot or they were making sure they were not in the vicinity when it was carried out—to maintain plausible deniability later. Josephus gives the explanation that the Praetorian Guard let them by because they would not want to inconvenience such dignified individuals. This is naïve, considering it is just such dignified individuals who murder emperors. No one was expecting John Q. Public to push through with a knife. Those who argue the goal of the conspirators was to wipe out the imperial dynasty and end the hereditary transfer of power suggest the conspirators must have intended to murder Claudius along with Caligula, in which case he should have been guarded as well as Caligula.[139] If this were an attempt to wipe out the imperial family, Claudius could have been hunted down later. There are those who argue that the conspirators were willing to let Claudius go in the beginning because they did not want to alert Caligula to the plot but, considering what happened shortly thereafter, it seems more likely that Claudius was in on the plot or took advantage of it to everyone's surprise (see chapter 6).

While Claudius and the two others proceeded along a main corridor lined with servants, Caligula, now flanked by Chaerea and Sabinus, turned into another corridor, where some dancers had assembled to rehearse a performance to be given in his honor. Caligula engaged the young men in conversation. It was at this moment that the emperor met his end.[140] The precise details of Caligula's death have been handed down in different traditions, and the accounts diverge on the details of the actual murder. Suetonius himself gives two different versions. In one, the Praetorian tribune, Cassius Chaerea, came up behind him and slashed Caligula in the neck, saying, "Take that!"[141] Then the tribune Cornelius Sabinus, facing the emperor, stabbed him in the chest. In the second version, Sabinus stepped smartly forward to ask the emperor for the password of the day, which it was his duty to request. As the emperor paused to think of a reply, Sabinus split his jaw with a blow of his sword. Other officers then crowded around to finish him off with thirty blows as he lay bleeding on the ground.[142] Josephus gives still another account, in which Chaerea "the freedom fighter" comes off somewhat better. In this version, it is Chaerea who asked for the watchword. Caligula gave him one of his insulting terms, whereupon Chaerea showered abuse on the emperor (something I am quite sure he had wanted to do for a long time), and struck a deep but not fatal wound. The blow fell between the neck and shoulder and was stopped by his collarbone. Josephus writes that he purposely did not strike a fatal blow so he could have more fun inflicting further torture on this man whom he hated so much. Josephus rightly adds that this was a very foolish thing to do because, in order to save their own lives, the assassins had to get away immediately. Assassins kill and kill quickly; they do not toy with their victims like a cat with a mouse.[143]

Caligula neither shouted nor called for help, but only let out a loud groan and tried to flee. He was confronted by Cornelius Sabinus, who pushed Caligula to the ground and brought him down on one knee. Then a number of assailants encircled the emperor and, at a single word of encouragement, struck at him with their swords, cheering one another on and even competing with one another. Josephus is sure that it was Aquila who delivered the fatal blow. In Seneca's version, Chaerea managed to decapitate the emperor with one blow, but many of the conspirators surrounded the emperor and thrust their swords into the corpse, anyway. Whatever version is true, the deed was done. Few would quarrel with Seneca's closing observation that on this day Caligula received a practical demonstration that he was *not* a god.[144]

THE GETAWAY

Part of any successful assassination plot is the escape. According to Josephus, the passageways along the corridor where the assassination occurred were narrow and blocked by a great crowd of the emperor's attendants and whatever soldiers were on duty that day as the emperor's bodyguard.[145] (One might ask why they had not been in front of and behind the emperor, as a good, full-time bodyguard should be.) So the conspirators took another escape route through the palace, finding refuge in the "House of Germanicus," named after Caligula's father, one of the individual houses that made up the palace complex.[146]

Most of the conspirators seem to have escaped by the time Caligula's German bodyguard arrived. They were trailing behind (quite unprofessionally) their master in a crowd of theater spectators and had to force their way through the crowd to arrive at the murder scene. They should have been on the scene already. Modern standards of security would have had bodyguards on all four sides of Caligula, making access impossible, but this was ancient Rome, not Washington, DC. The members of the German bodyguard were the first to discover the dead Caligula. They were led by Sabinus, a military tribune and former Thracian gladiator.[147] When the Germans saw what had happened, mayhem broke out. Several of the assassins were cut down, as well as some quite innocent bystanders.[148] The first person they set upon and killed was Asprenas. It was said his toga had been spattered with blood during the earlier religious sacrifice, but its presence on his toga attracted the attention of the bodyguard, who assumed he was one of the assassins. If he did have blood on him from another source, it is not clear why he would have stayed near the body.[149] Then they attacked Norbanus, who tried to fight back but stood no chance against the great mob of assailants.[150] The third victim was Anteius, described by Josephus as a distinguished senator. Josephus tells us that he was caught because he could not resist the pleasure of looking at the emperor's dead body, and he pulled himself away too late to escape.[151] A number of conspirators who succeeded in evading the German bodyguard owed their lives to the ingenuity of a physician called Alcyon. He was treating some wounded men and managed to smuggle some of the conspirators out of the passageway on the pretext of looking for supplies.[152] In the confusion, Vinicianus was seized, presumably by Praetorians not involved in the plot, and had the good fortune to be hauled before Clemens, who allowed him to leave unharmed.[153] This account, which stresses the great personal danger to which Vinicianus was supposedly exposed, may cover the reality that he, in fact, sought Clemens's protection at the first sign of danger.

Meanwhile, a small breakaway group of assassins had been sent by Chaerea, led by a tribune named Julius Lupus, to kill Caligula's wife, Caesonia, and his baby daughter, Drusilla. Reports say that the empress faced the blow courageously and that the little girl was dashed against a wall. Then Chaerea and Sabinus, fearful of what would follow, fled into the interior of the palace complex and then into the city, by a different route.[154]

The Germans clearly realized that they had not caught all of the assassins. They guarded the exits to the theater; a number of them rushed in while carrying the heads of Anteius and others, which they placed on the altar, which in turn led to scenes of utter confusion. It is interesting that Josephus concedes that there was not, by any means, universal joy at the news of the assassination and that many people were, in fact, stunned by the event.[155] People were horrified by the news that the emperor had been attacked. The situation was further confused by conflicting rumors: that Caligula was alive and being tended by his doctors, that he had escaped to the Forum and was addressing the people, or even that he had made up the story of his death to test their loyalty. It was not until a well-known wealthy auctioneer named Arruntius Euaristus entered the theater in mourning attire and announced that the emperor was dead that the people dispersed. The Germans were finally brought to order, probably because they were persuaded that the anguish of the ordinary people over Caligula's death was genuine, and now they had no emperor to protect.[156]

The Senate acted with a coordination and speed that suggested detailed preparation.[157] They met and gave instructions for the contents of the emperor's treasury to be carried to the capital (because one guards the money first).[158] The Senate instructed the urban cohorts to take up positions around the capital and the Forum, to secure the capital.[159] Then the senators spent most of the day discussing the possibility of a return to the republic or of a new princeps to be elected by the Senate.[160] The whole afternoon and night of January 24 were wasted in political indecision, and not even the entire Senate was there. Most of the senators had discreetly absented themselves and run off to the country in fear.[161] Josephus's account is certainly not very flattering to them:

Once they foresaw how the whole matter would turn out, he says, they despaired for their freedom and assumed that it would be far better to live their lives slothfully in the security of slavery than to exert any effort and risk their personal safety in an attempt to recover the prestige of their ancestors.[162]

By the morning of January 25 it was clear that, if the ultimate aim of the senatorial conspirators had been to restore the republic, their goal was unattainable. On the other hand, if the plot had involved choosing a new princeps, who was the new emperor to be? In the end, none of these discussions would be relevant, because the troops could not be rallied to their cause, and the Praetorian Guard had already designated its own candidate. In the most stunning surprise of all, while they were debating, Claudius was being proclaimed the new emperor in a suspiciously fast and smooth transition. Claudius did not hesitate for a second. He immediately named Rufrius Pollio as his new Praetorian prefect, because the emperor and his head of security were the two most powerful people in the government. He removed the two prefects who had participated in the conspiracy. After the Senate recognized him as emperor the next day, one of his first acts was to get rid of Caligula's assassins. Chaerea was executed, and Sabinus took his own life.[163] Not long afterward, the two most important figures close to Caligula after Callistus—that is, the freedman, Protogenes, and the Egyptian slave, Caligula's bodyguard, Helicon—were also killed.[164]

THE AFTERMATH

One of the reasons it is exceedingly difficult to recover the facts of Caligula's short, four-year reign is that the entire historiographical tradition has been distorted against him.[165] His successor, Claudius, came to the throne as a result of an assassination in which Claudius may have been complicit. Claudius had to prove that Caligula—not the assassins and not the system of the principate itself—was evil. In other words, Caligula was not murdered because he was a monster; he was turned into a monster because he was murdered.[166] Tacitus himself spoke of how the histories of Tiberius and Caligula were falsified through cowardice when they lived and composed in hatred after they died.[167] It is telling that none of the conspirators themselves ever accused Caligula of being insane or suggested they were serving a mad emperor. It certainly was not the reason they assassinated him.

Although maligned by the ancient sources, modern biographies of Caligula by classical scholars have been able to draw a more balanced picture of this emperor as a rational ruler. He was a shrewd manipulator of people who lived "in a hostile world of jealous, disgruntled senatorial aristocrats, and a scheming, ruthless family, riddled with dynastic ambition."[168] That would be enough to make anyone paranoid. This is not to say he was an innocent, charming young man. Aristocrats found his megalomania repugnant. His pretentious munificence,[169] extravagance in providing entertainments,[170] and the pageantry with which he surrounded himself[171] reminded them not only that they were subservient to the principate, but that, if he depleted the treasury, they would be subject to confiscation and extortion.[172] The revival, in the very year of the conspiracy, of the *lex maiestatis* must have been an important source of antagonism, and it was all the more ironic because Caligula himself had revoked it upon his succession.[173] The alienation had to be great if his own heir, Lepidus, could be convinced to conspire against him.[174] Once a ruler has incurred such hostility and loss of respect, a single injustice, real or imagined, could be enough to ignite a plot. If Chaerea had not killed him, no doubt someone else would have.

We should not underestimate the role of the Senate in its complicity. In a frightening speech made to the Senate in 39, Caligula reminded those assembled that all the executions that had occurred under Tiberius were done with their cooperation. It was senators who made the accusations, senators who bore witness and testified, and the Senate that had voted for condemnation. He even had his freedmen read passages from the documents that he had supposedly destroyed.[175] His attempts to assert imperial power over the Senate created much of the hostility from that quarter. Pointing out the Senate's own hypocrisy only made it worse.

No matter what his personality, lack of morals, bizarre behavior, or state of mind, Caligula, like every other emperor, had to manage the populace, the aristocracy, the army, the Senate, and his own household. Although there is evidence that he remained popular with the people, when the last three groups turned against him, no security force in the world could have saved him.[176] Caligula's goal should have been the same as any emperor's. In any imperial system, a successful emperor would come to the throne, produce an heir or at least adopt one, and then die in bed of natural causes. None of the first three emperors produced a son who was alive at the time of his death, and the succession problem persisted. Caligula had not designated an heir, nor did he die a natural death.

The series of plots against Caligula's life is presented by Josephus with such vividness that it gives the impression that his reign was one long, perpetual bloodbath. The list of people he actually had killed is not that long, and if they were indeed engaged in treasonous acts, then their removal was both legal and wise. An emperor certainly has the right to defend himself and his regime. It has been suggested that not all these eliminations were for national security; some of Caligula's tortures were reserved for people he just did not like.[177] He had exhibited this behavior long before he was emperor. In 32, Marcus Cotta Messalinus had been accused of expressing doubts about Caligula's masculinity and was saved only by the intervention of Tiberius. His friend Sextus Vestilius, who made similar charges, was informed that he was no longer welcome with Tiberius. No trial was held, but he killed himself by opening his veins.[178] If Caligula was willing to kill people over a personal insult before he was even emperor, imagine what he would do with a real case of treason once he was on the throne.

Contrary to the image we often get of Caligula as a mad and capricious ruler, if we concentrate on the security issues, we see a young emperor coming to the throne as an Augustan princeps and securing his power by eliminating his rivals. He took specific measures to stabilize his position as ruler with different segments of the population, without making too many concessions to the aristocracy. At one point, however, when his life had been threatened by a senatorial conspiracy, he dropped the Augustan façade of there being both a republic and a monarchy and came down solidly on the side of monarchy. He continued to impose traditional modes of behavior on the aristocracy, but its members were incapable of expressing their enmity for him openly because he held all the power. Much of his mockery toward the Senate may have been a response to the unexpected attempts on his life. Instead of issuing orders to have heads roll indiscriminately, he took aim at their positions in the Senate, in relationships of patronage, and in the hierarchy of their society. He confronted them with the unpleasant reality of autocratic rule, pointing out their own duplicitous behavior, and highlighting their lack of real power. He forced them to humiliate themselves. He dishonored them with cynicism and symbolic acts. He left them to their impotence and absurdity.[179]

Unlike with Caesar's murder, which had taken place in an open meeting of senators, Caligula was killed by a hit squad, privately in the palace, and his family was targeted along with him. Most importantly, the assassins included members of his own troop of bodyguards. This amplifies another trend in Roman imperial history, that is, the role played by the Praetorian Guard. The Guard had been developed by Augustus first and foremost for his own protection. Although these soldiers became involved in many other tasks after the establishment of the unit, the security of the emperor still remained their primary function. Yet in just over half a century after its founding, the Guard would become responsible for the assassination of the man they had sworn to protect. By 41 CE the Guard was so firmly established as a vital part of the management of the state that several of its members were willing to risk their positions to eliminate a dangerous emperor and put forth a better candidate. The close association of these men to the emperor and the administration meant that they saw themselves as the people who could cause a political change.[180]

Although the plot that killed Caligula succeeded largely through the efforts of a tribune of the Praetorian Guard, we must not forget that it was supported, or possibly led, by a movement of senators, and one faction may have included the man who became Caligula's successor. The fact that officers in the Guard were willing to go along with an assassination plot suggests that this was more than a personal vendetta. They had a stake in eliminating this particular emperor—perhaps to protect themselves from his vindictiveness and cruelty. We do not have details about their complaints, but Josephus records that Chaerea, in a comment directed to one of the Praetorian prefects, Marcus Arrecinus Clemens, and to Papinius, a fellow tribune, referred to the Guard as "torturers and executioners."[181] This may give us a clue as to the grievances held by at least some of the officers. Perhaps they resented the abuse of power wielded by an emperor who used loyal and moral men to put innocent people to death.

A significant part of any plot to kill an emperor is the dynastic linkage. By Caligula's time, the imperial system had been in place for two generations. The right of an heir to succeed to power solely by virtue of his descent had already taken hold. Another trend that was becoming evident was that the women of the imperial family could publicly play the sort of role played in the more private sphere by the daughters, sisters, and wives of Roman aristocrats.[182] They had the important role of producing the heir apparent, and, since there were many collateral relatives, there would also be jockeying for position. Emperors and their extended families were now a permanent fixture of Roman life, so killing Caligula had no significant impact except producing another emperor.

The plot against Caligula was a complex one involving many individuals, some perhaps acting out of idealism, perhaps others out of self-interest. J. V. P. D. Balsdon describes the conspirators of 41 as cherishing "the illusion that in some marvelous way the future would look after itself."[183] At the center of this conspiracy there must have been a small group that had a clear idea of where events should lead, and these men were happy to exploit and manipulate the others to their own ends. The Praetorian Guard and the imperial freedmen would not have been served by abolishing the principate. They might, however, have seen the merit of removing a specific princeps whose behavior threatened to discredit the whole institution and of replacing him with a more suitable incumbent. Although the actual deed was restricted to only a few officers of the Guard, that is all it would take. These were the people with easy access to Caligula. Taking this kind of initiative themselves or allowing themselves to be manipulated by others must have sent a sign that the political life in Rome could be changed by the Praetorians. It was not unthinkable now that they could become a threat to the emperor himself. The key to the future lay not just with the Senate or the people but also with the Praetorian Guard.

The most important element in the plot, and the one that has been most successfully covered up, is the ambition of members of the ruling house. Claudius himself may or may not have been party to such a plot from the outset, but at some point he joined in. Once the deed was done, however, he would have been anxious to prevent any general knowledge about it and to foster the notion that the principate came to him only in an accidental twist of fate.[184] While Chaerea and his colleagues performed the bloody deed, the high leadership of the Praetorians, prominent senators, and just possibly Claudius himself played some part in arranging Caligula's assassination. If this is true, the plot was a complete success. The unexpected elevation of Claudius against the will of the other factions, however, intensified the dissatisfaction with the new emperor and would only lead to more conspiracies.

6

Claudius the Fool?

The popular view, given to us by Suetonius and Dio and amplified in modern times by Robert Graves, of the drooling Claudius being found behind a curtain by the Praetorians and made emperor, must be radically altered once we see the role he played in the conspiracy against Caligula. In spite of his physical afflictions, Claudius was neither reluctant to accept the role when it was thrust upon him nor totally unprepared for supreme rule.[1] The man whom so many had underestimated seems to have had a consummate grasp of political realities, which he demonstrated by the achievement of managing his way to the throne and staying on it for fourteen years.[2] The historiographical tradition, so hostile to Caligula, has covered up Claudius's part in one of the best preplanned transitions of the principate. Claudius seized power in the wake of Caligula's assassination in an opportunistic coup that shocked everyone. Even the Senate had not considered him a possible contender. He marked out a route to the throne for any potential successor to follow and spent his entire reign seeing that no one else could topple him by the same means.[3]

There had been no substantive model for succession established by 41 CE. If there were any rules to follow, they would involve getting the support of the military and neutralizing any rival claims to the throne. Once in power, Claudius set out to deliberately minimize his role in the plot that had brought him to power by encouraging the belief that the outcome was due to a series of chance events over which he had no control.[4] Claudius succeeded in taking the reins of power within twenty-four hours of his nephew's death in 41 in an operation so remarkably smooth that it provokes immediate questions about how much planning went into it. Although none of the sources speaks directly of his involvement, Josephus does reflect a tradition that his rise to power came through a cohesive plan in the immediate aftermath of the assassination. The events surrounding the transition put Claudius's claims that he was innocent "of any desire to rule" in serious doubt.[5]

The traditional story is that Gratus, a Praetorian, supposedly found Claudius behind a curtain while the soldiers were "milling about" the Palatine area.[6] They carried him to their barracks nearly two miles away, just outside the city wall. Eyewitnesses thought he was being taken to his execution—which would explain the later story, obviously encouraged by Claudius himself, that he had been kidnapped against his will and forced to become emperor in order to avoid a civil war. Of course, Gratus could have been in on the takeover and was simply telling Claudius the coast was clear. The entire scene could have been staged for the benefit of those Senate elements who opposed the takeover of Claudius.[7]

THE TAKEOVER

Once Claudius had reached the barracks, he made sure that the Praetorians were entirely loyal. In effect, Claudius bypassed the Senate and was proclaimed ruler by the troops. The price was a bribe of 15,000 sesterces for each Guardsman—the equivalent of five years' pay.[8] With his access to funds, his family connections, a good source of inside information, and military support, he had outmaneuvered his rivals. To what extent Claudius was party to the plot against Caligula from the outset can never be known for sure, but once he had the throne, he would have been anxious to prevent any general knowledge of his involvement in the coup and would help to foster the notion that the principate came to him only by a twist of fate.[9]

With the death of Caligula, the senators were enjoying a brief moment of euphoria when they convinced themselves that they were once more in charge, but this was only an illusion. The Senate sent two tribunes, Veranius and Brocchus, to demand that Claudius relinquish all claims to the principate and submit to the Senate's authority.[10] Once in camp, they realized that the key to the future lay with neither the Senate nor the Roman people but with the Praetorian Guard. Claudius sent his own clear message to the Senate while he was still at the barracks with the Guard. He promised senators he would share power with them. With the armies behind him and appropriate measures taken to protect himself around the palace, Claudius felt he could, by diplomacy and flattery, reconcile the senators to his rule. He issued an amnesty for the events following

Caligula's murder. Exiles were recalled, prisoners freed, incriminating papers burned, constitutional courtesies ostentatiously observed, and new honors were devised for the Senate as a body; in addition, Claudius advertised a return to Augustan standards.[11] Claudius tried to convert the underground hostility of the senators to healthy criticism in the open, but at this he would fail. In spite of his auspicious announcements, the senators were not won over, and Claudius spent much of his reign protecting himself against attacks on his authority.[12] In fact, it has been argued that a split between the Julians and the Claudians had caused a great deal of turmoil in the past and continued to exist.[13]

The situation within the emperor's own household was no less shaky. The first crack in the façade of a stabilized dynastic rule came when Julia Livilla, Caligula's sister, was restored from exile only to be banished again.[14] The official charge was adultery, but as we have seen with previous emperors, such charges were often used to cover up a different form of treachery. When members of the imperial house, or people closely linked to it, fell from grace, it was common to blame their demise on their own moral failings.[15] The genetic link, however, was the key. Since Livilla was a great-granddaughter of Augustus and married to Marcus Vinicius, a potential candidate for the throne, it has not passed the notice of historians that they might have been caught hatching a plot against the emperor.[16]

A similar situation occurred in 42 with the death of C. Appius Silanus, who had been governor of Spain and was married to Domitia Lepida, the mother of Claudius's wife, Messalina.[17] Claudius reported his execution to the Senate. We are told the sentence was carried out because of a "dream by Narcissus" that Silanus was killing Claudius. Since Silanus was a member of a family whose record was one of constant conflict with the emperors, it is likely he came under suspicion for something more concrete. The charge of *maiestas* had actually been brought against him in 32.[18] The imperial reaction would not be out of place for a court that felt itself under threat.[19]

Suetonius mentions several attempts on Claudius's life. A commoner was caught near his bedchamber in the middle of the night with a dagger in his hand. How did he get into the palace? What was his motive? It was certainly not to make himself emperor, unless he was the kind of deranged person we read about almost daily who are trying to kill famous people.[20] It is Suetonius again who reports that two equestrians were found lying in wait for the emperor in a public place, one ready to attack Claudius with a sword-cane as he came out of the theater, and the other with a hunting knife as he was making a sacrifice in the Temple of Mars.[21]

THE REVOLT OF 42 CE

Within less than a year from his accession, Claudius had to face his first documented conspiracy—an attempt to replace him mounted by one of the members of the great conspiracy of 39 CE. Annius Vinicianus, a man who had been considered a candidate for the throne himself, evidently had not stopped his quest for the position of princeps even though he had been thwarted by Claudius.[22] He spent the months after Caligula's death secretly gathering allies around himself. Lacking any substantial military force, he co-opted L. Arruntius Camillus Scribonianus, the governor of Dalmatia, into the plot.[23]

Once the revolt was declared, senators and equestrians flocked to Vinicianus, but then everything went awry in Dalmatia. Scribonianus talked about restoring the republic, but this rallying cry failed completely.[24] After only five days the soldiers decided to stick with their oath of allegiance to the current princeps. Although initially they had accepted the proposal of revolt, what caused them to change their minds was not their guilty conscience (because they had planned to break their oath to the emperor) but the unacceptable political program of their new leader. When Scribonianus started asking for restoration of freedom and the republic, they could only think about trouble, disorder, and civil war; there was really nothing in it for them.[25] Scribonianus fled to the island of Issa and committed suicide.[26]

The attempted coup was put down in only five days, presumably at the point when the legions deserted.[27] According to Suetonius, who portrays the entire movement as an attempted civil war, Scribonianus had actually thought he was going to write a letter to Claudius demanding that he step down and go into retirement, as if this were enough to intimidate the emperor. It would take more than that to get Claudius off the throne. The account of Pliny the Younger adds the name of another conspirator, Caecina Paetus, the former consul.[28] Paetus joined the plot and was with Scribonianus in Dalmatia when he killed himself.[29] Paetus was taken prisoner and sent back to Rome.[30] Once there, he was allowed to commit suicide but not before his wife, Arria, threw herself on the sword first, saying the now legendary words: "See Paetus, it does not hurt."[31] Other equestrian and senatorial conspirators were either prosecuted, tortured, and compelled to leave Rome; made to resign; or forced to commit suicide.[32]

Just because this revolt came to nothing in the end does not mean it could not have developed into a serious and widespread danger. Suetonius characterized the events as a "civil war" for a reason. The fact that the uprising included some of the people who had been involved in the conspiracy against Caligula in 39 meant that there was a definite undercurrent of senatorial dissatisfaction with Claudius as emperor.[33] The plot had been afoot since his succession and not just in response to the death of Appius Silanus. In fact, Silanus may have been part of the plot. It is significant that the plot involved four men of consular rank and military units: they are more high-ranking people than are known to have taken part in any other plot against a Julio-Claudian emperor.[34] The actions of this senatorial opposition put Claudius in a very difficult position. He had no choice but to immediately launch an investigation.

Claudius was both willing and able to use any means necessary to find out how far the conspiracy had spread. He demanded that anyone with relevant information should come forward immediately, not just senators but also their wives, freedmen, and slaves. Suspects were imprisoned and tortured to get intelligence. Pliny says that one of the people willing to come forward was Vinicia, the wife of Scribonianus, who had been with him in Dalmatia and in whose arms he died. Her testimony implicated a whole group of prominent individuals in Rome, most notably Annius Vinicianus, who took his own life.[35] She also named the consul of 41 CE, Q. Pomponius Secundus, whose brother had suffered at the hands of Caligula and may have preferred the restoration of the republic to any principate.[36] Citizens were tortured, and a praetor was compelled to abdicate and was executed. The bodies of those killed in Rome were exposed on the Gemonian steps; those killed outside the city had their heads removed, brought to Rome, and displayed on the steps. Their burials were forbidden, and *damnatio memoriae* was decreed.[37]

Scholars have often characterized Claudius's response as an "inquisition" or a "witch hunt," but, in truth, the sequence of trials and executions illustrates that Claudius was serious about keeping his job, his life, and the principate.[38] From the senatorial point of view, however, this was not an auspicious start to the new reign. Some historians believe Claudius erred in responding so repressively to this threat, because it "evaporated quickly." But a widespread senatorial conspiracy backed by provincial governors with legions at their disposal is not a small matter, and it would not have disappeared had Claudius not taken immediate steps and made it clear he would not tolerate such resistance to his rule.[39] A "small" conspiracy had just killed Caligula. Had the legions not remained loyal, this conspiracy may have well succeeded.[40] Yes, Claudius's response may have lost him his reputation for clemency, but it might also have set the tone for anyone else planning to make a move on the throne or at least killing the emperor in some dream of restoring the republic.[41] In the end, the plot failed because the emperor's donatives (cash bonuses to the soldiers) had done their work. Claudius further showed his indebtedness to the army when he gave Scribonianus's two legions fresh rewards and renamed them *Claudia Pia Fidelis* ("Claudian, Loyal and Patriotic").[42]

The populace certainly felt there had been a threat to the throne. At one point a rumor spread that Emperor Claudius had been killed in an ambush on his way to Ostia. The news caused consternation among the people. With dreadful curses they abused both the army for its treachery and the senators for having murdered him. The crowds became silent only when the magistrates had one after another ascended the rostra and testified that the emperor was in good health and approaching the city.[43]

TIGHTENING SECURITY

The atmosphere around the palace changed permanently because of these attempts. Claudius tightened security around himself immediately. Every visitor had to undergo a body search before being admitted into his presence. Even when the emperor visited ailing, bedridden senators at their homes, the rooms, including the bedding and the pillows, were searched ahead of time. The fact that Claudius had all the poisons stored in the palace destroyed says a lot about the atmosphere surrounding the new princeps. The common practice of the emperor and senators mingling together at banquets created the kind of access an assassin would need and an environment in which an informer could collect intelligence.[44] So Claudius never dared go to a banquet unless he was surrounded by *speculatores* with lances. *Speculatores* were promoted Praetorians with special duties, such as carrying messages or escorting the emperor.[45] Other soldiers replaced the slaves who served his meals.[46]

The emperor was never free of apprehension. Not too long after Scribonianus's rebellion, we are told that in 43 an equestrian was thrown from the Tarpeian Rock for plotting against the emperor.[47] Also eliminated around the same time was Julia, daughter of Claudius's late sister Livilla. We do not know why she was done away with, only that she was denounced by the infamous informer Suillius Rufus. Tacitus tells us that Suillius claimed to be acting for Claudius and his wife, Messalina.[48]

POPPAEA AND ASIATICUS

The next victim was Valerius Asiaticus, a wealthy man from Gallia Narbonensis who was the first Gaul to be admitted to the Senate. He was a longtime friend of the emperor Claudius.[49] During his brilliant consular career, he had amassed enough wealth to buy a luxurious villa and park-like gardens in Rome that were formerly owned by Lucullus.[50] In 47, the notorious professional informer, Publius Suillius Rufus, brought capital charges against Asiaticus before the Senate. The charges included adultery with Poppaea Sabina the Elder.[51] Tacitus says that Messalina engineered the fall of Valerius Asiaticus because she wanted the gardens of Lucullus and to get back at Poppaea Sabina, now her rival for the actor Mnester, but this account has been questioned. Suetonius is simply silent.[52]

Asiaticus, in chains, was brought from a holiday in Baiae to the palace by the Praetorian prefect, Crispinus, and he faced Claudius in a private hearing (*in cubiculum*). Sosibus the freedman and Suillius brought the charges of failure to maintain discipline among his troops and homosexual acts.[53] Tacitus includes political material in Sosibus's revelations: Asiaticus was accused of extortion and then using the money to buy political influence. Were the charges really just a screen for Messalina's pettier motives, or was there a possibility of a plot against Claudius? What about Dio's claim of trumped-up charges by a soldier?

Some facts are known. Asiaticus was another of those involved in the plot against Caligula. He was fabulously wealthy, and he was accused of tampering with the troops. If a charge of *maiestas* could be proven, there should have been a trial before his colleagues. In many ways this resembled the trial of Appius Silanus in 42. Although Emperor Claudius was inclined to acquit him, Asiaticus, according to Tacitus, maintained that he had been both grievously insulted and a victim of womanish deceit (*fraude muliebre*). Then in a final act befitting his illustrious predecessor, Lucullus, Asiaticus ordered that the funeral pyre be moved so the flames would not hurt the trees in his beloved gardens. After his suicide, his wife, Lollia Saturnina, also killed herself.[54] At that point a trial was no longer necessary or even possible. Tacitus reports that they awarded Crispinus a large sum of money and the insignia of a praetor. Sosibus was also awarded a large sum of money.[55]

Was there a conspiracy? Even if Asiaticus was not a threat in his own right, he was in a position to deploy decisive wealth and manpower to any conspiracy. If Claudius thought ridding Rome of Asiaticus was a security measure, the Senate was not convinced. This was the most famous *intra cubiculum* hearing of the reign, and the Senate was summoned only afterward to hear what had happened. The condemnation of an ex-consul without a hearing from his peers hardened opinion against Messalina, her freedmen, and Suillius. The emperor came off as Messalina's dupe, but still he remained guarded. In 47 a Roman equestrian, Cn. Nonius, was discovered armed with a sword among the morning callers. He was tortured but gave up no names. Perhaps he was seeking revenge for a relative, since Asiaticus's wife was one of the Nonii.[56]

The fall of the ex-conspirators continued. Marcus Vinicius, who had put himself forward as one of the candidates for consul in 41 and who had won a consulship in 45 with Asiaticus, died the following year in circumstances that aroused suspicion.[57] Asinius Gallus was banished in 46 on the grounds of conspiracy, and along with him was accused Titus Statilius Taurus Corvinus, consul of 45.[58] Suetonius tells us that they were aided by a number of Claudius's own freedmen and slaves. Their attempts were labeled as "harmless" because Gallus made neither military nor financial preparations but relied rather on the nobility to win the consent of the Romans to his rule.[59] The aristocracy was getting nervous watching members of Claudius's own family being eliminated, not to mention members of their own order being prosecuted.[60] Tacitus recounts tales of a series of prosecutions launched by Suillius, who was to become fabulously wealthy through them. There was no guarantee of fair legal proceedings for the accused.[61] Claudius tried to administer justice fairly and efficiently but, in the eyes of the Senate, he remained a fraud.[62]

One of the widespread complaints against Claudius has always been the undue influence that his wives and freedmen had over him. On this point even Tacitus, Dio, and Suetonius agree. While it is true that he relied more on his freedmen than the equestrians and senators, this should not be seen as a sign of weakness. Already under Augustus the imperial household had become a form of bureaucracy. This is an anachronistic use of the term in the Weberian sense, but it is used to indicate the growth of an office staff around the palace. Governmental functions were becoming concentrated as each emperor was obliged to choose mainly from among his personal retinue of slaves and ex-slaves for people to do the work that, in modern states, would be carried out by senior civil servants or government ministers. It was Claudius who ran the government. In order to achieve his ambitious plans, he needed a large staff of people, and whether they were *equites*, freedmen, slaves or whether they came from his *domus* or the *res publica* did not matter as long as they were loyal to him.[63] The immense power that these men wielded annoyed the traditional elite, who did not appreciate being upstaged by this new and powerful servile class, whom they considered as acting "above their station."[64]

The imperial household emerged as a political entity in its own right. It was both a source of intelligence and a group that could be Claudius's front line of internal security. Each member of the household was sworn to protect it. With the princeps at the apex of the patronage system, this created a new dimension of prosecution. If one could not aspire to power by other means, one could gain influence by gaining access to the imperial ear.[65] To the emperor, loyalty was a black-and-white matter: either you were for the emperor or you were against him. Claudius had to think in these terms if he wished to survive, given the circumstances of his early life and accession. The question of loyalty became particularly acute when the people closest to him professed their undying loyalty but were lying. They were not exactly a reliable group where security was concerned. They often played upon the emperor's fears and turned in people they did not like on charges of disloyalty. His household staff was not accountable in ways that senatorial or even equestrian officers would have been, nor was there a clear chain of command. By using his household staff for administration, intelligence, and security, he created a monster that was potentially strong enough to bring him down.[66]

THE FALL OF MESSALINA

If Claudius is accused of being a fool, his third wife Messalina has become a byword for the lowest form of depravity.[67] Few figures in ancient history have had such a lurid picture painted of them. The accounts written about her after her death make it difficult to dislodge from one's mind the portrait of her we get in popular literature and even some of the older scholarly treatments.[68] As we have seen already, women of the imperial house were condemned for trying to usurp power, and they were usually accused of moral transgression to cover their political exploits.[69] This is particularly true when there has been an attempt to remove the emperor.[70] Allegations of sexual misconduct were the easiest way to discredit women. They should be viewed, therefore, with great skepticism, and in the end they are mostly irrelevant to internal security matters, anyway.[71] The relevant questions for this study are: Was there a threat to Claudius, and was his wife involved? The sexual adventures are, in some ways, a red herring. Traitors should be condemned for the right reasons, not cheap gossip.

Claudius married Messalina for very practical reasons. The marriage provided him with a genetic link to the house of Augustus, and he needed all the legitimacy he could conjure up to keep his throne. Messalina was the great-granddaughter of Augustus's sister, Octavia.[72] Claudius had been married twice before. Each of his marriages got him closer to the Augustan house.[73] A second motivation for marrying Messalina was that Claudius needed an heir for his dynasty. Shortly after marrying Claudius in 38 or 39, Messalina produced two children, Tiberius Claudius Caesar Britannicus and Claudia Octavia.[74] A son would ensure the survival of imperial rule and help secure Claudius's own position. It was the job of imperial women to secure the continuity of the imperial house and embody its moral integrity. In fact, ever since Augustus, a claim to morality was one of the justifications for imperial rule. There was no real power in the position of the emperor's wife except for the ability to influence one's husband and other members of the household and produce, protect, and influence the heir. She also had access to the emperor's presence, the imperial bedchamber, and the emperor's food. This made her a key player in any discussion of internal security.

What some refer to as a "plot" began in 48 CE, seven years after Claudius's accession, when it was said Messalina conceived an *amour fou* for a personable and very handsome aristocrat, the consul-designate, Gaius Silius.[75] The empress forced him to divorce his wife, Junia Silana, to ensure his faithfulness. Supposedly, Gaius then told her he wanted to marry her and adopt Britannicus. While Claudius was away supervising construction works at the port of Ostia, about fifteen miles from Rome, the two celebrated a "wedding" of sorts complete with a witnessed contract, celebratory supper, and a honeymoon.[76]

If there was indeed a plot, it was an extraordinarily inept one. What either one of them was planning to do after the "marriage" is unclear. Perhaps Messalina sensed that the regime was in danger and decided to be part of a new regime.[77] Or there is the distinct possibility that she was being manipulated by an older group of people who, anxious to overthrow her husband, convinced her that with Claudius doomed she could survive as empress if she married Silius.[78] In none of the sources do we get a clear picture of what Messalina's intentions were. Perhaps her motive was wanting to clear the path to ultimate power for her small son, Britannicus, by a preemptive strike.

The wedding seems so incongruous and foolish that it has led at least one scholar to suggest that perhaps the ceremony was some sort of bacchanalian revel while Claudius was out of town. She played the part of the sacred bride to her aristocratic boyfriend's role as the god Dionysius or one of his votaries. They dressed up in animal skins and capered about.[79] It is an attractive idea that would solve the basic problem of the implausibility of Tacitus's narrative, but why should the lovers take such a gigantic risk by getting married without moving to secure their position?[80]

Modern scholars have not been short of theories about what was really going on here.[81] The possibilities for a good conspiracy are endless. Perhaps Silius and Messalina *were* really plotting to overthrow Claudius together. Perhaps Silius was plotting to overthrow Claudius and was using Messalina as a pawn in his scheme. Perhaps Silius was part of a larger senatorial plot to overthrow Claudius. Claudius was certainly unpopular enough in those quarters. Perhaps Messalina turned to Silius only after her position was endangered. Less likely, though nevertheless suggested, was that Messalina was aiming to marry Silius and establish a more elective principate. Perhaps the freedman fabricated the whole episode to bring down Messalina. All are plausible; none is provable.[82] None of them supplies the most important piece of the puzzle: How were they going to eliminate Claudius? No princeps was going to have power taken away from him while he was still in office.

Many scholars have rejected any suggestion of this being a coup attempt.[83] The goals and membership of this supposed "conspiracy" are totally unclear, although it is in the nature of conspiracies to be opaque. If it were a conspiracy, it was a staggeringly inept one. The affair between Messalina and Silius was conducted openly, but adultery is one thing and usurpation quite another. We know that the plotters tried to get the support of the *vigiles* and possibly some gladiators, but they would have been no match for regular troops or the Praetorian Guard, although at least one of the two Praetorian prefects, Lusius Geta, was a supporter of the empress.[84] Had they succeeded in killing Claudius and seizing the throne, the others might have followed suit. The fact that it was detected early means that none of what they planned was carried out. Yet when it was over, there were no charges of treason, not even against Silius, and also missing was the usual round of denunciations, interrogations, suicides, and executions such as followed the attempted revolt by Scribonianus.

Silius certainly had the breeding to be a plausible candidate for a throne. He was a patrician with five consuls in his family tree, and he was about to be a sixth at the start of the new year, 49, only about two or three months away. His father had commanded part of Germanicus's Rhine army, so he would have reason to hope for support from the military, as well as from his natural allies in the Senate. If the marriage was part of an attempted coup, then why, after having "married" Messalina, did he not immediately act to take control of the city in Claudius's absence?

It was the powerful freedman, Narcissus, who decided to inform on Messalina and Silius. He had reason to be paranoid about the empress. A close colleague of his, the freedman Polybius, had recently been executed, and he may have feared he was next on her list. Narcissus left for Ostia after consulting two other highly placed freedmen, Pallas and Callistus, in a series of confidential meetings within the imperial household. The household shuddered when it received the news of the marriage. According to Tacitus, there is no doubt they interpreted the events for what they were: an attempted coup d'état. Clearly the parties surrounding Messalina at the time interpreted events in political terms and as an attempted usurpation.[85] All those who feared for their own positions scrambled to give Claudius a report of what they had found out. The idea that he stayed ignorant of the events is not entirely believable, especially since he found out early enough to prevent the coup.[86] We are told the preliminary intelligence was delivered by two concubines who then began the mobilization of the real power-holders. The freedman Narcissus led the charge and warned Claudius that many people had witnessed Messalina's marriage to Silius.

Once apprised of the situation, Claudius held a council in Ostia to plan his response. Tacitus portrays Claudius as so scared that he could only ask his advisors repeatedly whether he was still emperor and Silius a private citizen.[87] In reality, he and his staff snapped into action quickly and effectively. The emperor was brought back to Rome from Ostia, accompanied by Vitellius, Narcissus, and Claudius's friend, Caecina Largus, and kept safe. It was decided that he would go to the Praetorian camp, assure himself of the loyalty of the Guard, and think first of his own security. He is criticized for seeking refuge among his trusted Praetorians, but this is exactly what they were supposed to do: keep the emperor safe in case of an attempted coup.[88] Claudius doubted the loyalty of the prefect of the Guard, Geta, who may have been part of the plot, and removed him from office immediately. He temporarily entrusted the command to Narcissus.[89]

Messalina's revel, whatever it was, ended abruptly when a messenger brought news that Claudius was on his way back to Rome from Ostia, seeking revenge. Messalina, deserted by all but three companions, walked to the outskirts of Rome and hitched a ride along the road to Ostia on a rubbish cart. She managed to get within pleading distance of Claudius's carriage after it came in sight toward her. Narcissus prevented her from reaching the emperor, and he also shut out Britannicus and his sister, Octavia, from reaching their father. He took Claudius directly to Silius's mansion to show him the wide range of Claudius's own possessions that had been transferred there from the palace.[90]

Claudius, enraged, stormed off to the Praetorian barracks, where he had Silius, along with eight senators and equestrians, quickly eliminated.[91] He then went back to his palace for dinner, where he said Messalina should be brought before him in the morning to defend herself. Narcissus knew that if she lived, he would die. He sent a senior Praetorian officer to kill Messalina—assuming she had not already killed herself. The officer found her in her gardens with her mother, and he ran her through with his sword. There would be no trial. Claudius was still dining when news of her death arrived. He simply called for more wine and went on with the meal.[92]

Some kind of official version was disseminated at the time.[93] The Senate voted that Messalina's name and images be removed from all public and private places.[94] She is the first empress for whom there is extant physical evidence that her portraits were deliberately mutilated as a result of *damnatio memoriae*.[95] The blackening of her memory and using her as a scapegoat to explain all of Claudius's shortcomings soon followed. As always, the emphasis was on immorality, not conspiracy. Given the absence of a public trial and the very real condemnation of her memory, it is very difficult to determine what actually happened. Seneca makes no mention of it in his parody of Claudius, the *Apocolocyntosis*, where Messalina is presented as an innocent victim of both Claudius's fears and Narcissus's dealings.[96]

One can argue that these events are entirely a literary construct with no historical content whatsoever.[97] Most historians put more faith in Tacitus, especially since many of the details, like her passion for Silius, the marriage, and the machinations of the freedmen, are corroborated by other authors. But Tacitus, writing sixty years after Messalina's death, was dealing with a hostile senatorial tradition that was critical of Claudius.[98] As more than one scholar has pointed out, Tacitus was simply drawing on a commonplace of Roman moral rhetoric that associates uncontrolled female sexuality with chaos. Tacitus creates an adulterous wife whose desire creates disorder in the family, the household, and the social hierarchy.[99] What we do know is that the new role played by women was resented and that Messalina's reputation was blackened. A high-status woman-turned-whore was a familiar literary trope even during the republic. In the empire it simply went to new extremes.[100]

We will never be able to recover the real Messalina or her motives. Was she just a teenager married to a much older Claudius and looking only for fun? Was her affair with Silius a silly prank? Or was she just looking for a way out? The image of the depraved Messalina certainly accords with Roman male expectations of powerful women, but this still does not explain their actions. She may have deliberately ruined rivals, both men and women, during her marriage to Claudius, thereby revealing her ruthlessness and political acumen, but she was already empress. What did she hope to gain by marrying Silius? The marriage scene is so unbelievable that even Tacitus calls it *fabulosus*—"story-like," "theatrical."[101]

How could anyone hope to keep these affairs secret? Why, for example, didn't the freedmen, who knew about the affair, tell Claudius when imperial goods and personnel were being transferred to Silius's house?[102] Even Tacitus realized it seemed fantastic to believe any mortal beings could have supposed themselves safe and secure in a city where everybody's business was known and nothing could be kept quiet—much less when it involved the consul-designate and the emperor's wife getting together on a prearranged day before invited witnesses.[103]

If Messalina conducted an affair with a prominent senator, much less contracted a marriage, Claudius would have known about it and been foolish not to consider the alliance at least a *potential* threat.[104] Perhaps there was a plot revolving around Silius, and Messalina was simply the pawn in the scheme. Tacitus's account, stripped of its lurid sexual detail seems to make clear that Messalina was attempting to divorce her husband and marry Silius. This would make Claudius's grip on the empire suddenly more tenuous. Whether or not we detect an attempt on his life, Claudius would have responded to the threat in exactly the way he did: to condemn her without a trial. And so her statues were taken down, her name chiseled out of inscriptions, and stories were circulated that would blacken her reputation and good name for all eternity.[105]

The one person to benefit from this entire affair was Claudius's next wife, Agrippina, and not surprisingly, it has been suggested that she was behind the whole affair in a conspiracy to push forward her own agenda and her son's position. Why not? It is as plausible as any other guess. But as one author has pointed out, the "multiplicity of the schemes shows the futility of the exercise."[106]

AGRIPPINA

The palace must have convulsed at the execution of Messalina. Claudius had to come to terms with the infidelity and possible treason of his wife and now the hatred of his children for killing their mother. He would be faced with a threat to his power from a whole new generation. Claudius had been facing down threats, real or perceived, ever since he took over the throne. And although there were still senators who would have been happy to eliminate him and take his place, the biggest threat now came from those closest to him: the people with access.

Was Messalina executed so that he could arrange for a better alliance with someone whose blood was connected to the Augustan house? He had such a person at hand; Julia Agrippina was the eldest daughter of Claudius's brother, Germanicus.[107] Her mother, Vipsania Agrippina, was the daughter of Agrippa and Julia, the daughter of Augustus. Agrippina and her sister, Drusilla, had been exiled in the aftermath of the execution of Drusilla's late husband, Marcus Aemilius Lepidus.[108] They were brought back early in Claudius's reign. Livilla was exiled again within a year, but Agrippina stayed put with her young son, anxious to get back into the game.

The success of Agrippina in thrusting herself into the forefront of political activity and of public consciousness became evident immediately upon her marriage to Claudius.[109] This was a woman determined to have her authority publicly recognized and institutionalized. She began by having her ten-year-old son, Nero, betrothed to Claudius's daughter, Octavia. Octavia was already betrothed to Lucius Silanus, a great-grandson of Augustus. Silanus was easily eliminated; he was accused of incestuous relations with his sister, Calvina, and Agrippina persuaded Claudius to break the engagement and remove Silanus from political office, even from membership in the Senate.[110] The marriage of Claudius to Agrippina took place, and Silanus took his life on the same day, while his sister was banished from Italy.[111]

The clue to the importance of this marriage can be seen in the trouble Claudius went through to make it happen. He flouted the taboo on incestuous unions by marrying his niece. Why? Agrippina had something more to offer than just any wife. She was a blood relative of Augustus, and she had a son approaching maturity who also had the blood of Augustus. Claudius could not risk having someone else become Nero's stepfather.[112] This could give Claudius the legitimacy he so desperately needed, and by adopting Nero he would settle the succession to almost everybody's approval while removing a major incentive for senatorial opponents to assassinate him.

Messalina and Britannicus had been unable to create for Claudius a dynasty that could stave off the threats that Claudius had faced since 41 CE. Now with Messalina dead and disgraced and with general doubts about Britannicus's physical condition and his level of intelligence, a new dynastic line could be created. The hope for the new marriage was that, with Agrippina married to Claudius and her son Nero married to Claudius's daughter, they would be able to succeed where the previous wife had failed. It seems like an entirely rational response to the long-term security problems of his reign. The principate was still in a shaky position. Rulers had not yet divorced themselves from the idea that they needed a connection to the charismatic founder, Augustus. On the other hand, neither had they openly acknowledged the principle of succession.

Claudius's next step after the marriage was to adopt Agrippina's son, Nero. Having the boy transferred into the Claudian family was another way of shoring up his dynasty.[113] This marked Nero as a possible successor to Claudius. At the same time, Agrippina was given the title "Augusta." She was the first wife of a ruling emperor to bear it, and thus it elevated her over her predecessor Messalina.[114] A goodly number of portraits, coins, and gems were created to send the message of the imperial marriage and the strength of the dynasty.[115]

Modern historians, taking their lead from Tacitus, write about Claudius's last years as dominated by the figure of Agrippina eliminating anyone who might be a threat to the new arrangement.[116] For this reason posterity would see her as a powerful force behind the scenes.[117] But it was not the title of "Augusta" that made Agrippina dangerous or the fact that she received foreign delegations or that she wore a military cloak decorated with gold embroidery. She could never really accumulate power for herself except the power to make her son emperor. She was dangerous because she was willing to murder her husband to accomplish this.[118] The real "risk" that Claudius took was in making himself redundant. Once Nero had reached manhood, the heir was in place.[119] Nero headed a parade of the Praetorians. It was announced that a gift to the soldiers and the people of Rome would be given in his name.[120] He was given the title *princeps iuventutis* (young princeps), which made him symbolic head of the equestrian order.[121] In 51 he was given proconsular *imperium* outside of the city, and he was awarded permanent membership in all of Rome's priestly colleges.[122] In 53 he married Claudius's daughter, Octavia.[123]

Claudius saw to it that Nero got all the training that Claudius had never gotten. He helped Nero secure the relationships with all of the most important elements of the Roman world beyond the imperial court. Nero was given priority in Rome through ritual, costume, honors, and the like. Claudius started no new building projects but rather finished only those that had been started. The rest of the money was used for donatives (cash bonuses) in Nero's name while still leaving the young man a surplus in the treasury.[124] It was Nero's title as princeps designate that may have been a bit too much. Promoting Nero as the "heir apparent" was dangerous for both Claudius and Nero. To designate the young boy as Claudius's successor would offend senators who still did not recognize hereditary rule. Princes were known to have disappeared before. Britannicus and his adult supporters were being pushed out in favor of Nero as Claudius sealed the fate of his own son and himself.

Did Claudius suppose that during the long summer of 54 his wife would simply lie back in the shade waiting for the natural course of events? He ought to have understood her better. At the very least, he and Narcissus should have inquired into the reason for the sudden close relationship that had developed between Agrippina and the emperor's personal doctor, Gaius Xenophon. According to Tacitus, Agrippina was worried that Claudius was having second thoughts about his marriage to her and even about his adoption of Nero. She decided to poison Claudius, but it took some time for her to make up her mind about what type of poison to use. It should not work too fast, because that would arouse suspicion. On the other hand, it must not take too long, either, because then Claudius might suspect there was something amiss. She or one of her underlings supposedly contacted Locusta, a notorious dealer in poisons. The poison was then given to Claudius by Halotus, a eunuch who usually tasted Claudius's food before serving it to him.[125]

DEATH OF CLAUDIUS

According to the official record, on October 13, 54 CE, an announcement was made that Claudius was dead following a short illness. He was sixty-three and had ruled thirteen years, eight months, and twenty days.[126] Although there are a few scholars who still argue that Claudius died of natural causes, we will never know for sure what happened behind those palace walls. Later historians had many sinister stories to tell, but even those stories conflict with one another. The only thing they agree upon is that Claudius was a victim of foul play.

Suetonius wrote that everyone agreed Claudius was killed by poison, but when and by whom were disputed points.[127] We should not rule out the possibility that Agrippina administered the poison herself. Suetonius claimed she soaked his favorite mushrooms in poison and served them to him. The choice of which mushroom was used has also been endlessly debated by scholars.[128] Any attempt to identify the poison is a waste of time. There is not enough reliable information in the ancient sources for a CSI investigation. Since sources disagree with one another, in the end all they can tell us is what was suspected at the time or later. It caused Nero to joke that mushrooms were a divine food, because, thanks to eating them, Claudius became a god. It is not reported in the sources how long Claudius lived after ingesting the mushrooms. It was rumored that he immediately lost the ability to speak and died the next morning, following a night of unbearable pain, but there are other possibilities. Perhaps the poison worked well but not as well as was hoped, because as often happened, Claudius had gotten drunk during the meal and vomited it all up or had had diarrhea. Agrippina was thrown into a state of panic. She appealed to Xenophon, who masqueraded as a "helpful" doctor. According to this scenario, it was Xenophon who actually poisoned Claudius once and for all by feeding him a bowl of poisoned gruel or by injecting a fast-acting poison into his throat.[129] We know that emperors had official tasters, so we must ask what happened to that first line of defense in this version.[130]

The problem with both these stories is that the accounts were written much later, after Agrippina's reputation had been blackened. The charge of poisoning was frequently leveled during the Julio-Claudian period, especially against women. She might well have been innocent, and Claudius's death may have stemmed from natural causes. On the other hand, some have argued that in order to secure her own position and that of her son, how could she have acted any differently?[131] All we can do is look for motive and opportunity. The classic question of cui bono—who benefitted from the death?—has the obvious answer: Agrippina and Nero. The picture of Agrippina that has survived is of the ultimate schemer who perfectly copied Claudius's example of how to achieve supreme power. She did it on Nero's behalf, by eliminating the incumbent emperor completely by herself. The fact that Claudius's will was never read has caused people to suggest it was because Nero and Britannicus were to be made joint heirs.[132] Although Agrippina did not need an elaborate web of conspiracy to succeed, she did need cooperation, especially from the army. She held up the announcement of his death until she was ready to put her program in place.[133]

Claudius's death was kept secret until all arrangements had been made for Nero's succession. The official story was that the emperor was ill and the gods were being implored to spare his life. When it came time for the news to be made public, Agrippina conspicuously sought solace with Claudius's son, Britannicus, embracing him and saying how much he looked like his father, but she made sure that he did not leave the room until after Nero had presented himself as the new emperor. Around noon, the doors of the palace were flung open, and Nero emerged with the Praetorian prefect, Burrus, at his side. The sixteen-year-old was hailed by the Praetorians assembled there, placed on a litter, and taken to the Praetorian camp.[134]

THE REIGN OF CLAUDIUS AND THE PRINCIPATE

It is of no importance what Claudius looked like, what ailments he might have suffered from, or what his personality was like. In the end, as Fergus Millar famously wrote, the emperor *was* what the emperor *did*.[135] And what Claudius did was grab the principate, hold onto it for fourteen years, and reinforce the concept of an inherited monarchy. Once there, however, his security concerns were much the same as for every other emperor. A would-be assassin could penetrate the defenses of the most security-minded emperor. Starting with the most banal attack, a commoner was found outside of Claudius's own bedroom. How he penetrated so deeply into the palace is never explained by Suetonius.[136] Would a commoner have enough money to bribe his way into the palace? Was he deranged, or was he someone else's dupe?

Unlike the traditional image of a bumbling Claudius being abducted by the Praetorian Guard and forced to become emperor, it seems quite clear that Claudius was up to his neck in the conspiracy. Although it cannot be proven, he may very well have played a role in the assassination of Caligula. Not everyone in the conspiracy backed the same candidate as successor. Chaerea seems to have been opposed to Claudius having succeeded Caligula, but he was the first person eliminated, along with Lupus, the tribune who killed Caligula's wife and daughter.[137] One of the first rules of hiding the true architect of an assassination is kill the assassin. We do not know whether it was one of the prefects of the Guard or Claudius himself who betrayed a number of their coconspirators. What we do know is that the Praetorians accepted Claudius as *imperator*, swore allegiance to him, and forced the Senate to accept their acclamation. There can be no doubt that cooperation between the Praetorians and Claudius was essential. Together they forged a Caesar who was not a Julius. This was a move of great consequence. Although Claudius was a member of Augustus's family through marriage, the Senate had to vote him the bundle of legal powers that had been gradually accumulated by Augustus, along with a number of miscellaneous honors and titles, including those of "Augustus" and "Caesar." It is also apparent that the Senate put their collective weight behind Claudius, giving him those magical legitimizing honors, powers, and names only because they were forced to by the Praetorians. For the time being the only alternative was civil war.

Claudius was a usurper who depended for support on the army and the people. The army's demand for his installation meant more than any constitutional powers conferred on him by the Senate. All the Senate did was give formal ratification of powers Claudius already possessed.[138] In order to stay in power, Claudius had to destroy potential rivals and confer favors and powers on groups and individuals outside the Senate to a degree unknown before. Claudius thus arrogated power to himself at the expense of the Senate. This alienated members of the aristocracy and created an opposition that the emperor then had to suppress. It was Seneca's view that Claudius represented two traits: a hypocritical reverence for tradition and autocratic license.[139]

Claudius maintained power for almost fourteen years—which was not easy considering he was not the designated heir, that he suffered from physical disabilities, and that he spent most of his reign fighting off plots against his life—and the opposition to Claudius was more serious than the sources are prepared to admit.[140] Unlike during the reign of Tiberius, where Agrippina was the only rival claimant to the imperial house, a generation later there were numerous descendants who could press their claims, which caused insecurity and anxiety for the sitting princeps.[141] Claudius was only the fourth emperor in the Julio-Claudian line, and yet his entire life had been dominated by his fear of being murdered; he could never let his guard down. With the Praetorian Guard on duty and extra security measures taken, he nipped every attempted assassination in the bud (except the last one) and meted out severe punishments for those involved. The frequent trials of important men attest to the strength of the opposition. He tried to avoid Caligula's error by spending as little time as possible away from Rome, although his military triumph in 43 added southeast Britain to the Roman Empire where Julius Caesar had failed. His grasp of power became more practiced with the passage of time, but not necessarily any firmer.

Those who resented both Claudius and the Praetorians had a conspiracy under discussion from the beginning. Within the year there would be a move on the throne in a coup attempt that has not always been well understood. Claudius, of all people, should have known that even with the titles his position was precarious. His policies were all aimed at strengthening the principate and mending relations with all the vital constituencies. It was in this vein that he granted amnesty to all those senators who initially opposed him, and he sought no vengeance. But they were still alive, still resentful, and they still saw themselves on his throne.

Claudius tried to maintain good relations with the Senate, treating that institution and its members with respect, but any whiff of treason that threatened his life had to be stomped out immediately, and the perpetrators shown no mercy. During his reign, no fewer than thirty-five senators and three hundred equestrians were killed.[142] Among that number were definitely men who had tried to oust him, but there were certainly those who may have done no wrong. Such is the weakness of a system that relies on personal accusation and the personal trust of the emperor. Men fell victim to the accusations of Claudius's third and fourth wives, Messalina and Agrippina. Senators were also falsely accused by freedmen who enjoyed the emperor's implicit trust.

Some scholars have plausibly argued that the reason Claudius had so much opposition was that he was never really recognized as emperor at all, that there was never any such thing as a Julio-Claudian dynasty and this term is an anachronism in itself.[143] They state that there was only a *Julian* dynasty, and Claudius did not belong to it, so he spent so much time setting up marriage arrangements and trying to produce a Julio-Claudian heir.[144] There was constant senatorial resistance from those who felt they had a better link, and the pushback was imperial persecution. Because of the position the emperor was in, he had to take understandable precautions and sometimes justifiable measures against treason, committed or contemplated. In Claudius's case this led to the execution of many charged with political crimes and imperial intrigue.[145] Compare this to Tiberius, who executed no senators in the first seventeen years of his reign. If we see Claudius as inheriting the aspirations and grudges of the last regime and having to deal with much passive or active resistance by certain groups within the Senate, then we begin to see his situation as a security problem. Claudius had to secure his survival by extreme measures because of his uncertain claim to the throne. The reign of Claudius, therefore, contributed to a change in the principate in two ways: (1) the manner of his accession and (2) his success in surviving in power and arranging for the peaceful transmission of it to an heir. The first made his reign a turning point from the constitutional point of view because of the open role played in it by the army. The second became a standard practice.

Wiseman's interpretation makes much more sense than attributing the casualties of the reign to the wives and freedmen, as the sources have us believe. It is only in the ancient propaganda that Claudius comes across as a weakling and a fool. Claudius had never been forgiven for seizing power the way he did. He was resented for the manner in which he delegated imperial responsibilities. In relying on his household and in trying to fashion a new dynasty, he offended many key elements of Roman society. Having to deal with freedmen ensured that the hostility rankled on a daily basis. How must the senators have felt when they realized that, in spite of his occasional fine words, the Senate had been reduced to impotence in all matters deemed important, not simply by the emperor but by his wife and even his former slaves. His favored freedmen grew rich by exploiting their offices for profit, and the ancient writers protest with every show of righteousness at the humiliation involved for gentlemen (read: slave-owners) having to defer to former slaves. Claudius presided over a society in flux. The old nobility in Rome was being edged out. Slaves, freedmen, and women of the court seemed to have more power than the senators.

Claudius had not begun the trend of building a staff to run the government. Augustus had begun the trend of relying for practical help in administering the empire on his own household, including slaves and freedmen, as well as members of his immediate family and close friends in the ruling class. As the principate became more institutionalized, the emperor needed help to run his court. Claudius was thrust into power quickly and had fewer allies in the Senate; therefore, he had to rely even more heavily on the slaves and freedmen he believed he could trust. Claudius's challenge was to create a new and lasting dynasty. In his conception of things, there would be new public roles for freedmen with administrative tasks shifted onto more explicitly defined officials. This even included innovative public roles for his wives. His goal, like that of other emperors, was to keep multiple constituencies happy: the populace, the old aristocracy, the new aristocracy, the imperial family, the armies, and now even the provincials. In the end his experiment would prove a failure, and Claudius would end up assassinated like his predecessor.

Claudius did conceive of new public roles for women in his family, especially his wives. Many Romans resented this. Claudius was living through a civil war in which women played a huge role. Much good research has helped us to see that the influence of emperor's wives, however, was considerably exaggerated. Later writers created rhetorical constructs of women that were part of a larger critique of the Julio-Claudian system. The "power" of Agrippina serves to diminish the emperor and imply that he could not control his women. The dysfunctional family mirrored the dysfunctional state. An empress consorting with freedmen undermined the entire social hierarchy. And allegations of incest mask wider challenges to the Julio-Claudian dynasty. These were portraits painted long after the death of Claudius, and they were designed to discredit him.[146] The study of women in the Roman world, especially imperial women, has shown that recovering their real lives and motives is almost impossible from male-authored sources. Both the frivolous wanton and the fertile exemplar are literary creations created by men for their own purposes.

The idea that Claudius's weak spot was marrying the wrong women is as simplistic as it is wrong. What must really be made apparent is the relationship between gender and power.[147] To keep Augustus's bloodline going and to foster the idea of legitimacy, Claudius was willing to pass over his own son, Britannicus, marry his own niece, and adopt her son, Nero. This is one of Claudius's greatest achievements, and it is often overlooked. He provided for a smooth succession without even a threat of civil war. He had knitted together the two houses and presented it to his heir. Claudius accepted marriage to Agrippina and the succession of Nero because it worked. It was his best prospect for survival personally, but also for the principate. That Nero was an unproven adolescent who might not have been the best choice for the position is not Claudius's fault; he did not plan to die early. The idea of an inherited monarchy was the legacy of Augustus, but there was still no legal way of achieving it. However smooth Nero's succession, the cracks in the institution of the principate were still there. The succession problem would not go away, and as Claudius's own accession showed, if there was no clear designate, the army would step in to back its own candidate. The army could do this because it had force on its side. Not the Senate, not the Roman people, but the army had control because the principate was, if nothing else, a military monarchy.

The structural problems within the principate still persisted, and this affected how Claudius was viewed. The Roman emperor was a monarch, but he was not called one, and the idea that the princeps was still a citizen of a Republic meant that there was still no legal basis for an hereditary succession. As Claudius's own accession dramatically demonstrated, when there was no clear designate, soldiers would choose the *imperator* they wanted. The ideology of a civil leader existed alongside the reality of a military monarchy. This dissonance between the survival of the *res publica* and the realities of where power now lay was profound. This problem existed for all of Augustus's successors. Anyone in the position of emperor had to navigate his way between the resentment shown by the senators, the power of the armies, and the well-being of the Roman people all over the empire.

Claudius was forced to use manipulation as his main political weapon, but he did so to remain in power, stabilize his regime, and secure it for the next generation, averting for nearly three decades a civil war, the worst of all political evils to the Romans. The ruthlessness of Claudius's efforts to stay in power also centralized the government and allowed the social and economic constitution of the empire as a whole to continue to improve and stabilize itself. As a usurping emperor, he doubled his effort to conciliate the nobility, but his efforts proved inadequate against the resentment that his usurpation caused, and too many fissures developed among his own supporters that weakened his political position.

Claudius's claim to the throne had always been tenuous at best. He was not a great general, he was not a man of eloquence, and he was not a designated successor. The political culture of the principate was still very much developing, and there was still no established tradition of what to do about the succession when the emperor died.[148] What was clear is that Claudius's accession was due in no small part to the Praetorian Guard, and thus the Roman Empire was moving toward the establishment of a military monarchy. Other groups still had to be cultivated, but most fundamental were the armies.[149]

Although Claudius expressed lofty ideals, aimed at a just as well as viable government and a concern for justice, the underlying problem was still survival. Effecting reform was difficult, and there is no way to measure the effectiveness of Claudius's administration. In many ways he was powerless to change the flaws in the principate. Claudius could rail at the "iniquity of men," but there was little he could do about it. Surrounded by sycophants and suppliants, it was perfectly possible for the emperor to be insulated from many of the resentments his policies may have raised. Bruised feelings were an undeniable flaw of his reign.

Although Mommsen claimed that there were no major accomplishments during his reign, Josiah Osgood has recently shown in his excellent book on Claudius that most of what Claudius did was positive.[150] Claudius was not a passive emperor manipulated by women and freedmen. In spite of the fact that he had had no experience of warfare, oratory, or the law, he seems to have been paying attention. Although excluded from the men's world and raised by his mother and grandmother, he had a good sense of what the empire needed and what an emperor might do to improve the lives of his subjects. He wanted to create an image of himself as a mighty ruler who stood for strengthening the empire through hard work after years of neglect by Tiberius and Caligula. He seized the throne, established his priorities, made plans, and was extraordinarily active in keeping the principate moving forward. He made strategically related decisions about the boundaries of empire and staged an invasion of Britain.[151]

The reign of Claudius is a window on the developing political culture in the capital. Although he got the throne through intrigue and assassination, he helped to gradually move the development of the institution of the principate along. It was still an office that lay uneasily between hereditary monarchy and elected magistrates. With Claudius's reverence for Rome's republican past and traditions, a true monarchy with a fixed succession was not an option.[152] Sources of authority were developed on

republican traditions—wills, adoptions, artistic imagery, building projects, religious rituals, military campaigning, the distribution of honors.
On the other hand, his reign demonstrated that this was a military monarchy, no matter how much other groups had to be cultivated. All emperors
ruled fundamentally at the behest of their armies. While the support of
the people was important, it was the twenty-five legions stationed across
the empire that had to be kept happy. Any independently minded commander might easily lead a rebellion, especially any province with large
armies, such as Syria.[153] Therefore, it is no surprise that Claudius granted
all the troops substantial cash payments. He promised the Praetorian
Guard 15,000 sesterces—a sum five times their normal annual pay. This is
why control of the state finances was so important and why the first thing
Claudius did after leaving the Praetorian camp was to gain control of the
imperial property on the Palatine even though it was technically not his
by private law, since he was not a Julian. The slaves and freedmen would
make up his staff, and the treasury would pay them.

The Senate opposed him when he proposed having prominent Gauls
in the Senate. He implemented his plan to grant civil rights to the provinces on a large scale. Claudius did not have a personal relationship
with the military when he became emperor, but he made up for that by
personally visiting and leading his troops at the end of the first stage of
the conquest of Britain.[154] His annexation of southwest England resulted
in Britain's becoming a province. To safeguard the grain supply he had
the port of Ostia built. He offered the people amusement in the form of
gladiatorial matches, which also fed his own fondness for blood sport.
Even so, Claudius had problems with keeping the plebs in order. In 51
an extremely unusual security breach took place when disorderly and
hungry crowds set upon the emperor personally. An angry crowd surrounded Claudius in the Forum and pelted him with stale crusts of bread,
until soldiers rescued the emperor and hurried him away to the palace.[155]

Claudius survived by preventing political fragmentation. With limited
resources at his disposal, and while plagued by constant opposition, he
still carried out his policies effectively and offered the Roman people
a sense of renewal. In many ways, he strengthened the nascent institution of the principate. He left his imprint across the empire in the form
of roads, temples, statues, decrees, speeches, and diplomas. He tried to
serve the needs of provincials as well as citizens in an empire where the
two were becoming more alike. As long as they accepted imperial rule,
his subjects were treated well. The achievements of Claudius are many.
The conquest of Britain, the conquest and organization of Mauretania, his
colonial foundations and the extension of the citizenship, and the many
sensible pronouncements accidentally preserved for us in inscriptions
and on papyri should enable us to paint a new picture of Claudius as

perhaps the wisest fool in the empire. Tacitus shows little appreciation for this imperial policy, but then, as Balsdon has charged, "Tacitus had little imperial sense himself."[156] The wisdom that Claudius displayed was his, not the schemes of his freedmen and wives. And his security system succeeded for fourteen years. If the rumors of his poisoning are true, however, then his assassination was a security breach that brought another famous "monster" to the throne.

7

The "Mad" Emperor, Nero

If Claudius and his wives were the subject of a negative publicity campaign after their deaths, then Nero is the ultimate problem in ancient spin-doctoring. The Nero of Hollywood kitsch is the archetypal sadistic monster, a pretentious buffoon, the tyrant who killed his mother, fiddled while Rome burned, and threw Christians to the lions. Killing such a man was practically a public service. Despite recent efforts to rehabilitate his reputation, Nero has gone down in history as one of the worst of all emperors. His administration was steeped in treachery and assassination. Everyone, high or low, family or stranger, lived in fear of his bloodthirsty regime. Not surprisingly, his own life was under threat as people tried to remove the emperor to save their own lives.[1]

HIS CHILDHOOD AND MOTHER

Considering Nero's early life, it would have been perfectly understandable if he *had* been driven insane.[2] He was a sensitive child who had known practically from infancy that some people wanted to kill him—and that one false move on his part might result in disaster for both him and his mother, Agrippina. Nero was only two years old when his mother was left to rot on a prison island forty miles off the Italian coast, thanks to the Emperor Tiberius (see chapter 3). Nero was left in the care of his sick and notoriously brutal father, Cn. Domitius Ahenobarbus.[3] Nobody wanted to know them. When his father died, his inheritance was seized by his wicked uncle, Caligula, and he was sent as a pauper to live with his aunt Lepida. When Caligula died, Nero's mother and his wealth were returned to him. Suddenly at the age of three, everyone loved him again, except the evil empress, Messalina. But then the evil empress was executed, and the Emperor Claudius married his mother and adopted him as his son and heir. As at least one scholar has pointed out, the Brothers Grimm could not have made up a better story.[4] In writing about Nero, we encounter all the same source problems and later hostile traditions that plagued us with the first four emperors. In Nero's case, however, it is worse because everything about Nero is portrayed as larger than life: his loves, his hates, his appetites. In addition, no one's reputation has been more blackened after death.[5]

Having been forced to become emperor at the age of sixteen whether he wanted to or not, Nero had little experience to help him rule. His first line of defense at this point was probably his mother, Agrippina, a formidable woman who had acquired political allies at all levels during Claudius's reign. She knew how to exploit these connections, and she was fiercely protective of her young son. She used her Augustan lineage and descent from Germanicus to justify the new emperor's right to the succession. Whether or not she actually killed her husband Claudius may be debated, but she never stopped reminding Nero of how her efforts had gotten him to the throne.[6]

As mother of the young princeps, and as his primary protector, Agrippina set out to eliminate any rivals to herself and her son. In 54 she had the proconsul of Asia, Marcus Junius Silanus, poisoned without the emperor's knowledge.[7] It was called the first crime of the new principate. Five years earlier she had destroyed his brother to facilitate Nero's marriage to Claudius's daughter, Octavia. Marcus Silanus was a descendant of Augustus and could have been a possible rival to Nero. Agrippina may have feared the vengeance of the Junii Silanii now that she was no longer protected by Claudius. Not long after this, Narcissus, Claudius's loyal freedman and the strongest supporter of Claudius's son Britannicus's claim to the throne, was forced to commit suicide. Agrippina was a master at eliminating the competition surreptitiously to protect her son and settle old scores.

Agrippina had stage-managed her son's accession and its acceptance by the Praetorian Guard, the Senate, and the people, but this was the height of her accomplishments. When it came to true power, women in Rome did not have any, really.[8] Her only connection to power was her son, and he was too young and uninterested in affairs of state to be of much help. Her position began to collapse within the first few months of his reign. Her power rested on the position she occupied under Claudius, her son's dependence on her, and whatever gratitude he felt for what she had done. She had provided the genetic link to the throne, which is what gave Julio-Claudian women their influence, but there was no way that the men with the actual power were going to let her hold the reins of state or appear in a public role.

It is Tacitus who gives us the myth that the first five years of Nero's reign were regarded as a golden age. Nero certainly made some moves that were popular with the Senate, like denouncing delation.[9] In truth, however, there was trouble in paradise from the beginning.[10] Factions began developing quickly with Agrippina and her supporters on the one side and Nero and his advisors on the other. Within a year of Nero's coming to power, there was dissension between mother and son; Nero's advisors—Seneca and the Praetorian prefect, Burrus—naturally sided with the young emperor. Seneca and Burrus wanted to make the decisions themselves and sought to push Agrippina into the background while encouraging the young Nero to enjoy himself.[11]

As Nero's mother, Agrippina could certainly try to control her seventeen-year-old son's personal life, but remember that he was a teenage boy. The first big crisis arose when Nero embarked on a passionate love affair with a freedwoman named Acte, openly insulting his wife, Octavia, in the process and bringing his mother's disapproval down on himself. His advisors tried to cover up the affair by providing a shill. Annaeus Serenus, one of Seneca's protégés, pretended to be Acte's lover in order to explain her much-improved circumstances and presence around the palace. But secrets of this sort cannot be kept long in the hothouse atmosphere of an imperial court. Agrippina became enraged when she discovered what was happening. She stormed at Nero, screaming, "I made you emperor!" as if she had the power to take the title back. Nero called her bluff by threatening to abdicate and run off to Rhodes with his mistress. Nero was a naïve teenager in love. He should have realized, of course, that the Roman people might accept a divorce—after all, he had been married to Octavia for ten years and they had produced no children. They were not, however, ready for an empress who had been a slave.[12]

AGRIPPINA'S DEMISE

Agrippina's continued, violent opposition alienated Nero's affection. At this point he threw off the maternal yoke and put his trust in Seneca. When Agrippina realized she had pushed Nero too far, she tried to win him back, but Nero was not fooled. He must have realized that a woman who would murder so many aristocratic opponents while in the pursuit of power would not hesitate to eliminate a freedwoman who got in her way. Nero began the slow process of moving her away from power, away from the court, and eventually away from Rome.

In 55 Nero moved against her chief supporter at court, the financial secretary (*a rationibus*), Pallas. Angry at the dismissal of Pallas and realizing that her influence was waning, she threatened to present Claudius's natural son, Britannicus, to the troops in the Castra Praetoria as Claudius's legitimate heir.[13] The use of the Praetorians in Nero's accession and her threat illustrate that at least the empress knew that the Praetorian Guard was of paramount importance in determining the legitimacy of the rule and keeping the emperor alive. In the end, Agrippina's attempt at intimidation backfired. Nero banned her from the palace and withdrew her contingent of Praetorian Guardsmen and the German bodyguard that accompanied her.[14] The dismissal of her bodyguard meant she could no longer influence the soldiers.[15]

Agrippina had overplayed her hand. Nero may have been young, but he was no fool. As long as Britannicus was alive, the young but infirm boy could be used as a pawn in any move on the throne. Nero, with the help of the infamous poisoner Locusta, arranged to have Britannicus poisoned at the children's table in the palace. The official version was circulated that Britannicus had had an epileptic fit. Dio reports that the appearance of the body at the funeral was a dead giveaway.[16] The poison had turned the body livid, so they smeared it with gypsum, but when they transported it through the Forum a heavy rain fell and the gypsum washed off, revealing the truth.

Agrippina herself never stopped being seen as a threat to the emperor. On the rare occasions when he paid her a visit, he came surrounded by his own armed guard and did not stay long. This may have been a legitimate move involving internal security, since shortly after her isolation, no doubt bolstered by the obvious change in her status, a charge of inciting revolution was brought against her by a former friend, Junia Silana.[17] Agrippina was outraged at the charge, fought back, and won. Junia Silana was banished, one of her henchmen executed, and two others were given lesser punishments. But no matter how successfully Agrippina fought off accusations of conspiring against Nero, her days were numbered.

Agrippina survived another four years before Nero decided that he had to get rid of her. Thus 59 CE became the year when the most famous assassination of his reign occurred, and that event would change everything. Nero was afraid to murder his mother in a way that would become publicly known. He was very afraid that the assassination attempt would be uncovered and would enrage the soldiers, the people, and the Senate.[18] His first attempt at having her drowned by rigging her boat failed; she swam back madder than hell.[19] When a large group of people streamed to the seashore at Baiae to congratulate Agrippina on being saved from certain death, Nero understood its true meaning. She was popular with the public, could draw crowds, and those crowds could be turned against him. He quickly sent an army unit to disperse the crowd, which stopped the demonstrations immediately. Tired of her constant interference and urged on by certain members of court, including Seneca and Poppaea Sabina, his new mistress since 58, he had Agrippina clubbed to death by a group of sailors from the Misenum fleet who were dispatched to her lakeside villa. The official story was that the messenger who came to tell Nero of the boat accident was carrying a sword and intended to kill Nero, and, thus exposed, his mother committed suicide out of guilt for her attempt to murder her son.[20]

There is no indication in the sources of the Praetorian Guard's response to the news that Agrippina was dead. The official version—that Nero had escaped an assassin sent by his mother—was accepted without hesitation.[21] The absence of the Praetorians from this event is significant. The Guard was not being used as the agent of the matricide, although by this time executions of a political nature, including eliminating members of the imperial family, had become one of its functions. Burrus could certainly have found some of his men willing to perform the deed, although it has been suggested that the Guard remained loyal to the imperial house, which meant the memory of Germanicus, Agrippina's father. The day after the murder, the Praetorians demonstrated their loyalty to the emperor in a display of affection arranged by Burrus that was designed as well to assuage Nero's fear.[22] According to Dio, the emperor granted the Praetorians a donative (cash bonus) after Agrippina's death, though the author's rationale for this—that they might expect more crimes to be committed—has not convinced everyone.[23] Nero may have been simply acknowledging the importance of the Praetorians to his rule and ensuring their continued support. Burrus continued in his position until his death in 62 CE.[24]

The year 62 marked another turning point of Nero's reign. Burrus died, and Ofonius Tigellinus was appointed Praetorian prefect.[25] It was the end of the partnership that had guided him since his accession. Nero, now a bit older, felt he did not have to pay attention to appearances and could do what he wanted. What he wanted was to divorce his barren wife, Octavia, and marry his mistress, Poppaea Sabina. Nero could not come up with a charge against his wife plausible enough to counteract her popular appeal and spotless reputation.[26] Octavia was relegated to the island of Pandateria, the place of exile for imperial ladies that had started with Augustus's own daughter, Julia. Octavia was put under military supervision—the first step to her destruction. There were vociferous popular protests and riots in the capital that verged on civil revolt.[27] It was the most pronounced mass disturbance in Nero's reign.

Realizing that his adultery charge against Octavia was not going to fly, Nero had to find someone to confess to the same crime and prove collusion.

Such a person was found in Anicetus, his former preceptor and the prefect of the Misenum fleet. Upon the promise of a secret reward and a handsome retirement arrangement, Nero's henchman, who had cooperated in Agrippina's murder, obliged and made a guilty confession of adultery with Octavia in the presence of Nero's entourage. This was followed by an imperial edict denouncing Octavia for having joined in a conspiracy with the naval prefect to seize power.[28] Nero threw in a charge of procuring an abortion just for good measure—foolish, when one realizes it contradicted the earlier charge of sterility. She was ordered to die, June 9, 62, despite her protests of innocence and insignificance.[29] She was forced to cut her veins and then was suffocated in the vapors of an overheated bath. Her head was severed and delivered to Poppaea Sabina. The sycophantic Senate voted national thanksgiving.[30]

Nero was now free to marry his mistress, although Poppaea Sabina would not fare any better. She died in the summer of 65; the cause and timing of her death are uncertain.[31] Suetonius says Nero personally kicked the pregnant Poppaea to death when she criticized him for coming home late from the chariot races. Tacitus believed Nero's personal grief over the loss of his wife was sincere, since he loved her and wanted children.[32] The loss of the unborn child and heir must have weighed on his mind, because he remarried within the year. He consoled himself in Naples while sending letters back to the Senate ordering prosecutions for treason.[33] He was a man obsessed with violence. It was whispered that he would comb the streets and public houses at night with friends in order to find people to beat up. He was also no stranger to sexual violence. He was a menace to men as well as women. His most notorious affair was with a man, Sporus, whom it is said he loved passionately. Nero had him castrated and treated him as his wife.[34]

Although the spontaneous reaction of the populace to Octavia's death was negative in the face of what they perceived as an injustice, Nero's public relations remained relatively good. Of course, the public was fed official versions of events and had no clue as to what the real goings-on in the palace were. Nero always made himself accessible to the public. He attended the games, appeared in public, and mingled with the crowds. How ironic that the populace could express their discontent with Nero more than the Senate could. Unfortunately, there was no group that could harness this energy and take advantage of it against the emperor.

Public violence against the emperor or his representatives was not unheard of. A violent incident occurred in 61 CE when the city prefect (*praefectus urbi*), Pedanius Secundus, was murdered in Rome by one of his slaves. The reason was personal, not political. Either he had refused the slave's emancipation after agreeing on the price, or, if the rumor is true, he and the slave competed for the love of a catamite. It was customary in such cases not only to execute the guilty slave but to kill every slave in the household as a warning to other slaves who might raise their hand to their owner.[35] People gathered to protest the shedding of so much blood and the taking of innocent lives. This brought matters to the point of sedition, and the Senate was besieged. The Senate wished for the sentence to be served and not to listen to the crowd. The emperor had to issue an edict reprimanding the people, and he lined the route along which the condemned were led to their execution with detachments of soldiers.[36]

THE SENATE

Nero's lack of popularity with the Senate was another story. Like his mother's approach to security, Nero simply eliminated people who opposed him in any way. Although he had begun his reign in 54 by committing himself to a modus vivendi with the Senate and discouraging *maiestas* trials altogether, it was not long before his reign began a long descent into imperial misconduct, senatorial resentment, and mutual suspicion. Trials within the palace had been considered a particularly offensive characteristic of Claudius's reign. Both Caligula and Claudius had promised not to have such trials, but both went back on their word. Nero kept his word for the first eight years. Then it all changed in 62, when the *maiestas* trials began again. Murder had been used as a security measure against the immediate members of the imperial family; now it was aimed at men with ties to the imperial blood, those who enjoyed too much popularity and success, or who were simply perceived as better candidates for the supreme power. Whether they were an actual threat or were only perceived as a threat did not matter much; it was enough that Nero saw their elimination as a matter of his own survival.[37] Even the freedman, Pallas, was eliminated in 62, possibly to gain access to his large fortune.[38]

To make things worse, these accusations ran against entire families. Indeed, the danger came from men whose relationship to the founding father of the dynasty was no more distant than Nero's. One such family that perpetually paid a price for providing possible candidates for the throne were the Junii Silani.[39] Marcus Junius Silanus had been murdered in 54 (see above).[40] His son Lucius Junius Silanus Torquatus was raised in the house of the famous jurist, Cassius Longinus, by his aunt, Junia Lepida. Longinus supposedly honored his ancestor, the tyrannicide C. Cassius, on whose statue he was alleged to have inscribed, "To the leader of the cause." Marcus's plan was supposedly to raise his nephew, Lucius Junius Silanus Torquatus, a descendant of Augustus, to the throne. Lucius himself was accused of following the plan in 64. His uncle, Decimus, had been convicted the previous year.[41] Because the accusation was so thin, another charge was added: incest with his aunt Junia Lepida, the wife of Cassius, who was also accused of using black magic. Her fate is unknown.[42] Lucius was exiled to Naxos, but later was confined to the town of Barium (Bari) in Apulia. At the end he rather bravely showed resistance to his executioners.[43] Seized by some guards and a centurion bearing the imperial sentence of death, he was ordered to open his veins. He refused and fought them off with his bare fists and fell fighting, wounded only in the front. Cassius, Junia's husband, was banished as a concession to his age; he was exiled to Sardinia.[44]

Denounced as their accomplices were senators Vulcacius Tullinus and L. Cornelius Marcellus and the equestrian L. Calpurnius Fabatus.[45] In the end all three managed to save themselves, perhaps because Nero was concentrating on other, more serious cases. Nero had his sights set on Thrasea Paetus, a senator of high social standing and a follower of Stoic philosophy. Paetus had disapproved of the murders of Agrippina and Octavia and had withdrawn publicly over the matter. This included general nonattendance in the Senate after 63 and nonparticipation in the senatorial oath taken every January 1 to uphold the acts of past and present emperors. He was absent from his priestly college when vows for the emperor's safety were taken each January 3 and absent again from Poppaea's funeral and consecration in 65.[46] These acts identified him as a dissident who openly defied the emperor. In early 63 Nero renounced his friendship (*amicitiae renuntiato*) with Paetus. For people who existed on imperial favor, this was a signal of disgrace.[47]

THE PISONIAN CONSPIRACY

All this senatorial discontent finally came to a head when, on April 19, 65, an attempt was made on Nero's life. The plot was planned without the cooperation of governors, provincial armies, or indeed anyone outside of Rome. The conspirators made no contact with sympathetic generals, though they clearly expected the armies to welcome, or at least accept, the deed. And although we have better documentation for this conspiracy than any other against a Julio-Claudian emperor, it has not produced a scholarly consensus.[48]

The conspiracy was fairly widespread judging by the cast of characters, which included senators, *equites*, Praetorian tribunes, centurions, and eventually one of the Praetorian prefects. The list resembles closely that of the assassins of Caligula in January 41, except that no imperial freedmen are named. The plan was modeled closely on the murder of Caesar: the senator Plautius Lateranus, who had earlier enjoyed Nero's clemency, was to present a petition to the emperor and, by grasping his knees, prevent him from avoiding the daggers of the others. As with most conspiracies, the motives for each person varied: some participated out of patriotism, others out of pique, and no doubt some out of ambition. Various conspirators reacted to various wrongs. We can see themes emerging in Tacitus through the speeches of the participants. They allude to the resurgence of the power of the freedmen and the fact that the Senate had no power. The Praetorian officers stressed Nero's crimes—the domestic murders, his embarrassing public performances, and an attempt to destroy the capital.[49]

The difference between the plots against Caesar and Caligula and the one against Nero was that the first two succeeded. The plot against Nero failed because the emperor had a good security staff that got intelligence of the plot before it was carried out. Tacitus marvels at the fact that the secret was kept as long as it was.[50] There were no more people involved than there had been with Caesar's assassination, but knowledge of this plot leaked out. Nero, unlike Caesar, would not refuse to read a list of his possible assassins (see chapter 1).[51] And, unlike the plot against Caesar, this one seems to have been poorly planned and poorly executed. To have succeeded, they would have needed a small, dedicated group of people willing to kill the emperor quickly. And, of course, it goes without saying that one has to succeed on the first try; one never gets a second chance—especially not with Nero. Some participants must have had to be willing to die in the attempt. With Nero's security being so tight, they had to plan the deed at a location where they could neutralize his bodyguards and have a viable escape route. Most importantly, they needed a plausible candidate who could be put forth as the next emperor. That person would need to have the support of the Praetorian Guard and the Senate initially and then win over the army and the populace.

The plot against Nero in 65 intended to replace the dead emperor with Gaius Calpurnius Piso, a descendant of the republican nobility who enjoyed widespread popularity, and thus the event is called the Pisonian conspiracy.[52] Piso himself had been in exile when Caligula was killed, but now was his chance at the top job. He was well aware of the fact that there were rival candidates.[53] We cannot adequately explain how he got to be the nominal head of a plot that he neither initiated nor actively directed.[54] Even when the plot had been detected and his confederates were urging him, as a last resort, to rouse the populace or the troops to revolt, he did absolutely nothing.[55] He may just have been the figurehead chosen as a transitional princeps. He was of consular rank, popular, and related to many senatorial families. If diminution of the Senate's position was the chief complaint of the conspirators, he would be a good face for the new regime.[56] Tacitus notes that he feared the ambitions of other senators, including the consul, M. Julius Vestinus Atticus; this is why the consul was not informed of the plot, lest he become a rival or give his support to another candidate.[57]

In choosing the spot for the deed, Piso refused to have the murder carried out at his own villa at Baiae, ostensibly because it would taint him with sacrilegious disregard of the duties of hospitality. He also wanted the deed to be done publicly with an audience. Committing the murder in Baiae would also have allowed others to take control of the situation in Rome.[58] Piso did not want to leave the capital and allow the initiative to be taken by some other aspirant to power.

The contradictions of the sources make it difficult to know the truth about who started the conspiracy, how many people actually participated, or even what their plan was. Rudich, for example, identifies two groups as a conspiracy within a conspiracy.[59] The inner group was made up of a tightly knit cell of Praetorian officers who were acting independently of the senatorial group and pursued different goals. This would explain Dio's version of the story, where Piso is not even mentioned. Dio names both Tigellinus's colleague, the Praetorian prefect L. Faenius Rufus, and Seneca as the culprits.[60] Polyaenus calls it the conspiracy of Piso and Seneca.[61] In Suetonius, *Nero* 36.1, Seneca is not mentioned, which may be significant in itself since the Senate may have wanted it covered up. Tacitus does not gloss over the incriminating accusation against Seneca by Antonius Natalis, nor does he try to cover it up.[62] He does not withhold the report that Subrius Flavus and certain centurions of the Praetorian Guard intended, with Seneca's cognizance, to overthrow Nero with Piso's help and then slay Piso and confer the principate on Seneca. Others have the two-headed plot consisting of Seneca and the Stoic republicans on one side and Piso and the monarchical group on the other. This does not work, since there is virtually no evidence that the Stoics (or anyone else) were pursuing a restoration of the republic.[63] It is just as easy to follow Tacitus when he says that the plot grew quickly because of Piso's popularity and a hatred of Nero.[64]

The key group, whatever it was, seems to have had a final round of negotiations. The conspirators decided that Nero would be attacked when attending chariot races during the games in honor of Ceres, which lasted from April 12 to April 19.[65] Nero would be attacked at the Circus Maximus, just as Caligula had been killed, on his way to or at a theatrical performance. Access to the emperor at such a time was easy, and Nero's movements would be restricted by the crowds around him. The emperor would be in a good mood with his guard down. The lesson about first securing the allegiance of the Praetorian Guard had been learned. There was to be no Claudius found by the soldiers hiding behind the curtain and spirited off. Piso himself, right after the murder in the Circus Maximus, was to be escorted from the Temple of Ceres nearby to the Praetorian camp by Faenius Rufus, one of the Praetorian prefects, and the other officers.[66]

It does seem clear that the junior Praetorian officers were the ones who drove the plot forward, because they would be the ones to commit the bloody act. It could be, and Tacitus confirms, that Piso was drawn into a conspiracy already in progress; he certainly showed no leadership in the course of the plot.[67] The most active members were Subrius Flavus, the tribune of the Praetorian cohort, and Sulpicius Asper, a centurion. Subrius Flavus had more than once expressed his eagerness to kill Nero.[68] He seemed ready to kill the emperor while Nero sang on stage (critics!). He could also have killed Nero during the great fire, while the emperor was running around, unescorted, helping with relief efforts. Tacitus says Subrius restrained himself only because he needed to plan a safe escape.[69] Among his allies were two other Praetorian tribunes, C. Gavius Silvanus and Statius Proximus, together with two centurions, Maximus Scaurus and Venetus Paulus.[70]

They planned the attack so that Lateranus, a man of enormous size and unwavering spirit, would pretend to be pleading for a subsidy for his estate. He would fall at the knees of the emperor in the position of a suppliant and then, taking him by surprise, throw him on the ground and pin him. While he was still prostrate and unable to move, the tribunes and centurions and any of the others with enough audacity, were to run up and stab him. How could they be sure those particular officers would be in place unless Faenius Rufus was involved?[71]

The plan sounded good on paper, but in the end their plan was a huge failure. The weak link was the disloyalty of Milichus, freedman of the senator Flavius Scaevinus, who reported his patron's suspicious preparations to the emperor. Scaevinus and Natalis were examined separately and then chained and threatened with torture. Natalis confessed first and named Piso and Seneca, in that order. Scaevinus named Lucan, Quintianus, and Claudius Senecio.[72] The plan was also wrecked by the indecision of Piso, who immediately lost heart and could not be persuaded to appeal to the Praetorians and people to seize the city. Treason is not a hobby for the hesitant.

Abject confessions and dishonorable accusations followed. Nero learned with growing alarm the numbers that were involved and the extent of the betrayal. The disloyalty of the Praetorian officers was particularly distressing; Nero could only trust new recruits to deliver the death order to Piso. After the revelations and punishments, he felt it necessary to buy the loyalty of the Guard with a handsome donative of 2,000 sesterces per man and a free grain allowance.[73] In addition to the tribune Subrius Flavus and the centurion Sulpicius Asper, who were guilty and suffered execution, four Praetorian tribunes were dismissed. Two other tribunes were spared for cooperating in the punishment of their fellow conspirators, but they killed themselves.[74] In all, a total of forty-one persons were named in connection with the conspiracy. There were nineteen senators, seven equestrians, eleven soldiers, and four women. Of these twenty were found guilty, and nineteen were noted as innocent. Of the twenty guilty conspirators, sixteen were executed and four were pardoned or acquitted. Four others escaped, but two of them later committed suicide.[75]

All of these reactions were normal. Nero's intelligence network had done its duty, and he had powerful support in uncovering the plot. The consular Petronius Turpilianus, the praetor-designate Cocceius Nerva, the loyal prefect Tigellinus, and the imperial freedman Epaphroditus all received honors befitting a military victory. The conspirators were revealed, and the punishments they received should have been expected. In order to answer the public outcry that the charges against the conspirators were counterfeited, Nero had the information against the condemned and their confessions collected in booklets and published.[76]

Nero treated the exposure and punishment of the conspirators as a serious event, as well he should have. At first he retained a modicum of balance: some of the accused were pardoned, others ignored. The Senate felt confident enough to stop the malicious prosecution of Seneca's brother, Gallio, by one of its members, and Nero refused a temple to himself, an unprecedented honor for the living emperor at Rome. Tacitus claims, however, that Nero used the plot to accuse many innocent men who were punished on inadequate evidence. Tacitus believed that Vestinus Atticus, Seneca, and Rufrius Crispinus were done away with because Nero simply hated them. Others believed they were eliminated because they were falsely accused by conspirators trying to help themselves by giving information. According to Miriam Griffin, it was only later in 65, after the death of Poppaea and her unborn child, that the "unprovoked" persecution of influential senators on treason charges began in earnest.[77] Tacitus also detected financial motives behind some of the political convictions that followed Poppaea's death later in the year.[78] Nero was having financial problems; we can see this in 66, when the condemned were advised to make the emperor or Tigellinus part heir in order to save the rest of the estates for their family.[79]

There is always the possibility that many of these prosecutions were linked to real attempts on the emperor's life.[80] It is not clear whether Nero believed that Lucius Silanus had been considered as a possible alternative to Piso earlier in 65. The next to be accused were three people: L. Anistius Vetus, his mother-in-law, Sextia, and his daughter, Antistia Pollitta, who had been the wife of Rubellius Plautus. Rubellius Plautus had been executed in 62, and, therefore, any hint of friendship or family ties would be an excuse for more persecution.[81] Antistia Pollitta had been with her husband when he was murdered three years before and ever since had practiced that form of ostentatious widowhood that had become so fashionable in the early empire.[82] She went to Naples to plead with Nero, but in vain. The three anticipated condemnation and they committed suicide. And, as always, there was no shortage of senators willing to turn up and condemn their peers.[83]

One set of condemnations has been portrayed as reflecting Nero's new fear of able military men.[84] The wealthy Anteius Rufus was accused by Nero's old victim Antistius Sosianus, still in exile and seeing a possible ticket home, of consulting an astrologer about the death of the emperor. Antistius also implicated Ostorius Scapula, a war hero of the Claudian conquest of Britain, who had refused to give hostile evidence at Antistius's trial in 62.[85]

THE AFTERMATH

A number of prominent literary men fell in the aftermath of the Pisonian conspiracy. Annaeus Mela was accused with his son, Lucan, in conspiratorial plans. Again, with regard to the senatorial ringleaders, Lucan may have been banned from writing and publishing his poetry in 64 and may have turned to treason for vengeance.[86] Tacitus is clear in asserting that Lucan's motives were private rather than republican, Stoic, or even public.[87] Petronius, Nero's *arbiter elegentiae* (master of ceremonies), was similarly linked with Scaevinus (see above), but Rufrius Crispinus, who had been exiled at the time of the detection, was not sentenced to death.

Tacitus's history of the period breaks off with the deaths of Barea Soranus and Thrasea Paetus, men whom Nero had long distrusted. Barea was accused of treasonable collusion with Rubellius Plautus.[88] Barea's daughter was implicated in a further charge, that of dabbling in magic, and it was recalled that her husband Annius Pollio had been exiled as an associate of Piso.[89]

There has been much made of Nero's attack on a small group of Stoic philosophers.[90] There is no evidence that C. Calpurnius Piso himself or any of the senators, *equites*, and Praetorian officers who planned the conspiracy with Lucan were Stoics. While Lucius Silanus is described as a pupil of Heliodorus, the Stoic, there is nothing to suggest that Cassius Longinus was an adherent of the same creed; his ancestors certainly were not. And the victims that perished in 66 before Thrasea Paetus, Barea Soranus, and even Seneca's brother, Annaeus Mela, were not Stoics.[91] Whatever their shared philosophical sentiments were, either you took concerted action against the emperor or you did not. Stoics had been condemned in the past on political charges, but not because they were Stoics.[92] If the entire school was under suspicion by Nero as purveying treasonous ideas, then was there anything distinctively Stoic about the opposition, real or alleged, that caused these men to confront the emperor? The Stoics showed no doctrinaire opposition to monarchy. Even a king was capable of displaying Stoic virtues. The accuser of Thrasea Paetus claimed that, if they destroyed the emperor's power, they would go on to attack the republic afterward.[93] The Stoics did not ascribe to specific tenets of government. They simply condemned tyranny and distinguished it from good kingship.[94] This was done not by constitutional criteria but by the morality of the ruler. The moral disapproval of Thrasea Paetus, Helvidius Priscus, and Paconius Agrippinus toward Nero's conduct was political only in the sense that, if the qualification for kingship was virtue, Nero failed the test and had no right to the throne. Stoics were accused of being arrogant and censorious. These are irritating qualities to a ruler who wants obedience. We may not think of disapproval as opposition, but it all depends on how the disapproval is implemented. Stoicism was not exactly a call to action. If anything, Stoics justified their acquiescence to the rule of a dictator while trying not to compromise their virtue. Of course, tyrannicide, like suicide, could be justified in Stoic terms as one of those duties imposed by special circumstances.[95] While Stoic teaching did not offer support for political sedition, turning a blind eye to an assassination plot is still treason, even if many historians want to get Seneca off the hook.[96]

Stoics would withdraw from a corrupt state. That was the safest way to protest. This remedy was not unique nor confined to Stoics. As they watched the Senate lose even a modicum of freedom compatible with what they thought the principate should be, they used the language of Stoicism to formulate their moral choices and justify their decisions. Seneca was afraid that if political disapproval and defiance were cast in Stoic language, the entire sect itself would be persecuted. There was enough substance to the charge that Nero expelled Musonius Rufus and Demetrius the Cynic from Rome, and under later emperors, like Vespasian and Domitian, more philosophers were expelled.[97]

Tacitus leaves the verdict against Seneca as rumor (*fama*) and, at least, "unproved."[98] Dio, on the other hand, says he was a participant.[99] The evidence from Tacitus does make him look complicit. Seneca returned to his villa near Rome on the very day set for the murder. Was this by chance or intention? He had just come from Campania, where Epicharis, the mistress of his brother, Annaeus Mela, was attempting to bribe the imperial fleet to join the cause.[100] Polyaenus says flat out that it was Seneca himself who persuaded Epicharis to join the conspiracy.[101] Seneca admitted to exchanging messages with Piso through a conspirator, Antonius Natalis, in which he showed previous friendship with Piso and a disinclination to have him visit at the time. These facts could certainly lead one to believe

that Seneca knew of the conspiracy but not that he was an active participant. From the emperor's point of view, however, this was close enough.
Knowing about a conspiracy and its participants and not telling the emperor is treason. That is what the oath of loyalty to the emperor taken by
soldiers and civilians was all about. He denied having written to Piso in
treasonous terms. He did write that their meetings were not frequent and
that his "safety depended on that of Piso."[102] Even Tacitus himself reports
that at the time there was a rumor going around that the Praetorian officers, with Seneca's knowledge, planned to make Seneca emperor after
killing Nero and disposing of Piso. Subrius Flavus was supposed to have
remarked that the disgrace would remain if the lyre player (Nero) were
replaced by a tragic actor (Piso).[103] The death sentence was delivered to
Seneca by Gavius Silvanus, a Praetorian officer who himself was part of
the conspiracy. He could not refuse the order, but he could not bring himself to read the death sentence to Seneca; instead, he sent in a centurion
to do it.[104]

Tacitus has tried to make it look otherwise, but it has been argued
that the majority of the deaths and suicides after Piso's plot involved the
guilty.[105] Nero was badly frightened by the Pisonian conspiracy. The plot
had just narrowly failed getting to him. It is understandable, albeit unpalatable, that his attitude toward his rivals remained less than generous,
even vindictive, for the rest of his reign. He did, however, handle all this
legally; there were judicial proceedings.[106] The cases were tried in Nero's
court. We read of arrests, questionings, presented evidence, tortures
(especially of slave witnesses, which was the law), state witnesses, and
confessions. After the trial there was a full publication of the proceedings by Nero, addressed to the Senate and the Roman people, including
testimony and confessions. Tacitus states categorically that those at the
time who knew the truth did not doubt that a conspiracy had taken place
and that those who had been exiled admitted to their guilt when they returned.[107] In all, nineteen men and women lost their lives in the aftermath
of the conspiracy, and thirteen were banished into exile.[108]

THE DEATH OF THRASEA PAETUS

Tacitus considered the trials and death of Thrasea Paetus and Barea Soranus as the culmination of the Neronian terror.[109] Thrasea Paetus's doom
was precipitated by the intrigues of the Praetorian prefect, Tigellinus, and
his son-in-law, Cossutianus Capito.[110] In 66 Capito launched a vociferous
attack on Paetus in the Senate. The charge was treason for not taking the
public oath of loyalty or attending the presentation of prayers for the
prosperity of the nation.[111] The attack on Thrasea Paetus coincided with

the impending visit to Rome of Tiridates I, the newly installed King of Armenia. Tacitus says the timing of the dissident trial was deliberate to show the emperor's power through the murder of illustrious men, as if he were some royal potentate.[112] Paetus was banned from the ceremonies involving Nero and Tiridates. At this point he foresaw his own doom.

As can be expected, no one volunteered to act as Paetus's defense counsel. His defiance and honorable death would distinguish his memory from the spineless who watched in silence. Indeed, Paetus was admired but not much imitated. Thrasea Paetus, Helvidius Priscus, Paconius Agrippinus, and Curtius Montanus were indicted on a charge of *maiestas*, but it is worth noting that at no point was any attempt made to implicate them in an active plot against the government.[113] Thrasea Paetus chose to commit suicide. The last extant chapters of Tacitus's *Annals* with the description of Paetus's death are among the finest pages of Latin prose. We will never know what his last words were because Tacitus's text breaks off in midsentence.[114]

EVEN MORE DEATHS

The effect of the conspiracy was that Nero was now afraid of people who were not related to him. He believed that any one of the old republican nobility could be dangerous. That section of society was much more of a threat than the Stoic philosophers, and over the next two years there were several more victims: M. Crassus Frugi, Antistius Vetus, and Sulpicius Camerinus.[115]

Nero was being advised by his security staff that there might be a threat to his reign from the provincial armies. Tigellinus had already suggested in 62 that Rubellius Plautus in Asia might seek the support of the eastern armies and that he was in touch with Corbulo. He also warned Nero about Faustus Cornelius Sulla in Marseilles, who he said might have the support of the Rhine legions.[116] Tacitus plays down these charges, but both men had been under suspicion before. It would have taken little persuading for Nero to eliminate them.[117] But after the Pisonian conspiracy, Nero's attitude began to change. Corbulo and the Scribonii brothers who governed the German provinces were removed in the winter of 66–67.[118] In 66 one of the charges against Barea Soranus that led to his conviction was that he had tried to rouse the province of Asia to rebellion when he was proconsul. He was also friends with the previously condemned Rubellius Plautus.[119]

Tacitus leaves out lots of the details that would link together all of these participants. Many of the deaths were due to family connections. Antistius Vetus was Plautus's father-in-law. He had urged his son to resistance in 62. Antistius was proconsul in Asia in 63–64 when Corbulo was in the East, and gossip claimed they were in collusion. Annius Pollio, the husband of Barea Soranus's daughter, Servilia, was also the brother of Corbulo's son-in-law, Annius Vinicianus. They were both sons of the Annius Vinicianus who was active against the plot against Caligula and afterward instigated the armed revolt of the governor of Dalmatia against Claudius.[120] Slowly but surely, Corbulo must have felt the net closing in on him. His father-in-law, Cassius Longinus, had been condemned in 65. A son of his half-brother had been exiled with Annius Pollio after the Pisonian conspiracy, and the other brother perished probably in 66–67.[121] With the loss of Tacitus's account of these years we have to guess that the last death may have been connected to the conspiracy that led to Corbulo's execution.[122]

THE VINICIAN CONSPIRACY

There is a conspiracy of Vinicius mentioned only by Suetonius, who says it was conceived and detected at Beneventum.[123] The place was probably chosen because it would have been easier to assassinate Nero outside of Rome. He left for a trip to Greece in September 66, and Beneventum would be the natural stopping-off place.[124] Nero's plans for the Greek tour were made well in advance; the conspirators could have easily found out when he would leave Rome and when he would arrive at Beneventum. It has been inferred by the name of the conspiracy that it was led by Annius Vinicianus, the son-in-law of Corbulo.[125]

Once the conspiracy was detected and the culprits eliminated, Nero continued on with his Greek trip. The only thing he seemed to fear was personal assassination, and being away from Rome might actually protect him. He could deal with the generals in the East when he got there. Corbulo was summoned to Greece and given the order to die. His last words, "Your due!" have been interpreted to mean that he regretted not challenging Nero when he had the chance.[126]

This was the first time the emperor had left Italy since Claudius participated in his British invasion in 43–44. But whereas the conspiracy against Claudius had been an army revolt in a province, not a plot at Rome, Nero's problem was his reputation at home. Claudius had traveled to bolster his military reputation. Nero was traveling because he thought artistic glory was waiting for him in Greece. Miriam Griffin has suggested that Nero had a diminishing grasp on political reality and what it took to survive.[127] When Claudius went on campaign, he would take with him many of the men who might have been a threat to him, so they could be watched; then he would leave an experienced military man in charge of Rome.[128] Nero, on the other hand, left his freedman Helius in charge, with the power to banish, confiscate, and execute men of all ranks. The Praetorian prefect, Tigellinus, was with the emperor, leading his escort to Greece. The other prefect, Nymphidius Sabinus, controlled the Guard in Rome. Most of the people traveling with him were freedmen, a fact that created the impression that freedmen and flatterers ruled the empire and that the days of respect for the Senate were gone. Helius did his job at Rome well and kept an eye on security for Nero. He sent letters to the emperor reporting that there was another great conspiracy brewing. When Nero did not respond to his letters, Helius went to Greece himself to impress upon the emperor the importance of coming back to Rome to take care of business and protect his own interests.

Nero seemed to think he could keep himself adequately safe and prevent a revolt by summoning suspected commanders to Greece and executing them.[129] Although Nero had had senatorial enemies before, he now began to increasingly view the entire Senate as his enemy. He threatened to fire them all and turn the provinces over to the *equites* and freedmen. One of his *delatores* was said to have taunted Nero for being lazy because he eliminated the senators one at a time when he should have wiped out the entire body.[130] We have no more evidence of any conspiracy in Rome, but perhaps Helius had received intelligence of what was happening in Gaul.

THE *BELLUM NERONIS*

The revolt that would succeed in overthrowing Nero was now in motion.[131] It began in Gaul with a revolt by Gaius Julius Vindex, the Roman governor of Gallia Lugdunensis. There are many questions about how the secret conspiracy was set up, how it played out, and whether Nero could have survived it with the help of his security services. Contacting other possible conspirators is always the first move. According to Plutarch, Vindex began by sending letters to the neighboring governors and military commanders to win their support for an uprising.[132] He avoided naming himself as Nero's replacement. Perhaps he thought that, as a first-generation senator, he would be perceived as an upstart if he nominated himself. This was not a mere secessionist rebellion by the Gauls but a revolt against Nero's regime.[133] Perhaps Vindex did not want to alienate any of his potential supporters yet by putting all his eggs in one basket. We are not informed of the responses Vindex received, but we do know governors and commanders generally remained loyal and instead turned the letters over to Nero. The one exception was Servius Sulpicius Galba, governor of Hispania Tarraconensis; he neither replied to Vindex nor notified Rome.[134] There was always the chance that the letters were forgeries set up by Nero to test the loyalty of his commanders. Or perhaps Galba rated Vindex's chance of success so small that he preferred to wait and see what happened—a smart move, considering he would be the ultimate choice and the new emperor. He did not decide to join until he intercepted letters from Nero's agents and discovered that the emperor had put a "hit" out on him. The failed attempt on his life convinced him that he was compromised in Nero's eyes, anyway, so he might as well join the conspiracy.[135]

Vindex certainly should have been smart enough to know that, once he contacted any other commanders, at least some of them would have let Nero know. He had to move forward and do it quickly.[136] He does not seem to have expected any opposition from Verginius Rufus or Fonteius Capito, the commanders of Upper and Lower Germany, respectively. Since they had seven legions between them, he must have believed he had their tacit consent to go ahead with the revolt. There is no way a sensible person like Vindex would throw off his loyalty without having rational grounds for counting on the cooperation, or at least the connivance, of the German legates.[137] Verginius's loyalty should have been settled by security considerations alone. If Nero had had the German legions behind him, he could have put down any revolt.[138] This uprising could not have been just a revolt by the Gauls, because the Rhine legions would never have joined in such an operation. Their function was to defend the empire from German tribes to their east and Gallic uprisings to their west.[139] This was a revolt specifically against the reign of Nero.[140]

The emperor's response would have been needed to put down the revolt as quickly as possible before it grew. Unfortunately, Nero did not take the revolt seriously until Galba publicly proclaimed his willingness to become the leader of the revolt.[141] Once Galba, Vindex, and Verginius Rufus were in on it together, it became a major conspiracy.[142] When you stand back and look at what everyone was doing in the larger context, you can see the modus operandi of the conspiracy. It had everything a revolutionary movement needed and can certainly be seen as organized effort to terminate the Julio-Claudian dynasty.

Galba's freedman, Icelus, was in Rome when the news arrived that his master had accepted Vindex's offer to head the revolt.[143] Suetonius tells us Nero threw the man in chains immediately, which would make sense if Icelus were acting as an intermediary between Galba and members of the Senate.[144] Actually, no prominent members of the Senate swung their support to Galba this early.

Galba then set out on what Tacitus calls his "long and bloody march" and sent out proclamations to the provinces urging everyone to aid the common cause in any way they could. He had to raise troops and raise money.[145] What he did not want to do was come to the aid of Vindex. Vindex's march through Gaul reached Besançon (Vesontio) by the end of April, a week or so after L. Verginius Rufus, the commander of Upper Germany, arrived there. The chronology is muddled, and historians disagree on whether Rufus was working for Vindex or Nero. We are told that Vindex and Verginius met and parleyed at Vesontio.[146] We do not know what the agreement was or if either man understood the agreement in the same manner.[147] Did they agree to join forces against Nero, or was Verginius defending Vesontio as a loyal general to Nero? The resulting clash between the two forces has been explained in many ways. If there was an agreement, the officers may have been informed, but the rank and file may not have been. Vindex ordered his men to march into Vesontio and take possession of the town, presumably to indicate that the siege was over and to reassure the town's inhabitants. Verginius's men interpreted the Gauls' march toward them as a sign that a battle was imminent. Vindex's men acted as if an agreement had been reached; Verginius's men acted as if it had not. Without waiting for orders, the legionaries attacked the "rebels" before they could deploy into a battle line. Plutarch tells a similar story, but he stresses the helplessness of both commanders, likening them to charioteers who lose control of their horses in a race. Whatever the real cause, the result was a massacre. Some thirty thousand Gauls were said to have been slaughtered, and Vindex committed suicide. It is said Verginius was as disconsolate over the results as the surviving rebels were.[148] The victorious legionaries took it upon themselves to proclaim Verginius emperor, and this act has provoked endless speculation to the effect that this was his plan all along.[149]

Scholars have suggested that this Machiavellian plot was later covered up by spin doctors who wanted to present Verginius in a better light:[150] that Verginius had marched against Vindex as a loyal soldier of Nero and had every intention of wiping the rebels out but later pretended the battle was a mistake because he did not want to be connected with an emperor whose memory was being condemned.[151] This story does not work; being unable to control your troops is surely not something a general would admit. We should not attribute too much cleverness to Verginius. He had been appointed to the command because he was a mediocrity, and he was later treated as such by Galba, Otho, Vitellius, and the three Flavian emperors who followed. He was probably caught off guard by the events of May 68 and was neither crafty enough to manipulate the troops nor ambitious and enterprising enough to take advantage of the situation. In the end, he was neither king nor kingmaker.[152] Verginius Rufus could have disposed of all the dissidents easily, but he did not, which is why his motives have always been questioned. Because of the troops he commanded, he was always necessary to the revolt. The movement needed a candidate, which they had in Galba, but only Verginius had the eight legions needed to depose an incumbent and install the insurgent.[153] Vesontio was a setback, but only temporarily. Verginius regained control, and Galba marched on Rome. This was a group effort, not just the provincial legions declaring an emperor.

Back in Rome, Nero, who had treated the news of Vindex's revolt with indifference, now acted vigorously when he was told that Galba had joined the revolt. He recalled forces that were earmarked for the eastern campaign he had been contemplating.[154] He probably attempted to bring forces up from Africa. He set about forming a new legion (Legio I Adiutrix) from the marines of the imperial fleet stationed at Misenum, but this went so slowly they could not take part in the ensuing events. In Rome he called for volunteers from the citizenry. The bulk of the troops were placed in northern Italy under the command of P. Petronius Turpilianus and Rubrius Gallus.[155]

He initially threatened to turn the Gallic provinces over to his armies to ravage, but what troops would these have been?[156] Suetonius's account is filled with silly plans he claims Nero had contemplated, like poisoning the entire Senate or turning loose wild beasts on the citizenry.[157] Nero was said to have offered to go before his troops and cry, and to have packed wagons to escape, carrying his theatrical equipment, surrounded by his concubines dressed as Amazons. Most of this is scandalmongering, and it is picked up by too many people who wish to attribute his behavior to the deranged mental state of a man who had a very tenuous grip on reality in the first place. His initial efforts at defense seem quite rational, but, by the end of May, Nero lost his nerve and was contemplating flight. He was unsure of his destination, but his first choice was Alexandria in Egypt. So what preparations did he *really* take in the thirty days left to him? Nero seems to have swung from overconfidence to complete cowardice. Tacitus may be correct that his overthrow was due more to a war of intelligence and rumors than force of arms. Of course, anyone would have been unnerved by news that they had just been deserted by all their commanders. Rubrius Gallus eventually went over to the rebels, and Turpilianus seems to have been abandoned by his troops.

When the news of Vesontio and the troop defections reached Rome, it also triggered an abrupt rush of the Senate and Praetorians to forsake their distraught princeps.[158] Even Verginius Rufus, the eternal fence-sitter, came out publicly for Galba at this point. Galba's henchmen in Rome managed to win over many a senator to their cause. It was only a matter of time before Galba would march on Rome and be appointed emperor. The defection of Gaius Nymphidius Sabinus, the commander of the Praetorian Guard, was the final blow for Nero.[159] This was the same prefect who had been awarded an honorary consulship for his role in bringing the Pisonian conspiracy to light.[160] We do not know why his co-prefect Tigellinus did nothing to save Nero. It has been suggested that he was seriously ill.[161]

Nymphidius had the troops on the spot at his command, and he negotiated with the Senate on the loyalty of the Praetorian troops, while painting Tigellinus as the main offender regarding the excesses of recent years.[162] Nymphidius thus seized the opportunity to put Galba in his debt by bringing the Praetorian Guard over to his side. Plutarch makes him the villain.[163] He subverted the Guard by convincing them that they were not abandoning Nero but their emperor was abandoning them by embarking on a ship and going to Alexandria. For any soldiers who still did not think Nero's total failure in recent weeks was sufficient grounds to ignore the oath sworn to protect the princeps and his house, the prefect offered them 7,500 denarii each, which was an enormous sum—ten times their annual pay. This was twice the amount Claudius and Nero had promised them upon their succession. To do this, Galba would have to live up to Plutarch's description of him as "the richest private citizen ever to enter the House of the Caesar."[164]

Nero could have gained control in Rome if the Praetorians had stayed loyal to him and the status quo, as they had in the past, rather than risk their privileged position.[165] Why were they so willing to abandon the man they were sworn to protect? Tacitus claims that the Guardsmen were led to desert Nero because they were deceived by their prefect rather than by their own impetus. The Praetorians had always maintained their loyalty to the Julio-Claudian house. But Nero was either unwilling or unable to negotiate with his household troops in a timely fashion and, as a result, they were left with only the word of their prefect that the emperor had deserted *them*, which made their decision that much easier.

Nymphidius is one of the most controversial figures in the story. He has been painted as an ambitious turncoat trying to feather his own nest. No sooner had he promised the Guard a sizable donative in Galba's name than he turned on Galba when the new emperor appointed Cornelius Laco as the new Praetorian prefect instead of him.[166] Plutarch accused him of subverting Galba's authority in order to be proclaimed emperor in his own right. The Guard refused to take part in the coup, and Nymphidius was murdered in the Castra Praetoria.[167] It has been argued that, rather than trying to stage a coup, he may have just found himself in the position of having to act in the place of an absent emperor and was trying to keep the situation stable in Rome.[168] Since Plutarch says "it was decided" to take Nymphidius to the Praetorian camp around midnight and proclaim him emperor, one might ask, "Decided by whom?" There may well have been someone more high-ranking behind the whole affair. If it really was an attempted coup, the soldiers did not go along with it.[169]

Once the Guard had been persuaded to abandon Nero, the Senate found the courage to declare him an enemy of the state and declare Galba their new ruler. In his palace on June 9, Nero sensed that the end was near and that he should not count on clemency. He knew that his enemies would be looking for him and that his only option was flight, but that hope quickly vanished when he realized that his palace guard had deserted him. He sent slaves to call his friends in the guest wings, but they returned with no one. Then he walked past the doors of the sleeping chambers himself, but everyone had fled. He went back to his bedroom only to discover that even his personal bodyguards had now left him, and they had taken away the little box of poison he always kept on hand. He toyed with the idea of throwing himself into the Tiber, but he decided against it in the end.[170]

The freedman Phaon, Nero's *a libellis*, offered the fleeing emperor use of his villa, which was located between the Via Salaria and the Via Nomentana, approximately six kilometers from the palace. The emperor gratefully accepted the offer. In the company of Epaphroditus, a freedman with whom he had been close, and his beloved eunuch Sporus, he rode there on horseback. His companions may very well have been in on the plot and were simply luring Nero away from the palace so they could do the deed in private. Nero may have thought he was regrouping to a safer place to fight against Galba. Instead he was galloping toward his own death.[171]

It was certainly an ignomious retreat for Nero. Dressed only in simple clothes and with his head covered so as not to be recognized, he looked nothing like the flamboyant emperor he once was. On his way to Phaon's, there was a small earthquake—a dark omen that reminded him his end was near (not that he needed any reminding, of course). It seemed to him that the earth was splitting open and the spirits of all those he had killed were rising up to take revenge.[172] He was recognized by a passerby who hailed him as emperor, but bereft of any illusions he rode on. The company left the horses at the side of the road and made their way through the underbrush, bramble bushes, and reeds to Phaon's estate. When they reached the wall of the house, Phaon asked Nero to hide temporarily in a sandpit until he could be brought into the villa unseen. Nero balked at the idea of being buried while he was still alive and waited by a pool of water instead. Finally, he was smuggled into the house. He rested for a time on a mattress and drank a glass of lukewarm water. He refused the coarse brown bread that was offered to him.

Presently it became clear to Nero that he was not going to escape his pursuers. He asked his companions to kill him, but they refused. Execution might produce a martyr. Nero heaved a deep sigh and said, "Have I neither friend nor foe?" While Nero debated about whether to take his own life, Phaon received a note from a messenger. Nero snatched it out of his hands and read that, if caught, he would be punished in the manner of his ancient ancestors: he would be tied to a post and whipped to death. It was then that he planned his suicide. He took out two daggers and tested the sharpness of the steel but kept postponing the final deed with the excuse that his time had not yet come. At the same time, he cursed the cowardice that kept him from administering the coup de grace. "This does not become you, Nero, get a hold of yourself," he kept muttering. When he heard the horsemen riding into the grounds of the villa, he jabbed the dagger into his throat, crying out, "What an artist the world is losing in me!" The wound was probably not fatal, and in the end it was Epaphroditus who put him out of his misery. He was barely thirty years old and had been emperor for fourteen years.[173]

He was interred in the family tomb of the Domitii, on the Pincian Hill, visible from the field of Mars. A porphyry sarcophagus and a marble altar surrounded by a stone balustrade kept his memory alive.[174] For although he was despised by the Senate, the common people, whom he had regaled with imposing spectacles, had loved him. Years later, in the spring and summer, flowers could still be found decorating his tomb.[175]

THE SUCCESSION PROBLEM

In what way did weaknesses in the principate and its security system contribute to Nero's fall? The ancient sources talk only about Nero's monstrousness; they rarely critique their own system (Tacitus being the exception). Even by the fifth emperor of the dynasty, the position of princeps was still not fully defined. The upper classes were not resigned to a monarchy or their diminishing role in running the state. The emperor needed a staff to run the government, yet if he used freedmen, the upper classes would chafe at being ordered around by their social inferiors. The same strain had been put on previous emperors, and they all reacted differently. Nero's artistic personality meant he had no interest in or ability for politics and military operations, which were the basis of running the Roman state.

Both Nero and his mother have been accused of paranoia, but they faced a greater problem than all previous emperors. They were surrounded by the descendants of republican families as old and illustrious as the Julii and Claudii. With each emperor, the number of men who could claim descent from past emperors naturally increased as the dynasty continued. Agrippina had done her best to destroy them, and Nero continued her work. As Tacitus says of Marcus Junius Silanus, whom Agrippina destroyed on her son's accession, "He was the great-great grandson of

Augustus. That was the cause of his death."[176] There were also men more remotely connected with the first princeps by marriage.[177]

The succession problem can be seen very clearly in the assassination attempts against Nero. In the conspiracy to put C. Calpurnius Piso on the throne, there were two dynastic rivals. Tacitus notes that Piso feared competition from Lucius Junius Silanus, but he rejects the story in the Elder Pliny that Piso was to be accompanied by Claudius's daughter Antonia when he entered the Praetorian camp after Nero's murder.[178] The fact that one of them had kinship with the imperial house put merely republican lineage in the shade. L. Junius Silanus was a direct descendant of Augustus. The marriage with Antonia would have given Piso a similar dynastic claim. Tacitus rejects the story in the end, saying that Piso loved his wife (as if that ever mattered) and that Antonia would not have given her name to such a dangerous venture. Suetonius goes on to say that she refused to marry Nero after Poppaea's death. (It may have happened in the part of Tacitus that was lost, or surely he would have mentioned it).[179] If she had been complicit in the Pisonian conspiracy, this would have been her chance for amnesty. She would have reached the same goal if her husband, Faustus Sulla, had been successful in his plot against Nero, or if Piso had succeeded and set aside his wife for a more suitable empress. Then there's the obvious reason: she said no to Nero because he had displaced her brother as heir, come to the throne by assassinating her father, poisoned her brother, had banished and later executed her husband, and had divorced, banished, and finally executed her half-sister. Surely that is enough reason. When Antonia refused to marry him, Nero had her executed on a charge of treason.[180] Had he allowed her to remain alive, she could always have married one of his rivals.

THE ARMY

It has been fashionable to blame the revolt against Nero, and thus the downfall of the Julio-Claudians, on the army. Plutarch certainly saw the undisciplined soldiers as the original cause of the uprising.[181] Was it the legions who deserted Nero? Or his Praetorians? Or did his troubles come from the upper classes? The nobles were the men Nero could not trust, which is why the emperor saw to it that the larger armies were led by senators less capable of aspiring to greater power. Paola Zancan, following Tacitus, argues that the prime movers were to be found in the governing class, who failed to identify with the good of the state, as opposed to their own self-interest. The problem was, therefore, faction from above and not revolution from below.[182]

ABSOLUTISM

Much has been made of the possibility that Nero was establishing a ruler cult patterned on the Hellenistic monarchies or that he had aspirations to divine monarchy on the Eastern model, but there is not much evidence to support this.[183] In any event, if he had tried, either his divine status did not protect him or he should have set up a much tighter security system on Eastern models.

Nero's regime was certainly autocratic and harsh to many. The followers of Vindex, Galba, and Clodius Macer complained about heavy taxes and forced levies in Gaul and Britain. There are numerous stories told about Nero's exactions. He supposedly put to death six landowners in Africa who together owned one half of the land of the province.[184] Sufferings in Judaea at the hands of Gessius Florus had caused a revolt in 66. Losing the support of the provincials certainly contributed to Nero's problems.

CHANGING THE CULTURE OF ROME

Some historians see the reign of Nero as a "time of terror and a crisis of values."[185] Others see it as the creation of an extravagant artist and "public relations man ahead of his time with a shrewd understanding of what the people wanted."[186] The fact that Nero chose to be different from all his predecessors—an artist and a philhellene rather than a soldier or statesman—made many of those around him angry, confused, or simply hostile. Nero drew on Greek mythology and its reenactment on the theatrical stage to shape an image of himself that enjoyed much success, especially with the populace in Rome and with the Greeks.[187] On the other hand, we have been warned not to make too much of Nero's patronage of the arts, considering three of the most famous literary figures of the age, Seneca, Lucan, and Petronius, lost their lives because of Nero's jealousy.

Nero's extravagant standard of living was tied up with his self-image and concept of what the princeps was supposed to be. He was a young emperor with no achievements to justify his assumption of power, and so he created his own persona. He would have had to have been much more secure as a person to play the *civilis princeps*, one among equals. Instead, he chose an artistic path. He was an artist and a beneficent benefactor, a superaristocrat, a magnificent monarch, and the plebs loved him for it. It also set up a standard for successors to follow. Wealth became equated with power, and those who accumulated it were thought to be ambitious. But he was also someone who intentionally aimed at the mockery and subversion of the *mos maiorum*. And anything that stripped the dignity from the imperial office could lead to a revolt by senatorial conservatives.

The public image of the emperor had always been that of a military leader. The title *imperator* was a republican title conferred on a commander by his troops after a dazzling victory. The title was also used to denote a magistrate or pro-magistrate holding a command outside of Rome. When it was attached to the titles of the princeps, it kept its military connotations. Even Claudius, with his physical disabilities, had a deep sense of this Roman tradition when he decided to lead the expedition to Britain himself. As Fergus Millar has written, "Society demanded of the emperor military protection, and if possible resounding victories over foreign enemies."[188] But Nero never led an army. If anything, Nero's reign was a travesty of the Roman conceptions of military glory. Perhaps this is why it is during his reign that a military revolt topples an emperor for the first time.

SECURITY MISTAKES

Could Nero's security staff have saved him? Piso's aborted conspiracy shows that Nero's intelligence network functioned properly. Nero's security staff was generally loyal, but when they received no direction from their leader and then realized every other constituency was turning against them, they were the last to jump ship to save themselves. Nero made a number of short-term mistakes. He underestimated the defections of 68 CE and overreacted by fleeing Rome when his doom could still be averted; after all, he did have nine thousand troops guarding him. Even Tacitus tells us he was driven from his throne "by messages and rumors, rather than by [force of] arms."[189] Not only did he have the Praetorian Guard but he had the loyalty of most of the legions. Some commanders may have wavered, but neither the governor of Upper Germany, Verginius Rufus, nor his colleague, Fonteius Capito, failed Nero at the start. The seven legions belonging to those two German commands proved loyal up to the defeat of Vindex at Vesontio. Even when his troops offered to raise him to the purple, Verginius declined and brought the troops back to their allegiance to the emperor. Had Nero himself appeared before the German troops or his forces in northern Italy, his resolution might have inspired more prompt and decisive action, but Nero was no general.[190] What made the last rebellion against Nero different was that it started not as a rebellion of the provincials but at the initiative of Roman commanders and officials in the provinces.[191] Nero had offended members of the ruling class deeply and irrevocably.

The security situation in Rome itself could also have been controlled. The Senate had dutifully declared Galba a public enemy. It reversed its position only once the Guard changed allegiance and proclaimed Galba emperor. It is easy to blame the Praetorian Guard for what happened, but we must look at what brought the Guard to desert Nero, to whom they had sworn allegiance. Tacitus claims the men were brought over by "deceit and incitement" rather than their own inclination.[192] It was the leadership that brought them over; it had to be. Nymphidius Sabinus knew about the emperor's sailing to Alexandria. All he had to tell them was that the emperor was as good as gone and offer them a huge donative to declare for Galba. Why would they stay loyal to Nero if he was running away? Nero was already in flight from Rome when he heard the declaration for Galba in the Praetorian camp as he approached the northeast gate.[193] Had Nero been a real leader, he could have gone to the camp and kept them loyal. After all, they were much more likely to follow the emperor than a prefect who had betrayed Praetorian officers in the Pisonian conspiracy some three years before.[194] Had Nero kept his cool and not panicked and run, he could have retained his position at home and suppressed the revolts of Galba and Clodius Macer, who were not acting in concert and had no forces of any size.[195]

Nero made a huge mistake by ignoring all three components of the system set up by Augustus. He did not take care of the material needs of the army; he let pay and retirement rewards get in arrears. He did not establish a personal relationship with the soldiers, and through extravagant behavior he antagonized important members of the centurionate. He also not only made bad selections for governors but arbitrarily put to death some successful commanders. This decisively alienated his corps of generals. It is surprising not that the system broke down but that it lasted as long as it did. The attempt of the German legions to proclaim Verginius as emperor, the revolt of the Spanish troops under Galba, and the subsequent civil wars may have been a bit uncoordinated, but they were logical and inevitable. The armies were finding their political role.[196]

OVERREACTION AND CRUELTY

Some scholars have suggested that trying to find any conscious strategy in Nero's policies of persecution is useless because neither the reasons nor the timing nor the responses are consistent.[197] During Nero's reign of more than thirteen years, he executed or forced to commit suicide about thirty named people who either plotted to kill him or gave him good reason to suspect of having done so. There were probably others, but our sources for the last two years of his reign are incomplete. The same fate befell three adult male members of his family—his brother-in-law and two cousins—who may or may not have been guilty of conspiracy but who were potentially dangerous rivals. His worst personal crimes, although both had political dimensions, were the murder of his mother, Agrippina, and his first wife, Octavia. He has also been accused of murdering his thirteen-year-old stepbrother Britannicus (after sodomizing him). No emperor has a good record on this account. An absolute ruler who holds the power of life and death over all his subjects will not refrain from using it to protect himself. The usual question arises as to how much of this bloodshed was due to internal security, how much to dynastic necessity, and how much to the emperor's paranoia.

Some people see no consistency in Nero's policies of persecution, but I think the common theme is survival. Whether or not the threats were real, the products of Nero's paranoid mind, or the imaginings of a noxious sycophant, if Nero believed there was a threat, he would strike quickly. Although Suetonius remarked that Nero was indifferent to criticism, ridicule, and similar forms of personal offense, I think this cannot be true. He was a performer, and performers care about audience response. And Nero had his image as imperial ruler to defend. Can any ruler be mocked publicly and not strike back? In the aftermath of the Pisonian conspiracy, Nero's brutal retaliation against some of Rome's most talented writers of the day came to symbolize the harsh circumstances of life under tyranny.

THE END OF A DYNASTY

When Nero died, the Julio-Claudian dynasty was almost one hundred years old. No other dynasty would last this long. There would only be more assassinations and shorter dynasties, but they would face different challenges. By the time the Flavian dynasty was established by Vespasian, the remnants of the old republican nobility were gone. They had been killed off by Nero, the civil war, or natural attrition. The link with Augustus had been broken. The policy of intermarriage within the governing class would still remain and cause trouble by producing potential rivals, but it would take a very long dynasty indeed to produce the numbers of rivals who appeared under Nero.

8

The End of the Julio-Claudians

The death of Nero brought the end to the nearly one-hundred-year-old dynasty of the Julio-Claudians that had been established by Augustus. During the year of civil war called the Year of the Four Emperors, Italy would be invaded twice by Roman armies, its cities and the capital would be taken by storm, and three successive emperors would die by assassination, suicide, or lynching. Even a Praetorian prefect made a move on the throne. The events of 68–69 showed that the armies both on the frontiers and in the city of Rome were generally not more loyal to the princeps than to their commanders and were ready to pursue their own advantage. The provinces became convulsed and fell into disarray. The fateful year of 69 brought a spectacle of calamity, endurance, and survival such as the Roman Empire had never seen. The principate, as Augustus designed it, was being tested and yet somehow the empire survived.

Most of the problems that came to a head in 69 CE can be traced back to the arrangements Augustus had made. He had eliminated the factionalism of the governing class that had plagued the last century of the republic. He had ended the civil war, and created rule by one person, hiding behind the claim that the emperor was merely the "first citizen" (princeps). His claims of restoring liberty and removing tyranny, however, were just rhetoric. This was a military monarchy. There could be no free interplay of opinions by senators or competition for offices and honors as there had been in the republic. The emperor was holding all the cards—the military, the police, and the political informers. Even the laws were differently interpreted; the *crimen maiestatis* of the republic that protected the "diminution of the majesty of the Roman people" now covered any

lack of respect for the emperor that could be manifest in spoken or written words or even gestures. It even included sedition and betrayal of the
army. What might have once cost a senator loss of status or financial ruin
could now cost him his life. The outcome of a trial no longer depended on
arguing well in court or the exercise of free will by one's peers but solely
on the whim of the emperor.[1]

Augustus portrayed himself as embodying the old republican virtues:
courage, dignity, self-discipline, high moral standards, and the manly
virtues: truthfulness and fidelity, as expressed in his speeches, public
monuments, and laws. In order to cover the reality with a new, benign
image, he had to be a master politician, a genius at delegating authority,
and a superb actor. He was as much the "Godfather" of the nation as its
pater patriae. He never left home without his sinister escort of Praetorians
and made a series of offers to the Senate and the Roman people that they
could not refuse.[2] While Caesar had spared the lives of his senatorial enemies but treated them with calculated contempt, Augustus killed them en
masse and then treated the surviving senators with exaggerated respect.[3]
The principate could become a system of institutionalized hypocrisy because Augustus raised humbug to the level of great art. His legacy was an
empire that would encompass the entire Mediterranean world. He controlled the historical record in a way that made sure we would never find
out the whole truth about his wife, his daughter, or his granddaughter.[4]

No matter how safe Augustus had made Rome, however, the reality
was that he had established a system that was autocratic yet unstable.[5] Although some scholars have rejected the idea of there being "opposition"
to Augustus, there can be no doubt, as Barbara Levick has written, that
the political and social changes he brought were not acceptable to all his
peers or even his own family. Even after his death, the deified Augustus
did not remain exempt from the criticisms of ancient writers.[6] Augustus
had also made it easier to change the system. Assassination only needed
one target—the emperor.

Senators resented the Augustan system for its falsity, because they
wanted to continue to believe that power resided with the Senate and the
Roman people, whereas a realist would see that Augustus wanted a monarchy.[7] The principate had been accepted in the beginning as a last-ditch
effort to restore the republic after a series of disastrous civil wars. No one
knew for sure whether his system was a stop-gap measure, meant to be
temporary. Once he made plans to pass it on to his heirs, it became a piece
of intentional hypocrisy, the proverbial velvet glove over the iron fist, and
Tacitus portrayed it that way.

The problem was that in order to create this military monarchy, Augustus still needed large segments of the upper class to help him run his
empire. The senators who had been skillful or lucky enough to survive

the civil wars could still act as an advisory body, but Augustus had to convince them that he was sharing civil and military power with them. It was the work, however, and not the power that fell to them. Even though Augustus preserved as much as possible the republican magistracies, they retained only their prestige but not their influence.

Much has been written about the "stability" brought by the Augustan system.[8] He controlled the workings of patronage and who in the oligarchy would rule. He controlled promotion for loyalty and merit in Rome, Italy, and the provinces. He set up a system of monarchy that changed personnel but not its character. Why, then, did it remain so unstable?

The instability occurred because a once powerful ruling class was trying to hold on to its ancient privileges while in opposition to an emperor whose powers were becoming more autocratic with each reign. It was the emperor's right to defend himself and his position, but the manner in which the ruler responded to challenges to his authority always seemed high-handed to members of the Senate. Tiberius and Claudius tried to dignify the Senate, but that body was, in many ways, too far gone down the road of sycophancy to suddenly take an independent role. Caligula and Nero saw the hypocrisy of it all and basically taunted senators as powerless complainers. Senators used accusations of treason against each other to stay in good stead with the emperor. They were complicit in their own persecution. The relations between the Senate and the emperor continued to deteriorate throughout the early principate. The oath of allegiance to the Senate and the Roman people was nothing more than a transparent fiction.

The very nature of the principate thus encouraged fear on one side and ambition on the other. The more the ruler clamped down on freedom of speech, thought, and political activity, the more frustrated the upper classes became, and the only way of removing what they perceived as a bad emperor was to kill him. Like any monarch, the princeps could be removed only against his will. There was no restricted length of office, no mandatory retirement age. And while he remained on the throne, he could not destroy or disgrace all of the possible candidates for the throne while waiting to produce a legitimate heir himself. The more male progeny he produced, the safer the hereditary line would be, but even the mortality rate for young successors was high.

NOVUS ORDO SECLORUM

Augustus depicted himself as the personal guarantor of domestic peace and stability.[9] The public's overall receptiveness to this image of stability and order continued under Augustus's successors, who themselves perpetrated this Augustan-style propaganda. His principate concretely molded the way his successors maintained power and their own safety. The security measures that the first princeps laid down in Rome and Italy continued growing, eventually becoming an elaborate military/police apparatus. But even this was not enough. Since there was no written constitution, the workings of Augustus's unsystematic system also depended heavily on the personality and character of each emperor to keep the system going, even with all the enforcement mechanisms.

One of the major problems the Julio-Claudian dynasty had was that Augustus's four successors lacked his prestige, his talent, his acting abilities, his self-control, and most importantly his ability to reconcile hypocrisy. It is not surprising, therefore, that, under Tiberius (14–37), Caligula (37–41), Claudius (41–54), and Nero (54–68), the situation slowly deteriorated. All five emperors had the same problem: how to effect the Senate's adaptation to a new political order. The smoke and mirrors under Augustus seem to have obfuscated things so well that the nobility did not yet quite realize what the new institution was going to be like—or its possibilities for despotism—until sometime after Augustus's death. Under each of his four successors, senators hoped for more power and freedom, but instead their position deteriorated. Emperors were simply not going to give power back to the Senate, and it became evident that the only way to restore their powers was to bring back the republic or replace the emperor with someone who would be willing to share power with them. Unfortunately, no emperor would do either; autocrats do not negotiate their one-man rule. It was only a matter of time before the usual discontent set in, and then, depending on how widely or deeply it spread among the upper classes, a conspiracy would always develop. While the rhetoric of public order held great importance for Augustus and all his successors, stability continued to elude them. Emperors would be removed and replaced at a higher rate than any other world monarchy.[10] Once the principate had left the grasp of the Julio-Claudians, every other emperor simply became a usurper.

SENATORIAL OPPOSITION

It took nearly a century of struggle with the princeps for the former ruling class to find its political place in the new order as civil servants. The tension caused by these two incompatible sources of power fighting each other ensured that the task of ruling the empire could never simply be a case of issuing commands and expecting them to be obeyed without question. What ensued was due in no small part to the disappearance of the old republican nobility with their hereditary principles and their outmoded ideas regarding the Senate's functions. They had to resign themselves to the new reality—the monopoly of power in the hands of emperors and the administrative concentration in the hands of freedmen and slaves. Senators who chafed under this new imperial restriction and mourned their lost "freedom" were not talking about democracy but were talking about what they thought of as their immemorial right to compete within their own exclusive circle for the great offices of state, which they could use to enrich themselves and their families. They believed that their fathers and grandfathers had put together an empire by the valor of their arms and the favor of the gods and that the empire had been taken away from them by a tyrant who now maintained his power with the help of their social inferiors.

By the time we get to the Year of the Four Emperors, the new ruling class was being drawn from new men all over Italy and the Romanized elites of the provinces.[11] These new men would be the senators, magistrates, and commanders. They were willing to serve the state, but they had no experience or family history of political dominance. The throne would not belong to the person who deserved it, either by genetic inheritance or by strict justice. The throne went to the one who could hold it, sometimes at a bloody price.

The official fiction was that the Senate was the nation's government with the emperor as its partner, but the truth was just the opposite. The power was always in the hands of the princeps, and he made sure the Senate was filled with his supporters. The Senate underwent at least three substantial purges in 28 BCE, 8 BCE, and 14 CE, with Augustus acting as censor. The boldest champions of the republic had perished on the battlefield or in the course of proscriptions. There were still men willing to fight for the old senatorial ideal, but the symbiosis that Augustus tried to institute was uneven and awkward, and it was never clearly defined in constitutional terms.

On the surface it may have seemed that the Senate was conducting business as usual in the first century CE, and the Senate was certainly involved in affairs of state. They received embassies, made laws, sat as a court, supervised the state religion, kept public order, and elected numerous magistrates. They still competed for the same offices just as they had done in the republic, but Tacitus knew the reality. He and his senatorial colleagues had seen the system from the inside and, according to him, the rule of the Julio-Claudians was, at best, only "the shadow of a republic" (*imago rei publicae*).[12] The Senate continued to be the symbol of the Roman state, but in reality it was subservient to a tyrant, no matter how benevolent he was. The free interplay of politics and ambition, freedom of speech, and all the rest of the things that represented *libertas* to them were gone. The Senate had been stripped of control over financial and military matters. Once there is a state policed by the emperor, freedom begins to shrivel. As Epictetus observed, "No one is afraid of Caesar himself; but he is afraid of death, exile, loss of property, prison, disenfranchisement." Senators might not love Caesar, but he played on the fact that they "loved wealth, a tribuneship, a praetorship, a consulship."[13]

Certainly there were ways for senators to survive in the new regime. The emperor was at the top of the power pyramid, and he acted as the supreme patron to the upper classes. He could promote their careers, bestow upon them rewards and honors in the form of ranks, office, decorations, or even financial assistance. There were rewards for being quiet and docile, and many senators considered their new situation to actually be an improvement. The new nobility that had been recruited from the municipal and provincial gentry now filled vacancies and began to replace the old senatorial families. Even though they might have tried to ape the old nobles or pay lip service to the old values, most imperial senators were acutely aware of one thing, their debt and dependence on the emperor, and therefore they owed their loyalty to him.[14] So, in a sense, they were in power but powerless—burdened by the sham of routine administration but ultimately excluded from high-level decision-making and from active governance of the empire.

Their ambiguous status could be seen in all of their political behavior. They were required to pursue a public career, the *cursus honorum*, and take part in senatorial proceedings that were devoid of practical import and even occasionally required them to take action against their peers. Serving on the jury condemning other senators to death certainly must have created some cognitive dissonance in many men of honor. They could find themselves forced into a shameless contest for sycophancy. Are we to treat the flattered as honest cooperators with the new order or denounce them as sycophants? Do we see the dissidents as noble men fighting a corrupt system or impractical dreamers trying to reinstitute a republic that was never coming back?

THE SUCCESSION PROBLEM

The emperor also had to find a way to survive at the top. It was the emperor's job to stay alive, stay in command of the political process, maximize his own prestige and authority, and maintain in his own hands the choice of who would get the position after his death. This became increasingly difficult under the Julio-Claudians. Few future emperors found themselves in total control with as little difficulty as Augustus and with the ability to hand over the principate as Augustus did to Tiberius.[15] The sheer instability of the principate was what threw up so many conspiracies, and this is what the security services had to battle against.[16]

The moment at which monarchical power is transferred from one man to his successor is a critical point. If the transition is caused by an assassination, we see the elements that constitute the political system and its weaknesses most clearly. It is this question that Tacitus writes into the events he describes, which may betray his concern over the accessions of much later emperors, but the problem was always the same. The new emperor had to exercise control over many constituencies: his family, the imperial household (the *domus Caesaris*),[17] and then, in an ever-widening circle, the Praetorian Guard, the urban cohorts and *vigiles*, the magistrates, the Senate, the people of Rome, and the Roman armies in the provinces.[18]

The imperial household emerged under the Julio-Claudians as a political entity in its own right. All members, including freedmen, were sworn to protect the emperor and his family, which added a political dimension and security function to a job that had started out as a domestic task.[19] Having senators, ambitious *novi homines*, and imperial freedmen all at odds with each other for rewards and political influence certainly kept things interesting around the palace.

Besides the constant pull between the emperor and his ruling class was the structural problem of the Augustan system itself. There was little discussion of this problem in the ancient sources. Tacitus only asked whether an imperial government could ever deliver justice, but not whether the structure of the imperial system itself was to blame. Considering the eccentricities of the Julio-Claudians and the need to remove them by assassination, it is surprising that there was so little criticism of hereditary succession in the Augustan Principate.

The problem with the method of succession in the Roman Empire was that there *was no method for succession*.[20] Because of Rome's reverence for its republican past, a truly typical monarchy with fixed rules for succession did not develop. Since the principate was not presented as an overt monarchy, there could be no acknowledgment of a hereditary principle. As hard as emperors tried to get their blood relatives on the throne, there was no law of succession that recognized hereditary claims to power. In theory, the choice belonged to the Senate and the Roman people; in fact, there was no obligation for SPQR to choose a princeps at all. In theory, they could always go back to the republican system, but they never did. Each time an incumbent died, there was the opportunity to revert back. They tried after Caligula's assassination, but they failed. Part of the reason for this is that whoever inherited the *domus Caesaris* controlled the Praetorian Guard, the palace staff, and had a vested interest in the imperial system working against any reversion back. Once on the throne, a man might announce that he was only a servant of the Senate and the Roman people, but this was merely paying lip service to the actual theory of the principate itself. It might not have been more than the appearance of republican sympathies, but many still attached importance to that appearance. Emperors like Caligula and Nero who tried to strip away the veneer paid for it with their lives.

The lack of legitimacy did not stop emperors from trying to hand down the position to their own kin. Even those with Stoic views, like Seneca, were prepared to justify selection by blood. The dynastic principle was strong; time and again it happened that the emperor's relatives were perceived by many as worthier candidates for the throne, and their position might have been envied by outsiders, but being in the imperial family itself could be the cause of death as emperors, whether out of fear or paranoia, depleted the lists of their relatives in the attempt to stay alive.

Since there was no recognized mechanism for choosing a new princeps and no agreed-upon rules of eligibility, one only needed for the Senate to confer power on a candidate. The inherent weakness of the system was that, in theory, anyone could himself become eligible and get the approval of the Senate. But if one got the approval of the Guard first, what choice did the Senate have? This also meant that no candidate had to be tolerated forever, because the Senate or the Guard could change its mind. Continued armed usurpations could be justified on constitutional grounds. It is in this sense that Mommsen was right to call the principate "not only in practice but in theory, an autocracy tempered by legally permanent revolution."[21] The idealized dream of an elective monarchy was unattainable.

Later rulers, like the Five Good Emperors, worked out a system of selection based on merit, but the Julio-Claudians were trying to establish selection based on blood ties. This might stifle some ambition and soften the envy, but because the upper classes were so intermarried, senators with connections to the imperial family were not lacking. The princeps was a Roman aristocrat whose family married within the Roman governing class. The result was an ever-increasing number of senators who had some tie of kinship with the ruling family. The longer the Julio-Claudian dynasty continued, the greater the number of people came forth with some claim to the throne. Every generation brought more descendants of Tiberius or Claudius or more Junii Silani. The common motif in most of the killings under the Julio-Claudians was consolidating their position and getting rid of those rivals with claims to a relationship with the emperor. In many cases there seems to have been some measure of justification.[22] There was always factional strife at court organized around rival claimants to the throne and involving senators, many of whom might reasonably expect to command armies.

DOMUS AUGUSTA

Being a blood relative of the princeps could put one closer to the throne, but to actually get on the throne one had to escape disgrace, exile, or premature death. Augustus created a new family unit called the *domus Augusta* ("House of Augustus") with himself as *paterfamilias*. His family endured for six generations.[23] Access to the princeps was one of the first requirements for an assassination, and who had more access than his own family? The *domus Augusta* by definition provided potential competitors for the throne, as well as possible assassins, as factions within the family fought for position. This is where the role of women becomes very important. The Romans never put a woman on the throne, but this did not mean women could not work behind the scenes to make or break an emperor.

Family factionalism is present in all royal families, and it started early in Augustus's reign. Since Augustus had no brothers or sons, he could provide a legitimate male descendant only with the help of his female relatives. His sister Octavia provided him with a nephew, and his wife Livia gave him two stepsons. With an abundance of female relatives in his family (a daughter and four nieces) he could manage all the possibilities that could be arranged through marriage, divorce, remarriage after divorce or widowhood, and adoption. The potential danger represented by the widows who had children and who might remarry was well understood.[24] Augustus built alliances among his kin by marrying his daughter Julia to his nephew Marcellus in 25 BCE and continued with the marriage of his younger stepson Drusus to his younger niece Antonia Minor. This led to a multibranched imperial family over four generations. After Augustus's death, this also created two competing sources of legitimacy: one through relationship with the founder himself and one through a relationship with the current ruler (Tiberius or Claudius).[25]

These multiple sources of legitimacy, and therefore competition, resulted in danger for any sitting emperor. The Julio-Claudians eliminated not only possible competing legitimate heirs but anyone who could potentially produce a rival legitimate heir. Augustus had demonstrated this soon after Actium, when he had Cleopatra's (presumed) son by Caesar eliminated as well as Antony's elder son by his wife, Fulvia. When Tiberius came to power, the first thing he did was have Agrippa Postumus eliminated, even though he had already been disinherited. Less than a year after Caligula acceded to the throne, he had his cousin, Tiberius Gemellus, driven to suicide. Claudius's son, Britannicus, did not live beyond the first six months of his adoptive brother's reign.

Conspiracies almost always involved women who could provide a legitimate blood link with the throne. There were conspiracies involving both Augustus's daughter and granddaughter. Tiberius had to deal with the wife of Germanicus and her sons; Caligula had to deal with conspiracies involving his own sisters. Claudius had his wives and their sons, and the last wife successfully removed him in favor of her son, Nero. Imperial women thus plotted on behalf of their offspring. Praetorian prefects tried to marry them; equestrians and senators lost their lives through involvement in plots real or alleged, but all such events always revolved around the imperial succession.

THE IMPERIAL COURT

Tacitus is quite clear on the problems caused by the rise of an imperial court.[26] Already under Augustus there was something very much like a monarch's court. To a large degree it overlapped with the emperor's household, comprising members of his own immediate family and his slaves and freedmen, but it could also include highly trusted friends from the senatorial and equestrian orders. All members of the court fought for influence with the emperor to advance their own position or simply secure their survival. The result was a perpetual contest for the emperor's ear, and, at its worst, the contest could degenerate and even turn on itself.[27] None of this was open to public scrutiny, and sometimes the system appeared opaque even to insiders.

From Augustus on, as Cassius Dio noted, politics ceased to be public. Important political choices were debated or voted upon only in the private *consilium* of the emperor and his *amici*, but not in public. Consequently, historians both ancient and modern lack public records of how decisions came to be made by the emperor. We do not get firsthand reports directly from the palace. The absence of reliable information meant that the decision-making process was portrayed by historians through rumors, jokes, and anecdotes—that is, the hostile reminiscences of bitter and disillusioned men and women who hated the principate largely because it had not given them the rewards they thought they deserved.

One aspect of the new imperial bureaucracy was that the Julio-Claudians added a whole new cast of characters around the palace by using freedmen as their civil servants. As with all bureaucrats, in order to safeguard their positions the freedmen would either have to side with the incumbent or go over to a possible successor. The palace became the principal scene of intrigue, where even lowlier inhabitants were not immune to ambition. Freedmen were slowly replacing the aristocracy as the civil servants of the new regime, and even well-placed slaves could be part of the intrigue that went on behind the curtains. Anyone could be the carrier of intelligence about a plot.

The irony is that although the emperor had a court as a source of strength and consultation, it was also the source of his most immediate danger. The court comprised people who found themselves in the presence of the emperor frequently and therefore had access and proximity. As the principate grew into more of an institution, those carryovers who survived from court to court might come to see themselves as less dependent on the survival of the emperor himself than on the principate as an institution. If they thought they could guarantee their survival by joining a conspiracy to remove an emperor, then this was a viable option. All monarchs fear their court, but because Rome's monarchy was still quasi-disguised as a Republic, the court could not be regulated by formal rules that could regulate powers.

THE MILITARY

Although there were many groups that had to be cultivated to keep the new monarchy stable, all emperors ruled most fundamentally at the behest of the armies.[28] The threat came from two obvious realities: (1) the loyalty of the troops was not always a given; (2) the most serious problem was not the troops but their commanders.[29] Civil wars became a possibility when soldiers and their commanders united in their interests and decided to take a political role to remove an emperor.

The army took its oath of allegiance to the emperor on the first of January every year from the time of Tiberius on. The troops took the sanctity of this oath seriously and they remained true to him even when others thought him mad, incompetent, or vicious. The Praetorian Guard was equally loyal. Although one of their members murdered Caligula in January 41, it was the Guard who applied the rule of dynastic succession and proclaimed Claudius, the late emperor's uncle, while the Senate debated what to do.

The support of the military took precedence over everything else, and a successful emperor would have to gain the goodwill of the soldiers. Plutarch would later portray the Roman Empire as overtaken by disasters and upheavals because of the greed and lack of discipline among the soldiers, who were untrained and given to "irrational impulses." He pictured the soldiery as ushering one emperor after another into the palace just like characters in a stage play.[30] This was not yet true, however, in the first century CE.[31] While it is true that the army played a significant role in the upheavals of 68–69, it was not the cause of the upheavals. The assassination of the last Julio-Claudian emperor and the scramble for his position were the cause. Military discipline became undermined by the civil war as soldiers had to make the dangerous choice of which officials to obey and when to obey them as the scramble for power took form.

THE PRAETORIAN GUARD

Augustus had set up the Praetorian Guard with the express purpose of guarding his own life and the lives of his family. With nine thousand men dedicated to keeping him alive, how could anyone expect to get close enough to the emperor to kill him? If we were to believe popular sources, it was the Guard itself that represented the biggest threat to the emperor. How do we reconcile these two images? Was the Guard a protector or a threat?

The image of the Guard as a threat that connects it to greedy, ambitious men doing nefarious deeds is depicted in such popular media, such as the *I, Claudius* series, broadcast by the BBC and PBS in the 1970s. This portrayal showed the Guardsmen in most episodes intimidating individuals or acting like executioners. This image was made worse by *Gladiator*, where they appeared in black like Gestapo agents doing the bidding of a fascist emperor.[32] Novels on the Praetorian Guard have been even less accurate.[33] This image, however, is not entirely a media creation. Even Edward Gibbon talked about "Praetorian bands, whose licentious fury was the first symptom and cause of the decline of the Romans Empire."[34]

The placement of the Praetorians in Rome and their close relationship with the emperor did indeed make them the lynchpin of the internal security apparatus. The principate was a military dictatorship relying on the military for support. As Sandra Bingham has argued, the Praetorians' duties related to imperial security were many and varied. As a body, they did their duty well and loyally, but they also became aware of their privileged position. They received higher pay, better working conditions, numerous donatives, and a closer relationship with the emperor. As time went on, they became very protective of that position and did not want it put at risk. If they felt their position was being threatened, they might take action, which included betraying the emperor himself.[35]

Since we are discussing only the Julio-Claudians in this book, we can look at the first hundred years of the principate and say that for half that time the Guard was completely loyal. It took fifty years after their introduction by Augustus for them to assassinate the man they were sworn to protect. The involvement of the Guard in Caligula's murder was certainly significant in the history of the Julio-Claudians, since this was the first time that the emperor's personal unit had taken part in an overtly political action. There had been previous plots against Caligula's life before the one in 41 that killed him, and the Guard may well have had a hand in putting them down, although we lack detail.[36] Discontent would have to be widespread before it would have been in the best interests of the Guard to join in. The reason given in Josephus's account was that Caligula mocked Cassius Chaerea, the centurion who eventually slew him. The emperor had offended the honor and dignity of the very people who guarded him and guaranteed his safety. This was foolish, and it did put the emperor's life in jeopardy.[37]

This betrayal had as much to do with the nature of the Roman state as it did with the Guard itself.[38] It was in response to the political events of the times that soldiers were drawn into an intrigue and driven to break their oaths of loyalty. The broadening of their scope of activities inserted them into the administration of the city in a way that made them visible and likely to be influenced. After all, if there was no constitutional way to remove an emperor, then, when it became necessary to forcibly remove one, the Guard had only two choices: to prevent the move or participate in it.

What made them both effective and dangerous was that Guard had even more access to the emperor than other groups. The Praetorians formed the emperor's principal bodyguard; they guarded his chamber at night, escorted him in Rome even into the Senate house, and they accompanied him on journeys. They were under the direct command of the princeps, who gave them their password and appointed their higher officers—for example, the tribunes and centurions—himself. From 2 BCE on, it was customary for two men of equestrian rank, the Praetorian prefects, to command the Guard. They served the princeps in an increasing number of ways, from guarding his person to appearing on the panel of advisors when he exercised jurisdiction. The double prefecture, like the direct imperial appointment of the officers, was no doubt partly devised as a curb on the ambitions of the prefect, who might be tempted to use his command of the Guard against the princeps. There were four cases in which emperors veered from this Augustan arrangement and allowed just one man to hold the post. None of these exceptions turned out well. Burrus and Seneca both got compromised by trying to be a good influence on Nero but ultimately losing control. Burrus acquiesced to Nero's murder of Agrippina the Younger but lost his influence over Nero anyway. He died in 62, some say from poison.

Agrippina had Claudius appoint Burrus to the prefecture in 51 CE. She argued that there was a need for stricter discipline with respect to the Praetorians and that this could be accomplished more easily through the command of a single prefect.[39] Tiberius had had to remove Sejanus by a combination of stealth and force. Macro had met a similar fate early in the reign of Caligula, as did Tigellinus during the reign of Nero.

That the Praetorians got caught up in the political life of Rome is not surprising. Their duties placed both the officers and regular soldiers in close proximity to the center of power, and they obviously took an interest in the affairs of state. The most discernible illustration of this involvement in politics was during the transition of power. The grant of sizable donatives to the Guard at such times provides the strongest evidence of a tacit understanding that the soldiers had to be well rewarded for their acceptance of the new regime. This is a bad precedent. People should not be paid for their loyalty; it just leads to open bidding. Success in carrying out an assassination had to include the leadership of the Guard, and the recognition of this fact by all involved meant they knew the Guard was a political force to be reckoned with. This meant that the emperor's life was held in the balance between the Guard's loyalty and the ability of a small group of conspirators to convince the Praetorian prefect that coming over to them would be in the interests of the entire Guard and to him specifically.

At those moments when the security of the emperor was most tenuous, the attitude of the Praetorian Guard and its prefects would naturally be of crucial importance. At the accession of a new princeps or when a serious conspiracy threatened the throne, the loyalty of the Praetorians could determine the course of history. For this reason they became involved in intrigue regarding the succession. The emperor's personal troops had played an important role in the transition of power between Augustus and Tiberius and between Tiberius and Caligula. They participated in the murder of Caligula and they were the primary means by which the succession to Claudius could even be accomplished. The influence of the Guard and its sense of its own importance as a key player in the transition to a new emperor became blatantly obvious when troops in the field recognized Galba as emperor, but he refused to give them the donative promised by Nymphidius. This mistake, added to his cruel treatment of the soldiers on his march to Rome and his dismissal of several officers from the city cohorts, set the military against him. Otho, one of Galba's confidants in Rome, read this situation correctly. He ingratiated himself with the Praetorians and even stooped to bribery—100 sesterces for each member of the cohort attending Galba.[40]

It is ironic that all the conspirators against emperors, whether they were high-ranking government officials, soldiers, or even family members, had taken oaths of loyalty and had enjoyed benefactions from the emperor whom they plotted against. That some of them were members of the very security organizations tasked with protecting the emperor's life—members of the Praetorian Guard or the Praetorian prefect himself—is even more disturbing. The Guard could not act in its own interests since no Praetorian prefect could succeed an emperor. They were certainly not the "kingmakers" portrayed in books, movies, and websites that focus on the Praetorians, although it serves to make the story more dramatic.[41] They did, however, have to be key players in any assassination attempt, and they could play one of two roles. Any conspirators would have to overcome the Guard to get to the emperor, because it was his first line of defense. Once a conspiracy was successful, the choice of successor had to be accepted by the Guard to have any chance of the usurper's remaining on the throne. So the Praetorians helped members of the senatorial class kill Caligula, and they placed Claudius on the throne, daring the Senate to oppose their decision. Of course, later emperors would have a much bigger problem with the Guard than the Julio-Claudians. Once they realized their power to make emperors, they were more willing to initiate a change in regime. A calculated uprising of Praetorians led by Casperius Aelianus against Emperor Nerva, for example, forced the emperor to adopt the more popular Trajan as his son and successor.

We should also separate the rank and file of the guard from the ambitious men who headed up the unit. If the Praetorian prefect was willing to use the Guard to help advance his political aims, it would have been difficult for men following his orders to stop him without seeming disloyal themselves. In the case of Sejanus, however, Tiberius was able to remove him and replace him with Macro and other loyal members of the Guard and the *vigiles*. Even when a conspiracy involved both the leadership and the officer corps, it was usually restricted for the most part to a few officers. These few men were those who had the closest association with the emperor and with the administration and would have been affected by the political situation around them. Certainly individual men were corruptible, but such conspirators by no means represented the attitude of the entire force. The average soldier probably remained loyal as long as his needs were being met. The rank and file generally fared well either way. If the conspiracy failed, they would be rewarded for their loyalty. If it succeeded, they would be offered incentives to follow the new emperor. The average soldier probably remained ambivalent about the various machinations of the powerful. The Praetorians as a whole remained pragmatic about their relationship with the emperor because the vast majority of them had little to gain by challenging the status quo. This is why they never would have joined in a conspiracy to return to the republic. With no emperor, there would be no need for a Praetorian Guard.

The Guard may have been ordered to carry out some dastardly deeds at the command of the emperor, but that does not mean that every member agreed with the policy or enjoyed his work. Josephus records a comment made by Chaerea to one of the Praetorian prefects, Arrecinus Clemens, and to Papinius, a fellow tribune, that the Guard had been turned into "torturers and executioners." Guardsmen were tasked with doing the exact deeds that were to cause people to want to overthrow the emperor. The most sinister duties assigned to the Guard were the confinement and execution of those whom the emperor considered a risk. Generally these people came from the nobility, and most cases were political in nature. There are numerous examples of the use of Praetorians to detain individuals who were simply thought to be a threat as well as those who had actually been charged and were waiting to be tried. In several instances, the intimidating presence of the soldiers was enough to force the individual to commit suicide. Such an act removed the responsibility of the emperor and allowed him to claim that he would have interceded on behalf of the accused and been lenient toward him if only he had not killed himself.

The Guard provided intelligence about potential threats even from the emperor's own family. Members of the imperial family were guarded by the Praetorians, but they were also spied upon by the same men. Having a Guard provided protection and prestige, as we see when Agrippina lost hers and then turned up dead, but Praetorians could also report back to their superiors the conversations and events that they witnessed. This was one of the few ways the emperor could keep an eye on another of his major threats—his own family.

The organization of the Guard did not change much after Augustus's arrangement, since it worked well and needed little improvement. The one change that had significance was when Tiberius brought all the cohorts together in a single camp, the Castra Praetoria. This made the basis of imperial power evident to all; the camp was a clear manifestation of imperial power, and it was permanent.[42] Tacitus claims it was done for disciplinary reasons, that having the soldiers together made for better control, but the expanded use of the Praetorians for other tasks, primarily in Rome, meant their duties went far beyond just guarding the emperor and his family. The Praetorians had a huge impact in the political arena at Rome; therefore, their power remained a two-edged sword. The Praetorian officers had to be carefully chosen and carefully monitored. The emperor needed to know that someone he could trust implicitly was in command of his Guard, for the greatest danger he could potentially encounter would come from the armed men who had sworn to protect him.

WAS ANYONE HAPPY?

Our approach to security may seem to imply that everyone was out to kill the emperor. This is, of course, not true. There were broad swaths of the population who were quite pleased with the new arrangement. The political position of the equestrian class was different: since they were gaining status, their attitudes were not quite as contradictory or ambivalent as those of the senatorial class. They actually competed with senators for public influence, especially in the courts. Since the equestrians never regarded themselves as being in possession of the government, they had not really lost anything under the new regime. The arrival of the principate enhanced, rather than diminished, their social status.[43] Most of them acquired their sense of accomplishment by following the *cursus equitum*—the ladder of military and civil posts reserved for equestrians in the public realm. Of course, there was always the possibility of someone like Sejanus trying to rise higher. After all, by the mere exercise of his will, the emperor could advance to the Senate those who were covetous of privilege and honor, but this was a dangerous route. As the people who administered the imperial domain and administered the imperial bureaucracy, the *equites* served the emperor loyally, recognizing their full dependence on him and identifying their interests with their own. They were spared the painful moral and political choices that faced senators.

The same can be said of the wealthy provincial class that benefited from the rule of the emperors. As long as the emperor lavished grants of Roman citizenship on them, kept a tight control over the conduct of senatorial proconsuls, and prosecuted those who abused their positions, the provincials generally remained quiet.[44] Emperors used two main strategies to bolster their position and stabilize the empire. They could strengthen their personal relationship with soldiers, and they could act as a patron toward the population of the provinces, specifically the municipal aristocracies of the empire. The provincials themselves do not really figure in this story. They had no access to the emperor. For many of his subjects, the emperor was more of a symbol, almost a fiction, but a powerful symbol who could inspire and unite people, bring justice or punishment. Assassination requires access, and most provincials would never see Rome, let alone the emperor.

The urban plebs in the capital were generally quiet except in cases of bread shortages. They did not generally side with the senators because of the mutual rancor that had arisen between the upper and lower classes after a century of civil war. So whereas the senators rejoiced over the killing of Caligula and Nero, the populace generally mourned. The plebs saw the emperor as a curb on the Senate's greed and arrogance.[45] Through their bread-and-circuses policy, which was a major aspect of their patronage, the Julio-Claudian emperors were successful in reaching the "man on the street" and ensuring their favor with him despite the occasional riot caused by theatrical performances of the arena. The government could prevent neither the threat nor an outburst of violence on the part of the common people. The plebs were a raucous bunch and would express their opinion in the face of what they perceived as a brutal injustice. But the plebs also never assassinated an emperor. Not every outburst of public dissatisfaction is a threat to the emperor. If anything, being able to express yourself publicly without being beaten or killed was a healthy expression of freedom of speech.

THE "GOLDEN AGE" OF AUGUSTUS

The Augustan Principate is praised for producing a strong central government that lasted for over two hundred years, from 30 BCE until 180 CE. The political structures Augustus put in place survived "mad" emperors and civil wars, foreign wars, and foreign invasions. Even after the great days of the Roman Empire, Augustus's rule represented a model to aspire to. Yet the cracks that would appear in the Late Empire were already present in the Augustan system. The trends were all in place: the growth of autocracy that produced rulers who could be cruel and arbitrary, senatorial discontent at the loss of power and prestige, lack of a succession system, and the politicizing of the Praetorian Guard. From the point of view of internal security, how could Augustus's reign be a "golden age" if three out of five (all five if you believe the rumors) of the Julio-Claudians were assassinated? So although later senators prayed that their emperors would be "more fortunate than Augustus and better than Trajan" (*Felicior Augusto, melior Traiano*),[46] their wish was seldom granted. Augustus ruled relatively well and died in his bed, poisoned or not, at the ripe old age of seventy-six. Few of his successors reached this happy end.

9

Conspiracies and Conspiracy Theories

An Empire in Blood

There were many elements that could contribute to an emperor's safety. Some places like Egypt and China had sacred dynasties and sacrosanct emperors. In China the emperor had the Mandate of Heaven, was a god on earth, and was responsible for weather, crops, and so forth. The emperor in Rome was just a citizen. Running the empire was just a job. The imperial cult did not keep the emperor alive, and he was much more accessible to his people. Rome was an open society. Rome did not revert to secret poisonings as much as China did. It was not that big a deal to kill a Roman emperor; you just had to replace him.

DID ROME HAVE ADEQUATE INTERNAL SECURITY?

Although it would indeed be anachronistic to look at all the security organizations in Rome as a coordinated "team," we do not even have that today in America, despite calls for reform and better cooperation after each intelligence failure. The personnel that Augustus put together still all had to report to the emperor or one of his representatives, and this required collection, analysis, and coordination by whoever was going to give them orders. What were the security services doing? How would their activities affect the mortality rate of Roman emperors? Were they good at what they did? Were they effective enough to keep the emperor alive? Or were they so bad and disloyal that they earned Rome the dubious honor of having the highest death rate of any monarchy?

Augustus had invented any number of internal security organs to protect the state and himself. It would be unfair—and anachronistic—to compare them with modern security services. Even by the standards of their own times, however, these organizations had too much to do and could not be everywhere at once. Protecting the Roman emperor was a full-time job and then some. The Praetorian Guard, for example, fought in the field as regular soldiers, guarded Rome, guarded the palace, acted as intelligence agents, guarded the relatives of the emperor, and guarded the emperor himself when he traveled, when he appeared in public, and when he was most "at home."[1] The emperor was expected to appear in public at games, in processions, in the Senate house, and in the streets of Rome, and he had to be made safe in all these venues. Even within the confines of the palace, it is not certain that the emperor always had Praetorians with him. For most of the Julio-Claudian period, they did an excellent job, but to quote the well-known, fictional Godfather, Michael Corleone: "If anything in this life is certain, if history has taught us anything, it is that you can kill anyone."[2] Sandra Bingham, in her book, *The Praetorian Guard*, had to admit that even the Praetorian prefects often proved ineffective at stopping all conspiracies against the princeps.[3]

Sometimes simple ineffectiveness was the problem. Emperors had more specialized personnel for protection who were obviously not always competent.[4] Lictors, for example, did not have training as bodyguards, and they were usually absent from violent imperial death scenes. The German bodyguard was effective, but its members had to be on the scene surrounding the emperor when an attempt was made on his life. Separating the emperor from his bodyguards, be they Germans or Praetorians, had to be one of the first goals of a conspirator.[5]

We cannot hold these security men to too high a standard. Even today with our vast array of security organizations, modern weapons, and electronic communications, leaders are assassinated. Even highly professional police do not succeed in preventing crimes, solving all crimes, or arresting the perpetrators. No matter how conscientious police forces are in enforcing the law, serious criminals will find room to operate—outmaneuvering and outnumbering the forces of public order—by finding weak spots within the thin security patchwork of various officials, guards, and soldiers.[6] It is the very basis of all terrorist operations. Build a better mousetrap, and the world will build a better mouse.

Following are ten considerations that made guarding the emperor a difficult job.

1. Flaws in the Augustan Template

Augustus had founded the principate, and from that point a reaction arose immediately. When looked at as a whole, these conspiracies form a pattern: whether it was to restore the republic, to replace a madman, to satisfy private animosity, or to make room for someone else's ambition, there was never a lack of people willing to kill an emperor.

Part of the problem with the Roman state was that the "Augustan template," as it has been called, was flawed. Although it was solid in some ways, in others it was a precarious balancing act. Most perilously, it never solved the problem of succession. Dynasty based on heredity came to be the accepted model of succession, but no state-based formula for the choice of candidates was ever established. The succession thus became a source of uncertainty, conspiracy, and violence as various candidates and their supporters, even in peace, vied with one another to reach the throne.

Every conspiracy against an emperor had the same motive—an attempt to take his job and rule in his place. If the emperor's position was of dubious legitimacy in the first place, then there was no reason the princeps could not be challenged by those who felt they had a better claim to the throne. The essential components of a successful conspiracy generally included membership from both the senatorial and equestrian orders, the allegiance of at least one of the Praetorian Guard commanders, and, if the candidate for princeps was not of the Julio-Claudian line, provincial legionary support.[7]

The instability of the principate and its lack of a clear dynastic principle mean the job was always up for grabs, even when there was a sitting emperor. If everyone has the potential to be a ruler, then someone will always try. Plots to remove the emperor, even later in Roman history, never went away. A good emperor was one who could keep enough constituencies happy enough to not try to murder him, and a smart emperor would also use his security services wisely—by keeping them happy and out of politics.[8] Finally, detecting and killing would-be usurpers never hurt.

The role of the Senate and the relationship between the emperor and the upper classes remained highly contested. All the Julio-Claudian emperors had to grapple with those dilemmas that lurked below the surface of every assassination attempt, whether it be the poisoning of imperial heirs, show trials for treason, or murder to effect a regime change. Even those who were not murdered had rumors of murder surrounding them. Some of the stories may be real, and some may be fabricated, but they point to the fact that succession almost never happened without a struggle or a victim.[9] Not one case exists in the history of the principate when a princeps's power was removed from him while he was still alive. That means that regime change requires a natural death or an assassination.[10]

2. Growing Needs of Installation Security

The expansion of imperial power meant an expansion of the palatial headquarters of the ruler, his staff of imperial administrators, and his family. The palace had to be kept safe, and there were many more people to keep an eye on. Not only did emperors acquire luxurious suburban estates and gardens, but the entire Palatine Hill was taken over as "the palace."[11] The complex included audience chambers, dining rooms, reception halls, baths, and accommodations for family, staff, and slaves. Senators who had once lived on the Palatine were now edged out and sent to the Aventine, a place that had been the headquarters of radical plebeians back in republican days. The message this sent about the growth of imperial power was not lost on them.[12] Hand in hand with the expansion of the imperial palace came the expansion of the imperial administration. We have little detail about how Augustus organized his staff, but we do know it had a vastly expanded scale. By the time of Claudius, an entire bureau had been established to deal with administration—correspondence, petitions to the emperor, accounts, and legal cases.[13]

The emperor's bodyguard and the Praetorians had to keep the emperor safe as he moved around in this complex. Since the Praetorian Guard had sworn an oath to protect the entire imperial family, this meant an extension of its responsibilities with each new family member. It was the *Domus Augusta* that the Praetorians were sworn to protect, and it was from the *Domus Augusta* that their rewards would come. One recent biographer of Nero claimed that a princeps could do just about anything he wanted without risking the loyalty of the Praetorians, and he calls their loyalty naïve.[14] This is unfair; loyalty to the emperor was their job. The motivations of men like Burrus and other Praetorian prefects were largely service to the *civitas*. They were not supposed to be motivated by private interests, and they certainly were not supposed to pick and choose which emperors they would protect or which ones they would sacrifice. For the most part, their attitudes were positive and constructive toward the state. It was not unusual for them to be co-opted into a conspiracy for moral reasons if they really thought the emperor had gone too far, had abused members of the Praetorian Guard personally, or was destroying the state. After all, any attempt on the emperor's life had to get through the Praetorian Guard, and this not only made it the first line of defense but also made the prefect the first man the conspirators would have to suborn. By the end of the Julio-Claudian period, the prefecture was still a long way from being the developed institution of the second and third centuries, but it is equally true that it had come a long way from the purely military posting it had been under Augustus.[15] There can be no doubt that the careers of Macro and Sejanus were instrumental in the extension of the role and influence of the prefecture.[16] The ambitions of a strong prefect like Macro or Sejanus were a source of danger to any emperor. On the other hand, as Durry has pointed out, the suspicions of a princeps were more often fatal to the prefect.[17]

3. Too Many Dissidents to Watch

Augustus's reign is always portrayed as calm compared to his successors, and yet there were three major conspiracies against his life that we know of and perhaps others for which we have no evidence. All of his successors down through Nero faced conspiracies and the threat of armed revolt. There is no such thing as "the beginning of conspiracies," the "beginning of troops being involved," or the beginning of when "the Guard got involved." The threat of conspiracy was always there, and a successful conspirator needed loyal allies, someone who represented the military, the cooperation of the Praetorian prefect or Guardsmen, and a successor waiting in the wings. Many segments of the power elite were involved, whether by actively plotting or just turning a blind eye. On two occasions actual legions were involved, but, fortunately for the emperor, these uprisings were quickly squashed. Such attempts included the conspiracy against Caligula in 39 CE, which included among its members Cn. Lentulus Gaetulicus, commander of the troops stationed in Upper Germany, but that ended as soon as Caligula headed for the German camp and ordered his execution. In 42 CE there was an uprising against Claudius by Furius Camillus Scribonianus, governor of Dalmatia, that collapsed within five days because the troops remained loyal to the emperor.[18]

As we have argued above, the problems with the principate were structural. The principate proved to be a strong institution—strong enough to overpower the old republican constitution—because it addressed the needs of many more people in Italy and the provinces. The drag of the old republic, however, prevented them from drawing up a new and explicit constitution. This was perilous to a civil society because an autocracy brought about through military usurpation does not lead to freedom. When a government becomes willing to enforce its own beliefs by any and all means necessary, liberty is crushed, demoralization sets in; along with that goes creativity and loyalty, which are then replaced by apathy. When a society is held together by no values beyond knee-jerk loyalty to the government or simply fear for one's own existence, there is no reason to fight to protect such an institution. When an emperor, the head of such an institution, falls, there is no clear reason for anyone to mourn except a few old faithful servants.[19]

4. The Loyalty of the Security Services and Their Politicization

There is no security service that cannot be subverted. For all the passage of time, people spy and subvert for the same reasons: (1) they can be subverted with money and power; (2) they act on personal grudges; (3) they get seduced by a different ideology. The betrayers had modern-day counterparts in terms of their motivations, such as a Kim Filby or Guy

Burgess (ideology), Aldrich Ames or Johnny Walker (money), or Robert Hanssen (personal grudge or ego).

When we look at the careers of men like the prefect Burrus, we see modern historians making value judgments about their character. They are portrayed as sycophants and tools of a corrupt emperor. Both Praetorian prefects were *equites*, as were all future holders of the post.[20] They are condescended to by those who equate class with worth; their origin is of little importance. They were civil servants hired to do a job. Fagan has argued that their first loyalty was to the maintenance of their privileges above the performance of their duty as soldiers.[21] This remains unproven for the Julio-Claudian era. They did not back Sejanus over Tiberius. Certainly they would prefer a principate over a republic simply for the maintenance of their jobs, but they had a striking loyalty to their emperor long after someone like Caligula stopped deserving it. Thus the news of Caligula's death was not greeted with rejoicing in the Castra Praetoria.[22] Any individual can be motivated by personal gain, but the Praetorians were no more a victim of these motives than were any other Romans, senators included. So when Fagan says, "The Guardsman's motives were thus entirely selfish: preservation of his privileged position, and the opportunity of personal gain," he does them a disservice.[23] At no stage did they represent a distinct political entity in the Roman state, and they adhered to no particular political doctrine beyond their desire to ensure the continuance of the principate and to protect the life of the emperor.

Similarly, historians create a dichotomy between the loyalist imperial officials, of whom the Praetorian prefect was an eminent example, and the imperial henchmen, such as the *delatores*, seen as their opponents (moral opposites). As modern author Vassily Rudich has noted, these men are really on the same side. Tacitus often favorably distorts the portraits of the loyalists and heavily maligns the *delatores*.[24] If you trace the careers of these two groups through the *cursus honorum*, there is little difference in their success in making their careers. There are examples of opportunism and moral misconduct in both groups.

5. Paranoia, Self Defense, and Insanity

The effect on an individual's personal life of struggling to found a dynasty and maintaining power should not be underestimated. Augustus's success in public was not mirrored in a successful private life. His family disintegrated largely as a result of his machinations to perpetuate his power through ill-conceived dynastic marriages, taking his and their personal happiness with it. This fight between individuals and institutions would plague every Julio-Claudian. Julius Caesar and Caligula were stabbed to death by republican conspirators. Claudius was poisoned for dynastic reasons. Augustus and Tiberius were lucky to survive assassination plots. They became so suspicious of possible rivals that they virtually exterminated the direct bloodlines of their own imperial clan.[25]

The pressure and insecurities of the position of emperor must have made great demands on the mental state of any man who held the office. How could a child be raised in a palace surrounded by aristocratic bloodbaths like those in the reigns of Tiberius, Caligula, and Claudius and not be affected? How could anyone ever feel secure? How could one *not* be paranoid about one's safety? If Claudius alone is credited with the deaths of thirty-five senators and over two hundred knights, how could anyone at court be left unaffected?[26]

What effect does it have on a young prince to know that every advance in his position exposes him to further jealousy and disloyalty? Surrounded by immense ambition, children could observe the ruthless methods of their parents and relatives. It would be hard not to associate political power with malice, intrigue, and distrust. Being emperor was a tough job for anyone to do well. Some were more successful than others and sometimes for reasons beyond their control. In the Julio-Claudian dynasty alone, Tiberius, in the end, walked away from the position; Caligula, Claudius, and Nero tried to refashion the emperor's role and were murdered for it.

No emperor manipulated the smoke and mirrors as well as Augustus. Tiberius delegated much of his power to Sejanus which almost led to his downfall. His withdrawal to Capri implied he did not care to rule and led to a widespread belief in his personal misconduct. Nor were Claudius's eccentricities well received despite his professed conservatism. Caligula and Nero were too extravagant and did things seen as clearly tyrannical.

Even one attempt on an emperor's life could drastically change his psyche. Most emperors did try conscientiously to solve perceived problems within the imperial government and to dispense justice fairly, but the more defensive an emperor got and the more senators he killed, the more his efforts to rule would be seen as hypocritical—as Tiberius soon found out. Yet the actions of emperors often baffled contemporaries, and what they found unable to explain was liable to be dismissed as lunatic or condemned as monstrous by the ancient sources.[27] Catherine Edwards has written that "mad emperors are an embarrassment to serious historians."[28] It seems, however, that "mad emperors" sell a lot better than a story about morally weak and cowardly aristocrats, especially if the historian writing about them is an aristocrat. Considering the fact that the last four Julio-Claudian emperors were turned into "hate figures" by the sources does not make getting at the truth any easier.[29] Tiberius, in spite of his outstanding achievements as a general and a statesman, was damned to posterity as a reclusive pederast. Caligula has come down in history as a homicidal maniac, and Claudius is caricatured as a slobbering dimwit. Nero is simply buried under so much "literary and ecclesiastic manure" it is hard to dig him out.[30] Tacitus's loathing and contempt for Tiberius, Caligula, Claudius, and Nero run like a dark thread through the tapestry of his prose. When emperors were overthrown, they were charged with crimes that so obviously transgressed the hallowed and instinctively understood codes of sexual and moral conduct that it justified their murder in the eyes of the general public. Once a person suffered *damnatio memoriae*, there was little that would have survived with a favorable view of him or her in the written record. Two millennia later, we become captive to these smear campaigns and are left to discern what really happened.

Rarely are the senators who participated in the conspiracies called out for what they really were: ambitious men willing to kill for their own ambition. Many others were willing to join a conspiracy in the hopes that, under a new leader, they might restore the ancient, esteemed position that they were losing because of rising *equites* and freedmen. Ancient historians, all sharing the same senatorial bias, present the idea that the charge of *maiestas* was to be considered false unless there was an actual rebellion and/or an assassination as proof, but we know that there was much jockeying for position behind the scenes. An emperor had to be ever on the alert for the possibility of disloyalty, and the cheapest and fastest way to eliminate a conspiracy was to nip it in the bud before an actual attempt was made.

6. The Absence of a Professional Prosecutorial Staff

Tacitus believed that *delatores* were, by the very nature of their activities, immoral and a force destructive to the entire social fabric, but what else did the emperor have?[31] Rudich has called *delatores* "court schemers whose energy was directed inwards and whose goal was self-aggrandisement at any cost, leading inevitably to nihilism and destruction."[32] But, as Steven Rutledge has shown, the *delatores* functioned in the place of a prosecutorial staff.[33] They were by no means neutral. They were loyal to their own careers and sometimes even the emperor. They were never entirely good or bad. Take, for example, A. Didius Gallus Fabricius Veiento, who was consul three times, admired as a brilliant orator, but hated as a *delator*.[34] As a praetor he showed strength of character in the way he handled cases. Under Nero's reign, he was charged with bribery, trading in imperial favors (as if that were uncommon) and the right to occupy public office. Nero took over the trial personally and convicted the defendant. Fabricius Veiento was banished from Italy, his books (he wrote satires) were burned, and, as a result, his writings took on a new popularity underground.[35] If anything, this shows why labels are inaccurate. One could be a dissident, an author, an opportunist, and a hero at the same time.

Opportunists with relativist ethics like the *delatores* can certainly be contrasted with those senators who avoided making capital charges of treason against their colleagues, even for the sake of vengeance. The opportunists did not hesitate to resort to a *maiestas* prosecution if they found it expedient or profitable—especially since a successful informer received a sizable portion of the property of the condemned. On such occasions, senatorial competition could turn into a slaughter. Prosecutors knew whom to turn in so that the emperor would approve. If they turned in someone and the emperor did not approve, they not only would lose their reward but might be punished themselves. If they uncovered an actual conspiracy, however, they could be termed patriots. Much of what they did had to occur with the passive cooperation of the Senate. During the revolt of Scribonianus against Claudius, Narcissus asked the freedman Galaesus what he would have done if Scribonianus had become emperor. His reply pretty much sums up the situation of most senators: "I would have stood behind him and kept my mouth shut."[36]

7. Lack of Professional Police, Secret Service, or Intelligence Organizations

Although the protection of property and personal security was the responsibility of the individual in ancient Rome, the one duty that did fall to the government was the protection of the emperor. The Romans had to achieve a certain level of security without a police force, professional secret service, or any formal intelligence-gathering organization. Elements of these activities were done by various magistrates and guards, but the Romans did not have the bureaucratic specialization we enjoy in modern times. The government obviously concentrated its limited forces on those things that seemed a direct threat to the government, like treason, sedition, and assassination. The political order in Rome seems, even by modern standards, to have been particularly vulnerable to conspiracies and sedition.

Some historians writing about internal security in Roman society even suggested that the absence of police apparatus jeopardized the stability of the political order.[37] German scholarship in the late nineteenth century took an interest in the institutionalization of police forces, and there was a tendency to see gross deficiencies in both the republican and the late imperial orders in contrast with the alleged efficiency of the principate.[38] While it is true that there was a distinctive development under Augustus, historians should avoid assuming any modern standards of policing in the ancient world.[39]

Standard works on the Praetorians all attempt to remedy the lack of concrete information on the actual security functions of these forces by making assumptions about "necessary tasks." But the fact of the matter is we know precious little about the inner workings of their duties.[40] The same can be said of the *vigiles*. J. S. Rainbird has argued that the *vigiles* were probably fully occupied with their duties as a fire brigade and therefore unable to do anything else.[41]

8. Ambitious Upper Classes—So Many Possible Usurpers

The most fundamental general cause of why senators were so persistently guilty of conspiratorial activity lay in the pressures exerted upon them by the political and social changes that were occurring under the early principate. These changes infringed upon the traditional position of the Senate and the senatorial class, jeopardizing their dignity, their fortunes, and the lives of their members. Augustus's creation of the principate made a permanent, drastic reduction in the powers of the Senate, in the government of the provinces, in control of the financial and military affairs of the state, and in foreign policy. This only got worse under Tiberius as the status of the Senate was eroded further. Tiberius ruled for eleven years without consulting the Senate in person once and by dealing with it through ministers who were of equestrian rank only (Sejanus and Macro). By condoning the abuses of the *Lex Iulia de maiestatis*, at least during the last years of his rule, he exposed the senatorial class to injury and harassment by informers who rose from among its own numbers. This further degenerated when Gaius's despotic treatment of the senators humiliated and antagonized them and made them acutely aware of their own impotence in the face of the power of the principate. Claudius was able to neutralize some of the antagonism by courting the loyalty of the *nobiles*. However, his extension of the imperial bureaucracy, particularly his employment of freedmen in positions of great power, and the political ascendancy of his wives further demeaned the Senate. Nero, once free of the influence of Seneca and Burrus, reduced all but the staunchest part of the Senate to unprecedented subservience.

As certain members of the Senate and the old ruling class watched as their powers were stripped away, given to their social inferiors, or assumed by the emperor, they had no choice but to adapt to this new political order. Although we should expect to see a gradual accommodation to the new reality with each emperor after Augustus, some people adjusted better than others. The reactions of individual senators ranged from servile acceptance of benefits from the regime to hereditary hatred of the system. Their behavior ranged from close collaboration, to reluctance, cooperation, or violent revolt.

How does one reconcile following old patterns of moral virtue while accommodating oneself to the new realities of restricted political action? Is this accommodation to a new reality enough to explain why things became so deadly for the emperor? In the beginning, there must have been members of the old ruling class who would have preferred a return to the days of the republic, when their illustrious ancestors had taken turns to share power. As time went on, however, most of them were realistic enough to acknowledge that this ambition was an impossible pipe dream. If they had to be ruled by an emperor, no doubt they wanted a competent military leader who would conform to the unwritten rules of the *mos maiorum*, the traditional moral ways of the worthiest Romans.[42] Frequently, this was the ideology under which they made their move against the emperor, even if it was strictly ambition they were acting on. Their stated motives were not always their real motives. The men trying to assassinate an emperor must have had pangs of conscience. After all, murdering anyone takes a psychological toll. What kind of self-excuses did they make in their own minds through defense mechanisms?

I think we get closer to the truth once we realize that the people who revolted against the emperor had no intention of restoring the republic. Their aims tended to be self-serving and immediate. The loyalists who defended the status quo did so to preserve or raise their status within the political elite.[43] They were simply eliminating the competition.

In an autocracy, a challenger needs to ensure the deposition of the incumbent; he must seize command of the instruments of state, including the army and the security services, and sufficiently reward a coalition of supporters so that they back him as the new incumbent.[44] Those who opposed the reigning emperor hoped to accelerate their own advancement within the elite, which wanted its own candidate on the throne. In both groups the overriding consideration was fear or ambition, not principle. After all, why should the throne not be theirs? With no clear criteria for eligibility or primacy, or even a certainty that a new princeps had to be appointed, those senators who were descendants of noble families that had been equals in birth, office, and status to the Julii and the Claudii in the republic would naturally see themselves as worthy candidates for the throne.[45] Seneca has Augustus address the traitor Cn. Cornelius Cinna, the grandson of Pompey, and point out that, if he had succeeded in killing Augustus, what made him think Paulus and Fabius Maximus and the Cossi and Servilii and other great lines of nobles would tolerate him?[46]

The supply of potential rivals was also increased by the number of imperial marriages. Children of previous wives were always a threat. Augustus wanted to make one-man rule permanent and keep it in his family, but the series of deaths among those marked as his heirs and the lack of any surviving sons from his marriage to Livia put the kibosh on these plans. Succession throughout the Julio-Claudian dynasty was fraught with different claims from different sides of the family tree. Would this have been different had there been sons? Possibly, but there was no presumption in Roman law that the firstborn would be the sole or principal heir. Primogeniture is a post-Roman invention. There was no legal way to pass on the principate. Much depended on someone being in the right place at the right time. Being related to Augustus was no guarantee—in fact, it was a reason for elimination, as Marcus Julius Silanus Torquatus and his relatives found out.

9. Are Historians Making the Problem Seem Worse?

Ronald Syme asked, "What is a conspiracy? When an individual or a group is incriminated for nefarious designs against the person of Caesar or the security of the State, the count can subsume anything from treasonable talk to daggers and poison. Verification is generally precluded, documents are forged or fallacious, and the inquirer must use his own judgment: did a plot exist, who formed it, and what was the precise purpose? Not all historians ask these questions."[47]

Questions like "Did Livia poison her husband in the year 14?" (as Tacitus and Dio say she did) have always been subjective. People claim to be weighing evidence, but in the end the "facts" of the murder depend on *how* you weigh the evidence. If people like Eisenhut do not accept them, it is because their general view of human nature and of human probabilities is different from those who believe in conspiracies.[48] Whether what a doctor and a *spado* said under torture is likely to be true, whether a wife is likely to have learned the secret of a husband who discarded her, and whether she is likely to have preserved her life and to have kept the secret (Drusus) for eight years depend upon one's views. There is an alarming variation between the versions of each conspiracy related by the sources. We have to rely too much on the accounts of writers with senatorial bias, accounts put out by the emperor himself or by the succeeding emperor, to cover his tracks. We should also not get caught up in the sweeping generalizations of the ancient sources or the modern historians who follow them about the irresponsibility of the Senate, the mutinous spirit of the armies, or the general decline in people's respect for the laws and the gods. People always think the world is going to hell in a handcart.

Historians of the principate belonged to the senatorial class, the very class that was deprived of its earlier role as head of affairs by the new regime. These historians/senators identified republican freedom with their own preeminent position. They were the ones who linked playing a part in decision-making with freedom of opinion and the ability to write history. This was the class that was on the losing side in the civil wars.

Many of them clung to an idealized vision of republican history even if they did not share the nostalgia of the *nobiles*.[49] Other historians, like Velleius Paterculus, who came from a pro-Roman Italian family, would have found the aristocratic republican traditions alien. Paterculus is much more the optimist, whereas Tacitus is a pessimist. The rise of *novi homines* into the ruling class during the republic and empire (i.e., the progressive assimilation of Italy into the Roman citizenship) means they are more likely to follow the Augustan program. Dio, on the other hand, approves of monarchy because there is no other choice and the Roman world had become accustomed to it.

What did the ancients think about the instability of their own empire? Latin historiography on the origins of the principate and on Augustus is the sphere of authors belonging to the senatorial class.[50] Every writer and every thinker has an ideological position, and that ideology affects the way a given writer understands history. There is also a reason for writing about conspiracies. Conspiracies generate fear—fear about impending chaos, about who is in charge, about the state being in control. By retelling the stories of how conspiracies were detected, suppressed, and punished, Roman readers were reassured order could be restored. No matter how praiseworthy tyrannicides may seem, assassins have to be punished, for while their motives may be pure, no state can tolerate violence against its leaders.[51]

The most authoritative source of information about the Julio-Claudians is, of course, Tacitus's *Annals*. One must be careful because he was writing a century after the death of Augustus, and some scholars believe many of his preoccupations were with the attitudes and actions of Trajan and Hadrian, under whom he lived.[52] In his *Annals* he sought to demonstrate that the principate of the Julii and the Claudii was a tyranny, starting from Tiberius down to Nero, as the emperors practiced the merciless extinction of the old aristocracy.[53]

The language that the senatorial writers use to express the relationship between emperor and the state is often framed as a contrast between "tyranny" and "freedom"—concepts inherited from the Late Republic. But this republican vocabulary should not mislead us into treating the history of the Julio-Claudian period as if the republic were recoverable. The competition that once existed between senators for magistracies and honors was gone. It had been replaced with competition for the emperor's favor.[54] Sallust had already pointed out during the republic that Roman politicians, whether they claimed to be defending the rights of the people or of the Senate, were acting on pretense. They were striving for power and nothing more.[55] Even when they mention the succession problem, it is criticized not because it allowed for hereditary monarchy but simply because it allowed evil principes to come to the throne. Cassius Dio, another senatorial writer, has been criticized for describing the atmosphere in his own time, the third century CE, and not that of Augustus. Some misrepresentation of the first emperor is inevitable, yet we still see the continuity of imperial policy and the constant reappearance of the same problems.[56]

10. The Sheer Difficulty of the Job

Stable rule under the Julio-Claudians would have required a monarchy that was well defined as a monarchy. It would have needed a clear succession policy, a professional internal security organization, and loyal supporters of the man on the throne. Unfortunately for the empire, Rome had none of these. What it had was a government transitioning from a republic to an autocracy, with too many people whose privileges were inherited from the old system. There was an internal security organization that was nowhere near as sophisticated as our modern counterparts are and no clear succession policy. And once people discovered its leadership could be suborned by promising money or power, there was nothing the rank and file could do but go along.

Historians describe the Augustan system as reliable, admired, and secure. Attitudes of honor, duty, and obedience added to force, authority, and patronage kept the empire going for hundreds of years.[57] But it had gotten off to a rocky start. Three of the first five rulers are murdered, and, if the rumors are to be believed, the other two were murdered also. In other words, most of the Julio-Claudians were murdered in a system that was designed to keep them safe. Yet it was no more salubrious to be Praetorian prefect. Out of the seventeen or so men who held the position under the Julio-Claudian emperors, six of them were executed or murdered on the job. Two were killed later on, and only two made it to the top equestrian post of the prefecture of Egypt. Two of them vied to become princeps—and both of them died in the attempt. This was probably the second most unsafe post after emperor.

One can see a progression through the coups. Julius Caesar's death was carried out by a widespread conspiracy and many senators. It was well planned and successful. Its aim was to restore the republic. As time went on, other conspiracies became more heterogeneous: temporary coalitions that united disaffected politicians, rebellious officers, and others with a grudge. In the case of Caligula, there was a group of senatorial opportunists closely linked to the regime who exploited the widespread hatred for him. They spouted republican slogans. The group behind Scribonianus that tried to overthrow Claudius showed how ineffectual republican ideology was. By the time the Pisonians came along to kill Nero, all republican slogans were gone. No one was trying to restore the *res publica vetus*. It was not until Galba's success in 68 that the *arcanum imperii*, the "secret of empire," was revealed—that emperors could be made not only in Rome but elsewhere.

BEING EMPEROR: IT'S A TOUGH JOB, BUT SOMEBODY HAS TO DO IT

All of Augustus's heirs inherited the same problem: how to be a civilian leader in a military monarchy. There was a dissonance between the survival of the perceived *res publica* and the realities of where power really lay. Emperors had to find different ways to deal with this dissonance. Ruling overtly created damaging opposition in the Senate. The emperor's monopolization of military campaigning, the chief source of new and rapid wealth in the republic, was gone. All the senators could do now was struggle to outdo each other in displays of wealth and imperial patronage.

Because the emperor's position was not explicitly spelled out constitutionally, the emperor had to work frantically to justify his existence to the Senate and the Roman people, the communities of Italy, and the provinces. Through public works, the passage of laws, statues and buildings, donatives and largesse, games and gladiatorial shows and wild beast hunts, religious rituals, and marriage and the adoption of heirs, they were in a frantic competition to stay on top and stay alive. Tiberius compared it to holding a wolf by the ears.[58] This was a tough job for anyone to do well, and some emperors fared better than others. Augustus seemed to love the sham of it all. Tiberius simply walked away from the job. Claudius worked desperately hard to keep the state from civil war but got little credit for his hard work. Caligula and Nero tried to refashion the emperor's role more radically and both paid with their lives.

To a great extent, emperors became prisoners—prisoners of their own entourage, prisoners of an old senatorial order that did not want to let go of power, and prisoners of the military. Arnaldo Momigliano saw ever so clearly how the republican past hindered the emergence of a new government with an explicit constitution.[59] The lack of a constitution made any transition dangerous, and thus, when an emperor was murdered, there was an immediate crisis. When a dynasty went extinct, as it did after Nero, it resulted in all-out civil war. A similar catastrophe was only narrowly avoided after the assassination of Domitian, the last of the Flavians.

The sheer difficulty of the role of princeps and its unresolved contradictions put a strain on all the emperors. Each acted differently, depending on age, intellect, interests, and character. None of the ancient sources rates emperors on the basis of institutions. The idea that their own system of government was flawed and could contribute to political disaster never seems to have occurred to them. They all wrote in terms of the emperor's character. They revered the republic and abhorred its fall, but they rarely discussed its instability.[60] They could blame its fall on Caesar or the greed and ambition of the Late Republic but not on the fact that the republic itself was not meeting the needs of the population or the provinces.

The great historian Michael Rostovtzeff, who is later quoted by an equally great historian, Arnaldo Momigliano, summed up the problem succinctly: "One of the most serious cares of Augustus and of the whole Julian line was the protection of the House against senatorial efforts at a restoration, or even the first suggestion of an attempt on the part of a usurper. This preoccupation, universal and inevitable in a family so weak in members and so insecurely established, explains the brooding atmosphere of conspiracy which never lifts from Tiberius to Nero; and it accounts for the mutual distrust that grew up within the family itself."[61]

The birth and development of the Roman Empire under the Julio-Claudians show the slow growth of a monarchical institution we have come to call the principate. The birth pangs were felt by the senators, who were watching their powers shrink, and an emperor, who was watching his power grow. The clash between the two resulted in bloodshed. Emperors had to protect themselves from those who wanted their position, acted on personal grudges, or got caught up in political movements aimed at regime change. The picture was never pretty. The emperor defended himself by means of a series of overlapping institutions set up by Augustus. None of them would seem efficient by our modern standards, and we might argue that, although numerous, they were not sufficient to do the job. There were too many tasks to accomplish and too many people to watch. Still, the empire continued. Perhaps that is the biggest mystery of all: that despite having the highest rate of attrition of any monarchy in the world, the Roman Empire survived another three centuries. It evolved, it struggled, it changed, but the desire for power is ultimately human, and the problem is that despotism will always breed dissent. Perhaps Daniel Mendelsohn was correct when he wrote, "When dealing with governance, individual responsibilities, enmities and friendships, except in scale, the machinations for power are about the same in a university as in the Roman Empire."[62]

Notes

PREFACE

1. F. Meijer, *Emperors Don't Die in Bed* (London: Routledge, 2001).

2. F. L. Ford, *Political Murder* (Cambridge, MA: HUP, 1985). For a more popular treatment, see R. G. Grant, *Assassinations: History's Most Shocking Moments of Murder, Betrayal and Madness* (Pleasantville, NY: Reader's Digest, 2004).

3. Walter Scheidel, in his talk "The Roman Emperor in the Wider World," given at the University of Cambridge, July 26, 2011, http://www.sms.cam.ac.uk/media/1174184.

4. F. Millar, *The Emperor in the Roman World* (Ithaca, NY: Cornell University Press, 1992), 59.

5. See the remarks of Werner Riess, "How Tyrants and Dynasts Die: The Semantics of Political Assassination in Fourth-Century Greece," in *Terror et Pavor: Violenza, intimidazione, clandestinità nel mondo antico*, ed. G. Urso (Pisa: ETS, 2006), 65, who writes, "Assassinations in the ancient world are under-researched."

6. E. Flaig, *Den Kaiser herausfordern: Die usurpation im römischen Reich* (Frankfurt: Campus Verlag, 1992); U. Vogel-Weidemann, "The Opposition under the Early Caesars: Some Remarks on Its Nature and Aims," *Acta Classica* 22 (1979): 91–107; F. Amarelli, *Trasmissione, rifiuto, usurpazione: Vicende del potere degli imperatori romani* (Naples: Jovene, 2008); K. Becker, "Studien zur Opposition gegen den römischen Prinzipat" (PhD diss., Tübingen, 1950); G. Boissier, *L'opposition sous les Césars* (Paris: Librairie Hachette, 1942); K. A. Raaflaub, "Grundzüge Ziele und Ideen der Opposition gegen die Kaiser im I. Jh. N. Chr.," in *Opposition et résistances a l'empire d'Auguste a Trajan*, ed. A. Giovannini and D. van Berchem (Geneva: Fondation Hardt, 1986), 1–63.

7. Vogel-Weidemann, "The Opposition under the Early Caesars," 93.

8. See V. Rudich, *Political Dissidence under Nero: The Price of Dissimulation* (London: Routledge, 1993); V. Rudich, *Dissidence and Literature under Nero: The Price of Rhetorization* (New York: Routledge, 1997).

9. N. J. E. Austin and B. Rankov, *Exploration: Military and Political Intelligence in the Roman World from the Second Punic War to the Battle of Adrianople* (New York: Routledge, 1995); R. M. Sheldon, *Intelligence Activities in Ancient Rome: Trust in the Gods, but Verify* (London: Frank Cass, 2005); F. S. Russell, "Finding the Enemy: Military Intelligence," in *Oxford Handbook on Warfare in the Classical World*, ed. J. B. Campbell and L. A. Tritle (Oxford: OUP, 2013), 474–92.

10. On policing, see C. J. Fuhrmann, *Policing the Roman Empire: Soldiers, Administration, and Public Order* (Oxford: OUP, 2012).

11. G. Boissier, "Les Délateurs," *Revue des Deux Mondes* 72 (1867): 305–40; Boissier, *L'opposition sous les Césars*, 160–217; G. Boissière, *L'accusation publique et les délateurs chez les Romains* (Niort, France: G. Clouzot, 1911); A. Dumeril, "Origine des Délateurs et Précis de leur histoire pendant la durée de l'empire romain," *Annales de la Faculté des Lettres de Bordeaux* 3 (1881): 262–81; T. Froment, "L'éloquence des délateurs," *Annales de la Faculté des Lettres de Bordeaux* 1 (1880): 35–57; J. Gaudemet, "La répression de la délation au bas-empire," in *Philias charin: Miscellanea di studi classici in onore di Eugenio Manni* (Rome: Bretschneider, 1980), 3:1065–83; A. Giovannini, "Pline et les délateurs de Domitien," in *Opposition et résistances à l'empire d'Auguste à Trajan*, 219–48; W. J. O'Neal, "Delation in the Early Empire," *CB* 55 (1978): 24–28; S. Rutledge, *Imperial Inquisitions: Prosecutors and Informants from Tiberius to Domitian* (New York: Routledge, 2001); J. S. A. Zijlstra, *De delatores te Rome tot aan Tiberius' regering* (Nijmegen, Netherlands: Berkhout, 1967); M. F. Petraccia, *Indices e Delatores nell'Antica Roma: Occultiore indicio Proditus; in Occulta Delatus Insidias* (Milan: LED Edizioni Universitarie, 2014).

12. S. Bingham, *The Praetorian Guard: A History of Rome's Elite Special Forces* (Waco, TX: Baylor University Press, 2013); see also H. Ceñal Martinez, "La Guardia Pretoriana: Composicíon, funciones e historia" (PhD diss., Universidad de Oviedo, 2009).

13. A good example would be Stephen Dando-Collins's book on the murder of Germanicus, *Blood of the Caesars* (Hoboken, NJ: Wiley, 2008). The detection of a conspiracy needs a more subtle hand, more evidence, and better use of the existing sources.

14. A. J. Woodman, *Rhetoric in Classical Historiography: Four Studies* (London: Croom Helm, 1988), ix–xiii, 197–212.

15. V. E. Pagán, *Conspiracy Narratives in Roman History* (Austin: University of Texas Press, 2004), 5.

16. Pagán, *Conspiracy Narratives*, 1–4.

17. Woodman, *Rhetoric in Classical Historiography*, ix–xiii, 197–212.

18. See the comments of J. Osgood, *Claudius Caesar: Image and Power in the Early Roman Empire* (Cambridge: CUP, 2011), 24. This has not stopped anyone from writing imperial biographies. See the series issued by publishers Routledge and Lancaster. I have listed these works separately at the beginning of each chapter of the appropriate emperor.

19. Pagán, *Conspiracy Narratives*; V. E. Pagán, *Conspiracy Theory in Latin Literature* (Austin: University of Texas Press, 2012); V. E. Pagán, "Toward a Model of

Conspiracy Theory for Ancient Rome," *New German Critique* 103 (2008): 27–49. On the study of conspiracy theory as a political and cultural phenomenon, see M. Fenster, *Conspiracy Theories: Secrecy and Power in American Culture* (Minneapolis: University of Minnesota Press, 2008), vii–19.

20. Pagán, "Toward a Model of Conspiracy Theory for Ancient Rome," 27–28, on marginalized groups and conspiracies in Roman literature. Just one example concerning women and scandal is A. Ferrill, "Augustus and His Daughter: A Modern Myth," in *Studies in Latin Literature*, ed. C. Deroux (Brussels: Latomus, 1980), 2:332–46.

21. On the attitude toward informers, see Rutledge, *Imperial Inquisitions*, passim.

22. Pagán, "Toward a Model of Conspiracy Theory for Ancient Rome," 30, 32–33.

23. M. Griffin, *Nero: The End of a Dynasty* (London: Routledge, 1984), 9.

24. Fuhrmann, *Policing the Roman Empire*, 247.

INTRODUCTION

1. R. Syme, *Tacitus* (London: OUP, 1958), 403.

2. M. Griffin, *Nero* (London: Routledge, 1984), 193.

3. On this instability, see especially I. Cogitore, *La légitimité dynastique d'Auguste à Néron à l'épreuve des conspirations* (Rome: École Française de Rome, 2002), 1–4.

4. On Nero, see chapter 7; on Commodus, see Dio 71–73; Herodian 1–2; *SHA*, Marcus Antonius Commodus; A. Birley, *Marcus Aurelius*, 2nd ed. (London: B. T. Batsford, 1993), 224–25.

5. Syme, *Tacitus*, 403.

6. Syme, *Tacitus*, 404.

7. Suet., *Dom.* 21.1: *Condicionem principum miserrimam aiebat, quibus de coniuratione comperta non crederetur nisi occisis.* A modern example of a skeptic would be J. A. Crook, "The Last Age of the Roman Republic," *CAH²*, 9: 70–112, who rejects virtually every conspiracy against Augustus and Tiberius.

8. J. Carcopino, *Passion et politique chez les Césars* (Paris: Hachette, 1958); V. Gardthausen, *Augustus und seine Zeit* (Leipzig: Teubner, 1904), vol. 3, on Julia, 1093–94. See the comments of E. Fantham, *Julia Augusti* (London: Routledge, 2006), xi. On the stereotype of the evil woman in Roman authors, see M. R. McHugh, "Manipulating Memory: Remembering and Defaming Julio-Claudian Women" (PhD diss., University of Wisconsin, Madison, 2004), chapters 2–4.

9. On the reasons behind the accusations of sexual impropriety against aristocratic women, see C. Edwards, *The Politics of Immorality in Ancient Rome* (Cambridge: CUP, 1993), 42–62; McHugh, "Manipulating Memory," chapters 2–4.

10. V. Rudich, *Political Dissidence under Nero* (London: Routledge, 1993), xxvii.

11. Maternus's words in Tacitus, *Dial.* 13: *Quod adligati omni adulatione nec imperantibus umquam satis servi videntur nec nobis satis liberi?* And see Rudich, *Political Dissidence under Nero*, xxvi.

12. Epictetus 4.1.48. Epictetus was a slave of Nero's freedman secretary, Epaphroditus.

13. Rudich, *Political Dissidence under Nero*, xxvii.

14. J. V. P. D. Balsdon, "The Principates of Tiberius and Gaius," *ANRW* 2, no. 2 (1975): 91.

15. Rudich, *Political Dissidence under Nero*, xxviii.

CHAPTER 1: THE REPUBLIC

1. See R. Alston, *Rome's Revolution* (Oxford: OUP, 2015), vii, on the transition from republic to empire. Alston calls the violence "cataclysmic" and writes about how we have lost sight of the violence of Rome's revolution (viii). See also J. W. Heaton, *Mob Violence in the Late Roman Republic 133–49 B.C.* (Urbana: University of Illinois Press, 1939).

2. For a discussion of Rome's regal period and its historicity, See M. Beard, *SPQR* (New York: W. W. Norton, 2015), 91–130. On the possibility of a connection between the violence of early Rome and the Late Republic, see A. W. Lintott, "The Tradition of Violence in the Annals of the Early Roman Republic," *Historia* 19, no. 1 (Jan. 1970): 12–29; T. P. Wiseman, *Remembering the Roman People: Essays on Late Republican Politics and Literature* (Oxford: OUP, 2009), 177–78, on the ethics of murder.

3. Wiseman, *Remembering the Roman People*, 178: "One oath that was kept for 360 years guaranteed the sacrosanct status of the tribunes and aediles of the plebs"; Livy 3.55.10 and note by B. O. Foster (p. 184); cf. 2.33.1; Dion. Hal. 6.89.3–4. On how the Romans established legitimacy, see H. Mouritsen, *Politics in the Roman Republic* (Cambridge: CUP, 2017), 3.

4. The Romans founded a temple to *Fides Publica* on the Capitol in 257 BCE. On the importance of the concept, see Wiseman, *Remembering the Roman People*, 178.

5. Ford, *Political Murder*, 49. On their restraint by custom rather than law, see Mouritsen, *Politics in the Roman Republic*, 1–5.

6. Alston, *Rome's Revolution*, ix; Beard, *SPQR*, 468–69.

7. Val. Max. 3.7.3; See Livy 2.23.14, for example, on the majesty of the consuls keeping an angry crowd in check. On Rome's idealized past, see T. J. Cornell, *The Beginnings of Rome* (London: Routledge, 1995), 1–30. B. Kelly, "Riot Control and Imperial Ideology in the Roman Empire," *Phoenix* 61, nos. 1–2 (Spring/Summer 2007):162, shows that a person of great moral standing quelling an angry mob single-handedly became somewhat of a *topos* in Roman literature. Cf. Vergil, *Aeneid*, trans. Sarah Ruden (New Haven, CT: YUP, 2008), 1.148–53; *Perseus* 4.6–8. On the idealization of earlier times in Livy, see Mouritsen, *Politics in the Roman Republic*, 108–11.

8. Harmodius and Aristogeiton were the tyrannicides celebrated by the Greeks for having killed the Peisistratid tyrant, Hipparchus, and were the preeminent symbol of democracy to ancient Athenians.

9. W. Nippel, *Public Order in Ancient Rome* (Cambridge: CUP, 1995), 4.

10. M. I. Finley, *Politics in the Ancient World* (Cambridge: CUP, 1983), 18; Nippel, *Public Order in Ancient Rome*, 4. Mouritsen, *Politics in the Roman Republic*, 167–68, on the *senatus consultum ultimum*.

11. The distinction between the military and civil capacities of the magistrates precluded any recourse to conscripts within the city, subject to military discipline by virtue of their oaths. See Dion. Hal. 11.43.2. Cf. Livy 7.16.8; Nippel, *Public Order in Ancient Rome*, 4.

12. W. Nippel, "Policing Rome," *JRS* 74 (1984): 20–29; W. Nippel, *Aufruhr und "Polizei" in der römischen Republik* (Stuttgart: Klett-Cotta, 1988), 7–9; Nippel, *Public Order in Ancient Rome*, 1; A. Riggsby, *Crime and Community in Ciceronian Rome* (Austin: University of Texas Press, 1999), 170–71; T. W. Africa, "Urban Violence in Imperil Rome," *Journal of Interdisciplinary History* 2, no. 1 (Summer, 1971): 7–8.

13. On the *nocturne*, A. Lintott, *Violence in Republican Rome* (Oxford: Clarendon Press, 1968), 104, following T. Mommsen, *Staatsr.* II, 1, 594n3, who uses the word *Sicherheitsdienst* and concurs with the idea of nocturnal policing. Nippel, "Policing Rome," 21, finds the evidence meager and uncertain. Alternatively, E. Gruen in his review of Nippel's *Public Order in Ancient Rome* (*Gnomon* 70, no. 6 [1998]: 566) says, "Nothing suggests that the *tresviri capitales* exercised summary judgments against lower class criminals." Cf. O. F. Robinson, "The Forces of Law and Order," in *Ancient Rome: City Planning and Administration* (London: Routledge, 1992), 173–80; Nippel, *Public Order in Ancient Rome*, 22–26; C. Fuhrmann, *Policing the Roman Empire*, 93–94. On the jail, the *carcer Tullianum* (the name Mamertine is postclassical), see Sallust, *Bell. Cat.* 55.3–4; L. Richardson Jr., *A New Topographical Dictionary* (Baltimore: Johns Hopkins University Press, 1992), 71; "Tullianum," *OCD*, 1558.

14. A Late Republican restriction on the number of followers (*sectatores*) who could attend a candidate for public office reflects a concern to limit the possibility of violent clashes. Cicero, *pro Murena* 71, on the *Lex Fabia* that regulated the number of escorts; T. E. Kinsey, "Cicero *pro Murena* 71," *RBPhil* 43 (1965): 57–59; Nippel, *Public Order in Ancient Rome*, 36.

15. Nippel, *Public Order in Ancient Rome*, 5–12; Nippel, "Policing Rome," 22. Gruen notes in his review of Nippel, however, that *coercitio* was more regularly employed against members of the ruling class than against disruptive commoners (566).

16. Only magistrates with *imperium* could issue orders to a citizen, summon a citizen, or have a citizen arrested without the magistrate being present in person. See Aul. Gell., *NA* 13.12.6, quoting book 21 of Varro's *Antiquitates Rerum Humanarum* [*Human Antiquities*]; Nippel, *Public Order in Ancient Rome*, 5.

17. For a discussion of *provocatio*, see J. Martin, "Die Provokation in der klassischen und späten Republik," *Hermes* 98 (1970): 72–96; A. W. Lintott, "Provocatio: From the Struggle of the Orders to the Principate," *ANRW* 1, no. 2 (1974): 226–67; Nippel, *Public Order in Ancient Rome*, 6.

18. Silius Italicus, *Punica* 8.483–84, who says they came from Vetulonia and held the twelve axes with their "silent menace" (*tacito terrore*); Livy 1.8.2; B. Gladigow, "Die sakralen Funktionen der Liktoren: Zum Problem von Institutioneller Macht und sakraler Praesentation," *ANRW* 1, no. 2 (1972): 295–314; A. J. Marshall, "Symbols and Showmanship in Roman Public Life: The Fasces," *Phoenix* 38 (1984): 120–41; R. Drews, "Light from Anatolia on the Roman Fasces," *AJPh* 93 (1972): 40–51; T. Shaefer, *Imperii Insignia: Sella curulis und Fasces. Zur Repraesentation römischer Magistrate* (Mainz: P. von Zaben, 1989); Nippel, *Public Order in Ancient Rome*, 13; Gladigow, "Die sakralen Funktionen der Liktoren," 295–314.

19. On terror abroad, Cicero, *de Lege Agr.* 1.9; on the axe blade removed when in the city, Cicero, *de Rep.* 2.55. And see H. Beck et al., *Consuls and Res Publica: Holding High Office in the Roman Republic* (Cambridge: CUP, 2011), 169.

20. Nippel, "Policing Rome," 22. A praetor being accompanied to the threshold of a brothel was warned that this would violate the dignity of his office. Also see Seneca, *Contr.* 9.2.17; Livy 31.29.9, on "rods threatening their backs"; Dion. Hal. 3.61.2–62, on their being symbols of the absolute power of a king. And see Beck et al., *Consuls and Res Publica*, 169.

21. Polybius 3.87.7.

22. See Val. Max. 2.2.4; Beck et al., *Consuls and Res Publica*, 170.

23. Nippel, *Public Order in Ancient Rome*, 14, quoting Mommsen, *Staatsr.* 1.376.

24. Nippel, *Public Order in Ancient Rome*, 13.

25. Livy 2.23.15, 2.27.12; Plut., *Publicola* 7.3; Nippel, "Policing Rome," 23; Livy 4.50.2 has a lictor sent to arrest a brawling soldier.

26. Livy 2.27.12 has lictors dragging a man away. In his account of the Volero Publilius conflict (2.55.3) in 473 BCE, he writes that it was "every man's own imagination that made them [the lictors] great and awe-inspiring." Shortly thereafter, however, the crowd stormed the lictors and broke their rods, 2.55.9.

27. Livy 2.55.9, 3.49.4; Dio Cassius 38.6.3; Asconius Pedianus 58.14–24; Florus 1.22.2. On the breaking of the rods as a "highly symbolic act" see Karl-Joachim Hölkeskamp, "The Roman Republic as Theatre of Power: The Consuls as Leading Actors," in Beck et al, *Consuls and Res Publica*, 169.

28. See Val. Max. 9.5.2 where a tribune of the plebs, M. Drusus, throttles a consul; Nippel, *Public Order in Ancient Rome*, 9–12, on the tribunate not used as bodyguards; see Nippel, "Policing Rome," 23.

29. The four occupational grades were *scribae* (scribes), *lictores* (lictors), *viatores* (messengers), and *praecones* (heralds). See W. Smith, W. Wayte, and G. Marindin's *Dictionary of Greek and Roman Antiquities* (London: J. Murray, 1914), under the appropriate headings. On the emperor's entourage during the Imperial period, see Millar, *Emperor in the Roman World*, 59.

30. Millar, *Emperor in the Roman World*, 59–61.

31. N. W. de Witt, "Litigation in the Forum in Cicero's Time," *CP* 21 (1926): 218–24; F. Millar, "Political Power in Mid-Republican Rome: *Curia* or *Comitium*?" *JRS* 79 (1989): 138–50; J. R. Patterson, "The City of Rome from Republic to Empire," *JRS* 82 (1992): 190–94; Nippel, *Public Order in Ancient Rome*, 15.

32. There is a disagreement between Nippel, who assumed the Roman machinery of government was adequate for the city to suppress criminality, and Kunkel, who believed that as the city grew, the increasing number of slaves and the urban proletariat caused order to degenerate and people to begin hiring their own retainers. See Nippel, *Public Order in Ancient Rome*, 24, and W. Kunkel, *Untersuchungen zur Entwicklung des römischen Kriminalverfahrens in vorsullanischer Zeit* (Munich: Beck, 1962), 71–79.

33. This pattern of suspicious associations extended to *collegia* suspected of organizing citizens beyond the authorities' reach, and the suppression of foreign and private cults. Nippel, *Public Order in Ancient Rome*, 29–30, 72–73, 82.

34. For the Twelve Tables ban, see VIII. 26 in M. H. Crawford, *Roman Statutes* (London: Institute for Classical Studies, 1996), vol. 2 with comments at 694–95;

P. O'Neill, "Going Round in Circles: Popular Speech in Ancient Rome," *ClAnt* 22 (2003), 135–63; Nippel, *Public Order in Ancient Rome*, 27–30; Nippel, "Policing Rome," 24.

35. See Livy 2.3.7: the Tarquins; 4.13.10: Spurius Maelius; 6.20.4: Manlius Capitolinus; and T. P. Wiseman, *The Myths of Rome* (Exeter: University of Exeter Press, 2004), 183. According to Beard, *SPQR*, 43, Livy's story of a nobleman leading a doomed revolution may be largely a projection of Catiline back into early Roman history.

36. For an assessment of the sources on early Rome, see Cornell, *Beginnings of Rome*, 1–30.

37. See Sallust, *Bell. Cat.*, passim, and the comments of Beard, *SPQR*, 27–36.

38. On paying informants, see Livy 39.19.4 on the crisis of 186 BCE.

39. On paying informants: Livy 32.26.14 (crisis of 198) and 39.19.4 (crisis of 186) mentions sums of 100,000 *asses* for a freedman. Such a sum would elevate the informer to membership in the first census class as compensation for the loss of a patron that might ensue from the informer's denunciation. See also J.-M. David, "La faute et l'abandon: Théories et pratiques judicaires à Rome à la fin de la république," in *L'Aveu: Antiquité et Moyen Age* (Rome: L'École Française de Rome, 1986), 71–87.

40. On state compensation: Livy 32.26.14.

41. On slaves not giving testimony: Cicero, *pro Reg. Dei.* 3. On this demonstrating how seriously alleged conspiracies were taken, see D. Liebs, "Der Schutz der Privatsfäre[sic] in einer Sklavenhaltergesellschaft: Aussagen von Sklaven gegen ihre Herren nach römischen Recht," *BIDR* 83 (1980): 147–89; L. Schumacher, *Servus Index: Sklavenverhör und Sklavenanzeige im republikanischen und kaiserzeitlichen Rom* (Wiesbaden: Steiner, 1982), 39–68; Nippel, *Public Order in Ancient Rome*, 28, who points out a similar practice among the Athenians for extreme cases like the profanation of the Mysteries and the mutilation of the Herms, which were treated like a great conspiracy in 415 BCE. See Thuc., 6.27.2; Andoc., On the Mysteries 1.11.

42. A. Watson, "Enuptio Gentis," in *Daube Noster* (Edinburgh: Scottish Academic Press, 1974), 331–41; Nippel, *Public Order in Ancient Rome*, 28.

43. The magistrates would confront further suspects with the evidence given by the informers; this often produced more confessions. See Livy 26.27.8–10, where the informing slave is awarded his freedom and 20,000 *asses*. See Cicero, *Att.* 2.24.3, on Vettius, his "famous informer." On the Vettius affair, see W. Allen Jr., "The Vettius Affair Once More," *TAPA* 81 (1950): 153–63; W. C. McDermott, "Vettius Ille, Ille Noster Index," *TAPA* 80 (1949): 351–67; L. R. Taylor, "The Date and Meaning of the Vettius Affair," *Historia* (1950): 45–51.

44. Nippel, *Public Order in Ancient Rome*, 30.

45. J. E. Allison and J. D. Cloud, "The Lex Julia Maiestatis," *Latomus* 21 (1962): 711–31, who have established that the vital innovations in widening the field of liability to prosecution for *maiestas* were made administratively by Augustus. On its role in politically charged prosecutions, see S. H. Rutledge, *Imperial Inquisitions*, 87–88.

46. Justinian, *Digest* 48.4.11 (Ulpian); "Perduellio," *OCD*, 1138.

47. Allison and Cloud, "Lex Julia Maiestatis," 711–31, contra B. Levick, "Poena Legis Maiestatis," *Historia* 28, no. 3 (1979): 358–79, who argues that Augustus never passed such a law.

48. Appian, *BC* 1.2.4–5; cf. 1.17; translation by Wiseman, *Remembering the Roman People*, 178.

49. Augustus was empowered by the Senate with an SCU early in his career (January 43 BCE). On the SCU see Lintott, *Violence in Republican Rome*, 149–74; Nippel, *Public Order in Ancient Rome*, 59, 63, 66, 68, 79–80. Lintott argues that political violence was already "a recognized political weapon" in 133 BCE (175); Wiseman, *Remembering the Roman People*, 187, disagrees.

50. Beard, *SPQR*, 216.

51. Nippel, *Public Order in Ancient Rome*, 47–60, on riot control. Also see Mouritsen, *Politics in the Roman Republic*, 167–70.

52. Beard, *SPQR*, 216.

53. Beard, *SPQR*, 217, 243–44, where she wisely notes that the violence was far more widespread than could possibly be attributed to one man.

54. Plut., *Caesar* 28.

55. Val. Max. 3.7.3. According to Cicero, *de Leg.* 3.42–43, a magistrate who could not control a turbulent meeting was obliged to dissolve it or be held responsible for the consequences, as the Senate had ruled in 92.

56. Vergil, *Aeneid* 1.148–53: "As often in a crowded gathering/Crude commoners in rage begin to riot/Torches and stones fly, frenzy finds its weapons—/But if they see a stern and blameless statesman/They all fall silent, keen for him to speak/Then he will tame their hearts and guide their passions." On the bodyguards, see C. Meier, "Review of F. E. Adcock, *Roman Political Ideas*," *GGA* 216 (1964): 44–48.

57. Nippel, *Public Order in Ancient Rome*, 51.

58. As did Cicero in 63 during the Catilinarian conspiracy. Cicero, *Cat.* 1.11, 3.5; Sallust, *Bell. Cat.* 26.4; Nippel, *Public Order in Ancient Rome*, 51.

59. Nippel, *Public Order in Ancient Rome*, 53. Cf. C. Meier, *Res Publica Amissa: Eine Studie zu Verfassung und Geschichte der späten römischen Republik* (Wiesbaden: Steiner, 1966), 157.

60. The *Lex Lutatia de Vi* of 78 and a *Lex Plautia* that passed before 63; Nippel, *Public Order in Ancient Rome*, 54. On the relationship between the two laws see Lintott, *Violence in Republican Rome*, 107–24, and R. A. Bauman, "Il 'sovversivismo' di Emilio Lepido," *Labeo* 24 (1978): 60–74.

61. Cicero, *pro Caelio* 1, on "seditious and wicked citizens [who] have made armed onslaught against the Senate [and] have laid violent hands on magistrates and have attacked the State," in *The Speeches of Cicero*, trans. R. Gardner (Cambridge, MA: HUP, 1965); Nippel, *Public Order in Ancient Rome*, 55.

62. Cicero, *de Har. Resp.* 15, on violence to public places; and 16, on violence to ambassadors.

63. Nippel, *Public Order in Ancient Rome*, 55, believed this clause was part of the Sullan law on murderers and poisoners—the *Lex Cornelia de sicariis et veneficis*—which he believed dated to pre-Sullan times. See Plautus, *Aulularia* 415–17, on carrying a knife and being reported to the police; See also Kunkel, *Untersuchungen zur Entwicklung des römischen Kriminalverfahrens*, 64–70; J. D. Cloud, "The

Primary Purpose of the Lex Cornelia de Sicariis," *ZRG* 86 (1969): 258–86; J. D. Cloud, "The Constitution and Public Criminal Law," in *CAH²*, ed. J. A. Crook, A. Lintott, and E. Rawson, 9:522–23; D. Nörr, *Causa Mortis: Auf den Spuren einer Redewendung* (Munich: Münchener Beiträge zur Papyrusforschung und antiken Rechtgeschichte, 1986), 86–115; J. L. Ferrary, "Lex Cornelia de Sicariis et Veneficiis," *Athenaeum* 69 (1991): 417–34.

64. On the carrying of weapons, Asc. Ped. 55, 12–13; Pliny *HN* 34.139; Dio 42.29.2, 44.51.1. The assembling of weapons within the city was banned by a law of Caesar (or possibly Augustus), the *Lex Iulia de Vi Publica*. This also included country houses but not hunting lodges. Cf. *Dig.* 48.6.1; cf. Dion. Hal. 4.48.1.

65. M. C. Alexander, *Trials in the Late Roman Republic 149 B.C. to 50 BCE* (Toronto: University of Toronto Press, 1990); Nippel, *Public Order in Ancient Rome*, 55.

66. Nippel, *Public Order in Ancient Rome*, 56, points out that we know very little of Late Republican trials except as they affect the elite, and most of the descriptions involve political maneuvering, not discussions of the points of law and procedure.

67. The SCU was a senatorial decree that authorized the consuls to employ any means necessary to solve a domestic crisis. The *optimates* did this because they were in need of a new emergency power that would not fall under the public rights of *provocatio* or *intercessio* or *veto*. On its unconstitutionality, see C. Kefeng, "A Perspective of the *Senatus Consultum Ultimum* in the Late Roman Republic from the Constitutional Point of View," *Journal of Ancient Civilizations* 19 (2004): 125–32.

68. On popular acts of justice, see Nippel, *Public Order in Ancient Rome*, 56–57. On the *populus* claimed as the basis of Roman society, see Mouritsen, *Politics in the Roman Republic*, 14–21 and passim.

69. On the violence surrounding the Gracchan crisis, see Nippel, *Public Order in Ancient Rome*, 57–65; Heaton, *Mob Violence in the Late Roman Republic*, 21–33.

70. Diod. 34/35.33.6–7; Nippel, *Public Order in Ancient Rome*, 62.

71. These developments are especially associated with the role played by P. Clodius Pulcher. On Clodius profiting from the deadlocks in the power struggle between Crassus, Pompey, and Caesar, see Nippel, *Public Order in Ancient Rome*, 70–75.

72. Lintott, *Violence in Republican Rome*, 173–74, 203, 208.

73. Nippel, *Public Order in Ancient Rome*, 83.

74. Appian, *BC* 3.3.6; Nippel, *Public Order in Ancient Rome*, 84.

75. Cicero, *Att.* 14.15.2 calls throwing people from the Tarpeian Rock and crucifixion "heroic deed"; Cicero, *Phil.* 1.5 on the destruction of private property and 1.12.30 on the punishment of "ringleaders"; and Nippel, *Public Order in Ancient Rome*, 84.

76. Appian, *BC* 5.18, 5.34; Nippel, *Public Order in Ancient Rome*, 84.

77. Appian, *BC* 4.12; Nippel, *Public Order in Ancient Rome*, 84.

78. Beard, *SPQR*, 15. The longest connected narrative of the event in a historical work is Appian's *Civil Wars*.

79. We know only twenty of the conspirators by name. On their numbers see B. Strauss, *The Death of Caesar* (New York: Simon & Schuster, 2015), 137–38.

80. Beard, *SPQR*, 94. On tyranny as a figure in Greek politics and in the Roman Republic, see Wiseman, *Remembering the Roman People*, 184–85, 189–191.

81. Suet., *Div. Jul.* 80.

82. Cicero, *Att.* 1.14; Ovid, *Fasti*, 5.634; Suet., *Div. Jul.* 80.4.

83. On the Tiber Island were troops under the command of Lepidus, a Caesar loyalist. He was with his legion on the morning of the Ides. Dio 44.19.2; Zon. 10.12; Strauss, *Death of Caesar*, 118.

84. Plut., *Caesar* 63.7–8; Appian, *BC* 2.118; Suet., *Div. Jul.* 87; he supposedly said this the night before his assassination, March 14, at a dinner with Lepidus. See C. Meier, *Caesar: A Biography* (New York: Basic Books, 1982), 485; Strauss, *Death of Caesar*, 106.

85. Listed in Plut., *Caesar* 63.

86. Dio 44.18.1. On Calpurnia's dreams, Plut., *Caesar* 63.8–9; Appian, *BC* 2.115.

87. Or so argues Strauss, *Death of Caesar*, 121.

88. Caesar as easily persuaded, Nic. of Dam. 23, 24; the passive Caesar, Plut., *Caesar* 64.6; the Caesar who cares about appearances, Appian, *BC* 2.116; Caesar the arrogant: Suet., *Div. Jul.* 81.4 and Dio 44.18.4; Caesar the risk taker, Appian, *BC* 2.115 and Strauss, *Death of Caesar*, 122–23.

89. There are different versions of what happened. Nic. of Dam. 24 says the soothsayers saw a curse in the victims. Caesar got angry and faced west—another bad omen since the west symbolized sunset and death. The other sources just leave out Decimus and simply speak of Caesar's hubris. Appian, *BC* 2.116 says Caesar reminded the soothsayer of another bad omen that had been predicted during his campaign in Spain, and yet he went on to crush Pompey's armies.

90. Nic. of Dam. 23.

91. Plut., *Caesar* 63.6.

92. Nic. of Dam. 23 says Decimus's gladiators were "at hand." Cf. Appian, *BC* 2.118; Dio 44.16. Also see Strauss, *Death of Caesar*, 116.

93. Gaius Trebonius, in Plut., *Brutus* 17.1; Appian, *BC* 2.17; Cicero, *ad. Fam.* 10.28. Plut., *Caesar* 66.4, identifies the friend as Brutus Albinus, but in *Antony* 13.2 he says only that "some" detained Antony. See also Dio 44.19.1–3; Cicero, *Phil.* 2.34; Strauss, *Death of Caesar*, 287n129.

94. This is one version of the story, Plut., *Caesar* 65. The other, Appian, *BC* 2.116, says that Artemidorus could not get close enough to Caesar to hand him the scroll. Suet., *Div. Jul.* 81.4, says he was handed the scroll but it was one of many he held in his left hand—an ill-omened hand for Romans (thus the word *sinister*, from the Latin for "left"); Dio 44.18.3.

95. Sheldon, *Intelligence Activities in Ancient Rome*, 5.

96. For a discussion of the sources, their dates, and reliability, see Wiseman, *Remembering the Roman People*, 214–15.

97. Nic. of Dam. 24; Plut., *Caesar* 66.5; Wiseman, *Remembering the Roman People*, 211.

98. The pulling down of the toga as a signal for attack: Plut., *Caesar* 66.4 and *Brutus* 17.4; Dio 44.19.4; Appian, *BC* 2.117; Suet., *Div. Jul.* 82.1; Wiseman, *Remembering the Roman People*, 212.

99. Suet., *Div. Jul.* 82.1, is the only one to record the phrase. Wiseman, *Remembering the Roman People*, 212, suggests the description might be a conflation of Casca's blow with that of his brother.

100. Plut., *Caesar* 66.7, on wounding Caesar in the neck near the shoulder. Appian *BC* 2.117 has him miss the neck and hit Caesar in the chest. Also see Wiseman, *Remembering the Roman People*, 212; Pagán, *Conspiracy Narratives*, 119.

101. Dio 44.19.5.

102. Nic. of Dam. 24.

103. Caesar caught the handle: Plut., *Caesar* 66.7 and *Brutus* 17.5.

104. Appian, *BC* 2.117 has Caesar respond to the attack with anger and shouting. Plut., *Caesar* 66.8, has him cry out, "Impious Casca! What are you doing?" Suet., *Div. Jul.* 82.2, claims that Caesar merely groaned without uttering a word in the attack. Dio 44.19.5 says that Caesar was unable to say anything.

105. Suet., *Div. Jul.* 82.3 and Dio 44.19.5; Strauss, *Death of Caesar*, 136. See also D. E. Gershenson, "Caesar's Last Words," *Shakespeare Quarterly* 43, no. 2 (Summer 1992): 218–19.

106. In Nic. of Dam. 24, Minucius Basilus missed Caesar and struck Rubrius in the thigh. Then Cassius tried for a second blow but struck Brutus's hand instead. Plut., *Caesar* 66.11, says Brutus stabbed him in the groin—perhaps all too appropriate from Caesar's alleged love child.

107. The sources all have different opinions on when this happened. Suet., *Div. Jul.* 82.2, states and Dio 44.19.5 implies that he made the gesture as soon as he realized that he was being attacked on all sides. Whether he did it for protection, modesty, or resignation is debated. Val. Max., 4.5.6 favors modesty. Plut., *Caesar* 66.12 and *Brutus* 17.6, has him cover himself only when he sees Brutus approach him with a dagger. Appian, *BC* 2.117 has Caesar do it after he is struck by Brutus.

108. Suet., *Div. Jul.* 82.2. This autopsy report is the earliest known postmortem report in history. It describes Caesar's death as mostly attributable to blood loss from his stab wounds. Cf. Plut., *Caesar* 66.14.

109. Suet., *Div. Jul.* 82.3; Plut., *Caesar* 67.1. Cicero was among them. He was delighted by Caesar's murder. See Cicero, *Att.* 14.9.2, 12.1, 13.2, 14.4, 22.2.

110. Plut., *Caesar* 64.1; Suet., *Div. Jul.* 83.2.

111. Suet., *Div. Jul.* 89.1.

112. Finley, *Politics in the Ancient World*, chapters 2, 6 passim; Nippel, "Policing Rome," 23; Mouritsen, *Politics in the Roman Republic*, 166.

113. Nippel, "Policing Rome," 26. On the monumentalization of public spaces, see Mouritsen, *Politics in the Roman Republic*, 98.

114. See n67 on the SCU.

115. Nippel, "Policing Rome," 29; Mouritsen, *Politics in the Roman Republic*, 168, describes a "ruling elite that appears to lose its collective sense of purpose and instinct for survival."

116. See W. O. Moeller's review of Lintott in *CW* 63, no. 1 (Sept. 1969): 24, on the police, contra S. I. Oost's review, *CP* 65, no. 4 (Oct. 1970): 280. And see E. S. Gruen's review *AJPh* 91, no. 3 (July 1970): 367–70; A. N. Sherwin-White's review *JRS* 59, nos. 1–2 (1969): 286–87.

117. Noted by A. H. McDonald in his review of Lintott in *CR* 23, no. 2 (December 1973): 239–41.

CHAPTER 2: THE AUGUSTAN SYSTEM

1. Although scholars frequently use the terms "Augustan model" or "Augustan system," they have been warned against using this "overly reified concept as a normative construct," and should remember the role of improvisation in the creation of what we call the principate. See A. G. G. Gibson, ed., *The Julio-Claudian Succession: Reality and Perception of the "Augustan Model* (Leiden: Brill, 2013). A thorough discussion of Augustus and the "system" he created is almost impossible in one volume, but D. Kienast, *Augustus: Prinzeps und Monarch*, 4th ed. (Darmstadt: Primus, 2009) with its monumental references is a good start. For other studies of Augustus and his age, see A. Goldsworthy, *Augustus* (New Haven, CT: YUP, 2014); P. Southern, *Augustus*, 2nd ed. (London: Routledge, 2013); K. Galinsky, *Augustus: Introduction to the Life of an Emperor* (Cambridge: CUP, 2012); K. Galinsky, ed., *Cambridge Companion to the Age of Augustus* (Cambridge: CUP, 2005); W. Eck, *The Age of Augustus*, 2nd ed. (Malden, MA: Blackwell, 2007); J. Edmondson, ed. *Augustus* (Edinburgh: Edinburgh University Press, 2009); K. A. Raaflaub and M. Toher, *Between Republic and Empire: Interpretations of Augustus and His Principate* (Berkeley: University of California Press, 1990); F. Millar and C. Segal, eds., *Caesar Augustus: Seven Aspects* (Oxford: Clarendon Press, 1984); on the Augustan template, Beard, *SPQR*. See F. Millar, "Triumvirate and Principate," in Edmondson, ed., *Augustus*, 89, on all the steps "towards, not away from monarchy; and no good evidence suggests that anybody at the time claimed, or supposed otherwise."

2. See Suet., *Div. Jul.* 77. On Augustus's creation of a new order based on a new mythology, see A. Wallace-Hadrill, *Augustan Rome* (London: Bristol Classical Press, 2007), 1–9 and 13 on Dio hating the lies in which "autocratic power wraps itself."

3. On the new administrative apparatus and nomenclature, see F. Millar, "The First Revolution: Imperator Caesar, 36–28 BC," in *La Révolution Romaine après Ronald Syme*, ed. A. Giovannini (Vandoeuvres-Genève: Fondation Hardt, 1999), 1–63. Also see Edmondson, *Augustus*, 2 on the coexistence of monarchy and the traditional Republican magistracies; T. E. J. Wiedemann, "Tiberius to Nero," *CAH²*, 10:198; Galinsky, *Augustus*, 63.

4. E. Gruen, "Augustus and the Making of the Principate," in Galinsky, ed., *The Cambridge Companion to the Age of Augustus*, 38. Gruen, unlike Syme, believes we should avoid seeing any overt signs of planning for a biological successor. More recently, see J. Osgood, "Suetonius and the Succession to Augustus," in Gibson, *Julio-Claudian Succession*, 19–40, who comes closer to Syme.

5. R. Syme believed the principate "baffled definition": *The Roman Revolution* (Oxford: Clarendon Press, 1939), 152. He considered Rome's written constitution to be no constitution at all, at least according to the canons of Greek political thought. Fergus Millar disagreed, in "The Political Character of the Classical Roman Republic," *JRS* 74 (1984): 1–19. For a discussion of the debate on Rome's constitution and a full bibliography, see Karl-Joachim Hölkeskamp, *Reconstructing the Roman Republic* (Princeton, NJ: PUP, 2010) and H. Mouritsen, *Politics in the Roman Republic* (Cambridge: CUP, 2017); Crook, "Last Age of the Roman Republic," 9:70, warned against viewing its institutions as "too much the product of deliberation

and the drawing-board." He finds the term "constitutional" (page 87) too schematic a description. German scholarship has tended toward legal, institutional, and administrative studies that tended to legitimize the Augustan regime. The exception is M. H. Dettenhofer, who sees Augustus as the ultimate Machiavellian prince, in *Herrschaft und Widerstand in augusteischen Principat: Die Konkurrenz zwischen res publica und domus Augustus* (Stuttgart: Steiner, 2000).

6. On the enigma, see B. Levick, *Augustus: Image and Substance* (London: Routledge, 2010), 8–9. For a selection of other opinions, see the essays in Edmondson, *Augustus*. For the works left out, see review of Edmondson by A. Dalla Rosa, *BMCR* 2011.06.60; E. Gabba, "The Historians and Augustus," in Millar and Segal, eds., *Caesar Augustus*, 61–88. Other noteworthy contributions include G. Rowe, "Reconsidering the *Auctoritas* of Augustus," *JRS* 103 (2013): 1–15; K. Galinsky, "Making Haste Slowly: New Books on the Augustan Age," *CJ* 93, no. 1 (1997): 93–99; J. Bleichen, *Augustus: The Biography* (London: Allen Lane, 2015), who spends 750 pages trying to turn back the hands of the clock to Mommsen.

7. Suet., *Div. Aug.* 28.2.

8. See P. A. Brunt, "The Role of the Senate in the Augustan Regime," *CQ* 34, no. 2 (1984): 423–44; Crook, "Last Age of the Roman Republic," 9:73. On what constituted the traditional republican state, see Mouritsen, *Politics in the Roman Republic*, 6–31.

9. R. Alston, *Aspects of Roman History, AD 14–117* (New York: Routledge, 1998), 38; Beard, *SPQR*, 358, writes, "A number of modern historians . . . [accuse] the Augustan regime of being based on hypocrisy and pretense and of abusing traditional Republican forms and language to provide a cloak and disguise for a fairly hard-line tyranny." She agrees that they have a point.

10. Wallace-Hadrill, commenting on Millar's "The First Revolution: Imperator Caesar, 36–28 BC," in A. Giovannini, ed., *La Révolution Romaine*, 35. On those who deny a monarchy, see W. Eder, "Augustus and the Power of Tradition," in Galinsky, ed., *Cambridge Companion to the Age of Augustus*, 13–32. See, most recently, W. V. Harris, *Roman Power: A Thousand Years of Empire* (Cambridge: CUP, 2016), 5, on the "tyrannous nature of the regime of Augustus."

11. See the comments of Alston, *Rome's Revolution*, 238–39.

12. F. K. Drogula, *Commanders & Command in the Roman Republic and Early Empire* (Chapel Hill: University of North Carolina Press, 2015), 345.

13. Syme, *Roman Revolution*, 316, who argues for a social revolution. On the political revolution, see A. Wallace-Hadrill, "Mutatio morum: The idea of a cultural revolution," in *The Roman Cultural Revolution*, ed. T. Habinek and A. Schiesaro (Cambridge: CUP, 1997), 3–22. On the political culture of the Roman Republic and how little changed culturally, see Mouritsen, *Politics in the Roman Republic*, 164.

14. On republican themes in the empire, see A. Gowing, *Empire and Memory: The Representation of the Roman Republic in Imperial Culture* (Cambridge: CUP, 2005). Even Tacitus admitted there were debates about Augustus's aims among his own contemporaries. On the new ideology, see Edmondson, *Augustus*, 2. On Augustus's military reforms, see K. Raaflaub, "Augustus' Military Reforms," in Edmondson, *Augustus*, 203–28, esp. 210, where he argues for the perpetuation of the split between armed and unarmed citizens.

15. For a full discussion of the powers of Augustus, see J.-L. Ferrary, "The Powers of Augustus," in Edmondson, *Augustus*, 90–136; cf. Fuhrmann, *Policing the Roman Empire*, 113; see Z. Yavetz, *Plebs and Princeps* (Oxford: Clarendon Press, 1969), 88–102; G. Rowe, *Princes and Political Cultures* (Ann Arbor: University of Michigan Press, 2002), chapter 1; R. Talbert, "'Germanicus and Piso': Review of *Princes and Political Cultures: The New Tiberian Senatorial Decrees* by G. Rowe," *CR* 54 (2004): 182.

16. Drogula, *Commanders and Command in the Roman Republic and Early Empire*, 370. Wallace-Hadrill, *Augustan Rome*, 14.

17. See, for example, Bleichen, *Augustus*. Ernst Badian warned against portraying Augustus as founding the principate almost accidentally—that is, by "lurching from crisis to crisis, with all the main decisions merely *ad hoc* responses to emergencies." See E. Badian, "'Crisis Theories' and the Beginning of the Principate," in *Romanitas, Christianitas* (Berlin: de Gruyter, 1982), 37. Certainly there were crises like his persistent ill health, attempts on his life, and the premature deaths of his successors. This is in opposition to Eck, *Age of Augustus*, 51, on the "slow development without any abrupt adjustments." See Crook, "Last Age of the Roman Republic," 9:91, who dismisses seeing this as a Machiavellian policy of *reculer pour mieux sauter*; J. V. P. D. Balsdon, *The Emperor Gaius* (Oxford: Clarendon Press, 1934), 108–9 on the weakness of the Senate; E. Cowan, "Tacitus, Tiberius and Augustus," *ClAnt* 28, no. 2 (Oct. 2009): 207, on Augustan precedent being developed over his lifetime in his dealings with diverse situations and groups of people. See Levick, *Augustus*, 14–15 and chapter 2, on the state of the subject.

18. Tacitus, *Ann.* 3.28. Of course, many have pointed out Tacitus was writing from the perspective of one who had already seen what the principate would become under emperors after Augustus. This argument does not touch upon the question of whether Augustus was a hypocritical politician or a sincere statesman of genius. For a thorough discussion on the views of both ancient and modern historians, see Z. Yavetz, "The Res Gestae and Augustus' Public Image," in Millar and Segal, eds., *Caesar Augustus*, 20–26. Cf. H. W. Benario, "Tacitus and the Principate," *CJ* 60, no. 3 (December 1964): 97–106.

19. Wiedemann, "Tiberius to Nero," 10:198. The polarization between the interests of the pro- and antimonarchic forces was the essential feature of Syme's interpretation of the principate. See J. H. Corbett, "The Succession Policy of Augustus," *Latomus* 33, no. 1 (1974): 87–97.

20. H. I. Flower, *Roman Republics* (Princeton, NJ: PUP, 2010) traces the political and especially constitutional changes in the decades from the 80s to Caesar's death that made restoring the old traditional republic of the *nobiles* nonrecoverable. Wallace-Hadrill, *Augustan Rome*, 19, calls it a "modern myth" that the key characteristic of the Roman Republic was ever the power of the Senate. Cf. P. A. Brunt, *The Fall of the Roman Republic* (Oxford: Clarendon Press, 1988), chapter 9, with regard to "factions," 443–502.

21. For a more detailed discussion of the relations between Augustus and the Senate, see P. Sattler, *Augustus und der Senat: Untersuchingen zur römischen Innenpolitik zwischen 30 und 17 v. Christus* (Göttingen: Vandenhoeck & Ruprecht, 1960). On the loss of "liberty," Beard, *SPQR*, 423.

22. Rudich, *Political Dissidence under Nero*, xvii, calls this a "schizophrenic state of affairs" where the *de iure* and *de facto* aspects of societal life meant there was a gap between words and deeds. It was a world of "illusion and delusion," of "ambivalencies and ambiguities on all levels of interaction." Also see Wiedemann, "Tiberius to Nero," 10:198, on the descendants of the republican aristocracy not having independent power.

23. Syme, *Roman Revolution*, 490–508; Alston, *Rome's Revolution*, 237. See the discussion in A. Wallace-Hadrill, "The Roman Revolution and Material Culture," in Giovannini, ed., *La Révolution Romaine*, 288–313, versus E. S. Gruen, *Culture and National Identity in Republican Rome* (Ithaca, NY: Cornell University Press, 1992).

24. C. G. Starr, *Civilization and the Caesars* (Ithaca, NY: Cornell University Press, 1954), 64.

25. For his organizing of opinion, see Syme, *Roman Revolution*, 459–75, and "The Apologia for the Principate," in his *The Augustan Aristocracy* (Oxford: Clarendon Press, 1986), 439–54. For his ability to influence what was written and disseminated, see P. White, *Promised Verse: Poets in the Society of Augustan Rome* (Cambridge, MA: HUP, 1993), passim. F. Millar, "State and Subject: The Impact of Monarchy," in Millar and Segal, eds., *Caesar Augustus*, 1–36, on the other hand, argued that emperors had little scope for the active dissemination of "policy" or "propaganda."

26. Breastplate: Suet., *Div. Aug.* 35.1; Dio 54.12.3; A. A. Barrett, *Caligula: The Corruption of Power* (New Haven, CT: YUP, 1989), 159.

27. Fuhrmann, *Policing the Roman Empire*, 92.

28. Wallace-Hadrill, *Augustan Rome*, 46.

29. Policing became a significant factor in the evolution of the principate. Christopher Fuhrmann wrote his book *Policing the Roman Empire* in reaction to claims that the Romans and premodern societies did not have or seek recourse to state institutions for enforcement; see pages 7–9.

30. Fuhrmann, *Policing the Roman Empire*.

31. W. Nippel, *Public Order in Ancient Rome* (Cambridge: CUP, 1995), preface. His work is essential because it avoids the two opposite extremes: assuming Rome had a modern police force and assuming Rome had no police force due to a weakness of the state. See the comments of Beard, *SPQR*, 462–65.

32. On the development of the Roman Secret Service, see Sheldon, *Intelligence Activities in Ancient Rome*, 250–60, with earlier bibliography.

33. As noted by Millar, *Emperor in the Roman World*, 59.

34. Dio 54.10.5; Fuhrmann, *Policing the Roman Empire*, 64.

35. See Pliny, *Paneg.* 23, where Trajan's lictors help him make his way through friendly crowds.

36. They were also used as reconnaissance officers. See Sheldon, *Intelligence Activities in Ancient Rome*, 166; M. Speidel, *Riding for Caesar* (Cambridge, MA: HUP, 1994), 33–35.

37. Sometime after 23 CE when all Praetorian cohorts were brought to Rome, the *speculatores* were incorporated into those cohorts and were thereafter not called "Augusti." The entire Praetorian Guard was the "emperor's," and therefore no distinction was made.

38. O. Hirschfeld, "Die Sicherheitspolizei im römischen Kaiserreich," in *Kleine Schriften* (Berlin: Weidmann, 1913), 586–88; Speidel, *Riding for Caesar*, 33–35. We know what the lance looked like from a grave relief. The long shaft ended in a knob, and the short, broad, heart-shaped blade had a crossbar. Both ends, therefore, were designed for crowd control. For a gravestone illustration see M. I. Rostovtzeff, "Ein Speculator auf der Reise," *Röm. Mitt.* 26 (1911): 267–83.

39. At banquets: Suet., *Claudius* 35, Dio 60.3.3. Crowded streets: Tacitus, *Ann.* 15.58.2.

40. Speidel, *Riding for Caesar*, 34, points out that since they were used on the battlefield, their numbers had to be at least three hundred, if not higher. See Tacitus, *Hist.* 1.59. on the strong force with Otho in 69. "Three hundred" carries through much of Roman history as well as elsewhere: Romulus's three hundred *celeres* horse guard, three hundred republican praetorian horse guards, three hundred late-Roman *excubitores*, Speidel, *Riding for Caesar*, 34.

41. Speidel, *Riding for Caesar*, 171; H. Bellen, *Die germanische Leibwache der römischen Kaiser des Julisch-Claudischen Hauses* (Wiesbaden: Steiner, 1981), 83.

42. Speidel, *Riding for Caesar*, 35; M. Clauss, "Untersuchungen zu den principales der römischen Heeres von Augustus bis Diocletian" (PhD diss., Ruhr-Universität Bochum, 1973), 58.

43. Marius had Bardyaei, Appian, *BC* 1.70-1; Suet., *Div. Jul.* 86. Antony as consul of 44 had a guard of Iturean archers, Cicero, *Phil.* 2.44/112; cf. 5.6/17–18. Client kings of Rome certainly had the same practice. Juba of Mauretania had Gallic and Spanish cavalry as a guard. See Caesar, *BG* 2.40.1. Cleopatra had four hundred Gauls whom Octavian presented as a gift to Herod the Great in 30 BCE; Josephus, *AJ* 15.7.3 (217). And see Millar, *Emperor in the Roman World*, 62.

44. Caesar, *BG* 7.13.1.

45. Suet., *Div. Jul.* 86, Appian, *BC* 2.109/455. Strauss, *Death of Caesar*, 100–105; Millar, *Emperor in the Roman World*, 62.

46. See most recently, Strauss, *Death of Caesar*, 100.

47. This type of unit was used only by the Julio-Claudians. See Suet., *Caligula* 58.3. They were permanently disbanded by Galba in 69 CE because he felt they had backed his opponent, Gnaeus Dolabella. Suet., *Galba* 12; Bingham, *Praetorian Guard*, 17.

48. The standard work on the German bodyguard is still Bellen, *Die germanische Leibwache*. See also Speidel, *Riding for Caesar*, 15–18; and R. Sablayrolles, "La rue, le soldat et le pouvoir: La garnison de Rome de César à Pertinax," *Pallas* 55 (2001): 136–37; M. Jallet-Huant, *La garde prétorienne: Dans la Rome antique* (Charenton-le-Pont, France: Presses de Valmy, 2004): 19–20.

49. Bingham, *Praetorian Guard*, 16, although neither M. Bang, *Die Germanen im römischen Dienst* (Berlin: Weidmann, 1906), 63, nor Bellen, *Die germanische Leibwache*, link "Caesar's Guard" with Augustus although the names are the same. Also see Speidel, *Riding for Caesar*, 165n6; on Batavi, Suet., *Caligula* 43. For inscriptions called the *equites singulari Augusti* "Batavi," see M. Speidel, *Die Denkmäler der Kaisereiter (Equites Singulari Augusti)* (Cologne: Rheinland Verlag, 1994), 688ff. Dio 55.24.6 calls Augustus's guard Batavi.

50. Speidel, *Riding for Caesar*, 16.

51. The exact size is unknown, but since it is described as a cohort in ancient sources, a strength of five hundred is usually suggested. Under Caligula the number may have been raised to a thousand. Speidel, *Riding for Caesar*, 50.

52. Tacitus, *Ann.* 15.58.2, who is referring to the reign of Nero.

53. Y. Le Bohec, *The Imperial Roman Army* (London: Hippocrene Books, 1994), 23; M. Grant, *Army of the Caesars* (New York: Charles Scribner & Sons, 1974), 91.

54. Sheldon, *Intelligence Activities in Ancient Rome*; Barrett, *Caligula*, 159.

55. Suet., *Div. Aug.* 49; Speidel, *Riding for Caesar*, 18, suggests that the *Germani* must have taken some steps that smacked of treason or they would not have been banished, but there is no evidence for this beyond a general Roman distrust for Germans. On the connection between the Batavians and the Cherusci, see G. Walser, *Rom, das Reich, und die fremden Volker in der Geschichtsschreibung der frühen Kaiserzeit* (Baden-Baden: Verlag für Kunst und Wissenschaft, 1951), 107; D. Timpe, *Arminiuss-Studien* (Heidelberg: C. Winter, 1970), 115. Millar, *Emperor in the Roman World*, 62.

56. The unit that eventually replaced the *Germani corporis custodies* in the second and third centuries comprised the *equites singulares Augusti*. See Speidel, *Riding for Caesar*, 35–37; F. Grosso, "Equites Singulari Augusti," *Latomus* 25 (1966): 900; Speidel, *Die Denkmäler der Kaisereiter*. This was a unit of one thousand cavalry individually recruited mainly from auxiliary units on the Rhine and Danube. They had their own barracks in Rome, formed a mounted complement to the praetorian cohorts, and like them accompanied the emperor on journeys and expeditions. See Millar, *Emperor in the Roman World*, 63.

57. Even Livy's history reminded Augustus and senators that Romulus kept his three hundred *celeres* around him in both war and peace, but the senators had torn him to pieces for being a tyrant. Livy 1.15ff.; Dio 53.16.7; Speidel, *Riding for Caesar*, 17; Syme, *Roman Revolution*, 313ff. and 464.

58. Cicero, *Att.* 13.52.

59. Tacitus, *Ann.* 13.18.3; Dio 61.8.6; Suet., *Nero* 34.

60. See the comments of Wallace-Hadrill, *Augustan Rome*, 46. The standard older works on the Guard are M. Durry, *Les cohorts pretoriennes* (Paris: E. Boccard, 1938); A. Passerini, *Le coorti pretorie* (Rome: Signorelli, 1939); S. J. De Laet, "Les pouvoirs militaires des Préfets du Prétoire et leur développement progressif," *Revue belge de philologie et d'histoire* 25, nos. 3–4 (1946): 509–54. For more recent studies, see Bingham, *Praetorian Guard*; Jallet-Huant, *La garde prétorienne*; H. D. Stöver, *Die Prätorianer: Kaisermacher, Kaisermörder* (Munich: Langen Müller, 1994); Fuhrmann, *Policing the Roman Empire*, 115. Notice that Karl Galinsky's *Augustus* does not even mention them.

61. On the history of the Republican praetorians, see Jallet-Huant, *La garde prétorienne*, 9–10; Bingham, *Praetorian Guard*, 9–15.

62. There is some modern controversy over the organization and strength of the Guard, based on the evidence of Tacitus, *Ann.* 4.2.5; Tacitus, *Hist.* 2.93; Hyginus 30; and Dio 55.24.6 and the epigraphic record. See J. Coulston, "'Armed and Belted Men': The Soldiery in Imperial Rome," in *Ancient Rome: The Archaeology of the Eternal City*, ed. J. Coulston and H. Dodge (Oxford: Oxford School of Archaeology, 2000), 76–78; on their organization and strength see also Durry, *Les cohorts*, 77–89; Passerini, *Le coorti pretorie*, 46–70, 208; L. Keppie, *The Making of the Roman*

Army from Republic to Empire (New York: Barnes & Noble, 1984), 153–54, 187–88; L. Keppie, "The Praetorian Guard before Sejanus," *Athenaeum* 84 (1996): 109–12; B. Rankov, *The Praetorian Guard* (London: Osprey, 1994), 7–8; Jallet-Huant, *La garde prétorienne*, 16–18.

63. The emergence of their police functions was gradual. See Wallace-Hadrill, *Augustan Rome*, 47.

64. At first they served only twelve years, but after 5 CE their term of service was raised to sixteen. Their pay had been doubled by the Senate in 27 BCE and, by the time of Augustus's death, it amounted to 750 *denarii*, more than three times what the legionaries earned at 225 *denarii*. A. H. M. Jones, *Augustus* (New York: W. W. Norton, 1970), 113; Bingham, *Praetorian Guard*, 1; K. Wellesley, *The Year of the Four Emperors* (London: Routledge, 2000), 8, editorializes and calls the rate "disgracefully higher" than the ordinary soldiers who faced the danger and monotony of frontier duty. Dio 53.11.5 makes the sinister connection between money and loyalty immediately. Of course, Dio is writing at a time when the monarchy had long been established.

65. On the pay of the Guard, see G. Powell, "The Praetorian Guard," *History Today* 18 (1968): 859.

66. The reluctance to delegate responsibility for the Guard to any one individual in the early years of his reign may have resulted from a desire to deflect criticism for having stationed troops in the city. By 2 BCE there would have been less concern about their presence; Durry, *Les cohorts*, 158. It is not impossible that Augustus created the two praetorian prefects in response to the scandal of 2 BCE with Julia, feeling a greater need for security. See P. Southern, *Augustus*, 179.

67. Bingham, *Praetorian Guard*, 21; Powell, "Praetorian Guard," 859.

68. Bingham, *Praetorian Guard*, 16, also points out that the unit played a major role in the funeral of Augustus, on which see Dio 56.31–42; Tacitus, *Ann.* 1.8.6; Suet., *Div. Aug.* 99.2–100.4. Cf. Dio 75.4–5.6 on the funeral of Pertinax.

69. On the development of the Guard, see M. Absil, "Le rôle des préfets du prétoire pendant les règnes de Néron, Galba, Othon et Vitellius: Aspects Politiques," *Neronia VI*, 229–47; M. Absil, *Les préfets du prétoire d'Auguste à Commode: 2 avant Jésus-Christ–192 après Jésus Christ* (Paris: De Boccard, 1997). P. A. Brunt, "Princeps and Equites," *JRS* 73 (1983): 59–60. Brunt asks whether the establishment of a permanent prefecture was not the culmination of a process in which Augustus had from time to time delegated supreme command to one or more of the tribunes. The first two prefects were Postumius Scapula and P. Satrius Aper. Cf. Fuhrmann, *Policing the Roman Empire*, 117; R. Bauman, *Crime and Punishment in Ancient Rome* (London: Routledge, 1996), 106–14; Bingham, *Praetorian Guard*, 19.

70. Bingham, *Praetorian Guard*, 19; L. L. Howe, *The Praetorian Prefects from Commodus to Diocletian* (Chicago: University of Chicago Press, 1942), 10, 32, argues that the initial function for these men was military. Cf. Brunt, "Princeps and equites," 60; Absil, *Les préfets*, 14. Syme, *Tacitus*, 591 strikes the best compromise: the praetorians were "military in rank, but political in significance." Pliny, *Paneg.* 67.8 notes that Trajan armed his prefect in case he, as emperor, did not act in the interests of the state, but the evidence is inconclusive as to whether this was standard practice. Herodian 3.11.7 does suggest that Severus's prefect, Plautianus, carried a sword at his side.

71. Bingham, *Praetorian Guard*, 19; on the relationship, see A. E. Hanson, "Publius Ostorius Scapula: Augustan Prefect of Egypt," *ZPE* 47 (1982): 252. On the issue of patronage in the appointment of the equestrian prefectures, see Millar, *Emperor in the Roman World*, 64; A. N. Sherwin-White, "Procurator Augusti," *PBSR* 15 (1939): 17; R. P. Saller, *Personal Patronage in the Early Empire* (Cambridge: CUP, 2002), 49. Saller notes (p. 62) that it cannot be doubted that praetorian prefects, whose very appointments testified to the emperor's confidence in their loyalty and friendship, were among the most influential figures in imperial circles.

72. Dio 60.23.

73. Dio's speech 52.24.1–6 to Maecenas on this subject may be hindsight, and there may have not yet been any fear when the position was first established. Dio's dislike of Fulvius Plautianus may have colored his interpretation (see 76.15). And see Bingham, *Praetorian Guard*, 20.

74. On guarding imperial villas on the outskirts of Rome and beyond, see Coulston, "Armed and Belted Men," 87–88. Powell, "Praetorian Guard," 859, rejects Dio's numbers of one thousand men and argues for cohorts of five hundred. On the dispute, see P. M. Swan, *The Augustan Succession* (Oxford: OUP, 2004), 169–70, with the relevant bibliography.

75. Bingham, *Praetorian Guard*, 2. On the duties of the Guard generally, see Jallet-Huant, *La garde prétorienne*, 47–57.

76. Bingham, *Praetorian Guard*, 1–2, points out their expanding role, which has received little attention in the literature.

77. Suet., *Div. Aug.* 49.1; Tacitus, *Hist.* 1.38.2, *Ann.* 4.2.1. There seems to be some ambiguity regarding whether their swords were normally displayed openly, as in Tacitus, *Ann.* 16.27.1, when Nero wishes to intimidate the Senate. There a throng of Praetorians is described as "wearing togas, but swords unconcealed."

78. On the *speculatores*, see A. M. Liberati and E. Silverio, *Servizi Segreti in Roma Antica: Informazioni e sicurezza dagli initia Urbis all'impero universal* (Rome: Bretschneider, 2010), 117–18; Clauss, "Untersuchungen zu den principales der römischen Heeres von Augustus bis Diocletian"; W. Krenkel, "Speculatores," in *Lexicon der Alten Welt* (Zurich: Artemis Verlag, 1990), 2855; F. Lammert, "Speculatores," *R-E*: 1583–86. The *speculatores* were also involved in the confinement and execution of those convicted of treason. They assisted the *vigiles* in firefighting and provided security at the games. See Bingham, *Praetorian Guard*, 2 and 106–13 on the *vigiles*.

79. Bingham, *Praetorian Guard*, 2; J. B. Campbell, *The Roman Army 31 B.C.–A.D. 337: A Sourcebook* (London: Routledge, 1994), 183.

80. Tacitus, *Ann.* 1.13.6, 12.69.1. On the presumably military functions of the urban cohorts in the time of Domitian and Trajan, see F. Bérard, "Le rôle militaire des cohorts urbaines," *MEFR* 100 (1988): 159–82, but also the objections by M. Roxan and W. Eck, "A Military Diploma of AD 85 for the Rome Cohorts," *ZPE* 96 (1993): 67–74.

81. On the *Res Gestae*, Augustus's list of "What I Did," see Beard, *SPQR*, 360–67.

82. Durry, *Les cohorts*, 10. Passerini, *Le coorti pretorie*, 210, has argued, however, that Augustus included the Praetorians among those referred to generally as *milites* in the *Res Gestae*. While it is impossible to know whether his audience would

make this assumption, it does allow Augustus to mask the significance of the Guard; Bingham, *Praetorian Guard*, 18.

83. Tacitus, *Ann.* 6.15.2.

84. Tacitus, *Ann.* 15.52.1.

85. On the bodyguard for the princes, see Bellen, *Die germanische Leibwache*; M. Speidel, "Germani Corporis Custodes," *Germania* 62 (1984): 31–45. On the succession and the princes, see Rowe, *Princes and Political Cultures*, 1–7.

86. Coulston, "Armed and Belted Men," 86 and 104n61, who notes that attempts have been made to identify guard stations and accommodations in the rooms and corridors around the great atrium facing the Roman Forum.

87. Grant, *Army of the Caesars*, 130–66; J. B. Campbell, *The Emperor and the Roman Army 31 B.C.–A.D. 235* (New York: OUP, 1984), 118-20; Flaig, *Den Kaiser herausforden*, 132–68.

88. Nippel, *Public Order in Ancient Rome*, 91; Sablayrolles, "La rue, le soldat et le pouvoir," 135; Bingham, *Praetorian Guard*, 17. Coulston, "Armed and Belted Men," 97, writes, "In actual fact, the military forces in Rome, belying the proverbial reputation of 'Praetorian Guards' in modern politics, were generally loyal to reigning emperors and established dynasties."

89. The numbers of the cohorts gradually became jumbled as various cohorts were deleted or added. H. Freis, *Die cohortes urbanae* (Cologne: Böhlau, 1967) remains the leading discussion. See Freis's entry "Cohortes Urbanae" in *R-E* Suppl. 10, col. 1125–40; Fuhrmann, *Policing the Roman Empire*, 117. B. Rankov, *Guardians of the Roman Empire* (Oxford: Osprey, 1999), 5, says that the three urban cohorts were raised around the end of Augustus's reign, so it seems likely that the last three Praetorian cohorts were simply redesignated for duty in the city.

90. Tacitus, *Ann.* 4.5.3. On their pay and service see Freis, *Die cohortes urbanae*; H. Lieb, "Die constitutiones für die stadtrömischen Truppen," in *Heer und Integrationspolitik: Die römischen Militärdiplome als historische Quelle*, ed. W. Eck and H. Wolff (Cologne and Vienna: Böhlau, 1986), 322–46.

91. Le Bohec, *Imperial Roman Army*, 21; also according to Nippel, *Public Order in Ancient Rome*, 92. A cohort became a thousand strong temporarily in 69 CE, according to Tacitus, *Ann.* 2.93.2, and then permanently after the reorganization of Septimius Severus in 193 CE on the occasion of his dissolving the existing Praetorian Guard and establishing an entirely new one.

92. Tacitus, *Ann.* 6.10.3. F. Della Corte, "La breve praefectura urbis di Messala Corvino," in *Philias charin: Miscellanea di studi classici in onore di E. Manni* (Rome: Bretschneider, 1980), 2:667–77; Fuhrmann, *Policing the Roman Empire*, 117; Nippel, *Public Order in Ancient Rome*, 92.

93. Vell. Pat. 2.98.1; Cf. Statius, *Silvae* 1.4. During the crises of 41 and 68 (December) CE, however, this command structure sometimes led to confrontation between urban and Praetorian cohorts. See Flaig, *Den Kaiser herausforden*, 224–28, 393–98; Nippel, *Public Order in Ancient Rome*, 92.

94. On close supervision, Dio Cassius 52.21.6-7; on more latitude, Tacitus, *Hist.* 3.75.1; Juvenal 4.75–81; Statius, *Silvae* 1.4.; Nippel, *Public Order in Ancient Rome*, 92.

95. N. Purcell, "Rome and Its Development under Augustus and His Successors," *CAH²*, 10:782–811, on more personnel for policing.

96. Fuhrmann, *Policing the Roman Empire*, 116; Millar, *Emperor in the Roman World*, 33, 61; C. Ricci, *Soldati delle milizie urbane fuori da Rome: La documentazione epigrafica*, Opuscula Epigrafica 5 (Rome: Quasar, 1994), 17–18. We do not know exactly when the urban cohorts were created. See Freis, *Die cohortes urbanae*, 4–5, and Sablayrolles, "Le rue, le soldat et le pouvoir," 133–34. They did do some campaigning outside of Italy: Bérard, "Le rôle militaire des cohorts urbaines," 159–82.

97. They were similar enough that ancient observers often did not bother to differentiate between the two in their accounts of the period. L. Keppie, "The Army and the Navy," *CAH*, 10:385, believed urban cohorts served as a police force for the city, but see Fuhrmann, *Policing the Roman Empire*, 116; Nippel, *Public Order in Ancient Rome*, 93.

98. Dio 57.3.2; Bingham, *Praetorian Guard*, 16; Campbell, *Emperor and the Roman Army*, 27, 30, where it is pointed out that in the third century, at least, the oath was considered "a holy secret." See also Herodian 8.7.4.

99. Nippel, *Public Order in Ancient Rome*, 29, against seeing them as a modern police force; Fuhrmann, *Policing the Roman Empire*, 98, on seeing them in a larger context.

100. Tacitus, *Ann.* 6.11.4; A. Valvo, "M. Valerio Messalla Corvino negli studi più recenti," *ANRW* 2.30.3 (1983): 1673–74; Syme, *Augustan Aristocracy*, 211–12; C. Ando, *Imperial Ideology and Provincial Loyalty in the Roman Empire* (Berkeley: University of California Press, 2000), 140; Fuhrmann, *Policing the Roman Empire*, 117; Wallace-Hadrill, *Augustan Rome*, 46.

101. O. Hirschfeld, *Die Kaiserlischen Verwaltungsbeamten bis auf Diocletian* (Berlin: Weidmann, 1905), 252–57; J. S. Rainbird, "The Fire Stations of Imperial Rome," *PBSR* 54 (1986): 147–69; P. K. Baillie Reynolds, *The Vigiles of Imperial Rome* (Oxford: OUP, 1926); O. F. Robinson, "Fire Prevention at Rome," *RIDA* 24 (1977): 377–88; Robinson, *Ancient Rome: City Planning and Administration*, 184–88.

102. Dio 54.2.4, 55.8.6–8.

103. Dio 55.24.4–5.

104. Dio 55.26.4. The only source that refers to them as soldiers is Ulpian, Justinian, *Digest* 37.13.1. On the number of *vigiles*, Rainbird, "Fire Stations of Imperial Rome," 150; Bingham, *Praetorian Guard*, 106–7. On Augustus's organization of the regions of the city, see C. Nicolet, *Space, Geography and Politics in the Early Roman Empire* (Ann Arbor: University of Michigan Press, 1991), 210–13.

105. Gaius, *Institutes* 1.32b.

106. Wallace-Hadrill, *Augustan Rome*, 46.

107. Strabo 5.3.7 = C235; Tacitus, *Ann.* 15.43.4; Justinian, *Digest* 1.15.3.4.

108. Their numbers are disputed. See Rainbird, "The Fire Stations of Imperial Rome," 150; Nippel, *Public Order in Ancient Rome*, 97. Nippel does not believe that street patrolling was among their regular duties. It is questionable whether they were able to undertake effective searches, and any long-term implementation of the law enabling them to search for fugitive slaves was probably not possible. The idea that the *vigiles* performed ordinary police functions is based on the juridical competences of their commanding officer, the *praefectus vigilum*. He was authorized to arrest runaway slaves, as had been the *tresviri capitales*. The duty to pursue *fugitivi* was assigned to the *praefectus vigilum* by the emperor Septimius

Severus, Justinian, *Digest* 1.15.4. Cf. H. Bellen, *Studien zur Sklavenflucht im rö-mischen Kaiser des julisch-claudischen Hauses* (Wiesbaden: Steiner, 1971), 13–15, 121.

109. See, for example, Suet., *Div. Aug.* 25.2. Reynolds, *Vigiles of Imperial Rome*, 2, believed Augustus was reluctant to introduce "anything which might appear to be military force and an instrument of tyranny." Considering the other military institutions discussed in this chapter, this seems unlikely.

110. On the definition of these terms, see Rutledge, *Imperial Inquisitions*, 9–16.

111. Rutledge, *Imperial Inquisitions*, 3.

112. Much of this is due to the presentation of Tacitus. See P. Sinclair, *Tacitus the Sententious Historian* (University Park, PA: Penn State University Press, 1995) on his rhetoric. On the older literature, mostly devoid of source criticism, see Bois-sier, "Les Délateurs," 305–40; Boissière, *L'accusation publique et les delateurs chez les Romains*; Dumeril, "Origine des Délateurs et Précis de leur histoire pendant la durée de l'empire romain," 262–81; O'Neal, "Delation in the Early Empire," 24–28; Zijlstra, *De delatores te Rome tot aan Tiberius' regering*.

113. More recently on the *delatores*, see Lucia Fanizza, *Delatori e Accusatori: L'iniziativa nei processi di Età imperiale* (Rome: L'Erma di Bretschneider, 1988); Libe-rati and Silverio, *Servizi Segreti in Roma Antica*, 43–47; Rutledge, *Imperial Inquisi-tions*; Petraccia, *Indices e Delatores nell'Antica Roma*.

114. For a description of how such prosecutions worked, see Rutledge, *Imperial Inquisitions*, 16–19.

115. See Rudich, *Political Dissidence under Nero*, 15–16 on Cicero, Tacitus, and Pliny.

116. K. Raaflaub, "Grundzüge, Ziele und Ideen der Opposition gegen die Kaiser," 19, notes the large number of *novi homines* among the *delatores*; Rutledge, *Imperial Inquisitions*, 24.

117. Rutledge, "Delatores and the Tradition of Violence in Roman Oratory," *AJPh* 120 (1999): 555–73.

118. On the political advancement of *delatores* during the empire, see esp. Rut-ledge, *Imperial Inquisitions,* chapter 2.

119. For an exhaustive prosopographical survey of the *delatores*, see Rutledge, *Imperial Inquisitions*, 185–301.

120. Rutledge, *Imperial Inquisitions*, 178. He notes that the noun *delator* does not appear under the republic with the meaning that it came to have under the empire.

121. Starr, *Civilization and the Caesars*, 73; Vell. Pat. 2.88.3.

122. Appian, *BC* 5.128.

123. Appian, *BC* 3.95.394; Starr, *Civilization and the Caesars*, 73; Syme, *Roman Revolution*, 187, who suggests pirates or shipwreck.

124. Tacitus, *Ann.* 4.36.

125. Tacitus, *Ann.* 4.71.

126. Rudich, *Political Dissidence under Nero*, xxvi.

127. Tacitus, *Ann.* 6.3.

128. Rutledge, *Imperial Inquisitions*, 86, who points out that how much of a threat the opposition really was is highly debated.

129. Rutledge, *Imperial Inquisitions*, 88; R. A. Bauman, *Impietas in Principem* (Munich: Beck, 1974), 55–56, citing Tacitus, *Hist.* 1.2, 1.3 on the slaves; B. Levick, *Tiberius the Politician* (London: Routledge, 1976), 185, on the juries.

130. On the *delatores* and law enforcement, see Rutledge, *Imperial Inquisitions*, chapter 3.

131. See Rutledge, *Imperial Inquisitions*, 12–15 on the social marginalization of informers.

132. On senatorial opposition to the emperor, see Rutledge, *Imperial Inquisitions*, chapter 4.

133. The bibliography concerning Augustus's legislation is vast. For some of the more significant studies, see Rutledge, *Imperial Inquisitions*, 335n6.

134. Wallace-Hadrill, *Augustan Rome*, 96. The republican concept of treason was commonly referred to in the last century of the republic as *laesa maiestas*. According to Cicero, this term referred to a lessening of *dignitas*, majesty, or the authority of the people or of those to whom the people had given authority. The problem was that already by the Late Republic, the definition of *maiestas* was becoming hazy. See Cicero, *De Inventione* 2.17.53. The term *laesa maiestas* appears frequently in legislation of the first century BCE, especially in a not very well-known law of Sulla. Cf. R. S. Rogers, "The Emperor's Displeasure: *Amicitiam renuntiare*," *TAPA* (1959): 224–37, who argues that the law of treason did not extend to criticism or disrespect to the emperor.

135. Starr, *Civilization and the Caesars*, 75.

136. On *maiestas*, see Tacitus, *Ann.* 1.72–75. Censorship included any form of communication that challenged the established order. Disloyal writings, abusive speeches, unsettling predictions by soothsayers, and maleficent magic were all seen as threats. See Sheldon, *Intelligence Activities in Ancient Rome*, 157; R. Macmullen, *Enemies of Roman Order* (Cambridge, MA: HUP, 1966), 152, on Augustus and Tiberius, and 163; Syme, *Roman Revolution*, 486; K. A. Raaflaub and L. J. Samons, "Opposition to Augustus," in Raaflaub and Toher, eds., *Between Republic and Empire*, 443n110.

137. Rutledge, *Imperial Inquisitions*, 58.

138. Tacitus, *Ann.* 4.34 claims Augustus's relative tolerance of dissent compared to Tiberius, but he may be retrojecting Domitian's behavior. See Dio 57.9.1–3; Fuhrmann, *Policing the Roman Empire*, 109. Of course, this was a gradual process. See R. Bauman, *The Crimen Maiestatis in the Roman Republic and Augustan Principate* (Johannesburg: Witwatersrand University Press, 1967); and Bauman, *Impietas in Principem*, 1–24.

139. S. Price, *Rituals and Power: The Roman Imperial Cult in Asia Minor* (Cambridge: CUP, 1986), 248. See also Edmondson, *Augustus*, 295–99, and Wallace-Hadrill, *Augustan Rome*, 79–81.

140. Starr, *Civilization and the Caesars*, 59–60. In Rome, the lower orders were allowed to worship the genius of Augustus at the *Lares Compitales*, the shrines of the city wards now renamed *Lares Augusti*, but all overt worship of the emperor was banned. See Jones, *Augustus*, 151–52; J. R. Fears, *Princeps a Diis Electus: The Divine Election of the Emperor as a Political Concept at Rome* (Rome: American Academy at Rome, 1977); Galinsky, *Augustus*, 169–73.

141. Starr, *Civilization and the Caesars*, 61.

142. As Jon Lendon has pointed out, although the imperial cult is central to an understanding of Roman government, it may be as much a part of the question of how the emperors ruled rather than the answer. See J. Lendon, *Empire of Honour* (Oxford: OUP, 1997), 10; and J. Scheid, "To Honour the Princeps and Venerate the Gods: Public Cult, Neighbourhood Cults, and Imperial Cult in Augustan Rome," in J. Edmondson, *Augustus*, 295–96.

143. W. Scheidel, "The Emperor in the Wider World," lecture at Cambridge University, July 26, 2011, provided by generosity of the author. See especially J. E. Lendon's article, "The Legitimacy of the Roman Emperor against Weberian Legitimacy and Imperial 'Strategies of Legitimation,'" in *Herrschafsstrukturen und Herrschaftspraxis: Konzepte, Prinzipien und Stratagien der Administration im römischen Kaiserreich*, ed. E. Kolb (Berlin: Akademie Verlag, 2006), 53–63.

144. See Nippel, *Public Order in Ancient Rome*, 85–90, on the regulation of the corn supply, creating the *vici*, and the attempts to control the *plebs urbana*.

145. Levick, *Augustus*, 141–44; Starr, *Civilization and the Caesars*, 61-62; Syme, *Roman Revolution*, 349–68; Shotter, *Augustus Caesar* (London: Routledge, 2005), 46–50; all are referring to *equites* and not artisans, traders, and merchants. Although the term *middle class* is considered an anachronism by many, see E. Mayer, *The Ancient Middle Classes: Urban Life and Aesthetics in the Roman Empire 100 BCE–250 BCE* (Cambridge, MA: HUP, 2012), 1–21, on his redefinition. On the gradual concentration of local wealth, see W. Scheidel, *The Great Leveller* (Princeton, NJ: PUP, 2017), 71–80.

146. The most enthusiastic Latin praise for Augustus after his death came from Velleius Paterculus, a man of Italian equestrian origin who rose in the Senate under Augustus. On the new nobility, see Starr, *Civilization and the Caesars*, 62; Jones, *Augustus*, 83–84; J. Osgood, *Caesar's Legacy* (Cambridge: CUP, 2006), 251–97.

147. Starr, *Civilization and the Caesars*, 45.

148. On the lack of need for legitimation, especially in the Weberian sense, see especially Lendon, "The Legitimacy of the Roman Emperor," 53–63.

149. N. Mackie, "Ovid and the Birth of Maiestas," in *Roman Poetry and Propaganda in the Age of Augustus*, ed. A. Powell (London: Duckworth, 1992), 91.

150. Galinsky, *Augustus*, 81.

151. On the "wordless saturation by portraiture of the leader, in statuary and coins" see Levick, *Augustus*, 136. See Starr, *Civilization and the Caesars*, on the coinage, 45–47, and on inscriptions, 46–56; on sculpture see N. Hannestad, *Roman Art and Imperial Policy* (Aarhus, Denmark: Aarhus University Press, 1986); and T. Hölscher, *Staatsdenkmal und Publikum: Vom Untergang der Republik bis zur Festigung des Kaisertuns in Rome* (Xenia: Konstanzer althistorische Vorträge und Forschungen, 1984). That the buildings, art-objects, and coins are central and not merely corroboratory evidence, see Crook, "Last Age of the Roman Republic," *CAH* 9:72–73. On poets, see White, *Promised Verse*, passim.

152. On literature, see J. Griffin, "Augustus and the Poets: 'Caesar Qui Cogere Posset,'" in Millar and Segal, eds., *Caesar Augustus*, 189–218. On the material culture of the regime, see Wallace-Hadrill, "Roman Revolution and Material Culture," 288–313; White, *Promised Verse*, passim.

153. On the relationship between Augustus and poetic literary production, see White, *Promised Verse*, who does not see any direct instigation of literary output yet also admits, "The enormous power of Augustus is the fact from which very discussion must begin" (118). Although White does not believe there was a direct program to influence poets, he writes, "Yet in their different ways they all contribute to the chorus of Augustan panegyric" (206).

154. Levick, *Augustus*, 133, points out how the suppression of information is the negative side of "propaganda." See D. C. Feeney, "'*Si licet et fas est*': Ovid's Fasti and the Problem of Free Speech under the Principate," in *Roman Poetry and Propaganda in the Age of Augustus*, ed. A. Powell (London: Duckworth, 1992), 1–25, who calls freedom of expression under Augustus "a vexed issue" (7).

155. Dio 53.19.1–5. The quotation is from P. Green, "Carmen et error," chap. 13 in *Classical Bearings* (London: Thames & Hudson, 1989), 213.

156. O. S. Due, *Changing Forms: Studies in the Metamorphosis of Ovid* (Copenhagen: Gyldendal, 1974), 174n92. The strength of his power enabled him to permit a certain freedom of speech, but he arbitrarily and unpredictably reserved for himself the right of determining the limits of it, and in his later years he narrowed those limits. Feeney, "*Si licet et fas est*," 8, adds that it is the arbitrary and unpredictable element that is the key in every aspect of imperial power. White, *Promised Verse*, 118, mentions his control of the gazette that carried news of the city; his edicts, which made his opinions known and issued regulations; his direction of legislative action; and his ability to inject himself into the administration of justice.

157. Starr, *Civilization and the Caesars*, 72. It was Seneca who related the story of the inebriated senator who hoped that Augustus would not return from a journey he was about to make. The remark was noted by other guests, and in the morning the contrite guest had to run to the Forum to beg Augustus's forgiveness. Seneca, *de Bene.* 3.27.1.

158. A passing note in Suet., *Div. Aug.* 51.1 records that a letter circulated in the name of Agrippa Postumus was scathingly critical of Augustus, and Dio claims it spoke ill of Livia as a stepmother. Cf. Dio 55.32.2; J. S. Richardson, *Augustan Rome 44 BC to AD 14* (Edinburgh: Edinburgh University Press, 2012), 177.

159. Macrobius, *Sat.* 2.4.21; *SHA, Hadrian* 15.13.

160. A. Everitt, *Augustus* (New York: Random House, 2006), 234.

161. Seneca, *Rhet. Contr.* 10, praef. 6ff. Rudich, *Political Dissidence under Nero*, xxxiii; Syme, *Roman Revolution*, 486; Starr, *Civilization and the Caesars*, 78–79, 83–85, 214–15, 217, 332–33, 364. On freedom of thought, see Starr, 85–88, and Raaflaub and Samons, "Opposition to Augustus," 445. J. V. P. D. Balsdon, "The Successors of Augustus," *G&R* 2, no. 6 (May 1933): 164, writes, "There existed something that approximated closely to a censorship of the press."

162. Dio 56.27.1; Swan, *Augustan Succession*, 286, thus identifies Augustus as the author of this new form of *damnatio memoriae*. On Labienus: Seneca, *Contr.* 10, praef. 5–9. On Cassius Severus: Tacitus, *Ann.* 1.72.3, 4.21.3. For the uncertain dating of Severus's condemnation, see Swan, *Augustan Succession*, 287.

163. Raaflaub and Samons, "Opposition to Augustus," 445. There is a debate over Ovid's exile having more to do with his behavior than his writings, on which see chapter 3. On writers, see White, *Promised Verse*.

164. Dio Cassius 47.39.2–3.

165. On policing in Rome during the principate, see Keppie, "The Army and the Navy," 10:384–87; Nippel, *Public Order in Ancient Rome*, 85–98; Campbell, *Roman Army*, 38–45; C. Brélaz, "Lutter contre la violence à Rome," in *Les exclus dans l'Antiquté*, ed. C. Wolff (Paris: Boccard, 2007), 229–34; Kelly, "Policing and Security," in *A Cambridge Companion to the City of Rome*, ed. P. Erdkamp (Cambridge: CUP, 2013), 410–24; G. S. Aldrete, "Riots," in *A Cambridge Companion to the City of Rome*, ed. P. Erdkamp (Cambridge: CUP, 2013), 425–40; H. Ménard, *Maintenir l'Order: IIe-IVe siècles ap. J.-C* (Seysell: Champ Vallon, 2004); Fuhrmann, *Policing the Roman Empire*, 91.

166. Fuhrmann, *Policing the Roman Empire*, 93.

167. On riots, see B. Kelly, "Riot Control," 150–76, with further bibliography. He points out quite rightly that the ancient sources do not explain official responses to riots in terms of keeping officials, including the emperor, safe (156).

168. Other reasons are given by J. S. Rainbird, "The Vigiles of Rome" (PhD diss., University of Durham, 1976), chapter 3, esp. page 220, followed by Bingham, *Praetorian Guard*, 206: too few citizens were willing to do the job, using slaves might cause insurrection, and the *collegia* were not trustworthy. There is evidence, however, for citizens joining the corps, though this is rare.

169. On the hostility between the people and the military at these venues, see Campbell, *Roman Army*, 171. Their difficult relationship has already been noted in Coulston, "Armed and Belted Men," 76–118.

170. See M. Wistrand, *Entertainment and Violence in Ancient Rome* (Göteborg: Acta Universitatis Gothoburgensis, 1992), 35–36; A. Cameron, *Circus Factions* (Oxford: Clarendon Press, 1976), 223–24. There were even periods when actors were banished completely from Rome because of disruptive incidents. See, for example, Tacitus, *Ann.* 4.14.3; Suet., *Tiberius* 37.2; Dio 57.21.3 (under Tiberius, recalled by Caligula); cf. Dio 59.2.5; Suet., *Nero* 16.2 (under Nero though they had been recalled by 60 CE); cf. Tacitus, *Ann.* 14.21.4.

171. Val. Max. 2.4.1. He was writing in the early part of the first century CE. Also see Bingham, *Praetorian Guard*, 202.

172. This happened in 15 CE. See Tacitus, *Ann.* 1.77.1. See also Suet., *Tiberius* 37.2. It is possible that the violence resulted from restrictions put on actors after previous disruptions. See Tacitus, *Ann.* 1.54.2. Cameron, *Circus Factions*, 225, notes that the theater was notorious for "rowdyism" whereas events at the circus did not promote "regular and violent brawls." Also see Bingham, *Praetorian Guard*, 202.

173. J. V. P. D. Balsdon, *Life and Leisure in Ancient Rome* (London: Bodley Head, 1969), 418n117, argues that the urban cohorts were not used in this instance because "the city prefecture, with command of the urban cohorts, was not yet established." Yet Tacitus has Lucius Calpurnius Piso as urban prefect by 14 CE at least, and probably a year earlier, and therefore the option of using the urban cohorts clearly was available. See Tacitus, *Ann.* 6.11.3. When the first urban prefect was appointed is not clear. C. Ricci, "*In Custodiam Urbis.* Notes on the *Cohortes Urbanae*," *Historia* 60, no. 4 (2011): 486n7, claims the earliest was Marcus Valerius Messalla Corvinus (26 BCE), as does Fuhrmann, *Policing the Roman Empire*, 117; Bingham, *Praetorian Guard*, 202.

174. Tacitus, *Ann.* 14.61.

175. Starr, *Civilization and the Caesars*, 66.

176. Gabba, "Historians and Augustus," 75, 78.

177. See the comments of Gabba, "Historians and Augustus," 71.

178. Gabba, 72.

179. D. Shotter, *Tiberius Caesar* (London: Routledge, 2004), 17.

180. See Julian the Apostate in his *Caesares* 309A, where Silanus calls Augustus a chameleon.

181. See Wallace-Hadrill, *Augustan Rome*, 35.

182. The breastplate: Suet., *Div. Aug.* 35.1; Dio 54.12.3; Levick, *Augustus*, 178–79. Crook, "Last Age of the Roman Republic," 9:76, warns against making "incautious inferences" from this fact.

183. Suet., *Div. Aug.* 27.4.

184. Edmondson, *Augustus*, 5. His granddaughter Julia's son, Aemilius Paullus, died in 11 BCE. He also had his granddaughter's child, born during her exile to Trimerus, murdered (see chapter 3).

185. Millar, *Emperor in the Roman World*, 63.

186. Beard, *SPQR*, 371, claims there were "very few troops" and that Rome was otherwise a "demilitarized zone." She admits that Augustus took a monopoly on military force, but claims "his regime was nothing like a modern military dictatorship." This is simply an anachronism. The Augustan regime does not have to be like a modern dictatorship for the people of Rome to realize something had changed. There were ten thousand more troops in their vicinity, and Augustus was in charge of them. Nor does Beard mention the urban cohorts. If one must make a modern comparison in 1929, the number of active SS members acting as Nazi bodyguards had only grown to one thousand. Cf. Coulston, "Armed and Belted Men," 76–86, on how many troops there were and where they were stationed. Coulston also discussed their representation in Roman art (91–97).

187. On how the Senate slavishly advertised its loyalty to the imperial house, see Syme, *Roman Revolution*, 3; Rudich, *Political Dissidence under Nero*, xx–xxviii; Southern, *Augustus*, 142–44.

188. Momigliano claimed that Rostovtzeff failed to grasp this point. See A. Momigliano, "M. I. Rostovtzeff," in *Studies on Modern Scholarship* (Berkeley: University of California Press, 1994), 42; Edmondson, *Augustus*, 218.

189. See Syme, "The Nobiles in Eclipse," in *Augustan Aristocracy*, 32–49.

190. Ferrary, "Powers of Augustus," 129.

191. C. Nicolet, "Augustus, Government, and the Propertied Classes," in Millar and Segal, eds., *Caesar Augustus*, 111.

192. Jones, *Augustus*, 83.

193. Jones, *Augustus*, 81.

194. Lendon, *Empire of Honour*, 11. On patronage see Syme, *Roman Revolution*, 349–86.

195. Seneca, *de Clem.* 1.13.5; Cf. Dio 53.4.1.

196. Lendon, *Empire of Honour*, 9; Dio Chrys. 3.889. On fear of bodyguards: Josephus, *AJ* 19.6; Herodian 4.13.3–6.

197. Suet., *Div. Aug.* 51.3: *satis est enim, si hoc habemus ne quis nobis male facere possit.*

198. Pliny, *Ep.* 9.5 calls this characteristic *humanitas.*

199. For a survey of the forms of publicity available to emperors, see Campbell, *Emperor and the Roman Army*, 142–55; D. S. Potter, *Prophets and Emperors: Human and Divine Authority from Augustus to Theodosius* (Cambridge: CUP, 1994), 110–30. On the argument against "propaganda" see Galinsky, *Augustus*, 148–52.

200. S. Forbes and J. Prevas, *Power, Ambition, Glory: The Stunning Parallels between Great Leaders of the Ancient World and Today . . . and Lessons You Can Learn* (New York: Crown Business, 2009).

201. Galinsky, *Augustus*, 184.

202. Alston, *Aspects of Roman History*, 38.

CHAPTER 3: AUGUSTUS AND THE OPPOSITION

1. On the opposition to Augustus and his successors, see K. A. Raaflaub and L. J. Samons II, "Opposition to Augustus" in *Between Republic and Empire*, ed. K. Raaflaub and M. Toher (Berkeley: University of California Press, 1990), 433–47; A. Luisi, "L'opposizione sotto Augusto: Le due Giulie, Germanico e gli amici," in *Fazioni e congiure nel Mondo antico*, ed. M. Sordi (Milan: Vita e Pensiero 1999), 181–92. On the relationship to Augustus, see Kienast, *Augustus*, 126–51, with literature; Brunt, "The Role of the Senate in the Augustan Regime," 423–44; B. Levick, *Augustus: Image and Substance* (London and New York: Routledge, 2010), 164–201.

2. We should note that B. Levick, in *Augustus: Image and Substance*, is arguing against an organized, continuous opposition, a unified party that opposed the principate itself and existed throughout the Julio-Claudian period, instead of individual conspiracies. She notes that the idea of an organized opposition has recently lost ground (164). Raaflaub and Samons, "Opposition to Augustus," 417, write "that there existed opposition under Augustus and that much of it was aimed no less at the new system and individual solutions introduced by Augustus than at the *Princeps* himself cannot be doubted."

3. J. Crook, "Political History 30 BC to AD 14," *CAH²*, 10:73, in contradiction to Sattler, *Augustus und der Senat*, and W. Schmitthenner, ed., *Augustus. Wege der Forschung* 128 (Darmstadt: Wissenschaftliche Buchgesellschaft, 1969), 404–85.

4. Raaflaub and Samons, "Opposition to Augustus," 454.

5. W. Allen Jr., "The Political Atmosphere of the Reign of Tiberius," *TAPA* 72 (1941): 14. Allen also says the plots seem to have involved individuals with "no definite platform" except to kill the emperor. Surely those responsible gave some thought to replacing the emperor.

6. See the remarks of Suet., *Domitian* 21; Raaflaub and Samons, "Opposition to Augustus," 421.

7. Levick, *Augustus*, 173.

8. Southern, *Augustus*, 176; Levick, *Augustus*, 166.

9. They may also be literary creations. On the literary composition of the conspiracies under Augustus, see Cogitore, *La légitimité dynastique d'Auguste à Néron à l'épreuve des conspirations*, 20–26; on the sources, 26–33. On the subjectivity, see Levick, *Augustus*, 173.

10. Pliny, *HN* 7.45.149ff. Cogitore, *La légitimité dynastique d'Auguste à Néron à l'épreuve des conspirations*, 48–55, lists Quintus Gallius (44) and Q. Salvidienus

Rufus (40) as conspirators. Gallius, as praetor, was accused of attempting to assassinate Octavian, the consul, by smuggling in a weapon under his toga. Augustus had Gallius hustled from the tribunal by centurions and soldiers, tortured him, and supposedly tore his eyes out with his own hands. See Suet., *Div. Aug.* 27.4.

11. Sources on Lepidus: Dio 54.15.4; Appian, *BC* 4.50; Livy, *Per.* 133; Vell. Pat. 2.88; Suet., *Div. Aug.* 19.1. For the argument on the date with all the evidence, see P. M. D. Swan, "A Study of the Conspiracies against Emperors of the Julio-Claudian Dynasty" (PhD diss., Harvard University, 1964), 2; Crook, "Political History 30 BC to AD 14," 74, however, calls the story "unconvincing."

12. On Lepidus's background, family, and republican sentiments, see Swan, "Study of the Conspiracies," 2–11.

13. Vell. Pat. 2.88.3; Appian, *BC* 4.50.217–19; Livy, *Per.* 133; Dio 54.15.4; Raaflaub and Samons, "Opposition to Augustus," 422. See Cogitore, *La légitimité dynastique d'Auguste à Néron à l'épreuve des conspirations*, 55–62; Swan, "Study of the Conspiracies," 11.

14. On fighting for family glory, see Raaflaub and Samons, "Opposition to Augustus," 422. They also doubt the story of a conspiracy by the grandson of another triumvir, M. Licinius Crassus, 422–23. Contra, Kienast, *Augustus*, 96ff.

15. Levick, *Augustus*, 173–74; Syme, *Augustan Aristocracy*, 35.

16. On conspiracies, see Vell. Pat. 2.91.2.L; on Murena and Fannius Caepio, Suet., *Div. Aug.* 19; Vell. Pat. 2.91–92. Dio 54.3 gives the date, which would be 22 BCE. This date has been doubted because of an entry in the *Fasti Capitolini* for 23 BCE (*CIL* 1², 1). See the discussion in R. A. Bauman, "Tiberius and Murena," *Historia* 15, no. 4 (1966): 420–32. On the sources, see G. Cresci Marrone, "La congiura di Murena e le 'forbici' di Cassio Dione," in *Fazione e congiure nel mondo antico*, ed. M. Sordi (Milan: Vita e Pensiero, 1999), 193–203. Cf. Suet., *de Gramm.* 16.

17. See comments of Crook, "Political History 30 BC to AD 14," 87–88; Levick, *Augustus*, 176–77.

18. Dio 54.3.2–4; Vell. Pat. 2.91.2; Suet., *Div. Aug.* 19.1; *Tib.* 8; Tacitus, *Ann.* 1.10.4; Swan, "Study of the Conspiracies," 12. The literature on the conspiracy of Murena and Caepio is extensive. On the chronology and personnel, see Levick, *Augustus*, 100–103; Kienast, *Augustus*, 86n72, with the literature; J. S. Arkenberg, "Licinii Murenae Terentii Varrones, and Varrones Muranae," *Historia* 42, no. 4 (1993): 471–91; Raaflaub and Samons, "Opposition to Augustus," 425–26; Cogitore, *La légitimité dynastique d'Auguste à Néron à l'épreuve des conspirations*, 123–35.

19. Vell. Pat. 2.91.2. Syme, *Augustan Aristocracy*, 40n47, suggests he was the son of C. Fannius, a republican among the last companions of Sex. Pompeius in 35. See Appian, *BC* 5.139.579; Swan, "Study of the Conspiracies," 33.

20. See Arkenberg for the full bibliography and the prosopography: "Licinii Murenae Terentii Varrones, and Varrones Muranae," 326–51 (part 1); also Arkenberg, 471–91 (part 2), analyzes the literature on the subject. See L. J. Daly, "Varro Murena, cos. 23 B.C.," *Historia* 27, no. 1 (1978): 83–94, on Augustus engineering the death and disgrace of his consular colleague. Daly describes it as "a morass of inferences, conjectures, assumptions, and speculations, overgrow with well-worn truisms, which rarely are rooted in solid evidence." The problem revolves around whether one dates the conspiracy to 24, 23, or 22. For those arguing that the consul and the conspirator were *not* the same, See M. Swan, "The Consular

Fasti of 23 B.C. and the Conspiracy of Varro Murena," *HSCPh* 71 (1967): 235–47; Badian, "Crisis Theories and the Beginning of the Principate," 18–41; Swan, "Study of the Conspiracies," 4, 11–38. It was Syme, *Roman Revolution*, 225, who represented the traditional view that the consul was the conspirator. Cf. Syme, *Augustan Aristocracy*, 40. Dio 54.3 dates the conspiracy of Caepio and Murena to 22, but many modern scholars have placed it in early 23. See Strabo 14.670; Vell. Pat. 2.91.2, 93.1; Suet., *Div. Aug.* 19.1, 56.4, 66.3, and *Tib.* 8, with no indication of date; Tacitus, *Ann.* 1.10.5. It is also mentioned by Seneca, *de Brev. Vit.* 4.5, and *de Clem.* 1.9.6; Macrobius, *Sat.* 1.11.21. Also see Richardson, *Augustan Rome*, 103; S. Jameson, "22 or 23?" *Historia* 18, no. 2 (1969): 204–29; D. Stockton, "Primus and Murena," *Historia* 14, no. 1 (1965): 18–40.

21. Raaflaub and Samons, "Opposition to Augustus," 426. On the conspiracy, W. C. McDermott, "Varro Murena," *TAPA* 72 (1941): 255–65.

22. On Castricius: Suet., *Div. Aug.* 56.4.

23. On Maecenas: G. Williams, "Did Maecenas 'Fall from Favor'? Augustan Literary Patronage," in Raaflaub and Toher, eds., *Between Republic and Empire*, 258–75, argues against Maecenas's fall from grace, as does Levick, *Augustus*, 177. Even the name of the conspirators differs in the sources: Dio 54.3.4; Suet., *Div. Aug.* 19, 66; *Tib.* 8; Tacitus, *Ann.* 1.10; Vell. Pat. 2.91.2; Seneca, *de Clem* 1.9.6, *de Brev. Vit.* 4.5; Macrobius, *Sat.* 1.11.21; Jones, *Augustus*, 68; Everitt, *Augustus*, 215. Syme, *Roman Revolution*, 333–35, argues for the importance of this conspiracy as does Stockton, "Primus and Murena," 18–40, esp. 26ff.

24. Dio 54.3.4, where he uses the words *hetero* and *allo* (others).

25. Crook, "Political History 30 BC to AD 14," 88.

26. Dio 54.3.5, 7. The slaves' names are not given.

27. Dio 54.3.6; Cf. Macrobius, *Sat.* 1.11.21 has Caepio killed in Naples after the conviction. Strabo 14.5.4 tells of Athenaeus, who fled with Murena but was proven innocent and released by Augustus. Dio 54.3.8 introduces a skeptical note about the complicity of Murena. He has Maecenas and Proculus pleading on Murena's behalf. This seems unlikely, although the historicity of the plot itself is accepted by Strabo, Velleius, Seneca, Suetonius, and Macrobius.

28. On sacrifices, Dio 54.3.8.

29. On Egnatius Rufus: Vell. Pat. 2. 91.3–4. Also see Cogitore, *La légitimité dynastique d'Auguste à Néron à l'épreuve des conspirations*, 136–41; D. A. Phillips, "The Conspiracy of Egnatius Rufus and the Election of Suffect Consuls under Augustus," *Historia* 46, no. 1 (1997): 103–12.

30. Dio 53.24.6, 54.2.4. On the date, see Swan, "Study of the Conspiracies," 41n78.

31. Vell. Pat. 2.91.3, 92.4; Dio 53.24.4–5. Swan, "Study of the Conspiracies," 40.

32. Dio 53.24.5. See Crook, "Political History 30 BC to AD 14," 89, who objects to this being listed as a conspiracy.

33. Dio 53.24.6; Starr, *Civilization and the Caesars*, 65, 71.

34. Dio 53.24.6; Swan, "Study of the Conspiracies," 41n78.

35. Dio 54.2.3–4; Swan, "Study of the Conspiracies," 42.

36. See Vell. Pat. 2.92.4 and Phillips, "Conspiracy of Egnatius Rufus," 109–11, who argues that he was aedile in 21 and praetor in 20. If that is the case, not only was his candidacy for consul probably illegal, but his quick succession to prae-

torship was likewise contrary to the customs of the *cursus honorum*. It should be noted, however, that such breaches had become common over the previous one hundred years.

37. Dio 54.10.1–2.

38. Vell. Pat. 2.91.3–4. Beard, *SPQR*, 375, says there could be no plot because Augustus was not in Rome, but he could have easily been killed on his return voyage. Cf. Raaflaub and Samons, "Opposition to Augustus," 427.

39. Dio 54.10.1–2; Although Dio does not named Egnatius, Swan, "Study of the Conspiracies," 39–44, makes the connection between the disturbances and the conspiracy.

40. Vell. Pat. 2.91.4; Tacitus, *Ann.* 1.10.4; Suet., *Div. Aug.* 19.1. Cf. Seneca, *de Clem.* 1.9.6, *de Brev. Vit.* 4.5. Also see Swan, "Study of the Conspiracies," 44; Everitt, *Augustus*, 227.

41. Beard, *SPQR*, 376. On the social and economic milieu, see P. Badot, "À propos de la conspiration de M. Egnatius Rufus," *Latomus* 32 (1973): 606–15. Also see Phillips, "Conspiracy of Egnatius Rufus," 103–12.

42. Cogitore, *La légitimité dynastique d'Auguste à Néron à l'épreuve des conspirations*, 141–45; Crook, "Political History 30 BC to AD 14," 80–81.

43. Dio 53.23.5; Suet., *Div. Aug.* 66.2; Starr, *Civilization and the Caesars*, 71; Jones, *Augustus*, 49–50; Raaflaub and Samons, "Opposition to Augustus," 423–24; Kienast, *Augustus*, 85n68, which cites the literature; L. J. Daly and W. L. Reiter, "The Gallus Affair and Augustus' Lex Iulia Maestatis: A Study of Historical Chronology and Causality," in *Studies in Latin Literature and Roman History*, ed. C. Deroux (Brussels: Latomus, 1979): 289–311; Crook, "Political History 30 BC to AD 14," 74; Levick, *Augustus*, 175–76.

44. Both the date and place of the plot assigned to the conspiracy are imprecise. Dio 55.14.1 puts it before 5 BCE; Seneca, *de Clem.* 1.9 between 16 and 13 BCE. See also Swan, "Study of the Conspiracies," 44–48. It seems more likely that Seneca was trying to inculcate a moral lesson to his pupil Nero about clemency than relating a historical event. On the entire episode being doubtful, see Raaflaub and Samons, "Opposition to Augustus," 427–28.

45. D. C. A. Shotter, "Cn. Cornelius Cinna Magnus and the Adoption of Tiberius," *Latomus* 33 (1974): 306–13; A. A. Barrett, *Livia: First Lady of Imperial Rome* (New Haven, CT: YUP, 2002), 132; Bauman, *Crimen Maiestatis*, 196–97.

46. Suet., *Div. Aug.* 19.2. See Gibson, *Julio-Claudian Succession*, 4, on someone else being involved.

47. Suet., *Div. Aug.* 19.2; *PIR* T, 41; Cogitore, *La légitimité dynastique d'Auguste à Néron à l'épreuve des conspirations*, 105–6; B. Baldwin, *The Roman Emperors* (Montreal: Harvest House, 1980), 8, considers the toga "one of the silliest garments ever invented," but it was a great place to hide a dagger.

48. Dio 54.12.3, 54.15.1.4, 55.4.4.

49. Whether or not these statements are accurate has been questioned. See Raaflaub and Samons, "Opposition to Augustus," 421, who also discusses the chronological problems that make it impossible to be sure how many conspiracies there really were. Levick, *Augustus*, 178–79, accepts Dio's account saying the victims may not have been men of distinction, but who else would try to kill Augustus?

50. On the "independence" of Augustan poets, see White, *Promised Verse*.

51. Various theories have been suggested as to Augustus's theory of succession. On the "regency" or "caretaker" theory see Seager, *Tiberius*, 18–22, 24–26, 29–35, 35–38; on "dynastic collegiality," see B. Levick, "Tiberius' Retirement to Rhodes in 6 BC," *Latomus* 31 (1972): 779–813, esp. 781–86; Levick, *Tiberius the Politician*, 19–67. Arguing for a more flexible system: G. G. Fagan, "The Roman Imperial Succession under the Julio-Claudians, 23 BC–AD 69" (MA thesis, School of Classics, Trinity College, Dublin, 1987), 18; Gruen, "Augustus and the Making of the Principate," 38, believes we should avoid seeing any overt signs of planning for a biological successor. Syme believed there were such signs. More recently, see Osgood, "Suetonius and the Succession to Augustus," 19–40, who comes closer to Syme, *Roman Revolution*, 341.

52. Wiseman, *Myths of Rome*, 235.

53. For a fuller discussion of women in the Augustan Principate, see R. A. Bauman, *Women and Politics in Ancient Rome* (London: Routledge, 1992), 99–129. On Augustus's "genetic" conception of the succession, see Crook, "Political History 30 BC to AD 14," 83. See McHugh, "Manipulating Memory," 119, on scholars who have linked the major honors granted to Livia in her lifetime to her role in Augustus's dynastic strategy. On the legal aspects of inheritance, see V. L. Johnson, "The Factor of Inheritance in the Julio-Claudian Succession" (PhD diss., University of Wisconsin, 1955).

54. Dio 55.10.15; Vell. Pat. 2.100.3–5.

55. Pliny, *HN* 7.149. For a discussion of Pliny's evidence, see H. Tränkle, "Augustus bei Tacitus, Cassius Dio, und dem alteren Plinius," *WS* 82 (1969): 108–30; Swan, "Study of the Conspiracies," 52–62; R. Till, "Plinius über Augustus (*Hist. Nat.* 7.147–150)," *WJA.* 3 (1977): 127–37; Ferrill, "Augustus and His Daughter," 332–46, accepts the gossip. R. Bauman, *Crimen Maiestatis*, 198–245, argues there was no political conspiracy and yet Julia and her paramours were convicted of a form of treason.

56. On their role in the power structure and how this role was portrayed by historians, see S. Fischler, "Social Stereotypes and Historical Analysis: The Case of the Imperial Women at Rome," in *Women in Ancient Societies: An Illusion of the Night*, ed. L. J. Archer, S. Fischler, and M. Wyke (New York: Routledge, 1994), 115–33. On the other hand, Bleichen, *Augustus*, writes as if women do not exist. T. A. Dorey, "Adultery and Propaganda in the Early Roman Empire," *University of Birmingham Historical Journal* 8 (1961): 1–6, believes Livia was behind the smear campaign against Julia.

57. Or so argued by B. Levick, "Julians and Claudians," *G&R* 22 (1975): 29–38.

58. On the scheme to murder Augustus, see Pliny, *HN* 7.149; Dio 55.10.12; Seneca, *de Brev Vit.* 4.6. The standard study on Julia's conspiracy remains R. Syme's "The Crisis of 2 B.C.," *Sitzungsberichte der Bayerische Akademie der Wissenschaften* 7 (1974): 3–34. See also Green, "Carmen et Error," 217; Raaflaub and Samons, "Opposition to Augustus," 428–30.

59. Macrobius, *Sat.* 1.11.17, says she was having an adulterous affair but does not hint at conspiracy. Pliny, *HN* 7.149 says there were many assassination attempts. He refers to Julia's adultery and plotted parricide, which suggests that the adultery charge brought on her by Augustus was to cover up the conspiracy. Tacitus, *Ann.* 1.10.4, 4.44, notes that Iullus Antonius was executed while everyone else

was exiled, suggesting he was more dangerous. No plot is alluded to in Vell. Pat. 88.1.3, 93.1–2, 100.3–5; nor in Seneca, *de Bene.* 6.32. See Luisi, "L'opposizione sotto Augusto," 182–91, on the factional strife between the Julio-Claudians. Raaflaub and Samons, "Opposition to Augustus," 429, think it was neither. Crook, "Political History 30 BC to AD 14," 100–101, rejects the entire interpretation of factional strife between the Julians and the Claudians as too simple.

60. Dio 55.10.12–16; Syme, "Crisis of 2 B.C.," 10–16; W. K. Lacey, "2 B.C. and Julia's Adultery," *Antichthon* 14 (1980): 127–42.

61. See the comments of Fantham, *Julia Augusti*, 130.

62. Fantham, *Julia Augusti*, 131, puts to rest Jerome Carcopino's portrait of Julia as out to murder anyone in her way. See Carcopino, "La Véritable Julie," in his *Passion et politique chez les Césars*, 83–142. It was J. V. P. D. Balsdon, *Roman Women* (London: Bodley Head, 1962), 84–86, who first tried to give a sympathetic portrait of Julia and suggested that Augustus's precipitous reaction is what makes one believe the charges were political. Perhaps best at separating history from myth is Wiseman, *Myths of Rome*, 232–35.

63. Syme, *Roman Revolution*, 427; Barrett, *Livia*, 50; Bauman, *Women and Politics*, 126. These are all arguments *ex silentio* since the literary sources give us no information whatsoever—not even speculation—on Livia's reaction to Julia's disgrace. Even Tacitus, who never misses an opportunity to slander Livia, is silent.

64. Green, "Carmen et Error," 218; B. Levick, "The Fall of Julia the Younger," *Latomus* 35 (1976): 301–39; Raaflaub and Samons, "Opposition to Augustus," 430–33, say it was a palace conspiracy gone wrong. Galinsky, *Augustus*, 126, dismisses the idea without discussion. It is also rejected by Southern, *Augustus*, 305, but see Cogitore, *La légitimité dynastique d'Auguste à Néron à l'épreuve des conspirations*, 165–72; Balsdon, *Roman Women*, 87; E. Groag, "Studien zur Kaisergeschichte III: Der Sturz der Julia," *WS* 41 (1919): 74–88; Carcopino, *Passion et politique chez les Césars*, 83–142, esp. 129ff.

65. McHugh, "Manipulating Memory," 148, on the standard accusations used to defame Roman women: attempted poisoning, sexual voracity, independence from masculine authority, desire for power, involvement in military action, lack of compassion, and cruelty. See Fantham, *Julia Augusti*, 85–87, for how this applies to Julia. For a male scholar who accepts every lascivious detail, see Ferrill, "Augustus and His Daughter," 332–33.

66. Syme, *Roman Revolution*, 427, bases his judgment on a prosopographical analysis of the group supposedly involved in the conspiracy. See also Levick, "Fall of Julia the Younger," 301–39.

67. Vell. Pat. 2.100.5; S. T. Cohen, "Augustus, Julia and the Development of Exile *ad Insulam*," *CQ* 58, no. 1 (2008): 206–17, argues that this was the first time exile to a specific place was used as punishment and that Augustus invented the penalty to deal with this particular crisis. On the deaths of Julia and Gracchus, see R. S. Rogers, "The Deaths of Julia and Gracchus, A.D. 14," *TAPA* 98 (1967): 383–90. B. Levick, *Tiberius the Politician*, 41–42 suggests Scribonia was part of the plot. Although there is no evidence, she argues for: "an air of family faction."

68. Tacitus, *Ann.* 3.24.4; R. S. Rogers, "The Emperor's Displeasure: *Amicitiam renuntiare*," *TAPA* 90 (1959): 229–30, who finds this extraordinarily lenient consid-

ering the *Lex Julia de adulteriis* called for relegation to an island and confiscation of half of the man's property.

69. Tacitus, *Ann.* 4.44.3; cf. 1.10.4; Dio 55.10.15. See Rogers, "The Emperor's Displeasure: *Amicitiam renuntiare*," 230–31, and references there on the trial.

70. There were other senators and equestrians, some named and unnamed—a certain Demosthenes, for example. Macrobius 1.11.17; Cf. Vell. Pat. 2.100.4ff; Dio 55.10.15; Tacitus, *Ann.* 3.18.1, 1.10.3; Pliny, *HN* 7.149; Suet., *Div. Aug* 65.2. We should note the famous names and their connections to prominent republican families. For the identity and family connections of these men, see Groag, "Der Sturz der Julia," *WS* 41 (1919): 86; R. Billows, "The Last of the Scipios," *AJAH* 7 (1982): 53–68, esp. 62.

71. Tacitus, *Ann.* 1.53. Syme accepts the story of Tiberius having Gracchus executed: *Roman Revolution*, 493n3 and *Tacitus*, 423. Rogers does not: "Death of Julia and Gracchus," 388. Rogers believes Augustus's daughter Julia, Agrippa Postumus, and Sempronius Gracchus all died of natural causes and the stories of their death were circulated by the Julian party to defame Tiberius (390). The others were Quintus Crispinus, Appius Claudius, and Cornelius Scipio. Whether one sees these lovers grouped together as a "formidable faction" or a "sordid lot of degenerate aristocrats" depends on how one interprets the evidence. See Ferrill, "Augustus and His Daughter," 341, or R. S. Rogers, "The Conspiracy of Agrippina," *TAPA* 62 (1931): 147, and Rogers, "Death of Julia and Gracchus," 383–90, who points out that Gracchus had been Julia's paramour even when she was Agrippa's wife and he remained so after her marriage to Tiberius, toward whom he kindled Julia's scorn and hatred.

72. This is found in Seneca, *de Brev. Vit.* 4.5, supported by Pliny, *HN* 7.149, and Dio 55.10.12–16. Vell. Pat. 2.100.4 has him commit suicide. Tacitus, *Ann.* 1–10 does not mention the conspiracy. On the idea that this was a smear campaign by Livia, see Fantham, *Julia Augusti*, 88, 127. A good discussion of the source of these stories can be found in Charlesworth, "Tiberius and the Death of Augustus," *AJPh* 44, no. 2 (1923): 145–57. There is a large literature on the subject, for which see Kienast, *Augustus*, 111n179. For those arguing against the conspiracy, see Ferrill, "Augustus and His Daughter," 332–46, with a survey of the literature on 333–37, and Lacey, "2 B.C. and Julia's Adultery," 127–42, esp. 128–36. Syme supports the conspiracy theory in *Roman Revolution*, 426ff., following E. Groag, "Der Sturz der Julia," *WS* 40 (1918): 150–67, and 41 (1919): 74–88. See also R. Syme, *Roman Papers*, vol. 3 (Oxford: OUP, 1984), 926–30; E. Meise, *Untersuchungen zur Geschichte der Julisch-Claudischen Dynastie* (Munich: Beck, 1969), 40–42. For modern attempts to rehabilitate Julia's reputation, beginning with C. M. Wieland, see Fantham, *Julia Augusti*, 126–27.

73. Dettenhofer, *Herrschaft und Widerstand im augusteischen Principat*, 176–79, suggested that Augustus knew of Julia's offenses and kept them quiet until he was installed as *Pater Patriae* and ready to strike. This is rejected by Levick, *Augustus*, 185–86, who also argues that even if there was not a conspiracy, Augustus may have chosen to treat adultery as treason against his regime.

74. Fantham, *Julia Augusti*, 89, making a parallel with Ovid's description of his own departure.

75. Suet., *Div. Aug.* 65; See Fantham, *Julia Augusti*, 92–93; J. Linderski wrote a learned and sympathetic study of Julia's last years based on inscriptions from former members of her household in Rhegium: "Julia in Rhegium," *ZPE* 72 (1988): 181–200.

76. Raaflaub and Samons, "Opposition to Augustus," 430–31; Rogers, "Conspiracy of Agrippina," 147; Syme, *Augustan Aristocracy*, 412; Cogitore, *La légitimité dynastique d'Auguste à Néron à l'épreuve des conspirations*, 172–75; Fantham, *Julia Augusti*, 109. Note that Swan, "Study of the Conspiracies," 52, 62, always identifies the conspiracy with the males involved.

77. Suet., *Div. Aug.* 19.1; *Schol. Iuv.* 6.158; Dio 55.27.1–3. On the troubles of the time, see R. Syme, *History in Ovid* (Oxford: Clarendon Press, 1978), 209; Syme, *Augustan Aristocracy*, 123, contra Levick, "Fall of Julia the Younger," 307–9. On the prosopographical problems caused by disagreements in the sources, see Swan, "Study of the Conspiracies," 63–69. The fact that Dio's account for the year 8 CE is lost only complicates the issue.

78. Richardson, *Augustan Rome*, 176; Levick, *Tiberius the Politician*, 54–61, but see Syme, *Augustan Aristocracy*, 115–27. For a detailed prosopographical study of the faction, see Levick, "Fall of Julia the Younger," 301–39. Cogitore, *La légitimité dynastique d'Auguste à Néron à l'épreuve des conspirations*,172–75; Green, "Carmen et Error," 219.

79. Suet., *Div. Aug.* 19. There is some debate over whether Paullus was exiled or executed. The only evidence for his survival is the entry of a man with the same name in the list of Arval brethren for 14 CE; see Levick, *Tiberius the Politician*, 187; Fantham, *Julia Augusti*, 111. Syme, *History in Ovid*, 206–11 argues for exile, not execution, as he does in Syme, *Augustan Aristocracy*, 122–23, with the inscriptional evidence. Raaflaub and Samons, "Opposition to Augustus," 431. Those who believe he was executed follow the Scholia of Juvenal. See Green, "Carmen et Error," 219.

80. The ancient sources are unanimous in saying Agrippa was banished because of his ferocious character and bad behavior. See Dio 55.32.1; Suet., *Div. Aug.* 65, on his temperament; *Tib.* 22, on his death; Tacitus, *Ann.* 1.6. This comes across to some as a smoke screen: Fagan, "Roman Imperial Succession," 32; Barrett, *Livia*, 59–60, on the possibility of a Julian party and Postumus's connection with it. Also see Levick, "Julians and Claudians," 29–38. Other scholars have attacked the notion of a Julian and Claudian split: Charlesworth, "Tiberius and the Death of Augustus," 153; A. E. Pappano, "Agrippa Postumus," *CP* 36, no. 1 (January 1941): 40.

81. Crook, "Political History 30 BC to AD 14," 105, says all the ancient sources describe him as truculent and retarded: Vell. Pat. 2.112.7; Suet., *Div. Aug.* 65.1 and 4; Dio 55.32.1–2; Tacitus, *Ann.* 1.5. Certainly Augustus may have considered the young man an unsuitable successor for these reasons. On the severity of the punishment, see Levick, "Abdication and Agrippa Postumus," *Historia* 21, no. 4 (1972): 674–97. For a different view of the inheritance, see S. Jameson, "Augustus and Agrippa Postumus," *Historia* 24, no. 2 (1975): 287–314. Cf. Seager, *Tiberius*, 37. Violent propaganda against Augustus had been circulating in Agrippa's name, if not actually by him. See Suet., *Div. Aug.* 51.1, and Green, "Carmen et Error," 219.

82. We know nothing more of the plot or of their fate. See Suet., *Div. Aug.* 19.2; cf. 65.4; Vell. Pat. 2.112.7; Tacitus, *Ann.* 1.3.4; Dio 55.32.1; Barrett, *Livia*, 65. The

secondary literature on the plot is cited by Kienast, *Augustus*, 120n217. Cf. Pappano, "Agrippa Postumus," 41.

83. Tacitus, *Ann.* 1.5; Dio 56.30; Zon. 10.38; Plutarch, *de Garul.* 508A (who says Postumus was exiled on a "false accusation"); Pliny, *HN* 7.150, Aur. Vic., *Epitome* 1.27. Pappano, "Agrippa Postumus," 40, calls it "a piece of propaganda." Charlesworth, "Tiberius and the Death of Augustus," 145–57, shows its extreme improbability and connects it to the rumor of Livia poisoning Augustus. Cf. Syme, *Roman Revolution*, 433; Levick, *Tiberius the Politician*, 64. See Crook, "Political History 30 BC to AD 14," 99, on antiquity being given to "novelettes about poisoning."

84. There is disagreement on whether Agrippa was murdered before or after the death of Augustus. Syme, *Roman Revolution*, 439, says it was done via Gaius Sallustius Crispus (grandnephew of the historian) on the orders of the dead princeps. Also see Tacitus, *Ann.* 1.6; Wiedemann, "Tiberius to Nero," 202. On the other hand, Charlesworth, "Tiberius and the Death of Augustus," 145–57, attacked the entire idea of a conspiracy. The accounts are inconsistent on who ordered the death. Tacitus, *Ann.* 1.6 has Tiberius dispatching the centurion. Suet., *Tiberius* 22 has Tiberius disavowing all knowledge of the event. W. Allen Jr., "The Death of Agrippa Postumus," *TAPA* 78 (1947): 131–39, argued for a natural death.

85. Pliny, *HN* 7.149, as Syme points out (*Augustan Aristocracy*, 122) and warns that the lack of evidence invites speculation.

86. On the political climate see Green, "Carmen et Error," 222; Fantham, *Julia Augusti*, 109, on the sexual stories.

87. F. Norwood, "The Riddle of Ovid's 'Regelatio,'" *CP* 58, no. 3 (July 1963): 153, is not the only scholar to have suggested that the Tacitean tradition has misrepresented the facts based on propaganda from Julia's party; R. S. Rogers, "The Emperor's Displeasure and Ovid," *TAPA* 97 (1966): 373–78, makes the case for treason. Also see Raaflaub and Samons, "Opposition to Augustus," 430; Syme, *Augustan Aristocracy*, 412–13; and Green, "Carmen et Error," 210–22, who writes that "on our available evidence, *only* a political solution to the problem is acceptable" (210). He proposes a *delator* was involved in the plot, who then turned state's evidence in return for immunity (221). Crook, "Political History 30 BC to AD 14," 108, finds many of the interpretations of treason "too close to fiction." The story was turned into fiction by Benita Kane Jaro in *Betray the Night* (Mundelein, IL: Bolchazy-Carducci, 2009). The many fanciful explanations for his relegation are collected in J. C. Thibault, *The Mystery of Ovid's Exile* (Berkeley: University of California Press, 1964).

88. Suet., *Div. Aug.* 65. See Raaflaub and Samons, "Opposition to Augustus," 454, who view these events as more personal rebellion than a broadly based attempt at overthrow.

89. Raaflaub and Samons, "Opposition to Augustus," 433.

90. Raaflaub and Samons, "Opposition to Augustus," 432.

91. Gibson, *Julio-Claudian Succession*, 4.

92. Suet., *Div. Aug.* 99.2. On the portrayal of Augustus's death in Velleius Paterculus, see A. J. Woodman, *Velleius Paterculus: The Tiberian Narrative* (Cambridge: CUP, 1977), 215–16.

93. Surprising deaths from undiagnosed natural causes were often attributed to poisoning. Poison scares often coincided with plagues. People died of food

poisoning regularly. See L. Cilliers and F. P. Retief, "Poisons, Poisoning and the Drug Trade in Ancient Rome," *Akroterion* 45 (2000), 88–100, for a list of the poisons available. For a more balanced view of Livia's career, see Barrett, *Livia*; A. Fraschetti, "Livia the Politician," in A. Fraschetti (ed.), *Roman Women* (Chicago: University of Chicago Press, 2001), 100–117; N. Purcell, "Livia and the Womanhood of Rome," in J. Edmondson, *Augustus*, 191–92. On the accusations against Livia, see McHugh, "Manipulating Memory," 147; C. Gafforini, "Livia Drusilla tra storie e letteratura." *Rendiconti, Classe di Lettere e Scienze morali e storiche. Istituto Lombardo* 130 (1996): 122–44.

94. In the ancient world, as in fairy tales, stepmothers were often portrayed as evil schemers. They must have felt that they could only protect their futures by advancing their sons' interests. Enough of them lived up to the stereotype, persecuting the children of their husband's first marriage that fathers sometimes had their children adopted and brought up in another family. See Everitt, *Augustus*, 221; Barrett, *Livia*, 62–64; A. A. Barrett, "Tacitus, Livia and the Evil Step-mother," *Rh. Mus.* 144 (2001): 171–75 who notes that Tacitus's assessment in the fifth book of the *Annals* (5.1) is negative as opposed to the measured criticisms of Seneca, *de Clem.* 1.9, *Cons. Marcia* 2–5; Pliny, *HN* 7.150. Only Aur. Vict. *Epit. Caes.* 1.27 as the source of Tacitus's criticism.

95. For non-American readers, Dr. Jack Kevorkian was America's best known euthanasia activist. It is Dio who introduces the charge that Livia resorted to murder to clear the way for her son. On the poisoned figs, see Dio 56.30.1–3; Barrett, *Livia*, 36 and 112–13; Suet., *Div. Aug.* 99.2; on euthanasia, Everitt, *Augustus*, 316. See D. Wardle, "Perfect Send-off: Suetonius and the Dying Art of Augustus (Suet., *Aug.* 99)," *Mnemosyne* 60, no. 3 (2007): 443–63, on the way Suetonius presents Augustus's final hours as reflecting his character or the model saintly death an emperor should have.

96. See Galinsky, *Augustus*, 113 on the image of the "wicked step-mother on the Palatine." He also points out her interest in medicines and cures could have added to her reputation as a poisoner (115). Cf. A. Fraschetti, "Livia the Politician," in *Roman Women*, ed. A. Fraschetti (Chicago: University of Chicago Press, 2001), 100–117.

97. Tacitus, *Ann.* 1.10 on the deification of Augustus. And see Levick, *Tiberius the Politician*, 75; Ferrary, *Powers of Augustus*, 125–29. Richardson, *Augustan Rome*, 194.

98. Gibson, *Julio-Claudian Succession*, 4.

99. Tacitus, *Ann.* 1.5.3–4. Bingham, *Praetorian Guard*, 21. Note the precedent: Tanaquil, the Etruscan wife of Tarquinius Priscus, was also said to have hidden her husband's death until she was sure that the succession would pass to Servius Tullius, the man she considered worthy of succeeding her husband. Dio 2.10 frag. (Zon. 7, 9).

100. Tacitus, *Ann.* 1.5.3–4; Bingham, *Praetorian Guard*, 21.

101. Bingham, *Praetorian Guard*, 21–22, 138n81.

102. Syme, *Roman Revolution*, 410; Gabba, "Historians and Augustus," 81.

103. Tacitus, *Ann.* 1.8 on the armed guard. He commits a substantial portion of Book 1 to the two mutinies that followed immediately after Tiberius's accession.

104. Pliny, *HN* 7.147–50. On the implausibility of a plot against Gaius Caesar and Lucius Caesar, see Barrett, *Livia*, 50–51.

105. Dio 55.16.3; Gabba, "Historians and Augustus," 74. Raaflaub and Samons, "Opposition to Augustus," 432, make a distinction between the attempts on Augustus's life and those against Tiberius, Claudius, Nero, and Domitian.

106. Wallace-Hadrill, *Augustan Rome*, 42.

107. Matthew D. H. Clark, *Augustus: The First Emperor* (Exeter: Bristol Phoenix Press, 2010), 4.

CHAPTER 4: THE REIGN OF TIBERIUS

1. R. S. Rogers, *Criminal Trials and Criminal Legislation under Tiberius* (Middletown, CT: American Philological Association, 1935) lists fifty-four people having been tried for *perduellio* (high treason), a charge that usually includes a plot to kill the emperor. For a discussion of the laws under which this was done, see C. W. Chilton, "The Roman Law of Treason under the Early Principate," *JRS* 45, nos. 1–2 (1955): 73–81, who argues that the very term *perduellio* was obsolete by the time of Tiberius, and that all the treason trials were conducted under the *Lex Julia*. R. S. Rogers, "Treason in the Early Empire," *JRS* 49, nos. 1–2 (1959): 90–94, defends himself against Chilton.

2. On the poisoned figs, see Dio 56.30.1–3 and Swan, *Augustan Succession*, 303. Rejecting the story: Everitt, *Augustus*, 315–16; Barrett, *Livia*, 36 and 112–13; and see my chapter 3, note 95. R. H. Martin, "Tacitus and the Death of Augustus," *CQ* 5, nos. 1–2 (January–April 1955): 123–28, has Tacitus believing the circumstances of Tiberius's accession being as dubious as those surrounding the accession of the emperor Nero.

3. Meijer, *Emperors Don't Die in Bed*, 21.

4. The sources do not agree on who eliminated Agrippa Postumus: Augustus alone, Livia in Augustus's name and with Tiberius's knowledge, Livia without the knowledge of Tiberius, or Tiberius alone. Tacitus, *Ann.* 1.6, wanted to exculpate Augustus and states firmly that Tiberius was lying when he said Augustus ordered the execution. Suet., *Tiberius* 22 is undecided between the three candidates. Dio 57.3.5 unhesitatingly blames Tiberius alone. There has also been a heated controversy in the secondary literature. See Seager, *Tiberius*, 41; Rogers, *Criminal Trials*, 2–4; E. Hohl, "Primum Facinus Novi Principatus," *Hermes* 70, no. 3 (1935): 350–55; Pappano, "Agrippa Postumus," 30–45; Allen, "Death of Agrippa Postumus," 131–39. On Tiberius's responsibility, see R. Detweiler, "Historical Perspectives on the Death of Agrippa Postumus," *CJ* 65, no. 7 (1970): 289–95.

5. The argument about there being Julian and Claudian factions belongs to Levick, "Julians and Claudians," 29–38, and B. Levick, "The Fall of Julia the Younger," *Latomus* 35 (1976): 301–39. Also accepting the escalating rivalry: D. C. A. Shotter, "Agrippina the Elder: A Woman in a Man's World," *Historia* 49, no. 3 (2000): 341–57, esp. 348; and D. C. A. Shotter, "Julians, Claudians and the Accession of Tiberius," *Latomus* 30 (1971): 1117–23. Those not accepting the argument: Raaflaub and Samons, "Opposition to Augustus," 429; and J. A. Crook, "The Last Age of the Roman Republic," *CAH²*, 9:100–101.

6. Fantham, *Julia Augusti*, 91.

7. Tiberius had been named as heir to two-thirds of Augustus's estate in his will. See Tacitus, *Ann.* 1.8; Dio 56.32.1, and Suet., *Div. Aug.* 101. Fagan, "Roman Imperial Succession under the Julio-Claudians," 98 and 98n8; Swan, *Augustan Succession*, 310–11.

8. On the relationship between Tiberius and Livia, see Barrett, *Livia*, 74, and Fischler, "Social Stereotypes and Historical Analysis," 128. For a bibliography and analytical essay on the subject of women in Tacitus, see K. G. Wallace, "Women in Tacitus," *ANRW* 2.33.5 (1991): 3556–74. B. Baldwin, "Women in Tacitus" *Prudentia* 4 (1972): 91, on the other hand, believed "Tacitus exhibited no unique attitude toward women."

9. The issue of his disposition was perhaps overargued by Gregorio Marañon, *Tiberius: A Study in Resentment* (London: Hollis & Carter, 1956). More recently, Stephanie Romkey has suggested a more up-to-date diagnosis in "OCPD and the Enigmatic Personality of Emperor Tiberius" (MA thesis, McMaster University, Hamilton, Ontario, 2006). For a balanced account and one that shrewdly concludes that we will never know the real Tiberius, see Balsdon, "Principates of Tiberius and Gaius," 87–90.

10. On Tiberius's relationship with the public, see Yavetz, *Plebs and Princeps*, 108ff.

11. On his arrogance, see Levick, *Tiberius the Politician*, 85.

12. Levick, *Tiberius the Politician*, 42 and 44.

13. As he did, for example, at a funeral in Pollentia. See Suet., *Tiberius* 37; Yavetz, *Plebs and Princeps*, 11.

14. Pliny, *HN* 34.62.

15. A tribune of one of the Praetorian cohorts was wounded when trying to stop the vituperation that rained on the magistrates; see Tacitus, *Ann.* 1.77. On efforts to maintain the grain supply see Tacitus, *Ann.* 2.87.1; Vell. Pat. 3.126.3; Levick, *Tiberius the Politician*, 121, 218.

16. On fires in 16: Dio 57.14.8. In 27: Tacitus, *Ann.* 4.6.1; Vell. Pat. 2.130.2; Suet., *Tiberius* 48. In 36: Tacitus, *Ann.* 6.45.1. And see Levick, *Tiberius the Politician*, 105 on floods, 218 on fires.

17. Suet., *Tiberius* 37; Tacitus, *Ann.* 4.27.3.

18. For the powers and the chronology, see Levick, *Tiberius the Politician*, 68–81, esp. 75, citing earlier bibliography. No matter how much hesitation was detected by later ancient historians, Levick sees none (76).

19. Tacitus, *Ann.* 1.12.1; Vell. Pat. 2.124.2; and the commentary of A. Woodman, *Velleius Paterculus. The Tiberian Narrative* (Cambridge: CUP, 1977), 223; Dio 57.2.4.

20. On the importance of this transition period and the chronology, see Levick, *Tiberius the Politician*, 68–81.

21. All the ancient sources report the offer to Germanicus: Tacitus, *Ann.* 1.16.4 and 1.31.4; Dio 57.5.1; Suet., *Tiberius* 25.2, *Caligula.* 1.1; Vell. Pat. 2.125.2. Levick, *Tiberius the Politician*, 71 and 247n6 thinks the attempt to proclaim Germanicus was "not seriously meant." Seager, *Tiberius*, 53–54, believes the offer "has significance." On the cause of the mutiny, see J. J. Wilkes, "A Note on the Mutiny of the Pannonian Legions in A.D. 14," *CQ* 13, no. 2 (1963): 268–71. As Levick points out, there is no specific evidence that Germanicus contemplated a premature

and hazardous bid for supremacy, when his future position was guaranteed by ancestry, adoption, experience, and powers.

22. Tacitus, *Ann.* 1.46.1. Levick, *Tiberius the Politician*, 71.

23. The official charge appears in the *Fasti Amiternini, CIL* IX:4192. The main literary accounts are those of Tacitus, *Ann.* 2.27–32 and Dio 57.15.4. Cf. Suet., *Tiberius* 25; Vell. Pat. 2.129.2, 130.3. See Rogers, *Criminal Trials*, 12; F. B. Marsh, "Tacitus and Aristocratic Tradition," *CP* 21, no. 4 (1926): 289–310; F. B. Marsh, *The Reign of Tiberius* (Oxford: OUP, 1931), 58–60. On the literary composition of the story, see Cogitore, *La légitimité dynastique d'Auguste à Néron à l'épreuve des conspirations*, 10–11, 181–91; Rutledge, *Imperial Inquisitions*, 158–62.

24. Seneca, *Epis.* 70.10. His mother was the granddaughter of Pompey, and Scribonia, wife of Augustus and mother of Julia, was his great-aunt. On Tacitus's portrayal, see Sinclair, *Tacitus the Sententious Historian*, 137–38.

25. Allen, "The Political Atmosphere of the Reign of Tiberius," 23. For those who take him and his astrology more seriously, see F. H. Cramer, *Astrology in Roman Law and Politics* (Chicago: Ares, 1954), 101–3. On there being little agreement on how grave the threat to Tiberius was, see Rutledge, *Imperial Inquisitions*, 160, who also thinks the charges were serious.

26. Suetonius has this contact made before Tiberius's accession, but in Tacitus, *Ann.* 2.28, it was made afterward.

27. See I. Cogitore, *La légitimité dynastique d'Auguste à Néron à l'épreuve des conspirations*, 116–23; see Cramer, *Astrology in Roman Law and Politics*, 81–146, on the power behind the throne from Augustus to Domitian. D. C. A. Shotter, "The Trial of M. Scribonius Libo Drusus," *Historia* 21, no. 1 (1972): 92, stresses this aspect. Rutledge, *Imperial Inquisitions*, 160, points out how seriously Tiberius took such charges (cf. Dio 57.19.2–3) and the fact that astrologers were banned from Rome shortly after the trial.

28. Rutledge, *Imperial Inquisitions*, 89. A. A. Barb, "The Survival of the Magic Arts," in *The Conflict between Paganism and Christianity in the Fourth Century*, ed. A. Momigliano (Oxford: Clarendon Press, 1963), 104–6.

29. Rutledge, *Imperial Inquisitions*, 160, considers the documents a "smoking gun." He also points out that the continuation of the prosecution after Libo's death is telling.

30. Tacitus, *Ann.* 2.27.2, 29, 30.2, 31.4. Cf. Seneca, *Epis.* 70.10; Dio 57.15.4. Cf. Suet., *Tiberius* 25; Vell. Pat. 2.129.2, 130.3. They all confirm the testimony of the *Fasti Amiternini*. Swan, "Conspiracies against Emperors of the Julio-Claudian Dynasty," 89, does not see a large disparity between Tacitus and the *Fasti Amiternini* (*CIL* IX 4192).

31. The most complete recent treatment is A. Pettinger, *The Republic in Danger: Drusus Libo and the Succession of Tiberius* (New York: OUP, 2012). The plot is also accepted by L. Freytag, *Tiberius und Germanicus* (Berlin: Henschel, 1870); later rejected by A. Lang, "Beiträge zur Geschichte des Kaisers Tiberius" (PhD diss., Jena, 1911), 32; resurrected by Marsh, "Tacitus and Aristocratic Tradition," 289–310, who uses the *Fasti Amiternini* as proof of an important plot and considered the Tacitean version simply the propaganda of the Scribonian family. He is followed closely by R. S. Rogers, *Studies in the Reign of Tiberius* (Baltimore: Johns Hopkins University Press, 1943), 115–16; E. F. Leon, "Notes on the Background

and Character of Libo Drusus," *CJ* 53 (1957): 77–80. For a defense of Tacitus's account see A. Passerini, "Per la storia dell'imperatore Tiberio, II: Il processo di Libone Druso," in *Studi giuridici in Memoria di Pietro Ciapessoni* (Pavia: Tipografia del Libro, 1948), 219–33, particularly 228; Syme, *Tacitus* 1:399–400; Levick, *Tiberius the Politician*, 149, 270n6. E. J. Weinrib, "The Family Connections of M. Livius Drusus Libo," *HSCPh* 72 (1968): 247–78. Swan, "Conspiracies against Emperors of the Julio-Claudian Dynasty," 85. Rejecting the plot completely is P. A. Brunt, "Did Emperors Ever Suspend the Law of Maiestas?" in *Sodalitas: Scritti in onore di Antonio Guarino*, Labeo VIII (Naples: Jovene, 1984), 469–80.

32. It has been suggested by Seager, *Tiberius*, 76, that Libo's body was exposed on the Gemonian steps—a custom he suggests was instituted by Tiberius and was well established by 20 CE. The stairs themselves were built some time immediately before the rule of Tiberius (14–37 CE), as they were not mentioned by name in any ancient texts that predate this period. On trials before the Senate see E. J. Weinrib, "The Prosecution of Roman Magistrates," *Phoenix* 22, no. 1 (Spring 1968): 32–56. Cf. W. D. Barry, "Exposure, Mutilation, and Riot: Violence at the *Scalae Gemoniae* in Early Imperial Rome," *G&R* 55, no. 2 (October 2008): 222–46.

33. These were the astrologers L. Pituanius and P. Marcius. See Tacitus, *Ann.* 2.32.3.

34. Tacitus, *Ann.* 2.32.

35. There are three accounts of Clemens's plotting: Tacitus, *Ann.* 2.39-40; Dio, who gives a briefer account in 57.16.3–4; and Suet., *Tiberius* 25. There are no important contradictions in the accounts although Dio and Suetonius only treat the plot of 16. Velleius omits the episode entirely, probably to avoid embarrassing Tiberius. J. Mogenet, "Le conjuration de Clemens," *AntCl* 23 (1954): 321–30, has called into question the trustworthiness of Tacitus's account. He accepts the plot of 16 but doubts the abortive rescue attempt of 14. Cf. J. A. Crook, "The Last Age of the Roman Republic," *CAH*², 9:109, who finds historians trying to be "too clever" in concocting conspiracy theories.

36. M. L. Paladini, "La morte di Agrippa Postumo e la congiura di Clemente," *Acme* 7 (1954): 313–29, saw this event as an important manifestation of the struggle all through Tiberius's reign between the emperor and the senatorial oligarchy.

37. Tacitus, *Ann.* 2.39.1. Paladini, "La morte di Agrippa Postumo e la congiura di Clemente," 328–29, tries to graft the Clemens incident onto the military attempt to rescue Postumus in 14 and take him "to the German armies." This connection has also been made by Pettinger, *Republic in Danger*, 213–14, although he admits there is no "manifest evidence."

38. Tacitus, *Ann.* 2.39ff.; on Tacitus's portrayal of Crispus, see Sinclair, *Tacitus the Sententious Historian*, 7; Suet., *Tiberius* 25; Dio 57.16.3. Cf. Mogenet, "Le conjuration de Clemens," 321–30; Seager, *Tiberius*, 77; Rogers, "Conspiracy of Agrippina," 148–49; Pappano, "Agrippa Postumus," 30–45. On the role of Clemens, see Hohl, "Primum Facinus Novi Principatus," 350–55; Cogitore, *La légitimité dynastique d'Auguste à Néron à l'épreuve des conspirations*, 179–81; Barrett, *Livia*, 68–72.

39. Tacitus, *Ann.* 6.51.5; on the rhetoric of Tacitus concerning Germanicus, see Sinclair, *Tacitus the Sententious Historian*, 117–18; Dio 57.13.6. On the reliability of Tacitus, see D. C. A. Shotter, "Tacitus, Tiberius and Germanicus," *Historia* 17, no. 2 (April 1968): 194–214.

40. On the atmosphere of mistrust at Tiberius's court, see C. Vout, "Tiberius and the Invention of Succession," in *The Julio-Claudian Succession*, ed. A. G. G. Gibson (Leiden, Netherlands: Brill, 2013), 59–77. On the loyalty of Germanicus, see Barrett, *Livia*, 78. Added to this was the dowager empress's hatred of Germanicus's wife, Agrippina. On the suggestion that Augustus had, at one point, planned to put Germanicus on the throne with Tiberius merely as regent, see Johnson, "Factor of Inheritance in the Julio-Claudian Succession." This plan was changed in a later, last-minute will (125).

41. See Tacitus, *Ann.* 2.2.2, where Germanicus left his name off a trophy set up after a victory, hoping not to set off Tiberius's suspicions about his ambition.

42. Tacitus, *Ann.* 2.41.5.

43. Tacitus, *Ann.* 2.43.4; Shotter, "Tacitus, Tiberius and Germanicus," 205. E. Koestermann proposed, in "Die Mission des Germanicus im Orient," *Historia* 7, no. 3 (July 1958): 352, that Piso must have had orders from Augustus to Tiberius to check Germanicus, but according to Seager, *Tiberius*, 256n140, there is no cogent reason for making such an assumption. Also see Barrett, *Caligula*, 14.

44. Tacitus, *Ann.* 2.57. Piso may have been insulted, not because his Republican sensibilities were being offended but because Germanicus was offered a larger crown.

45. Shotter, "Tacitus, Tiberius and Germanicus," 206.

46. Marsh, *Reign of Tiberius*, 93–94, points out that if Piso was not dismissed it was because he was doing what he was sent to do. And see Shotter, "Tacitus, Tiberius and Germanicus," 208.

47. Tacitus, *Ann.* 2.70ff. According to Marsh, *Reign of Tiberius*, 95, Tacitus does not believe the poisoning charge; he is simply reporting it. Other historians do believe the poisoning charge. See Suet., *Tiberius* 52; *Caligula* 2; Dio 57.18.9; Josephus, *AJ* 18.54; B. Walker, *The Annals of Tacitus* (Manchester: Manchester University Press, 1952), 96.

48. For a very levelheaded assessment of the Piso affair, see D. C. A. Shotter, "Cnaeus Calpurnius Piso, Legate of Syria," *Historia* 23, no. 2 (1974): 229–45. Cf. Barrett, *Livia*, 81–90; Levick, *Tiberius the Politician*, 156. On the poisoning of Germanicus, see Barrett, *Caligula*, 257n41. As Barrett, *Livia*, xi, points out, "Even in a modern murder investigation, conducted by a professional police force, aided by forensic science and chemical analyses and tried by a systematic court procedure, it is often impossible to reach a secure verdict where poisoning is suspected."

49. On the political use of the Gemonian stairs, see Barry, "Exposure, Mutilation, and Riot," 222–46. On the epigraphic evidence relating to the trial of Piso in 20 CE and to the role of his wife, Plancina, see Barrett, *Livia*, 168–69. On the Piso decree, see W. Eck, A. Caballos, and F. Fernandez, *Das Senatus Consulto de Cn. Pisone Patre* (Munich: Beck, 1996), 222; J. González, "Tacitus, Germanicus, Piso and the Tabula Siarensis," *AJPh* 120, no. 1 (Spring 1999): 123–42, with bibliography. On Piso's punishment: J. Bodel, "Punishing Piso," *AJPh* 120, no. 1 (Spring 1999): 43–63; that special issue of *AJPh* was entirely devoted to the Piso inscription.

50. Tacitus, *Ann.* 2.83; Suet., *Caligula* 6. McHugh, "Manipulating Memory," 168, points out that Agrippina did not have to stage anything; the popular grief

was genuine. On the expression of anger, Suet., *Caligula.* 5, tells of temples being stoned, altars of the gods being thrown down, and household gods being flung into the street.

51. Tacitus, *Ann.* 3.56. On the position of Drusus and Germanicus, see J. Bellemore, "The Identity of Drusus: The Making of a *Princeps*," in *The Julio-Claudian Succession*, ed. A. G. G. Gibson (Leiden, Netherlands: Brill, 2013), 79–94. On the succession plan: B. Levick, "Drusus Caesar and the Adoptions of A.D. 4," *Latomus* 25 (1966): 227–44; and G. V. Sumner's response, "Germanicus and Drusus Caesar," *Latomus* 26, no. 2 (April–June 1967): 413–35.

52. Political influence exercised by women through their children and other male relatives was a normal part of Roman aristocratic and dynastic life. See J. Hallett, *Fathers and Daughters in Roman Society: Women and the Elite Family* (Princeton, NJ: PUP, 1984), 29 and passim. As Barrett, *Livia*, x, has pointed out, however, women did not play a public role in the Roman state no matter how much power and influence they might exercise informally behind the scenes. Any attempt at usurpation of power was condemned, especially by Tacitus. See F. S. Santoro L'Hoir, "Tacitus and Women's Usurpation of Power," *CW* 88 (1994): 5–25, who attributes the suspicion toward Agrippina to Tacitus rather than Tiberius.

53. On the rhetoric used by Tacitus for Tiberius and Germanicus, see Sinclair, *Tacitus the Sententious Historian*, 97–103, 117–18. On the use of Sejanus by later literary figures, see https://en.wikipedia.org/wiki/Sejanus#Literary_interpretations.

54. Sejanus was born in 20 BCE at Volsinii, Etruria, to the family of Lucius Seius Strabo. See Vell. Pat. 2.127.3; Tacitus, *Ann.* 1.24, 4.1. On the evidence for his family ties, see F. Adams, "The Consular Brothers of Sejanus," *AJPh* 76, no. 1 (1955): 70–76; G. V. Sumner, "The Family Connections of L. Aelius Seianus," *Phoenix* 19 (1965): 134–45.

55. Dio 57.19; Bingham, *Praetorian Guard*, 43.

56. Tacitus, *Ann.* 4.2. Syme believed Tacitus delayed mention of these reforms until the year 23, for stylistic reasons. The actual date the Castra Praetoria was founded may have been 20 CE. See Syme, *Tacitus*, 1:286; Coulston and Dodge, eds., *Ancient Rome*, 82, with illustration of the camp on page 83.

57. Tacitus, *Ann.* 4.2; Suet., *Tiberius* 37.1; Dio 57.19.6.

58. Bingham, *Praetorian Guard*, 50.

59. Tacitus, *Ann.* 4.2.2; Bingham, *Praetorian Guard*, 60.

60. Tacitus, *Ann.* 4.2. On the portrayal of Sejanus in Velleius Paterculus, see Woodman, *Velleius Paterculus: The Tiberian Narrative*, 245–49.

61. Dio 57.19.

62. On the statue, see Seneca, *Cons. Marcia* 22.4–6. The honor was not unearned. When the Theatre of Pompey was destroyed by fire in 22, Tiberius lavished praise on Sejanus for his hard work and vigilance in restricting the damage done. He and the Praetorians had fought the fire and, although they could not save the theater, they prevented the blaze from spreading. The Senate responded by decreeing a statue to Sejanus set up in the theater itself. See Tacitus, *Ann.* 3.72; Suet., *Claudius* 21.1; Dio 60.6.8. For more on the statue, see Dio 57.21.3. On Sejanus parading his ambitions on the Aventine, see R. Syme, "Seianus on the Aventine," *Hermes* 84, no. 3 (1956): 257–66.

63. The number of people Sejanus would ultimately destroy is too long to discuss in detail. Among the writers of the time who fell victim to the regime of Sejanus and its aftermath were the historians Aulus Cremutius Cordus, Velleius Paterculus, and the poet Phaedrus. Cordus was brought to trial in 25 by Sejanus under accusations of treason brought by Satrius Secundus and Pinarius Natta. See Rutledge, *Imperial Inquisitions*, 50. He was charged for having eulogized Marcus Junius Brutus and spoke of Gaius Cassius Longinus as the last of the true Romans, which was considered an offense under the *Lex Maiestas*, and the Senate ordered the burning of his writings. His fall is elaborated upon by Seneca the Younger in his letter to Cordus's daughter, Marcia, *To Marcia, on Consolation*. Seneca, however, tells us that her father most likely incurred Sejanus's displeasure for criticizing him, because he had commissioned a statue of himself. We also know from this source that Cordus starved himself to death. Marcia was instrumental in saving her father's work so that it could be published again under Caligula. Phaedrus was suspected of having alluded to Sejanus in his *Fables* and received some unknown punishment short of death (Cf. *Fables* I.1, I.2.24, and I.17). Velleius Paterculus was a historian and contemporary of Sejanus, whose two-volume *The Roman History* details a history of Rome from the fall of Troy until the death of Livia Augusta in 29. In his work he praises both Tiberius and Sejanus, even defending the latter's high position in the government despite his equestrian rank. How much of Paterculus's writing is due to genuine admiration, prudence, or fear remains an open question, but it has been conjectured that he was put to death as a friend of Sejanus. See R. S. Rogers, "The Case of Cremutius Cordus," *TAPA* 96 (1965): 351–59; Raaflaub and Samons, "Opposition to Augustus," 442; M. R. McHugh, "Historiography and Freedom of Speech: The Case of Cremutius Cordus," in *Proceedings of the 2nd Penn-Leiden Colloquium on Ancient Values in 2002* (Leiden, Netherlands: Brill, 2004), 391–408.

64. On the betrothal, see Tacitus, *Ann.* 3.29; on the death Suet., *Claudius* 27.

65. Tacitus, *Ann.* 3.29; Suet., *Claudius* 27.1; Dio 58.11.5; Seager, *Tiberius*, 100, 152.

66. Tacitus, *Ann.* 1.24 and see chapter 2.

67. Tacitus, *Ann.* 2.44, 2.62.

68. Tacitus, *Ann.* 4.1.

69. Suet., *Tiberius* 55, 61.1 is nearer to the truth. Also see Cogitore, *La légitimité dynastique d'Auguste à Néron à l'épreuve des conspirations*, 212–21.

70. Tacitus, *Ann.* 4.7.

71. Tacitus, *Ann.* 4.3.

72. On the seduction see Tacitus, *Ann.* 4.3; on the poisoning, Tacitus, *Ann.* 4.8. For contrasting views on the reliability of Tacitus see J. V. P. D. Balsdon, "The 'Murder' of Drusus, son of Tiberius," *CR* 1, no. 2 (June, 1951): 75, versus W. Eisenhut, "Der Tod des Tiberius-Sohnes Drusus," *Museum Helveticum* 7 (1950): 123–28. D. Hennig, *L. Aelius Seianus. Untersuchungen zur Regierung des Tiberius* (Munich: Beck, 1975), 76–79 and the review of Hennig by D. Fishwick, in *Phoenix* 31, no. 3 (1977): 284–86.

73. Tacitus, *Ann.* 4.8.12.

74. Tacitus, *Ann.* 4.8.

75. Tacitus, *Ann.* 4.8, 4.12

76. Dio 58.10.

77. Not every scholar is in agreement as to the extent of the threat to Tiberius posed by Agrippina. See Rutledge, *Imperial Inquisitions*, 138–40. Cf. M. Kaplan, "Agrippina semper atrox," in *Studies in Latin Literature and Roman History*, ed. C. Deroux (Brussels: Latomus 1979), 1:410–17; Rogers, *Criminal Trials*, 98n311; H. W. Bird, "Aelius Sejanus and His Political Significance," *Latomus* 28 (1969): 69; J. I. McDougall, "Tacitus and the Portrayal of the Elder Agrippina," *EMC* 25 (1981): 104–7.

78. Tacitus, *Ann.* 4.39.

79. Tacitus, *Ann.* 4.1; Dio 57.22.4b. For a detailed discussion of the polarized views on this subject see Hennig, *L. Aelius Seianus*, passim, who synthesizes recent and older scholarship in search of a balance.

80. Tacitus, *Ann.* 4.40.

81. Tacitus, *Ann.* 4.57, 4.67.

82. Tacitus, *Ann.* 4.41.

83. Tacitus, *Ann.* 5.3. On whether the move against Agrippina and Nero Caesar happened after Livia's death or before is not agreed upon. See Barrett, *Caligula*, 21.

84. Barrett, *Livia*, 221 and appendix 19. R. H. Martin, *Tacitus* (London: Batsford, 1981), 141, does not believe Sejanus was hindered by Livia.

85. Dio 58.3; D. C. A. Shotter, "Tiberius and Asinius Gallus," *Historia* 20, no. 4 (1971): 443–57.

86. On the political and personal relationship between Tiberius and Gallus, see Shotter, "Tiberius and Asinius Gallus," 443–57. Among the others were Vallius Syriacus, Drusus Caesar, Fufius Geminus, his wife Mutilia Prisca, and their two daughters.

87. R. Holland, *Nero: The Man behind the Myth* (Stroud, UK: Sutton Publishing 2000), 19.

88. Tacitus, *Ann.* 4.68–70, 6.4. Dio 58.1, 1b–3; Pliny, *HN* 8.145; Rogers, "Conspiracy of Agrippina," 144.

89. On Silius and Sosia, see Rogers, "Conspiracy of Agrippina," 141–68. On Sejanus's attempts to remove Agrippina and her partisans, see Shotter, "Agrippina the Elder," 341–57. On the prosecution of the case by Visellius Varro and his possible personal motives, see Rutledge, *Imperial Inquisitions*, 86 and chapter 6.

90. Tacitus, *Ann.* 4.67.

91. On the reactions of individual senators see Rogers, "Conspiracy of Agrippina," 192–93.

92. We only know about it from a reference in Pliny, *HN* 8.145, to the trial of Sabinus "ex causa Neronis" and a statement in Philo, *in Flacc.* 3.9, that the chief prosecutor was Avillius Flaccus, who later became prefect of Egypt.

93. Suet., *Tiberius* 54.2; *Caligula* 7 and 15.1; Tacitus, *Ann.* 6.23–6.25. Also see E. R. Varner, "Portraits, Plots and Politics: 'Damnatio Memoriae' and the Images of Imperial Women," *MAAR* 46 (2001): 62.

94. On the chronology, see M. P. Charlesworth, "The Banishment of the Elder Agrippina," *CP* 17, no. 3 (1922): 260–61.

95. S. Wood, "Memoriae Agrippina: Agrippina the Elder in Julio-Claudian Art and Propaganda," *AJA* 92, no. 3 (July 1988): 409, shows how her images in art and coinage show how she was honored in her lifetime and afterward.

96. Tacitus, *Ann.* 6.3.4. D. C. A. Shotter, "The Fall of Sejanus: Two Problems," *CP* 69, no. 1 (January 1974): 42–46. There is evidence for a plot against Caligula

suggested by the fate of Sextius Paconianus, who was brought to trial later as one of those who had joined the conspiracy of Sejanus after Caligula. See Tacitus, *Ann.* 6.3.4; Barrett, *Caligula*, 27, which also addresses Caligula's move to Capri.

97. Holland, *Nero*, 18.

98. In the accounts of Josephus and Dio, the evidence for Sejanus's misdeeds was smuggled to Tiberius on Capri from the house of Antonia, his sister-in-law. The role of Antonia in this is accepted by most studies that treat the fall of Sejanus, including Marsh, *Reign of Tiberius*, 304n1; E. Koestermann, "Der Sturz Seianus," *Hermes* 83 (1955): 352ff.; Syme, *Tacitus*, 752–53; Sumner, "Family Connections of L. Aelius Seianus," 144; Bird, "L. Aelius Seianus and His Political Significance," 83; Seager, *Tiberius*, 180–88; A. Boddington, "Sejanus: Whose Conspiracy?" *AJPh* 84, no. 1 (January 1963): 8; Barrett, *Caligula*, 26–27, defending Josephus's account. Arguing against: J. Nicols, "Antonia and Sejanus," *Historia* 24, no. 1 (1975): 48–59, who believes it was an invention of the Claudian and Flavian eras.

99. The message: Josephus, *AJ* 18.182; Dio 65.14. On the important role ascribed to Antonia herself in exposing Sejanus: Seager, *Tiberius*, 216ff.; Nicols, "Antonia and Sejanus," 48–59. On Gaius's moves: Suet., *Caligula* 10.1; Caligula's birthday (as stated in Suet., *Caligula* 8.1) is confirmed by the *Fasti Vallenses*; see Levick, *Tiberius the Politician*, 278n132, with evidence.

100. Josephus, *AJ*, 18.179–80. Rutledge, *Imperial Inquisitions*, 162, even admits we do not know anything about the role the delators like Secundus played in this case.

101. Juvenal, *Sat.* 10.70.

102. Suet., *Tiberius* 65. On the operations against Sejanus, see Barrett, *Caligula*, 27–29.

103. For the inscription that identifies him as Q. Naevius Cordus Sutorius Macro, see *AE* (1957), 219n250; F. de Visscher, "L'amphithéâtre d'Alba Fucens et son fondateur Q. Naevius Macro, préfet du prétoire de Tibère," *RAL* 12 (1957): 39-49; Bingham, *Praetorian Guard*, 63.

104. Dio 58.9.

105. Dio 58.11. On the Gemonian stairs, see Barry, "Exposure, Mutilation, and Riot," 222–46.

106. On donatives in general, see Bingham, *Praetorian Guard*, chapter 3.

107. On Memmius Regulus, see Shotter, "Fall of Sejanus," 44.

108. On the repression see Cogitore, *La légitimité dynastique d'Auguste à Néron à l'épreuve des conspirations*, 221–28. The term *damnatio memoriae* is actually modern. The term is used in modern scholarship to cover a wide array of official and unofficial sanctions whereby the Romans removed physical remnants of a deceased individual. See Varner, "Portraits, Plots and Politics," 41–93, and McHugh, "Manipulating Memory," 9–13, for examples; E. Varner, "Tyranny and Transformation of the Roman Visual Landscape," in *From Caligula to Constantine: Tyranny and Transformation in Roman Portraiture*, ed. E. Varner (Atlanta: Emory University, 2000), 10; and on the removal of inscriptions, see H. Flower, "*Damnatio Memoriae* and Epigraphy," in *From Caligula to Constantine: Tyranny and Transformation in Roman Portraiture*, ed. E. Varner (Atlanta: Emory University, 2000), 58–69.

109. It is usually argued that Apicata committed suicide after having seen her sons exposed on the Gemonian stairs. J. Bellemore, "The Wife of Sejanus," *ZPE* 109

(1995): 255–66, argues against this identification as the woman mentioned in the *Fasti Ostienses*. See Sumner, "Family Connections of L. Aelius Sejanus," 139–41. The ancient writers who agree that Drusus was poisoned by Sejanus and Livilla: Tacitus, *Ann.* 4.3, 4.7.11; Suet., *Tiberius* 62.1; Dio (epitome of Xiph.) 57.22.1–4; Dio (Zonaras) 57.22.4a–4b; Dio 58.11.6–7; Seneca, *Octavia* 941–43. M. P. Charlesworth, "Gaius and Claudius," *CAH* (1934), 10:683; and Marsh, *Reign of Tiberius*, 162–65 accept Sejanus's guilt. Sejanus chose poison that was administered by the eunuch Lygdus, but the details only came to light under torture eight years later. Tacitus, *Ann.* 4.8.1, 4.11.2. Cf. Dio (Xiph.) 57.22.2.

110. Val. Max. 9.11, ext. 4; on Blaesus: Tacitus, *Ann.* 5.7.2; on Strabo and the children, *Fasti Ost.* 13.1.186ff. Also see Tacitus, *Ann.* 5.9; Dio 58.11.5; Hennig, *L. Aelius Seianus*, 14n40.

111. Dio 58.11.6 attributing responsibility for her death to Tiberius. Suet., *Tiberius* 62.1, reports a story that Tiberius spared her and she was starved. Hennig, *L. Aelius Seianus*, 38, posits death by natural causes.

112. Val. Max. 9.11, ext. 4, attacks him bitterly as a would-be usurper; cf. Philo, *Leg.* 24.159–60. An inscription on a monument describing Sejanus's punishment is recorded in *ILS* 157; cf. *ILS* 6044. Swan, "Conspiracies against Emperors of the Julio-Claudian Dynasty," 109, points out these were government documents. Juv., *Satires* 10.66–77 seems to say Sejanus aimed at overthrowing Tiberius. Cf. Tacitus, *Ann.* 6.8.6 and Val. Max. 9.11, ext. 4. Stöver, *Die Prätorianer*, 187, 240, called Sejanus "Kaiser ohne Purpur"—an emperor without the purple.

113. Koestermann, "Der Sturz Seianus," 350–73; Swan, "Conspiracies against Emperors of the Julio-Claudian Dynasty," 94.

114. Suet., *Tiberius* 61.1 and 65. Tacitus, *Ann.* books 3, 4 passim.

115. Dio 58.6.4, 8.2, Syme, *Tacitus*, 402, 404–6—cf. 752–54—believed we should be skeptical about the conspiracy and that the events were the result of realizing he had promoted Sejanus into a dangerous position. Sealey, following Syme, added that Sejanus belonged to a powerful group of senators dominated by the Cornelii Lentuli and that is why Tiberius had to remove Sejanus himself without warning the faction. See R. Sealey, "The Political Attachments of L. Aelius Sejanus," *Phoenix* 15, no. 2 (1961): 97–114. Boddington, "Sejanus," 1–16, suggests a "secret revolt by powerful members of the governing oligarchy" but cannot identify them.

116. Boddington, "Sejanus," 15.

117. Suet., *Tiberius* 48.2; Dio 58.9.5–6. On the Syrian legions Suet., *Tiberius* 48.2; Swan, "Conspiracies against Emperors of the Julio-Claudian Dynasty," 108.

118. Josephus, *AJ* 18.6.6 and Suet., *Tiberius* 65 argued for the plot against Tiberius. This has been rejected by Marsh, *Reign of Tiberius*, 304–10, and Syme, *Tacitus*, 752–54. Cf. Sealey, "Political Attachments of L. Aelius Sejanus," 97. Balsdon, "Principates of Tiberius and Gaius," 92, with further bibliography. I. Cogitore, "Les conspirations comme 'coups d'État' chez Gabriel Naudé: L'exemple antique," in *Complots et conjurations dans l'Europe moderne*, ed. Y. Bercé and E. Fasano Guarini (Rome: Coll. M.E.F.R. 220, 1996), 193–202, shows why Sejanus is not a good model for a coup d'état.

119. Dio 58.8.1.

120. This is the total calculated from Tacitus alone. See Swan, "Conspiracies against Emperors of the Julio-Claudian Dynasty," 5 and the full list on 113n34.

121. Swan, "Conspiracies against Emperors of the Julio-Claudian Dynasty," 116.

122. See Marañon, *Tiberius*; Romkey, "OCPD and the Enigmatic Personality of Emperor Tiberius."

123. Suet., *Tiberius* 42–45.

124. There is a great deal of confusion and speculation in the literary sources. There is a general sense that Tiberius was not happy with the prospect of giving the throne over to Caligula: Suet., *Tiberius* 55; *Caligula* 11.19.3; Dio 58.23.3. Tacitus, *Ann.* 6.46.9, claims he recognized that Caligula would have all the cruelty of a Sulla with none of his good qualities.

125. There were rumors that Tiberius found neither of them acceptable candidates and wanted them both killed: Philo, *Leg. ad Gaiam* 24.33–34, *in Flacc.* 24; Josephus, *AJ* 18.215; Tacitus, *Ann.* 6.46.9; Suet., *Tiberius* 55; *Caligula* 11.19.3; Dio 58.23.3.

126. There was no precedent for a dual principate. Was this what Tiberius intended? E. Kornemann, *Doppelprinzipat und Reichstellung im Imperium Romanum* (Leipzig-Berlin: Teubner, 1930), 37, believed it was. See also Levick, *Tiberius the Politician*, 209–10. Dio 59.1.1 speaks of leaving the *autarchia* to both young men. Philo describes Gemellus as being bequeathed "a share of the rule." Philo, *Leg. ad Gaiam* 23, *in Flacc.* 10. Both these sources are much less interested in the constitutional niceties than they are in Caligula's claim to be sole ruler.

127. Meijer, *Emperors Don't Die in Bed*, 22.

128. Tacitus, *Ann.* 6.50. Historians have debated whether Tacitus's obviously negative portrait of Tiberius is factual. On this see R. Syme, foreword to Marañon, *Tiberius*, v.

129. It seems that Charicles was acting as an agent of Macro: Tacitus, *Ann.* 6.50.6; Barrett, *Caligula*, 41.

130. Tacitus, *Ann.* 6.50; Seager, *Tiberius*, 206–7.

131. One might ask how Seneca, or anyone, could know this if Tiberius were alone in the room. The accounts of Tiberius's death are well discussed by Seager, *Tiberius*, 244ff.

132. Suet., *Tiberius* 73.2. On Caligula trying to stab Tiberius to death, see Barrett, *Caligula*, 31; Suet., *Caligula* 12.3.

133. Suet., *Tiberius* 75.

134. For an example of this older interpretation, see M. Grant, *The Twelve Caesars* (New York: Charles Scribner, 1975), 88.

135. The Julian and Claudian lines were brought together when Augustus married Livia. See my chart with the family tree. On Sejanus's attempt to marry into it, see Boddington, "Sejanus," 1–16.

136. On the Castra Praetoria, see n53.

137. While it is unproven that Sejanus ever did intend to overthrow and replace Tiberius, later prefects of the Guard did aspire to become emperor themselves. Upon the suicide of the emperor Nero in 68, the Guard prefect Gaius Nymphidius Sabinus attempted to have himself declared emperor on the pretense that he was the illegitimate son of Caligula. The attempt failed and Sabinus was killed by his own soldiers. In the early third century, Plautianus was executed after a failed conspiracy against Septimius Severus. According to sources, the downfall of Plau-

tianus was largely due to suspicion of Severus's son Caracalla, who was himself later murdered and replaced by his Praetorian prefect Marcus Opellius Macrinus.

138. Sejanus's fall is depicted in the section in Juvenal's *Satire X*, on the emptiness of power. See D. C. Boughner, "Juvenal, Horace and Sejanus," *Modern Languages Notes* 75, no. 7 (November 1960): 545–50. Swan, "Conspiracies against Emperors of the Julio-Claudian Dynasty," 121, believes Juvenal's words imply that Sejanus's aim was to assassinate Tiberius.

139. There had been suicides before prosecution under Augustus, and his reign is much more poorly documented. Could that be because Tacitus and Dio are hostile senatorial sources and Suetonius is a lover of gossip? Levick suggests that although there had been such cases under the republic, the diminishing freedoms of the principate turned up fewer chances of rehabilitation or survival: Levick, *Tiberius the Politician*, 188; also see Meijer, *Emperors Don't Die in Bed*, 21. On treason trials under Tiberius, see E. S. Gruen, *Roman Politics and the Criminal Courts 149–7 BC* (Cambridge, MA: HUP, 1968), 304ff., who records six republican suicides.

140. Seager, *Tiberius*, 137.

141. Seager, *Tiberius*, 137; E. Koestermann, "Die Majestätsprozesse unter Tiberius," *Historia* 4, no. 1 (1955): 97.

142. See, for example, the prosecution of Gaius Junius Silanus in 22 CE. To the alleged crime of misconduct the Senate added charges of treason. Tacitus suggests the charge was added in order to intimidate Silanus's friends from defending him. Silanus, abandoned by his friends, abandoned his defense: Tacitus, *Ann.* 3.67, 68, 71. Seager argues that the stiff sentence was justified by Augustus's memorandum on the similar case of Volesus Messalla. Cf. D. C. A. Shotter, "The Trial of C. Junius Silanus," *CP* 67, no. 2 (April 1972): 126–31, on why his senatorial friends turned on him.

143. Tacitus, *Ann.* 3.10.2; 19.1 (Trio); 4.29.4 (Serenus); 52.7 (Afer). Tacitus, *Ann.* 3.56.1, accused Tiberius of avoiding the outcry against delation, 54.1. Also see Rutledge, *Imperial Inquisitions*, 161–62.

144. Tiberius is defended by Seager, *Tiberius*, 138; Rogers, *Criminal Trials*, 83; Marsh, *Reign of Tiberius*, 60.

145. Tacitus, *Ann.* 4.20.3. See L. R. Taylor, *Party Politics in the Age of Caesar* (Berkeley: University of California Press, 1949), 112–13.

146. Tacitus, *Ann.* 1.74.1, 2.28.4, 6.38.2; Dio 58.25.2. On Tiberian *delatores* see Marsh, *Reign of Tiberius*, 107–15; Syme, *Tacitus*, 1.326ff.

147. On the rewards, see Tacitus, *Ann.* 4.28.4ff.; Levick, *Tiberius the Politician*, 104, 190; Syme, *Tacitus*, 2:693–94. For Tiberius encouraging delation, see Furneaux, *Annals of Tacitus*, 1.143ff.; Koestermann, "Die Majestätsprozesse unter Tiberius," 83–106.

148. See Tacitus, *Ann.* 1.74.2, 3.66.4, 4.52.2; Levick, *Tiberius the Politician*, 190.

149. Tacitus, *Ann.* 4.6.7.

150. Seneca, *de Bene* 3.26.1, says there was a greater loss of life than was caused by the civil wars. There is a similar passage in Tacitus, *Ann.* 6.7.4. Cf. Dio 58.7.4.

151. On the dynastic plotting behind the scenes by the women of the family, see Levick, *Tiberius the Politician*, 148–79 passim.

152. On Tiberius's *clementia*, see Levick, *Tiberius the Politician*, 91, 152, 197, 207.

153. Tacitus, *Ann.* 6.25.4. Levick, *Tiberius the Politician*, 88, includes a discussion of the coin evidence for *clementia* and its significance.

154. Levick, *Tiberius the Politician*, 183–92; Seager, *Tiberius*, 125–38; Alston, *Aspects of Roman History*, 123–25.

CHAPTER 5: THE CONSPIRACY THAT KILLED CALIGULA

1. We shall refer to the emperor by his nickname, "Caligula," ("little boots") after part of the soldier's uniform he had worn in his youth: Beard, *SPQR*, 389; Barrett, *Caligula*, 7. He was also called Gaius, but according to Seneca, *Constant.* 18.4 he did not like either name. Cf. Tacitus, *Ann.* 1.41.3, 3.69.5; Suet., *Cal.* 9.1; Dio 57.5.6; Aur. Vic., *Caes.* 3.4; *Epit.* 3.2; Eutropius, *Brev.*, 7.12.1. The name, Caligula, is not attested epigraphically: D. W. Hurley, *An Historical and Historiographical Commentary on Suetonius' Life of C. Caligula* (Oxford: OUP, 1993), 25. For a critique of the story concerning his early camp life, see D. W. Hurley, "Gaius Caligula in the Germanicus Tradition," *AJPh* 110 (1989): 316–38.

2. See Barrett, *Caligula*, 42–49. For other biographies, see A. Ferrill, *Caligula: Emperor of Rome* (London: Thames and Hudson, 1991); A. Winterling, *Caligula: A Biography* (Berkeley: University of California Press, 2011); P. Renucci, *Caligula l'Impudent* (Paris: Editions Memoria, 2007); S. Wilkinson, *Caligula* (London: Routledge, 2005); D. Nony, *Caligula* (Paris: Fayard, 1986). For older biographies see R. Auguet, *Caligula, ou le pouvoir à vingt ans* (Paris: Payot, 1984); J. V. P. D. Balsdon, *The Emperor Gaius (Caligula)* (Oxford: Clarendon Press, 1934); H. Sachs, *Caligula* (London: Elkins, Mathews & Marrot, 1931). Caligula has been the subject of a number of dissertations: J. Bissler, "Caligula Unmasked: An Investigation of the Historiography of Rome's Most Notorious Emperor" (MA thesis, Kent State University, 2013); A. M. Dabrowski, "Problems in the Tradition about the Principate of Gaius" (PhD diss., University of Toronto, 1972); U. Linnert, "Beiträge zur Geschichte Caligulas" (PhD diss., University of Jena, 1908).

3. Pagán, *Conspiracy Narratives in Roman History*, 94, says Josephus used his murder to reassure his readership that morality cannot be overrun by tyranny. Also see Juv., *Satires* 6.614–17, and Suet., *Cal.* 51 (mental weakness), 55 (madness). The debate is over whether the fever caused his later behavior. Only Philo, *Leg. ad Gaiam* 14 argues that the illness caused his aberrations. See Hurley, *Commentary*, 180. On Caligula's "insanity" or "illness" see D. T. Benedickton, "Caligula's Madness or Interictal Temporal Lobe Epilepsy," *CW* 82 (1989): 370–75; R. S. Katz, "The Illness of Caligula," *CW* 65 (1971–1972): 223–25; R. S. Katz, "Caligula's Illness Again," *CW* 70 (1977): 451; V. Massaro and I. Montgomery, "Gaius—Mad, Bad, Ill or All Three," *Latomus* 37 (1978): 894–909; M. G. Morgan, "Caligula's Illness Again," *CW* 66 (1973): 327–29; M. G. Morgan, "Once Again Caligula's Illness," *CW* 70 (1977): 452–53; A. T. Sandison, "The Madness of the Emperor Caligula," *Medical History* 2 (1958): 202–9; Z. Yavetz, "Caligula, Imperial Madness and Modern Historiography," *Klio* 78 (1996): 105–29. In the end, the answer is unknowable.

4. When Willrich used this line of reasoning, Balsdon called it a "white wash." See H. Willrich, "Caligula," *Klio* 3 (1903): 85–118, 288–317, 397–470, Balsdon, *Emperor Gaius*, xv; Balsdon, "The Principates of Tiberius and Gaius," 93.

5. Pagán, *Conspiracy Narratives*, 94, describes his reign as "riddled with intrigue from the outset."

6. Barrett, *Caligula*, 29; Philo, *ad Leg*. 35–38.

7. Tacitus names five senators, ex consuls against whom charges of treason were brought: Gaius Annius Pollio, his son Lucius Annius Vinicianus, Gaius Appius Silanus, Mamercus Aemilius Scaurus, and Calvisius Sabinus. There were lingering hints they had all plotted against Caligula. Scaurus was driven to suicide by Macro in 34. The remaining three survived. See Tacitus, *Ann*. 6.9.5–7, 14.2, 29.4–6; Z. Stewart, "Sejanus, Gaetulicus and Seneca," *AJPh* 74 (1953): 73; Levick, *Tiberius*, 202–3; Barrett, *Caligula*, 66; Rogers, *Criminal Trials and Criminal Legislation under Tiberius*, 138–40, and sources for each case.

8. On Caligula's popularity, see Tacitus, *Ann*. 6.46; Suet., *Cal*. 13–14; Ferrill, *Caligula*, 94–104; Barrett, *Caligula*, 38–41; Winterling, *Caligula*, 46; Balsdon, *Emperor Gaius*, 27–28.

9. A. G. G. Gibson, "'All Things to All Men': Claudius and the Politics of AD 41," in Gibson, ed., *Julio-Claudian Succession*, 115.

10. See Barrett, *Caligula*, 54, on the history of the loyalty oath since Augustus and for the inscriptional evidence for such oaths.

11. Suet., *Tib*. 76; Philo, *Leg. ad Gaiam* 5; Suet., *Cal*. 14, speaks of *consensus senatus*, but it is doubtful whether the consensus would have been so easily achieved had the masses not broken into the Senate. On this, see Yavetz, *Plebs*, 28; Hurley, *Commentary*, 39; Willrich, "Caligula," chapter 3, "Regierungsanfang," 85ff.

12. He became the first Roman emperor who could claim a link by bloodline, rather than simply by marriage or adoption, to both the two great families—the Julians and the Claudians. See Barrett, *Caligula*, 51; Beard, *SPQR*, 390.

13. Stöver, *Die Prätorianer*, 56–61, argues that this is the beginning of the "perversion" of the Guard.

14. Philo tells us that the Roman people, the whole of Italy, and the nations of both Asia and Europe rejoiced at his succession: Philo, *Leg. ad Gaiam* 2.11ff; cf. Suet., *Cal*. 13. Even Sejanus had hesitated to move against him: Dio 58.8.2.; Ferrill, *Caligula*, 94–104. Winterling, *Caligula*, 52–72, takes a dimmer view.

15. Suet., *Cal*. 16.3. On restoring the voting rights of the *comitia centuriata* and the *comitia tributa*, see Dio 59.9.6.

16. Jones, *Augustus*, 49; Yavetz, *Plebs*, 104.

17. Yavetz, *Plebs*, 104; Winterling, *Caligula*, 68; Barrett, *Caligula*, 230–31.

18. Brunt, "Did Emperors Ever Suspend the Law of Maiestas?" 469–80, who is highly critical of the contortions that Bauman, *Impietas in Principem*, chapter 8, goes through to prove that *maiestas* was the law suspended.

19. On "Ears for delatores" see Suet., *Cal*. 15.4; Dio 59.4.3, 6.3, says he burned copies instead. These would have been private documents, not those of the Senate. They reappeared in 39 CE (Dio 59.10.8, 16.3) and Claudius finally got rid of them (Dio 60.4.5). See Hurley, *Commentary*, 52; Barrett, *Caligula*, 65; Ferrill, *Caligula*, 98; Winterling, *Caligula*, 54.

20. Suet., *Cal.* 15.4; Hurley, *Commentary*, 52.

21. There were other criminal charges that could still be used. See Bauman, *Impietas in Principem*, 19; Barrett, *Caligula*, 66.

22. On the illness see Philo, *Leg. ad Gaiam* 14–21; Suet., *Cal.* 14.2; Dio 59.8.1–2. Modern speculation has included nervous breakdown: Barrett, *Caligula*, 73; epidemic encephalitis: Sandison, "Madness of the Emperor Caligula," 202–9; hypothyroidism: Katz, "Illness of Caligula," 223–25, and Katz, "Caligula's Illness Again," 451; various viral infections: Massaro and Montgomery, "Gaius—Mad, Bad, Ill or all Three," 894–909; or epilepsy: Benedickston, "Caligula's Madness or Interictal Temporal Lobe Epilepsy," 370–75. All of these speculations are unprovable and rely on descriptions of symptoms that may have been distorted by source transmission.

23. Philo, *Leg ad Gaiam* 14–21. For scholars who believe that the illness was the cause of Caligula's erratic behavior see, Charlesworth, "Gaius and Claudius," 656. For critics of this view, see Morgan, "Caligula's Illness Again," 327–29, and "Once Again Caligula's Illness," 452–53.

24. As with the reign of all emperors, our investigation is hampered by the usual source problems. We have lost the relevant sections of Tacitus and are left with only Dio and Suetonius, whose material tends toward the anecdotal and the trivial. Seneca the Younger was a witness to the events of the reign and would have known Caligula personally, but he did not write a history. On the sources for Caligula's reign and death, see Barrett, *Caligula*, 168–69.

25. Per Suet., *Cal.* 56.1, *in quadam coniuratione*. Also see Hurley, *Commentary*, 198–99.

26. Josephus, *AJ* 19.14. Feldman translation.

27. Dio 59.8.1–8 places the deaths of Gemellus and Silanus among the last events of 37, immediately after the illness. Macro's is placed at the beginning of 38 CE.

28. Philo, *Leg ad Gaiam* 14; Philo, *in Flacc.* 16; Dio 59.8.1, 10.6; Suet., *Cal.* 23.3; Hurley, *Commentary*, 95; Winterling, *Caligula*, 62–66; Barrett, *Caligula*, 74–76; Fagan, "Roman Imperial Succession," 102.

29. Anticipating the death of the emperor: Dio 59.8.3. See Winterling, *Caligula*, 62–64; Fagan, "Roman Imperial Succession," 102.

30. Suet., *Cal.* 23.3; Hurley, *Commentary*, 96.

31. For all the scholarly theorizing about a "Gemellus party" in Rome, his only named supporter was Avillius Flaccus, the prefect of Egypt: Philo, *in Flacc.* 9; Suet., *Cal.* 13. Flaccus had been involved in the prosecution of Agrippina, so his future under Caligula would have been dim. See Meise, *Untersuchungen . . . Julisch-Claudischen*, 116.

32. Philo, *Leg. ad Gaiam* 30–31, preserves the longest account of his death, whereby the doomed Gemellus was ordered to commit suicide under the supervision of Praetorian Guard and, pathetically, had to be guided through the act by those more skilled in killing than himself. He was buried in the mausoleum of Augustus and his tombstone was found in that vicinity. See *ILS* 172.

33. See Wilkinson, *Caligula*, 66.

34. Father-in-law's interference: Philo, *Leg. ad Gaiam* 62–65; Dio 59.8.5. Cf. Seneca, *Apoc.* 11.2. Dio's account is particularly inaccurate here. See Barrett, *Caligula*, 272n16.

35. Tacitus, *Agricola* 4.1; Barrett, *Caligula*, 77, 272n18.

36. His new wife's name is uncertain. Suet., *Cal.* 25.1 gives it as Livia Orestilla, Dio 59.8.7 as Cornelia Orestilla. See M. Kajava, "The Name of Cornelia Prestina/ Orestilla," *Arctos* 18 (1984): 23–30, who cites the evidence for both names. See Winterling, *Caligula*, 66–67; Hurley, *Commentary*, 52. D. Wardle, "Caligula and His Wives," *Latomus* 57, no. 1 (1998): 114, points out that the idea that the marriage led to the plots should also be considered. He reconstructs events differently than Barrett, *Caligula*, 76–77.

37. Barrett, *Caligula*, 78; Bingham, *Praetorian Guard*, 146n124.

38. Philo, *Leg. ad Gaiam* 52–59; Barrett, *Caligula*, 78.

39. On other executions: Dio 59.10.7.

40. Prefect of Egypt: Dio 59.10.6. This is the only mention of the appointment in the sources. See Bingham, *Praetorian Guard*, 142n122; Barrett, *Caligula*, 79; Winterling, *Caligula*, 64–65.

41. The sources disagree on almost every aspect of this story. Tacitus, *Ann.* 6.45.4, Philo, *Leg. ad Gaiam* 9, and Suet., *Cal.* 12.2 have Junia Claudilla die in childbirth. See Hurley, *Commentary*, 33. In Dio 59.8.7 they are divorced. Tacitus and Dio both say that Macro induced his wife to have an affair with Caligula to curry favor with the next emperor. Philo, *Leg. ad Gaiam* 39.6.1 places the blame on Ennia, saying that she deceived Macro, who was in the dark about the affair. Suet., *Cal.* 12.2, blames Caligula, saying he seduced Ennia. See Hurley, *Commentary*, 34. Tacitus, *Ann.* 6.45.5, says Caligula seemed to be happy to go along with the scheme since he needed Macro's support. Suetonius even says Caligula planned on marrying Ennia once he became emperor. Winterling, *Caligula*, 48–49, does not believe there was any relationship between Ennia and Caligula; cf. Barrett, *Caligula*, 79.

42. On the rhetoric of sexual misconduct, see Edwards, *Politics of Immorality in Ancient Rome*, esp. 11, on the unreliability of what was said about Roman emperors.

43. Philo and Dio have Caligula charging both Macro and Ennia, but neither one specifies any charge that would explain their fates. Bauman has suggested that since the *maiestas* laws had been suspended, Caligula had to use a different charge than treason: Bauman, *Impietas in Principem*, 176.

44. On Alba Fucens: Suet., *Cal.* 26.1; Philo, *Leg. ad Gaiam* 61; *AE* 1957, n250. Philo, *in Flacc.* 14 is the only source to claim his children were killed also. For more speculation about the reasons behind Macro's death, see F. de Visscher, "La politique dynastique sous la règne de Tibère," in *Synteleia*, ed. V. Arangio-Ruiz (Naples: Jovene, 1964), 54–65; Meise, *Untersuchungen . . . Julisch-Claudischen*, 252. Dabrowski, "Problems in the Tradition about the Principate of Gaius," argues that Macro, Gemellus, and Silanus were put to death by Caligula's sisters and Lepidus. On the evidence in the *Acts of the Pagan or Alexandrian Martyrs* for the prosecution of Macro by one Isidorus, see Barrett, *Caligula*, 79–80.

45. Despite the assertion of several scholars that it was immediately after Macro's dismissal that the command of the Guard reverted to being shared by two men, this is not supported by the sources. Dio 59.11.2 speaks of only one Praetorian prefect at the funeral of Drusilla in 38 CE, contra Barrett, *Caligula*, 80. By 41 CE there were definitely two prefects, one of whom was Clemens. See Suet., *Cal.* 56.1: *praefectorum praetori*; Hurley, *Commentary*, 198. Dio 59.25.8 has Caligula

playing one off the other. And see Bingham, *Praetorian Guard*, 143n126; Balsdon, *Emperor Gaius*, 39–40.

46. Suet., *Cal.* 56.1: *praefectorum praetori* (plural); Dio 59.25.8: *tous hyparchous*. See Bingham, *Praetorian Guard*, 143n126; Fagan, "Roman Imperial Succession," 112; Ferrill, *Caligula*, 107.

47. The evidence is so sketchy that some have even doubted a conspiracy at all. Rutledge, *Imperial Inquisitions*, 163, also points out we do not know who the informers were. Ferrill, *Caligula*, 121, sees a genuine conspiracy. C. J. Simpson, "The 'Conspiracy' of A.D. 39," in *Studies in Latin Literature and Roman History*, ed. C. Deroux (Brussels: Latomus, 1980), 347, says there is no support in the sources at all. Barrett, *Caligula*, 101–6, and *Agrippina* (New Haven, CT: YUP, 1996), 62–70, takes the middle ground; and see M. P. Charlesworth, "The Tradition about Caligula," *Cambridge Historical Journal* 4 (1933): 113–14. J. C. Faur, "La Première Conspiration contre Caligula," *RBPh* 51 (1973): 13–50, argues for the conspiracy. See Pagán, *Conspiracy Narratives*, 95–97. Rutledge, *Imperial Inquisitions*, 162–63, accepts the conspiracy but cannot name the informer.

48. Tacitus, *Ann.* 14.2.2.

49. There is no consensus about the date of the marriage of Caligula to Caesonia. Dio 59.23.7 locates it during the northern expedition of 39 CE, and this was accepted by Gelzer, "Iulius," *R-E*, 10: 404, and Charlesworth, "Gaius and Claudius," 663. Willrich, "Caligula," 296–97, and Balsdon, *Emperor Gaius*, 48, placed it in the summer before the expedition, based on the story that when Caesonia gave birth thirty days after the marriage, Caligula took the child to the Capitoline and entrusted her upbringing to Jupiter and Minerva, meaning he was in Rome. The anecdote survives in Josephus, *AJ* 19.11, Suet., *Cal.* 25.4, and Dio 59.23.7. This puts the marriage date and the birth in advance of his departure in September. Cf. Linnert, "Beiträge zur Geschichte Caligulas," 81; Faur, "La Première Conspiration contre Caligula," 16; Meise, *Untersuchungen . . . Julisch-Claudischen*, 121–22; Swan, "Conspiracies," 147–50.

50. On the role and image of the women in Caligula's family see S. Wood, "Diva Drusilla Panthea and the Sisters of Caligula," *AJA* 99, no. 3 (July 1995): 458–82; McHugh, "Manipulating Memory," 184–205.

51. As suggested by Balsdon, *Emperor Gaius*, 70–71.

52. For Gaetulicus's career, see *PIR²*, C 1390. Not all scholars accept that Lepidus and Gaetulicus acted together in a concerted and organized fashion. See Linnert, "Beiträge zur Geschichte Caligulas," 61–82; Willrich, "Caligula," 308; Meise, *Untersuchungen . . . Julisch-Claudischen*, 108–15; Faur, "La Première Conspiration contre Caligula," 19; Cogitore, *La légitimité dynastique d'Auguste à Néron*, 191–200. D. Fishwick and B. D. Shaw, "Ptolemy of Mauretania and the Conspiracy of Gaetulicus," *Historia* 25, no. 4 (1976): 491–92, suggest there was a family connection. On the establishment of the new legions, see J. V. P. D. Balsdon, "Notes Concerning the Principate of Gaius," *JRS* 24 (1934): 13–16.

53. Holland, *Nero*, 20.

54. On the fate of Lepidus and Gaetulicus: Dio 59.21.4 (executing rebels), 22.5 (executing both Lentulus and Gaetulicus). Suet., *Claudius* 9.1 makes no reference to Gaetulicus connected with a plot. Stewart, "Sejanus, Gaetulicus and Seneca," 70–85, argued that Gaetulicus's downfall was due to his earlier associations with

Sejanus. This is refuted by Swan, *Conspiracies*, 134–44. Some see him as part of a much larger group of old adherents of Tiberius who were unhappy with Caligula's behavior. Some see him as an adherent of the old pro-Gemellus party. See Meise, *Untersuchungen . . . Julisch-Claudischen*, 114–15; A. Bergener, *Die Führende Senatorenschicht im Frühen Prinzipat 14-68 n. Chr.* (Bonn: Habelt, 1965), 119; Faur, "La Première Conspiration contre Caligula," 19. We know nothing of the role of the *delatores* in this episode. See Rutledge, *Imperial Inquisitions*, 147.

55. Dio 59.20.1 claimed Caligula did this because they had failed to proclaim a thanksgiving on his birthday. This, at least, secures the date of August 31 for us. See Suet., *Cal.* 26.3; Hurley, *Commentary*, 109.

56. Bergener, *Die Führende Senatorenschicht*, 120. It has been argued by Bergener that Lepidus became involved in some sort of intrigue but not because of his own ambitions: he became the leader of a faction that came to oppose Caligula. This group was made up of old adherents of Tiberius and probably involved at least one of the consuls removed in 39. Cf. Barrett, *Caligula*, 108.

57. Winterling, *Caligula*, 108; Barrett, *Caligula*, 119.

58. There is a debate over whether the planned campaign to Britain ever came off. R. W. Davies, "The Abortive Invasion of Britain by Gaius," *Historia* 15 (1966): 124–28, suggested a continuation of the maneuvers on the Channel coast in the spring of 40 CE. P. Bicknell, "The Emperor Gaius' Military Activities in A.D. 40," *Historia* 17 (1968): 496–505, believed there were actual operations against the Canninefates conducted from the Insula Batavorum. E. J. Philips, "The Emperor Gaius' Abortive Invasion of Britain," *Historia* 19 (1970): 369–74, thinks that Gaius planned to invade Britain but the troops mutinied and refused to go; see Balsdon, "The Principates of Tiberius and Gaius," 94.

59. Barrett, *Caligula*, 159; Suet., *Aug.* 49.1; Suet., *Cal.* 43.1; Hurley, *Commentary*, 159; Dio 55.24.8, 56.23.4. Keune, "Custos," (2) *R-E* 4 (1901): col. 1902, says he filled out the numbers from prisoners of war. The standard modern work on the subject is Bellen, *Die germanische Leibwache der römischen Kaiser des Julisch-Claudischen Hauses*. There seems to be no parallel for the publicly appointed guard for the statues. See *CIL* 8.9052 for a private guard. See T. Pekary, *Das Römische Kaiserbildnis in Staat, Kult und Gesellschaft* (Berlin: Mann, 1985), 114; he thinks it may have been honorary (140).

60. This reconstruction also solves the problem of why he would bring his sisters and Lepidus with him to Germany, where the other conspirators would be waiting. See Swan, *Conspiracies*, 133. For another reconstruction of the events, see Balsdon, "Notes Concerning the Principate of Gaius," 16–17.

61. The Arval record (*CIL* 6.32346) for that day says "because of the wicked plots of Cn. Lentulus Gaetulicus against Gaius Germanicus." Suet., *Claudius* 9.1 links Lepidus and Gaetulicus. It is generally assumed that the execution took place in Mainz, at Gaetulicus's headquarters, but it might also have taken place at Lyon. Lyon was suggested by Faur, "La Première Conspiration contre Caligula," 13–50, esp. 32–35, developing the idea of G. Teubner, *Beiträge zur Geschichte der Eroberung Britanniens durch die Römer* (Breslau: Trewendt & Granier, 1909), 1–15, 82–86. For an excellent reconstruction, see Winterling, *Caligula*, 108–12. Dio 59.22.5 says some were executed for rebelling or plotting, but the real reason was that they were rich and Gaetulicus was too popular.

62. Swan, *Conspiracies*, 130.

63. Dio 59.18.4. On Calvisius Sabinus: Tacitus, *Ann.* 6.9.5–6. He is not mentioned by Suetonius. Cf. Barrett, *Caligula*, 100–101; Swan, *Conspiracies*, 135. On the "consulars' conspiracy" and the elimination of Gaius Calvisius Sabinus, Junius Priscus, and Gnaeus Domitius Afer, see Winterling, *Caligula*, 90–107; Ferrill, *Caligula*, 117.

64. On the execution of Lepidus: Seneca, *Epis.* 4.7, who says Lepidus had his throat cut by a tribune, and the Senate decreed that his remains should not be given proper burial. See Josephus, *AJ* 19.20; Tacitus, *Ann.* 14.2.2. All accept the validity of the charges against Agrippina and Lepidus; see Rut. Nam. 1.305–6; Dio 59.22.6–8 states that Caligula accused Lepidus and his sisters in the Senate; this implies there was no formal trial but merely a statement from the emperor of the grounds on which he had acted. This is probably the *causa Lepidi* to which Suetonius refers: Suet., *Claudius* 9.1; *Cal.* 24.3. See Hurley, *Commentary*, 101; T. P. Wiseman's commentary in Flavius Josephus, *Death of an Emperor* (Exeter: University of Exeter Press, 1991), 48. For a discussion of where the condemnation took place, see Barrett, *Caligula*, 107, who believes it was in Mevania, contra Willrich, "Caligula," 307, and M. Gelzer, "Ilius Caligula," 402; Swan, *Conspiracies*, 133.

65. Suet., *Cal.* 24.3; Dio 59.22.8. It has been doubted that two intelligent women, who knew what their brother was capable of doing, would have implicated themselves by writing incriminating letters that might be intercepted. Perhaps they were forced to write them to provide Caligula with evidence and in return he spared their lives. See Ferrill, *Caligula*, 121; Balsdon, *Emperor Gaius*, 75, takes it as "documentary evidence."

66. On Agrippina carrying the ashes: Dio 59.22.8; Barrett, *Caligula*, 107; Winterling, *Caligula*, 110.

67. On donatives to the soldiers: Dio 59.22.7. On donatives in general, see Bingham, *Praetorian Guard*, chapter 3. Both Dio 59.22.7–8 and Suet., *Cal.* 24.3 mention that Caligula sent three daggers to the Temple of Mars Ultor in Rome. Nero repeated the gesture when he put down the conspiracy in 65 CE and dedicated the dagger of Scaevinus in the Temple of Jupiter on the Capitoline. See Barrett, *Caligula*, 108; Hurley, *Commentary*, 101–2; Barrett, *Agrippina*, 66; Auguet, *Caligula, ou le pouvoir à vingt ans*, 106.

68. On the Arval Brethren inscription: *CIL* 6.2029.d; Barrett, *Caligula*, 104.

69. Suet., *Cal.* 48, on decimating the legions that had him and his mother in the mutiny of 14 CE. Also see Hurley, *Commentary*, 172.

70. Dio 59.23.8.

71. Wilkinson, *Caligula*, 65, dismisses the charges by Suet., *Cal.* 38, Josephus, *AJ* 19.3, and Philo, *Leg. ad Gaiam* 105, that Caligula did it for the money. He argues for the fact that Caligula was not bankrupt and points out that the emperor reduced the fee for informers from a quarter to one-eighth of the convicted man's property. This does not tie in with the allegation that Caligula encouraged false allegations.

72. Barrett, *Caligula*, 98. On the use of freedmen, Winterling, *Caligula*, 165.

73. Josephus, *AJ* 19.64. On his house, Pliny, *HN* 36.60; Barrett, *Caligula*, 98.

74. On Protogenes's sword and dagger: Suet., *Cal.* 28; Dio 59.26.1.2; Orosius 7.5.10. The story is rejected by Balsdon, *Emperor Gaius*, 100. Protogenes is mentioned in Juvenal 3.120 among the famous *delatores*. He was executed in the first

year of Claudius's reign, per Dio 60.4.5, and his books were supposedly destroyed. See Barrett, *Caligula*, 158–59.

75. Helicon first appears in Philo's account of the initial reception of the Jewish embassy that he headed from Alexandria. See Philo, *Leg. ad Gaiam* 166–77, 181, 203, 206 (in interpolation in the text, perhaps by Philo himself); Barrett, *Caligula*, 274n47. Helicon was the leader of a large group of Alexandrian Greeks in Caligula's service whom Philo calls "Egyptians."

76. Seneca, *Ira* 3.19.2; Suet., *Cal.* 49.1–2; "He was returning only to those who wanted him, the equestrians and the people, but not to the senators, whom he could never again regard as fellow citizens." It may be at this point that he made his famous remark about eliminating the entire Senate. See Dio 59.23.7, 25.5; Barrett, *Caligula*, 139; Hurley, *Commentary*, 174, on the tactlessness of putting such open hostility in an openly circulated edict.

77. On the influence of freedmen, see Barrett, *Caligula*, 85. Unfortunately, the role of the *delatores* in partisan politics under Caligula is not documented. See Rutledge, *Imperial Inquisitions*, 147.

78. Suet., *Cal.* 49.1; Barrett, *Caligula*, 139.

79. On soldiers released on the crowd: Dio 59.28.11.

80. On guards around his statues: Dio 59.26.3. This is the first reference to this practice, and it suggests that there was a problem with vandalism or demonstrations centering around the images. See Barrett, *Caligula*, 294n29.

81. Tacitus, *Ann.* 16.17.6.

82. On Anicius Cerialis and Sextus Papinius: Dio's somewhat muddled account in 59.25.5b (Zonaras *Epitome* [of Dio]). Rutledge, *Imperial Inquisitions*, 163, notes Dio is trying to link father and son conspirator stories. He makes a double error since Anicius does not die but takes part in the later Pisonian conspiracy.

83. Dio 59.25.5b (Zonaras *Epitome*). Note that Zonaras and the Vatican epitome of John Patricius summarize somewhat differently. The latter states that Cerialis said nothing, thus only implying that Papinius talked.

84. Barrett, *Caligula*, 156–57 does not accept this story; he believed Dio confused the story and added the touch of having the father murdered before the son. Also see Balsdon, *Emperor Gaius*, 99, contra Swan, *Conspiracies*, 153, 153n74.

85. Dio 59.25.6–7 (who gives the name as Betilinus); Seneca, *Ira* 3.18.3; Suet., *Cal.* 26.3, speaks of the scourging—but not the execution—of a quaestor who some assume to be Bassus. See Pagán, *Conspiracy Narratives*, 97.

86. Swan, *Conspiracies*, 153–54; Barrett, *Caligula*, 157.

87. Dio 59.25.6–7. Getting the chronology right is very important. Those who argue that the conspiracy against him started with his marriage to Caesonia in the spring of 39 CE are thwarted if we date the marriage to the fall after the conspiracy was uncovered. See Barrett, *Caligula*, 157; Ferrill, *Caligula*, 122; Rutledge, *Imperial Inquisitions*, 163, on the informing.

88. Dio 59.18.5; Wilkinson, *Caligula*, 66–67. Wilkinson also points out that since the tradition of treason trials is absent from Seneca and Philo but present in Suetonius and Dio, the trials may all be retrojections of events from later principates used to blacken the memory of Caligula.

89. Seneca, *Tranquil* 14.4–10; Seneca, *Epis.* 73.1, 103.5; P. A. Brunt, "Stoicism and the Principate," *PBSR* 43 (1975): 9; Barrett, *Caligula*, 157.

90. Seneca, *Tranquil* 14.4–10; Seneca, *Epis.* 73.1, 103.5; Tacitus, *Ann.* 3.51.3, and Boethius, *Consol. Phil.* 1.4.94, seem to reflect a tradition in which Canus was actually involved in a plot. Also see Barrett, *Caligula*, 157 and notes.

91. Seneca, *Epis.* 29.6, *de Bene* 2.21.5; Tacitus, *Agricola* 4.1; Balsdon, *Emperor Gaius*, 98; Barrett, *Caligula*, 158. Winterling, *Caligula*, 135, rejects this as a motive; see Ferrill, *Caligula*, 133.

92. The main source is Josephus, *AJ* 19.32–36; Suet., *Cal.* 16.4; Dio 59.26.4; Seneca, *Bene* 2.12.1. Barrett, *Caligula*, 158 and 293n24, with other sources on Pomponius. On the connection between Timidius's betrayal of Pomponius and Chaerea's plot, see Rutledge, *Imperial Inquisitions*, 163.

93. Suet., *Cal.* 16.4, who related the story without mentioning the names; Hurley, *Commentary*, 60–61. Josephus, *AJ* 32–36 provides the names of Timidius and Quintilia and calls the accused man Pompedius. Dio 59.26.4 gives the name as Pomponius. Scholars have debated the identities of the participants. See Barrett, *Caligula*, 293, for the references; Wiseman's commentary in Josephus, *Death of an Emperor*, 51–52.

94. Barrett, *Caligula*, 158; Cogitore, *La légitimité dynastique d'Auguste à Néron*, 63–65.

95. On Seneca, *OCD*, 96. Stewart, "Sejanus, Gaetulicus and Seneca," 70–85; G. W. Clarke, "Seneca the Younger under Caligula," *Latomus* 24 (1965): 62–69; M. Griffin, *Seneca: A Philosopher in Politics* (Oxford: Clarendon Press, 1976), 367–68; E. Wilson, *The Greatest Empire: A Life of Seneca* (Oxford: OUP, 2014), 205–7.

96. Dio 59.19.7–8, 60.8.5, 61.12.1. Tacitus, *Ann.* 14.63.2; Suet., *Claudius* 29.1; Barrett, *Caligula*, 112; Clarke, "Seneca the Younger under Caligula," 62–69.

97. Suet., *Cal.* 28; Dio 59.26.1–2; Orosius 7.5.10; Barrett, *Caligula*, 159. Protogenes is mentioned by Juvenal 3.120 among the famous *delatores*. He was executed in the first year of Claudius's reign (Dio 60.4.5), and the books were destroyed.

98. Dio 59.26.3. The arrangement did not continue after his death, and Claudius sat on the consul's tribunal or on the tribune's bench in the body of the house. See Baldwin, *Roman Emperors*, 8.

99. On the German bodyguard, see chapter 2. Although Augustus had dismissed them after the Varian disaster in 9 CE, the unit is attested again in 14 CE, when the pick of the unit was sent north in the quelling of the Pannonian revolt after the death of Augustus. See Tacitus, *Ann.* 1.24.2.

100. Barrett, *Caligula*, 159; Tacitus, *Ann.* 6.15.5; Suet., *Div. Aug.* 35.2; *Tib.* 65.1.

101. An inscription predating the Claudian invasion of Britain shows that the increase had certainly taken place by 43. Barrett, *Caligula*, 159. See Willrich, "Caligula," 306; M. Durry, "Praetoriae Cohortes," *R-E* 22 (1954), col. 1613.

102. Barrett, *Caligula*, 160; Dio 59.25.7 (*Epitome*).

103. Wiseman's commentary in Josephus, *Death of an Emperor*, 54; Barrett, *Caligula*, 160. Josephus, *AJ* 19.64-69 implicates Callistus specifically. Tacitus, *Ann.* 11.29.1, 12.1.3, also implies he had a major role in Caligula's death in one of his earlier (lost) books. Suet., *Cal.* 56.1, suggests that Callistus found allies among the other important freedmen. Dio 59.29.1 has him as part of the conspiracy. See Hurley, *Commentary*, 198–99.

104. Josephus, *AJ* 19.64–69. Josephus also reports that at one point Callistus had been instructed to poison Claudius but found excuses to constantly postpone the deed—a claim that provokes skepticism from Josephus.

105. Suet., *Cal.* 56.1; Hurley, *Commentary*, 198–99; Dio 59.29.1.

106. Josephus, *AJ* 19.44–47.

107. On Sabinus, Lupus, and Papinius: Suet., *Cal.* 58.2; Hurley, *Commentary*, 209–12; Josephus, *AJ* 19.46; Dio 59.29.1; Wiseman's commentary in Josephus, *Death of an Emperor*, 52, for Sabinus.

108. Josephus, *AJ* 45; Barrett, *Caligula*, 160.

109. Dio 59.25.7.

110. Tacitus, *Hist.* 3.68.5.

111. Josephus, *AJ* 19.60–62. Barrett, *Caligula*, 292n10; D. Timpe, *Untersuchungen zur Kontinuät des frühen Prinzipats* (Wiesbaden: Steiner, 1962), 80–81, believed the conspiracy was known much more widely.

112. Josephus, *AJ* 19.18–200, for the entire story of the assassination. We know little about Chaerea except that by 41, at the latest, he held a tribunate in the Praetorian Guard. Tacitus, *Ann.* 1.32.5, calls him an *adulescens* (up to about thirty years old) at the time of the mutinies in 14. At the time of the assassination he is called a *senior* by Suet., *Cal.* 56.2. See Hurley, *Commentary*, 200; Cogitore, *La légitimité dynastique d'Auguste à Néron*, 69–73.

113. P. A. Rogers, "The Stigma of Politics: Imperial Conspirators and Their Descendants in the Early Roman Empire" (PhD diss., University of Washington, 1979), preface, 2, who writes, "Genuine Republican motives did not exist in either the conspiracy of 41 against Caligula or in the Pisonian conspiracy of 65 against Nero."

114. Josephus, *AJ* 19.21. On the insults: Josephus, *AJ* 19.29–31; Tacitus, *Ann.* 1.32.2; Swan, *Conspiracies*, 156. The other sources: Seneca, *Constant.* 183; Suet., *Cal.* 56.2; Dio-Xiph. 59.29.2; Pagán, *Conspiracy Narratives*, 99–103.

115. According to the versions of Dio 59.29.2 and Josephus, *AJ* 19.29–31, when asked for the daily watchword by Chaerea, the emperor chose suggestive expressions such as "Venus" or "Priapus," causing much ribaldry among Chaerea's fellow Praetorians. When Chaerea had occasion to thank him for anything, Caligula would offer his hand to be kissed, and then at the last moment move it in obscene gestures. Cf. Suet., *Cal.* 56.2; Hurley, *Commentary*, 201.

116. Seneca, *Constant.* 18.3; Josephus, *AJ* 19.29; Suet., *Cal.* 56.2; Barrett, *Caligula*, 161; Swan, *Conspiracies*, 156; Winterling, *Caligula*, 177.

117. Josephus, *AJ* 19.34.

118. He was made fun of by Caligula, who called him a *gynnis* ("womanish man"). Even the fourth-century poet Ausonius writes of *Caerea mollis* ("effeminate Chaerea") *De Caesar.* 4.4. Balsdon, *Emperor Gaius*, 103, sees Chaerea as a "lady's man"!

119. Dio 59.29.1a. On the other participants, see Swan, *Conspiracies*, 156–58.

120. Josephus, *AJ* 19.46; Suet., *Cal.* 58.2; Dio 59.29.1; Swan, *Conspiracies*, 157.

121. See B. J. Kavanagh, "The Conspirator Aemilius Regulus's Aunt's Family," *Historia* 50, no. 3 (2001): 379–84, who suggests Regulus is really Aemilius Rectus, a relative of Seneca's. See also B. J. Kavanagh, "The Identity and Fate of Caligula's Assassin, Aquila," *Latomus* 69, no. 4 (2010): 1012.

122. Josephus, *AJ* 19.20, 49, 52. Tacitus, *Ann.* 6.9.5–7; Dio 60.15.1. The manuscripts of Josephus create difficulties since throughout them the name "Minucianus" is used where "Vinicinus" is clearly meant. See *PIR*² A 701; Barrett, *Caligula*, 161.

123. On the passages in Josephus and possible emendations, see M. Swan, "Josephus, *A.J.* 19. 251–52: Opposition to Gaius and Claudius," *AJPh* 91 (1970): 149–64. See Swan, *Conspiracies,* 158, 164–68, for a thorough discussion of the role of Vinicianus. Among the other senators involved was an ex-praetor Vatinius, whom Josephus calls Bathybius (Josephus, *AJ* 19.91–92). See R. Hanslik, "Vatinius," no. 5, *R-E* 2 (1955), Reihe line 8, col. 520 makes this identification. It is rejected by L. H. Feldman, Loeb edition of *AJ,* 258, but see Swan, *Conspiracies,* 158. Another senator was Cluvius, a consular possibly identified with the historian Cluvius Rufus (Josephus, *AJ* 19.91–92). Cf. Fagan, "Roman Imperial Succession," 106–7.

124. It is Dio 60.15.1 who supplies the motive of imperial ambition. V. M. Scramuzza, *The Emperor Claudius* (Cambridge, MA: HUP, 1940), 51–54, saw Chaerea and Sabinus as mere dupes of the senatorial conspiracy. Balsdon, *Emperor Gaius,* 101–3, also saw the Senate as the driving force, but see Timpe, *Untersuchungen zur Kontinuät des frühen Prinzipats,* 89; Bergener, *Die Fürhrende Senatorenschicht,* 125; J. Scheid, *Les Frères Arvales: Recruitement et origine sociale sous les empereurs Julio-claudiens* (Paris: Presses Universitaires de France, 1975), 200–201; M. Gelzer, "Ilius Caligula," 414; Barrett, *Caligula,* 162 and Swan, *Conspiracies,* 5–6 believe he remained a republican but was trying to frustrate the attempts of Vinicius and Valerius Asiaticus to grab the throne. Swan, "Josephus, *A.J.* 19. 251–52," 157, sees Vinicianus as the core of the opposition, and finds it more united and determined than is generally recognized.

125. Valerius Asiaticus: Suffect in 35, followed by a second in 46. See Josephus, *AJ* 19.159; Barrett, *Caligula,* 162.

126. Seneca, *Cons.* 18.2. On the grudge but not the story, Josephus, *AJ* 19.159; Tacitus, *Ann.* 11.1–3. Barrett, *Caligula,* 162.

127. Seneca, *Constant.* 18.2; Josephus, *AJ* 19.159; Tacitus, *Ann.* 11.1–3.

128. He was the brother of Lucius Cassius Longinus, who had been married to Drusilla and had an unfortunate habit of boasting that his ancestor had assassinated Julius Caesar. He did escape with his life (perhaps being recalled too late) since he went on to become governor of Syria and was eventually exiled by Nero: *CIL* 10.1233; Suet., *Cal.* 57.1; Suet., *Nero* 37.1; Josephus, *AJ* 20.1; Tacitus, *Ann.* 12.11.4, 12.12.1, 16.7.3, 9, 1.22.9; Dio 59.29.3; Barrett, *Caligula,* 162, 294n45.

129. Norbanus: Josephus, *AJ* 19.123. Two of the Norbani brothers held consulships—L. Norbanus Flaccus in 19 and L. Norbanus Balbus in 15—and either might have been the father of the Norbanus who died in 38 CE. See Barrett, *Caligula,* 162, 294n45; Ferrill, *Caligula,* 161.

130. Barrett, *Caligula,* 163; Coulston and Dodge, *Ancient Rome,* 219–21, on temporary theaters.

131. Winterling, *Caligula,* 179.

132. Or on Publius Nonius Asprenas, according to Josephus, *AJ* 19.87. Suet., *Cal.* 57.4 has the blood spurt onto Caligula. Also see Hurley, *Commentary,* 205; Barrett, *Caligula,* 164.

133. Dio 59.29.5. Both Cn. Sentius Saturninus and Q. Pomponius Secundus were newly elevated to the consulship. They also had knowledge of the plot that bordered on complicity. See Swan, *Conspiracies,* 159. Once Caligula was dead, Pomponius joined his colleagues in decisive actions to seize control of the city and the government.

134. On exotic birds and fruit: Josephus, *AJ* 19.93.

135. Josephus, *AJ* 19.91–92. Cluvius (or Josephus) slightly misquotes Homer's *Iliad* 14.90–91 omitting "this" (*touton*) before "report." See Barrett, *Caligula*, 164.

136. On Vinicianus trying to leave: Josephus, *AJ* 19.96; Suet., *Cal.* 56.2, 58; Suet., *Claudius* 10.1. The senator is named in one text as Minucianus but has been identified as Lucius Annius Vinicianus. See Wiseman's commentary on Josephus, *Death of an Emperor*, 47–48; Feldman, Josephus *AJ*, Loeb edition, 261n*e*.

137. Josephus has him leave at the ninth hour (2:00 p.m.), whereas Suetonius says the sixth. See Josephus, *AJ* 19.99; Suet., *Cal.* 58.1; Hurley, *Commentary*, 208; Dio 59.29, for murder with no time stamp. The reading of the name of Asprenas in the Josephus manuscripts is far from certain. Some manuscripts have Ambronas or Ampronas. See the Loeb Josephus, vol. 9, p. 262. On C. Nonius Asprenas as the decoy, see Scramuzza, *Emperor Claudius*, 51.

138. On the plotters' exit: Josephus, *AJ* 19.102–5; Suet., *Cal.* 58.1; Dio 59.29.6–7. Josephus is the only one to mention the shortcut. Dio adds that some of the youths came from Greece (59.29.6).

139. This was the interpretation of those who believed there was to be a restoration of the republic. See Swan, *Conspiracies*, 160–62. This would all depend on whether one sees Josephus, *AJ* 19.92, 159; Tacitus, *Ann.* 11.1.2; Dio 59.30.2 as rhetoric or a real possibility.

140. Josephus, *AJ* 19.102–6; Suet., *Cal.* 58.1; Dio 59.29.6–7.

141. Suet., *Cal.* 58.2; Barrett, *Caligula*, 165.

142. Suet., *Cal.* 58.3.

143. Toying with Caligula: Josephus, *AJ* 19.106–7 although Josephus rejects it, saying, "Fear leaves no room for deliberation" (Feldman translation).

144. Seneca, *Constant.* 18.3; Suet., *Cal.* 58.2–3; Barrett, *Caligula*, 165.

145. Crowded corridor: Josephus, *AJ* 19.116. Barrett, *Caligula*, 165.

146. Although the palace was one large complex, it had been enlarged piecemeal with other additions that were named for members of the ruling family. On the House of Germanicus: Josephus, *AJ* 19.117; Barrett, *Caligula*, 165–66. For a detailed discussion of the location of Caligula's death, see Barrett, *Caligula*, appendix 3, 169–70.

147. Josephus, *AJ* 19.122; Suet., *Cal.* 55.2. Sabinus was later rescued from death in a gladiatorial combat by Messalina, whose lover he was; see Dio 60.28.2; Barrett, *Caligula*, 166.

148. Josephus, *AJ* 19.123–26; Suet., *Cal.* 58.3; Dio 59.30.1b; Barrett, *Caligula*, 166.

149. Blood on his toga: Josephus, *AJ* 19.87; Barrett, *Caligula*, 166. Josephus offers no explanation for Nonius Asprenas's presence by the body. Dabrowski, "Problems in the Tradition about the Principate of Gaius," 255–56, suggests that he may have been killed simply as a bystander and his role elevated by later tradition.

150. Josephus, *AJ* 19.123. This was probably L. Norbanus Balbus, the consul of 19 CE. Norbanus no. 8, *R-E* 1936, p. 931; Barrett, *Caligula*, 166.

151. Josephus, *AJ* 19.125. We do not know much about this Anteius, but his father, of the same name, had been driven by Caligula into exile and later executed. Barrett, *Caligula*, 296n61, suggests that Anteius was perhaps the brother of Publius Anteius, legate in Dalmatia in 51–52, who committed suicide in 66.

152. Josephus, *AJ* 19.157; Barrett, *Caligula*, 166.

153. Josephus, *AJ* 19.154.

154. On the death of Caesonia and her daughter: Josephus, *AJ* 19.190–200; Suet., *Cal.* 59; Barrett, *Caligula*, 166. Suetonius calls the murderer a "centurion" of the Praetorian Guard. Josephus has the murder carried out in the evening after the Senate had called its emergency meeting. It is also totally conceivable that the conspirators would have delayed until the evening and allowed her the opportunity to escape. Another even more serious problem is that Lupus was sent by Chaerea to the palace to murder her, yet the palace seems to have been under the control of the Praetorian Guard almost immediately after the assassination. The likelihood is that the murder of Caesonia had been decided upon well in advance to avoid the danger that she might become a focus of resentment and resistance, just as Agrippina and her sons had been in the previous reign, and that it had been planned to follow almost immediately after Caligula's. It will be recalled that the conspirators were said to have escaped "into the Palace." It had probably been arranged beforehand that Lupus was to kill Caesonia, and that the account of her body being draped over her dead husband's corpse (not mentioned in Dio or Suetonius) is a poetic elaboration. See Barrett, *Caligula*, 167.

155. Josephus, *AJ* 127–28; Winterling, *Caligula*, 182.

156. German guard: Josephus, *AJ* 19.148–52; Winterling, *Caligula*, 182.

157. See Scramuuzza, *The Emperor Claudius*, 51–52.

158. On the seizing of the state funds, see John of Antioch fr. 84; Barrett, *Caligula*, 172.

159. On urban cohorts: Dio 60.1 actually says "guards" (*phylakes*). See Winterling, *Caligula*, 183.

160. Senate meeting: Josephus, *AJ* 19.159–84; Tacitus, *Ann.* 11.1.2; Dio 59.30.2; Suet., *Cal.* 60.

161. Senators fleeing to the country: Josephus, *AJ* 19.248–49.

162. Josephus, *AJ* 19.248.

163. Chaerea's execution: Josephus, *AJ* 19.269; Sabinus's suicide: Josephus, *AJ* 19.273. Winterling, *Caligula*, 175.

164. We do not know how Callistus died. See Josephus, *AJ* 19.64–69; Dio 60.4.5, 59.26.1–2; and Barrett, *Caligula*, 176–77. On the death of Protogenes: Dio 60.4.5. On Helicon, Philo, *Leg. ad Gaiam* 206; Winterling, *Caligula*, 175; J. Osgood, *Claudius Caesar*, 41.

165. On the sources see Beard, *SPQR*, 395–98; See Barrett, *Caligula*, 213–41 for an extensive discussion of the sources and Caligula's historical reputation.

166. Winterling's biography of Caligula, esp. 188–92, explains in great detail the aristocratic bias of our sources and how the image of the "mad" Caligula was created. See also Beard, *SPQR*, 397, for the quip.

167. Tacitus, *Ann.* 1.1.2.

168. Ferrill, *Caligula*, 9.

169. Dio 59.2.1–3.

170. Dio 59.13.8–9.

171. Suet., *Cal.* 19; Dio 59.17.1–11; Josephus, *AJ* 19.5–6.

172. Dio 59.2.5–6, 10.7, 59.14–15.

173. Restoration of the *maiestas* laws: Dio 59.16.8.

174. Swan, *Conspiracies*, 145.

175. The speech is in Dio 59.16.2–7. For an attempt to rationalize this speech see J. C. Faur, "Un discours de l'empereur Caligula au Senat (Dion., *Hist. rom.* LIX, 16)," *Klio* 60 (1978): 439–47, who dates it later in the year in response to the conspiracy of Lepidus and Gaetulicus. Also see Ferrill, *Caligula*, 113.

176. For his popularity, see Wilkinson, *Caligula*, 68–69. Even Josephus, *AJ* 19.227, states that the will of the people and that of the Senate were at variance.

177. See the treatment of the son of Pastor mentioned by Seneca, *Ira* 33.3–7.

178. Tacitus, *Ann.* 6.3.4–4.1, 5–6, 6.5–6, 9.2–5.

179. Winterling, *Caligula*, 104. The author's biography focuses on the dissimulation and hypocrisy that lay at the heart of Roman imperial politics and had in a sense been the foundation of the governmental system established by Augustus. In making one-man rule work successfully at Rome, after almost half a millennium of (more or less) democracy, and establishing a "workable entente" between the old aristocracy and the new autocracy, Augustus resorted to a game of smoke and mirrors in which everyone, it seems, was play-acting. The senators had to act as if they still possessed a degree of power that they no longer had, while the emperor had to exercise his power in such a way as to dissemble his possession of it. On Winterling's model, successful emperors after Augustus were those who managed to exploit the doublespeak and turn it to their advantage; the unsuccessful were those who fought against it. Caligula's predecessor, Tiberius, never grew into the role. He took it all at face value, refused to master the game of "ambiguous communication," (24) and in the process repeatedly revealed the autocratic reality of imperial rule underneath the carefully constructed democratic veneer of the Augustan system. Caligula resisted imperial doublespeak in a subtly different way. He tried to fight the ambiguity of political communication that had become the norm in the imperial regime and to counter not only its insincere flattery and apparent emptiness, but also its systematic corruption of meaning. Swan, *Conspiracies*, 160–61 sees in this an actual attempt to return to the republic, an idea that should be rejected out of hand. See Wilkinson, *Caligula*, 73–78, on the emperor's relationship to the Senate, although Wilkinson, too, sees this as an attempt to restore the republic.

180. Bingham, *Praetorian Guard*, 23, believes they were influenced by "the political situation" and were "corruptible" but, in this case, we could ask, "Corruptible by whom?"

181. Josephus, *AJ* 19.41–42.

182. Wood, *Diva Drusilla*, 482.

183. Balsdon, *Emperor Gaius*, 102.

184. On the possible role of Claudius in the assassination, see H. Jung, "Die Thronerhebung des Claudius," *Chiron* 2 (1972): 367–86; Campbell, *Emperor and the Roman Army*, 81.

CHAPTER 6: CLAUDIUS THE FOOL?

1. On Claudius's physical afflictions, see Osgood, *Claudius Caesar*, 9; W. Valente et. al, "Caveat Cenans!" *American Journal of Medicine* 112 (2002): 392–98. For earlier views see B. Levick, *Claudius* (New Haven, CT: YUP, 1990), 13–14; and D. Fasolini, *Aggioramento bibliografico ed epigrafico ragionato sull'imperatore Claudio* (Milan: Vita

e Pensiero, 2006), 41–44; E. F. Leon, "The *Imbecillitas* of the Emperor Claudius," *TAPA* 79 (1948): 79–86.

2. T. Mommsen, *A History of Rome under the Emperors* (London: Routledge, 1992), 157–58, who sees him as a fool. See R. Saller, "Anecdotes as Historical Evidence for the Principate," *G&R* 27, no. 1 (April 1980): 79, who writes, "The anecdotes portraying Claudius as a buffoon seem to have been more a product of a stereotype, which circulated in the Roman aristocracy, than an accurate assessment of his character." Cf. A. Momigliano, *Claudius: The Emperor and His Achievement* (Oxford: Clarendon Press, 1934), 78–79. Rudich, *Political Dissidence under Nero*, 3, accepts the image of the reluctant Claudius.

3. The ancient accounts: Suet., *Cal.* 56–60, *Claudius* 10; Dio 59.29–60.2.1; Josephus, *AJ* 19.1–273, which has a much different interpretation of the events than the more abbreviated accounts of Suetonius and Dio. Tacitus, who has little to say about any of the Julio-Claudians, treats Claudius as a buffoon in books XI and XII. Seneca, *Apoc.*, presents him as a tyrant who arbitrarily executes people. See D. W. T. C. Vessey, "Thoughts on Tacitus' Portrayal of Claudius," *AJPh* 92, no. 3 (July 1971): 385–409. On Claudius taking an active role: Scramuzza, *Emperor Claudius*, 51–63; A. G. G. Gibson, "Claudius and the Politics of AD 41," in his *Julio Claudian Succession*, 107–32, esp. 111ff., on "A Paradigm for First Century Accession." See Barrett, *Livia*, 222, on the coup; and Osgood, *Claudius Caesar*, 29–32.

4. Holland, *Nero*, 27, on the "opportunistic coup." T. P. Wiseman, "Calpurnius Siculus and the Claudian Civil War," *JRS* (1982): 64, calls it "the military coup."

5. Osgood, *Claudius Caesar*, 30, writes, "one may even suspect that, while Chaerea and his colleagues performed the bloody deed, the high leadership of the Praetorians, prominent Senators, and just possibly Claudius himself played some part in arranging Caligula's assassination."

6. Suet., *Claudius* 10, says he was on a balcony not far from an apartment called the Hermaeum. Dio 60.2 simply say he was hidden away in "a dark corner." Josephus, *BJ* 2.204 says he was carried off by force, but does not say from where; Josephus, *AJ* 19.216 says a narrow alcove.

7. As suggested by A. Major, "Was He Pushed or Did He Leap? Claudius' Ascent to Power," *AH* 22 (1992): 26; Jung, "Die Thronerhebung des Claudius," 380–82; Stöver, *Die Prätorianer*, 83–145.

8. A Praetorian Guardsman made about 3,000 sesterces a year as opposed to 900 for a legionary foot soldier; Holland, *Nero*, 30. Claudius acknowledged his debt to the Guardsmen when he issued a significant series of gold and silver coins. One read *imper(ator) recept(us)*, showing the Praetorian camp with a soldier standing at a gate by a military standard. The other is inscribed *praetor(iani) recept(i)*. See Scramuzza, *Emperor Claudius*, 62, with references to coins on page 241, no. 4141.

9. On the possible role of Claudius in the assassination see Osgood, *Claudius Caesar*, 19; Jung, "Die Thronerhebung des Claudius," 367–86. We must be aware of the danger of using circular reasoning: because Claudius was involved in the assassination and his own accession, he suppressed the evidence and put out the "hapless accession" story; therefore, the absence of evidence for his active involvement is to be read as proof of it. On controlling the message, see E. S. Ramage, "Denigration of Predecessor under Claudius, Galba and Vespasian," *Historia* 32, no. 2 (1983): 201–14.

10. Josephus, *AJ* 19.229–35; R. S. Rogers, "Quinti Veranii, Pater et Filius," *CP* 26, no. 2 (April 1931): 172–77.

11. On all these measures and the amnesty, see Dio 60.3.5–4.6; Suet., *Claudius* 11.1.; Wiseman, "Calpurnius Siculus and the Claudian Civil War," 64; D. McAlindon, "Senatorial Opposition to Claudius and Nero," *AJPh* 77, no. 2 (1956): 113–32.

12. Osgood, *Claudius Caesar*, 31–32; Momigliano, *Claudius*, 41, on Claudius working against the Senate; Levick, *Claudius*, 35; Scramuzza, *Claudius*, 99–128.

13. See the chart of the Julio-Claudian family for the branches of the two houses that were brought together when Augustus married Livia. The argument for a civil war within the family factions was taken up by Wiseman, "Calpurnius Siculus and the Claudian Civil War," 57–67. Some of his argument has been doubted by Griffin, *Nero*, and Levick, *Claudius*, 44.

14. Suet., *Claudius* 1.1 and Dio 60.3.5-4.6. Cf. 60.18.4 and 60.27.4. Osgood, *Claudius Caesar*, 32; Levick, *Claudius*, 51.

15. Tacitus, *Ann.* 13.43.3. Edwards, *Politics of Immorality in Ancient Rome*, 34–62; Rutledge, *Imperial Inquisitions*, 147–48.

16. For Vinicius's pedigree, see C. Ehrhardt, "Messalina and the Succession to Claudius," *Antichthon* 12 (1978): 53.

17. On the Silanus affair see Suet., *Claudius* 37.2 (cf. 29.1) and Dio 60.14.2–15.1, who mentions plotting against the emperor. See also Seneca, *Apoc.* 11.5 and Tacitus, *Ann.* 11.29.1, who only mentions the charge of incest, but that is not mentioned by Suetonius nor Dio. Levick, *Claudius*, 58, points out that the other eliminations around the same time may not have been for the same reasons, but it was enough that Claudius deemed them a threat. See Osgood, *Claudius Caesar*, 43, on those suspicions.

18. Tacitus, *Ann.* 6.9. On the Iunii Silani being in conflict with the emperors, see McAlindon, "Senatorial Opposition to Claudius and Nero," 119–20. Rutledge, *Imperial Inquisitions*, 167.

19. McAlindon, "Senatorial Opposition to Claudius and Nero," 117, finds it hard to believe that Claudius, at this early stage, when the outstanding feature of his policy was extreme caution and clemency, would have permitted the death of a prominent senator against whom "no credible charge could be lodged" (Cf. Dio 60.14.4.); Ehrhardt, "Messalina and the Succession to Claudius," 51–77; Levick, *Claudius*, 57–59.

20. Suet., *Claudius* 13.1.

21. Suet., *Claudius* 13.1.

22. Dio 60.15–16 is our main source. The two other sources are Suet., *Claudius* 13.2 and 35.2, and Pliny, *Ep.* 3.16. See also Tacitus, *Ann.* 12.52.2 and 13.43.2; *Hist.* 1.89.2 and 2.75; and Orosius, *Histories* 7.6.6–8. The best modern discussions are Wiseman, "Calpurnius Siculus and the Claudian Civil War," 57–67; A. Galimberti, "La rivolta del 42 e l'opposizione senatoria sotto Claudio," in *Fazioni e congiure nel mondo antico*, ed. M. Sordi (Milan: Vita e Pensiero, 1999), 205–15; Swan, "Josephus, *A.J.* 19. 251–52," 159–60, 161. See also Levick, *Claudius*, 59–61; Osgood, *Claudius Caesar*, 45-46.

23. Suet., *Claudius* 13.2. On the conspiracy, see Rogers, "The Stigma of Politics," 86–89.

24. Dio 60.15.3. C. Wirszubski, *Libertas as a Political Idea at Rome during the Late Republic and Early Principate* (Cambridge: CUP, 1950), 126, believed Scribonianus's republican protestations were a sham and merely disguised his personal ambitions. Balsdon, *Emperor Gaius*, 107, also believed the cries of *libertas* were just propaganda. But see Galimberti, "La rivolta del 42 e l'opposizione senatoria sotto Claudio," 205–15; Harris, *Roman Power*, 72–73. Rutledge, *Imperial Inquisitions*, 164, refers to Vinicianus as the brains behind the conspiracy.

25. Raaflaub, "Augustus' Military Reforms," 215. Camillus might have wanted to revert to republican government, but Levick, *Claudius*, 60, notes that in the course of Galaesus's interrogation in the Senate, it was clear he would have simply replaced Claudius. See also Rutledge, *Imperial Inquisitions*, 164.

26. Dio 60.15.3.

27. Suet., *Claudius* 13, is very explicit in calling it a civil war to distinguish it from mere conspiracies like those of Asinius Gallus and Statilius Taurus Corvinus. Cf. Tacitus, *Ann.* 13.43.3. E. Champlin, "The Life and Times of Calpurnius Siculus," *JRS* 68 (1978): 98, wrote, "Under no circumstances is it possible to see the reign of Claudius as a period of civil war," in response to G. B. Townend, "Calpurnius Siculus and the Munus Neronis," *JRS* 70 (1980): 166. Wiseman, "Calpurnius Siculus and the Claudian Civil War," 63, disagrees.

28. On civil war: Suet., *Claudius* 13.2; Tacitus, *Ann.* 12.52.2; on Caecina's participation: Pliny, *Ep.* 3.16.7–9. On Vinicianus, Josephus, *AJ* 19.252; Dio 60.15.1–2; on Pomponius: Tacitus, *Ann.* 13.43.3; on Paetus (cos. suff. 37 [consul suffectus—a Roman consul elected to complete the term of one who vacated office before the end of the year]): Dio 60.16.5–6. On other senators and *equites*: Dio 60.15.3. For this episode in general, see Ehrhardt, "Messalina and the Succession to Claudius," 62–64.

29. It is said that Scribonianus fled to the island of Issa, where he was slain by a common soldier named Volaginius, who was subsequently promoted as a reward. On his flight: Dio 60.15.3. On his death: Tacitus, *Hist.* 2.75; Pliny, *Ep.* 3.16; Tacitus, *Ann.* 12.52.

30. Pliny, *Epis.* 3.16.8. Pliny adds the touching story of how Paetus's brave wife Arria begged to be allowed to accompany her husband back to Rome. When she was denied, she hired a small fishing boat to follow her husband's ship all the way back to Italy.

31. Pliny, *Epis.* 3.16.6; Levick, *Claudius*, 60.

32. Dio 60.15.4–16.8. See D. Hurley, *Suetonius: Divus Claudius* (Cambridge: CUP, 2001), 112–15.

33. McAlindon, "Senatorial Opposition to Claudius and Nero," 114. On the continuity of the membership of the two groups, see Swan, *Conspiracies*, 184.

34. As argued by McAlindon, "Senatorial Opposition to Claudius and Nero," 114.

35. Pliny, *Epist.* 3.16.9; Dio 60.15.5; Levick, *Claudius*, 60.

36. On Pomponius Secundus: Josephus, *AJ* 19.160 and 263–64 and *BJ* 2.205; Dio 60.1.4; Tacitus, *Ann.* 13.43.2. Also see Swan, *Conspiracies*, 184; Levick, *Claudius*, 60; Osgood, *Claudius Caesar*, 45.

37. On citizens tortured: Dio 60.15.6; on Praetor's suicide: Dio 60.15.4; on exposure of the bodies: Dio 60.16.1; Quint. 8.5.16. On the *damnatio memoriae* of Scribonianus: Fasti Nolani A.D. 32, ILS 6124, 157; Osgood, *Claudius Caesar*, 45; Levick,

Claudius, 60. On the use of the Gemonian steps for political reasons, see Barry, "Exposure, Mutilation, and Riot," 222–46.

38. Osgood, *Claudius Caesar*, 45, who sees the coordinated wings of this revolt, in Rome and Dalmatia, as a direct result of Claudius's accession. When Claudius struck back, denunciations poured in as some people took advantage of the situation to settle private scores.

39. The conspiracy has attracted little attention. See Swan, *Conspiracies*, 175; Rogers, "Quinti Veranii, Pater et Filius," 31–45, suggests that this conspiracy was the first in a history of opposition inherited from his adoptive father, L. Arruntius. Syme, *Tacitus*, 559, disagreed.

40. On Claudius promoting Volaginius and the slayers of the defecting officers: Tacitus, *Hist.* 2.75; Swan, *Conspiracies*, 173.

41. Swan, *Conspiracies*, 181; Gibson, "All Things to All Men," 118–32. Numismatic evidence shows that the ideal of *libertas* that motivated the assassins was co-opted by Claudius. His coinage uses the legend perhaps hoping to show that one could enjoy *libertas* within the principate. See M. Grant, *Roman Anniversary Issues* (Cambridge: CUP, 1959), 74; Swan, *Conspiracies*, 180–81.

42. *ILS* 2702 confirms the granting of these titles to those legions. See Swan, *Conspiracies*, 174; Osgood, *Claudius Caesar*, 45. On donatives in general, see Bingham, *Praetorian Guard*, chapter 3.

43. Suet., *Claudius* 12.

44. On the social mingling and the "place to see and be seen," see A. Wallace-Hadrill, "The Roman Imperial Court: Seen and Unseen in the Performance of Power," in *Royal Courts in Dynastic States and Empires: A Global Perspective*, ed. J. Duinden, T. Artan, and M. Kunt (Leiden, Netherlands: Brill, 2011), 91–102. For more on the imperial court, see A. Wallace-Hadrill, "The Imperial Court," in *CAH*[2] (1996): 283–301; Mario Pani, *La corte dei Caesari* (Rome: Laterza, 2003); A. Winterling, *Aula Caesaris: Studien zur Institutionalisierung der römischen Kaiserhofes in der Zeit von Augustus bis Commodus (33 v. Chr.-192 n. Chr.)* (Munich: Oldenbourg Verlag, 1999). On patronage during the early empire, see Saller, *Personal Patronage Under the Early Empire*.

45. Tacitus, *Hist.* 2.22.3; Millar, *Emperor in the Roman World*, 62; Sheldon, *Intelligence Activities in Ancient Rome*, 165–67; Austin and Rankov, *Exploration*, 54–60.

46. Suet., *Claudius* 35.1; Millar, *Emperor in the Roman World*, 62.

47. Dio 60.18.4. It is possible that the father of the future emperor Otho was involved in this plot. See Suet., *Otho* 1.3. Cf. Suet., *Claudius* 13.1 and 36. Also see Osgood, *Claudius Caesar*, 89; Rutledge, *Imperial Inquisitions*, 165.

48. Tacitus, *Ann.* 13.32.3 and 43. Cf. Suet., *Claudius* 29.1 and Dio 60.18.4. Also see Seneca, *Apoc.* 10.4 and 13.5; Osgood, *Claudius Caesar*, 89; Rutledge, *Imperial Inquisitions*, 148.

49. Tacitus, *Ann.* 11.3; Osgood, *Claudius Caesar*, 148–49.

50. Tacitus, *Ann.* 11.1.1; Dio 60.27.1–3; 60.61.29.4–6.

51. She was the mother of Poppaea Sabina the Younger, the woman who was to become the second wife of the Emperor Nero. See Tacitus, *Ann.* 13.45, 14.61–63. Dio offers a different version involving a trumped-up accusation by a soldier: Dio 60.29.4–6a; Suetonius—completely silent. See Levick, *Claudius*, 61–64; Rutledge, *Imperial Inquisitions*, 106–7.

52. Tacitus, *Ann.* 11.1–3. See M. T. Boatwright, "Luxuriant Gardens and Extravagant Women: The *Horti* of Rome between Republic and Empire," in *Horti Romani*, ed. M. Cima and E. La Rocca (Rome: Bretschneider, 1998), 71–82, on gardens as being emblematic of luxury, licentiousness, and perversity in political life and gender roles. Cf. K. T. Stackelberg, "Performative Space and Garden Transgressions in Tacitus' *Death of Messalina*," *AJPh* 130, no. 4 (2009): 595–624. Another example is given by Tacitus in the trial of the senator, Statilius Taurus, because Claudius's fourth wife, Agrippina, wanting his gardens. The senator was the brother of the conspirator of 46. See Scramuzza, *Emperor Claudius*, 93. On Messalina: Tacitus, *Ann.* 11.1.1; Dio 60.29.6a, and cf. 60.27.2. On Agrippina: Tacitus, *Ann.* 12.59.1. Also see Cogitore, *La légitimité dynastique d'Auguste à Néron à l'épreuve des conspirations*, 205–11.

53. Dragged from Baiae: Tacitus, *Ann.* 11.1–3; Osgood, *Claudius Caesar*, 148–49. The Senate was probably told something about Asiaticus and Poppaea in adultery . . . that a man so good-looking was sought after by other men, too; that Asiaticus had been tampering with some troops. And that upon hearing this from the vigilant Sosibius, Claudius sent Crispinus to bring him to Rome and that Claudius had investigated the threat. For discussions, see Scramuzza, *Emperor Claudius*, 93–97; Levick, *Claudius*, 61–64; M. Tagliafico, "I processi intra cubilculum: Il caso di Valerio Asiatico," in *Processi e politica nel mondo antico*, ed. M. Sordi (Milan: Vita e Pensiero, 1996), 249–59; Cogitore, *La légitimité dynastique d'Auguste à Néron à l'épreuve des conspirations*, 205–11; Rutledge, *Imperial Inquisitions*, 106–7.

54. On moving the pyre: Tacitus, *Ann.* 11.3.

55. Tacitus, *Ann.* 11.4; Scramuzza, *Emperor Claudius*, 93–97; Osgood, *Claudius Caesar*, 149.

56. Tacitus, *Ann.* 11.22.1ff. On Cn. Nonius: *PIR*[1] N 90; Swan, *Conspiracies*, 192; Levick, *Claudius*, 64.

57. Osgood, *Claudius Caesar*, 149. His wife, Caligula's sister Livilla, had already been eliminated in 41. Cassius Dio 60.27.4, of course, blames Messalina. Cf. Josephus, *AJ* 19.251. Also see A. Tortoriello, *I fasti consolari degli anni di Claudio* (Rome: Accademia Nazionale dei Lincei, 2004), 588–91. On Julia Livilla, see Osgood, *Claudius Caesar*, 42–43.

58. On Asinius Gallus and Statilius Corvinus, see, Suet., *Claudius* 13.2 and Dio 60.27.5. On the consulship of Statilius see Tortoriello, *I fasti consolari degli anni di Claudio*, 563–65; Cogitore, *La légitimité dynastique d'Auguste à Néron à l'épreuve des conspirations*, 202–5; Swan, *Conspiracies*, 192; Osgood, *Claudius Caesar*, 149.

59. Dio 60.27.5; Swan, *Conspiracies*, 192–93.

60. Claudius's own son-in-law, Pompeius Magnus, was killed when caught in the arms of a male lover, and his parents, M. Licinius Crassus Frugi and Scribonia, perished with him. See Seneca, *Apoc.* 11.2 and 11.5; Suet., *Claudius* 27.2 and 29.1–2; Tacitus, *Hist.* 1.48.1; Dio 60.29.6a. Also see Osgood, *Claudius Caesar*, 149–50.

61. Tacitus, *Ann.* 11.5–7; Osgood, *Claudius Caesar*, 150.

62. See Osgood, *Claudius Caesar*, 150–51, on the administration of justice under Claudius. This includes a discussion of the speech of Claudius made before the Senate. Cf. Levick, *Claudius*, 120–26; J. Wolf, "Claudius Iudex," in *Die Regierungszeit des Kaisers Claudius (41-54 n. Chr.): Umbruch oder Episode?* ed. V. Strocka (Mainz: Philipp von Zabern, 1994), 145–58; Hurley, *Suetonius*, 117–18, 160. On the

general administration of justice, see Millar, *Emperor in the Roman World*, 516–37, and H. Galsterer, "The Administration of Justice," in *CAH²*, 10:397–413.

63. Momigliano, *Claudius*, 41–42, saw Claudius as the first emperor to organize a secretariat, but Osgood, *Claudius Caesar*, 20, disagrees. On the development of the so-called civil service from Augustus to Claudius, see Sherwin-White, "Procuator Augusti," 11–26.

64. Beard, *SPQR*, 409.

65. Rutledge, *Imperial Inquisitions*, 53.

66. Osgood, *Claudius Caesar*, 204, 212–14; Levick, *Claudius*, 51–53. Griffin, *Nero*, 54, argues that one cannot dismiss "uxorial influence" by postulating the organization of Claudius's wives into a ministry. She also points out that the instances of recorded offensive activity by his freedmen seem to have little to do with their actual posts.

67. The events of her fall are covered by Tacitus, *Ann.* 11.12, 26–38. Messalina's death is mentioned by Suet., *Claudius* 26.2, 29.3, 36, 39.1; Dio 60.31.1–5; Seneca, *Octavia* 257–69; *Apoc.* 11, 13; Josephus, *AJ* 20.149; Juvenal, *Satires* 10.329–45; Aur. Vic., *Epit. de Caes.* 4.12–13.

68. On the reasons behind the accusations of sexual impropriety against aristocratic women, see Edwards, *Politics of Immorality in Ancient Rome*, 42–62. For modern attempts to rehabilitate Messalina's reputation, beginning with C. M. Wieland, see Fantham, *Julia Augusti*, 126–27.

69. Varner, "Portraits, Plots and Politics," 64; Edwards, *Politics of Immorality in Ancient Rome*, 642–62.

70. Juvenal 6.115–24. On his anti-Claudian sources, see J. Clack, "To Those Who Fell on Agrippina's Pen," *CW* 69, no. 1 (September 1975): 45–53. For a thorough discussion of the treatment of Agrippina and Messalina in the historiographical tradition, see J. Ginsburg, *Representing Agrippina: Constructing of Female Power in the Early Roman Empire* (Oxford: OUP, 2006); S. Wood, *Imperial Women: A Study in Public Images 40 BC–AD 68* (Leiden, Netherlands: Brill, 1999), 249–314; C. Questa, "Messalina, meretrix augusta," in *Vicende e figure femminili in Graecia e a Roma*, ed. R. Raffaelli (Ancona: Commissione per le pari opportunità tra uomo e donna della Regione Marche, 1995), 399–423. S. Joshel, "Female Desire and the Discourse of Empire: Tacitus's Messalina," *Signs* 21, no. 1 (Autumn 1995): 50–82.

71. See the comments of Wood, "Diva Drusilla Panthea and the Sisters of Caligula," 457; Edwards, *Politics of Immorality*, 42–62.

72. She was the great-granddaughter of Octavia through both her father, Marcus Valerius Messalla Barbatus, and her mother, Domitia Lepida; Levick, *Claudius*, 55.

73. Suet., *Claudius* 26.2. His first wife was Plautia Urgulanilla, daughter of a close personal friend of Livia. His second wife was Aelia Paetina, a relative of the ambitious Praetorian prefect, Sejanus.

74. Suet., *Claudius* 27.1–2 and Dio 60.12.5 (both curiously in error on the date). Cf. Tacitus, *Ann.* 12.15.1 and 13.15.1 on the acquisition of his name Britannicus, Cf. Osgood, *Claudius Caesar*, 91; Levick, *Claudius*, 55–56.

75. Tacitus, *Ann.* 11.26–38 (with background at 11.12). Suetonius, Cassius Dio, and Juvenal all corroborate Tacitus's basic narrative of Messalina's marriage to Silius and her subsequent execution without a trial: Suet., *Claudius* 26.2, 29.3, 36

and 39.1; Dio 60.31.1–5 and Juvenal, *Sat.* 10. 329.45. All ancient sources and a long list of modern treatments are given by A. A. Barrett, *Agrippina*, 274-275, note 86.

76. Tacitus, *Ann.* 11.25–38; Suet., *Claudius* 26.2; Juvenal 10.329–45; Dio 60.31.35; Aurelius Victor, *Epit. De Caes.* 4; Barrett, *Agrippina*, 91–94; R. Bauman, *Women and Politics in Ancient Rome* (London: Routledge, 1992), 176–79, take the account at face value. See Varner, "Portraits, Plots and Politics," 64.

77. This is suggested by Osgood, *Claudius Caesar*, 215; Levick, *Claudius*, 66–67.

78. Scramuzza, *Emperor Claudius*, 90. E. Meise, *Untersuchungen zur Geschichte der Julisch-Claudischen Dynastie*, 136ff., believes in the conspiracy theory.

79. J. Colin, "Les vendages dionysiaques et la légende de Messalina," *LEC* 24 (1956): 23–39. This explanation fits in with the long and sometimes turbulent history of the worship in Rome of the god of ecstasy and wine, whether under the name of Bacchus or Dionysius. On the references to the *Bacchae* of Euripides, see Holland, *Nero*, 41.

80. G. Fagan, "Messalina's Folly," *CQ* 52, no. 2 (2002): 577, who calls the wedding detail a "gratuitous and fabulous invention."

81. Osgood, *Claudius Caesar*, 210; "Messalina's Folly," 573n32, for a full bibliography.

82. See Osgood, *Claudius Caesar*, 211; N. Kampen, "Between Public and Private: Women as Historical Subjects in Roman Art," in *Women's History and Ancient History*, ed. S. Pomeroy (Chapel Hill: University of North Carolina Press, 1991), 218–48. Ehrhardt, "Messalina and the Succession to Claudius," 68, thinks that ten years of tedious marriage to Claudius would make the "handsomest man in Rome" an attraction, and that her plot might have succeeded had Narcissus not betrayed her.

83. Fagan, "Messalina's Folly," 573, for example. Why does Suetonius list various plots against Claudius in one chapter (Suet., *Claudius* 13), yet dismiss the Silius affair (*Claudius* 36) as a "baseless report"?

84. The evidence for this is that Decrius Calpurnianus, the prefect of the *vigiles*, was one of those executed by the Praetorians along with Sulpicius Rufus, procurator of a *ludus*. These were the very groups that deserted the Senate en masse when it suited them to do so. See Josephus, *AJ* 19.253–59; *BJ* 2.211–12.

85. See Joshel, "Female Desire and Discourse of Empire," on why the two cannot be separated. Cf. Levick, "Julians and Claudians," 33.

86. Tacitus, *Ann.* 11.12. On the role played by Pallas, see S. V. Oost, "The Career of M. Antonius Pallas," *AJPh* 79, no. 2 (1958): 113–39.

87. Suet., *Claudius* 36; Tacitus, *Ann.* 11.31.3. See Joshel, "Desire and Discourse of Empire: Tacitus's Messalina," 73, on the theme that "the man who holds the woman holds the power," thus making the marriage a symbolic transfer from Claudius to Silius.

88. Tacitus, *Ann.* 11.31.3; Suet., *Claudius* 36.

89. Tacitus, *Ann.* 11.33.1–2.

90. Tacitus, *Ann.* 11.35.

91. Tacitus, *Ann.* 11.35.5–36.5 gives us their names: C. Silius, Iuncus Vergilianus (the ex-praetor), the *equites* Titius Proculus, Vettius Valens, Pompeius Urbicus, and Saufeius Trogus. Cf. Suet., *Claudius* 26.2, 39. Dio 60.31.5.1. See Fagan, "Messalina's Folly," 566n4. On the plot, see also Bauman, *Impietas in Principem*, 177–88;

S. Wood, "Messalina, Wife of Claudius," *JRA* 5 (1992): 233–34; Barrett, *Agrippina*, 86–94; Wood, *Imperial Women*, 255.

92. Tacitus, *Ann.* 11.37–38.

93. Fagan, "Messalina's Folly," 570, who believes the similarity of the accounts may be due to their common usage of an official version of events put out shortly after her death that blamed the empress's fall on her moral failings.

94. Tacitus, *Ann.* 11.38; Varner, "Portraits, Plots and Politics," 64; G. Fagan, "Messalina's Folly," 572. See Furneaux, *Annals of Tacitus*, 2:207, for other examples. Also see Scramuzza, *Emperor Claudius*, 90; Wood, *Imperial Women*, 322.

95. Varner, "Portraits, Plots and Politics," 67.

96. The title means, literally, "The Pumpkinification" of Claudius. It is a play upon the idea of apotheosis, the process by which dead Roman emperors were recognized as gods. For the people executed in this work, see B. Baldwin, "Executions under Claudius: Seneca's Ludus de Morte Claudii," *Phoenix* 18, no. 1 (Spring 1964): 39–48.

97. Fagan, "Messalina's Folly," 568, points out parallel stories elsewhere in classical literature.

98. See esp. Joshel, "Female Desire and Discourse of Empire," 55 and 57, who points out how Tacitus's narrative resembles a stock comedy motif with Claudius in the role of the old man deluded by an adulterous wife and outwitted by his clever servants.

99. Joshel, "Female Desire and Discourse of Empire: Tacitus's Messalina," 60; Edwards, *Politics of Immorality in Ancient Rome*, 43.

100. Cicero's treatment of Clodia in his speech *For Caelius* is the classic example. See Osgood, *Claudius Caesar*, 309n3.

101. Ehrhardt, "Messalina and the Succession to Claudius," 55–77; Levick, *Agrippina*, 55–64.

102. Tacitus, *Ann.* 11.12.4; Suet., *Claudius* 26.2.

103. Tacitus, *Ann.* 11.27.

104. Osgood, *Claudius Caesar*, 212, and Meise, *Untersuchungen zur Geschichte der Julisch-Claudischen Dynastie*, 217–21.

105. Osgood, *Claudius Caesar*, 213; E. R. Varner, "Portraits, Plots and Politics," 64–68.

106. Osgood, *Claudius Caesar*, 211.

107. She was born in 15 CE in *Ara Ubiorum* on the Rhine frontier during her father's campaigns there. On the place of birth: Tacitus, *Ann.* 12.27.1; year inferred from Suet., *Cal.* 7 and Tacitus, *Ann.* 2.54.1.

108. See Suet., *Cal.* 15.3; *Nero* 5–6; Tacitus, *Ann.* 4.75; Dio 59.22.9.

109. She is shown on the obverse of *aurei* and *denarii* of 54 with her images equal to Claudius's in importance and her titles, not his, encircling the flan. See Wood, "Memoriae Agrippinae," 421.

110. Tacitus, *Ann.* 12.4; Suet., *Claudius* 27.1; Dio 60.5.7 and 60.31.8; and Osgood, *Claudius Caesar*, 96. On her use of *delatores* to achieve her ends, see Rutledge, *Imperial Inquisitions*, 148.

111. Tacitus, *Ann.* 12.8.1; cf. Suet., *Claudius* 29.2. See also Seneca, *Apoc.* 8.2, 10.4, and 11.5; and Dio 60.31.8.

112. Wiseman, *Myths of Rome*, 252–62.

113. Tacitus, *Ann.* 12.26.1. By this move the young boy went from being L. Domitius Ahenobarbus to Nero Claudius Caesar Drusus.

114. Tacitus, *Ann.* 12.16.1; Dio 60.33.2. Precious metal coinage of Rome minted around this time shows the new names and a suggestive set of juxtaposed portraits: Claudius with Agrippina and Claudius with Nero. *RIC* I (2nd ed.) Claudius nos. 80–83.

115. Osgood, *Claudius Caesar*, 216–23 accompanies his discussion of these objects with illustrations.

116. For a list of the eliminated rivals, see Osgood, *Claudius Caesar*, 227–28.

117. Griffin, *Nero*, 67; Levick, *Claudius*, 69–79. J. Aveline, "The Death of Claudius," *Historia* 53, no. 4 (2004): 458–64.

118. Among the people she murdered to get out of the way was Lepida, Nero's aunt and the mother of Messalina. See Tacitus, *Ann.* 12.64–65; Rutledge, *Imperial Inquisitions*, 149.

119. Nero assumed the *toga virilis* a year before the normal age; Tacitus, *Ann.* 12.41; Suet., *Nero* 7.2.

120. Tacitus, *Ann.* 12.41.1; Suet., *Nero* 7.2.

121. Tacitus, *Ann.* 12.41.1; and *RIC* I (2nd ed.) Claudius nos. 76–79, 82–83.

122. On proconsular *imperium*: Tacitus, *Ann.* 12.41.1; on priestly colleges: *RIC* I (2nd ed.) Claudius nos. 76–77, 107, and note. Also see E. Smallwood, *Documents Illustrating the Principates of Gaius, Claudius and Nero* (Cambridge: CUP, 2011), nos. 100 and 132; Osgood, *Claudius Caesar*, 229.

123. Tacitus, *Ann.* 12.58.1; Suet., *Nero* 7.2 and Dio 60.33.11.

124. On donatives in general, see Bingham, *Praetorian Guard*, chapter 3.

125. Dio 60.34.2–3; Osgood, *Claudius Caesar*, 243.

126. Tacitus, *Ann.* 12.67ff.; Suet., *Claudius* 45; Dio 60.34.3; Josephus, *AJ* 148. R. A. Pack, "Seneca's Evidence on the Deaths of Claudius and Narcissus," *CW* 36, no. 13 (February 8, 1943): 150–51.

127. Suet., *Claudius* 44.2.

128. Poisoning by *Amanita muscaria* causes lacrimation, vasodilation, salivation, rhinorrhea, intractable diarrhea, severe abdominal pain, loss of sphincter control, wheezing, brachycardia, and hypotension. It causes death within several hours. The symptoms fit, but one mushroom would not deliver enough of the poison to kill him. Another poison could have been added—perhaps aconite or cyanide. Muscarinic mushroom poisoning would have been particularly dangerous for Claudius because of his dystonia. He might have suffered a massive pulmonary aspiration or a fatal dystonic crisis. See Valente et al., "Caveat Cenans!" 396. V. Grimm-Samuel, "On the Mushroom that Deified the Emperor Claudius," *CQ* 41, no. 1 (1991): 178–82, argues for *Amanita phalloides*, the Death Cap mushroom. Avelline, "The Death of Claudius," 453–75, argues for the accidental ingestion of a poison mushroom.

129. Tacitus, *Ann.* 12.66–68.

130. Examples of imperial tasters come in both genders. See *CIL* 6.37752: Ti. Iulius Secundus; *ILS* 1734: Tiberius Claudius Alcibiades; *ILS* 1750: Ti. Claudius Quadratus; *ILS* 1781: Amoenus; *ILS* 1786: Paezusa; and Osgood, *Claudius Caesar*, 39.

131. Rudich, *Political Dissidence under Nero*, 5–6; Rutledge, *Imperial Inquisitions*, 150.

132. Tacitus, *Ann.* 12.69.5 cf. Dio 61.1.2. Also see Rutledge, *Imperial Inquisitions*, 150.

133. For the suggestion that she was planning this since her return from exile, see Holland, *Nero*, 32. On the fact that Agrippina was under investigation at the time of the poisoning, see Rutledge, *Imperial Inquisitions*, 149. Numerous *delatores* had sent in reports on her, per Suet., *Claudius* 44.1. R. Bauman, *Women and Politics in Ancient Rome* (London: Routledge, 1992), 186–87, comments on the burning of Narcissus's correspondence at the same time.

134. Josephus, *AJ* 20–152; Tacitus, *Ann.* 12.69; Suet., *Nero* 8; Dio 61.3.1.

135. Millar, *Emperor in the Roman World*, xi.

136. Suet., *Claudius* 13.1, *Aug.* 19.2, and *Tib.* 19 for similar episodes.

137. Dio 60.3.4, 5–7; Suet., *Claudius* 11; Josephus, *AJ* 19.2689–71. See Josephus, *AJ* 19.190–200 for Lupus's actions.

138. Levick, *Claudius*, 196.

139. Momigliano, *Claudius*, 74; Osgood, *Claudius Caesar*, 18.

140. So argues D. McAlindon, "Claudius and the Senators," *AJPh* 78, no. 3 (1957): 279.

141. Rutledge, *Imperial Inquisitions*, 150.

142. Suet., *Claudius* 29; Seneca, *Apoc.* 14. Baldwin, "Executions under Claudius," 39.

143. Wiseman, "Calpurnius Siculus and the Claudian Civil War," 57–67; Ehrhardt, "Messalina and the Succession to Claudius," 51–77. The term originated with Galba, Tacitus, *Hist.*, 1.16.1 "*unius familiae . . . Iuliorum Claudiorum domo*" is a rhetorical simplification. Contrast "*post Iulios Claudios Servios,*" in *Hist.* 2.48.2 Cf. V. M. Strocka, ed., *Die Regierungszeit des Kaisers Claudius (41–54 n. Chr.): Umbruch oder Episode?* (Mainz: Philipp von Zabern, 1994), on the continuities and disjunctions between the members of the Julio-Claudian imperial family.

144. McAlindon, "Senatorial Opposition to Claudius and Nero," 113–14.

145. The sources agree on the numbers: Suet., *Claudius* 29; Seneca, *Apoc.* 13; Baldwin, "Executions Under Claudius," 39.

146. E. S. Gruen, introduction to Ginsberg, *Representing Agrippina*, 8.

147. See, for example, K. Milnor, *Gender, Domesticity, and the Age of Augustus: Inventing Private Life* (Oxford: OUP, 2005).

148. Osgood, *Claudius Caesar*, 22. On the emerging political culture of the early principate, see Rowe, *Princes and Political Cultures*; Flaig, *Den Kaiser herausfordern*, 94–126. On the rituals of the emperor as a basis for his rule, see Lendon, *Empire of Honour*; and "The Legitimacy of the Roman Emperor against Weberian legitimacy and Imperial 'Strategies of Legitimation,'" 53–63, on the importance of prestige. See F. Hurlet, *Les collègues du prince sous Auguste et Tibère de la légalité républicaine à la légitimité dynastique* (Rome: CEFR, 1997), on the interplay between republican forms and dynastic realities. See Ando, *Imperial Ideology and Provincial Loyalty in the Roman Empire*, on provincial perceptions of the emperor; M. B. Roller, *Constructing Autocracy: Aristocrats and Emperors in Julio-Claudian Rome* (Princeton, NJ: PUP, 2001), on the development of ideology among senators; and H. I. Flower, *The Art of Forgetting: Disgrace and Oblivion in Roman Political Culture* (Chapel Hill: University of North Carolina Press, 2006), on the imperial construction and control of memory.

149. Osgood, *Claudius Caesar*, 23.

150. Osgood, *Claudius Caesar*, 17–19. See his discussion on the role that Arnaldo Momigliano's scholarship played in this reassessment.

151. Osgood, *Claudius Caesar*, 124.

152. On Claudius's reverence for the past, see Osgood, *Claudius Caesar*, 17–18, and Momigliano, *Claudius*, xv, who believed Claudius never successfully identified the problem nor solved it.

153. Philo, *Leg. ad Gaiam* 259.

154. Raaflaub, "Augustus' Military Reforms," 223.

155. Tacitus, *Ann.* 12.43; Suet., *Claudius* 18; Yavetz, *Plebs and Princeps*, 28; Africa, "Urban Violence in Imperil Rome," 13.

156. Balsdon, "The Successors of Augustus," 168.

CHAPTER 7: THE "MAD" EMPEROR, NERO

1. For a good, short essay on the source problems for Nero's reign, see A. Momigliano, "Nero," *CAH* (1966), 10:702–42. On his image, see E. Cizek, *Néron* (Paris: Fayard, 1982), "Néron et son Image," 15–24.

2. M. Grant, *Nero* (New York: American Heritage Press, 1970), 15 writes, "Nero was born of murderous parents, and brought up in a murderous atmosphere. And he, too, was murderous. But only when frightened; though unfortunately he got frightened easily." See also the comments of J. Drinkwater, "Nero Caesar and the Half-Baked Principate," in *The Julio-Claudian Succession: Reality and Perception of the "Augustan Model,"* ed. A. G. G. Gibson (Leiden, Netherlands: Brill, 2013), 155–74.

3. Suet., *Nero* 5, describes him as a murderer and a cheat. See K. R. Bradley, *Suetonius' Life of Nero: An Historical Commentary* (Brussels: Latomus, 1978), 14–15, on Suetonius's portrayal of Nero's character, and 23–28, on his ancestry.

4. Holland, *Nero*, 13.

5. Our most important source is Tacitus's *Annals* but the incomplete state of the manuscript means that the first nine years and last two years of Nero's life are missing. Suetonius's *Life of Nero* is largely a series of disconnected anecdotes that cannot be dated to a particular year and must be used cautiously. See Saller, "Anecdotes as Historical Evidence for the Principate," 69–83. For a popular attempt to extract a balanced picture of Nero from the ancient spin doctors, see Holland, *Nero*, v–xii; Bradley, *Suetonius' Life of Nero*, 17–18, on his sources.

6. Griffin, *Nero*, 73.

7. She admits to it openly in Tacitus, *Ann.* 13.14. *Ann.* 13.1 says the lethal drug was administered by an equestrian named P. Celer with the help of a freedman named Helius. Celer was eventually prosecuted for the deed, but Nero saw to it that the prosecution was delayed for so long that Celer died of old age: Tacitus, *Ann.* 13.33. Dio 61.6.4 says it was the same poison she had used on her husband. Pliny, *HN* 7.58, blames Nero for the death.

8. Tacitus, *Ann.* 13.12 was right about Agrippina's insecure grasp on power. She was honored publicly, but there was no real power. See Bauman, *Women and Politics in Ancient Rome*, 2, on women and political power, and 194–98, on Agrip-

pina. See McHugh, "Manipulating Memory," 192, on Agrippina as a "product of a society that encouraged women to act indirectly, through their familial and sexual roles." See Barrett, *Agrippina*, 150–53, on her honors and special privileges. For the republic, see T. Hilliard, "On the Stage. Behind the Curtain: Images of Politically Active Women in the Late Roman Republic," in *Stereotypes of Women in Power: Historical Perspectives and Revisionist Views*, ed. B. Garlick, S. Dixon, and P. Allen (New York: Greenwood Press, 1992), 37–64. Momigliano, "Nero," 708: "The authority of Agrippina could not last long, for it was incompatible with that sovereign height on which her son had been placed." And see D. C. A. Shotter, *Nero Caesar Augustus: Emperor of Rome* (Harlow, UK: Pearson Education Ltd., 2008), 57.

9. Rutledge, *Imperial Inquisitions*, 150.

10. On the myth of the so-called *Quinquennium Neronis* and how it was created, see Wiedemann, "Tiberius to Nero," 243–44.

11. J. Malitz, *Nero* (Malden, MA: Blackwell, 2005), 24–25; Shotter, *Nero Caesar Augustus*, 60; Holland, *Nero*, 76–77. On Seneca's position, see Griffin, *Seneca*, 67–128.

12. On Nero chafing under his mother's influence and Tacitus's treatment of this, see McHugh, "Manipulating Memory," 196–97; Momigliano, "Nero," 711; Tacitus, *Ann.* 13.12–13.

13. Tacitus, *Ann.* 13.14. Shortly after this episode, Britannicus died, though it is not clear whether he was murdered. As for the end of Pallas, see Oost, "Career of M. Antonius Pallas," 113–39.

14. Momigliano argues that Agrippina's threats not only weakened her own position but put Britannicus in harm's way. He also admits, however, that even without her threats, the boy's fate was sealed: "Suspicion against all possible rivals to the throne and the use of any means to be rid of them were becoming as much a tradition of the Julio-Claudian family as of any ancient monarchy." See Momigliano, "Nero," 709. Rutledge, *Imperial Inquisitions*, 150, accepts the story that Britannicus was poisoned.

15. The consequence for Agrippina of the deprivation of this bodyguard and of being denied quarters in the palace was that she was shunned. See Tacitus, *Ann.* 13.18; Dio 61.8.6; Suet., *Nero* 34.1; Millar, *Emperor in the Roman World*, 62.

16. Dio 61.7.4; Suet., *Nero* 33.3; Tacitus, *Ann.* 13.15–17; Josephus, *BJ* 2.250 and *AJ* 20.153; Barrett, *Agrippina*, 170–71.

17. On being denied quarters in the palace and her bodyguard: Tacitus, *Ann.* 13.19.1; Dio 61.8.6. Barrett, *Agrippina*, 174, does not see the removal of the bodyguard as a reduction of her power, but admits that "in the world of political intrigue, the appearance of power and influence is almost as important as the real thing." On Junia Silana: Tacitus, *Ann.* 13.19–21; Bingham, *Praetorian Guard*, 144; Griffin, *Nero*, 74; Malitz, *Nero*, 27–28; Holland, *Nero*, 85, 114.

18. Tacitus, *Ann.* 14.7. On the refusal of Burrus to involve the Praetorian Guards, see Holland, *Nero*, 106–7; Griffin, *Nero*, 74; Malitz, *Nero*, 33; Barrett, *Agrippina*, 189.

19. A. Dawson, "Whatever Happened to Lady Agrippina?" *CJ* 64, no. 6 (March 1969): 253–67, completely rejects the story of Agrippina's demise on chronological, logistical, and historical reasons. She argues for an actual conspiracy to put Otho on the throne with Agrippina.

20. On the murder, see Tacitus, *Ann.* 14.8; Suet., *Nero* 34; Dio 62.12; Malitz, *Nero*, 31–34; Barrett, *Agrippina*, 186–91; Holland, *Nero*, 108–9.

21. Barrett, *Agrippina*, 190, points out that the Praetorians' loyalty to Agrippina was tempered with realism. The official account was repeated in a letter to the Senate in which Nero claimed that his mother wanted to be co-ruler with him, symbolized by having the oath of allegiance sworn to her separately rather than being included with the imperial household. See Tacitus, *Ann.* 14.11.1; Bingham, *Praetorian Guard*, 145. On the murder as a political necessity, see E. Paratore, "Nerone (nel XIX centenaio della morte)," *Studi Romani* 17 (1969): 269–87.

22. Tacitus, *Ann.* 14.10.2, reports they "grasped his hand and wished him joy of escaping his unexpected danger and the criminal enterprise of his mother." J. Jackson translation, Loeb edition.

23. Dio 61.14.3; Bingham, *Praetorian Guard*, 32. This grant does not appear in other sources. On donatives in general, see Bingham, *Praetorian Guard*, chapter 3.

24. Most of the ancient sources record that he was poisoned, but Tacitus suggests the possibility of a natural death: Tacitus, *Ann.* 14.51.1–3. Cf. Suet., *Nero* 35.5 (poison sent as throat medicine). Dio 62.13.3 gives the reason for the murder as Burrus's opposition to Nero divorcing his wife Octavia in order to marry his mistress Poppaea. See L. Cotta Ramosino, "L'opposizione a Nerone e le 'partes' di Galba," in *Fazioni e congiure nel mondo antico*, ed. M. Sordi (Milan: Vita e Pensiero, 1999), 217–36; W. C. McDermott, "Sextus Afranius Burrus," *Latomus* 8 (1949): 253, accepts the story of the murder.

25. Nero had appointed Tigellinus *Praefectus Vigilum* sometime before 62: Tacitus, *Hist.* 1.72. On Tigellinus's earlier career and political ties to Caligula's sisters and the anti-Claudian faction, see T. Roper, "Nero, Seneca and Tigellinus," *Historia* 28, no. 3 (1979): 346–57.

26. Tacitus, *Ann.* 14.62; Suet., *Nero* 35.

27. In Tacitus, *Ann.* 14.60, Octavia is accused of having an affair with an Egyptian flute-player named Eucaerus. Her slaves refused to testify against her even under torture; one of them spat in Tigellinus's face saying, "My mistress' private parts are cleaner than your mouth." See Tacitus, *Ann.* 14.60; Dio 62.13.4. In Suet., *Nero* 35, the trumped-up affair is with Anicetus; *Octavia, Praetexta* 780ff.

28. Tacitus, *Ann.* 14.63; Suet., *Nero* 35; Griffin, *Nero*, 112; P. Murgatroyd, "Tacitus on the Death of Octavia," *G&R* 55, no. 2 (October 2008): 263–73, gives a vivid account of the story.

29. Tacitus, *Ann.* 14.64.

30. Tacitus, *Ann.* 14.64.

31. According to Suet., *Nero* 35.3, she quarreled fiercely with Nero over his spending too much time at the races. In a fit of rage, Nero kicked her in the abdomen and caused her death. Tacitus, *Ann.* 16.6, places the death after the *Quinquennial Neronia* and claims Nero's kick was a "casual outburst." Tacitus also mentions that some writers, now lost, claimed Nero poisoned her, though Tacitus does not believe them. Dio 62.27.4 claims Nero leapt upon her belly but admitted that he did not know if it was intentional or accidental.

32. Kicking a pregnant woman was a familiar literary *topos* commonly used in Greek rhetoric against tyrants. An example would be Herodotus 3.32.4, where the Persian king, Cambyses, does the same thing. See the comments of T. Wiede-

mann, *The Julio-Claudian Emperors* (London: Bristol Classical Press, 2002), 12, and R. Mayer, "What Caused Poppaea's Death?" *Historia* 31, no. 2 (1982): 248–49.

33. Tacitus, *Ann.* 16.7.2, 10.4.

34. Suet., *Nero* 28; E. Champlin, *Nero* (Cambridge, MA: HUP, 2003), 145; D. Woods, "Nero and Sporus," *Latomus* 68 (2009): 73–82; C. Vout, *Power and Eroticism in Imperial Rome* (Cambridge: CUP, 2007), "The Case of Nero and Sporus," 136–66; Bradley, *Suetonius' Life of Nero*, 161, on his life after Nero.

35. Tacitus, *Ann.* 14.42–45. The *senatus consultum Silanianum* was passed in 10 CE and said that all slaves in the household must be executed. See J. Harries, "The *Senatus Consultum Silanianum*: Court Decisions and Judicial Severity in the Early Roman Empire," in *New Frontiers: Law and Society in the Roman World*, ed. Paul J. du Plessis (Edinburgh: Edinburgh University Press, 2013), 51–72.

36. On crowd gathering with firebrands and clubs: Tacitus, *Ann.* 14.43.4; on lining the streets with soldiers: Tacitus, *Ann.* 14.45; Holland, *Nero*, 8. On Pedanius Secundus, see Syme, *Tacitus*, 591.

37. Tacitus, *Ann.* 13.2.

38. When Nero succeeded Claudius, Narcissus, who had backed Britannicus, was arrested and executed. Pallas had retained his position in the treasury for a time. It is suggested that he assisted Agrippina in murdering Claudius, since he was sure of his future security. This security did not last long. In 55, Nero dismissed Pallas from service, tired of having to deal with any allies of Agrippina. He further accused Pallas of conspiring to overthrow him and placed Faustus Sulla, the husband of Claudius's daughter Claudia Antonia, on the throne. Seneca, who was prominent in Nero's circle, came to Pallas's defense at the trial and got him acquitted, but Pallas did not elude Nero's wrath for long. Part of the money was Nero's by right as Pallas's official patron. Some money must have gone to Pallas's family, because a descendant of his became consul in 167. Tacitus, *Ann.* 14.65.1. Polybius, his fellow freedman, has been executed for treason for backing Sulla Felix as a candidate for the throne. For the details, see Oost, "Career of M. Antonius Pallas," 113–39.

39. Malitz, *Nero*, 77–78; Cogitore, *La légitimé dynastique d'Auguste à Néron à l'épreuve des conspirations*, 234–43; Griffin, *Nero*, 169, 192, 195. See B. Baldwin, "Executions, Trials and Punishment in the Reign of Nero," *La Parola del Passato* 22 (1967): 427, on the difficulty of disentangling the individual Silanii.

40. Tacitus, *Ann.* 13.1, exonerates Nero of the crime and pins it on Agrippina. It was called the "first crime of the new principate." Dio 61.6.4 says she used the same poison she had used on her late husband, Claudius.

41. *PIR* 1:558, brother of Marcus Junius Silanus, consul in 53.

42. Tacitus, *Ann.* 16.8. We do not know what happened to Junia Lepida; we just have the enigmatic remark that Nero himself pronounced on her case.

43. Tacitus, *Ann.* 16.7–9; Suet., *Nero* 37.

44. Tacitus, *Ann.* 16.9. Cassius Longinus managed to survive Nero as triumphantly as he had survived Caligula. He was recalled to Rome by Vespasian and died in honor at a venerable old age. See R. S. Rogers, "Heirs and Rivals to Nero," *TAPA* 86 (1955): 210; R. S. Rogers, "A Tacitean Pattern in Narrating Treason-Trials," *TAPA* 83 (1952): 303–5.

45. Tacitus, *Ann.* 16.8; L. Calpurnius Fabatus was the client of one of the condemned. He was the grandfather of Calpurnia Hispulla, the younger Pliny's wife.

Fabatus may have been the source of additional information on the whole affair and was an acquaintance of Tacitus. Nine of Pliny's letters are addressed to him.

46. Tacitus, *Ann.* 14.12. Cogitore, *La légitimité dynastique d'Auguste à Néron à l'épreuve des conspirations*, 78–85; Malitz, *Nero*, 35–36; T. E. Strunk, "Saving the Life of a Foolish Poet: Tacitus on Marcus Lepidus, Thrasea Paetus, and Political Action under the Principate," *Syllecta Classica* 21 (2010): 119–39, with bibliography on the subject.

47. Tacitus, *Ann.* 15.23. Paetus immediately interpreted this as "prophetic of his impending slaughter" (Jackson trans.). V. Rudich, *Political Dissidence under Nero*, 79, suggests that Thrasea Paetus's disgrace was due to the intrigues of Tigellinus and his son-in-law, Cossutianus Capito. Strunk argues that Thrasea was not a reckless adversary of the princeps, who died a martyr for an abstract cause, but a thoughtful dissident whose persecution revealed the extremism and decadence of the Neronian principate. See Strunk, "Saving the Life of a Foolish Poet," 120.

48. We have accounts by Dio 62.24.1–29.4; Suet., *Nero* 36.1; and Tacitus, *Ann.* 15.48–74. See Swan, *Conspiracies*, 195–96, who discusses the interpretations of B. W. Henderson, *The Life and Principate of the Emperor Nero* (London: Methuen, 1903), 260–74; E. Ciaceri, "La congiura pisoniana contro Nerone," in *Processi politici e relazioni internazionali* (Rome: A. Nardecchia, 1918), 363–86; Momigliano, "Nero," 726–31; G. Walter, *Nero* (London: Allen & Unwin, 1957): 176–82; H. de la Ville de Mirmont, "C. Calpurnius Piso et la conspiration de l'an 818/65," *Revue des Études Anciennes* 15 (1913): 405–20. See also Rogers, "Heirs and Rivals to Nero," 207–12; Griffin, *Nero*, 166–70; Shotter, *Nero Caesar Augustus*, 146–52; Holland, *Nero*, 181–96.

49. Tacitus, *Ann.* 15.51.3, 15.67; Bingham, *Praetorian Guard*, 61–62. On the varying motives, see Rutledge, *Imperial Inquisitions*, 167.

50. Tacitus, *Ann.* 15.54. His observation is completely contradicted by Plutarch, *Moralia* 505 C, D, which relates the story of a man giving away the secret to Nero.

51. Tacitus provides the names of at least twenty members of the conspiracy. Senatorial conspirators: C. Calpurnius Piso, of consular rank; Plautius Lateranus, consul designate; Annaeus Lucanus, ex-quaestor; Afranius Quintianus and Flavius Scaevinus, of unknown rank. Equestrian conspirators: Antonius Natalis; Cervarius Proculus; Claudius Senecio; Iulius Augurinus; Marcius Festus; Munatius Gratus; Vulcacius Araricus. The plot infiltrated the heart of the Praetorian camp; among the military conspirators: Faenius Rufus, Praetorian prefect; Gavius Silvanus, Statius Proxumus, and Subrius Flavus, tribunes of the Praetorian Guard; Maximus Scaurus, Sulpicius Asper, and Venetus Paulus, centurions of the Praetorian Guard. Freedwoman: Epicharis. As if this were not enough, he mentions twenty-one other people whose guilt was less certain but who were suspected of being involved. Senatorial rank: L. Annaeus Seneca, Annius Pollio, Caesennius Maximus, P. Glitius Gallus, M. (Iulius) Vestinus Atticus, Novius Priscus. Of equestrian rank: Rufrius Crispinus. Tribunes of the Praetorian Guard: Cornelius Martialis, Flavius Nepos, Pompeius, Statius Domitius, who were later demoted to suspected complicity. Others: Blitius Catulinus, Cluvidienus Quietus, Iulius Agrippa, Iulius Altinus, Musonius Rufus, Petronius Priscus, Verginius Flavus, Acilia (the mother of Lucan), Antonia (daughter of the emperor Claudius), Caedicia (wife of Flavius Scaevinus). Many of the names are obscure.

52. On Piso, see R. Rees, "The Lousy Reputation of Piso," in Gibson, *Julio-Claudian Succession*, 95–106. On the fact that we know so little about the chronology and the course of the conspiracy, see D. C. Earl, "Two Passages of Sallust," *Hermes* 91, no. 1 (1963): 126–27. Tacitus himself admits this; see V. Pagán, *Conspiracy Narratives*, 68.

53. Suet., *Cal.* 25.1. The exile was in 40, not 37, as Dio 59.8.7–8 has it.

54. Tacitus, *Ann.* 15.49.1, 49.4; Swan, *Conspiracies*, 220. His only recorded part in the planning was to veto the suggestion that the assassination be carried out in his villa at Baiae.

55. Tacitus, *Ann.* 15.59, says he secluded himself in his house and steeled his spirits until the end. When the troops arrived, he opened his veins.

56. Walker, *Annals of Tacitus*, 131–37, has written on the "general demoralization of the Senate" as a theme in Tacitus's treatment of the Pisonian conspiracy. Thus he prefers Lateranus's patriotism over Lucan's private grudge.

57. Tacitus, *Ann.* 15.50. How ironic then that Vestinus Atticus, excluded from the plot because of his republican leanings, gets caught up in the aftermath of the Pisonian conspiracy. When the Praetorian Guard arrived at his house during a dinner party, he committed suicide. See Tacitus, *Ann.* 15.68.2–69.3; Bingham, *Praetorian Guard*, 194n72; Malitz, *Nero*, 81; Rutledge, *Imperial Inquisitions*, 167.

58. On the relationship of the conspiracy to the city of Rome, see I. Cogitore, "Rome dans la Conspiration de Pison," in *Neronia VI* (Brussels: Latomus, 2002), 261–72.

59. Rudich, *Political Dissidence under Nero*, 98; contra Swan, *Conspiracies*, 211, who finds this idea inconsistent with Tacitus's description of the plot.

60. Dio 62.24. People have questioned Dio's account because it is riddled with errors. Perhaps it reflects a popular, and much later, view of military participation in the affair. Cf. Rudich, *Political Dissidence under Nero*, 114–17, on his motives.

61. Polyaenus, *Stratagems of War*, 8.62.

62. Tacitus, *Ann.* 15.56.2, who names Cluvius Rufus, Fabius Rusticus, and Pliny the Elder. See Swan, *Conspiracies*, 195–96; Henderson, *Life and Principate of the Emperor Nero*, 260–74; Griffin, *Seneca*, 367–68, who believes he knew of the conspiracy but did not participate; commentary by Wiseman, in Josephus, *Death of an Emperor*, 111–18, appendix 2: "Cluvius Rufus."

63. On the two-headed conspiracy, Ciaceri, "La congiura pisoniana contro Nerone," 363–86; rejected by Swan, *Conspiracies*, 212–13. Momigliano, "Nero," 726–31, sees two groups but with the Pisonian one dominating. He thinks that Seneca without a doubt was in on the conspiracy. Walter, *Nero*, 176–82, sees the conspiracy as a patchwork of private intrigues. Roper, "Nero, Seneca and Tigellinus," 351, says the evidence implicating Seneca in the conspiracy is simply too weak to stand up under scrutiny. For an older interpretation of "the hatred between Nero and those uncompromising Stoic philosophers," see G. Charles-Picard, *Augustus & Nero* (New York: Thomas Crowell, 1965), 153. On the idea that love for the *res publica* meant the principate not the old republic, see Rogers, "Stigma of Politics," 159.

64. Tacitus, *Ann.* 15.49.

65. Tacitus, *Ann.* 15.53.

66. Tacitus, *Ann.* 15.53.

67. See Rutledge, *Imperial Inquisitions*, 167.

68. Tacitus, *Ann.* 15.49ff., 58, 65, 67ff.; Dio 62.24.

69. Tacitus, *Ann.* 15.50.

70. Tacitus, *Ann.* 15.50.

71. Tacitus, *Ann.* 15.53.

72. Tacitus, *Ann.* 15.54.1–55.3., who makes no secret of what he thinks of Milichus. Malitz, *Nero*, 82, attributes the failure to "vanity and weak nerves." Tacitus, *Ann.* 15.67, has Scaevinus brag that nobody knew more about the conspiracy than he did. Tacitus, rather oddly, felt that the security had been astonishingly well kept until Scaevinus's boasting. See Baldwin, *Roman Emperors*, 7. Rutledge, *Imperial Inquisitions*, 169, disagrees with Rudich, *Political Dissidents under Nero*, 103, who believes Milichus's denunciation represents a perversion of values.

73. Tacitus, *Ann.* 15.62.1.

74. Tacitus, *Ann.* 15.71.

75. See the table in Henderson, *Life and Principate of the Emperor Nero*, 486; Rogers, "Stigma of Politics," 157–58.

76. Tacitus, *Ann.* 15.73.1. Tacitus never records what punishment befell the four *equites*—Vulcacius Araricus, Iulius Augurinus, Munatius Gratus, and Marcius Festus—although he does name them as conspirators in 15.50.1.

77. Griffin, *Nero*, 168–69.

78. Suet., *Nero* 32; Tacitus, *Ann.* 16.7. Griffin, *Nero*, 205–6.

79. Tacitus, *Ann.* 15.62.1, 16.11, 16.14.3, 16.19. Dio 62.28.4 dates to the period after Poppaea's death the practice of buying safety from Tigellinus. On the financial crisis, see Griffin, *Nero*, 197–205.

80. Baldwin, "Executions, Trials and Punishment in the Reign of Nero," 439, argued that there was no sustained "terror" under Nero and that *maiestas* trials were not indiscriminately employed.

81. Rudich, *Political Dissidence under Nero*, 70, 141, 159; Cogitore, *La légitimité dynastique d'Auguste à Néron à l'épreuve des conspirations*, 228–34. Plautus had been executed while exercising. He was decapitated in the presence of his wife. See Tacitus, *Ann.* 14.59.3, 16.10.4. Suetonius never mentions him at all, but see Dio 62.14.1 (epitome).

82. Griffin, *Nero*, 170n26. See Tacitus, *Ann.* 16.10, on her lamentations, which included going to Naples in her bloodstained robe and pounding on the door to see the emperor. He declined to reply.

83. Tacitus, *Ann.* 16.10. Thrasea's absence at the senatorial sessions when Lucius Silanus and Antistius Vetus were condemned was unusual and remarked upon: Tacitus, *Ann.* 16.22.1. On Thrasea's slow secession, see Rudich, *Political Dissidence under Nero*, 78–81.

84. Tacitus, *Ann.* 16.14, cf. 14.48; Griffin, *Nero*, 170. On Anteius Rufus, see Rudich, *Political Dissidence under Nero*, 144–46.

85. Tacitus, *Ann.* 16.14–16; Griffin, *Nero*, 170; Wiedemann, "Tiberius to Nero," 253; Rutledge, *Imperial Inquisitions*, 112–13, 170, 374.

86. It is Dio who attributes the quarrel to Nero's envy of Lucan: Dio 62.29.4. Suet., *Vita Lucani* may suggest that Lucan was insulted by Nero, but the text is corrupt. See Tacitus, *Ann.* 15.49.3; Swan, *Conspiracies*, 218n72. G. K. Gresseth, "The Quarrel between Lucan and Nero," *CP* 52 (1957): 24–27, believes the quarrel

between Lucan and Nero was an invention of the following age to explain how the most brilliant poet of Nero's age could have conspired against him and be executed. See Rudich, *Political Dissidence under Nero*, 94–96.

87. Tacitus, *Ann*. 15.49.3. Ciaceri, "La congiura pisoniana contro Nerone," 363–86, believes the accusations put forth in the literary sources are invalid, but he says nothing to support this rejection. He needs this out of the way to assert later that republican and Stoic influences were dominant in the plot. See Wiedemann, "Tiberius to Nero," 253.

88. *PIR* R 85, son of Rubellius Blandus and Julia, granddaughter of Tiberius.

89. Annius Pollio, *PIR²* A 678, brother of Annius Vinicianus. They were sons of Lucius Annius Vinicianus (*PIR²* A 701), who conspired against Gaius and Claudius.

90. G. Boissier, *L'opposition sous les Césars*, 91–105; Allen, "Political Atmosphere of the Reign of Tiberius," 19.

91. Griffin, *Nero*, 171 and 171n35 with references. See also Rogers, "Stigma of Politics," preface and 160.

92. For example, Julius Canus under Gaius: Barrett, *Caligula*, 157–58. Boethius, *Consol. Phil*. 1.4.94 seems to reflect a tradition in which Canus was actually involved in a plot. On Julius Graecinus, father of Agricola, see Seneca, *Tranquil* 14.4; Tacitus, *Agricola* 4; Seneca, *Epis*. 29.6; Barrett, *Caligula*, 76, 158.

93. Tacitus, *Ann*. 16.22.4.

94. This point is thoroughly argued by Brunt, "Stoicism and the Principate," 7–35.

95. Tyrannicide is described as *a moral duty* in Cicero, *de Off*. 3.32, perhaps following Posidonius *Att*. 6.11.4. For such duties in general, see Diog. Laert 7.109; Griffin, *Nero*, 173.

96. Griffin, *Nero*, 174–75. For a full discussion of Seneca and his predicament, see J. Romm, *Dying Every Day: Seneca at the Court of Nero* (New York: Alfred Knopf, 2014).

97. The question is whether the emperors were reacting against individual Stoics or the entire sect. Helvidius Priscus was put to death by Vespasian, who also expelled Demetrius and others: Dio 66.12.3–13. In 93 Arulenus Rusticus and Herennius Senecio were condemned, and there was an expulsion of philosophers including Artemidorus, Epictetus, and possibly Plutarch. See Tacitus, *Agricola* 2; Pliny, *Epistles* 3.11.2; Suet., *Domitian* 10.3; Dio 67.13.3. The expulsions were linked to political trials of men related by birth and doctrine to Nero's senatorial victims. See Momigliano, "Nero," 730–31.

98. Tacitus, *Ann*. 15.60.2; Romm, *Dying Every Day*, 190–94.

99. Dio 62.24.1 is rejected by Rudich, *Political Dissidence*, 107. Henderson, *Life and Principate of the Emperor Nero*, 260–74, argues for Seneca being part of the plot. Romm, *Dying Every Day*, 187–94, says he at least knew of the plot. Malitz, *Nero*, 83, absolves him, as does Griffin, *Nero*, 168. Holland, *Nero*, 182–84, has him involved.

100. Dio 62.24.1; Polyaenus, *Stratagems of War* 8.62. Volusius Proculus, commander of the fleet at Misenum, had helped Nero in Agrippina's murder. Perhaps he felt he had not gotten enough of a reward. See Rutledge, *Imperial Inquisitions*, 167.

101. Polyaenus, *Stratagems of War* 8.62.

102. Tacitus, *Ann.* 15.60; Rudich, *Political Dissidence*, 107.

103. Tacitus, *Ann.* 15.65. Cf. Juvenal, 8.211–14: "If a free vote were given to the people, who would be so depraved as to waver in his preference for Seneca over Nero?"

104. Tacitus, *Ann.* 15.61; Malitz, *Nero*, 83.

105. Baldwin, "Executions, Trials and Punishment in the Reign of Nero," 439, who does not accuse Tacitus of outright fabrication but sees contradictions in his narrative. He reminds us that the key to understanding the early principate is always the personal relationships and family politics.

106. Starr, *Civilization and the Caesars*, 161, compared them to Hitlerian and Stalinist purges.

107. Tacitus, *Ann.* 15.73.1, on evidence and the confessions. Annius Pollio was one of the returnees, mentioned in Tacitus, *Ann.* 15.73.3, who admitted guilt.

108. Malitz, *Nero*, 84.

109. Tacitus, *Ann.* 16.21; Dio 62.26ff. On the prosecutions, see Rutledge, *Imperial Inquisitions*, 115–21.

110. Capito had a grudge against him for supporting the Cilician charge of extortion against him back in 57. See Tacitus, *Ann.* 16.21.

111. Tacitus, *Ann.* 16.22.

112. Tacitus, *Ann.* 16.23, also suggests that diverting public curiosity to foreign affairs would take their minds off the domestic crimes.

113. Rudich, *Political Dissidence under Nero*, 174, points out how ironic it is that Antistius Sosianus was convicted of publishing scurrilous verse against the emperor yet has his life spared, but Thrasea Paetus, who does nothing untoward, gets death.

114. Rudich, *Political Dissidence under Nero*, 178.

115. Tacitus, *Hist.* 4.42, who implies you were only safe if you were too young to hold office, had nothing Nero could covet, or had nothing Nero could fear. On Camerinus: Dio 63.18.2; J. Malitz, *Nero*, 91; Griffin, *Nero*, 178.

116. *PIR*[2] C 1464. Faustus Cornelius Sulla was the last descendant of the famous dictator and heir to his famous name. He was half-brother of the late empress Messalina. Griffin, *Nero*, 178.

117. Roper, "Nero, Seneca and Tigellinus," 355. Sulla had been under suspicion twice before, once in 56, when Burrus and Pallas were charged with conspiracy to make him emperor (Tacitus, *Ann.* 13.23), and again in 58, when a second charge of conspiracy was brought against him (Tacitus, *Ann.* 13.47). Similarly Rubellius Plautus had been denounced in 55 as the man whom Agrippina was plotting to put on the throne (Tacitus, *Ann.* 13.19.3, 14.21). See also, Cogitore, *La légitimité dynastique d'Auguste à Néron à l'épreuve des conspirations*, 228–34. Griffin, *Nero*, 178, prefers the Tacitean version.

118. Sulpicius Scribonius Rufus and P. Sulpicius Scribonius Proculus were the governors of Lower and Upper Germany, respectively: Dio 63.17.1–4. Cf. Tacitus, *Hist.* 4.41.3, and see Griffin, *Nero*, 178; Grant, *Nero*, 221.

119. Griffin, *Nero*, 178. Barea Soranus had been proconsul in 61 CE and Plautus was executed in Asia at the close of his term: Tacitus, *Ann.* 14.57–58, 16.23. For the date of Barea's proconsulship and attendant problems, see Griffin, *Nero*, 256n10.

120. On the senior Vinicianus (*PIR*[2] A 700), see Josephus, *AJ* 19.49, 52. Dio 60.15.1; Pliny, *Epistles* 3.16.7; Griffin, *Nero*, 178.

121. On Corbulo's wife and family connections see R. Syme, "Domitius Corbulo," *JRS* 60 (1970): 27.

122. Momigliano ("Nero," 731) goes as far as to suggest the aim of the conspiracy was to replace Nero with Corbulo. Cf. Holland, *Nero*, 207. Cf. M. Hammond, "Corbulo and Nero's Eastern Policy," *HSCPh* 45 (1934): 101–2; Fagan, *Roman Imperial Succession*, 174, who believes Corbulo was in on the plot but recognizes this is only speculation.

123. Suet., *Nero* 36.1, gives us no date but simply says it happened after the Pisonian conspiracy. The Arval Brethren offered thanks "for the detection of the wicked plot" at some point after mid-May 66. On the conspiracy: Suet., *Nero* 36; E. Mary Smallwood, *Documents*, no. 26; *Acta Arvalium*, in *CIL* VI 2044. Calling it *coniuratio Viniciana* suggests that its leader may have been Annius Vinicianus (*PIR*[2] A 700), probably the son of the conspirator against Gaius and Claudius, L. Annius Vinicianus, and a brother of Annius Pollio (*PIR*[2] A 678), who was exiled in connection with the Pisonian conspiracy.

124. Suet., *Nero* 36.

125. Griffin, *Nero*, 177–78. On Corbulo, see Syme, "Domitius Corbulo," 27–39; Rutledge, *Imperial Inquisitions*, 171.

126. Dio 63.17.5–6 on the last words; Fagan, *Roman Imperial Succession*, 174. Corbulo's participation is questionable at best, but he had too many incriminating family members. We know he was denounced by Arrius Varus. See Rutledge, *Imperial Inquisitions*, 172.

127. Griffin, *Nero*, 179. He was just finishing his second term as *consul ordinarius*: Dio 60.21.2. For Nero's entourage, see K. R. Bradley, "Nero's Retinue in Greece, AD 66/67," *Illinois Classical Studies* 4 (1979): 152–57.

128. Dio 62.14.3 tells us Nero took many prominent men with him to Greece to kill them. The only senators he names are Vespasian and Cluvius Rufus. Another member of his entourage—Paccius Africanus—is known because he informed against the two Scribonii. See H. W. Benario, "Paccius Africanus," *Historia* 4 (October 1959): 496–98; Syme, *Tacitus*, 333n, 594.

129. Dio 63.19.1; Suet., *Nero* 23.1. Rudich, *Political Dissidence under Nero*, 206–7.

130. Suet., *Nero* 37.3; Aquilius Regulus's victims: Tacitus, *Hist.* 4.42.1; Pliny, *Epistles* 1.5.3.

131. The *Bellum Neronis*, as it was dubbed by Tacitus, has been called the first successful revolt against the Julio-Claudian dynasty. Unfortunately, the versions of Cassius Dio 63.22–29, Plut., *Galba* 6–11, and Suet., *Nero* 40–49, vary considerably. See the discussion in L. J. Daly, "Verginius at Vesontio: The Incongruity of the '*Bellum Neronis*,'" *Historia* 24, no. 1 (1975): 75–100. J. van Ooteghem, "Verginius et Vindex," *Et.Cl.* 36 (1968): 27, called the problem of reconciling the sources "insoluble." The reasons for Nero's fall are multifarious and have been covered in detail by Griffin, *Nero*, 185–234.

132. Plut., *Galba* 4.

133. We can see this in the coins and the literary evidence: C. M. Kraay, "The Coinage of Vindex and Galba A.D. 68," *NC* 9 (1949): 129, and G. E. F. Chilver,

"The Army in Politics A.D. 68–70," *JRS* 47 (1957): 29. Some nineteenth-century historians, followed by Henderson, attempted to explain the uprising in Gaul as a matter of Gallic nationalism, especially since some Gallic tribes attempted to found an empire of the Gauls two years later. Swan, *Conspiracies*, 231, discusses both Mommsen's theory that the revolters wanted a return to the republic, and Henderson's theory that it was nationalistic. The tribes who rose in 70 were not the ones following Vindex, who was backed mostly by Basques. The program being espoused by Vindex was a return to Roman government on the Augustan model and a liberation from tyranny, not from Rome. On their program and its slogans, see Wiedemann, *Julio-Claudian Emperors*, 66. Cf. Momigliano, "Nero," 739; G. B. Townend, "The Reputation of Verginius Rufus," *Latomus* 20 (1961): 337; Daly, "Verginius at Vesontio," 79; P. A. Brunt, "The Revolt of Vindex and the Fall of Nero," *Latomus* 18 (1959): 543n3; J. B. Hainsworth, "Verginius and Vindex," *Historia* 11 (1962): 86–96; and the exhaustive study of M. Raoss, "La rivolta di Vindice ed il successo di Galba," *Epigraphica* 20 (1958): 46–120, 22 (1960): 37–151.

134. Tarraconensis was the largest of the three provinces into which Spain was divided. Galba may have wanted to be the lead candidate for the job, but he knew his wealth, birth, and position were enough to make Nero suspicious without adding treason. See Rudich, *Political Dissidence under Nero*, 223. The fact that Nero sent Galba there for the rest of his career suggests Nero was trying to get him out of the picture. See Wiedemann, "Tiberius to Nero," 248.

135. Suet., *Galba* 9. Malitz, *Nero*, 101; Rudich, *Political Dissidence under Nero*, 223. In addition, there was another attempt on his life by one of Nero's freedmen: Suet., *Galba* 10.

136. Plut., *Galba* 4, says outright that they sent the letters to Nero purposely trying to ruin the enterprise of Vindex.

137. See Hainsworth, "Verginius and Vindex," 89. Vindex's communications with exiled senators is asserted by Dio's epitomator, John of Antioch, *fr.* 91. Vindex's tampering with provincial governors is asserted by Plut., *Galba* 4.4. The fact that Nero wanted all governors and exiles executed because they had turned against him suggests he believed a revolt would come to pass. Hainsworth (p. 90) suggested that Vindex had already made overtures to the Scribonii, Verginius's predecessors.

138. See Daly, "Verginius at Vesontio," 81. He believes Verginius was involved as a silent partner in a joint effort with Vindex and Galba to overthrow Nero.

139. As Syme, *Tacitus*, 179, pointed out, if the defeat of Vindex saved Rome, then it should also have saved Nero. The Rhine legions were the single most powerful military force available in the West for the defense of Rome's authority.

140. Suet., *Galba* 9 says Galba joined the revolt because Nero had sent instructions to the procurators in Tarraconensis to kill him. Some, like Henderson, *Life and Principate of the Emperor Nero*, 196n31, believed this was a story made up later to justify Galba's behavior. See Swan, *Conspiracies*, 240n63, with bibliography and discussion.

141. In Plutarch's version, *Galba* 4 has the Praetorian prefect Titus Vinius as the evil genius who talked Galba into revolting. Galba was hailed by a crowd assembled for the occasion at Carthago Nova. He denounced Nero, stressed the number of prominent men murdered or exiled by the mad emperor, and declared

that he himself was acting as a lieutenant of the Senate and the Roman people. See Swan, *Conspiracies*, 241–42.

142. See C. L. Murison, *Galba, Otho and Vitellius: Careers and Controversies* (New York: Georg Olms, 1993), 46–50, who connects Galba with other anti-Neronian elements. R. Syme, "The Partisans of Galba," *Historia* 31 (1982): 460–83, sees him as isolated.

143. On Galba's agents in Rome, see Murison, *Galba, Otho and Vitellius*, 47–50. What specifically impelled Galba to accept Vindex's invitation and join the conspiracy is uncertain. For possible factors, see Swan, *Conspiracies*, 235–38. R. Syme, "The Partisans of Galba," *Historia* 31 (1982): 469.

144. Plut., *Galba* 7; Suet., *Galba* 14; Rudich, *Political Dissidence under Nero*, 225.

145. On the source problems concerning Galba's journey from Spain to Rome, see Murison, *Galba, Otho and Vitellius*, 27–30. Tacitus, *Hist.* 1.6, describes it as "slow and bloody."

146. Some say Vindex timed his revolt to coincide with the Ides of March. See B. Levick, "L. Verginius Rufus and the Four Emperors," *RhM* 128 (1985): 325; Shotter, *Nero Caesar Augustus*, 162–65; Rudich, *Political Dissidence under Nero*, 212–13; M. Griffin, *Nero*, 181–82.

147. We do not even know if there *was* an agreement. At first, historians assumed that Verginius Rufus suppressed the revolt of Vindex as a loyal officer of the emperor Nero: Syme, *Tacitus*, 179, 462; Kraay, "The Coinage of Vindex and Galba, A.D. 68," 144–46; Chilver, "Army in Politics A.D. 68–70," 32–33; Hainsworth, "Verginius and Vindex," 90, 92, 94–95. Then P. A. Brunt published a carefully argued and highly persuasive paper on the *Bellum Neronis* that shifted scholarly opinion to the idea that by the time of Vesontio, Verginius had abandoned Nero and had tacitly joined the rebellion. See Brunt, "Revolt of Vindex and the Fall of Nero," 537–43. Syme, "Partisans of Galba," 469, later reiterated his earlier view. Also see Levick, "L. Verginius Rufus and the Four Emperors," 330–41.

148. Plut., *Galba* 6. On the intractable problem of the date of Vesontio, see Murison, *Galba, Otho and Vitellius*, 2; Malitz, *Nero*, 101–2.

149. This depends on the chronology. Chilver ("Army in Politics A.D. 68–70," 33) has argued that Verginius's troops did not proclaim him until after Nero was dead.

150. See Pliny's defense of Verginius Rufus in *Epistles* 9.19. G. Morgan, *69 A.D.: The Year of the Four Emperors* (Oxford: OUP, 2006), 24, calls this a fantasy. Cf. Townend, "The Reputation of Verginius Rufus," 337–41. On Verginius's background, see Levick, "L. Verginius Rufus and the Four Emperors," 322–23.

151. Wiedemann, *Julio-Claudian Emperors*, 67.

152. Views are sharply divided over Verginius's motives. See Shotter, *Nero Caesar Augustus*, 375; contra Daly, "Verginius at Vesontio," 83. Swan, *Conspiracies*, 244, says the idea that Verginius was still loyal to Nero at the battle of Vesontio should be abandoned.

153. Daly, "Verginius at Vesontio," 95. Levick, "L. Verginius Rufus and the Four Emperors," 318–46, still argued for Verginius's loyalty to Nero. For a detailed discussion of the sources and the problem of Verginius, see Murison, *Galba, Otho and Vitellius*, 17, on the loyalty (or lack thereof) of the German legions. Also see Swan, *Conspiracies*, 247–48; Fagan, *Roman Imperial Succession*, 177–78.

154. He mobilized units that were waiting in Italy to be sent to the eastern front, including the XIV Gemina Martia Victrix.

155. Tacitus, *Hist.* 1.6; Dio 63.27; Griffin, *Nero*, 181–82.

156. Suet., *Nero* 40.4; Griffin, *Nero*, 181.

157. Suet., *Nero* 41, panic; 42, fainting; 43, assassinating the army commanders and the governors of the provinces, massacring all exiles, killing all the Gauls in the city, poisoning the Senate. See Dio 63.27.2 on killing senators.

158. Suet., *Nero* 47.1, tells us that although the revolts of Vindex and Galba were taken in stride, once he heard about the neutrality of Verginius he panicked straight away. On Vesontio being decisive, see Brunt, "Revolt of Vindex and the Fall of Nero," 537. On the Guard defecting after Vesontio, see D. Shotter, "Tacitus and Verginius Rufus," *CQ* 17, no. 2 (November 1967): 375.

159. On this event, see Tacitus, *Hist.* 1.5; Suet., *Galba* 11, 14; Plut., *Galba* 2; Bingham, *Praetorian Guard*, 32.

160. Rudich, *Political Dissidence under Nero*, 130; Bingham, *Praetorian Guard*, 32; and on the conspiracy see Bingham, *Praetorian Guard*, chapter 3.

161. Plut., *Otho* 2, takes the illness as fact; he was certainly ill by January of 69. See Morgan, *69 A.D.*, 29; Malitz, *Nero*, 103 and 105. Holland, *Nero*, 221–22, asks whether he was keeping information from Nero. Tacitus, *Hist.* 1.72, has him later saved by Galba. See Griffin, *Nero*, 182; Rudich, *Political Dissidence under Nero*, 232–33.

162. Plut., *Galba* 8; Malitz, *Nero*, 105; Rudich, *Political Dissidence under Nero*, 232. Roper, "Nero, Seneca and Tigellinus," 346–57, does an admirable job of trying to save Tigellinus's reputation from the negative picture Tacitus paints of him. Tacitus sees Tigellinus as advisor to Nero as a replica of Sejanus to Tiberius. See Syme, *Tacitus*, 263; E. Cizek, *L'Époque de Néron et ses controversies idéologiques* (Leiden, Netherlands: Brill, 1973), 20n1, citing Syme, *Tacitus*, 261ff. Cizek traces the anti-Tigellinus writings to Greek authors who try to make the prefect the evil genius behind Nero in order to absolve Nero of crimes because he was popular with the Greeks (160n5). On the other hand, Walker, *Annals of Tacitus*, 78–79, believed making out Tigellinus to be the evil genius just emphasized Nero's rottenness.

163. Plut., *Galba* 13, 14.

164. Plut., *Galba* 2, on the amount offered the soldiers; 3, on being the richest man to hold the throne.

165. Tacitus, *Hist.* 1.5.1. As noted by Campbell, *The Emperor and the Roman Army 31 B.C.–A.D. 235*, 85, a speech to the Guard when there were exceptional circumstances was seen as an opportunity to test the loyalty of the army. Also see Bingham, *Praetorian Guard*, 146n152.

166. Plut., *Galba* 2.2; Cf. Suet., *Galba* 16.1, where he reneges on the offer. See Tacitus, *Hist.* 1.5.1; Josephus, *BJ* 4.492–93; Champlin, *Nero*, 4; Griffin, *Nero*, 185–86; Rudich, *Political Dissidence under Nero*, 232–33. G. E. F. Chilver, *A Historical Commentary on Tacitus' Histories I and II* (Oxford: Clarendon Press, 1979), 50, points out the amount of the donative has been challenged as being too large to be believable.

167. Plut., *Galba* 13–14; Tacitus, *Hist.* 1.5; this puts the Guard in the center of events of the so-called Year of the Four Emperors. See Bingham, *Praetorian Guard*, 146. For a different interpretation of the event—that Nymphidius had changed allegiance from Galba to another senator rather than desiring power for himself—

see S. Ottley, "The Coup of Nymphidius Sabinus," *AHB* 24 (2010): 95. Rudich, *Political Dissidence under Nero*, 232–33, believes he was aiming for the throne. The period is discussed in detail by S. Ottley, "The Role Played by the Praetorian Guard in the Events of AD 69, as Described by Tacitus in His *Historiae*" (Unpublished PhD diss., University of Western Australia, 2009).

168. Ottley, "Coup of Nymphidius Sabinus," 95–113, dissects the events with great care.

169. Plut., *Galba* 14.3-6. Ottley, "Coup of Nymphidius Sabinus," 109, asks how a man of humble origins thought he had any chance of being accepted as an alternative emperor to the aristocratic Galba or a successor to the blue-blooded Julio-Claudians. See also Ottley's commentary on Nero's popularity with the troops and their attitude toward Nymphidius through all this (110–11).

170. Suet., *Nero* 47ff., has the fullest account of Nero's end. See also Dio 63.27.3.

171. Suet., *Nero* 48. On the "air of treachery," see Bradley, *Suetonius' Life of Nero*, 274.

172. Suet., *Nero* 47–49; Meijer, *Emperors Don't Die in Bed*, 32. D. Sansone, "Nero's Final Hours," *ICS* 18 (1993): 179–89 points out that the details of this escape are highly improbable and that both Suetonius and Dio's account (63.26–29) may have used a common source that was highly fictionalized. Cf. Bradley, *Suetonius' Life of Nero*, 273–74.

173. Suet., *Nero* 49; Zon. 11, 13, on the date.

174. Suet., *Nero* 50. His ashes were deposited by his two nurses, Ecloge and Alexandria, and by his faithful mistress, Acte. Acte's epitaph was found at Velitrae: *CIL* 10.6599. See Attilio Mastino and Paola Ruggeri, "*Claudia Augusti liberta Acte*, la liberta amata da Nerone ad Olbia," *Latomus* 54, no. 3 (July/September 1995): 513–44.

175. Suet., *Nero* 50; Dio 63.27–29. See M. P. Charlesworth, "Nero: Some Aspects," *JRS* 40, nos. 1–2 (1950): 69–76, on Nero's popularity. He notes that since Nero's death was sudden and mysterious, witnessed by no more than five people, and followed by no state funeral or impressive ceremony, it allowed stories of his survival to grow and circulate.

176. Tacitus, *Ann.* 13.1.1.

177. See Griffin, *Nero*, 194–95.

178. Tacitus, *Ann.* 15.52.2–3, 53.3–4.

179. Suet., *Nero*, 35.4. Poppaea was supposedly kicked to death by Nero when she was pregnant. See Tacitus, *Ann.* 16.6.1; Suet., *Nero* 35.3; Dio 62.27.4.

180. Suet., *Nero* 35.4; Dio 61.1.2.

181. Plut., *Galba* 2.

182. P. Lancan, *La crisi del Impero nell'anno 69 D.C.* (Padova: CEDAM, 1939), 98–106.

183. For example, Cizek, *L'Époque de Néron et ses controversies idéologiques*, 242–43. Griffin, *Nero*, 215–20, rejects the idea.

184. Pliny, *HN* 18.3, does not tell us who the six men were.

185. Rudich, *Political Dissidence under Nero*, xxiv–xvii.

186. Champlin, *Nero*, 236. Cf. Drinkwater, "Nero Caesar and the Half-Baked Principate," 161.

187. Champlin, *Nero*, 25–27; Osgood, *Claudius Caesar*, 27.

188. Millar, *Emperor in the Roman World*, 11.

189. Tacitus, *Hist.* 1.89. Moore translation, Loeb edition.

190. He had recruited the I Italica less than two years before. The I Adiutrix was raised for the current crisis. The British legion XIV Gemina was famed for its loyalty to him even after his death. See Tacitus, *Hist.* 2.11ff., 2.27.2. For Nero's sake, they were quick to join Otho against Galba. Nothing suggests these legions would have favored Galba over a descendant of Augustus.

191. Griffin, *Nero*, 180, 187. On the allies Galba collected before his recognition, see Chilver, "Army in Politics A.D. 68–70," 29–35.

192. Tacitus, *Hist.* 1.5.1, 1.30; Plut., *Galba* 2, 7, 14.

193. Suet., *Nero* 48.2. He left Rome by the Via Nomentana.

194. Tacitus, *Ann.* 15.72.

195. Griffin, *Nero*, 186.

196. Raaflaub, "Augustus' Military Reforms," 223.

197. Rudich, *Political Dissidence under Nero*, xxx.

CHAPTER 8: THE END OF THE JULIO-CLAUDIANS

1. Rudich, *Political Dissidence under Nero*, xxv.

2. Dettenhofer, *Herrschaft und Widerstand im augusteischen Principat*, portrays him as the quintessential Machiavellian prince.

3. See Alston, *Rome's Revolution*, 215, who describes Augustus as "notably brutal, even by the blood-soaked standards of the time."

4. On this, see Fantham, *Julia Augusti*, xi.

5. Those who have concentrated on economy, society, and administrative machinery often lose sight of this. See, for example, A. Wallace-Hadrill, "The Imperial Court," 285. German scholarship with its emphasis on law, institutions, and administration also had a tendency to legitimize the Augustan regime in all its aspects. See Dettenhofer, *Herrschaft und Widerstand im augusteischen Principat*, 27; Eck, *Age of Augustus*, 124–25; Levick, *Augustus*, 7 finds it stable.

6. Levick, *Augustus*, 6 and chapter 7.

7. Tacitus, *Ann.* 1.1–2, 4.33; Dio 53.17. Griffin, *Nero*, 188; Levick, *Augustus*, 5–6.

8. Implied in the very title of T. Rice Holmes, *Architect of the Roman Empire* (Oxford: OUP, 1928); Levick, *Augustus*, 5, presents him as the first Roman politician to aim right from the start at permanent sole supremacy. See her comments on the effect of German scholarship on the justification of Augustus's regime, 7.

9. On Augustus's "New World Order" see Wallace-Hadrill, *Augustan Rome*, 1.

10. Several full-length studies have been written on the so-called Year of the Four Emperors, which actually lasted eighteen months: a popular treatment by P. Greenhalgh, *The Year of the Four Emperors* (London: Weidenfeld and Nicolson, 1975); B. W. Henderson, *Civil War and Rebellion in the Roman Empire* (London: Macmillan, 1908); which concentrates on the military aspects of the civil war; Morgan, *69 A.D.*, which is best at analyzing the ancient sources; Murison, *Galba, Otho and Vitellius*; Wellesley, *The Year of the Four Emperors*. Also see Fuhrmann, *Policing the Roman Empire*, 113; P. Zancan, *La crisi del Impero nell'anno 69 D.C.* (Padova: CE-DEM, 1939), and see *JRS* 20 (1940): 199ff.

11. On the non-Roman oligarchy, see A. Momigliano in his review of Ronald Syme's *Roman Revolution*, *JRS* 30 (1940): 75–80.

12. Tacitus, *Ann.* 13.28; Rudich, *Political Dissidence under Nero*, xx.

13. Epictetus, 4.60; Rudich, *Political Dissidence under Nero*, xxi.

14. Rudich, *Political Dissidence under Nero*, xx.

15. Wiedemann, "Tiberius to Nero," 200.

16. See Cogitore, *La légitimité dynastique d'Auguste à Néron à l'épreuve des conspirations*, 1–4.

17. With later emperors, once they had control of the imperial household, the award of public titles and offices by the Senate and the people were just a formality. See Wiedemann, "Tiberius to Nero," 203.

18. Wiedemann, "Tiberius to Nero," 200.

19. Rutledge, *Imperial Inquisitions*, 53.

20. Seneca, *de Bene* 4.31.1; Griffin, *Nero*, 191.

21. Mommsen, *Römische Staatsrecht*, II:1133.

22. For a detailed list, see McAlindon, "Senatorial Opposition to Claudius and Nero," 123–130.

23. Roughly a century counting from the murder of Caesar in 44 BCE to the suicide of Nero in 68 CE. Tacitus refers to the House of the Caesars; it was an intentional construction. See M. Corbier, "A propos de la Tabula Siarensis: Le Sénat, Germanicus et la domus Augusta," in *Roma y las provincias; realidad administrative e ideologia imperial*, ed. J. González (Madrid: Ediciones Clásicas, 1994), 39–85; M. Corbier, "La maisons de Césars," in *Épouser au plus proche: Inceste, prohibitions et stratégies matrimoniales autour de la Méditerranée*, ed. P. Bonte (Paris: Éditions de l'École des hautes études en sciences sociales, 1994), 243–91; Levick, *Augustus*, 294–95.

24. Note that Tiberius took the opposite tack than had Augustus. Agrippina the Elder and Livilla, the two daughters-in-law of Tiberius, were not allowed to remarry when, in 19 CE and 23 CE, respectively, their husbands Germanicus and Drusus the Younger died. Tiberius was especially adamant in not allowing Livilla to marry Sejanus, the ambitious Praetorian prefect. See Tacitus, *Ann.* 4.39–41. Cf. M. Corbier, "Male Power and Legitimacy through Women: The *domus Augusta* under the Julio-Claudians," in *Women in Antiquity: New Assessments*, ed. R. Hawley and B. Levick (London: Routledge, 1995), 187–88.

25. Corbier, "Male Power and Legitimacy through Women," 178–93, traces all the family ties created by Augustus in an attempt to provide an heir.

26. See A. Mehl, *Tacitus über Kaiser Claudius: Die Ereignisse am Hof* (Munich: Wilhelm Fink Verlag, 1974), for the drama Tacitus creates around this theme. Tacitus makes Claudius look more like a victim than Suetonius or Dio does. See Wallace-Hadrill, *Augustan Rome*, 25–42, on the palace and court.

27. Osgood, *Claudius*, 212.

28. Osgood, *Claudius*, 23.

29. Raaflaub, "Augustus' Military Reforms," 213–22.

30. Plut., *Galba* 1–4. On the military history of the year, see Henderson, *Civil War and Rebellion in the Roman Empire*. Wellesley, *The Year of the Four Emperors*, who served in military intelligence during World War II, focuses mostly on topography.

31. Historians have also argued that the specious antithesis between the emperor on one side and the soldiery on the other is a modern construct. See Morgan, *69 A.D.*, 5, on his predecessors' use of the ancient sources.

32. Bingham, *Praetorian Guard*, 6.

33. See, for example, P. M. Prescott, *Optimus: Praetorian Guard* (P. M. Prescott Enterprises, 2006); S. Scarrow, *Praetorian* (London: Headline, 2011); and references in the twenty-one novels in the Falco series by Lindsey Davis from 1989 to 2012.

34. E. Gibbon, *The Decline and Fall of the Roman Empire* (New York: Modern Library, 1983), 1:91.

35. Bingham, *Praetorian Guard*, 3, 123.

36. Suet., *Gaius* 56.1; Dio 59.25.5b. Scholars have argued over whether there were two separate conspiracies in 40–41 CE or, as Barrett, *Caligula*, 155, argues, a single plot. See chapter 5 of this volume.

37. Lendon, *Empire of Honour*, 13.

38. Bingham, *Praetorian Guard*, 23.

39. Tacitus, *Ann.* 12.42.2; Durry, *Les cohorts pretoriennes*, 158; Bingham, *Praetorian Guard*, 19.

40. Tacitus, *Hist.* 1.24. Most scholars already have Otho's seduction of the Guard, beginning with his march on Rome, based on this passage of Tacitus, but it is not clear whether the troops he was suborning were Praetorians or regular legionaries. See Bingham, *Praetorian Guard*, 146n157. C. Damon, *Tacitus: Histories Book I* (Cambridge: CUP, 2003), 152; Morgan, *69 A.D.*, 58; Chilver, "Army in Politics A.D. 68–70," *JRS* 47 (1957): 33. They all assume the soldiers to be men of the VII Galbiana.

41. Bingham, *Praetorian Guard*, 7–8.

42. Bingham, *Praetorian Guard*, 117. On the Castra Praetoria, see Coulston, "Armed and Belted Men," 76–118.

43. Rudich, *Political Dissidence under Nero*, xxiii.

44. Tacitus, *Ann.* 1.2, on the happiness of the provinces that were conciliated by "amenities of peace."

45. See, for example, Josephus, *AJ* 19.227ff.

46. A third-century prayer to the Roman Senate. Eutropius, *Breviarum* 8.5.3.

CHAPTER 9: CONSPIRACIES AND CONSPIRACY THEORIES

1. The closest the Guardsmen came to active duty in the field was when Germanicus used them as reserves in his German wars of 16–17. See Tacitus, *Ann.* 2.16. We heard of them restraining crowds, extinguishing major fires, and combating Italian brigands: Tacitus, *Ann.* 16.27; Dio 61.8.3 (crowds); Tacitus, *Ann.* 3.72, Dio 57.14.10, 59.9.4 (fire); Dio 76.10; Suet., *Tiberius* 37 (brigands).

2. Michael Corleone, *The Godfather: Part II*, directed by Francis Ford Coppola (1974, Paramount Pictures).

3. Bingham, *Praetorian Guard*, 123.

4. Fuhrmann, *Policing the Roman Empire*, 114; Suet., *Nero* 43.2; *SHA, Pertinax* 11.

5. Note that the German bodyguard did not survive the Julio-Claudians. See Suet., *Galba* 12 on the unit that eventually replaced the *Germani corporis custodes*, the *equites singulari Augusti*. See Bingham, *Praetorian Guard*, 135.

6. See the comments of Fuhrmann, *Policing the Roman Empire*, 86.

7. Rogers, "Stigma of Politics," preface, 2.

8. On the autocatalytic process and the cycle of violence, see W. Scheidel, "The Roman Emperor in the Wider World," http://www.sms.cam.ac.uk/media/1174184. On the argument for stability, see G. Woolf, *Rome: An Empire's Story* (Oxford: OUP, 2012), 163–84.

9. Beard, *SPQR*, 415, has pointed out that even when writing their earlier history, the Romans projected this violence into their own past. Although the seven traditional kings of Rome enjoyed long reigns, only two of the seven enjoyed natural deaths.

10. Fagan, "Roman Imperial Succession under the Julio-Claudians, 23 BC–AD 69," 14.

11. Wallace-Hadrill, *Augustan Rome*, 26–28; Galinksy, *Augustus*, 142–43; Wiseman, in Flavius, *Death of an Emperor*, 105–10, appendix I: "The Augustan Palatine."

12. Beard, *SPQR*, 408.

13. The archaeological remains of a *columbarium* (communal tomb) found on the Appian Way in 1726 contained the ashes of more than a thousand slaves and ex-slaves that had belonged to Livia. It listed their names and their jobs. Of course, not all of these lived in the palace. See S. Treggiari, "Jobs in the Household of Livia," *PBSR* 43 (1975): 48–77; Beard, *SPQR*, 336.

14. Malitz, *Nero* (Malden, MA: Blackwell, 1999), 78.

15. Fagan, *Roman Imperial Succession under the Julio-Claudians*, 113.

16. Durry, *Les cohorts pretoriennes*, 156, called Sejanus *"la vrai fondeur du pretoire."*

17. Durry, *Les cohorts pretoriennes*, 181–85.

18. Suetonius says it was because the omens were unfavorable. Dio says they were unimpressed by their general's announced intention of restoring the republic. Both could be possible, but it is more likely they were unwilling to follow a rebellious general against their emperor.

19. Osgood, *Claudius, Caesar*, 259.

20. Passerini, *Le coorti pretorie*, 275–360, provides a list of the prefects. Cf. Durry, *Les cohortes pretoriennes*, 163–65 and appendix II.

21. Fagan does note that the average Praetorian soldier was dedicated to the imperial house since it was his employer. See Tacitus, *Ann.* 14.7.

22. Suet., *Cal.* 58; Dio 59.29–30.

23. Saying they were all like the Praetorians who auctioned off the throne in 193 under Pertinax is an anachronism and denies any development of the office over time. Referring to them as "pampered" (Fagan, *Roman Imperial Succession under the Julio-Claudians*, 114) is the judgment of someone who does not understand the realities of military service. Campbell, *Emperor and the Roman Army*, 117–18, shares the same prejudice and sees all soldiers as being "guided by lucre."

24. Rudich, *Political Dissidence under Nero*, 63.

25. Holland, *Nero*, 2. Syme, *Tacitus*, 485: "A Princeps was fortunate if he did not have to remove rival claimants."

26. Seneca, *Apoc.* 10.3–14.1. Griffin, *Nero*, 193.

27. Wiedemann, "Tiberius to Nero," 199.

28. C. Edwards, "The Truth about Caligula," *CR* 41 (1991): 407.

29. On the development of the principate, its movement toward autocracy, and the effect on the holders of the office, see M. Pani, "Lotte per il potere e vicende dinastiche: Il principato fra Tiberio e Nerone," in *Storia di Roma*, ed. A. Momigliano and A. Schiavone (Torino: Einaudi, 1991), vol. 2, part 2, 221–252.

30. Holland, *Nero*, 12.

31. Tacitus, *Ann.* 1.72–74, 4.34.

32. Rudich, *Political Dissidence under Nero*, 64.

33. Rutledge, *Imperial Inquisitions*, 39–53.

34. Dio 61.6; Rudich, *Political Dissidence under Nero*, 58–59.

35. Tacitus, *Ann.* 14.50. His work, entitled *Codicilli* (*Codicils*, or "Testaments") may have been styled like testamentary documents. He was prosecuted by Tullius Geminus, possibly identified with the suffect consul, Terentius Tullius Geminus.

36. Dio Cassius 60.16.4, E. Cary translation; Levick, *Claudius*, 60.

37. Nippel, *Public Order in Ancient Rome*, 120.

38. Hirschfeld, *Kleine Schriften*; Lintott, *Violence in Republican Rome*.

39. R. W. Davies in his works, "Augustus Caesar: A Police System in the Ancient World," in *Pioneers in Policing*, ed. P. J. Stead (Montclair, NJ: Patterson Smith, 1977), 12–32, and "The Daily Life of the Roman Soldier under the Principate," in *ANRW* 2, no. 1 (1974): 229–338, suggested there was a breakthrough in policing during the principate. W. Nippel criticized this approach and the concentration on "police" forces as represented by E. Echols in his article, "Roman City Police," *CJ* 53 (1957/8): 377–85. Nippel believed a standing police force was inconceivable under the Republican constitution, and that the works of Davies and Echols overestimated their use.

40. On Praetorians, Durry, *Les cohortes prétoriennes*; on the urban cohorts, Freis, *Die cohorts urbanae*; and on the *vigiles*, Reynolds, *Vigiles of Imperial Rome*. All aspects of the administration of the city of Rome are dealt with by Robinson, *Ancient Rome*.

41. Rainbird, "Fire Stations of Imperial Rome," 147–49. The police functions of the Roman army throughout the empire are placed in perspective by B. Isaac's *The Limits of Empire* (Oxford: OUP, 1992).

42. See Rudich, *Political Dissidence under Nero*, xxii, on why this traditional republican behavior was incompatible with the new imperial reality. The need for dissimulation acquired paramount importance in the Julio-Claudian empire. In fact, it became a prerequisite not only for political success but even for physical survival. The toll this took on the psyche of senators can never be measured. We will never know how many nervous breakdowns were caused by living under a Caligula or a Nero, but we also do not know the psychological toll of living under constant death threats on the affected members of the imperial family.

43. Morgan, *69 A.D.*, 7, points this out for the Year of the Four Emperors, but it was equally true under the first five emperors.

44. Bruce Bueno de Mesquita and Alastair Smith, *The Dictator's Handbook* (New York: Public Affairs, 2011), 41.

45. On the fall of the old great families and the emergence of new ones, see Pani, "Lotte per il potere e vicende dinastiche," 238–42.

46. Seneca, *de Clem.* 1.9.3–9; Griffin, *Nero*, 191.

47. Syme, *Tacitus*, 403.

48. See Eisenhut, "Der Tod des Tiberius-Sohnes Drusus," 123–28.

49. Gabba, "Historians and Augustus," 79.

50. Gabba, "Historians and Augustus," 77.

51. Pagán, *Conspiracy Narratives*, 125.

52. Wiedemann, "Tiberius to Nero," 199; Syme, *Tacitus*, 1:131, 150, 217–52.

53. Syme, *Roman Revolution*, 5.

54. Wiedemann, "Tiberius to Nero," 199.

55. Sallust, *Bell. Cat.* 38.3.

56. Gabba, "Historians and Augustus," 75.

57. Lendon, *Empire of Honour*, 1–29.

58. Suet., *Tib.* 25.1.

59. Momigliano, *Claudius*, 69–73.

60. For exceptions, see Tacitus, *Ann.* 1.2, 3.27–29 and his *Dialogus de Oratoribus*, passim.

61. M. Rostovtzeff, *A History of the Ancient World* (Oxford: Clarendon Press, 1927), 2:212, quoted by Momigliano, *Claudius*, xi.

62. Daniel Mendelsohn, review of John William's novel, *Augustus*, *New York Review of Books*, August 14, 2014, 66.

Bibliography

ANCIENT SOURCES

Andocides. In *Minor Attic Orators*. Translated by K. J. Maident. 2 vols. Cambridge, MA: HUP, 1960.

Appian. *Roman History*. Translated by Horace White. 4 vols. (*Civil Wars* in vols. 3 and 4). Cambridge, MA: HUP, 1913.

Asconius Pedianus, Quintus. *Asconius: Commentaries on Five Speeches of Cicero*. Translated and edited by Simon Squires. Mundelein, IL: Bolchazy-Carducci Publishers, 2006.

Aulus Gellius. *The Attic Nights of Aulus Gellius*. Translated by J. C. Rolfe. 3 vols. Cambridge, MA: HUP, 1993.

Aurelius Victor, Sextus. *Epitome de Caesaribus*. Translated with an introduction and commentary by H. W. Bird. Liverpool: Liverpool University Press, 1994.

Ausonius, Decimus Magnus. *Ausonius*. Translated by Hugh G. Evelyn-White. 2 vols. Cambridge, MA: HUP, 1919.

Cassius Dio. *The Augustan Settlement*. Edited, with translation and commentary, by J. W. Rich. Warminster, UK: Aris & Phillips, 1990.

Cassius Dio. *Dio: The Julio-Claudians*. Translated by Jonathan Edmondson. London: London Association of Classical Teachers, 1992.

Cassius Dio. *Dio's Roman History*. Translated by E. Cary. 9 vols. Cambridge, MA: Loeb Classical Library, 1954.

Cicero. *De Haruspicum Responsis*. Translated by N. H. Watts. Cambridge, MA: HUP, 1961.

Cicero. *De Inventione Rhetorica*. Translated by H. M. Hubble. Cambridge, MA: HUP, 1949.

Cicero. *De Lege Agraria*. In Cicero, *The Speeches*. Translated by John Henry Freese. Cambridge, MA: HUP, 1961.

Cicero. *De Legibus.* Translated by Clinton Walker Keyes. Cambridge, MA: HUP, 1970.

Cicero. *de Officiis.* Translated by Walter Miller. Cambridge, MA: HUP, 1961.

Cicero. *De Re Publica.* Translated by Clinton Walker Keyes. Cambridge, MA: HUP, 1970.

Cicero. *In Calpurnium Pisonem.* Translated by N. H. Watts. Cambridge, MA: HUP, 1958.

Cicero. *In Catilinam.* In Cicero, *Orations.* Translated by C. MacDonald. Cambridge, MA: HUP, 1976.

Cicero. *Letters to Atticus.* Translated by E. O. Winstedt. 3 vols. Cambridge, MA: HUP, 1967.

Cicero. *On the Responses of the Haruspices.* Translated by C. D. Yonge. Perseus Digital Library. http://www.perseus.tufts.edu/hopper/text?doc=Cic.%20Har.

Cicero. *Philippics.* Translated by Walter C. A. Ker. Cambridge, MA: HUP, 1963.

Cicero. *Pro Caelio.* In *The Speeches of Cicero.* Translated by R. Gardner. Cambridge, MA: HUP, 1965.

Cicero. *Pro Murena.* In *In Catilinam, Pro Murena, Pro Sulla, Pro Flacco.* Translated by C. MacDonald. Cambridge, MA: HUP, 1976.

Cicero. *Pro Rege Deiotaro.* Translated by N. H. Watts. Cambridge, MA: HUP, 1958.

Diodorus of Sicily. *Diodorus of Sicily.* Translated by C. H. Oldfather (vols. 1–6), Charles L. Sherman (vol. 7), C. Bradford Welles (vol. 8), Russel M. Geer (vols. 9, 10, and 12), Francis R. Walton (vols. 11 and 12). 12 vols. Cambridge, MA: HUP, 1933.

Diogenes Laertius. *Lives of the Eminent Philosophers.* Translated by R. D. Hicks. 2 vols. Cambridge, MA: HUP, 1925.

Dionysius of Halicarnassus. *Roman Antiquities.* Translated by E. Cary. 7 vols. Cambridge, MA: HUP, 1960.

Epictetus. *The Discourses as Reported by Arrian, the Manual, and Fragments.* Translated by W. A. Oldfather. 2 vols. Cambridge, MA: HUP, 1995.

Eusebius. *The Ecclesiastical History.* Translated by Kirsopp Lake. 2 vols. Cambridge: Loeb Classical Library, 1959.

Eutropius. *Breviarum.* Translated with an introduction and commentary by H. W. Bird. Liverpool: Liverpool University Press, 1993.

Festus Historicus. *The Breviarum of Festus.* Translated with commentary by John W. Eadie. London: Athlone Press, 1967.

Florus, Lucius Annaeus. *Epitome of Roman History.* Translated by J. C. Rolfe. Cambridge, MA: HUP, 1960.

Frontinus. *The Stratagems.* Translated by Charles E. Bennett. Cambridge, MA: HUP, 1925.

Gaius. *The Institutes.* Translated by Francis de Zulueta. 2 vols. Oxford: Clarendon Press, 1946.

Herodian. *History.* Translated by C. R. Whittaker. 2 vols. Cambridge, MA: HUP, 1969.

Hyginus (Pseudo). *The Fortification of the Roman Camp.* Translated and edited by M. C. J. Miller and J. G. de Voto. Chicago: Ares Publishers, 1994.

John of Antioch. *Ioannis Antiocheni fragmenta quae supersunt.* Edited by Sergei Mariev. Berlin: de Gruyter, 2008.

Josephus, Flavius. *Jewish Antiquities*. Books 1–8 translated by H. St. J. Thackeray. Cambridge, MA: HUP, 1991.

Josephus, Flavius. *Jewish Antiquities*. Books 9–14 translated by Ralph Marcus. Cambridge, MA: HUP, 1987.

Josephus, Flavius. *Jewish Antiquities*. Books 15–17 translated by Ralph Marcus and Allen Wikgren. Cambridge, MA: HUP, 1980.

Josephus, Flavius. *Jewish Antiquities*. Books 18–20 translated by Louis Feldman. Cambridge, MA: HUP, 1981.

Josephus, Flavius. *The Jewish War*. Translated by H. St. J. Thackeray. 2 vols. Cambridge, MA: HUP, 1956.

Justin. *Justin, Cornelius Nepos and Eutropius*. Literally translated by John Selby Watson. London: G. Bell, 1876.

Justinian. *Digest of Justinian*. Edited by Paul Krueger and Alan Watson. Translated by Theodor Mommsen. 4 vols. Philadelphia: University of Pennsylvania Press, 1985.

Justinus, Marcus Junianus. *Epitoma historiarum Philippicarum Pompei Trogi*. Translated by Otto Seel. Stuttgart: Teubner, 1972.

Justinus, Marcus Junianus. *Epitome of the Philippic History of Pompeius Trogus: Books 11–12*. Translation and appendices by J. C. Yardley; introduction and commentary by Waldemar Heckel. Oxford: Clarendon Press, 1997.

Juvenal. *The Satires*. Translated by G. G. Ramsay. Cambridge, MA: HUP, 1961.

Juvenal. *Scholia in Iuvenalem Vetustiora*. Edited by P. Wessner. Leipzig: Teubner, 1931.

Livy (Titus Livius). *From the Founding of the City*. Translated by B. O. Foster. 14 vols. Cambridge, MA: HUP, 1988.

Macrobius. *Saturnalia*. Translated by Robert A. Kaster. 2 vols. Cambridge, MA: HUP, 2011.

Nicolaus of Damascus. *Life of Augustus: A Historical Commentary Embodying a Translation by Clayton Hall*. Northampton, MA: Smith College Classical Studies, 1923.

Ovid. *Fasti*. Translated by James George Frazer. Cambridge, MA: HUP, 1931.

Perseus Flaccus, Aulus. *The Satires of Persius*. Translated by G. G. Ramsay. Cambridge, MA: HUP, 1961.

Phaedrus. *Fables*. In *Babrius, Phaedrus, Fables*, translated by Ben Edwin Perry. Cambridge, MA: HUP, 1965.

Philo of Alexandria. *The Works of Philo*. Translated by C. D. Yonge, with a foreword by David M. Scholer. Peabody, MA: Hendrickson Publishers, 1993.

Plautus. *Aulularia*. Translated by Palmer Bovie. Baltimore: Johns Hopkins University Press, 1995.

Pliny the Elder. *Natural History*. Translated by H. Horace Rackham. 10 vols. Cambridge, MA: HUP.

Pliny the Younger. *Panegyricus*. In Pliny, *Letters and Panegyricus*, translated by Betty Radice. 2 vols. Cambridge, MA: HUP, 1969,

Plutarch. *Lives*. Translated by Bernadotte Perrin. 11 vols. Cambridge, MA: HUP, 1959.

Plutarch. *Moralia*. Vols. 1–5, translated by Frank Cole Babbit. Cambridge, MA: HUP, 1927.

Plutarch. *Moralia*. Vol. 6, translated by W. C. Helmbold. Cambridge, MA: HUP, 1939.

Plutarch. *Moralia*. Vol. 7, translated by Phillip H. DeLacy and Benedict Einarson. Cambridge, MA: HUP, 1959.

Plutarch. *Moralia*. Vol. 8, translated by Paul A. Clement and Herbert B. Hoffleit. Cambridge, MA: HUP, 1969.

Plutarch. *Moralia*. Vol. 9, translated by Edwin L. Minor, Jr., F. H. Sandbach, and W. C. Helmbold. Cambridge, MA: HUP, 1961.

Plutarch. *Moralia*. Vol. 10, translated by Harold North Fowler. Cambridge, MA: HUP, 1936.

Plutarch. *Moralia*. Vol. 11, translated by Lionel Pearson and F. H. Sandbach. Cambridge, MA: HUP, 1965.

Plutarch. *Moralia*. Vol. 13, parts 1 and 2, translated by Harold Cherniss. Cambridge, MA: HUP, 1976.

Plutarch. *Moralia*. Vol. 14, translated by Benedict Einarson and Philip H. DeLacy. Cambridge, MA: HUP, 1967.

Plutarch. *On the Fortune of the Romans*. In *Moralia*, Vol. 4, translated by F. C. Babbitt. Cambridge, MA: HUP, 1957.

Polyaenus. *Stratagems of War*. Translated and edited by Peter Krentz and Everett L. Wheeler. Chicago: Ares, 1994.

Polybius. *The Histories*. Translated by W. R. Paton. 6 vols. Cambridge, MA: HUP, 1979.

Roman Imperial Coinage. Vol. 1, edited by C. H. V. Sutherland. London, 1923 (revised 1984).

Sallust. *Bellum Catilinae*. Translated by J. C. Rolfe. Cambridge, MA: HUP, 1985.

Scriptores Historiae Augustae. *Historia Augusta*. Translated by David Magie. 3 vols. Cambridge MA: HUP, 1967.

Seneca. *Apocolocyntosis*. In *Petronius, Satyricon; Seneca, Apocolocyntosis*, translated by Michael Heseltine and W. H. D. Rouse, revised by E. H. Warmington. Cambridge, MA: HUP, 1913.

Seneca the Elder. *Controversiae*. In *Declamations*, translated by M. Winterbottom. 2 vols. Cambridge, MA: HUP, 1974.

Seneca. *De Beneficiis*. In *Moral Essays*, Vol. 3, translated by John W. Basore. Cambridge, MA: HUP, 1989.

Seneca. *De Brevitate Vitae*. In *Moral Essays*, Vol. 2, translated by John W. Basore. Cambridge, MA: HUP, 1932.

Seneca. *De Consolatione ad Helviam*. In *Moral Essays*, Vol. 2, translated by John W. Basore. Cambridge, MA: HUP, 1932.

Seneca. *De Constantia*. In *Moral Essays*, Vol. 1, translated by John W. Basore. Cambridge, MA: HUP, 1951.

Seneca. *De Ira*. In *Moral Essays*, Vol. 1, translated by John W. Basore. Cambridge, MA: HUP, 1951.

Seneca. *De Tranquilitate Animi*. In *Moral Essays*, Vol. 2., translated by John W. Basore. Cambridge, MA: HUP, 1932.

Seneca. *Dialogues and Essays*. Translated by John Davie, with an introduction by Tobias Reinhardt. Oxford: OUP, 2009.

Seneca. *Epistles*. Translated by Richard M. Gummere. 3 vols. Cambridge, MA: HUP, 1917–1925.

Seneca. *Natural Questions*. Translated by Thomas H. Corcoran. 2 vols. Cambridge, MA: HUP, 1972.

Seneca the Younger. *Octavia*. In *Tragedies*, Vol. 2, translated by John G. Fitch. Cambridge, MA: HUP, 2004.

Silius Italicus. *Punica*. Translated by J. D. Duff. 2 vols. Cambridge, MA: HUP, 1996.

Statius. *Silvae*. Edited and translated by D. R. Shackleton-Bailey. Revised by Christopher A. Parrot. Cambridge, MA: HUP, 2015.

Suetonius. *Lives of the Caesars*. Translated by J. C. Rolfe. 2 vols. Cambridge, MA: HUP, 1960.

Tacitus. *Agricola*. Translated by M. Hutton. Revised by R. M. Ogilvie. Cambridge, MA: HUP, 1980.

Tacitus. *The Annals*. Translated by J. Jackson. 3 vols. Cambridge, MA: HUP, 1956.

Tacitus. *Dialogus de Oratoribus*. Revised by M. Winterbottom. Translated by Sir W. Peterson. Cambridge, MA: HUP, 1980.

Tacitus. *The Histories*. Translated by Clifford H. Moore. Cambridge, MA: HUP, 1962.

Thucydides. *The Peloponnesian Wars*. Translated by Charles Forster Smith. 4 vols. Cambridge, MA: HUP, 1980.

Valerius Maximus. *Memorable Doings and Sayings*. Translated by D. R. Shackleton Bailey. 2 vols. Cambridge, MA: HUP, 2000.

Varro, Marcus Terentius. *Antiquitates Rerum Humanarum*. Edited, with German commentary, by Burkhart Cardauns. 2 vols. Mainz: Akademie der Wissenschaften und Literatur, 1976.

Velleius Paterculus. *The Roman History*. Translated by Frederick W. Shipley. Cambridge, MA: HUP, 1961.

Vergil. *The Aeneid*. Translated by Sarah Ruden. New Haven, CT: YUP, 2008.

Zonaras, Johannes. *Epitome Historiarum*. Edited by L. Dindorf. 6 vols. Leipzig: Teubner, 1868.

Zosimus. *Historia Nova* [New History]. Translated with commentary by Ronald T. Ridley. Sydney: Australian Association for Byzantine Studies, 1982.

COMMENTARIES AND LITERATURE

Baldwin, Barry. "Women in Tacitus." *Prudentia* 4 (1972): 83–101.

Benario, H. W. "Tacitus and the Principate." *CJ* 60 (1964): 97–106.

Bonamente, G. "Minor Latin Historians of the Fourth Century A.D." In *Greek and Roman Historiography in Late Antiquity: Fourth to Sixth Centuries A.D.*, edited by G. Marasco, 85–125. Leiden, Netherlands: Brill, 2003.

Bradley, K. R. *Suetonius' Life of Nero: An Historical Commentary*. Brussels: Latomus, 1978.

Chilver, G. E. F. *A Historical Commentary on Tacitus' Histories I and II*. Oxford: Clarendon Press, 1979.

Daitz, Stephen G. "Tacitus' Technique of Character Portrayal." *AJPh* 81 (1960): 30–52.

Damon, C. *Tacitus: Histories Book I*. Cambridge: CUP, 2003.

Furneaux, Henry. *The Annals of Tacitus*. 2nd ed. 2 vols. Oxford: Clarendon Press, 1968.

González, Julian. "Tacitus, Germanicus, Piso and the Tabula Siarensis." *AJPh* 120, no. 1 (1999): 123–42.

Goodyear, F. R. D. *The Annals of Tacitus*. Cambridge: CUP, 1972 (vol. 1), 1981 (vol. 2).

Haynes, Holly. *The History of Make-Believe: Tacitus on Imperial Rome*. Berkeley: University of California Press, 2003.

Humphrey, J. W. "An Historical Commentary on Cassius Dio's Roman History, Book 59 (Gaius Caligula)." PhD diss., University of British Columbia, 1976.

Hurley, Donna W. *An Historical and Historiographical Commentary on Suetonius' Life of C. Caligula*. Oxford: OUP, 1993.

Maurer, J. A. A Commentary on C. Suetoni *Tranquilli, Vita C. Caligulae Caesaris*, Ch. I–XXI." Ph.D. diss., University of Pennsylvania, Philadelphia, 1949.

Machiavelli, Niccolò. *The Historical, Political, and Diplomatic Writings*. Vol. 2, *The Prince, Discourses on the First Ten Books of Titus Livius, Thoughts of a Statesman*. http://oll.libertyfund.org/titles/machiavelli-the-historical-political-and-diplomatic-writings-vol-2.

Martin, R. H. *Tacitus*. London: Batsford, 1981.

Millar, F. *A Study of Cassius Dio*. Oxford: OUP, 1964.

Morgan, M. G. "The Three Minor Pretenders in Tacitus, Histories II." *Latomus* 52 (1993): 769–96.

Reinhold, Meyer. *From Republic to Principate: An Historical Commentary on Cassius Dio's Roman History Books 49–52 (36–29 BC)*. Atlanta: Scholars Press, 1988.

Santoro L'Hoir, Francesca. "Tacitus and Women's Usurpation of Power." *CW* 88 (1994): 5–25.

Sinclair, Patrick. *Tacitus the Sententious Historian*. University Park, PA: Penn State University Press, 1995.

Swan, P. M. D. *The Augustan Succession: An Historical Commentary on Cassius Dio's Roman History Books 55–56 (9 B.C.–A.D. 14)*. Oxford: OUP, 2004.

Syme, R. *Tacitus*. 2 vols. Oxford: OUP, 1958.

Tacitus. *The Annals: The Reigns of Tiberius, Claudius and Nero*. Translated by J. C. Yardley, with an introduction and notes by Anthony A. Barrett. Oxford: OUP, 2008.

Walker, B. *The Annals of Tacitus: A Study in the Writing of History*. 2nd ed. Manchester: Manchester University Press, 1960.

Wallace-Hadrill, Andrew. *Suetonius*. Bristol, UK: Bristol Classical Press, 1998.

Wardle, David. *Suetonius' Life of Caligula: A Commentary*. Brussels: Latomus, 1994.

White, Peter. *Promised Verse: Poets in the Society of Augustan Rome*. Cambridge, MA: HUP, 1993.

Woodman, A. J. *The Cambridge Companion to Tacitus*. Cambridge: CUP, 2009.

Woodman, A. J. *Rhetoric in Classical Historiography: Four Studies*. London: Croom Helm, 1988.

Woodman, A. J. *Velleius Paterculus: The Caesarian and Augustan Narrative (2.41–93)*. Cambridge: CUP, 1983.

Woodman, A. J. *Velleius Paterculus: The Tiberian Narrative (2.94–131)*. Cambridge: CUP, 1977.

REFERENCE WORKS

Hornblower, Simon, and Antony Spawforth. *Oxford Classical Dictionary*. 3rd ed. Oxford: OUP, 2005.
Prosopographia Imperii Romani, saec. I, II, III ediderunt P. von Rohden et H. Dessau. Berlin: Reimarus, 1897–1898.
Richardson, L., Jr. *A New Topographical Dictionary*. Baltimore: Johns Hopkins University Press, 1992.
Smith, William, William Wayte, and G. E. Marindin. *Dictionary of Greek and Roman Antiquities*. 3rd rev. ed. London: J. Murray, 1914.

FICTION

Jaro, Benita Kane. *Betray the Night*. Mundelein, IL: Bolchazy-Carducci, 2009.

MODERN HISTORY

Aaronovich, David. *Voodoo Histories. The Role of Conspiracy Theory in Shaping Modern History*. New York: Penguin, 2010.
Bercé, Yves Marie, and Elena Fasano Guarini, eds. *Complots et conjurations dans l'Europe modern*. Rome: Collection École Française de Rome 220, 1996.
Bueno de Mesquita, Bruce, and Alastair Smith. *The Dictator's Handbook*. New York: Public Affairs, 2011.
Butts, Edward. *Bodyguards! From Gladiators to the Secret Service*. Toronto: Annick Press, 2012.
Fenster, Mark. *Conspiracy Theories: Secrecy and Power in American Culture*. Minneapolis: University of Minnesota Press, 2008.
Forbes, Steve, and John Prevas. *Power, Ambition, Glory: The Stunning Parallels between Great Leaders of the Ancient World and Today . . . and Lessons You Can Learn*. New York: Crown Business, 2009.
Garlick, Barbara, Susan Dixon, and Pauline Allen, eds. *Stereotypes of Women in Power: Historical Perspectives and Revisionists Views*. New York: Greenwood Press, 1992.
Holden, Henry M. *To Be a U.S. Secret Service Agent*. St. Paul, MN: Zenith Press, 2006.
Horn, Eva, and Anson Rabinbach. "Dark Powers. Conspiracies and Conspiracy Theories in History and Literature." *New German Critique* 35 (Spring 2008): 1–8.
Priest, Dana, and William M. Arkin. *Top Secret America: The Rise of the New American Security State*. New York: Little, Brown & Co., 2011.
Stockwell, John. *The Praetorian Guard: The U.S. Role in the New World Order*. Boston: South End Press, 1991.

ASSASSINATION, OPPOSITION, CONSPIRACIES, VIOLENCE

Africa, Thomas W. "Urban Violence in Imperial Rome." *Journal of Interdisciplinary History* 2, no. 1 (Summer 1971): 3–21.

Allen, Walter, Jr. "The Vettius Affair Once More." *TAPA* 81 (1950): 153–63.

Amarelli, F. *Trasmissione, rifiuto, usurpazione: Vicende del potere degli imperatori romani.* Naples: Jovene, 2008.

Bauman, R. A. *Crime and Punishment in Ancient Rome.* London: Routledge, 1996.

Bauman, R. A. *The Crimen Maiestatis in the Roman Republic and Augustan Principate.* Johannesburg, South Africa: Witwatersrand University Press, 1967.

Bauman, R. A. *Impietas in Principem: A Study of Treason against the Roman Emperor with Special Reference to the First Century A.D.* Munich: Beck, 1974.

Becker, K. "Studien zur Opposition gegen den römischen Prinzipat." PhD diss., Tübingen, 1950. Phil. F., Diss. v. 28.

Béranger, J. "L'hérédité du Principat: Note sur la transmission du pouvoir impérial aux deux premiers siècles." *REL* 17 (1939): 171–87.

Boissier, Gaston. *L'opposition sous les Césars.* Paris: Librairie Hachette, 1942.

Brecht, C. H. *Perduellio: Eine Studie zu ihrer begrifflischen Abgrenzung im römischen Strafrecht zum Ausgang der Republik.* Munich: Beck, 1938.

Brélaz, C. "Lutter contre la violence à Rome: Attribution étatiques et tâches privées." In *Les exclus dans l'Antiqué*, edited by C. Wolff, 229–34. Paris: Boccard, 2007.

Brunt, Peter A. "Did Emperors Ever Suspend the Law of Maiestas?" In *Sodalitas: Scritti in onore di Antonio Guarino*, 469–80. Naples: Jovene, 1984.

Cogitore, I. "Les conspirations comme 'coups d'État' chez Gabriel Naudé: L'exemple antique." In *Complot et conjurations dans l'Europe modern*, edited by Y. M. Bercé and E. Fasano Guarini, 193–202. Rome: Coll. M.E.F.R. 220, 1996.

Cogitore, I. *La légitimité dynastique d'Auguste à Néron à l'épreuve des conspirations.* Rome: École Française de Rome, 2002.

Flaig, E. *Den Kaiser herausfordern: Die usurpation im römischen Reich.* Frankfurt: Campus Verlag, 1992.

Ford, Franklin L. *Political Murder: From Tyrannicide to Terrorism.* Cambridge, MA: HUP, 1985.

Grant, R. G. *Assassinations: History's Most Shocking Moments of Murder, Betrayal and Madness.* Pleasantville, NY: Readers Digest, 2004.

Gruen, Erich S. "Review of Lintott, *Violence in Republican Rome.*" *AJPh* 91, no. 3 (July 1970): 367–70.

Heaton, John Wesley. *Mob Violence in the Late Roman Republic 133–49 B.C.* Urbana: University of Illinois Press, 1939.

Lintott, A. W. "The Tradition of Violence in the Annals of the Early Roman Republic." *Historia* 19, 1 (January 1970): 12–29.

Lintott, A. W. *Violence in Republican Rome.* Oxford: Clarendon Press, 1968.

Luisi, Aldo. "L'opposizione sotto Augusto: Le due Giulie, Germanico e gli amici." In *Fazioni e congiure nel Mondo antico*, edited by M. Sordi, 181–92. Milan: Vita e Pensiero, 1999.

Marshall, Bruce A. "Pompeius's Fear of Assassination." *Chiron* 17 (1987): 119–33.

McDermott, W. C. "Vettius Ille, Ille Noster Index." *TAPA* 80 (1949): 351–67.

McDonald, A. H. "Review of A. W. Lintott, *Violence in Republican Rome*." *CR* 23, no. 2 (December 1973): 239–41.

Meijer, F. *Emperors Don't Die in Bed*. London: Routledge, 2001.

Moeller, Walter O. "Review of Lintott, *Violence in Republican Rome*." *CW* 63, no. 1 (September 1969): 24.

Oost, Stewart Irvin. "Review of Lintott, *Violence in Republican Rome*." *CP* 65, no. 4 (Oct. 1970): 280–81.

Pagán, Victoria Emma. *Conspiracy Narratives in Roman History*. Austin: University of Texas Press, 2004.

Pagán, Victoria Emma. *Conspiracy Theory in Latin Literature*. Austin: University of Texas Press, 2012.

Pagán, Victoria Emma. "Toward a Model of Conspiracy Theory for Ancient Rome." *New German Critique* 103 (2008): 27–49.

Pagán, Victoria Emma. "Shadows and Assassinations: Forms of Time in Tacitus and Appian." *Arethusa* 39, no. 2 (Spring 2006): 193–218.

Pani, M. "Lotte per il potere e vicende dinastiche: Il principato fra Tiberio e Nerone." In *Storia di Roma*, edited by A. Momigliano and A. Schiavone, vol. 2, part 2, 221–52. Torino: Einaudi, 1991.

Porter, Lindsay. *Assassination: A History of Political Murder*. New York: Overlook Press, 2001.

Raaflaub, K. A. "Grunzüge Ziele und Ideen des Opposition gegen die Kaiser im I Jh. N. Chr.: Versuch einer Standortbestimmung." In *Opposition et résistances a l'empire d'Auguste a Trajan*, edited by A. Giovannini and D. van Berchem, 1–63. *Entretiens sur l'antiquité classique*, edited by O. Reverdin and B. Grange, no. 33. Geneva: Fondation Hardt, 1986.

Reverdin, O., and B. Grange, eds. *Entretiens sur l'antiquité classique*. Geneva: Fondation Hardt, 1973–.

Riess, Werner. "How Tyrants and Dynasts Die: The Semantics of Political Assassination in Fourth-Century Greece." In *Terror et Pavor: Violenza, intimidazione, clandestinità nel mondo antico*, edited by Gianpaolo Urso, 65–88. Pisa: ETS, 2006.

Rogers, Perry McAdow. "The Stigma of Politics: Imperial Conspirators and Their Descendants in the Early Roman Empire." PhD diss., University of Washington, 1979.

Sherwin-White, A. N. "Review of A. W. Lintott, *Violence in Republican Rome*." *JRS* 59, nos. 1–2 (1969): 286–87.

Sordi, Marta, ed. *Fazione e congiure nel mondo antico*. Milan: Vita e Pensiero, 1999.

Swan, P. M. D. "A Study of the Conspiracies against Emperors of the Julio-Claudian Dynasty." PhD diss., Harvard University, 1964.

Taylor, Lily Ross. "The Date and Meaning of the Vettius Affair." *Historia* (1950): 45–51.

Urso, Gianpaolo. *Terror et Pavor: Violenza, intimidazione, clandestinità nel mondo antico*. Pisa: ETS, 2006.

Ville de Mirmont, H. de la. "C. Calpurnius Piso et la conspiration de l'an 818/65." *Revue des Études Anciennes* 15 (1913): 405–20.

Vogel-Weidemann, Ursula. "The Opposition under the Early Caesars: Some Remarks on Its Nature and Aims." *Acta Classica* 22 (1979): 91–107.

Woolf, Greg. *Et tu Brute? A Short History of Political Murder*. Cambridge, MA: HUP, 2007.

MEDICAL EVIDENCE

Bloch, H. "Poisons and Poisoning." *Journal of the National Medical Association* 79, no. 9 (1987): 761–63.

Cilliers, L., and F. P. Retief. "Poisons, Poisoning and the Drug Trade in Ancient Rome." *Akroterion* 45 (2000): 88–100.

Edwards, Catherine. *Death in Ancient Rome*. New Haven, CT: YUP, 2007.

Frohne, D., and H. J. Pfander. *A Colour Atlas of Poisonous Plants*. Translated by N. G. Bissett. London: Wolfe, 1983.

Golden, Cheryl L. *Poisons in the Roman World*. London: Routledge, 2011.

Horstmanshoff, Manfred. "Ancient Medicine between Hope and Fear: Medicament, Magic and Poison in the Roman Empire." *European Review* 7, no. 1 (1999): 37–51.

Kaufman, D. B. "Poisons and Poisoning among the Romans." *CP* 27 (1932): 166ff.

Macinnes, Peter. *Poisons: From Hemlock to Botox to the Killer Bean of Calabar*. New York: Arcade Publishing, 2005.

Mayor, Adrienne. *Greek Fire: Poison Arrows and Scorpion Bombs: Biological and Chemical Warfare in the Ancient World*. Woodstock, NY: Overlook Duckworth, 2003.

Nutton, V. "The Drug Trade in Antiquity." *Journal of the Royal Society of Medicine* 78 (1985): 138–45.

Smith, S. "Poisons and Poisoners through the Ages." *Medico-Legal Journal* 20 (1952): 153–67.

Thompson, C. J. S. *Poisons and Poisoners, with Historical Accounts of Some Famous Mysteries in Ancient and Modern Times*. London: H. Shaylor, 1931.

Valente, W., R. Talbert, J. P. Hallett, and P. A. Mackowiak. "Caveat Cenans!" *American Journal of Medicine* 112 (2002): 392–98.

Van Hooff, A. J. L. "Ancient Euthanasia: 'Good Death' and the Doctor in the Graeco-Roman World." *Social Science and Medicine* 58 (2004): 975–85.

Van Hooff, A. J. L. "The Imperial Art of Dying." In *The Representation and Perception of Roman Imperial Power*, edited by P. Erdkamp, O. Hekster, G. de Kleijn, Stephan T. A. M. Mols, and L. De Blois, 99–116. Amsterdam: Brill, 2003.

ROMAN HISTORY—GENERAL

Adcock, Frank E. *Roman Political Ideas and Practice*. Ann Arbor: University of Michigan Press, 1959.

Alexander, M. C. *Trials in the Late Roman Republic 149 B.C. to 50 BCE*. Toronto: University of Toronto Press, 1990.

Allison, J. E., and J. D. Cloud. "The Lex Julia Maiestatis." *Latomus* 21 (1962): 711–31.

Alston, Richard. *Aspects of Roman History, AD 14–117*. New York: Routledge, 1998.

Alston, Richard. *Rome's Revolution: Death of the Republic & Birth of the Empire*. Oxford: OUP, 2015.

Ando, C. *Imperial Ideology and Provincial Loyalty in the Roman Empire*. Berkeley: University of California Press, 2000.

Archer, Léonie J., Susan Fischler, and Maria Wyke, eds. *Women in Ancient Societies: An Illusion of the Night*. New York: Routledge, 1994.

Aubert, Jean-Jacques. "A Double Standard in Roman Criminal Law? The Death Penalty and Social Structure in Late Republican and Early Imperial Rome." In *Speculum Iuris. Roman Law as a Reflection of Social and Economic Life in Antiquity*, edited by Jean-Jacques Aubert and Boudewijn Sirks, 94–133. Ann Arbor: University of Michigan Press, 2002.

Badian, Ernst. "'Crisis Theories' and the Beginning of the Principate." In *Romanitas, Christianitas: Untersuchungwen zu Geschichte und Literatur der römischen Kaiserzeit: Joannes Straub zum 70 Geburstag am 18 Oktober 1982 gewidmet*, 18–41. Berlin: de Gruyter, 1982.

Badian, Ernst. "Tiberius Gracchus and the Beginning of the Roman Revolution." *ANRW* 1.1 (1972): 668–731.

Balsdon, J. V. P. D. *Life and Leisure in Ancient Rome*. London: Bodley Head, 1969.

Balsdon, J. V. P. D. *Roman Women: Their History and Habits*. London: Bodley Head, 1962.

Barb, A. A. "The Survival of the Magic Arts." In *The Conflict between Paganism and Christianity in the Fourth Century*, edited by A. Momigliano, 100–125. Oxford: Clarendon Press, 1963.

Barry, W. D. "Exposure, Mutilation, and Riot: Violence at the *Scalae Gemoniae* in Early Imperial Rome." *G&R* 55, no. 2 (October 2008): 222–46.

Bauman, R. A. "Il 'sovversivismo' di Emilio Lepido." *Labeo* 24 (1978): 60–74.

Bauman, R. A. *Women and Politics in Ancient Rome*. London: Routledge, 1992.

Beard, Mary. *SPQR: The History of Ancient Rome*. New York: W. W. Norton, 2015.

Beck, Hans, Antonio Duplá, Martin Jehne, and Francisco Pina Polo. *Consuls and Res Publica: Holding High Office in the Roman Republic*. Cambridge: CUP, 2011.

Bellen, Heinz. *Studien zur Sklavenflucht im römischen Kaiser des julisch-claudischen Hauses*. Wiesbaden: Steiner, 1971.

Béranger, J. *Principatus: Études de notions et d'histoire politiques dans l'Antiquité gréco-romaine*. Geneva: Librairie Droz, 1973.

Béranger, J. *Recherches sur l'aspect idéologique du principat*. Basel: Friedrich Reinhardt, 1953.

Bergener, A. *Die Führende Senatorenschicht im Frühen Prinzipat 14-68 n. Chr*. Bonn: Habelt, 1965.

Birley, Anthony. *Marcus Aurelius*. 2nd ed. London: B. T. Batsford, 1993.

Boatwright, Mary T. "Luxuriant Gardens and Extravagant Women: The *Horti* of Rome between Republic and Empire." In *Horti Romani*, edited by M. Cima and E. La Rocca, 71–82. Rome: Bretschneider, 1998.

Brunt, P. A. *The Fall of the Roman Republic*. Oxford: Clarendon Press, 1988.

Brunt, P. A. "Stoicism and the Principate." *PBSR* 43 (1975): 7–35.

Cameron, Alan. *Circus Factions: Blues and Greens at Rome and Byzantium*. Oxford: Clarendon Press, 1976.

Cloud, J. D. "The Constitution and Public Criminal Law." In *CAH²*, edited by J. A. Crook, A. Lintott, and E. Rawson, 9:522–23.

Cloud, J. D. "The Primary Purpose of the Lex Cornelia de Sicariis." *ZRG* 86 (1969): 258–86.

Cornell, T. J. *The Beginnings of Rome*. London: Routledge, 1995.

Coulston, J. J., and H. Dodge, eds. *Ancient Rome: The Archaeology of the Eternal City*. Oxford: Oxford School of Archaeology, 2000.

Cramer, F. H. *Astrology in Roman Law and Politics*. Chicago: Ares, 1954.

Crawford, M. H. *Roman Statutes*, vol. 2. London: Institute for Classical Studies, 1996.

Crook, J. A., Lintott, J. A., and Rawson, E., eds. "The Last Age of the Roman Republic." *CAH²*, 9:70–112.

David, J.-M. "La faute et l'abandon: Théories et pratiques judicaires à Rome à la fin de la république." In *L'Aveu: Antiquité et Moyen Age*, 69–87. Rome: École Française de Rome, 1986.

Deroux, C., ed. *Studies in Latin Literature and Roman History*. Brussels: Coll. Latomus 164, 1979.

De Witt, N. W. "Litigation in the Forum in Cicero's Time." *CP* 21 (1926): 218–24.

Dorey, T. A. "Adultery and Propaganda in the Early Roman Empire." *University of Birmingham Historical Journal* 8 (1961): 1–6.

Drews, R. "Light from Anatolia on the Roman Fasces." *AJPh* 93 (1972): 40–51.

Edwards, C. *The Politics of Immorality in Ancient Rome*. Cambridge: CUP, 1993.

Ferrary, J. L. "Lex Cornelia de Sicariis et Veneficiis." *Athenaem* 69 (1991): 417–34.

Finley, Moses I. *Politics in the Ancient World*. Cambridge: CUP, 1983.

Fischler, Susan. "Social Stereotypes and Historical Analysis: The Case of the Imperial Women at Rome." In *Women in Ancient Societies: An Illusion of the Night*, edited by Léonie J. Archer, Susan Fischler, and Maria Wyke, 115–33. New York: Routledge, 1994.

Fishwick, Duncan. "Review of D. Hennig, *L. Aelius Seianus. Untersuchungen zur Regierung des Tiberius.*" *Phoenix* 31, no. 3 (1977): 284–86.

Flower, Harriet I. *The Art of Forgetting: Disgrace and Oblivion in Roman Political Culture*. Chapel Hill: University of North Carolina Press, 2006.

Flower, Harriet I. "*Damnatio Memoriae* and Epigraphy." In *From Caligula to Constantine: Tyranny and Transformation in Roman Portraiture*, ed. E. Varner, 58–69. Atlanta: Emory University Press, 2000.

Flower, Harriet I. *Roman Republics*. Princeton, NJ: PUP, 2010.

Fraschetti, Augusto. *Roman Women*. Translated by Linda Lappin. Chicago: University of Chicago Press, 2001.

Galsterer, H. "The Administration of Justice." In *CAH²*, 10:397–413.

Garlick, Barbara, Suzanne Dixon, and Pauline Allen. *Stereotypes of Women in Power: Historical Perspectives and Revisionist Views*. New York: Greenwood Press, 1992.

Gibbon, Edward. *The Decline and Fall of the Roman Empire*. 3 vols. New York: Modern Library, 1983.

Gladigow, B. "Die sakralen Funktionen der Liktoren: Zum Problem von Institutioneller Macht und sakraler Praesentation." *ANRW* 1, no. 2 (1972): 295–314.

Gowing, A. *Empire and Memory: The Representation of the Roman Republic in Imperial Culture*. Cambridge: CUP, 2005.

Grant, Michael. *Roman Anniversary Issues*. Cambridge: CUP, 1959.

Grant, Michael. *The Twelve Caesars*. New York: Charles Scribner, 1975.

Green, Peter. "Carmen et Error." In *Classical Bearings: Interpreting Ancient History and Culture*, chapter 13. London: Thames & Hudson, 1989.

Gruen, Erich S. *Culture and National Identity in Republican Rome*. Ithaca, NY: Cornell University Press, 1992.

Gruen, Erich S. "Review of A. W. Lintott, *Violence in Republican Rome*." *AJPh* 91, no. 3 (July 1970): 367–70.

Gruen, Erich S. *Roman Politics and the Criminal Courts 149–7 BC*. Cambridge, MA: HUP, 1968.

Habinek, Thomas, and Alessandro Schiesaro, eds. *The Roman Cultural Revolution*. Cambridge: CUP, 1997.

Haeuber, Chrystina. *The Eastern Part of the Mons Oppius in Rome*. Rome: Bretschneider, 2014.

Hallett, Judith P. *Fathers and Daughters in Roman Society: Women and the Elite Family*. Princeton, NJ: PUP, 1984.

Hallett, Judith P., and M. Skinner, eds. *Roman Sexualities*. Princeton, NJ: PUP, 1997.

Hammond, M. "The Transmission of Powers of the Roman Emperor from the Death of Nero to that of Alexander Severus in A.D. 235." *MAAR* 24 (1956): 61–131.

Hannestad, N. *Roman Art and Imperial Policy*. Jutland Archaeological Society Publications 19. Aarhus, Denmark: Aarhus University Press, 1986.

Harries, Jill. "*The Senatus Consultum Silanianum*: Court Decisions and Judicial Severity in the Early Roman Empire." In *New Frontiers: Law and Society in the Roman World*, edited by Paul J. du Plessis, 51–72. Edinburgh: Edinburgh University Press, 2013.

Harris, William V. *Roman Power: A Thousand Years of Empire*. Cambridge: CUP, 2016.

Hilliard, Tom. "On the Stage. Behind the Curtain: Images of Politically Active Women in the Late Roman Republic." In *Stereotypes of Women in Power. Historical Perspectives and Revisionist Views*, edited by Barbara Garlick, Suzanne Dixon, and Pauline Allen, 37–64. New York: Greenwood Press, 1992.

Hirschfeld, Otto. *Kleine Schriften*. Berlin: Weidmann, 1913.

Hölkeskamp, Karl-Joachim. *Reconstructing the Roman Republic: An Ancient Political Culture and Modern Research*. Translated by Henry Heitzmann-Gordon. Princeton, NJ: PUP, 2010.

Hölkeskamp, Karl-Joachim. "The Roman Republic as Theatre of Power: The Consuls as Leading Actors." In *Consuls and Res Publica: Holding High Office in the Roman Republic*, edited by H. Beck et. al, 161–81. Cambridge: CUP, 2011.

Hopkins, Keith, and Graham P. Burton. "Ambition and Withdrawal: The Senatorial Aristocracy under the Emperors." In *Death and Renewal: Sociological Studies in Roman History*, edited by Keith Hopkins, 2:120–200. Cambridge: CUP, 1983.

Hurlet, F. *Les collègues du prince sous Auguste et Tibère de la légalité républicaine à la légitimité dynastique*. Rome: CEFR, 1997.

Isaac, Benjamin. *The Limits of Empire*. Oxford: OUP, 1992.

Kefeng, Chen. "A Perspective of the *Senatus Consultum Ultimum* in the Late Roman Republic from the Constitutional Point of View." *Journal of Ancient Civilizations* 19 (2004): 125–32.

Keune, J. B. "Custos" (2). *R-E* 4, no. 2 (1901): col. 1902.

Kinsey, T. E. "Cicero *pro Murena* 71." *RBPhil* 43 (1965): 57–59.

Kleiner, D. E. E., and S. B. Matheson, eds. *I Claudia: Women in Ancient Rome*. New Haven, CT: YUP, 1996.

Kolb, E., ed. *Herrschafsstrukturen und Herrschaftspraxis: Konzepte, Prinzipien und Stratagien der Administration im römischen Kaiserreich*. Berlin: Akademie Verlag, 2006.

Lendon, Jon E. *Empire of Honour: The Art of Government in the Roman World*. Oxford: OUP, 1997.

Lendon, Jon E. "The Legitimacy of the Roman Emperor against Weberian Legitimacy and Imperial 'Strategies of Legitimation.'" In *Herrschafsstrukturen und Herrschaftspraxis: Konzepte, Prinzipien und Stratagien der Administration im römischen Kaiserreich*, edited by E. Kolb, 53–63. Berlin: Akademie Verlag, 2006.

Liebs, D. "Der Schutz der Privatsfäre[sic] in einer Sklavenhaltergesellschaft: Aussagen von Sklaven gegen ihre Herren nach römischen Recht." *BIDR* 83 (1980): 147–89.

Lintott, A. W. "Provocatio: From the Struggle of the Orders to the Principate." *ANRW* 1, no. 2 (1974): 226–67.

Lobur, John Alexander. *Consensus, Concordia and the Formation of Roman Imperial Ideology*. London: Routledge, 2008.

Lott, J. Bert. *Death and Dynasty in Early Imperial Rome*. Cambridge: CUP, 2012.

Macmullen, Ramsay. *Enemies of Roman Order*. Cambridge, MA: HUP, 1966.

Marshall, A. J. "Symbols and Showmanship in Roman Public Life: The Fasces." *Phoenix* 38, no. 2 (Summer 1984): 120–41.

Martin, J. "Die Provokation in der klassischen und späten Republik." *Hermes* 98 (1970): 72–96.

Mayer, Emanuel. *The Ancient Middle Classes: Urban Life and Aesthetics in the Roman Empire 100 BCE–250 BCE*. Cambridge, MA: HUP, 2012.

McDonald, A. H. "Review of A. W. Lintott, *Violence in Republican Rome*." *CR* 23, no. 2 (December 1973): 239–41.

McDougall, J. I. "Tacitus and the Portrayal of the Elder Agrippina." *EMC* 25 (1981): 104–8.

McHugh, Mary R. "Historiography and Freedom of Speech: The Case of Cremutius Cordus." In *Proceedings of the 2nd Penn-Leiden Colloquium on Ancient Values in 2002*, 391–408. Leiden, Netherlands: Brill, 2004.

McHugh, Mary R. "Manipulating Memory: Remembering and Defaming Julio-Claudian Women." PhD diss., University of Wisconsin, Madison, 2004.

Meier, C. *Res Publica Amissa: Eine Studie zu Verfassung und Geschichte der späten römischen Republik*. Wiesbaden: Steiner, 1966.

Meier, C. "Review of F. E. Adcock, *Roman Political Ideas*." *GGA* 216 (1964): 44–48.

Mendelsohn, Daniel. "Hail Augustus! But Who Was He?" *New York Review of Books*, August 14, 2014, 64–66.

Millar, Fergus. *The Emperor in the Roman World*. Ithaca, NY: Cornell University Press, 1992.

Millar, Fergus. "The Political Character of the Classical Roman Republic." *JRS* 74 (1984): 1–19.

Millar, Fergus. "Political Power in Mid-Republican Rome: *Curia* or *Comitium*?" *JRS* 79 (1989): 138–50.

Milnor, Kristina. *Gender, Domesticity, and the Age of Augustus: Inventing Private Life.* Oxford: OUP, 2005.

Moeller, W. O. "Review of A. W. Lintott, *Violence in Republican Rome.*" *CW* 63, no. 1 (September 1969): 24.

Momigliano, Arnaldo. "Introduction to R. Syme, *The Roman Revolution.*" In *Studies on Modern Scholarship*, 72–79. Berkeley: University of California Press, 1994.

Momigliano, Arnaldo. *The Conflict between Paganism and Christianity in the Fourth Century.* Oxford: Clarendon Press, 1963.

Momigliano, Arnaldo. "M. I. Rostovtzeff." In *Studies on Modern Scholarship*, 32–43. Berkeley: University of California Press, 1994.

Mommsen, Theodor. *A History of Rome under the Emperors.* Translated by C. Krojzl. London: Routledge, 1992.

Mommsen, Theodor. *Römische Staatsrecht.* 3 vols. in 5. Leipzig: S. Hirzel, 1887– 1888. https://archive.org/details/rmischesstaatsr01mommgoog.

Mouritsen, Henrik. *Politics in the Roman Republic.* Cambridge: CUP, 2017.

Nicolet, Claude. *Space, Geography and Politics in the Early Roman Empire.* Ann Arbor: University of Michigan Press, 1991.

Nörr, D. *Causa Mortis: Auf den Spuren einer Redewendung.* Munich: Münchener Beiträge zur Papyrusforschung und antiken Rechtsgeschichte, 1986.

O'Neill, P. "Going Round in Circles: Popular Speech in Ancient Rome." *ClAnt* 22 (2003): 135–65.

Oost, S. I. "Review of A. W. Lintott, *Violence in Republican Rome.*" *CP* 65, no. 4 (October 1970): 280–81.

Osgood, Josiah. *Caesar's Legacy: Civil War and the Emergence of the Roman Empire.* Cambridge: CUP, 2006.

Pani, Mario. *La corte dei Caesari.* Rome: Laterza, 2003.

Patterson, J. R. "The City of Rome from Republic to Empire." *JRS* 82 (1992): 186–215.

Pekary, Thomas. *Das Römische Kaiserbildnis in Staat, Kult und Gesellschaft.* Berlin: Mann, 1985.

Plessis, Paul J. du., ed. *New Frontiers: Law and Society in the Roman World.* Edinburgh: Edinburgh University Press, 2013.

Pomeroy, Sarah, ed. *Women's History and Ancient History.* Chapel Hill: University of North Carolina Press, 1991.

Premerstein, Anton von. *Vom Werden und Wesen des Prinzipats.* Munich: Beck, 1937.

Price, S. *Rituals and Power: The Roman Imperial Cult in Asia Minor.* Cambridge: CUP, 1986.

Puett, M. "Ghosts, Gods, and the Coming Apocalypse. Empire and Religion in Early China and Ancient Rome." In *State Power in Ancient China and Rome*, edited by W. Scheidel, 230–59. Oxford: OUP, 2015.

Raaflaub, Kurt. "Grundzüge, Ziele und Ideen der Opposition gegen die Kaiser im I Jh. N. Chr.: Versuch einer Standortbestimmung." In *Opposition et résistances a l'empire d'Auguste a Trajan*, edited by A. Giovannini and D. van Berchem, 1–63.

Entretiens sur l'antiquité classique, edited by O. Reverdin and B. Grange, no. 33. Geneva: Fondation Hardt, 1986.

Robinson, O. F. *Ancient Rome: City Planning and Administration*. London: Routledge, 1992.

Rogers, R. S. "Treason in the Early Empire." *JRS* 49, nos. 1–2 (1959): 90–94.

Roller, Matthew B. *Constructing Autocracy: Aristocrats and Emperors in Julio-Claudian Rome*. Princeton, NJ: PUP, 2001.

Rostovtzeff, M. I. *A History of the Ancient World*. 2 vols. Oxford: Clarendon Press, 1927.

Rostovtzeff, M. I. "Ein Speculator auf der Reise." *Röm. Mitt.* 26 (1911): 267–83.

Saller, Richard. "Anecdotes as Historical Evidence for the Principate." *G&R* 27, no. 1 (1980): 69–83.

Saller, Richard. *Personal Patronage in the Early Empire*. Cambridge: CUP, 2002.

Santoro L'Hoir, Francesca. "Tacitus and Women's Usurpation of Power." *CW* 88 (1994): 5–25.

Scheidel, Walter. "Emperors, Aristocrats, and the Grim Reaper: Towards a Demographic Profile of the Roman Elite." *CQ* 49, no. 1 (1999): 254–81.

Scheidel, Walter. *The Great Leveller*. Princeton, NJ: PUP, 2017.

Scheidel, Walter. *State Power in Ancient China and Rome*. Oxford: OUP, 2015.

Scheidel, Walter. "The Roman Emperor in the Wider World." http://www.sms.cam.ac.uk/media/1174184.

Schumacher, Leonhard. *Servus Index: Sklavenverhör und Sklavenanzeige im republikanischen und kaiserzeitlichen Rom*. Wiesbaden: Steiner, 1982.

Shaefer, Thomas. *Imperii Insignia: Sella curulis und Fasces. Zur Repraesentation römischer Magistrate*. Mainz: P. von Zaben, 1989.

Sherwin-White, A. N. "Procurator Augusti." *PBSR* 15 (1939): 11–26.

Sherwin-White, A. N. "Review of A. W. Lintott, *Violence in Republican Rome*." *JRS* 59, nos. 1–2 (1969): 286–87.

Starr, Chester G. *Civilization and the Caesars*. Ithaca, NY: Cornell University Press, 1954.

Syme, Ronald. *History in Ovid*. Oxford: Clarendon Press, 1978.

Syme, Ronald. *Roman Papers*, vol. 3. Oxford: OUP, 1984.

Syme, Ronald. *The Roman Revolution*. Oxford: Clarendon Press, 1939.

Taylor, Lily Ross. *Party Politics in the Age of Caesar*. Berkeley: University of California Press, 1949.

Teubner, Georg. *Beiträge zur Geschichte der Eroberung Britanniens durch die Römer*. Breslau: Trewendt & Granier, 1909.

Timpe, Dieter. *Arminiuss-Studien*. Heidelberg: C. Winter, 1970.

Timpe, Dieter. *Untersuchungen zur Kontinuät des frühen Prinzipats*. Historia Einzelschrift 5. Wiesbaden: Steiner, 1962.

Treggiari, Susan. "Jobs in the Household of Livia." *PBSR* 43 (1975): 48–77.

Varner, Eric R., ed. *From Caligula to Constantine: Tyranny and Transformation in Roman Portraiture*. Atlanta: Emory University, 2000.

Varner, Eric R. "Portraits, Plots and Politics: 'Damnatio Memoriae' and the Images of Imperial Women." *MAAR* 46 (2001): 41–93.

Varner, Eric R. "Tyranny and Transformation of the Roman Visual Landscape." In *From Caligula to Constantine: Tyranny and Transformation in Roman Portraiture*, edited by E. Varner, 9–26. Atlanta: Emory University, 2000.

Wallace, K. G. "Women in Tacitus." *ANRW* 2.33.5 (1991): 3556–74.

Wallace-Hadrill, Andrew. "The Imperial Court." In *CAH²* (1996), 10:283–308.

Wallace-Hadrill, Andrew. "Mutatio morum: The idea of a cultural revolution." In *The Roman Cultural Revolution,* edited by T. Habinek and A. Schiesaro, 3–22. Cambridge: CUP, 1997.

Wallace-Hadrill, Andrew. "Propaganda and Dissent?" *Klio* 67 (1985): 180–84.

Wallace-Hadrill, Andrew. "The Roman Imperial Court: Seen and Unseen in the Performance of Power." In *Royal Courts in Dynastic States and Empires: A Global Perspective,* edited by Jeroen Duinden, Tülay Artan, and Metin Kunt, 91–102. Leiden, Netherlands: Brill, 2011.

Wallace-Hadrill, Andrew. "The Roman Revolution and Material Culture." In *La Révolution Romaine après Ronald Syme,* edited by A. Giovannini, 288–313. Vandoeuvres-Genève: Fondation Hardt, 1999.

Walser, Gerold. *Rom, das Reich, und die fremden Völker in der Geschichtsschreibung der frühen Kaiserzeit.* Studien zur Glaubwürdigkeit des Tacitus. Baden-Baden: Verlag für Kunst und Wissenaschaft, 1951.

Watson, P. A. *Ancient Stepmothers: Myth, Misogyny and Reality.* Leiden: Brill, 1995.

Weaver, P. R. C. *Familia Caesaris: A Social Study of the Emperor's Freedmen and Slaves.* Cambridge: CUP, 1972.

Winterling, Aloys. *Aula Caesaris: Studien zur Institutionalisierung der römischen Kaiserhofes in der Zeit von Augustus bis Commodus (33 v. Chr.-192 n. Chr.).* Munich: Oldenbourg Verlag, 1999.

Winterling, Aloys. *Politics and Society in Imperial Rome.* Translated by Kathrin Lüddecke. Oxford: Wiley-Blackwell, 2009.

Wirszubski, C. *Libertas as a Political Idea at Rome during the Late Republic and Early Principate.* Cambridge: CUP, 1950.

Wiseman, T. P. *The Myths of Rome.* Exeter: University of Exeter Press, 2004.

Wiseman, T. P. *Remembering the Roman People: Essays on Late Republican Politics and Literature.* Oxford: OUP, 2009.

Wistrand, Magnus. *Entertainment and Violence in Ancient Rome.* Studia Graeca et Latina Gothoburgensia 56. Göteborg: Acta Universitatis Gothoburgensis, 1992.

Wood, Susan. *Imperial Women: A Study in Public Images, 40 BC–AD 68.* Leiden, Netherlands: Brill, 1999.

Wood, Susan. "Memoriae Agrippinae: Agrippina the Elder in Julio-Claudian Art and Propaganda." *AJA* 92, no. 3 (1988): 409–26.

Woolf, Greg. *Rome: An Empire's Story.* Oxford: OUP, 2012.

Wyke, M. "Augustan Cleopatras: Female Power and Authority." In *Poetry and Propaganda in the Age of Augustus,* edited by A. Powell. Bristol: Bristol Classical Press, 1992.

Yavetz, Zvi. *Plebs and Princeps.* Oxford: Clarendon Press, 1969.

ROMAN EMPERORS—GENERAL

Baldwin, Barry. *The Roman Emperors.* Montreal: Harvest House, 1980.

Brunt, P. A. "Princeps and Equites." *JRS* 73 (1983): 42–75.

Campbell, J. B. *The Emperor and the Roman Army 31 B.C.–A.D. 235.* New York: OUP, 1984.

Carcopino, Jérome. *Passion et politique chez les Césars*. Paris: Hachette, 1958.

Davies, Penelope J. E. *Death and the Emperor: Roman Imperial Funerary Monuments from Augustus to Marcus Aurelius*. Cambridge: CUP, 2000.

Hirschfeld, Otto. *Die Kaiserlischen Verwaltungsbeamten bis auf Diocletian*. Berlin: Weidmann, 1905.

Josephus, Flavius. *Death of an Emperor*. Translation and commentary by T. P. Wiseman. Exeter: University of Exeter Press, 1991.

Khmaladze, E., R. Brownrigg, and J. Haywood. "Stable Rule or Brittle Power? On Exponential Rule Lengths and Roman Emperors." School of Mathematics, Statistics and Computer Science, Victoria, University of Wellington, Wellington, New Zealand, February 12, 2007. http://sms.victoria.ac.nz/foswiki/pub/Main/ResearchReportSeries/mscs07-02.pdf.

Millar, Fergus. *The Emperor in the Roman World*. Ithaca, NY: Cornell University Press, 1992.

Potter, D. S. *Prophets and Emperors: Human and Divine Authority from Augustus to Theodosius*. Cambridge: CUP, 1994.

Scheid, John. *Les Frères Arvales: Recruitement et origine sociale sous les empereurs Julio-claudiens*. Paris: Presses Universitaires de France, 1975.

Scheid, John. "To Honour the Princeps and Venerate the Gods: Public Cult, Neighbourhood Cults, and Imperial Cult in Augustan Rome." In *Augustus*, edited by J. Edmondson, 295–96. Edinburgh: Edinburgh University Press, 2009.

Shotter, D. C. A. "Tacitus' View of the Emperors and the Principate." *ANRW* 2.33.5 (1991): 3263–3331.

Watson, A., ed. *Daube Noster: Essays in Legal History for David Daube*. Edinburgh: Scottish Academic Press, 1974.

Watson, A. "Enuptio Gentis." In *Daube Noster: Essays in Legal History for David Daube*, 331–41. Edinburgh: Scottish Academic Press, 1974.

Wiedemann, T. *Emperors and Gladiators*. London & New York: Routledge, 1992.

ROMAN ARMY—GENERAL

Black, Jeremy, ed. *Elite Fighting Forces: From the Ancient World to the SAS*. London: Thames & Hudson, 2011.

Busch, A. W. "Militia in Urbe. The Military Presence in Rome." In *The Impact of the Roman Army (200 BCE–AD 476): Economic, Social, Political, Religious and Cultural Aspects*, edited by L. de Blois and E. Lo Cascio, 315–41. Leiden: Brill, 2007.

Busch, A. W. *Militär in Rom: Militärische und paramilitärische Einheiten im kaiserzeitlischen Stadbildf*. Wiesbaden: Steiner, 2011.

Campbell, Brian. *The Roman Army 31 B.C.–A.D. 337: A Sourcebook*. London: Routledge, 1994.

Campbell, J. B. *The Emperor and the Roman Army 31 B.C.–A.D. 235*. New York: OUP, 1984.

Chilver, G. E. F. "The Army in Politics A.D. 68–70." *JRS* 47 (1957): 29–35.

Clauss, Manfred. "Untersuchungen zu den principales des römischen Heeres von Augustus bis Diocletian: Cornicularii, speculatores, frumentarii." PhD diss., Ruhr-Universität Bochum, 1973.

Coulston, J. "'Armed and Belted Men': The Soldiery in Imperial Rome." In *Ancient Rome: The Archaeology of the Eternal City*, edited by J. Coulston and H. Dodge, 76–118. Oxford: Oxford University School of Archaeology, 2000.

Cowan, R. "The Praetorian Guard: Easy Soldiering in Rome." *Ancient Warfare* 2, no. 1 (2007): 30–35.

Davies, R. W. "The Daily Life of the Roman Soldier under the Principate." *ANRW* 2, no. 1 (1974): 229–338.

Drogula, Fred K. *Commanders & Command in the Roman Republic and Early Empire.* Chapel Hill: University of North Carolina Press, 2015.

Grant, Michael. *Army of the Caesars.* New York: Charles Scribner & Sons, 1974.

Grosso, F. "Equites Singulari Augusti" *Latomus* 25 (1966): 900–909.

Keppie, L. J. F. "The Army and the Navy." In *CAH*, 10:371–96.

Keppie, L. J. F. *The Making of the Roman Army from Republic to Empire.* New York: Barnes & Noble, 1984.

Le Bohec, Yann. *The Imperial Roman Army.* London: Hippocrene Books, 1994.

Lieb, H. "Die constitutiones für die stadtrömischen Truppen." In *Heer und Integrationspolitik: Die römischen Militärdiplome als historische Quelle*, edited by W. Eck and H. Wolff, 322–46. Cologne: Böhlau, 1986.

Speidel, Michael P. *Die Denkmäler der Kaisereiter (Equites Singulari Augusti).* Cologne: Rheinland Verlag, 1994.

Speidel, Michael P. "Exploratores: Mobile Elite Units of Roman Germany." *Epigraphische Studien* 13 (1983): 63–78.

Speidel, Michael P. *Riding for Caesar.* Cambridge, MA: HUP, 1994.

THE JULIO-CLAUDIANS

Baldwin, Barry. *The Roman Emperors.* Montreal: Harvest House, 1980.

Boatwright, Mary T. "The Imperial Women of the Early Second Century A.C." *AJPh* 112 (1991): 513–40.

Dando-Collins, Stephen. *Blood of the Caesars: How the Murder of Germanicus Led to the Fall of Rome.* Hoboken, NJ: Wiley, 2008.

Fagan, Garrett G. "The Roman Imperial Succession under the Julio-Claudians, 23 BC–AD 69." MA thesis, School of Classics, Trinity College, Dublin, 1987.

Gibson, Alisdair G. G. *The Julio-Claudian Succession: Reality and Perception of the "Augustan Model."* Mnemosyne Supplement 349. Leiden: Brill, 2013.

Johnson, Van Loren. "The Factor of Inheritance in the Julio-Claudian Succession." PhD diss., University of Wisconsin, 1955.

Levick, Barbara. "Julians and Claudians." *G&R* 22 (1975): 29–38.

Matyszak, Philip. *The Sons of Caesar: Imperial Rome's First Dynasty.* London: Thames and Hudson, 2006.

Meise, Eckhard. *Untersuchungen zur Geschichte der Julisch-Claudischen Dynastie.* Munich: Beck, 1969.

Ramage, Edwin S. "Denigration of Predecessors under Claudius, Galba and Vespasian." *Historia* 32, no. 2 (1983): 201–14.

Roller, M. B. *Constructing Autocracy: Aristocrats and Emperors in Julio-Claudian Rome.* Princeton, NJ: PUP, 2001.

Wiedemann, T. *The Julio-Claudian Emperors*. London: Bristol Classical Press, 2002.
Wiedemann, T. "Tiberius to Nero." In *CAH²*, 10:198–209.

JULIUS CAESAR

Canfora, L. *Julius Caesar*. Berkeley: University of California Press, 2007.
Gershenson, D. E. "Caesar's Last Words." *Shakespeare Quarterly* 43, no. 2 (Summer 1992): 218–19.
Meier, Christian. *Caesar: A Biography*. New York: Basic Books, 1982.
Strauss, Barry. *The Death of Caesar*. New York: Simon & Schuster, 2015.
Weinstock, Stefan. *Divus Julius*. Oxford: Clarendon Press, 1972.
Yavetz, Zvi. *Julius Caesar and His Public Image*. Ithaca, NY: Cornell University Press, 1983.

AUGUSTUS

Arkenberg, J. S. "The Enigma of Varro Murena." *Historia* 42 (1993): 471–91.
Arkenberg, J. S. "Licinii Murenae Terentii Varrones, and Varrones Muranae." *Historia* 42 (1993): 326–51 (part 1); 471–91 (part 2).
Atkinson, K. M. T. "Constitutional and Legal Aspects of the Trials of Marcus Primus and Varro Murena." *Historia* 9 (1960): 440–73.
Badot, Philippe. "À propos de la conspiration de M. Egnatius Rufus." *Latomus* 32 (1973): 606–15.
Balsdon, J. V. P. D. "The Successors of Augustus." *G&R* 2, no. 6 (May 1933): 161–69.
Barrett, A. A. *Livia: First Lady of Imperial Rome*. New Haven, CT: YUP, 2002.
Barrett, A. A. "Tacitus, Livia and the Evil Step-mother." *Rheinisches Museum für Philologie* 144 (2001): 171–75.
Bauman, R. A. "Tanaquil-Livia and the Death of Augustus." *Historia* 43, no. 2 (1994): 177–88.
Billows, Richard A. "The Last of the Scipios." *AJAH* 7 (1982): 53–68.
Bleichen, J. *Augustus: The Biography*. Translated by Anthea Bell. London: Allen Lane, 2015.
Bowman, A. K., E. Champlin, and A. Lintott. *The Augustan Empire 43 BC–A.D. 69*. Cambridge: CUP, 1996.
Brunt, P. A. "The Role of the Senate in the Augustan Regime." *CQ* 34, no. 2 (1984): 423–44.
Charles-Picard, Gilbert. *Augustus & Nero: Emperors of Glory and Decay*. New York: Thomas Y. Crowell, 1965.
Charlesworth, M. P. "The Banishment of the Elder Agrippina." *CP* 17, no. 3 (1922): 260–61.
Charlesworth, M. P. "Tiberius and the Death of Augustus." *AJPh* 44, no. 2 (1923): 145–57.
Chastagnol, André. "Leuers nouvelles sur la conjuration de Cinna." *MEFR* 106, no. 1 (1994): 423–29.

Clark, Matthew D. H. *Augustus: The First Emperor.* Exeter, UK: Bristol Phoenix Press, 2010.

Cohen, Sarah T. "Augustus, Julia and the Development of Exile *ad Insulam*." *CQ* 58, no. 1 (2008): 206–17.

Corbett, J. H. "The Succession Policy of Augustus." *Latomus* 33 (1974): 87–97.

Corbier, M. "A propos de la Tabula Siarensis: Le Sénat, Germanicus et la domus Augusta." In *Roma y las provincias; realidad administrative e ideologia imperial,* edited by J. González Fernandez, 39–85. Madrid: Ediciones Clásicas, 1994.

Corbier, M. "La maisons de Césars." In *Épouser au plus proche: Inceste, prohibitions et stratégies matrimoniales autour de la Méditerranée,* edited by P. Bonte, 243–91. Paris: Éditions de l'École des hautes études en sciences sociales, 1994.

Corbier, M. "Male Power and Legitimacy through Women: The *domus Augusta* under the Julio-Claudians." In *Women in Antiquity: New Assessments,* edited by R. Hawley and B. Levick, 178–93. London: Routledge, 1995.

Cresci Marrone, Giovanella. "La congiura di Murena e le 'forbici' di Cassio Dione." In *Fazione e congiure nel mondo antico: Contributi dell'Istituto di storia antica,* edited by M. Sordi, 193–203. Milan: Vita e Pensiero, 1999.

Crook, J. A. "Augustus, Power and Authority." In *CAH²* (1996), 10:113–46.

Dalla Rosa, A. "Review of J. Edmondson, *Augustus.*" *BMCR* 2011.06.60.

Daly, L. J. "Augustus and the Murder of Varro Murena (cos. 23 B.C.)." *Klio* 66 (1984): 157–69.

Daly, L. J. "The Report of Varro Murena's Death." *Klio* 65 (1983): 245–61.

Daly, L. J. "Varro Murena, cos. 23 B.C. [magistratu motus] est." *Historia* 27, no. 1 (1978): 83–94.

Daly, L. J., and Reiter, W. L. "The Gallus Affair and Augustus' Lex Iulia Maestatis: A Study of Historical Chronology and Causality." In *Studies in Latin Literature and Roman History,* edited by C. Deroux, 289–311. Brussells: Latomus, 1979.

Della Corte, F. "La breve praefectura urbis di Messala Corvino." In *Philias charin: Miscellanea di studi classici in onore di E. Manni,* 2:667–77. Rome: Bretschneider, 1980.

Dennison, Matthew. *Livia: Empress of Rome: A Biography.* New York: St. Martin's Press, 2011.

Dettenhofer, Maria H. *Herrschaft und Widerstand im augusteischen Principat: Die Konkurrenz zwischen res publica und domus Augusta.* Stuttgart: Steiner, 2000.

Detweiler, Robert. "Historical Perspectives on the Death of Agrippa Postumus." *CJ* 65, no. 7 (April 1970): 289–95.

Due, Otto Steen. *Changing Forms: Studies in the Metamorphosis of Ovid.* Copenhagen: Gyldendal, 1974.

Eck, Werner. *The Age of Augustus.* 2nd ed. Translated by Deborah Lucas Schneider. Malden, MA: Blackwell, 2007.

Eder, Walter. "Augustus and the Power of Tradition: The Augustan Principate as Binding Link between Republic and Empire." In *Between Republic and Empire: Interpretations of Augustus and His Principate,* edited by K. A. Raaflaub and M. Toher, 71–122. Berkeley: University of California Press, 1990.

Edmondson, Jonathan, ed. *Augustus.* Edinburgh: Edinburgh University Press, 2009.

Everitt, Anthony. *Augustus: The Life of Rome's First Emperor.* New York: Random House, 2006.

Fantham, Elaine. *Julia Augusti: The Emperor's Daughter.* London: Routledge, 2006.

Feeney, D. C. "'*Si licet et fas est*': Ovid's Fasti and the Problem of Free Speech under the Principate." In *Roman Poetry and Propaganda in the Age of Augustus,* edited by Anton Powell, 1–25. London: Duckworth, 1992.

Ferrary, Jean-Louis. "The Powers of Augustus." In *Augustus,* edited by J. Edmondson, 90–136. Edinburgh: Edinburgh University Press, 2009.

Ferrill, Arther. "Augustus and His Daughter: A Modern Myth." In *Studies in Latin Literature,* edited by C. Deroux, 2:332–46. Brussels: Latomus, 1980.

Fraschetti, Augusto. "Livia the Politician." In *Roman Women,* edited by A. Fraschetti, 100–117. Chicago: University of Chicago Press, 2001.

Gabba, Emilio. "The Historians and Augustus." In *Caesar Augustus: Seven Aspects,* edited by F. Millar and C. Segal, 61–88. Oxford: Clarendon Press, 1984.

Gafforini, C. "Livia Drusilla tra storie e letteratura." *Rendiconti, Classe di Lettere e Scienze morali e storiche. Istituto Lombado* 130 (1996): 122–44.

Galinsky, Karl. *Augustan Culture: An Interpretive Introduction.* Princeton, NJ: PUP, 1996.

Galinsky, Karl. *Augustus: Introduction to the Life of an Emperor.* Cambridge: CUP, 2012.

Galinsky, Karl, ed. *Cambridge Companion to the Age of Augustus.* Cambridge: CUP, 2005.

Galinsky, Karl. "Making Haste Slowly: New Books on the Augustan Age." *CJ* 93, no. 1 (1997): 93–99.

Gardthausen, Viktor Emil. *Augustus und seine Zeit.* 3 vols. Leipzig: Teubner, 1904.

Giovanini, Adalberto, ed. *La Révolution Romaine après Ronald Syme.* Vandoeuvres-Geneva: Fondation Hardt, 1999.

Goldsworthy, Adrian. *Augustus.* New Haven, CT: YUP, 2014.

Griffin, Jasper. "Augustus and the Poets: 'Caesar Qui Cogere Posset.'" In *Caesar Augustus: Seven Aspects,* edited by F. Millar and E. Segal, 189–218. Oxford: Clarendon Press, 1984.

Grimal, Pierre. "La Conjuration de Cinna, Mythe ou Realité?" In *Pallas. Mélanges offerts à Monsieur Michel Labrousse,* 49–57. Toulouse: Université de Toulouse-Le Mirail, 1986.

Groag, E. "Der Sturz der Julia." *WS* 40 (1918): 150–67.

Groag, E. "Studien zur Kaisergeschichte III: Der Sturz der Julia." *WS* 41 (1919): 74–88.

Gross, W. H. *Julia Augusta.* Göttingen: Vanderhoeck und Ruprecht, 1962.

Gruen, Erich. "Augustus and the Making of the Principate." In *The Cambridge Companion to the Age of Augustus,* edited by K. Galinsky, 33–51. Cambridge: CUP, 2005.

Hanson, A. E. "Publius Ostorius Scapula: Augustan Prefect of Egypt." *ZPE* 47 (1982): 243–53.

Holmes, T. Rice. *Architect of the Roman Empire.* Oxford: OUP, 1928.

Hölscher, Tonio. *Staatsdenkmal und Publikum: Vom Untergang der Republik bis zur Festigung des Kaisertuns in Rome.* Xenia: Konstanzer althistorische Vorträge und Forschungen, 1984.

Jameson, Shelagh. "22 or 23?" *Historia* 18, no. 2 (April 1969): 204–29.

Jameson, Shelagh. "Augustus and Agrippa Postumus." *Historia* 24, no. 2 (1975): 287–314.

Jones, A. H. M. *Augustus*. New York: W. W. Norton, 1970.

Kienast, Dietmar. *Augustus: Prinzeps und Monarch*. 4th ed. Darmstadt: Primus, 2009.

Kuttner, A. *Dynasty and Propaganda in the Age of Augustus*. Berkeley: University of California Press, 1994.

Lacey, W. K. "2 B.C. and Julia's Adultery." *Antichthon* 14 (1980): 127–42.

Lacey, W. K. *Augustus and the Principate: The Evolution of the System*. Leeds: Francis Cairns, 1996.

Levick, Barbara. "Abdication and Agrippa Postumus." *Historia* 21, no. 4 (1972): 674-97.

Levick, Barbara. *Augustus: Image and Substance*. London: Routledge, 2010.

Levick, Barbara. "The Fall of Julia the Younger." *Latomus* 35 (1976): 301–39.

Luisi, Aldo. "L'Opposizione sotto Augusto: Le due Giulie, Germanico e gli Amici." In *Fazioni e congiure nel mondo antico*, edited by M. Sordi, 181–92. Milan: Vita e Pensiero, 1999.

Mackie, Nicola. "Ovid and the Birth of Maiestas." In *Roman Poetry and Propaganda in the Age of Augustus*, edited by Anton Powell, 83–97. London: Duckworth, 1992.

Marrone, Giovanella Cresci. "La congiura di Murena e le 'forbici' di Cassio Dio." In *Fazioni e congiure nel mondo antico*, edited by M. Sordi, 193–203. Milan: Vita e Pensiero, 1999.

Martin, R. H. "Tacitus and the Death of Augustus." *CQ* 5, nos. 1–2 (January–April 1955): 123–28.

McDermott, W. C. "Varro Murena." *TAPA* 72 (1941): 255–65.

Millar, Fergus. "The First Revolution: Imperator Caesar, 36–28 BC." In *La Révolution Romaine après Ronald Syme*, edited by A. Giovannini, 1–38. Vandoeuvres-Genève: Fondation Hardt, 1999.

Millar, Fergus. "State and Subject: The Impact of Monarchy." In *Caesar Augustus: Seven Aspects*, edited by F. Millar and E. Segal, 1–36. Oxford: Clarendon Press, 1984.

Millar, Fergus. "Triumvirate and Principate." *JRS* 63 (1973): 50–67.

Millar, Fergus, and E. Segal. *Caesar Augustus: Seven Aspects*. Oxford: Clarendon Press, 1984.

Momigliano, Arnaldo. "Review of Ronald Syme's *Roman Revolution*." *JRS* 30 (1940): 75–80.

Norwood, Frances. "The Riddle of Ovid's 'Relegatio.'" *CP* 58, no. 3 (July 1963): 150–63.

Osgood, Josiah. "Suetonius and the Succession to Augustus." In *The Julio-Claudian Succession: Reality and Perception of the "Augustan Model,"* edited by A. G. G. Gibson, 19–40. Leiden: Brill, 2013.

Phillips, Darryl A. "The Conspiracy of Egnatius Rufus and the Election of Suffect Consuls under Augustus." *Historia* 46, no. 1 (1997): 103–12.

Powell, Anton, ed. *Roman Poetry and Propaganda in the Age of Augustus*. London: Duckworth, 1992.

Purcell, Nicholas. "Livia and the Womanhood of Rome." In *Augustus*, edited by J. Edmondson, 165–96. Edinburgh: Edinburgh University Press, 2009.

Purcell, Nicholas. "Rome and Its Development under Augustus and His Successors." *CAH*², 10:782–811.

Raaflaub, Kurt. "Augustus' Military Reforms." In *Augustus*, edited by J. Edmondson, 203–28. Edinburgh: Edinburgh University Press, 2009.

Raaflaub, Kurt A., and L. J. Samons II. "Opposition to Augustus." In *Between Republic and Empire: Interpretations of Augustus and His Principate*, edited by K. A. Raaflaub and M. Toher, 433–47. Berkeley: University of California Press, 1990.

Raaflaub, Kurt A., and M. Toher. *Between Republic and Empire: Interpretations of Augustus and His Principate*. Berkeley: University of California Press, 1990.

Richardson, J. S. *Augustan Rome 44 BC to AD 14: The Restoration of the Republic and the Establishment of Empire*. Edinburgh: Edinburgh University Press, 2012.

Rogers, R. S. "The Deaths of Julia and Gracchus, A.D. 14." *TAPA* 98 (1967): 383–90.

Rogers, R. S. "The Emperor's Displeasure and Ovid." *TAPA* 97 (1966): 373–78.

Rowe, G. "Reconsidering the *Auctoritas* of Augustus." *JRS* 103 (2013): 1–15.

Sattler, Peter. *Augustus und der Senat: Untersuchingen zur römischen Innenpolitik zwischen 30 und 17 v. Christus*. Göttingen: Vandenhoeck & Ruprecht, 1960.

Schmitthenner, W., ed. *Augustus. Wege der Forschung* 128. Darmstadt: Wissenschaftliche Buchgesellschaft, 1969.

Severy, B. *Augustus and the Family at the Birth of the Roman Empire*. New York: Routledge, 2003.

Shotter, David. *Augustus Caesar*. 2nd ed. London: Routledge, 2005.

Southern, Patricia. *Augustus*. London: Routledge, 2013.

Stockton, David. "Primus and Murena." *Historia* 14, no. 1 (January 1965): 18–40.

Sumner, G. V. "Varrones Murenae." *HSCPh* 82 (1978): 187–95.

Swan, Michael. "The Consular Fasti of 23 B.C. and the Conspiracy of Varro Murena." *HSCPh* 71 (1967): 235–47.

Syme, Ronald. *The Augustan Aristocracy*. Oxford: Clarendon Press, 1986.

Syme, Ronald. "The Crisis of 2 B.C." *Sitzungsberichte der Bayerischen Akademie der Wissenschaften* 7 (1974): 3–34.

Talbert, Richard J. A. "The Senate and Senatorial and Equestrian Posts." *CAH*² (1996), 10:324–43.

Thibault, John C. *The Mystery of Ovid's Exile*. Berkeley: University of California Press, 1964.

Till, R. "Plinius über Augustus (*Nat. Hist.* 7.147–150)." *WJA* 3 (1977): 127–37. [added to abbrev]

Toynbee, J. M. C. "Ara Pacis Augustae." *JRS* 51 (1961): 153–56.

Tränkle, H. "Augustus bei Tacitus, Cassius Dio, und dem alteren Plinius." *WS* 82 (1969): 108–30.

Valvo, A. "M. Valerio Messalla Corvino negli studi più recenti." *ANRW* 2.30.3 (1983): 1673–74.

Wallace-Hadrill, Andrew. *Augustan Rome*. London: Bristol Classical Press, 2007.

Wardle, David. "A Perfect Send-off: Suetonius and the Dying Art of Augustus (Suetonius, *Aug.* 99)." *Mnemosyne* 60, no. 3 (2007): 443–63.

Williams, G. "Did Maecenas 'Fall from Favor'? Augustan Literary Patronage." In *Between Republic and Empire: Interpretations of Augustus and His Principate*, edited by K. Raaflaub and M. Toher, 258–75. Berkeley: University of California Press, 1990.

Yavetz, Zvi. "The Res Gestae and Augustus' Public Image." In *Caesar Augustus: Seven Aspects*, edited by F. Millar and E. Segal, 20–26. Oxford: Clarendon Press, 1984.

Zanker, Paul. *The Power of Images in the Age of Augustus.* Ann Arbor: University of Michigan Press, 1988.

TIBERIUS

Adams, Freeman. "The Consular Brothers of Sejanus." *AJPh* 76, no. 1 (1955): 70–76.

Allen, Walter, Jr. "The Death of Agrippa Postumus." *TAPA* 78 (1947): 131–39.

Allen, Walter, Jr. "A Minor Type of Opposition to Tiberius." *CJ* 44, no. 3 (December 1948): 203–6.

Allen, Walter, Jr. "The Political Atmosphere of the Reign of Tiberius." *TAPA* 72 (1941): 1–25.

Balsdon, J. V. P. D. "The 'Murder' of Drusus, Son of Tiberius." *CR* 1, no. 2 (1951): 75.

Balsdon, J. V. P. D. "The Successors of Augustus." *ANRW* 2, no. 2 (1975): 86–94.

Bauman, R. A. "Tiberius and Murena." *Historia* 15, no. 4 (1966): 420–32.

Bellemore, Jane. "The Identity of Drusus: The Making of a *Princeps*." In *The Julio-Claudian Succession: Reality and Perception of the "Augustan Model,"* edited by A. G. G. Gibson, 79–94. Leiden, Netherlands: Brill, 2013.

Bellemore, Jane. "The Wife of Sejanus." *ZPE* 109 (1995): 255–66.

Bird, H. W. "Aelius Sejanus and His Political Significance." *Latomus* 28 (1969): 61–98.

Boddington, Ann. "Sejanus: Whose Conspiracy?" *AJPh* 84, no. 1 (January 1963): 1–16.

Bodel, John. "Punishing Piso." *AJPh* 120, no. 1 (1999): 43–63.

Boughner, Daniel C. "Juvenal, Horace and Sejanus." *Modern Languages Notes* 75, no. 7 (November 1960): 545–50.

Champlin, Edward. "Tiberius the Wise." *Historia* 57, no. 4 (2008): 408–25.

Charlesworth, M. P. "The Banishment of the Elder Agrippina." *CP* 17 (1922): 260–61.

Charlesworth, M. P. "Tiberius and the Death of Augustus." *AJPh* 44, no. 2 (1923): 145–57.

Chilton, C. W. "The Roman Law of Treason under the Early Principate." *JRS* 45, nos. 1–2 (1955): 73–81.

Ciaceri, E. *Tiberio: Successore di Augusto.* Milan: Società Anonima Editrice Dante Alighieri, 1934.

Cogitore, I. "Mancipii unius audacia, le faux Agrippa Postumus face au pouvoir de Tibère." *REL* 68 (1990): 23–35.

Corbier, M. "Male Power and Legitimacy through Women: The Domus Augusta under the Julio-Claudians." In *Women in Antiquity: New Assessments*, edited by R. Hawley and B. Levick, 178–93. London: Routledge, 1995.

Cowan, Eleanor. "Tacitus, Tiberius and Augustus." *ClAnt* 28, no. 2 (October 2009): 179–210.

Detweiler, R. "Historical Perspectives on the Death of Agrippa Postumus." *CJ* 65, no. 7 (1970): 289–95.

Eck, W., A. Caballos, and F. Fernandez. *Das Senatus Consulto de Cn. Pisone Patre.* Munich: Beck, 1996.

Eisenhut, Werner. "Der Tod des Tiberius-Sohnes Drusus." *Museum Helveticum* 7 (1950): 123–28.

Fishwick, Duncan, and Brent D. Shaw. "Ptolemy of Mauretania and the Conspiracy of Gaetulicus." *Historia* 25, no. 4 (1976): 491–94.

Freytag, L. *Tiberius und Germanicus.* Berlin: Henschel, 1870.

Grant, M. "Aspects of the Principate of Tiberius." In *Numismatic Notes and Monographs,* 116. New York: American Numismatic Society, 1950.

Griffin, Miriam. "Tacitus, Tiberius and the Principate." In *Leaders and Masses in the Roman World,* edited by I. Malkin and Z. Rubinsohn, 33–57. Leiden, Netherlands: Brill, 1995.

Hawley, R., and B. Levick. *Women in Antiquity: New Assessments.* London: Routledge, 1995.

Hennig, D. *L. Aelius Sejanus: Untersuchungen zue Regierung des Tiberius.* Munich: Beck, 1975.

Hohl, Ernst. "Primum Facinus Novi Principatus." *Hermes* 70, no. 3 (1935): 350–55.

Jones, C. P. "Sex on Capri." *TAPA* 141, no. 2 (2011): 315–32.

Kaplan, M. "Agrippina semper atrox." In *Studies in Latin Literature and Roman History,* edited by C. Deroux, 1:410–17. Brussels: Latomus, 1979.

Koestermann, E. "Der Sturz Seianus." *Hermes* 83 (1955): 350–73.

Koestermann, E. "Die Majestätsprozesse unter Tiberius." *Historia* 4, no. 1 (1955): 72–106.

Koestermann, E. "Die Mission des Germanicus im Orient." *Historia* 7, no. 3 (July 1958): 331–75.

Kornemann, Ernst. *Tiberius.* Stuttgart: W. Kohlhammer, 1960.

Kornemann, Ernst. *Das Prinzipat des Tiberius und der "Genius Senatus."* Vorgelegt von Albert Rehm am 11. Jan. 1947. *Sitzungsberichte der Bayerischen Akademie der Wissenschaften,* Philosophisch-Historische Klasse Jahrg. 1947, Heft 1.

Kornemann, Ernst. *Doppelprinzipat und Reichstellung im Imperium Romanum.* Leipzig-Berlin: Teubner, 1930.

Lang, Arno. "Beiträge zur Geschichte des Kaisers Tiberius." PhD diss., Jena, 1911.

Leon, E. F. "Notes on the Background and Character of Libo Drusus." *CJ* 53 (1957): 77–80.

Levick, Barbara. *Tiberius the Politician.* London: Routledge, 1976.

Levick, Barbara. "Poena Legis Maiestatis." *Historia* 28, no. 3 (1979): 358–79.

Levick, Barbara. "Tiberius' Retirement to Rhodes in 6 BC." *Latomus* 31 (1972): 779–813.

Levick, Barbara. "Drusus Caesar and the Adoptions of A.D. 4." *Latomus* 25 (1966): 227–44.

Linderski, Jerzy. "Julia in Rhegium." *ZPE* 72 (1988): 181–200.

Lindsay, H. *Suetonius: Tiberius.* Bristol, UK: Bristol Classical Press, 1995.

Marañon, Gregorio. *Tiberius: A Study in Resentment.* London: Hollis & Carter, 1956.

Marsh, F. B. *The Reign of Tiberius.* Oxford: OUP, 1931.

Marsh, F. B. "Tacitus and Aristocratic Tradition." *CP* 21, no. 4 (October 1926): 289–310.

Meissner, Erhard. *Sejan, Tiberius und die Nachfolge im Prinzipat.* Erlangen: Dissertationsdruck, 1968.

Menéndez Argüín, A. Raúl. "La Guardia Pretoriana en combate, I: Equipamiento." *Habis* 41 (2010): 241–61.

Menéndez Argüín, A. Raúl. "La Guardia Pretoriana en combate, II: Rutinas de entrenamiento, operaciones, tácticas y despliegues." *Habis* 42 (2011): 229–52.

Menéndez Argüín, A. Raúl. *Pretorianos.* Madrid: Almena Ediciones, 2006.

Mogenet, Joseph. "Le conjuration de Clemens." *AntCl* 23, no. 2 (1954): 321–30.

Nicols, John. "Antonia and Sejanus." *Historia* 24, no. 1 (1975): 48–58.

Paladini, M. L. "La morte di Agrippa Postumo e la congiura di Clemente." *Acme* 7 (1954): 313–29.

Pappano, A. E. "Agrippa Postumus." *CP* 36, no. 1 (January 1941): 30–45.

Passerini, A. "Per la storia dell'imperatore Tiberio II: Il processo di Libone Druso." In *Studi giuridici in memoria di Pietro Ciapessoni,* 219–33. Pavia: Tipografia del Libro, 1948.

Perkounig, Claudia Martina. *Livia Drusilla-Iulia Augusta: Das politische Porträt der ersten Kaiserin.* Vienna: Böhlau, 1995.

Pettinger, Andrew. *The Republic in Danger: Drusus Libo and the Succession of Tiberius.* New York: OUP, 2012.

Rogers, R. S. "The Case of Cremutius Cordus." *TAPA* 96 (1965): 351–59.

Rogers, R. S. "The Conspiracy of Agrippina." *TAPA* 62 (1931): 141–68.

Rogers, R. S. *Criminal Trials and Criminal Legislation under Tiberius.* Middletown, CT: American Philological Association, 1935.

Rogers, R. S. "The Emperor's Displeasure: *Amicitiam renuntiare.*" *TAPA* 90 (1959): 224–37.

Rogers, R. S. *Studies in the Reign of Tiberius.* Baltimore: Johns Hopkins University Press, 1943.

Rogers, R. S. "A Tacitean Pattern in Narrating Treason-Trials." *TAPA* 83 (1952): 279–311.

Rogers, R. S. "Tiberius' Reversal of an Augustan Policy." *TAPA* 71 (1940): 532–36.

Romkey, Stephanie. "OCPD and the Enigmatic Personality of Emperor Tiberius." MA thesis, McMaster University, Hamilton, Ontario, 2006.

Rowe, G. *Princes and Political Cultures: The New Tiberian Senatorial Decrees.* Ann Arbor: University of Michigan Press, 2002.

Sage, M. M. "Tacitus and the Accession of Tiberius." *Ancient Society* 13/14 (1982/1983): 293–321.

Seager, Robin. *Tiberius.* Oxford: Blackwell, 2005. First published 1972 by Methuran (London).

Sealey, R. "The Political Attachments of L. Aelius Sejanus." *Phoenix* 15, no. 2 (Summer 1961): 97–114.

Shotter, D. C. A. "Agrippina the Elder: A Woman in a Man's World." *Historia* 49, no. 3 (2000): 341–57.

Shotter, D. C. A. "Cn. Cornelius Cinna Magnus and the Adoption of Tiberius." *Latomus* 33 (1974): 306–13.

Shotter, D. C. A. "Cnaeus Calpurnius Piso, Legate of Syria." *Historia* 23, no. 2 (1974): 229–45.

Shotter, D. C. A. "The Fall of Sejanus: Two Problems." *CP* 69, no. 1 (January 1974): 42–46.

Shotter, D. C. A. "Julians, Claudians and the Accession of Tiberius." *Latomus* 30 (1971): 1117–23.

Shotter, D. C. A. "Tacitus, Tiberius and Germanicus." *Historia* 17, no. 2 (1968): 194–214.

Shotter, D. C. A. "Tiberius and Asinius Gallus." *Historia* 20, no. 4 (1971): 443–57.

Shotter, D. C. A. *Tiberius Caesar*. 2nd ed. London: Routledge, 2004.

Shotter, D. C. A. "The Trial of C. Junius Silanus." *CP* 67, no. 2 (1972): 1226–31.

Shotter, D. C. A. "The Trial of M. Scribonius Libo Drusus." *Historia* 21, no. 1 (1972): 88–98.

Simpson, Chris. "The 'Conspiracy' of A.D. 39." In *Studies in Latin Literature and Roman History*, edited by C. Deroux, 347–66. Volume 168 of Collection Latomus. Brussels: Latomus, 1980.

Stewart, Zeph. "Sejanus, Gaetulicus and Seneca." *AJPh* 74, no. 1 (1953): 70–85.

Sumner, G. V. "The Family Connections of L. Aelius Seianus." *Phoenix* 19 (1965): 134–45.

Sumner, G. V. "Germanicus and Drusus Caesar." *Latomus* 26, no. 2 (April–June 1967): 413–35.

Syme, Ronald. "History or Biography: The Case of Tiberius Caesar." *Historia* 23, 4 (1974): 481–96.

Syme, Ronald. "Seianus on the Aventine." *Hermes* 84, no. 3 (1956): 257–66.

Talbert, R. A. "Germanicus and Piso" (review of *Princes and Political Cultures: The New Tiberian Senatorial Decrees* by G. Rowe). *CR* 54 (2004): 180–82.

Vass, George. *Tiberius: Reluctant Caesar*. Leicester, UK: Upfront Publishing, Ltd., 2002.

Visscher, F. de. "L'amphithéâtre d'Alba Fucens et son fondateur Q. Naevius Macro, préfet du prétoire de Tibère." *RAL* 12 (1957): 39–49.

Visscher, F. de. "Macro, préfet des vigiles et ses cohorts contre la tyrannie de Séjan." *Mélanges A. Piganiol* II, 761–68. Paris: S.E.V.P.E.N., 1966.

Visscher, F. de. "La politique dynastique sous la règne de Tibère." In *Synteleia*, edited by Vincenzo Arangio-Ruiz, 54–65. Naples: Jovene, 1964.

Vout, Caroline. "Tiberius and the Invention of Succession." In *The Julio-Claudian Succession: Reality and Perception of the "Augustan Model*," Mnemosyne Supplement 349, edited by A. G. G. Gibson, 59–77. Leiden, Netherlands: Brill, 2013.

Weinrib, E. J. "The Family Connections of M. Livius Drusus Libo." *HSCPh* 72 (1968): 247–78.

Weinrib, E. J. "The Prosecution of Roman Magistrates." *Phoenix* 22, no. 1 (Spring 1968): 32–56.

Wiedemann, T. E. J. "Tiberius to Nero." In *CAH*², 10:198–255. Cambridge: CUP, 1996.

Wilkes, J. J. "A Note on the Mutiny of the Pannonian Legions in A.D. 14." *CQ* 13, no. 2 (November 1963): 268–71.

Yavetz, Zvi. *Tiberius. Der traurige Kaiser*. Munich: Beck, 1999.

CALIGULA

Auguet, Roland. *Caligula, ou le pouvoir à vingt ans*. Paris: Payot, 1984.

Balsdon, J. V. P. D. *The Emperor Gaius (Caligula)*. Oxford: Clarendon Press, 1934.

Balsdon, J. V. P. D. "Notes Concerning the Principate of Gaius." *JRS* 24 (1934): 13–24.

Balsdon, J. V. P. D. "The Principates of Tiberius and Gaius." *ANRW* 2, no. 2 (1995): 86–94.

Barrett, Anthony A. *Agrippina, Mother of Nero*. New Haven, CT: YUP, 1996.

Barrett, Anthony A. *Caligula: The Corruption of Power*. New Haven, CT: YUP, 1989.

Benedicktson, D. T. "Caligula's Madness or Interictal Temporal Lobe Epilepsy." *CW* 82 (1989): 370–75.

Bicknell, P. "The Emperor Gaius' Military Activities in A.D. 40." *Historia* 17 (1968): 496–505.

Bissler, Joseph. "Caligula Unmasked: An Investigation of the Historiography of Rome's Most Notorious Emperor." MA thesis, Kent State University, 2013.

Charlesworth, M. P. "Gaius and Claudius." *CAH* (1934), 10:652–701.

Charlesworth, M. P. "The Tradition about Caligula." *Cambridge Historical Journal* 4 (1933): 105–19.

Clarke, G. W. "Seneca the Younger under Caligula." *Latomus* 24 (1965): 62–69.

Dabrowski, A. M. "Problems in the Tradition about the Principate of Gaius." PhD diss., University of Toronto, 1972.

Davies, R. W. "The Abortive Invasion of Britain by Gaius." *Historia* 15 (1966): 124–28.

D'Ecré, F. "La Mort de Germanicus et les poisons de Caligula." *Janus* 56 (1969): 123–48.

Edwards, Catherine. "The Truth about Caligula" (review of Ferril's *Caligula*). *CR* 41 (1991): 406–8.

Faur, J. C. "La Première Conspiration contre Caligula." *RBPh* 51 (1973): 13–50.

Faur, J. C. "Un discours de l'empereur Caligula au Senat (Dion., *Hist. rom.* LIX, 16)." *Klio* 60 (1978): 439–48.

Ferrill, Arther. *Caligula: Emperor of Rome*. London: Thames and Hudson, 1991.

Gelzer, Matthias. "Iulius 133 (Caligula)." *R-E*, 10:381–423.

Griffin, Miriam. *Seneca: A Philosopher in Politics*. Oxford: Clarendon Press, 1976.

Hanslik, R. "Vatinius." *R-E* 2, no. 5 (1955).

Hurley, Donna W. "Gaius Caligula in the Germanicus Tradition." *AJPh* 110 (1989): 316–38.

Hurley, Donna W. *An Historical and Historiographical Commentary on Suetonius' Life of C. Caligula*. Oxford: OUP, 1993.

Josephus, Flavius. *Death of an Emperor*. Translation and commentary by T. P. Wiseman. Exeter: University of Exeter Press, 1991.

Kajava, M. "The Name of Cornelia Prestina/Orestilla." *Arctos* 18 (1984): 23–30.

Katz, R. S. "Caligula's Illness Again." *CW* 70 (1977): 451.

Katz, R. S. "The Illness of Caligula." *CW* 65 (1971–1972): 223–25.

Kavanagh, B. J. "The Conspirator Aemilius Regulus's Aunt's Family." *Historia* 50, no. 3 (2001): 379–84.

Kavanagh, B. J. The Identity and Fate of Caligula's Assassin, Aquila." *Latomus* 69, no. 4 (2010): 1007–17.

Keaveney, Arthur, and John A. Madden. "The *Crimen Maiestatis* under Caligula: The Evidence of Dio Cassius." *CQ* 48, no. 1 (1998): 316–20.

Lindsay, H. *Suetonius: Caligula.* London: Bristol Classical Press, 1993.

Lindsay, Hugh. "Revenge of the Tyrant: The Assassinations of Philip II and Caligula." *Eranos* 82, no. 2 (1994): 73–84.

Linnert, U. "Beiträge zur Geschichte Caligulas." PhD diss., University of Jena, 1908.

Massaro, V., and I. Montgomery. "Gaius—Mad, Bad, Ill or All Three." *Latomus* 37 (1978): 894–909.

Morgan, M. G. "Caligula's Illness Again." *CW* 66 (1973): 327–29.

Morgan, M. G. "Once Again Caligula's Illness." *CW* 70 (1977): 452–53.

Nony, Daniel. *Caligula.* Paris: Fayard, 1986.

Philips, E. J. "The Emperor Gaius' Abortive Invasion of Britain." *Historia* 19 (1970): 369–74.

Renucci, Pierre. *Caligula l'Impudent.* Paris: Editions Memoria, 2007.

Sachs, Hans. *Caligula.* Translated by Hedvig Singer. London: Elkin, Matthews & Marrot, 1931.

Sandison, A. T. "The Madness of the Emperor Caligula." *Medical History* 2 (1958): 202–9.

Simpson, Chris. "The 'Conspiracy' of A.D. 39." In *Studies in Latin Literature and Roman History*, edited by C. Deroux, 347–66. Volume 168 of Collection Latomus. Brussels: Latomus, 1980.

Smallwood, E. M. *Documents Illustrating the Principates of Gaius, Claudius and Nero.* Cambridge: CUP, 2011.

Swan, Michael. "Josephus, *A.J.* 19. 251–52: Opposition to Gaius and Claudius." *AJPh* 91 (1970): 149–64.

Wardle, David. "Caligula and His Wives." *Latomus* 57, no. 1 (1998): 109–26.

Wilkinson, Sam. *Caligula.* London: Routledge, 2005.

Willrich, Hugo. "Caligula." *Klio* 3 (1903): 85–118, 288–317, 397–470.

Winterling, Aloys. *Caligula: A Biography.* Translated by Deborah Lucas Schneider, Glenn W. Most, and Paul Psoinos. Berkeley: University of California Press, 2011.

Wiseman, T. P. "Killing Caligula." *Pegasus* 16 (1988): 1–9.

Wood, Susan. "Diva Drusilla Panthea and the Sisters of Caligula." *AJA* 99, no. 3 (1995): 457–82.

Woods, D. "Caligula's Seashells." *G&R* 47 (2000): 80–87.

Yavetz, Zvi. "Caligula, Imperial Madness and Modern Historiography." *Klio* 78 (1996): 105–29.

CLAUDIUS

Aveline, John. "The Death of Claudius." *Historia* 53, no. 4 (2004): 453–75.

Baldwin, Barry. "Executions under Claudius: Seneca's Ludus de Morte Claudii." *Phoenix* 18, no. 1 (1964): 39–48.

Champlin, Edward J. "The Life and Times of Calpurnius Siculus." *JRS* 68 (1978): 95–110.

Clack, Jerry. "To Those Who Fell on Agrippina's Pen." *CW* 69, no. 1 (September 1975): 45–53.

Colin, J. "Les vendages dionysiaques et la légende de Messalina." *LEC* 24 (1956): 23–39.

Ehrhardt, C. "Messalina and the Succession to Claudius." *Antichthon* 12 (1978): 51–77.

Fagan, Garrett. "Messalina's Folly." *CQ* 52, no. 2 (2002): 566–79.

Fasolini, D. *Aggioramento bibliografico ed epigrafico ragionato sull'imperatore Claudio.* Milan: Vita e Pensiero, 2006.

Galimberti, A. "La rivolta del 42 e l'opposizione senatoria sotto Claudio." In *Fazioni e congiure nel mondo antico*, edited by M. Sordi, 205–15. Contributi dell'Istituto di storia antica 25. Milan: Vita e Pensiero, 1999.

Gibson, Alisdair G. G. "'All Things to All Men': Claudius and the Politics of AD 41." In *The Julio-Claudian Succession: Reality and Perception of the "Augustan Model,"* 107–32. Leiden, Netherlands: Brill, 2013.

Ginsburg, Judith. *Representing Agrippina: Constructions of Female Power in the Early Roman Empire.* Oxford: OUP, 2006.

Grimm-Samuel, V. "On the Mushroom that Deified the Emperor Claudius." *CQ* 41, no. 1 (1991): 178–82.

Hurley, D., ed. *Suetonius: Divus Claudius.* Cambridge: CUP, 2001.

Joshel, Sandra. "Female Desire and Discourse of Empire: Tacitus's Messalina." *Signs* 21, no. 1 (Autumn 1995): 50–82.

Jung, Helmut. "Die Thronerhebung des Claudius." *Chiron* 2 (1972): 367–86.

Kampen, N. "Between Public and Private: Women as Historical Subjects in Roman Art." In *Women's History and Ancient History*, edited by S. Pomeroy, 218–48. Chapel Hill: University of North Carolina Press, 1991.

Leon, E. F. "The *Imbecillitas* of the Emperor Claudius." *TAPA* 79 (1948): 79–86.

Levick, Barbara. *Claudius.* New Haven, CT: YUP, 1990.

Major, A. "Was He Pushed or Did He Leap? Claudius' Ascent to Power." *AH* 22 (1992): 25–31.

McAlindon, D. "Claudius and the Senators." *AJPh* 77 (1956): 113–32 and *AJPh* 78 (1957): 279–86.

McAlindon, D. "Senatorial Opposition to Claudius and Nero." *AJPh* 77, no. 2 (1956): 113–32.

Mehl, A. *Tacitus über Kaiser Claudius: Die Ereignisse am Hof.* Munich: Wilhelm Fink Verlag, 1974.

Momigliano, A. *Claudius: The Emperor and His Achievement.* Translated by W. D. Hogarth. Oxford: Clarendon Press, 1934.

Mottershead, J. "Claudius' Physical Appearance and Health." In *Suetonius, Claudius*, 145–47. Bristol, UK: Bristol Classical Press, 1986.

Murgatroyd, Paul. "Tacitus on the Deaths of Britannicus and Claudius." *Eranos* 103, no. 2 (2005): 97–100.

Osgood, Josiah. *Claudius Caesar: Image and Power in the Early Roman Empire.* Cambridge: CUP, 2011.

Pack, Roger. "Seneca's Evidence on the Deaths of Claudius and Narcissus." *CW* 36, no. 13 (February 8, 1943): 150–51.

Questa, C. "Messalina, meretrix augusta." In *Vicende e figure femminili in Graecia e a Roma*, edited by R. Raffaelli, 399–423. Ancona: Commissione per le pari opportunità tra uomo e donna della Regione Marche, 1995.

Rogers, R. S. "Quinti Veranii, Pater et Filius." *CP* 26, no. 2 (April 1931): 172–77.

Scramuzza, V. M. *The Emperor Claudius.* Cambridge, MA: HUP, 1940.

Stackelberg, K. T. "Performative Space and Garden Transgressions in Tacitus' *Death of Messalina*." *AJPh* 130, no. 4 (2009): 595–624.

Tagliafico, M. "I processi intra cubilculum: Il caso di Valerio Asiatico." In *Processi e politica nel mondo antico*, edited by M. Sordi, 249–59. Milan: Vita e Pensiero, 1996.

Tortoriello, Annalisa. *I fasti consolari degli anni di Claudio.* Rome: Accademia Nazionale dei Lincei, 2004.

Vessey, D. W. T. C. "Thoughts on Tacitus' Portrayal of Claudius." *AJPh* 92, no. 3 (July 1971): 385–409.

Wiseman, T. P. "Calpurnius Siculus and the Claudian Civil War." *JRS* (1982): 57–67.

Wolf, J. "Claudius Iudex." In *Die Regierungszeit des Kaisers Claudius (41-54 n. Chr.): Umbruch oder Episode?* edited by V. Strocka. Internationales Interdisziplinäres Symposion aus Anlaß des hundertjährigen Jubiläums des Archäologischen Instituts der Universität Freiberg i. Br.,16.-18. Februar 1991. Mainz: Philipp von Zabern, 1994.

Wood, Susan. "Messalina, Wife of Claudius." *JRA* 5 (1992): 219–34.

NERO

Baldwin, Barry. "Executions, Trials and Punishment in the Reign of Nero." *La Parola del Passato* 22 (1967): 425–39.

Barton, T. "The *Inventio* of Nero." In *Reflections of Nero: Culture, History and Representation.* Edited by J. Elsner and J. Masters, 48–66. Chapel Hill: University of North Carolina Press, 1994.

Benario, Herbert W. "Paccius Africanus." *Historia* 4 (October 1959): 496–98.

Bradley, Keith Richard. "The Chronology of Nero's Visit to Greece in A.D. 66/67." *Latomus* 37 (1978): 61–72.

Bradley, Keith Richard. "Nero's Retinue in Greece, AD 66/67." *Illinois Classical Studies* 4 (1979) 152–57.

Bradley, Keith Richard. "Two Notes Concerning Nero." *GRBS* 16 (1975): 305–8.

Brouzas, Christopher G. "The George Washington of Rome, Lucius Verginius Rufus." *TAPA* 62 (1931): 41–42.

Brunt, P. A. "The Revolt of Vindex and the Fall of Nero." *Latomus* 18 (1959): 531–59.

Brunt, P. A. "Stoicism and the Principate." *PBSR* 43 (1975): 7–35.

Buckley, Emma. "Constructing Neronian Identity." In *The Julio-Claudian Succession: Reality and Perception of the "Augustan Model."* Edited by A. G. G. Gibson, 133–54. Leiden, Netherlands: Brill, 2013.

Buckley, Emma, and Martin T. Dinter. *A Companion to the Neronian Age.* London: Wiley-Blackwell, 2013.

Champlin, E. "The Life and Times of Calpurnius Piso." *MH* 46 (1989): 101–24.

Champlin, E. *Nero.* Cambridge, MA: HUP, 2003.

Champlin, E. "Nero Reconsidered." *New England Review* 19, no. 2 (Spring 1998): 97–108.

Charlesworth, M. P. "Nero: Some Aspects." *JRS* 40, nos. 1–2 (1950): 69–76.

Ciaceri, Emanuele. "La congiura pisoniana contro Nerone." In *Processi politici e relazioni internazionali,* 363–86. Rome: A. Nardecchia, 1918.

Cizek, Eugen. *L'Époque de Néron et ses controversies idéologiques.* Leiden, Netherlands: Brill, 1973.

Cizek, Eugen. *Néron.* Paris: Fayard, 1982.

Cogitore, I. "Rome dans la conspiration de Pison." In *Neronia VI: Rome à l'époque néronienne,* 261–72. Société international d'études neroniennes, Actes du VIe Colloque international de la SIEN (Rome 19–23 Mai, 1999). Brussels: Latomus, 2002.

Corsi-Zoli, D. "Aspetti inavvertiti della congiura pisoniana." *Stud. Rom.* 20 (1972): 329–39.

Cotta Ramosino, Laura. "L'opposizione a Nerone e le 'partes' di Galba." In *Fazioni e congiure nel mondo antico,* edited by M. Sordi, 217–36. Milan: Vita e Pensiero, 1999.

Daly, L. J. "Verginius at Vesontio: The Incongruity of the '*Bellum Neronis.*'" *Historia* 24, no. 1 (1975): 75–100.

Dawson, Alexis. "Whatever Happened to Lady Agrippina?" *CJ* 64, no. 6 (March 1969): 253–67.

Dowling, L. "Nero and the Aesthetics of Torture." *The Victorian Newsletter* 66 (Fall 1984): 1–5.

Drinkwater, J. "Nero Caesar and the Half-Baked Principate." In *The Julio-Claudian Succession: Reality and Perception of the "Augustan Model,"* edited by A. G. G. Gibson, 155–74. Leiden, Netherlands: Brill, 2013.

Earl, D. C. "Two Passages of Sallust." *Hermes* 91, no. 1 (1963): 126–27.

Elbern, Stephan. *Nero: Kaiser, Künstler, Antichrist.* Mainz: von Zabern, 2010.

Elsner, J., and J. Masters, eds. *Reflections of Nero: Culture, History and Representation.* Chapel Hill: University of North Carolina Press, 1994.

Fagan, Garrett. "Messalina's Folly." *CQ* 52, no. 2 (2002): 566–79.

Fears, J. Rufus. *Princeps a Diis Electus: The Divine Election of the Emperor as a Political Concept at Rome.* Rome: American Academy at Rome, 1977.

Fishwick, D. *The Imperial Cult in the Latin West: Studies in the Ruler Cult of the Western Provinces of the Roman Empire.* Leiden: Brill, 1991.

Grant, M. *Nero: Emperor in Revolt.* New York: American Heritage Press, 1970.

Gresseth, G. K. "The Quarrel between Lucan and Nero." *CP* 52 (1957): 24–27.

Griffin, Miriam T. *Nero: The End of a Dynasty.* London: Routledge, 1984.

Griffin, Miriam T. *Seneca: A Philosopher in Politics.* Oxford: Clarendon Press, 1976.

Gwyn, W. B. "Cruel Nero: The Concept of the Tyrant and the Image of Nero in Western Political Thought." *History of Political Thought* 12 (1991): 421–55.

Hainsworth, J. B. "Verginius and Vindex." *Historia* 11 (1962): 86–96.

Hammond, Mason. "Corbulo and Nero's Eastern Policy." *HSCPh* 45 (1934): 101–2.

Hannestad, N. "Nero, or the Potentialities of an Emperor." In *Ritratto ufficiale e ritratto private. Atti della II conferenza internazionale sul ritratto romano,* edited by N. Bonacusa and G. Rizzo, 325–29. Rome: Consiglio Nazioale della Ricerche, 1988.

Henderson, B. W. *The Life and Principate of the Emperor Nero.* London: Methuen, 1903.

Holland, Richard. *Nero: The Man behind the Myth.* Stroud, UK: Sutton Publishing, 2000.

Kraay, C. M. "The Coinage of Vindex and Galba, A.D. 68, and the Continuity of the Augustan Principate." *NC* 9 (1949): 129–49.

Lancan, Paola. *La crisi del Impero nell'anno 69 D.C.* Padova: CEDAM, 1939.

Levick, Barbara. "L. Verginius Rufus and the Four Emperors." *Rheinisches Museum für Philologie* 128 (1985): 318–46.

Malitz, Jürgen. *Nero.* Translated by Allison Brown. Malden, MA: Blackwell, 2005.

Mastino, Attilio, and Paola Ruggeri. "*Claudia Augusti liberta Acte,* la liberta amata da Nerone ad Olbia." *Latomus* 54, no. 3 (July/September 1995): 513–44.

Mayer, R. "What Caused Poppaea's Death?" *Historia* 31, no. 2 (1982): 248–49.

Momigliano, A. "Nero." In *CAH* (1966), 10:702–42.

Murgatroyd, P. "Tacitus on the Death of Octavia." *G&R* 55, no. 2 (October 2008): 263–73.

Oost, Stewart V. "The Career of M. Antonius Pallas." *AJPh* 79, no. 2 (1958): 113–39.

Ottley, Sandra. "The Coup of Nymphidius Sabinus." *AHB* 24 (2010): 95–113.

Paratore, Ettore. "Nerone (nel XIX centenaio della morte)." *Studi Romani* 17 (1969): 269–87.

Rees, Roger. "The Lousy Reputation of Piso." In *The Julio-Claudian Succession: Reality and Perception of the "Augustan Model,"* edited by Alisdair G. G. Gibson, 95–106. Leiden, Netherlands: Brill, 2013.

Rogers, R. S. "Freedom of Speech in the Empire: Nero." In *Laudatores temporis acti: Studies in Memory of Wallace Everett Caldwell,* edited by M. F. Gyles and E. W. Davis, 91–98. Chapel Hill: University of North Carolina Press, 1964.

Rogers, R. S. "Heirs and Rivals to Nero." *TAPA* 86 (1955): 190–212.

Romm, James. *Dying Every Day: Seneca at the Court of Nero.* New York: Alfred Knopf, 2014.

Roper, Theresa K. "Nero, Seneca and Tigellinus." *Historia* 28, no. 3 (1979): 346–57.

Rudich, Vasily. *Dissidence and Literature under Nero: The Price of Rhetorization.* New York: Routledge, 1997.

Rudich, Vasily. *Political Dissidence under Nero: The Price of Dissimulation.* London: Routledge, 1993.

Sansone, D. "Nero's Final Hours." *ICS* 18 (1993): 179–89.

Shotter, D. C. A. *Nero Caesar Augustus: Emperor of Rome.* Harlow, UK: Pearson Education Ltd., 2008.

Shotter, D. C. A. "Tacitus and Verginius Rufus." *CQ* 17, no. 2 (November 1967): 370–81.

Shotter, D. C. A. "A Timetable for the *Bellum Neronis.*" *Historia* 24 (1975): 59–74.

Strocka, V., ed. *Die Regierungszeit des Kaisers Claudius (41–54 n. Chr.): Umbruch oder Episode?* Internationales Interdisziplinäres Symposion aus Anlaß des hundertjährigen Jubiläums des Archäologischen Instituts der Universität Freiberg i. Br., February 16–18, 1991. Mainz: Philipp von Zabern, 1994.

Strunk, Thomas E. "Saving the Life of a Foolish Poet: Tacitus on Marcus Lepidus, Thrasea Paetus, and Political Action under the Principate." *Syllecta Classica* 21 (2010): 119–39.

Sullivan, J. P. *Literature and Politics in the Age of Nero.* Ithaca, NY: Cornell University Press, 1985.

Syme, R. "Domitius Corbulo." *JRS* 60 (1970): 27–39.

Townend, G. B. "Calpurnius Siculus and the Munus Neronis." *JRS* 70 (1980): 166–74.

Townend, G. B. "The Reputation of Verginius Rufus." *Latomus* 20 (1961): 337–41.

Van Ooteghem, J. "Verginius et Vindex." *Et.Cl.* 36 (1968): 18–27.

Vout, C. *Power and Eroticism in Imperial Rome.* Cambridge: CUP, 2007.

Walter, Gérard. *Nero.* Translated by Emma Craufurd. London: Allen & Unwin, 1957.

Warmington, B. H. *Nero: Reality and Legend.* New York: W. W. Norton & Co., 1969.

Warmington, B. H. *Suetonius' Nero.* London: Bristol Classical Press, 1995 (originally published 1977).

Wilson, Emily. *The Greatest Empire: A Life of Seneca.* Oxford: OUP, 2014.

Woods, D. "Nero and Sporus." *Latomus* 68 (2009): 73–82.

YEAR OF THE FOUR EMPERORS

Greenhalgh, Peter. *The Year of the Four Emperors.* London: Weidenfeld and Nicolson, 1975. [Appeared as *The Long Year*, Boulder, CO, 1976].

Henderson, Bernard W. *Civil War and Rebellion in the Roman Empire.* London: Macmillan, 1908. https://archive.org/details/civilwarrebellio00henduoft.

Last, Hugh. "Review of: Paola Zancan, *La Crisi del Impero nell' Anno 69 D.C.*" *JRS* 30, no. 2 (1940): 199–200.

Morgan, Gwynn. *69 A.D.: The Year of the Four Emperors.* Oxford: OUP, 2006.

Murison, Charles L. *Galba, Otho and Vitellius: Careers and Controversies.* New York: Georg Olms, 1993.

Raoss, M. "La rivolta di Vindice ed il successo di Galba." *Epigraphica* 20 (1958): 46–120; 22 (1960): 37–151.

Syme, Ronald. "The Partisans of Galba." *Historia* 31 (1982): 460–83.

Wellesley, Kenneth. *The Year of the Four Emperors.* 3rd edition. London: Routledge, 2000.

Zancan, Paola. *La crisi del Impero nell'anno 69 D.C.* Padova: CEDEM, 1939.

INTERNAL SECURITY—TREASON

Bauman, Richard A. *Crime and Punishment in Ancient Rome.* London: Routledge, 1996.

Bauman, Richard A. *The Crimen Maiestas in the Roman Republic and Augustan Principate.* Johannesburg, South Africa: Witwatersrand Univesity Press, 1967.

Bauman, Richard A. *Impietas in Principem: A Study of Treason against the Roman Emperor with Special Reference to the First Century A.D.* Mun. Beitrage zur Papyrus Forschungen & Antike Rechtsgeschichte 67. Munich: Beck, 1974.

Rutledge, Steven H. *Imperial Inquisitions: Prosecutors and Informants from Tiberius to Domitian*. New York: Routledge, 2001.

INTERNAL SECURITY—POLICING IN ROME AND OTHER ANCIENT SOCIETIES

Aldrete, Gregory S. "Riots." In *A Cambridge Companion to the City of Rome*, edited by P. Erdkamp, 425–40. Cambridge: CUP, 2013.

Davies, R. W. "Augustus Caesar. A Police System in the Ancient World." In *Pioneers in Policing*, edited by P. J. Stead, 12–32. Montclair, NJ: Patterson Smith, 1977.

Davies, R. W. "Police Work in Roman Times." *History Today* 18, no. 10 (October 1968): 700-707.

Echols, Edward. "The Roman City Police: Origin and Development." *CJ* 53 (1957–1958): 377–85.

Fuhrmann, Christopher J. *Policing the Roman Empire: Soldiers, Administration, and Public Order*. Oxford: OUP, 2012.

Gruen, Erich. "Review of W. Nippel, *Public Order in Ancient Rome*." *Gnomon* 70, no. 6 (1998): 566–68.

Harris, E. "Who Enforced the Law in Classical Athens?" In *Symposion 2005: Vorträge zur griechischen und hellenistischen Rechtsgeschichte* (Salerno, 14–18 September 2005) = *Comunicazioni sul diritto greco ed ellenistico* (Salerno, 14–18 settembre 2005), 159–76. Wien: Verlag der Österreichischen Akademie der Wissenschaften, 2007.

Hirschfeld, Otto. "Die Sicherheitspolizei im römischen Kaiserreich." In *Sitzungsberichte der könglischen Preussischen Akademie der Wissenschaften in Berlin*, 586–88. Berlin: Deutsche Akademie der Wissenschaften, 1891. Also in *Kleine Schriften*, 576–612. Berlin: Weidmann, 1913.

Hunter, V. *Policing Athens: Social Control in the Attic Lawsuits, 420–320 BC*. Princeton, NJ: PUP, 1994.

Kelly, Benjamin. "Riot Control and Imperial Ideology in the Roman Empire." *Phoenix* 61 (2007): 150–76.

Kelly, Benjamin. "Policing and Security." In *A Cambridge Companion to the City of Rome*, edited by P. Erdkamp, 410–24. Cambridge: CUP, 2013.

Kelly, Benjamin. "The Repression of Violence in the Roman Principate." PhD diss., Oxford University, 2002.

Kunkel, Wolfgang. *Untersuchungen zur Entwicklung des römischen Kriminalverfahrens in vorsullanischer Zeit*. Munich: Beck, 1962.

Lintott, A. W. *Violence in Republican Rome*. Oxford: Clarendon Press, 1968.

Ménard, H. *Maintenir l'Order: IIe-IVe siècles ap. J.-C*. Seysell: Champ Vallon, 2004.

Nippel, Wilfried. *Aufruhr und "Polizei" in der römischen Republik*. Stuttgart: Klett-Cotta, 1988.

Nippel, Wilfried. "Policing Rome." *JRS* 74 (1984): 20–29.

Nippel, Wilfried. *Public Order in Ancient Rome*. Cambridge: CUP, 1995.

Riggsby, Andrew M. *Crime and Community in Ciceronian Rome*. Austin: University of Texas Press, 1999.

Sablayrolles, R. "La rue, le soldat et le pouvoir: La garnison de Rome de César à Pertinax." *Pallas* 55 (2001): 127–53.

INTERNAL SECURITY—DELATION

Boissier, Gaston. "Les Délateurs." *Revue des Deux Mondes* 72 (1867): 305–40.

Boissière, Gustave. *L'accusation publique et les delateurs chez les Romains*. Niort, France: G. Clouzot, 1911.

Dumeril, A. "Origine des Délateurs et Précis de leur histoire pendant la durée de l'empire romain." *Annales de la Faculté des Lettres, Bordeaux* 3 (1881): 262–81.

Fanizza, Lucia. *Delatori e Accusatori: L'iniziativa nei processi di Età imperiale*. Studia juridica 84. Rome: Bretschneider, 1988.

Froment, Théodore. "L'éloquence des délateurs." *Annales de la Faculté des Lettres de Bordeaux* 1 (1880): 35–57.

Gaudemet, J. "La répression de la délation au bas-empire." In *Philias charin: Miscellanea di studi classici in onore di Eugenio Manni*, 3:1065–83. Rome: Bretschneider, 1980.

Giovannini, A. "Pline et les délateurs de Domitien." In *Opposition et résistances a l'empire d'Auguste a Trajan*, edited by A. Giovannini and D. van Berchem, 219–48. *Entretiens sur l'antiquité classique*, edited by O. Reverdin and B. Grange, no. 33. Geneva: Fondation Hardt, 1986.

O'Neal, William J. "Delation in the Early Empire." *CB* 55 (1978): 24–28.

Petraccia, Maria Federica. *Indices e Delatores nell'Antica Roma: Occultiore indicio Proditus; in Occulta Delatus Insidias*. Milan: LED Edizioni Universitarie, 2014.

Rutledge, Steven H. "Delatores and the Tradition of Violence in Roman Oratory." *AJPh* 120 (1999): 555–73.

Rutledge, Steven H. *Imperial Inquisitions: Prosecutors and Informants from Tiberius to Domitian*. New York: Routledge, 2001.

Zijlstra, J. S. A. *De delatores te Rome tot aan Tiberius' regering*. Nijmegen, Netherlands: Berkhout, 1967.

PRAETORIAN GUARD

Absil, M. *Les préfets du prétoire d'Auguste à Commode: 2 avant Jésus-Christ–192 après Jésus Christ*. Paris: De Boccard, 1997.

Absil, M. "Le rôle des préfets du prétoire pendant les règnes de Néron, Galba, Othon et Vitellius: Aspects Politiques." *Neronia VI*, 229–47.

Bingham, Sandra J. *The Praetorian Guard: A History of Rome's Special Elite Forces*. Waco, TX: Baylor University Press, 2013.

Birley, A. R. "Making Emperors. Imperial Instrument or Independent Force?" In *A Companion to the Roman Army*, edited by P. Erdkamp, 132–94. Malden, MA: Blackwell Publishing, 2007.

Ceñal Martinez, H. "La Guardia Pretoriana: Composicíon, funciones e historia." PhD diss., Universidad de Oviedo, 2009.

De Laet, S. J. "Les pouvoirs militaires des Préfets du Prétoire et leur développement progressif." *Revue belge de philologie et d'histoire* 25, nos. 3–4 (1946): 509–54.

Durry, M. *Les cohorts pretoriennes*. Paris: E. Boccard, 1938.

Durry, M. "Praetoriae Cohortes." *R-E* 22 (1954): col. 1613.

Howe, Laurence Lee. *The Praetorian Prefects from Commodus to Diocletian*. Chicago: University of Chicago Press, 1942.

Jallet-Huant, Monique. *La garde prétorienne: Dans la Rome antique*. Charenton-le-Pont, France: Presses de Valmy, 2004.

Keppie, L. J. F. "The Praetorian Guard before Sejanus." *Athenaeum* 84 (1996): 101–24.

McDermott, W. C. "Sextus Afranius Burrus." *Latomus* 8 (1949): 229–54.

Menéndez Argüín, A. Raúl. *Pretorianos*. Madrid: Almenas Ediciones, 2006.

Ottley, Sandra. "The Role Played by the Praetorian Guard in the Events of AD 69, as Described by Tacitus in His *Historiae*." Unpublished PhD diss., University of Western Australia, 2009.

Passerini, A. *Le coorti pretorie*. Rome: Signorelli, 1939.

Powell, Geoffrey. "The Praetorian Guard." *History Today* 18 (1968): 858–66.

Prescott, P. M. *Optimus: Praetorian Guard*. P. M. Prescott Enterprises, 2006.

Rankov, Boris. *Guardians of the Roman Empire*. Oxford: Osprey, 1999.

Rankov, Boris. *The Praetorian Guard*. London: Osprey, 1994.

Scarrow, S. *Praetorian*. London: Headline, 2011.

Stöver, Hans Dieter. *Die Prätorianer: Kaisermacher, Kaisermörder*. Munich: Langen Müller, 1994.

THE URBAN COHORTS

Bérard, F. "Le rôle militaire des cohorts urbaines." *MEFR* 100 (1988): 159–82.

Freis, Helmut. "Cohortes Urbanae." *R-E* Suppl., 10, col. 1125–40.

Freis, Helmut. *Die cohortes urbanae*. Epigraphische Studien 2; Beiheft des *Bonner Jahrbücher* 21. Cologne: Böhlau Verlag, 1967.

Ricci, Cecilia. "*In Custodiam Urbis*: Notes on the *Cohortes Urbanae*." *Historia* 60, no. 4 (2011): 484–508.

Ricci, Cecilia. *Soldati delle milizie urbane fuori da Rome: La documentazione epigrafica*. Opuscula Epigrafica 5. Rome: Quasar, 1994.

Roxan, Margaret, and Werner Eck. "A Military Diploma of AD 85 for the Rome Cohorts." *ZPE* 96 (1993): 67–74.

Vitucci, G. *Studi sulla praefectura urbi in età imperial (Sec. I-III)*. Rome: Bretschneider, 1956.

INTERNAL SECURITY—GERMAN BODYGUARD

Bang, Martin. *Die Germanen im römischen Dienst*. Berlin: Weidmann, 1906.

Bellen, H. *Die germanische Leibwache der römischen Kaiser des Julisch-Claudischen Hauses*. Wiesbaden: Steiner, 1981.

Frank, R. I. *Scholae Palatinae: The Palace Guards of the Later Roman Empire.* Rome: American Academy in Rome, 1969.
Speidel, M. "Germani Corporis Custodes." *Germania* 62 (1984): 31–45.

ESPIONAGE, INTELLIGENCE, SPIES AND SECRET SERVICE

Austin, N. J. E., and N. B. Rankov. *Exploration: Military and Political Intelligence in the Roman World from the Second Punic War to the Battle of Adrianople.* New York: Routledge, 1995.
Ezov, A. "Reconnaissance and Intelligence in the Roman Art of War Writing in the Imperial Period." In *Studies in Latin Literature and Roman History,* edited by C. Deroux, 299–317. Brussels: Latomus, 2000.
Fiebiger, H. O. "Exploratores." *R-E* 4 (1909): col. 122–25.
Gichon, M. "Military Intelligence in the Roman Army." In *Labor Omnibus Unus,* edited by H. E. Herzig and E. Frei-Stolba, 154–70. Festschrift Walser, Historia Einzelschriften 60. Stuttgart, 1989.
Krenkel, W. "Speculatores." In *Lexicon der Alten Welt,* 2855. Zurich: Artemis Verlag, 1990.
Lammert, F. "Speculatores." *R-E* 3, no. A2 (xxxx): 1583–86.
Liberati, Anna Maria, and Enrico Silverio. *Servizi Segreti in Roma Antica: Informazioni e sicurezza dagli initia Urbis all'impero universal.* Rome: Bretschneider, 2010.
Russell, Frank Santi. "Finding the Enemy: Military Intelligence." In *Oxford Handbook on Warfare in the Classical World,* edited by J. B. Campbell and L. A. Tritle, 474–92. Oxford: OUP, 2013.
Sheldon, Rose Mary. *Espionage in the Ancient World: An Annotated Bibliography.* Jefferson, NC: McFarland, 2003.
Sheldon, Rose Mary. *Intelligence Activities in Ancient Rome: Trust in the Gods, but Verify.* London: Frank Cass, 2005.

VIGILES

Rainbird, J. S. "The Vigiles of Rome." PhD diss., University of Durham, 1976.
Rainbird, J. S. "The Fire Stations of Imperial Rome." *PBSR* 54 (1986): 147–69.
Reynolds, P. K. Baillie. *The Vigiles of Imperial Rome.* Oxford: OUP, 1926. Reprint, Chicago: Ares Publishers, 1996.
Robinson, O. F. "Fire Prevention at Rome." *RIDA* 24 (1977): 377–88.
Sablayrolles, Robert. *Libertinus miles: Les cohortes de vigiles.* Rome: École Française de Rome, 1996.

Index

Note: Roman names are listed here by the cognomen (e.g., "Caesar") for the convenience of nonspecialists. Classicists usually list such people by their gens (e.g., Julius). Women, however, are listed gens first (e.g., Domitia Lepida).

About the Author

Colonel Rose Mary Sheldon received her PhD in ancient history from the University of Michigan. Her dissertation, on intelligence gathering in ancient Rome, won a National Intelligence Book Award in 1987. She is professor of history at the Virginia Military Institute and holder of the Henry King Burgwyn, Jr. Chair in Military History. She was made a fellow of the American Academy in Rome in 1980. Dr. Sheldon has been on the editorial boards of the *International Journal of Intelligence and Counterintelligence* and the *Journal of Military History*. She has written more than three dozen articles in such publications as *Studies in Intelligence*, the *American Intelligence Journal*, *Small Wars and Insurgencies*, the *Journal of Military History*, and the *Washington Post*. Her books include *Espionage in the Ancient World: An Annotated Bibliography*; *Intelligence Activities in Ancient Rome: Trust in the Gods, but Verify*; *Spies of the Bible*; *Rome's Wars in Parthia: Blood in the Sand*; and *Ambush! Surprise Attack in Ancient Greek Warfare*.